BRITISH SHIPPING LAWS

C.I.F. AND F.O.B. CONTRACTS

AUSTRALIA
The Law Book Company
Brisbane: Sydney: Melbourne: Perth

CANADA
Carswell
Ottawa: Toronto: Calgary: Montreal: Vancouver

Agents
Steimatzky's Agency Ltd, Tel Aviv
N.M. Tripathi (Private) Ltd, Bombay
Eastern Law House (Private) Ltd, Calcutta
M.P.P. House Bangalore
Universal Book Traders, Delhi
MacMillan Shuppan KK, Tokyo
Pakistan Law House, Karachi, Lahore

BRITISH SHIPPING LAWS

C.I.F. AND F.O.B. CONTRACTS

FOURTH EDITION
by

David M. Sassoon
M. JUR. (Jerusalem); D. PHIL. (OXON.); FCIArb.
Member of the Israeli Bar

LONDON
SWEET AND MAXWELL
1995

First Edition	(1968)	*By David M. Sassoon*
Second Edition	(1975)	*By David M. Sassoon*
Third Edition	(1984)	*By David M. Sassoon and H. Orren Merren*
Fourth Edition	(1995)	*By David M. Sassoon*

Published in 1995 by Sweet & Maxwell Limited of
South Quay Plaza, 183 Marsh Wall,
London E14 9FT
Computerset by Wyvern Typesetting, Bristol
Printed in Great Britain at
The Bath Press, Bath, Avon

No natural forests were destroyed to make this product;
only farmed timber was used and re-planted.

ISBN 0 421 51320 9
A CIP catalogue record for this book is available from the
British Library

1000726313

PREFACE

In preparing this fourth edition, I have not been unaware of suggestions that a more radical revision, than mere updating, might be called for in light of works such as the latest editions of Benjamin, *On the Sale of Goods* that, in contrast to the position that existed when this book first appeared, now contain extensive material on the subject matter covered by this work. If I have not opted to adopt such suggestions, it is because many of the reported cases are published in the Lloyd's (Law) Reports, that are not always easily available, or accessible, in many areas of the world, and because the book has gained a reading public not confined to the United Kingdom alone, where such particular reports are more readily obtainable. I have therefore decided, not without considerable doubt or hesitation, to remain with the earlier format, which I have endeavoured to correct and expand as well as update. Instead I had planned to add limited marginal notes to the various sections of the book in the expectation that this would facilitate the readers' task of finding or drawing the more general principle emerging from the case or topic under consideration, but this had to be discarded as technically unfeasible. I can only hope that my judgment in this matter was correct. References to over 100 new decisions are included in this edition. Additionaly the relevant legislative changes that have taken place since the last edition was published in 1984, for example, The Carriage of Goods by Sea Act 1992, as well as the possible impact of modern practices, such as the sea waybill, or technological innovations, such as EDI (Electronic Data Interchange), on the traditional characteristics of the classic terms under consideration (particularly c.i.f.) have also been briefly noted.

DAVID M. SASSOON

Herzlia-Pituach, Israel.

January 1995.

PREFACE TO FIRST EDITION

The great majority of international shipping contracts may be classified either as c.i.f. contracts or f.o.b. contracts and clearly the editors of the *British Shipping Laws* series were wise to decide that Volume 5 should cover both these classes of contract. This will mean that the subscriber to the series will have in one volume a statement of the law relating to these two main instruments of overseas trade covering the law and practice applicable thereto and indicating the salient characteristics from which their similarities and differences may be directly ascertained.

This volume is a successor to the two earlier books upon which it was based, the first being the late Judge Kennedy's book on *C.I.F. Contracts* and the second being my own on *F.O.B. Contracts*. Judge Kennedy's book was first published in 1924, and, while the second edition was revised by the original author in 1928, the most recent edition is the third prepared by Mr. Dennis C. Thompson in 1959. By that time Judge Kennedy's original work had achieved a recognised status and the publication of the third edition after a lapse of thirty years clearly testifies to its general acceptance. My own work was first published in 1960 and there has as yet been no revised edition.

Both original works were intended for the purpose best explained by Judge Kennedy in his own preface. This was the desire to present the reader, whether practitioner, student or business man, with a concise and complete guide to important commercial topics which, prior to these publications, had not received separate treatment. This new work consolidates the law relating to the two main types of international trade contracts. The two original works differed in various respects, particularly in that Judge Kennedy's book was confined to English authorities and contained little comparative material, nor did it contain any of the speculation and hypothesis that was to be found in my book. On the other hand Judge Kennedy quoted more extensively from the relevant judgments delivered by the courts.

In combining the statement of the law on the two subjects in a single volume one of my main concerns has been to introduce uniformity and cohesion. As a result, in addition to bringing the law on both subjects up to date and dealing with the development since the last two separate volumes were written. I have endeavoured to follow Judge Kennedy's example more closely and have in both parts adopted the practice of providing more extensive quotation from judgments and reports, thus allowing the explanation of the law to be given in the words of the judges themselves and reducing speculation and hypothesis to a minimum,

Because c.i.f. and f.o.b. law is the outgrowth of the customs and usages of merchants rather than the product of legislation, the value of foreign practice and experience is correspondingly greater. This means that the decisions of foreign courts and of arbitrators throughout the world are of more than usual importance. I have, therefore, made use of comparative material wherever this has appeared appropriate and reference to foreign cases and international trade practice will be found in both parts of the book. On the other hand it has been possible (and indeed has been found necessary in order to avoid an unwieldly book) to condense some of the material, and moreover to introduce certain older English decisions, particularly in relation to c.i.f. contracts, which were not previously considered or noted. This I have done in order to make the record as complete as possible and I hope that the utility of these additional authorities will justify their incorporation.

Where the principles governing one instrument have been found to be applicable to the other it has been possible to avoid repetition by relating these underlying principles in the context of one of the two types of contract and by providing the necessary cross-references in treating the other type of contract. In some cases this method has meant shifting material from one part of the work to another and in doing this I have been guided by my own judgment as to the appropriate location for the treatment of any particular topic. I trust that this will be accepted and that no difficulties will arise in view of the cross-references which have been incorporated. With the exception of the table of contents, which is in two parts, all the other tables and the index incorporate references to both c.i.f. and f.o.b. contracts alike.

Apart from these matters I have made as few changes as possible and this is especially true with respect to both the form and substance of Judge Kennedy's work. For obvious reasons I felt that I had greater freedom in dealing with f.o.b. contracts where the text is based on my own book and therefore large portions of this have been rewritten. Furthermore in order to remain consistent with this approach I have also included an entirely new chapter devoted to conflict of laws in relation to both forms of contract whereas previously the topic was considered in relation to f.o.b. contracts only.

C.i.f. and f.o.b. law is a branch of the general law relating to the sale of goods. Because of the enormous volume of trade which has been transacted on the basis of one or the other of these terms they have been the subject of considerable judicial attention and consideration for many years. But massive as it is, no separate treatment of this body of law can be entirely complete with some consultation of other sources. This is, of course, equally true with respect to the governing principles of insurance, banking, carriage, agency and other particular branches of the law to which certain aspects of these transactions commonly yield. This work is, however, designed to be as exhaustive and self-contained as possible.

Finally, there is one additional aspect to which I feel I ought to draw the reader's attention. The origin of these terms and the factors which have throughout the years influenced their development and, more particularly, the considerations underlying the choice or preference of one term over another seem nowhere to have been recorded. It is a well-known fact that during the course of the last 150 years or so certain periods witnessed a rise in the volume of c.i.f. trade and a decline in f.o.b. trade. While in others the reverse was true. Case-law provides little if any clue or guidance on the matter. A certain degree of speculation is therefore inevitable. The value of such speculation the reader must however determine for himself. Bearing this *caveat* in mind an attempt to set forth the origin of the respective terms and to explain the reasons for their fluctuating fortunes will be found in Part Two of the book in the Introductory section of the first chapter devoted to f.o.b. contracts (*post*, §§ 319 *et seq.*).

I should like to avail myself of the opportunity to express my thanks to the following persons for their valuable help and assistance: to Mr. D. Suratgar for reading and commenting on the manuscript, to Mrs. K. Morris for the typing thereof, and to my wife Sheila and daughters Thalia and Ronit, without whose patience and understanding the timely completion of this work would not have been possible.

DAVID M. SASSOON

Washington, D.C.

January 1, 1967

CONTENTS

Part One

C.I.F. CONTRACTS

xi

Contents

Contents

Part Two

F.O.B. CONTRACTS

Contents

TABLE OF CASES

All references are to paragraph numbers

Table of Cases

Table of Cases

Table of Cases

Table of Cases

TABLE OF STATUTES

Sections set out in the text are shown in **bold**

FOREIGN LEGISLATION

TABLE OF RULES OF THE SUPREME COURT

Rules set out in the text are shown in **bold**

THE SALE OF GOODS ACT 1893 AND 1979—
COMPARATIVE TABLE

1893	1979
s. 1 (1)	s. 2 (1) (2)
(2)	2 (3)
(3)	2 (4) (5)
(4)	2 (6)
2	3
3	4
5	5
6	6
7	7
8 (1)	8 (1)
(2)	8 (2) (3)
9	9
10 (1)	10 (1) (2)
(2)	10 (3)
11 (1)	11 (1)
(a)	11 (2)
(b)	11 (3)
(c)	11 (4)
(2)	11 (1) (5)
(3)	11 (6)
12	Sch. 1, para. 3
(1) (a)	s. 12 (1)
(b)	12 (2)
(2)	12 (3)
(a)	12 (4)
(b)	12 (5)
13 (1)	13 (1) (2)
(2)	13 (3)
14	Sch. 1, paras. 5, 6
(1)	s. 14 (1)
(2)	14 (2)
(3)	14 (3)
(4)	14 (4)
(5)	14 (5)
15	Sch. 1, para. 7
(1)	s. 15(1)
(2)	15(2)

1893	1979
s. 16	s. 16
17	17
18	18
19	19
20	20 (1)
proviso 1	20 (2)
proviso 2	20 (3)
21	21
22 (1)	22 (1)
(3)	22 (2)
23	23
25 (1)	24
(2)	25 (1) (2)
(3)	26
27	27
28	28
29 (1)	29 (1) (2)
(2)	29 (3)
(3)	29 (4)
(4)	29 (5)
(5)	29 (6)
30 (1)	30 (1)
(2)	30 (2) (3)
(3)	30 (4)
(4)	30 (5)
31	31
32	32
33	33
34	34
35	35
36	36
37	37
38	38
39	39
40	40
41	41
42	42
43	43
44	44

1893	1979
s. 45	s. 54
46 (1)	46 (1)–(3)
(2)	(4)
47	47
48	48
49	49
50	50
51	51
52	52
53	53
54	54
55	Sch. 1, paras. 11, 12
(1)	s. 55 (1)
(2)	55 (2)
55A	Sch. 1, para. 13 (1) (3)
56	s. 59
57	60
58	57
59	58
61	62
(6)	Sch. 1, paras. 11, 13 (1) (3)
62 (1)	ss. 39 (2), 41 (2), 61 (1) (2), Sch. 1, paras. 11, 13 (1) (3)
(1A)	ss. 14 (6), 15 (3), Sch. 1, para. 5
(2)	s. 61 (3)
(3)	61 (4)
(4)	61 (5)
63	1 (1)

Part One

C.I.F. CONTRACTS

CHAPTER 1

THE NATURE OF A C.I.F. CONTRACT

Introductory

1   A contract of sale c.i.f. (cost, insurance and freight) is a contract for the sale of goods on special and well-recognised terms. It is a contract which contemplates the carriage of goods by sea, and for the better part of this century has constituted the most important instrument of the overseas trade.[1] It is known as a c.i.f. contract, for the price which the buyer has to pay is the *cost* of the goods, together with the *insurance* of the goods during transit and the *freight* to the port of destination.

Under this form of contract the seller performs his obligations by shipping, at the time specified in the contract or, in the absence of express provision in the contract, within a reasonable time, goods of the contractual description in a ship bound for the destination named in the contract, or by purchasing documents in respect of such goods already afloat, and by tendering to the buyer, as soon as possible after the goods have been destined to him, the shipping documents, *i.e.* a bill of lading for carriage of the goods, a policy of insurance covering the reasonable value of the goods, together with an invoice showing the amount due from the buyer.

It is to be observed that in a contract of sale c.i.f. there are two subordinate contracts made by the seller. There is first the contract of carriage by sea which is known as the contract of affreightment, under which the shipowner (the carrier) signs a bill of lading on receipt of the goods. Secondly, there is the contract of insurance in accordance with which the underwriters deliver a policy of insurance.

But aside from the essential ancillary relationships which every c.i.f. contract creates with the shipowner and insurer, respectively, performance of a c.i.f. transaction normally entails the introduction of further parties and gives rise to additional relationships which are supplemental thereto. The documentary nature of the transaction, for example, lends itself readily to the introduction of bankers and other financing or forwarding agents who may act for either seller or buyer as intermediaries. Consequently, a variety of

---

[1] Certain periods have witnessed a reduction in the volume of trade transacted on c.i.f. terms with a corresponding increase in the volume of f.o.b. contracts becoming apparent. The factors which account for these periodic fluctuations and for the particular choice of term in question are discussed *post*, § 431 *et seq.*

parties often acquire rights and liabilities with respect to the subject-matter of the c.i.f. contract in question. It should be noted, however, that these various relationships are not governed and regulated by the sale contract. They are subject to their own terms; as are also the contract of affreightment and the marine policy which establish an independent contractual nexus between the carrier and the insurer and any party claiming thereunder.

Essence of c.i.f. contract

2   The essential feature of a c.i.f. contract is that delivery is satisfied by delivery of documents and not by actual physical delivery of the goods. "All that the buyer can call for is delivery of the customary documents. This represents the measure of the buyer's right and the extent of the vendor's duty. The buyer cannot refuse the documents and ask for the actual goods, nor can the vendor withhold the documents and tender the goods they represent."[2]

"The vital question . . ." said Lord Porter in an oft-cited opinion,[3] "is whether the buyers paid for the documents as representing the goods or for the delivery of the goods themselves." On the same occasion Lord Simonds stated[4] that the "salient characteristic" of a c.i.f. contract was that "the property in the goods not only may but must pass[5] by delivery of the documents against which payment is made."

On presentation of the shipping documents, if they are complete and regular, the buyer is bound to pay the price, irrespective of the arrival of the goods. And the same is apparently true where the seller agrees to provide a certificate of quality at the port of discharge. Payment in such a case was held to be due even without presentation of such a certificate, and the buyers' failure to pay was considered a wrongful repudiation absolving the seller from any further obligation with respect to conformity, except for the buyers' right (in case such lack of conformity was subsequently established) to reduce his liability for damages on account thereof.[6] But by paying, the buyer is not precluded from subsequently rejecting the goods or recovering damages for breach of the contract of sale if on examination the goods are found not to be in accordance with the contract. If the goods are lost in transit or arrive in a damaged condition the buyer ordinarily has his remedy under the policy of insurance or against the carrier under the contract contained in the bill of lading. Whether in any particular case either of these remedies is available to him depends upon the terms of the policy of insurance and the bill of

---

[2] *Manbre Saccharine Co. Ltd. v. Corn Products Co. Ltd.* [1919] 1 K.B. 198 at p. 202, *per* McCardie J.
[3] *Comptoir d'Achat et de Vente du Boerenbond Belge S.A. v. Luis de Ridder Limitada (The Julia)* [1949] A.C. 293 at p. 312.
[4] *Ibid.* at p. 317.
[5] Either conditionally or unconditionally, see *post*, § 81.
[6] *Gill & Duffus S.A. v. Burger & Co. Inc.* [1984] 1 Lloyd's Rep. 227 (H.L.), *post*, § 325a.

lading. Obviously, discharge of the goods in c.i.f. contracts is at the buyer's expense, and the cost thereof, if any, may be claimed as damages where he exercises his right of rejection. This complexity has given birth to the well known observation by Roche J. that in a c.i.f. contract "there are three stages of delivery", *i.e.* "provisional delivery" on shipment, "symbolical delivery" on tender of the documents, and "complete delivery" when the goods are handed over to the buyer.[7] While performance of the latter duty will not normally require any further act by the seller, because, as noted by Devlin J. in *Kwei Tek Chao v. British Traders and Shippers Ltd.*,[8] "a (c.i.f.) buyer who takes delivery from the ship at the port of destination is not taking delivery of the goods under the contract of sale, but merely taking delivery out of his own warehouse, as it were ...", the seller must at least abstain from doing anything which will prevent the buyer from taking possession of the goods.

3   *"The key to the warehouse."* In effect, transfer of the bill of lading, accompanied by the policy of insurance, operates as constructive delivery of the goods. Possession of the bill of lading places the goods at the disposal of the buyer. "In the case of goods which are at sea being transmitted from one country to another, you cannot deliver actual possession of them, therefore the bill of lading is considered to be a symbol of the goods, and its delivery to be a delivery of them."[9] In the words of Bowen L. J. in *Sanders v. Maclean*[10].

> "A cargo at sea while in the hands of the carrier is necessarily incapable of physical delivery. During this period of transit and voyage, the bill of lading by the law merchant is universally recognised as its symbol, and the indorsement and delivery of the bill of lading operates as a symbolical delivery of the cargo. Property in the goods passes by such indorsement and delivery of the bill of lading, whenever it is the intention of the parties that the property should pass, just as under similar circumstances the property would pass by an actual delivery of goods. And for the purpose of passing such property in the goods and completing the title of the indorsee to full possession thereof, the bill of lading, until complete delivery of the cargo has been made on shore to someone rightfully claiming under it, remains in force as a symbol, and carries with it not only the full ownership of the goods, but also all rights created by the contract of carriage between the shipper and the shipowner. It is a key which in the hands of a rightful owner is intended to unlock the door of the warehouse, floating or fixed, in which the goods may chance to be."

The shipping documents required under a c.i.f. contract have been recognised in the past to be a bill of lading, a policy of insurance and an invoice. Such documents are required today also unless the contract otherwise provides. Modern methods of business, however, often involve a bill of lading covering more than the goods sold,[11] and a floating or open policy[12] of insur-

---

[7] *Schmoll Fils & Co. Inc. v. Scriven Bros. & Co.* (1924) 19 Ll.L. Rep. 118, 119.
[8] [1954] 2 Q.B. 459, *post*, § 335.
[9] *Per* Lord Hatherley L.C., *Barber v. Meyerstein* (1870) L.R. 4 H.L. 317 at p. 329.
[10] (1883) 11 Q.B.D. 327 at p. 341 (C.A.).
[11] See *post*, § 135.
[12] As to floating policies, see *post*, § 210.

ance whereby the seller declares to his underwriters the goods that are on risk at any particular time. In these circumstances it is now common to find that the seller under a c.i.f. sale has contracted to fulfil his obligations by tendering a delivery order in place of the bill of lading, and a certificate or letters of insurance instead of the actual policy. Such contracts, although departing from the strict requirements, are still regarded as falling within the general description of c.i.f. contracts.[13] Unless it appears to be the contrary, the general conditions of a c.i.f. sale are not waived by the substitution of a delivery order for a bill of lading.[14]

Presumably the result is the same where the contract contains a provision such as was present in *S.I.A.T. Di Dal Ferro v. Tradax Overseas S.A.*[15] by which it was stipulated that "If any document whatsoever required to be furnished by Seller is missing or in apparent contradiction with the clauses and condition of the sale-contract and/or if such document contains errors or omissions of any kind, the Buyer must nevertheless perform and take up the documents if the Seller gives written or cable notice to the Buyer that Seller guarantees performance in accordance with the clauses and conditions of the contract."[16] Likewise, the provisions (in whole or in part) of a standard (c.i.f.) contract may survive even though the contract is later modified by the parties to an ex-warehouse contract save in so far as those of the c.i.f. provisions which could not apply to the new transaction.[17]

C.i.f. contracts do not extend to the carriage of cargo by air, and the Air Consignment Note required under the Carriage by Air Act 1932 is not a document of title, nor is it generally negotiable. As has been noted by a knowledgable commentator:

> "Despite some superficial similarities, airborne trade markedly differs from sea-borne commerce in operational speed, geographical span, freight rate structure, inter-line coordination, loading, stowing and packaging techniques, appropriation of the goods to the contract and their checking in transit, carrier's risk and liability ... documentary requirements ... the methods of ... insurance and export finance and in several other technical, economic and procedural facets."[18]

4   *Advantages of c.i.f. contracts.* The advantages of the c.i.f. contract which have made it an indispensable instrument of sea-borne commerce are manifest. Its object is to enable cargoes afloat to be dealt with by transferring the documents representing the goods. The price to be paid informs the buyer of the amount he has to pay for the goods delivered at their destination, whatever

---

[13] *Per* Lord Porter in *Comptoir d'Achat, etc. v. Luis de Ridder Ltda.* [1949] A.C. 293 at p. 309. See *post*, § 18.

[14] *Ginzberg and Others v. Barrow Haematite Steel Co. Ltd. and McKellar* [1966] 1 Lloyd's Rep. 343 where a delivery order was used to expedite delivery, but this was held not to affect rights of an unpaid seller under a c.i.f. contract.

[15] [1980] 1 Lloyd's Rep. 53 (C.A.).

[16] But a promise to bear the resulting costs and expenses of non-conforming documents is no such guarantee of performance, *id.*

[17] See, *e.g. Promos S.A.* v. *European Grain and Shipping Ltd.* [1979] 1 Lloyd's Rep. 375.

[18] Pal, "Air Trade Terms" [1973] J.B.L. 9.

may be their place of origin, or the freight rates that have to be paid. The seller, while taking the risk of the rise or fall in the price of the goods, the cost of carriage[19] and the rate of insurance before shipment, has the advantage of being able to obtain payment of the price of the goods before their arrival at their destination, and even in the event of their loss or damage in transit. By stipulating for payment by an irrevocable letter of credit the seller may obtain cash for the goods sold immediately after shipment; or, if the terms of payment are "cash against documents," or "net cash" (which is the same thing), he may still obtain payment from the buyer a considerable time before the goods arrive at their destination. On the other hand, the buyer, having received the documents, has the power of dealing with the goods for some time, which may be substantial, in advance of their actual arrival. His right to reject the goods if they turn out not to be in conformity with the contract remains. The risk which he takes is the risk that loss of or damage to the goods may not be covered by the bill of lading or policy of insurance.

The protection given to the buyer by transfer of the documents is generally, but not necessarily, sufficient. It is not complete where loss or damage has been caused by a peril excepted by the bill of lading (or in respect of which the carrier's liability is limited) and not covered by the policy of insurance. In such case, the buyer must pay the price against the documents though he receives no indemnity (or less than full indemnity) in respect of the loss or damage. But in the case of risks customarily excluded by the contract of carriage and the policy of insurance, such, for example, as war risks, the buyer can, and generally should cover his interests by supplementary insurance on his own account.

As against these advantages, there are certain problems or disadvantages that must be noted. Because the buyer must pay upon presentation of proper documents, he will generally be unable to reject the documents on the grounds that non conforming goods were shipped, and he will be in a position to reject non-conforming documents even when the seller has shipped confirming goods.

Judicial definition

5   It is now proposed to consider the views that have been expressed by judicial authority on the meaning to be attached in law to a c.i.f. contract.

Lord Blackburn. For judicial description of a c.i.f. contract, it is not necessary to look back further than to the well-known exposition of Blackburn J. (as he then was) in the case of *Ireland v. Livingston,*[20] where he said[21]:

---

[19] For an instance of a c.i.f. contract where the buyer took the risk of the rise of freight after the date of the contract, see *Acetylene Corporation v. Canada Carbide Co.* (1921) 6 Ll.L. Rep. 410 at p. 468; 8 Ll.L. Rep. 456 (C.A.).
[20] (1872) L.R. 5 H.L. 395.
[21] *Ibid.* at p. 406.

"The terms at a price 'to cover cost, freight and insurance, payment by acceptance on receiving shipping documents,' are very usual, and are perfectly well understood in practice. The invoice is made out debiting the consignee with the agreed price (or the actual cost and commission, with the premiums of insurance, and the freight, as the case may be), and giving him credit for the amount of the freight[22] which he will have to pay to the ship-owner on actual delivery, and for the balance a draft is drawn on the consignee which he is bound to accept (if the shipment be in conformity with his contract) on having handed to him the charterparty,[23] bill of lading, and policy of insurance. Should the ship arrive with the goods on board he will have to pay the freight, which will make up the amount he has engaged to pay. Should the goods not be delivered in consequence of a peril of the sea, he is not called on to pay the freight, and he will recover the amount of his interest in the goods under the policy. If the non-delivery is in consequence of some misconduct on the part of the master or mariners, not covered by the policy, he will recover it from the shipowner. . . .

In such a case it is obvious that if freight is high, the consignor gets the less for the goods he supplies, if freight is low he gets the more. But inasmuch as he has contracted to supply the goods at this price he is bound to do so, though, owing to the rise in prices at the port of shipment making him pay more for the goods, or of freight causing him to receive less himself, because the shipowner receives more, his bargain may turn out a bad one. On the other hand, if owing to the fall in prices in the port of shipment, or of freight, the bargain is a good one, the consignee still must pay the full agreed price. This results from the contract being one by which the one party binds himself absolutely to supply the goods in a vessel such as is stipulated for, at a fixed price, to be paid for in the customary manner, that is, part by acceptance on receipt of the customary documents, and part by paying the freight on delivery, and the other party binds himself to pay that fixed price. Each party there takes upon himself the risk of the rise or fall in price, and there is no contract of agency or trust between them, and therefore no commission is charged.''

6   *Lord Sumner.* In *Biddell Brothers v. E. Clemens Horst Company*[24] Hamilton J. (afterwards Lord Sumner) defined the obligations arising on a contract of sale on c.i.f. terms as follows[25]

"A seller under a contract of sale containing such terms has firstly to ship at the port of shipment goods of the description contained in the contract; secondly to procure a contract of affreightment, under which the goods will be delivered at the destination contemplated by the contract; thirdly to arrange for an insurance upon the terms current in the trade which will be available for the benefit of the buyer; fourthly to make out an invoice as described by Blackburn J. in *Ireland v. Livingston*[26] or in some similar form; and finally to tender these documents to the buyer so that he may know what freight he has to pay and obtain delivery of the goods, if they arrive, or recover for their loss if they are lost on the voyage. Such terms constitute an agreement that the delivery of the goods, provided they

---

[22] *Freight may however have to be prepaid, see post,* § 104.
[23] The obligation is to deliver a contract of affreightment. For this the bill of lading is normally sufficient, and accordingly the charterparty is not generally required. See *Finska Cellulosaforeningen v. Westfield Paper Co.* [1940] 4 All E.R. 473. *Post,* § 102.
[24] [1911] 1 K.B. 214.
[25] *Ibid.* at p. 220.
[26] *Ante* § 5.

are in conformity with the contract, shall be delivery on board ship at the port of shipment. It follows that against tender of these documents, the bill of lading, invoice, and policy of insurance, which completes delivery in accordance with that agreement, the buyer must be ready and willing to pay the price."

7   As to the first two of these requisites, Scrutton J. in *Landauer & Co. v. Craven & Speeding Bros.* said,[27] "I should add to the first requisite the words 'within the time named in the contract'; and to the second that such a contract must be procured on shipment. I should make the last addition for the reason that the seller must, as soon as possible after he has sent forward the cargo, send forward the documents to the vendee or consignee. See *per* Lord Esher in *Sanders v. Maclean.*"[28] Both additions were referred to with approval in *Hansson v. Hamel & Horley Ltd.*,[29] but with regard to the latter Lord Sumner, with whose judgment in the House of Lords the other Lords agreed, stated[30] "I do not understand this proposition as meaning that the bill of lading would be bad, unless it was signed contemporaneously with the actual placing of the goods on board. 'On shipment' is an expression of some latitude. Bills of lading are constantly signed after the loading is complete and, in some cases, after the ship has sailed. I do not think that they thereby necessarily cease to be procured 'on shipment,' nor do I suppose that the learned judge so intended his words."

In *C. Sharpe & Co. v. Nosawa & Co.*[31] Atkin J. said:

> "It is reasonably plain that such a contract is performed by the vendor taking reasonable steps to deliver as soon as possible after shipment the shipping documents, including the bill of lading and policy of insurance, and the buyer paying the price against the documents unless there is some other stipulation as to payment in the contract. . . . The contract is performed in fact, and the date of its performance is the date when the documents would come forward, the vendor making every reasonable effort to forward them."

8   *Lord Atkinson.* The effect of the authorities was summarised by Lord Atkinson in the House of Lords in *Johnson v. Taylor Bros.*,[32] in a statement that has been accepted as the modern definition of a c.i.f. contract.[33]

> "The authorities I shall presently cite establish clearly, I think, that when a vendor and purchaser of goods situated as they were in this case[34] enter into a c.i.f. contract, such as that entered into in the present case,[35] the vendor in the absence of any special provision to the contrary is bound by his contract to do

---

[27] [1912] 2 K.B. 94 at p. 105.
[28] (1883) 11 Q.B.D. 327 at p. 337.
[29] [1922] 2 A.C. 36.
[30] *Ibid.* at p. 47.
[31] [1917] 2 K.B. 814 at pp. 818, 819.
[32] [1920] A.C. 144 at p. 155.
[33] *e.g.* by Lord Merriman P. in *The Gabbiano* [1940] P. 166. *Post,* § 13.
[34] Seller in Sweden and buyers in England.
[35] Ordinary c.i.f. terms.

six things. First, to make out an invoice of the goods sold. Second, to ship at the port of shipment goods of the description contained in the contract. Third, to procure[36] a contract of affreightment under which the goods will be delivered at the destination contemplated by the contract. Fourth, to arrange for an insurance upon the terms current in the trade which will be available for the benefit of the buyer. Fifthly, with all reasonable despatch to send forward and tender to the buyer these shipping documents, namely, the invoice, bill of lading and policy of assurance, delivery of which to the buyer is symbolical of delivery of the goods purchased, placing the same at the buyer's risk and entitling the seller to payment of their price. These authorities are, *Ireland v. Livingston,*[37] *per* Blackburn J.; *Biddell Bros. v. E. Clemens Horst Co.*[38]; on appeal *E. Clemens Horst Co. v. Biddell Bros.*[39]; and *C. Sharpe & Co. v. Nosawa Co.*[40]. These cases also establish that if no place be named in the c.i.f. contract for the tender of the shipping documents they must prima facie be tendered at the residence or place of business of the buyer.''[41]

9   *Lord Wright.* A notable contribution to the judicial pronouncements on c.i.f. contracts was made in the House of Lords by Lord Wright in the case of *Ross T. Smyth & Co. Ltd. v. T. D. Bailey, Son & Co.*[42] His words are particularly illuminating on the commercial significance of the passing of the property in such a contract. In the course of his judgment he said:[43]

"The contract in question here is of a type familiar in commerce, and is described as a c.i.f. contract. The initials indicate that the price is to include cost, insurance and freight. It is a type of contract which is more widely and more frequently in use than any other contract used for purposes of seaborne commerce. An enormous number of transactions, in value amounting to untold sums, are carried out every year under c.i.f. contracts. The essential characteristics of the this contract have often been described. The seller has to ship or acquire after that shipment the contract goods, as to which, if unascertained, he is generally required to give a notice of appropriation.[44] On or after shipment, he has to obtain proper bills of lading and proper policies of insurance. He fulfils his contract by transferring the bills of lading and the policies to the buyer. As a general rule, he does so only against payment of the price, less the freight, which the buyer has to pay. In the invoice which accompanies the tender of the documents on the 'prompt'—that is, the date fixed for payment—the freight is deducted, for this reason. In this course of business, the general property in the goods remains in the seller until he transfers the bills of lading. These rules, which are simple enough to state in general terms, are of the utmost importance in commercial transactions. . . . The property which the seller retains while he or his agent, or the banker to whom he has pledged the documents, retains the bills of lading is the general property, and not a special property by way of security. In general, however, the importance of the retention of the property is not only to secure

[36] There might be added the words "on shipment," see *ante,* § 7.
[37] (1871) L.R. 5 H.L. 395 at p. 406.
[38] [1911] 1 K.B. 934 at p. 962.
[39] [1912] A.C. 18.
[40] [1917] 2 K.B. 814.
[41] Atkin J. *dubitante* as to place of tender in *Stein, Forbes & Co. v. County Tailoring Co.* (1916) 115 L.T. 215. See *post,* § 244.
[42] [1940] 3 All E.R. 60.
[43] *Ibid.* at p. 67.
[44] As to notice of appropriation, see *post,* § 279.

payment from the buyer but for purposes of finance. The general course of international commerce involves the practice of raising money on the documents so as to bridge the period between shipment and the time of obtaining payment against documents. These credit facilities, which are of the first importance, would be completely unsettled if the incidence of the property were made a matter of doubt. By mercantile law, the bills of lading are the symbols of the goods. The general property in the goods must be in the seller if he is to be able to pledge them. The whole system of commercial credits depends on the seller's ability to give a charge on the goods and the policies of insurance. A mere unpaid seller's lien would, for obvious reasons, be inadequate and unsatisfactory.''

10 A more recent statement of the definition was made by Lord Porter in the House of Lords in the case of *Comptoir d'Achat et de Vente du Boerenbond Belge S.A. v. Luis de Ridder Limitada (The Julia).*[45] He there expressed the view that a c.i.f. contract modified in the current way so as to suit modern requirements, with a delivery order substituted for a bill of lading, and a certificate of insurance for a policy, was none the less a c.i.f. contract.

Province of c.i.f. contracts

11 It is now necessary to consider how far the definition of a c.i.f. contract can extend, and to distinguish c.i.f. contracts from other forms of shipping contracts.

Contracts not strictly c.i.f. Not every contract of sale which is expressed to be c.i.f. is strictly a c.i.f. contract. Sometimes terms are introduced into contracts in that form which conflict with c.i.f. terms, and prevent them from being c.i.f. contracts proper.

The Parchim[46] is a notable instance of this. The contract there was in the nature of a cross between c.i.f. and f.o.b. (free on board). The price included cost and chartered freight to a European port, but did not include the premium for insurance. There were also provisions that in a certain event the buyer was to find another ship to take the goods, and in that event was to pay for storage until loading and for any excess freight over the chartered freight.

''The contract,'' said Lord Parker of Waddington in the House of Lords commenting thereon,[47] ''has far more of the characteristics of a contract f.o.b. Taltal [a port in Chile] than it has of a contract c.i.f. European port.''

It also frequently happens that forms of contract containing printed terms inapplicable to or unsuitable for c.i.f. contracts are used to carry out c.i.f. transactions. In such cases, unless the conflicting terms can either be recon-

---

[45] [1949] A.C. 293, set out fully, *post*, § 17.
[46] [1918] A.C. 157. See also *Comptoir d'Achat, etc. v. Luis de Ridder Ltda.* [1949] A.C. 293. *Post*, § 17.
[47] [1918] A.C. 157 at p. 164.

ciled with the essential provisions of c.i.f. contracts or disregarded or rejected as repugnant to the intended transaction, the character of the contract is changed. Thus, for example, contracts are to be found which, while expressed to be c.i.f., contain terms to the effect that the goods are to be at the risk of the seller until actual delivery to the buyer; that the contract is to be void for any portion shipped but not arriving; that an allowance is to be made for damaged condition on arrival; and that payment is to be on landing or landed weights. Some of these terms (and particularly the first) vitiate the meaning of the c.i.f. contract, whereas others merely impose additional obligations that can be reconciled with its basic pattern. In some cases the repugnant clause has been disregarded.

12   Thus, in *Law & Bonar Ltd. v. British American Tobacco Co. Ltd.*,[48] a printed clause in the contract that the goods were to be at the seller's risk until actual delivery to the buyers was treated by Rowlatt J. as repugnant to a transaction which was otherwise on c.i.f. terms, and the clause was held to be inapplicable.

While in *Denbigh, Cowan & Co. v. Atcherley & Co.*[49] the presence in a contract, expressed to be c.i.f., of the terms "net landing weights," "should the goods or any portion thereof not arrive from loss of vessel either before or after declaration this contract for such portion to be void," "payment cash (before delivery if required) against documents or delivery order," did not prevent the Court of Appeal, having regard to all its terms, from holding that the contract was to be treated as a c.i.f. contract.

So, too, where a c.i.f. contract provided that "insurance to be at [sellers'] risk" the Scottish Court of Session held in *A. Delaurier & Co. v. J. Wyllie & Others*[50] that the provision did not alter the nature of the contract in question, and that the property in the goods passed to the buyers when the bills of lading were forwarded. The clause held to imply no more than that the sellers had undertaken to obtain cover and had guaranteed to effect the necessary insurance.

And in *Petroleo Brasileiro, S.A., Petro v. Ameropan Oil Corp.*[51] the United States District Court in New York dismissed as wholly without merit the contention that the contract was not truly on c.i.f. terms, albeit so designated, because payment was not to be made until 30 days after delivery, and because the seller committed a breach by retaining the original bill of lading and certificate of insurance.

In *Congimex Companhia Geral de Comercia Importadora e Exportadora, S.à.r.l. v. Tradax Export S.A.*,[52] four c.i.f. contracts (on GAFTA terms) were subject to weighing and sampling in Lisbon. As a result of a supervening import prohibition imposed by the Portuguese Government, the buyers

---

[48] [1916] 2 K.B. 605. Approved in *comptoir d'Achat, etc. v. Luis Ridder Ltda.*, [1949] A.C. 293.
[49] (1921) 90 L.J.K.B. 836 (C.A.). See *post*, § 207.
[50] (1889) 17 R. (Ct. of Sess.) 167.
[51] 372 F. Supp. 503 (1974).
[52] [1983] 1 Lloyd's Rep. 250 (C.A.) affirming [1981] 2 Lloyd's Rep. 687.

attempted to justify cancellation of the contracts on the ground that they had been frustrated. Though the provisions in question (concerning weighing and sampling) imposed obligations to be performed at the port of destination (which were beyond the scope of the regular or classic c.i.f. contract) liability to discharge this obligation, in the circumstances considered, did not amount to frustration. First, because no proof was furnished that weighing or sampling was prohibited, if delivery at Lisbon would have been for the purpose of reshipment or transhipment to a non-Portuguese destination. Such a finding being an essential pre-requisite to any conclusion that the contracts were frustrated on the basis that some part of them had to be performed in Portugal, and that such performance was illegal by Portuguese law. Secondly, because even if such impossibility did obtain (in respect of some minor aspect of performance), it would amount to frustration only if it destroyed the commercial basis of the contracts.

As a general rule, the designation by the parties of a contract as a c.i.f. contract creates a strong inference in favour of its so being construed, and, unless that inference is overcome by express provisions showing that the parties intended otherwise, its meaning is not vitiated.

However, As Roskill L. J. Noted In *Concord Petroleum Corp. v. Gosford Marine Panama S.a. (The Albazero)*[53]:

> "It is a trite observation that what is sometimes called a true f.o.b. or a true c.i.f. contract is a comparative commercial rarity. Contracts vary infinitely according to the wishes of the parties to them. Though a contract may include the letters f.o.b. or c.i.f. amongst its terms, it may well be that other terms of the contract clearly show that the use of those letters is intended to do no more than show where the incidence of liability for freight or insurance will lie as between buyer and seller but is not to denote the mode of performance of the seller's obligations to the buyer or of the buyer's obligations to the seller. In other cases, though the letters c.i.f. are used, other terms of the contract may show that the property is intended to pass on shipment and not upon tender of and payment against the documents so tendered or though the letters f.o.b. are used, other terms may show that the property was not intended to pass on shipment but upon tender and payment, the seller by the form in which he took the bill of lading intending to reserve his right of disposal of the property until he was paid against the shipping documents. . . ."

Finally, it should be noted that the parties themselves may subsequently alter the terms of their contract, and agree to other terms in lieu of those originally stipulated. Thus, *e.g.* in *Redler Grain Silos Ltd. v. Bicc Ltd.*[54] a c and f contract for delivery of electrical cable and equipment to Iran was concluded between English sellers and buyers. Thereafter, the buyers agreed to pre-pay the contract price. Later events in Iran prevented shipment completely, and it was agreed that the buyers would take delivery of the goods in England against invoices, and that the sellers would repay the freight

---

[53] [1975] 2 Lloyd's Rep. 295 at p. 302. This decision was overruled by the House of Lords in [1977] A.C. 774, *post*, § 162 without, however, affecting the validity of the said observation.
[54] [1982] 1 Lloyd's Rep. 435 (C.A.).

charges. The Iranian Government then claimed delivery of the goods and the sellers wished to accommodate them. But the Court of Appeal held that the buyers were entitled to an injunction restraining the sellers from shipping goods to Iran as they admitted that the original c and f contract was varied, and that the property in the goods had unconditionally passed to the buyers.

13   *Conditional c.i.f. terms.* There may also be contracts on c.i.f. terms made subject to conditions which, when they are satisfied, will change the nature of the contract altogether. Until, however, these conditions come into operation the contract is to be treated as a c.i.f. contract.

In *Karinjee Jivanjee & Co. v. William F. Malcolm & Co.*[55] Roche J., affirming a decision of the umpire in an arbitration, held that a contract for the sale of a quantity of East African sisal c.i.f. U.K. and/or Continental port or ports which included the provision that "Should the goods or any portion thereof not arrive from loss of vessel or other unavoidable cause, this contract to be void for any such portion . . ." is a contingent c.i.f. contract. The meaning of the clause is that if before the contract is performed by the tender of the documents and payment, there is a loss of goods appropriated to the contract, the sellers are not entitled to claim performance in respect of the goods which have been lost. But after the tender of the documents neither the buyer nor the seller is entitled to claim rescission of the contract. In this case, a portion of the sisal covered by the contract was shipped on a vessel that caught fire. The buyer paid the price of the consignment against tender of the documents prior to the accident and recovered from the underwriters under the policy an amount which was larger than what they had paid the seller. The seller claimed this excess from the buyer relying on the above-mentioned clause, but the action failed.

In *The Gabbiano*,[56] a Prize case, there was a contract for the sale of iron ore from Sinai expressed to be c.i.f. Stettin. Clause 8(a) of the contract provided: "If, after loading, any steamer stemmed under this contract is lost, or is, for any reason, unable to deliver the cargo or any part thereof, the quantity of ore so undelivered by such steamer shall be written off the contract quantity. . . ." The risk during transit was thus to be borne not by the buyer, which would normally be the case in a c.i.f. contract, but by the seller. Lord Merriman P., considering how far this was a c.i.f. contract, said[57]:

"The essentials of a c.i.f. contract proper have been summarised authoritatively in several well-known judgments. I am content to refer, without quotation, to the recapitulation of them by Lord Atkinson in *Johnson v. Taylor Bros. & Co. Ltd.*[58] By this test, clause 8(a) of this contract is inappropriate to a c.i.f. contract proper (compare *Scrutton on Charterparties* (14th ed.) in the notes to Art. 59, at p.

---

[55] (1926) 25 Ll.L.Rep. 28.
[56] [1940] P. 166.
[57] *Ibid.* at p. 174.
[58] [1920] A.C. 144 at p. 155.

206,[59] and Judge Kennedy's book on c.i.f. contracts (2nd ed.) at p. 5),[60] for the goods are not at the buyers' risk in the events referred to in that clause. Nevertheless the contract may remain, as it is expressed to be, a c.i.f. contract but with variations: see for example *Denbigh Cowan & Co. v. Atcherley & Co.*[61] and *Karinjee Jivanjee & Co. v. William F. Malcolm & Co.*[62] For example, if the circumstances provided for in clause 8(a) never arose, the contract would, in normal conditions, be performed according to its tenor as an ordinary c.i.f. contract. Nor would any practical inconvenience result if the contract had to be resolved in whole or in part by a loss covered by the insurance policy after the buyer had taken up the documents, or even if he had taken them after, but in ignorance of, the loss. If, however, a total loss occurred to the knowledge of the parties before tender of the documents, the argument on both sides assumed, as I think correctly, that, contrary to the law applicable to a c.i.f. contract proper (see *Manbre Saccharine Co. v. Corn Products Co.*[63]), the sellers could not call upon the buyers to take up the documents, at any rate if the sellers still retained the bills of lading in their own possession at the material time.''

14 *Terms relating to delivery or arrival.* The mere fact that there is reference to delivery or arrival in a c.i.f. contract is not sufficient to alter the effect of the c.i.f. term.

Thus, in *Tregelles v. Sewell*[64] the contract was for the sale of ''300 tons of Old Bridge rails at £5 14s. 6d. per ton *delivered at Harburgh*, less freight and insurance; payment by net cash in London, less freight, upon handing bill of lading and policy of insurance,'' and it was held in the Court of Exchequer and the Exchequer Chamber that according to the true construction of the contract the seller did not contract to deliver the iron at Harburgh; that when he put it on a ship bound for Harburgh and handed to the buyers the policy of insurance and other documents, his liability ceased and the goods were at the risk of the buyer.

The parties, of course, contemplate the delivery of the goods sold at their destination, and it is, therefore, not unnatural that references to arrival of the ship or the goods or delivery of the goods should be found in many contracts expressed to be on c.i.f. terms. A common case is where the contract is expressed to be c.i.f. but provides for payment on arrival of the ship. In such a case if the ship is lost, unless the language used implies a condition of arrival before the liability to pay arises, payment is due at the time when the ship in ordinary course would have arrived. In other words, the term as to arrival of the ship denotes the time when payment is due and is not a condition of payment. In *Fragano v. Long*,[65] where an order was sent from Naples to Birmingham for goods ''to be dispatched on insurance being effected.

---

[59] See now (19th ed.), Art. 95, p. 187.
[60] See text ante, § 11.
[61] (1921) 90 L.J.K.B. 836.
[62] (1926) 25 Ll.L Rep. 28.
[63] [1919] 1 K.B. 198. *Post*, § 208.
[64] (1862) 7 H. & N. 574. And see *per* Kennedy L.J., *Biddell Bros. v. E. Clemens Horst* Co. [1911] 1 K.B. 934 at p. 963. For earlier cases where the contracts were in somewhat similar form, see 7 H. & N. at p. 586n.
[65] (1825) 4 B. & C. 219.

Terms to be three months' credit from the time of arrival," the goods were damaged in transit. It was held, that the property in the goods vested on dispatch, and that the terms of the order did not make the arrival of the goods at Naples a condition precedent to the liability to pay for them. "If, however, the goods were not to be paid for unless they arrived why should the plaintiff (buyer) insure them? That shows that the arrival was not considered as a condition precedent to the payment. . . . If they did not arrive, still the plaintiff would be bound to pay in a reasonable time after the arrival became impossible."[66]

15   A provision that payment is to be against documents "on arrival of the goods"[67] is also quite common. The effect frequently is to make arrival a condition of payment. In *Dupont v. British South Africa Co.*,[68] where there were sales of bullocks to be shipped at Buenos Aires c.i.f. Beira, and the contracts provided that half the price was payable on shipment in exchange for the documents and the balance was to be paid upon delivery of the shipments, Kennedy J. held that the balance of the price was payable only if and so far as the sellers were in a position to give delivery of the shipments, *i.e.* on the contingency of the goods actually arriving. Similarly, in *Polenghi v. Dried Milk Co.*,[69] where the contract, expressed to be c.i.f. London, contained the clause "payment to be made in cash in London on *arrival of the powders* against shipping or railway documents," Kennedy J. said that the sellers, to obtain payment, must show that the goods were *arrived goods*. But, unless the contract clearly requires otherwise, such a provision, it is submitted, ought to be construed as merely specifying the time when, and not stating a condition upon which, payment is to be made[70]; that is to say, if the goods shipped do not arrive, payment will be due against the shipping documents at the time when, but for the loss, the goods would have arrived. If this construction cannot be placed upon the words, the contract is not really a c.i.f. contract.[71]

---

[66] *Per* Bayley J., *ibid.* At p. 222.

[67] "Subject to safe arrival" was considered in *Barnett v. Javeri & Co.* [1916] 2 K. B. 390, where Bailhache J. held that the word "safe" showed that the event provided against was non-arrival of the goods *after shipment*, and therefore there was an absolute obligation on the seller to ship or to see that the goods were shipped, and, not having done so, he was liable for non-delivery.

[68] (1901) 18 T.L.R. 24. The decision in *Calcutta and Burmah Steam Navigation Co. v. De Mattos* (1863) 32 L.J.Q.B. 322; 33 *ibid.* 214 on a contract for delivery at Rangoon, containing similar terms as to payment, was to a similar effect.

[69] (1904) 10 Com.Cas. 42. In *Scriven Bros. & Co. v. Schmoll Fils & Co.* (1924) 40 T.L.R. 677, where a c.i.f. contract contained the clause "no claim shall be valid unless made within two weeks after the goods are delivered," the delivery contemplated by the clause was held to mean the actual delivery of the goods and not, as the sellers contended, delivery of the documents.

[70] *Cf. Fragano v. Long, ubi supra.* See also *Plaimar Ltd. v. Waters Trading Co. Ltd.* (1945) 72 C.L.R. 304 (Australia), c.i.f. terms not vitiated by the following stipulations: "Price . . . nett landed weight . . . terms nett cash against delivery order or bill of lading," the inference being that arrival and weighing were not conditions precedent to payment. For the facts of this case see *post*, § 96.

[71] In *Produce Brokers New Company (1924) Ltd. v. Wray, Sanderson & Co. Ltd.* (1931) 39 Ll. L. Rep. 257, the contract included a delivered weight clause and the court held that as regards "the right of payment . . . the goods remained at the sellers' risk". The decision notes that the

16   So in *Cundill v. A. W. Milhauser Corporation*[72] the Court of Appeals of New York held that a contract (designated as c.i.f. New York) that included the following provisions: "Insurance—For account of sellers"[73]; "Payment—Net cash against shipping documents payable upon arrival of steamer," and, finally, "No arrival—no sale," was not a c.i.f. contract. The action was for the purchase price of the goods shipped from Hamburg, and was lodged by the seller upon refusal of the buyer to pay against tender of the documents after arrival of the goods at New York.

Hubbs J. (with whose opinion the other members of the court, including Cardozo C. J. and Pound J., concurred) stated as follows:

> "Postponement of the time of payment alone would not prevent the contract from being a true c.i.f. contract, as provision for future payment of the price would not affect the vesting of title. Here, however, was more than a postponement of time of payment of the price and in effect an agreement that shipping documents were not to be forwarded but to be presented after arrival of the steamer, manifesting an agreement that if the steamer did not arrive, no payments were to be made and clearly indicating that the risk of the voyage was on the seller. So also the words "No arrival, no sale," are repugnant to the idea of a c.i.f. contract. . . .
>
> The letters c.i.f. in the contract created an inference that the instrument was in fact a c.i.f. contract. The express terms of the contract were, however, utterly inconsistent with such inference. The express terms must prevail, and the letters c.i.f. must be limited and applied to the price and not to the passing of title."

Consequently, the seller's action for the purchase price was denied, his remedy being limited to an action for damages for non acceptance.

17   *Comptoir d'Achat et de Vente du Boerenbond Belge S. A. v. Luis de Ridder Limitada (The Julia)*.[74] The whole question was considered at some length by the House of Lords in this case and the view plainly expressed that the criterion of a c.i.f. contract was that the buyer undertook to pay for and accept the documents as representing the goods rather than the goods themselves.

By a contract dated April 24, 1940, the sellers, a company in the Argentine, sold to a company in Belgium 500 tons of Plate rye for shipment "c.i.f. Antwerp." The printed contract of the London Corn Trade Association provided for payment in exchange for bills of lading and/or delivery orders, and policies and/or certificates of insurance. The contract also provided that the condition of the grain was to be guaranteed on arrival and any deficiency in

---

contract was of a "mixed character" since for some purposes it was a c.i.f. contract, and in other respects it was a contract for delivery of actual goods (at p. 260). As to such provisions see *post*, § 19. If the decision is based on the premise that the loss in that case was due to a transportation (or ordinary) as opposed to a marine (or extraordinary) risk it is in line with the general principles controlling conditional c.i.f. contracts. But if it goes further than that its correctness is, with respect, questionable since it is impossible to reconcile the term with the basic premise under which the risk of (extraordinary) loss in transit is, in a c.i.f. contract, on the buyer.
[72] 275 N.Y. 416; 178 N.E. 680 (1931).
[73] Which the court interpreted as meaning for the "benefit" of the seller.
[74] [1949] A.C. 293 (Lords Porter, Simmons, du Parcq, Normand and MacDermott).

the arrived grain below the bill of lading weights was to be paid for by the sellers. 1,120 tons of grain were shipped on board the *Julia*, the master having signed a bill of lading for delivery to the order of the seller's agents in Antwerp. On April 30, the sellers' agents sent to the buyers a form of delivery order addressed to Messrs. Van Bree of Antwerp, who acted as cargo superintendents for the sellers, requesting them to release the contract quantity of grain on arrival of the cargo, and this document was endorsed by Van Bree with an undertaking to honour the request. Insurance certificates were sent to Van Bree in accordance with the usual course of dealing between the parties. The buyers accepted the delivery order (together with an invoice) and paid the price to the sellers. In May 1940, while the *Julia* was at sea, Belgium was invaded by the Germans. The sellers thereupon directed the vessel to Lisbon, where the cargo was sold.

18   The buyers demanded the return of the price, claiming that there had been a total failure of performance. Morris J. upheld the award of the umpire in favour of the sellers on the ground that the contract was a modified form of c.i.f. contract under which the buyers had obtained a delivery order of some commercial value. His judgment was affirmed by the Court of Appeal (Lord Greene M. R. and Croom-Johnson J., Asquith L. J. dissenting). The buyers then appealed to the House of Lords. This appeal was allowed, it being held that, on its true construction, the contract was not an agreement for the sale of goods c.i.f. Antwerp but a contract to deliver to Antwerp.

Lord Porter in the course of his judgment said[75]:

> "The obligations imposed upon a seller under a c.i.f. contract are well known, and in the ordinary case include the tender of a bill of lading covering the goods contracted to be sold and no others, coupled with an insurance policy in the normal form and accompanied by an invoice which shows the price and, as in this case, usually contains a deduction of the freight which the buyer pays before delivery at the port of discharge. Against tender of these documents the purchaser may pay the price. In such a case the property may pass either on shipment or on tender, the risk generally passes on shipment or as from shipment, but possession does not pass until the documents which represent the goods are handed over in exchange for the price. In the result the buyer after receipt of the documents can claim against the ship for breach of the contract of carriage and against the underwriter for any loss covered by the policy. The strict form of c.i.f. contract may, however, be modified: a provision that a delivery order may be substituted for a bill of lading or a certificate of insurance for a policy would not, I think, make the contract concluded upon something other than c.i.f. terms, but in deciding whether it comes within that category or not, all the permutations and combinations of provision and circumstance must be taken into consideration. Not every contract which is expressed to be a c.i.f. contract is such. Sometimes, as in *The Parchim*,[76] terms are introduced into contracts so described which conflict with c.i.f. provisions. In the present case therefore it is not as if a usual form of delivery order had been given and accepted or an insurance certi-

---

[75] *Ibid.* at p. 309.
[76] [1918] A.C. 157.

ficate covering the parcel was in the hands of Van Bree as agents for the buyers, nor can a solution be found in the mere designation of the contract as c.i.f. This is not a case in which the overriding provision is the term c.i.f. under which antagonistic terms can be neglected on the ground that they are repugnant to the transaction, as was done by Rowlatt J. in *Law & Bonar Ltd. v. British American Tobacco Co. Ltd.*[77] The true effect of all its terms must be taken into account, though, of course, the description c.i.f. must not be neglected. . . .

"The object and the result of a c.i.f. contract is to enable sellers and buyers to deal with cargoes or parcels afloat and to transfer them freely from hand to hand by giving constructive possession of the goods which are being dealt with. Undoubtedly the practice of shipping and insuring produce in bulk is to make the process more difficult, but a ship's delivery order and a certificate of insurance transferred to or held for a buyer still leaves it possible for some, though less satisfactory, dealing with the goods whilst at sea to take place. The practice adopted between buyers and sellers in the present case renders such dealing well nigh impossible. The buyer gets neither propery nor possession until the goods are delivered to him at Antwerp, and the certificate of insurance, if it enures to his benefit at all, except on the journey from ship to warehouse, has never been held for or delivered to him. Indeed it is difficult to see how a parcel is at the buyers' risk when he has neither property nor possession except in such cases as *Inglis v. Stock*[78] and *Sterns Ltd. v. Vickers Ltd.*[79] where the purchaser had an interest in an undivided part of a bulk parcel on board ship, or elsewhere, obtained by attornment of the bailee to him.

"The vital question in the present case, as I see it, is whether the buyers paid for the documents as representing the goods or for the delivery of the goods themselves. The time and place of payment are elements to be considered but by no means conclusive of the question: such considerations may, on the one hand, indicate a payment in advance or, on the other, they may show a payment postponed until the arrival of the ship, though the property in the goods or the risk have passed to the buyer whilst the goods are still at sea, as in *Castle v. Playford*[80] But the whole circumstances have to be looked at and where, as, in my opinion, is the case here, no further security beyond that contained in the original contract passed to the buyers as a result of payment, where the property and possession both remained in the sellers until delivery in Antwerp, where the sellers were to pay for deficiency in bill of lading weight, guaranteed condition on arrival and made themselves responsible for all averages, the true view, I think, is that it is not a c.i.f. contract even in a modified form but a contract to deliver at Antwerp."

On somewhat similar grounds the Judicial Committee of the Privy Council, on appeal from Ceylon (as it was then known), held in *Holland Colombo Trading Society Ltd. v. Segu Mohamed Khaja Alawedeen*[81] that a contract expressed to be on c.i.f. terms permitting "any tender or delivery of the goods or of the bill of lading" was not a true c.i.f. contract since the tender of the goods was admitted as an alternative to the tender of the documents. So too in *Harper et al. v. Hochstim et al* (*post* § 221) it was held, by the United States Second Circuit Court of Appeals, that a c.i.f. seller does not perform his contract by tendering actual goods at the port of destination. And

---

[77] [1916] 2 K.B. 605, *post*, § 200.
[78] (1885) 10 App. Cas. 263, *post*, §§ 564–565.
[79] [1923] 1 K.B. 78.
[80] (1872) L.R. 7 Ex. 98.
[81] [1954] 2 Lloyd's Rep. 45.

in *Continental Imes Ltd. v. H. E. Dibble*,[82] where no documents were tendered (under a c.i.f. Liverpool contract), Byrne J. likewise justified the buyers' termination of the contract *inter alia* on the ground that "c.i.f. facilities were never available" to them. More recently, in *Vitol S. A. v. Esso Australia Ltd. (The "Wise")*[83] sellers under a c.i.f. contract that, *inter alia*, provided that vessel's nomination was "to be subject to buyers' acceptance" were unable to prove a custom whereby this term produced the result of postponing the transfer of title and risk until acceptance by the buyer of the sellers' nomination.

19   *Uniform commercial code.* An attempt to describe some of the variations of the c.i.f. contract (which are not inconsistent with its basic pattern) was undertaken in the American Uniform Commercial Code.[84] Section 2–321 of the Code provides as follows:

> "Under a contract containing a term c.i.f. or c. and f.
> (1) Where the price is based on or is to be adjusted according to 'net landed weights,' 'delivered weights,' 'out turn' quantity or quality or the like, unless otherwise agreed the seller must reasonably estimate the price. The payment due on tender of the documents called for by the contract is the amount so estimated, but after final adjustment of the price a settlement must be made with commercial promptness.[85]
> (2) An agreement described in subsection (1) or any warranty of quality or condition of the goods on arrival places upon the seller the risk of ordinary deterioration, shrinkage and the like in transportation but has no effect on the place or time of identification to the contract for sale or delivery or on the passing of the risk of loss.
> (3) Unless otherwise agreed where the contract provides for payment on or after arrival of the goods the seller must before payment allow such preliminary inspection as is feasible; but if the goods are lost delivery of the documents and payment are due when the goods should have arrived."

Where, however, the term "no arrival, no sale" or the like is stipulated, section 2–324(a) of the Code provides that unless otherwise agreed "the

---

[82] [1952] 1 Lloyd's Rep. 220.

[83] [1989] 1 Lloyd's Rep. 96, *per* Leggatt J. whose judgement (on other points) was reversed by the Court of Appeal in [1989] 2 Lloyd's Rep. 451.

[84] The normal c.i.f. and c. and f. terms are described in s. 2–320 of the Code which generally follows the Revised American Foreign Trade Definitions (1941) which at the time were recommended for general use by U.S. exporters and importers.

[85] In *Oricon Waren-Handels G.m.b.H.v. Intergraan N.V.* [1967] 2 Lloyd's Rep. 82, the contract provided that final settlement was to be made on the basis of "gross delivered weight" at the port of destination. Roskill J. described the contract as a "hybrid" c.i.f. contract (at p. 94), and held that the term required the buyers to weigh the goods upon discharge, that their failure to do so was a breach, and that the sellers were entitled to be put in the same position as if weighing had been carried out. In *Krohn & Co. v. Mitsui & Co.* [1978] 2 Lloyd's Rep. 419, the question was whether the c.i.f. buyers could invoke a delivered weight clause where they had agreed with the shipper, but not with the sellers, to discharge at a port other than the port of destination designated in the contract. Since the sellers agreed only to a final settlement on the basis of weight ascertained at the designated port of destination, "Rotterdam", the Court of Appeal held that there was no basis for adjusting the price when the cargo was landed in "Bremen".

seller must properly ship conforming goods and if they arrive by any means he must tender them on arrival but he assumes no obligation that the goods will arrive unless he has caused the non-arrival.''

The Coder thus makes clear that while parties may stipulate as to payment on the basis of delivered quantities, thus shifting to the buyer the transportation risk (*i.e.* loss resulting from evaporation, spillage or measurement or quantity error) without vitiating the essence of the c.i.f. bargain, they cannot shift the loss of the goods being destroyed in transit to the seller (freeing the buyer from the obligation to pay the full contract price) without altering the c.i.f. character of the transaction. In some respects the problem is similar to that of the goods deteriorating in transit, and to the risk assumed by the c.i.f. seller in respect of inevitable deterioration.[86] A difficulty may still persist as to who carries the burden of proving what kind of loss brought about the difference in quantity or quality. In the absence of an express stipulation on this matter, which the parties are well advised to adopt, it would appear that the onus would be on the buyer, since it is he who is maintaining the variation of the c.i.f. term.[87]

Scope of review

20   In these pages it is intended, in general, to refer only to contracts which are properly described as c.i.f. contracts, whether strict or modified. No useful purpose would be served by further attempting to distinguish between particular terms and expressions the presence of which—whether caused by inadvertence, or by misapprehension of the rights and duties of parties under c.i.f. contracts or otherwise—may or may not have the effect of converting a contract expressed to be c.i.f. into a different form of contract.

The fact, however, is to be noted that there is considerable laxity in the use of forms of contract for the sale of goods sent overseas, and the interpretation of any particular contract of sale expressed to be c.i.f. may present real difficulty. The statement of Lord Cairns that ''merchants are not in the habit of placing upon their contracts stipulations to which they do not attach some value and importance''[88] requires some qualification today. For, as Lord Atkin remarked[89]: ''Business men habitually adventure large sums of money on contracts which, for the purpose of defining legal obligations, are a mere jumble of words.''

In some of the cases referred to it will be observed that the contract of sale

---

[86] See *post*, §§ 319 *et seq.* See also Lightburn and Nienabar, ''Out-turn clauses in c.i.f. contracts in the oil trade'' [1988] L.M.C.L.Q. 177.
[87] See *Hawkland, Uniform Commercial Code Series* (1984), Vol. 2, Art. 2, p. 506. In France the position appears to be the reverse. See Lightburn and Nienaber, *op. cit.*
[88] In *Bowes* v. *Shand* (1877) 2 App. Cas. 455 at p. 463.
[89] *Phoenix Insurance Co. of Hartford* v. *De Monchy* (1929) 35 Com. Cas. 67 at p. 82. In the same case Scrutton L. J. expostulated: ''This document has to be seen to be believed'': (1928) 33 Com. Cas. 199.

is described as a c. and f. contract. Such a contract imports the usual obligations of a c.i.f. contract, but with the difference that the insurance is arranged by the buyer and not by the seller. In such a case it will be the duty of the seller, as in the case of f.o.b. contracts, to give the buyer such information as is necessary in order that he can arrange for insurance.[90]

21   In yet other cases the c.i.f. term may be supplemented by the addition of one or more initials. Thus, *e.g.* terms such as c.i.f. and e., c.i.f. and c. or c.i.f.c. and i. are sometimes encountered. Though all of these supplementary initials refer to cost items which the c.i.f. seller agrees to absorb, their precise meaning may be a matter of doubt as they have not been defined in any authoritative text. Thus, the first of these abbreviations which stands for "cost, insurance, freight and exchange" may mean one of two things. It is sometimes said to refer to a banker's commission or charge for collecting paper drawn on the buyer while others maintain that it indicates that the seller will absorb the exchange risk of converting the currency in which the purchase price is payable into another currency.[91] In view of this ambiguity, parties are well advised to clarify their intention in advance in order to avoid misunderstanding. The final "c" in the abbreviation c.i.f. and c. refers to "commission," and will normally be found in contracts concluded with, or through, indent or confirming houses indicating that the price quoted includes the commission of the house. Where the letter "i" is added to this abbreviation, the meaning is that the buyer shall not be called upon to reimburse the seller for the cost of discounting any bill with a bank. It is therefore usually used only when goods are exported to distant places where some time elapses before a bill drawn on the customer abroad is settled. If the buyer pays the bill before its prescribed maturity, he is sometimes allowed a rebate in respect of the amount paid on account of interest.

Finally, terms such as "c.i.f. and landed" are occasionally employed obligating the seller to bear the cost of discharge of the goods from the vessel. Because these additional initials are not always clearly understood they should not, as Note No. 2 to General Notes of Caution to the "Revised American Foreign Trade Definitions—1941" state, "be used unless there has first been a definite understanding as to the exact meaning thereof."

The foregoing notwithstanding, the c.i.f. term has a precise and definite meaning, and where the parties do not evince a clear intention to vitiate this meaning, the respective general obligations of the parties should no longer be a matter of doubt. This meaning is clearly recorded and reflected in the

---

[90] See *post*, § 662

[91] *Cf. National Mutual Life Association of Australasia Ltd. v. Att.-Gen. for New Zealand* [1956] A.C. 369 (P.C.). Exchange problems may arise in other ways also. Thus, *e.g.* where the agreement provides for the c.i.f. seller to transfer to the buyer the benefit of any export subsidy (as an allowance in the price), and the contract price is expressed in a currency other than the currency in which the subsidy is payable, difficulty may be encountered as to the exact date of conversion of the subsidy into the contract currency for the purpose of fixing the amount of the allowance. See *Compagnia Industriale Lavorazione Semi Oleosi S.p.a. v. Toepfer (Alfred C.)* [1974] 2 Lloyd's Rep. 148.

preceding citations from which it is apparent that the term has undergone little change of substance, if any, in the course of the past century. The exposition of the term as recorded in *Tregelles v. Sewell*[92] and *Ireland v. Livingston*,[93] the earliest reported cases, show a use which is fully consistent and in complete harmony with the principles invoked today in determining the rights and obligations of the parties to a c.i.f. contract, though formerly the initials were often spelled "c.f. and i."

The container revolution

22   With the advent of the container, and other modern cargo unitisation devices, a gradual switch from the customary "port to port" type of sea transport to a new "door to door" combined transport concept (involving several means or modes of transport and different carriers) is clearly evident. The effects of this technological change, which is often described as the "container revolution," on the traditional patterns of trade will be far reaching, since many of the existing trade terms cannot be applied in their present form to contracts (and the documentation relating thereto) whereby the goods are transported by one of the modern combined transport methods. Of the many problems which the new combined transport concept raises, perhaps the greatest difficulty relates to the documentary aspect of the c.i.f. term and the inability (where the sale comprises less than a full container load) to satisfy the bill of lading requirements of the transaction. As the goods are placed in a container (or similar unitisation device) at the inland point of origin never to be seen again until they are unpacked at the final inland point of destination, and, moreover, since the container, more likely than not, is (while transported on the sea leg portion of its journey) to be stowed "on" rather than "under" deck, it may be impossible to obtain the type of clean bill of lading (with direct privity between the holder and the carrier) which the c.i.f. term requires. And where the consignment consists of less than an entire container load, the shipper may even be prevented from obtaining any bill of lading relating to the individual package or packages in question. Under these circumstances it may be impossible to perform a c.i.f. contract. If the ocean carrier can in no way certify the receipt of the goods or their apparent good order and condition upon shipment, and there is no proof where or when damage occurred, the marine insurer may refuse to accept the risk.[94] To be sure, container operators have devised alternative or modified documents which attempt to overcome these difficulties,[95] but it is doubtful whether they satisfy the documentary requirements of the classic c.i.f. con-

---

[92] *Ante*, § 13.

[93] *Ante*, § 5.

[94] See Sassoon, "Cargo Insurance and the Container Revolution" *Donati Festschrift* [International Association for Insurance Law], Vol. I, 523 (Rome 1970).

[95] See also United Nations Convention on the International Multimodal Transport of Goods concluded in May 1980.

tract. Similarly, the land-bridge concepts or operating modes of container carriage may alter the predominantly maritime character of the customary c.i.f. and f.o.b. terms. The ever increasing growth in the volume of trade to which the new combined transport concept is being applied will no doubt express itself in the development and formulation of special trade terms designed to take account of the particular features of the intermodal age wherein carriage of goods from door to door may become the rule rather than the exception.

23   The International Chamber of Commerce, in the following extract from its 1980 edition of its Guide to Incoterms,[96] described the impact of this technological change thus:

> "The trend towards integrated (door to door) and multimodal transport—accelerated by the advent of the container—has made certain traditional practices virtually obsolete. In today's traffic system, the ship's rail—once the traditional 'critical point'under the f.o.b., c & f, and c.i.f. terms—no longer makes sense as a point for the division of functions, costs and risks between the contracting parties.
>
> "In addition, since a key function of the transport document is to evidence the good order and condition of the goods, it should be issued at a point where the carrier has reasonable means of conducting a check. In modern transport operations, this point has shifted from the ship's rail to seaport or inland terminals, where the goods are frequently stowed in containers or trailers, or on flats or pallets.
>
> "Consequently, there is a requirement for documents that specify received for shipment. A further consideration is that the principal carrier is frequently willing to assume a 'through liability' for the goods. This may apply even when he has contracted wholly or partly, with other parties. The ICC Rules for a Combined Transport Document (Brochure No. 298) are based on this principle. The combined transport document is invariably a received for shipment type of document and is also described in the ICC Guide to Documentary Credit Operations (Publication No. 305, article 23).
>
> "Costs of handling the 'paper flow' have in recent years become disproportionate to the costs of physical transportation. In an attempt to cope with this problem, organisations dedicated to the simplification of international trade procedures are currently investigating the possibility of replacing conventional transport documentation by electronic data processing systems. Trade terms themselves are being adapted to conform to the requirements of computer technology.
>
> "The new transportation techniques and the changed documentary practices receive special attention in the 1980 revision of Incoterms. In the new trade term 'Free Carrier . . . (named point)' (FRC)[97], the ship's rail has been replaced as a 'critical point' by the 'named point' where the carrier is to take the goods into his custody. As noted, this is likely to be a cargo terminal at the seaport or inland.
>
> "Under both the amended term 'Freight or Carriage Paid to' (d.c.p.)[98] and the new term 'Freight or Carriage and Insurance Paid to' (c.i.p.), the 'critical point' is the moment of the delivery of the goods into the custody of the first carrier.

---

[96] Now replaced by Incoterms 1990.
[97] Now discarded in favour of FCA.
[98] Now discarded in favour of CPT.

"In addition, there is no reference in these terms to a negotiable, on board bill of lading, but simply to the 'usual transport document.' In some traffic involving maritime transport, this document may still be a bill of lading, or a negotiable document with the same legal characteristics, but it is not likely to evidence shipment on board a designated vessel.[99]

"It is expected that f.r.c.[1] the amended d.c.p. and c.i.p. will gradually replace f.o.b., c & f and c.i.f. in the new type of traffic now evolving. The fact that the new terms have made it feasible for sponsors of the American Foreign Trade Definitions to discontinue the use of their terminology in favour of the revised Incoterms is most encouraging. It should contribute substantially to the unification of legal practices and procedures in international trading throughout the world."[2]

Although it would be inappropriate, within the present context, to speculate on the patterns of trade that will ultimately emerge as a result of the container revolution,[3] or other technological developments in the modes of transport, *e.g.* carriage by air,[4] there is little doubt that future trade terms will to the extent possibly draw on the rules underlying the traditional c.i.f. and f.o.b. terms. It is felt therefore that the relevance of these rules will not diminish with time.

International Chamber of Commerce definition

24 Because the c.i.f. term has not been the subject of legislative definition in the United Kingdom[5] but is rather the product and outgrowth of commercial custom and usage, it is of more than usual interest to note the interpretation of the term as recorded by the International Chamber of Commerce. The definition, which is of course not binding on English courts (unless expressly incorporated by the parties into their contract as the Chamber recommends), may nevertheless furnish prima facie evidence where the scope or onus of any particular duty is in doubt because of lack of authority or absence of agreement express or implied. According to "Incoterms"[6] the respective obligations of the parties are as follows:

A. The Seller Must:

1. *Provision of goods in conformity with the contract*

Provide the goods and the commercial invoice, or its equivalent electronic message, in conformity with the contract of sale and any other evidence of conformity which may be required by the contract.

---

[99] Or even a non-negotiable document, *post* § 161a.
[1] Now CPT.
[2] ICC, Guide to Incoterms (1980 ed.), pp. 8–9.
[3] See Sassoon, "Trade Terms and the Container Revolution," 1 J. Mar. L. & Comm. 73 (1969), where a shift from "shipment" to "destination" terms as a possible consequence of the container revolution is considered.
[4] See, *e.g.* the term fob Airport, defined in Incoterms, *post*, § 580.
[5] *Cf.* s. 2–320 of the American Uniform Commercial Code.
[6] ICC publication (1990 rev.).

2. *Licences, authorisations and formalities*

Obtain at his own risk and expense any export licence or other official authorisation and carry out all customs formalities necessary for the exportation of the goods.

3. *Contract of carriage and insurance*

(a) Contract of carriage. Contract on usual terms at his own expense for the carriage of the goods to the named port of destination by the usual route in a seagoing vessel (or inland waterway vessel as appropriate) of the type normally used for the transport of goods of the contract description.

(b) Contract of insurance. Obtain at his own expense cargo insurance as agreed in the contract, that the buyer, or any other person having an insurable interest in the goods, shall be entitled to claim directly from the insurer and provide the buyer with the insurance policy or other evidence of insurance cover.

The insurance shall be contracted with underwriters or an insurance company of good repute and, failing express agreement to the contrary, be in accordance with minimum cover of the Institute Cargo Clauses (Institute of London Underwriters) or any similar set of clauses. The duration of insurance cover shall be in accordance with B.5. and B.4. When required by the buyer, the seller shall provide at the buyer's expense war, strikes, riots and civil commotion risk insurances if procurable. The minimum insurance shall cover the price provided in the contract plus ten per cent (*i.e.* 110 per cent) and shall be provided in the currency of the contract.[7]

4. *Delivery*

Deliver the goods on board the vessel at the port of shipment on the date or within the period stipulated.

5. *Transfer of risks*

Subject to the provisions of B.5., bear all risks of loss of or damage to the goods until such time as they have passed the ship's rail at the port of shipment.

6. *Division of costs*

Subject to the provisions of B.6.
- pay all costs relating to the goods until they have been delivered in

---

[7] "Incoterms" provides for minimum insurance coverage. The basis of "Incoterms" is that, in matters on which there are major differences of practice, it provides that the contract-price will include minimum liabilities for the seller. Whenever the parties incorporate a reference to "Incoterms" in their agreement and the buyer wishes more than the minimum liability to be included in the contract, then he should take care to specify that the basis of the contract is to be "Incoterms" with whatever addition he requires. For instance, if he requires the equivalent of what used to be known as WA or All Risk insurance instead of the equivalent of FPA terms, the contract should specify "Incoterms CIF with WA or All Risk (as the case may be) insurance."

accordance with A.4. as well as the freight and all other costs resulting from A.3., including costs of loading the goods on board and any charges for unloading at the port of discharge which may be levied by regular shipping lines when contracting for carriage;

- pay the costs of customs formalities necessary for exportation as well as all duties, taxes and other official charges payable upon exportation.

7. *Notice to the buyer*

Give the buyer sufficient notice that the goods have been delivered on board the vessel as well as any other notice required in order to allow the buyer to take measures which are normally necessary to enable him to take the goods.

8. *Proof of delivery, transport document or equivalent electronic message*

Unless otherwise agreed, at his own expense provide the buyer without delay with the usual transport document for the agreed port of destination.

This document (for example, a negotiable bill of lading, a non-negotiable sea waybill or an inland waterway document) must cover the contract goods, be dated within the period agreed for shipment, enable the buyer to claim the goods from the carrier at destination and, unless otherwise agreed, enable the buyer to sell the goods in transit by the transfer of the document to a subsequent buyer (the negotiable bill of lading) or by notification to the carrier.

When such a transport document is issued in several originals, a full set of originals must be presented to the buyer. If the transport document contains a reference to a charter party, the seller must also provide a copy of this latter document.

Where the seller and the buyer have agreed to communicate electronically, the document referred to in the preceding paragraphs may be replaced by an equivalent electronic data interchange (EDI) message.

9. *Checking—packaging—marking*

Pay the costs of those checking operations (such as checking quality, measuring, weighing, counting) which are necessary for the purpose of delivering the goods in accordance with A.4.

Provide at his own expense packaging (unless it is usual for the particular trade to ship the goods of the contract description unpacked) which is required for the transport of the goods arranged by him. Packaging is to be marked approrpriately.

10. *Other obligations*

Render the buyer at the latter's request, risk and expense, every assistance in obtaining any documents or equivalent electronic messages (other than those mentioned in A.8.) issued or transmitted in the country of shipment and/or of origin which the buyer may require for the importation of the goods and, where necessary, for their transit through another country.

B. The Buyer must:

1. *Payment of the price*

Pay the price as provided in the contract of sale.

2. *Licences, authorisations and formalities*

Obtain at his own risk and expense any import licence or other official authorisation and carry out all customs formalities for the importation of the goods and, where necessary, for their transit through another country.

3. *Contract of carriage*

No obligation.

4. *Taking delivery*

Accept delivery of the goods when they have been delivered in accordance with A.4. and receive them from the carrier at the named port of destination.

5. *Transfer of risks*

Bear all risks of loss of or damage to the goods from the time they have passed the ship's rail at the port of shipment.

Should he fail to give notice in accordance with B.7., bear all risks of loss of or damage to the goods from the agreed date or the expiry date of the period fixed for shipment provided, however, that the goods have been duly appropriated to the contract, that is to say, clearly set aside or otherwise identified as the contract goods.

6. *Division of costs*

Subject to the provisions of A.3., pay all costs relating to the goods from the time they have been delivered in accordance with A.4. and, unless such costs and charges have been levied by regular shipping lines when contracting for carriage, pay all costs and charges relating to the goods whilst in transit until their arrival at the port of destination, as well as unloading costs including lighterage and wharfage charges.

Should he fail to give notice in accordance with B.7., pay the additional costs thereby incurred for the goods from the agreed date or the expiry date of the period fixed for shipment provided, however, that the goods have been duly appropriated to the contract, that is to say, clearly set aside or otherwise identified as the contract goods.

Pay all duties, taxes and other official charges as well as the costs of carrying out customs formalities payable upon importation of the goods and, where necessary, for their transit through another country.

7. *Notice to the seller*

Whenever he is entitled to determine the time for shipping the goods and/ or the port of destination, give the seller sufficient notice thereof.

8. *Proof of delivery, transport document or equivalent electronic message*

Accept the transport document in accordance with A.8. if it is in conformity with the contract.

9. *Inspection of goods*

Pay, unless otherwise agreed, the costs of pre-shipment inspection except when mandated by the authorities of the country of exportation.

10. *Other obligations*

Pay all costs and charges incurred in obtaining the documents or equivalent electronic messages mentioned in A.10. and reimburse those incurred by the seller in rendering his assistance in accordance therewith.

Provide the seller, upon request, with the necessary information for procuring insurance.

Finally it may be noted that the latest edition of "Incoterms" has replaced the c. and f. term or symbol by the term CFR, an undesirable substitution in light of the long and continued use of the more familiar term.

C.i.f. contract as a "sale of documents"

26   The suggestion that a contract for the sale of goods c.i.f. could be regarded as a sale of the documents is derived from the judgment of Scrutton J. in *Arnhold Karberg & Co. v. Blythe, Green, Jourdain & Co.*[8] when he declared:

> "I am strongly of the opinion that the key to many of the difficulties arising in c.i.f. contracts is to keep firmly in mind the cardinal distinction that a c.i.f. sale is not a sale of goods, but a sale of documents relating to goods. It is not a contract that goods shall arrive, but a contract to ship goods complying with the contract of sale, to obtain, unless the contract otherwise provides, the ordinary contract of carriage to the place of destination, and the ordinary contract of insurance of the goods on that voyage, and to tender these documents against payment of the contract price. The buyer then has the right to claim the fulfilment of the contract of carriage, or, if the goods are lost or damaged, such indemnity for the loss as he can claim under the contract of insurance. He buys the documents, not the goods, and it may be that under the terms of the contracts of insurance and affreightment he buys no indemnity for the damage that has happened to the goods. This depends on what documents he is entitled to under the contract of sale. In my view, therefore, the relevant question will generally be not 'what at the time of declaration or tender of documents is the condition of the goods?' . . . but 'what, at the time of tender of documents, was the condition of those documents as to compliance with the contract of sale?'."

For this reason the seller must tender documents and cannot claim performance of a c.i.f. contract by tendering, in lieu thereof, the goods themselves at

---

[8] [1915] 2 K.B. 379 at p. 388; [1916] 1 K.B. 495 (C.A.).

the port of destination unless of course the buyer waives compliance with the terms of the agreement.[9]

The statement that a c.i.f. sale is a sale of documents is a useful phrase to remember, particularly when questions as to damages for breach of contract arise. But it is a phrase only; as a legal interpretation, it was expressly dissented from in the Court of Appeal by Bankes and Warrington L. JJ. in the same case.[10] The contract is more correctly described as "a contract for the sale of goods to be performed by the delivery of documents."[11] The difference of view is one of language only, said McCardie J. in a later case[12]: ". . . the obligation of the vendor is to deliver documents rather than goods—to transfer symbols rather than the physical property represented thereby." And later Scrutton L. J. himself said[13]: "I need not discuss, what perhaps is merely a question of words, whether that sale is a sale of goods or of documents. One of the features of a sale c.i.f. is that, in the absence of special terms, the seller claims payment against presentation of shipping documents."

But whether or not this is merely a question of words, it is quite clear that a c.i.f. contract imposes upon the seller two sets of obligations which are quite distinct from each other. The one relates to the goods and the other to the documents. As Devlin J. noted in *Kwei Tek Chao v. British Traders and Shippers Ltd.*:[14]

> "A c.i.f. contract puts a number of obligations upon the seller, some of which are in relation to the goods and some of which are in relation to the documents. So far as the goods are concerned, he must put on board at the port of shipment goods in conformity with the contract description, but he must also send forward documents, and those documents must comply with the contract. If he commits a breach the breaches may in one sense overlap, in that they flow from the same act. If there is a late shipment . . . the seller has not put on board goods which conform to the contract description . . . He has also made it impossible to send forward a bill of lading which . . . conforms . . . Thus the same act can cause two breaches of two independent obligations."

Consequently, difficulties may arise where the seller delivers documents purporting to relate to goods of the contract description but which ultimately turn out to be incorrect. For, if the buyer refuses to pay against the presentation of the documents, his act may be considered a wrongful repudiation of the contract that releases the seller from performance.[15] On the other hand if the buyer is precluded from rejecting the documents (because of some term

---

[9] See *Holland Colombo Trading Society Ltd. v. Segu Mohamed Khaja Alawedeen* [1954] 2 Lloyd's Rep. 45 (P.C.); *Cohen v. Wood & Selick Inco.*, 212 N.Y.S. 31 (1925).
[10] [1916] 1 K.B. 495 at pp. 510, 514. The difference is "one of language rather than of substance": *Scrutton on Charterparties* (19th ed.), p. 191, n. 64. See also *The Gabbiano* [1940] P. 166 at p. 174, and *Ross T. Smyth & Co. Ltd. v. T. D. Bailey, Son & Co.* [1940] 3 All E.R. 60 at p. 70, *per* Lord Wright.
[11] *Id.*
[12] *Manbre Saccharine Co. v. Corn Products Co.* [1919] 1 K.B. 198 at p. 203.
[13] *Malmberg v. H. J. Evans & Co.* (1924) 30 Com. Cas. 107 at p. 112.
[14] [1954] 2 Q.B. 459 at p. 480.
[15] *Post*, §§ 338 *et seq.*

relating, *e.g.* to the conclusivity of an inspection certificate) he may lose his right to reject even if he can show that upon examination the goods are non-conforming and that the certificate was inaccurate.[16]

Where the seller tenders documents which purport to cover the contract goods but in fact do not, the buyer can usually recover the price, as well as damages for breach. In *Hindley & Co. v. East India Produce Co.*[17] sellers sold 50 tons of Siamese jute c. and f. Bremen at a price of £80 per ton for shipment during October, November and December, 1968, at sellers' option, cash against documents on or before arrival of the steamer. On January 27, 1969 the sellers tendered a bill of lading dated December 30, 1968, which they had obtained from a third party from whom they had purchased a quantity of jute and which stated that 275 bales of jute of the contract description had been shipped on board the steamship *Peramataris* at Bangkok. On March 5, 1969 the buyers paid the sellers the contract price of £3,960. When the vessel arrived at Bremen, no jute of the contract description was found to be on board because it had never been shipped. A dispute arose as to whether the buyers were entitled to return of the price and damages for breach. The sellers contended that:

(1) they were not liable because a contract of sale on c. and f. (or c.i.f.) terms was one for the sale of documents, or one to be performed by the delivery of documents, and in the present case the bill of lading was in all respects proper on its face;
(2) they were not the shippers of the goods, but were merely parties in a string who were unconnected with the circumstances giving rise to the issue of the bill of lading: and
(3) the buyers must be confined to the remedies which they had against the carrier.

All of these defences were rejected by Kerr J. who held that the sellers were in breach of their obligation to ship or procure the shipment of goods of the contractual description, for no goods had in fact been shipped. The fact that the sellers were not privy to the non-shipment was, in his opinion, immaterial and irrelevant. In his Lordship's view this was sufficient to enable the buyers to succeed in their claims. But Kerr J. further opined that "it is an implied term of a contract of this nature that the bill of lading shall not only appear to be true and accurate in the material statements which it contains, but that such statements shall in fact be true and accurate."[18] As in the present case the bill of lading which was tendered was not a proper one, the sellers were in breach on that ground also, and it was immaterial whether the buyers had a right of action against the carrier.

In other words, where no goods were ever shipped, or where the seller has

---

[16] *Gill and Duffus S.A. v. Berger & Co Inc.* [1984] 1 Lloyd's Rep. 227; *Alfred C. Toepfer v. Continental Grain Co.* [1979] 1 Lloyd's Rep. 11.
[17] [1973] 2 Lloyd's Rep. 515. And see further on the tender of invalid and ineffective documents, *post*, §§ 247 *et seq.*
[18] *Ibid.* at p. 518.

31

ordered the ship to go elsewhere,[19] the seller has not performed his contract, and cannot demand payment on the ground that the contract has been performed by tendering conforming documents. And of course if the seller is guilty of fraud, and the documents are false, even if they appear on their face to be in order, the buyer is likewise justified in non-payment or rejection of the same.

On the other hand, the c.i.f. buyer is entitled to reject documents that show carriage to a non-contract port, even though the actual contract of carriage made by the seller provided for carriage to the right destination. Altering the bill of lading, by inserting the agreed destination, and representing them, would not be able to cure the defect because that would amount to a variation of the original contract of carriage at some unknown date, while the buyer is entitled to have in the documents proper evidence of the contract from the time of shipment.[20]

Commission agent as consignor

27   The cases so far cited have dealt with the contract of sale c.i.f. *simpliciter*, in which case neither of the parties is the agent or trustee for the *other*.[21] But the consignor may be an agent to procure goods on commission for dispatch to the consignee. In such case, the legal position seems to be that the commission agent, while bound under the contract of agency to use reasonable skill and diligence to procure the goods ordered at or below the limit of price given to him by his principal, and to ship and insure them on terms as favourable as he can obtain, after shipment becomes in relation to his principal a quasi-seller with the rights of a seller, *e.g.* the right of stoppage *in transitu*. The legal position was thus defined by Blackburn J. in *Ireland v. Livingston*:[22]

> "It is also very common for the consignor to be an agent who . . . merely accepts an order by which he binds himself to use due diligence to fulfil the order. In that case he is bound to get the goods as cheap as he reasonably can, and the sum inserted in the invoice represents the actual cost and charges at which the goods are procured by the consignor, with the addition of a commission; and the naming of a maximum limit shews that the order is of that nature . . .
>
> The contract of agency is precisely the same as if the order had been to procure goods at or below a certain price, and then ship them to the person ordering them, the freight being in noways an element in the limit. But when, as in the present case, the limit is made to include cost, freight, and insurance, the agent must take care in executing the order that the aggregate of the sums which his principal will have to pay does not exceed the limit prescribed in his order; if it does, the principal is not bound to take the goods. . . . The agent, therefore, as is

---

[19] *Peter Cremer v. Brinkers Grondstoffen B.V.* [1980] 2 Lloyd's Rep. 605; *Empressa Exportadora Azucar v. Industria Azucarera Nacional S.A. (The Playa Larga)* [1983] 2 Lloyd's Rep 171 *post*, § 87.

[20] *S.I.A.T. Di Del Ferro v. Tradax Overseas S.A.* [1980] 1 Lloyd's Rep. 53 at p. 64 (C.A.).

[21] *Per* Blackburn J. in *Ireland v. Livingston* (1872) L.R. 5 H.L. 395 at p. 407.

[22] (1872) L.R. 5 H.L. 395 at p. 407.

obvious, does not take upon himself any part of the rise or profit which may arise from the rise and fall of prices, and is entitled to charge commission, because there is a contract of agency.... It is quite true that the agent who in thus executing an order, ships goods to his principal, is in contemplation of law a vendor to him. The persons who supply goods to a commission merchant sell them to him, and not to his unknown foreign correspondent, and the commission merchant has no authority to pledge the credit of his correspondent for them ... and just so does the property in the goods pass from the country producer to the commission merchant; and then, when the goods are shipped, from the commission merchant to his consignee. The legal effect of the transaction[23] between the commission merchant and the consignee, who has given him the order, is a contract of sale passing the property from the one to the other; and consequently the commission merchant is a vendor, and has the right of one as to stoppage *in transitu.* ...

My opinion is, for the reasons I have indicated, that when the order was accepted by the Plaintiffs [commission merchants] there was a contract of agency by which the Plaintiffs undertook to use reasonable skill and diligence to procure the goods ordered at or below the limit given, to be followed up by a transfer of the property at the actual cost, with the addition of the commission; but that this superadded sale is not in any way inconsistent with the contract of agency existing between the parties, by virtue of which the Plaintiffs were under the obligation to make reasonable exertions to procure the goods ordered as much below the limit as they could.''

28   It had previously been held, in the case of *Feise v. Wray*,[24] that a commission agent who had bought goods on account and by order of his principal on his own credit in a foreign port and had shipped the goods to London, drawing bills on his principal, was entitled to stop the goods *in transitu* on his principal becoming bankrupt; that for the purpose of stopping the goods *in transitu* the parties "stood in the relative situation of vendor and vendee; though perhaps not so as for all purposes." And the principle of this case had been recognised in other cases.[25]

In *Cassaboglou v. Gibb*[26] the Court of Appeal (Brett M.R., Lindley and Fry L.J.) held that, upon breach of an executory contract by a commission agent to supply his principal with goods, the damages were to be assessed as between principal and agent, and not as between seller and buyer. There the plaintiff, a London merchant, gave orders to the defendants, who were commission agents in Hong Kong, to buy for him ten cases of the finest "dry new crop Persian opium." Opium of this kind could not be then bought in Hong Kong, but the defendants, instead of so informing the plaintiff, by mistake informed him that they could procure it, and they purchased and shipped opium which they supposed to be of the contractual description but which was in fact of an inferior description. In an action for damages by the

---

[23] "By the legal effect of the transaction he means the legal effect of an analogous contract to that of purchase and sale": *per* Lindley L.J., *Cassaboglou v. Gibb* (1883) 11 Q.B.D. 797 at p. 807.

[24] (1802) 3 East 93.

[25] *e.g. Tucker v. Humphrey* (1828) 4 Bing. 516; *Hawkes v. Dunn* (1831) 1 C. & J. 519.

[26] (1883) 11 Q.B.D. 797; approved in *Chr. Salvesen & Co. v. Rederi Aktiebolaget Nordstjernan* [1905] A. C. 302. See also *Weiss, Biheller and Brooks Lts. v. Farmer* [1923] 1 K.B. 226.

London merchant it was held that he was entitled to recover not the difference between the value of the opium ordered and that shipped, but the loss actually sustained by him in consequence of the opium not being of the description ordered. Brett M.R. and Fry L.J. explained the statement of Blackburn J. in *Ireland v. Livingston*, cited ante, as to the legal effect of the transaction, saying that the contract between the commission agent and his principal is not one of seller and buyer, but a contract analogous thereto, placing the commission agent *after shipment* of the goods ordered in the position of a quasi-vendor for certain purposes only; that the contract of principal and agent is not turned into a contract of seller and buyer for the purpose of settling the damages for the breach of duty of the agent.

Likewise where the seller is merely the agent of the buyer, the buyer may be held to be subject to any exceptions contained in a charterparty which have not been incorporated into the bill of lading, so that he is barred from claiming from the carrier any benefits extending beyond those stipulated with his principal.

29   In *A. Delaurier & Co. v. J. Wyllie & Others*[27] iron was sold under a c.i.f. contract in pursuance of which the sellers chartered a vessel. The charterparty contained a clause exempting the shipowners from liability for loss arising from damages of navigation even when caused by the negligence of the master or the crew. However, the bills of lading, which were issued in respect of the shipment and tendered to the buyers, were construed as if this exception was not incorporated in them. The vessel having been lost through the negligence of the master, an action by the buyer against the shipowner was upheld on the grounds that the sellers were not agents of the buyers and therefore the buyers were not bound by the provisions of the charterparty as the shipowner had alleged. Nor was the shipowner entitled to raise as a defence to the claim the fact that the loss was covered by a policy, and that insurance had been paid in respect thereof. But it was further held that in respect of another cargo shipped on the same vessel by the sellers as agents for the buyers, the shipowners were entitled to claim the benefit of the exception in the charterparty that was not altered by the term of the bills of lading.

By section 38(2) of the Sale of Goods Act 1979, the rights of an unpaid seller as defined by that Act extend to a person:

> "who is in the position of a seller, as, for instance, an agent of the seller to whom the bill of lading has been indorsed, or a consignor or agent who has himself paid (or is directly responsible for) the price."

[The next paragraph is 41.]

---

[27] (1889) 17 R. (Ct. of Sess.) 167; of the 13 judges who heard the case 12 concurred and one dissented. The judgments contain many observations on the nature of c.i.f. contracts but they do not appear to add much to the observations from the English cases here before quoted.

CHAPTER 2

THE SHIPMENT

41   The seller under a c.i.f. contract has to ship at the place of shipment, within the time named in the contract, or within a reasonable time, goods of the contract description or to purchase afloat goods so shipped. "'Sales afloat' [contracts] in practice are synonymous with c.i.f. and c. and f. contracts."[1] The option of performing the contract by selection from these latter alternative methods, is, in the absence of a stipulation to the contrary,[2] with the seller. If, however, one method of performance becomes impossible, the contract normally is not discharged because the seller is usually under a duty to adopt the other alternative. So, for example, when the seller intends to ship the goods but cannot implement this intention due to events beyond his control (war, export prohibition, strikes or similar unforseen causes) then, except in so far as he is able to plead illegality as a defence for non-performance,[3] the seller is normally under an obligation to procure goods afloat. So that, as stated by McNair J. in *J. H. Vantol v. Fairclough Dodd & Jones Ltd.*[4]:

> "Generally, a seller cannot claim the protection of [a] clause which provides that the contract shall be cancelled if shipment is prevented by certain specific causes unless he proves both (a) that he was himself so prevented from shipping, and (b) that it was impossible for him to fulfil the contract by buying goods afloat which had been shipped during the contract period."[5]

---

[1] *Esteve Trading Corp. v. Agropee International (The Golden Rio)* [1990] 2 Lloyd's Rep. 273, 276.

[2] See *post, 52 et seq.*

[3] Under English law for a plea of illegality to succeed it must arise either by the proper law, or by the law of the place of performance. Other illegal acts are irrelevant and do not provide any defence. See, *e.g. post*, § 624. See also *Congimex S.à.r.l. (Lisbon) v. Continental Grain Export Corp.* [1979] 2 Lloyd's Rep. 346, and *Congimex Companhia Geral de Comercia Importadora e Exportadora S.à.r.l. v. Tradax Export S.a.* [1983] 1 Lloyd's Rep. 250 (C.A.); affirming [1981] 2 Lloyd's Rep. 687. The plea of illegality in the cases cited was made by the c.i.f. buyer, but the principles stated apply *mutatis mutandis.*

[4] [1955] 2 All E.R. 516, decision reversed by the Court of Appeal but affirmed by the House of Lords in [1956] 3 All E.R. 921, see *post*, § 52. In *Joseph Pyke & Son (Liverpool) Ltd. v. Richard Cornelius & Co.* [1955] 2 Lloyd's Rep. 747, the sellers failed to prove impossibility of export. The question whether any duty to purchase goods afloat persisted was therefore not considered. Sellers J., however, commented that he "... would not rule out the desirability of some evidence about practice and custom in this matter. I may be wrong—I do not know— because many years have gone by since trading on c.i.f. terms commenced, and I doubt whether it is a practice to buy afloat to fulfil a contract, or whether it is expected by a buyer" (at p. 751).

[5] [1995] 2 All E.R. 516 at p. 519. On the other hand in *P. J. Van Der Zijden Wildhandel N.V. v. Tucker & Cross Ltd.* [1975] 2 Lloyd's Rep. 240, Donaldson J. said (at p. 242) considering a

force majeure claim that failed, "The contract called for Chinese rabbits, c.i.f. Their [the sellers] obligation was, therefore, to tender documents, not to ship the rabbits themselves. If there were any Chinese rabbits afloat, they could have bought them, and it is for the sellers to show that no such rabbits were available." Likewise, where the seller in a string or chain transaction wishes to establish a *force majeure* excuse (within an exemption clause) he will generally have to show that the event relied upon obstructed the shipment of the very goods which he intended to appropriate to the contract. The burden on the seller in this situation was first described by Mustill J. in *Cook Industries Inc. v. Mucneric Ligeois S.A.* [1981] 1 Lloyd's Rep. 359 at p. 365 as follows:

> "The seller need go no further than prove the impact of the embargo on his intended source of supply; and this he can do by proving either that there was no shipper who had unappropriated goods which were free from the embargo or that the shipper from whom the seller intended to obtain the goods had none which were free from the embargo. Attention must therefore be focused on what has come to be called the 'relevant' shipper rather than on the individual consignment."

But in *Brenaer Handelsgesellschaft M.B.H. v. Westzucker G.M.B.H.* [1989] 1 Lloyd's Rep. 198, Phillips J. (at p. 204) expressed some doubt as to whether the first alternative suggested by Mustill J. (proof that there was no shipper who had unappropriated goods of the contract description free from the embargo) would be a viable one in circumstances such as those that arose in the cases mentioned hereunder. However, the Court of Appeal, who affirmed this decision in [1989] 1 Lloyd's Rep. 582, does not appear to have shared this view. And in *Bremer Handelsgesellschaft M.B.H. v. Continental Grain* [1983] 1 Lloyd's Rep. 269, Lord Ackner opined that for a seller to establish that (in a string transaction) a shipment had been prevented in any part by an embargo the seller must first, on the balance of probabilities, identify the shipper whose shipment has been delayed. Failure to meet this onus of proof will delay the immunity conferred by the export prohibition escape clause and expose him to liability for damages. See *Vanden Avenne-Izegen P.V.B.A. v. Fingrani S.A.* [1985] 2 Lloyd's Rep. 99, and further *post*, § 280, and the cases there cited. Where some goods could escape the operation of the event (imposition of absolute export ban subsequently modified, *inter alia*, not to affect goods already on lighters or in the course of loading prior to a specified date and thereafter lifted to the extent of 40 per cent of pre-existing export commitments) the seller is in default for his inability to prove that the goods he intended to appropriate did not escape the embargo loopholes. *André & Cie S.A. v. Ets. Michel Blanc & Fils* [1979] 2 Lloyd's Rep. 427 (C.A.); *Bunge S.A. v. Deutsche Conti Handelsgesellschaft mbH* [1979] 2 Lloyd's Rep. 435 (C.A.); *Avimex S.A. v. Dewulf & Cie* [1979] 2 Lloyd's Rep. 57; *Bremer Handelsgesellschaft mbH v. C. Mackprang Jr.* [1979] 1 Lloyd's Rep. 221 (C.A.); *Raiffeisen Hauptgenossenschaft v. Dreyfus (Louis) & Co.; Dreyfus (Louis) & Co. v. Becher (Kurt A.)* [1981] 1 Lloyd's Rep. 345; *Bremer Handelsgesellschaft mbH v. Continental Grain Co.* [1983] 1 Lloyd's Rep. 269; *Bremer Handelsgesellschaft mbH v. Bunge Corp.* [1983] 1 Lloyd's Rep. 476 (C.A.). The burden of proof required seems to have been relaxed somewhat as the upheaval caused by the embargo was fully realised. In *André & Cie S.A. v. Tradax Export S.A.* [1983] 1 Lloyd's Rep. 254 the Court of Appeal held that the seller avoids liability by showing that his failure to ship was excused by the embargo, that no shipper could lawfully enter into fresh export contracts at the time the contract was entered into and in the absence of evidence or knowledge about the availability of similar goods on the market. (This case as well as *Cook Industries Inc. v. Tradax Export S.A.* [1983] 1 Lloyd's Rep. 327, aff'd [1985] 2 Lloyd's Rep. 457 (C.A.), and *André & Cie S.A. v. Tradax Export S.A.* [1983] 1 Lloyd's Rep. 254 (C.A.) also considered the effect of a subsequent lifting of the embargo permitting exports under fresh contracts entered into after a certain date on some of the contracts in question.) On the option of purchasing goods afloat under such circumstances see *Tradax Export S.A. v. André & Cie S.A.* [1976] 1 Lloyd's Rep. 416, and the cases applying it (discussed hereunder) holding that no duty to purchase afloat is to be implied in string transactions (for the purchase of a commodity in short supply) and affected by an export prohibition subsequent to shipping arrangements being made. On the latter point see also *Continental Grain Export Corp. v. S.T.M. Grain Ltd.* [1979] 2 Lloyd's Rep. 460. And see further *Toepfer v. Schwarze* [1980] 1 Lloyd's Rep. 385 (C.A.); *Bunge S.A. v. Kruse* [1980] 2 Lloyd's Rep. 142 (C.A.); *Tradax Export S.A. v. Cook Industries Inc.* [1982] 1 Lloyd's Rep. 385, *inter alia*, with respect to the stage at which a buyer might have to raise certain pleas on the seller's ability to perform within a chain transaction in respect of such loopholes: where the dispute is referred to arbitration such issues cannot be raised for the first time before the court. See *Bremer Handelsgesellschaft mbH v. Raiffeisen Hauptgenossensch-*

But in *Tradax Export S.A. v. Andre & Cie S.A.*[6] the Court of Appeal (Lord Denning M.R. and Orr and Browne L.J.) held that, in certain types of c.i.f. transactions (string contracts in which the seller had already made arrangements to ship the goods and was thereafter prevented from so doing by an event of *force majeure* or export prohibition) the seller is not required to seek goods afloat so as to fulfil his contractual obligations. In other words, if the shipment arrangements have already been made (by the seller or some other shipper higher up in the string), a supervening event excusing his intended method of performance will act as a discharge without his also having to show that he could not have bought goods afloat to fulfil the contract, at any rate when there is only a small amount of alternative cargoes available.[7] For, as explained by Lord Denning M.R. in the *Tradax* Case (at page 423):

> "If there were to be an obligation to buy afloat, who is to do the buying? Is each seller to do so in order to fulfil his obligation to the buyer? If that were so, there would be . . . large numbers of buyers chasing very few goods and the price would reach unheard of levels."

In such circumstances, as was stated in a later case, "a duty to buy afloat is impracticable and commercially unsuitable."[8]

The *Tradax* decision involved a c.i.f. contract within a string transaction.

---

aft eg [1982] 1 Lloyd's Rep. 599 (C.A.), and *Raiffeisen Hauptgenossenschaft v. Louis Dreyfus & Co. Ltd.; Dreyfus v. Becher* [1981] 1 Lloyd's Rep. 345; *Bremer Handelsgesellschaft mbH v. Westzucker GmbH* [1981] 1 Lloyd's Rep. 207; *Bremer Handelsgesellschaft mbH v. Westzucker (No. 2); Westzucker GmbH v. Bunge GmbH* [1981] 2 Lloyd's Rep. 130 (C.A.); *Cook Industries Inc. v. Meunerie Liegeois* [1981] 1 Lloyd's Rep. 359; *Bremer Handelsgesellschaft v. C. Mackprang Jr.* [1981] 1 Lloyd's Rep. 292 (C.A.). All of these disputes involved chain transactions (and in certain cases circle ones with goods resold to the original seller) for soya meal under c.i.f. shipments from the U.S. in the summer of 1973. The U.S. government issued a series of export control measures with sellers desiring to take advantage of *force majeure* exemptions that gave them rights to extend, and, thereafter, cancel (without penalty) their commitments. In order to enjoy the benefit of such extension or exemption clauses, however, the seller may have to serve the required notice in terms of the relevant contract provision. Where he fails to provide the right type of notice—absent the buyer's waiver or acceptance of the defective notice—he will normally be unable to enjoy the protection afforded: see *Bunge GmbH v. (Alfred C.) Toepfer* [1978] 1 Lloyd's Rep. 506, affirmed [1979] 1 Lloyd's Rep. 554 (C.A.). However the contract may expressly provide for automatic (rather than conditional) cancellation as a result of an event preventing fulfilment occurring (*e.g.* the imposition of an export prohibition). In the latter case, the seller's failure to give the required notice will not prevent the cancellation and will only make him liable for any loss incurred in consequence. See *Bremer Handelsgesellschaft mbH v. Vanden Avenne-Izegem P.V.B.A.* [1978] 2 Lloyd's Rep. 109 (H.L.) followed in *Bremer Handelsgesellschaft mbH v. Finagrain Compagnie Commerciale Agricole et Financière S.A.* [1981] 2 Lloyd's Rep. 259 (C.A.).

[6] [1976] 1 Lloyd's Rep. 416, followed on this point in *Bremer Handelsgesellschaft mbH v. Vanden Avenne-Izegem P.V.B.A.* [1977] 2 Lloyd's Rep. 329 (C.A.) and [1978] 2 Lloyd's Rep. 109 (H.L.). See also *per* Kerr L.J. in *André & Cie S.A. v. Tradax Export S.A.* [1983] 1 Lloyd's Rep. 254 at pp. 265 *et seq.*

[7] *Bremer Handelsgesellschaft mbH v. Fingrain Compagnie Commerciale Agricole et Financière S.A.* [1981] 2 Lloyd's Rep. 259 (C.A.) (where the "string" was not long and there were no intermediate sellers) may suggest that the latter is the decisive criteria. However the judgment is based on a finding by an arbitration Board of Appeal that the contract there considered "was no different to the one considered in the *Tradax* case".

[8] *Per* Lord Wilberforce in the *Vanden* decision [1978] 2 Lloyd's Rep. 109 at p. 115.

Lord Denning M.R. (who delivered the main judgment) referred to the difficulties that would arise in such transactions if there were an obligation upon a seller who could not get his goods direct from the intended ports of shipment, after arrangements to ship had already been made, to have to buy them afloat, particularly where (as was the situation in the case under consideration) the only quantity of goods afloat of which there was evidence was a relatively very small quantity with many purchasers who would be obliged to seek to buy for themselves that small quantity in the event that purchase of goods afloat was required.

In light of the particular circumstances in *Tradax v. Andre*, the principle (there decided) was not extended to apply to a case where the seller—who could ship from one or more ports in various countries—wished to rely on an exception clause relieving him from liability in the event of an export prohibition which prevented him from shipping from a particular port or country from which he had made arrangements to ship. In *Warinco A. G. v. Fritz Mauthner*[9] the Court of Appeal (Megaw, Bridge and Waller L.JJs.) overruled Donaldson J. who decided he was bound by the *Tradax v. Andre* holding, and gave judgment for the seller. The facts in the *Warinco* decision were as follows: The sellers agreed to sell to the buyers 1,000 metric tonnes of U.S. soya bean meal c.i.f. Weser, shipment Mediterranean port between May 29 and June 16, 1973. The contract contained an exception clause in the case of "prohibition of export . . . on behalf of the government of the country of origin or of the territory where the port or ports of shipment named herein is/are situate. . . ." In order to perform the contract the sellers purchased a cargo of U.S. soya bean meal f.o.b. a Piraeus silo, and chartered a vessel to carry it to Weser. Export licences had been obtained, but they were suspended the day loading was about to begin, and it would have been illegal to ship throughout the remainder of the shipment period. The sellers took all reasonable steps to have the suspension lifted or a new licence granted but their efforts were in vain. The buyers claim for damages for non-delivery, which was denied by the lower court which considered itself bound by the *Tradax v. Andre* ruling, succeeded before the Court of Appeal. In the course of his judgment Megaw L. J. said:

> "It is clear law, based on many decided cases, that, in general, where the seller has undertaken to supply goods shipped from one or other of a number of ports, he cannot rely on an event included in an exception clause, if that event happens but affects only one of the ports: unless, at any rate, he can show the burden being on him, that, despite reasonable efforts (and . . . I do not stay to consider what is the standard of effort required), he could not have shipped goods complying with the contract description, and within the permitted time for shipment, from any one of the other ports."[10]

The result was very unfortunate for the seller, as he could obtain no similar

---

[9] [1978] 1 Lloyd's Rep. 151.
[10] At p. 153.

relief from his own supplier from whom he had in turn bought the soya bean meal on an f.o.b. Piraeus basis. The f.o.b. supplier was able to rely on a similar exception clause in his contract, and avoid any liability for non performance due to the export prohibition since his obligation was confined to delivery in Greece.[11]

In some c.i.f. cases (concerning string or chain transactions) the parties never intend the contract to be performed by the seller shipping the goods but from the start contemplate its being implemented by the purchase of goods afloat. In such cases the ability of the seller to plead impossibility of shipment, or to rely on an exception clause excusing performance as a result of an export prohibition, will apparently be curtailed.[12] And a similar result obtains in the case of "circle" contracts (within a string transaction) where the goods originally sold, or some part of them, are or may ultimately be resold back to the original seller. In such cases, the rights and obligations of the parties may be monetary only, and an attempt to invoke the exception clause by the original seller may be construed as an effort to rely on an inability to perform an act which he no longer has the right or obligation to do.[13]

42   Whether or not the contract is discharged through frustration where performance (under both alternatives) becomes a practical impossibility is however a different question which is beyond the scope of this work. Suffice it here to state[14] the general rule that where the contract contains no provision as to the consequences of impossibility to ship or of the purchase of goods afloat, the circumstances surrounding the contract will determine whether or not the seller is discharged from his contract. Certainly the mere fact that performance becomes more costly would not usually suffice to constitute frustration. In the American case of *Madeirense Do Brasil S/A v. Stulman-Emerick Lumber Co.*,[15] the Second Circuit Court of Appeals opined that a seller of Brazilian lumber sold on c. and f. terms would have been liable for breach if he was unable to secure shipping space as a result of scarcity caused by the Second World War. The contract was entered into after the Second World War had been under way for over a year, and although the seller was able to obtain shipping space there was an unexpected increase in freight and some of the lumber was shipped "on" instead of "below" deck. The seller alleged that he was not responsible for the increased freight or for breach in not procuring the required contract of carriage[16] on the grounds of *force*

[11] See *Provimi Hellas A. E. v. Warinco A. G.* [1978] 1 Lloyd's Rep. 373 (C.A.).
[12] See, *e.g. Bunge S.A.* v. *Deutsche Conti Handelsgesellschaft mbH* [1979] 2 Lloyd's Rep. 435 (C.A.).
[13] See, *e.g. Tradax Export S.A.* v. *Rocco Giuseppe & Figli* [1981] 1 Lloyd's Rep. 353. But *cf. Tradax Export S.A.* v. *Carapelli S.p.A.* [1977] 2 Lloyd's Rep. 157 where the "circle" transaction was the subject of an express term of the contract that did not oust the application of the exception clause in question.
[14] See further *post*, 53.
[15] 147 F. 2d 399 (1945).
[16] *Post*, 93 *et seq.*

majeure resulting from the scarcity of shipping space due to the war. The court dismissed these allegations on the grounds that it was a foreseeable risk willingly undertaken, adding that "even had there been no ships available, plaintiff was not, under the circumstances of this case, excused from performance."

43   In *Intertradex S.A. v. Lesieur-Turteaux S.A.R.L.*[17] Donaldson J. opined that:

> "whether or not a contract is frustrated is a mixed question of fact and law. . . . The sellers' basic obligation [under a c.i.f. contract] was to deliver the goods (or documents covering the goods) in accordance with their contract. The basic risks which they assumed were those of shortage of supply and a rise in price . . . a mere reduction in the supplies available, even from a sole supplier, due to such common-place events as a breakdown of machinery or the inadequacies of a railway [by means of which the goods are to be transported to the port of shipment] are far removed from [the] category [of events constituting frustration]."

In that case the contract was for the sale of 800 metric tonnes of Mali groundnut expellers c.i.f. Rouen, shipment in March 1973. The sellers intended to fulfil their obligation by purchasing from suppliers who, to their knowledge (but not the buyers') were the sole producers of Mali groundnut expellers, and whose factory was 10 days by rail from Abidjan and three or four days from Dakar, the only export ports. Due to a breakdown of the electrical distribution panel at the suppliers factory, the fact that a replacement part had to be obtained from Germany, and interruptions in the supply by rail of raw materials for the factory, the suppliers (and, as a result, the sellers) were unable to meet their commitments in full. The contract contained a *force majeure* clause, and the question arose as to whether the sellers could claim the protection of the clause, or, failing its application in the circumstances, defend the claim on the grounds that the contract was frustrated. The dispute went to arbitration, and the Board of Appeal of the GAFTA held in favour of the sellers but, on a case stated, Donaldson J. reversed their decision. He ruled that, in the circumstances, the sellers could neither claim the benefit of the *force majeure* clause (because their notice to the buyers alleging the *force majeure* was bad as it was based only upon breakdown of machinery whereas shortage of materials was also an effective cause of non shipment) nor succeed on the grounds that non performance was justified by frustration, albeit there being no alternative source of supply available at the time.

On shipment, or upon purchase of goods afloat, the seller must procure a bill of lading (or such other equivalent document in lieu thereof as the contract may prescribe), for tender to the buyer, under which the goods will be delivered at the destination provided in the contract.

Where loading was affected by or on behalf of the c.i.f. seller, but the vessel was struck and unable to depart or sail for its destination, the seller is

---

[17] [1977] 2 Lloyd's Rep. 146 at p. 154.

entitled to payment on tender of the documents, and any resulting damages due to the delay are for account of the buyer. Such a situation arose in *Badhwar v. Colorado Fuel & Iron Corp.*[18] where 2000 tons of caustic soda were sold "CIF Bombay". The vessel, on which the cargo was shipped, arrived in Bombay some months after it had been loaded in New Orleans, due to a strike by the engine room crew that prevented sailing as well as unloading and reloading it on board some other vessel that was free to sail. It was held, correctly it is submitted, that the contract was performed by the seller, and that he was under no duty to find a ship that would not be strike bound. The potential for strikes and their possible duration were (and usually are) always present, but they are not (in the absence malfeasance or an agreement to the contrary) matters of foreseeability for which the c.i.f. seller would be liable.

The duty of seller

44   The first duty of the seller is to see that the goods shipped correspond with the contractual description. He must then ensure that the shipment on board the vessel is in accordance with the terms of the contract. It is, of course, at all times the duty of the seller to comply with the terms of the particular contract of sale he has made. Whether as a general rule the express terms in a c.i.f. contract amount to conditions of the contract,[19] a breach of which entitles the buyer to reject the documents or the goods is, however, less clear. This was no doubt true in earlier times, but more recently the courts appear to have adopted a less stringent attitude. While stipulations made by either party are intended to be binding for, as Bailhache J. said,[20] considering a contract by correspondence, "commercial men in making contracts of this kind do not give each other pieces of news," the parties must have agreed, expressly or by implication, that any failure to perform a primary obligation, irrespective of the gravity of the event that has in fact resulted from the breach, shall entitle the other party to bring the contract to an end.[21] Nowdays the courts may be more inclined to view contracts as if they were meant to be performed, and to treat certain obligations as warranties or innominate terms, a breach of which may only give rise to damages.[22]

Where the seller personally or by his agent ships the goods it is his duty, as shipper, to enter into a contract of carriage with the carrier, or shipowner as he is usually called. The contract of carriage is known as the contract of affreightment. In some c.i.f. contracts, the seller may be required to give the buyer an advance notice of the vessel's arrival. This is particularly common

---

[18] (1955) 138 F. Supp. 595.
[19] See further *post*, § 60.
[20] *French Government v. Sunday & Co.* (1923) 16 Ll.L.Rep. 238 at p. 240.
[21] See *per* Lord Diplock in *Photo Production Ltd. v. Securicor Transport Ltd.* [1980] A.C. 427, and *per* Lord Wilberforce in *Bungee Corp. v. Tradax Export S.A.* [1985] Lloyd's Rep. 1 at p. 6.
[22] See *post*, § 316 *et seq.*

in commodity trades involving chain or string transactions.[23] On shipment of the goods, the seller, as shipper, is given a bill of lading which is, *inter alia*, a receipt for the goods stating the terms on which they are received. It is this document which is to be later tendered to the buyer.

If the seller does not himself ship the goods, but purchases goods afloat, he must ensure that the documents he obtains are such as to conform to the contract of sale with his buyer.

The goods

45   The goods shipped must correspond with the contract description. The Sale of Goods Act 1803, s. 13 (now section 13 of the Sale of Goods Act 1979), enacts that:

> "Where there is a contract for the sale of goods by description, there is an implied condition that the goods shall correspond with the description; and if the sale be by sample as well as by description, it is not sufficient that the bulk of the goods corresponds with the sample if the goods do not also correspond with the description."

There is a sale by description where the goods are described in the contract and the buyer contracts in reliance on that description. By section 2 of the Supply of Goods (Implied Terms) Act 1973, a new subsection (2) was added to the said section 13 providing that "A sale of goods shall not be prevented from being a sale by description by reason only that, being exposed for sale or hire, they are selected by the buyer." Prior to the passage of this amendment there was some doubt as to whether section 13 applied, and, if so, under what circumstances, where the purchaser had seen or selected the goods. In relation to the old section 13 it was said that: "the term 'sale of goods by description' must apply to all cases where the purchaser has not seen the goods, but is relying on the description alone."[24] This statement is of course still valid; and since the buyer under a c.i.f. contract seldom sees the goods before the contract is entered into, practically all c.i.f. contracts were sales by description even under the unamended Act. Thus, the amending provision merely reinforces this conclusion. The principle embodied in section 13 is nowhere more clearly stated than in the words of Lord Blackburn in *Bowes v. Shand*.[25] "If you contract to sell peas, you cannot oblige a party to take beans. If the description of the article tendered is different in any respect it is not the article bargained for, and the other party is not bound to take it." The extent of its application is well illustrated by the case of *Manbre Sac-*

---

[23] As was the case, *e.g.* in *Nova Petroleum International Establishment v. Tricon Trading Ltd.* [1989] 1 Lloyd's Rep. 312 where the provision in question was construed as a condition. See also *Transpetrol Ltd. v. Tansol Owerproduction B.V.* [1989] 1 Lloyd's Rep. 309.

[24] *Per* Channell J., *Varley v. Whipp* [1900] 1 Q.B. 513 at p. 516.

[25] (1877) 2 App. Cas. 455 at p. 480, see *post*, § 60.

charine Co. v. Corn Product Co.,[26] where the contract was for the sale c.i.f. of starch in 280 lb. bags and the starch shipped was partly in 280 lb. bags and partly in 140 lb. bags. It was argued by the sellers that the words "280 lb. bags" were not a material part of the bargain, but McCardie J. disagreed. He said[27]:

> "It is clear that such words were an essential part of the contract requirements. They constitute a portion of the description of the goods. The size of bags may be important to a purchaser in view of sub-contracts or otherwise. A man may prefer to receive starch either in small or large or medium bags. If the size of the bags was immaterial I fail to see why it should have been so clearly specified in the contract. A vendor must supply goods in accordance with the contract description, and he is not entitled to say that another description of goods will suffice for the purposes of the purchaser."

46   Similarly, in the case of *Re Moore & Co. and Landauer & Co.,*[28] a contract for the sale c.i.f. of cases of Australian canned fruits each being described as containing thirty tins, was held by the Court of Appeal (Bankes, Scrutton and Atkin L.JJ.), affirming Rowlatt J., not to have been satisfied by a tender of a consignment one half of which consisted of cases containing 24 tins only. In that case Scrutton L.J. adopted the above cited words of McCardie J. as part of his judgment.[29]

In *Arcos Ltd. v. E. A. Ronaasen & Son*[30] the sellers tendered goods that were merchantable under the description of the contract but which failed to conform with the exact contract specifications. An umpire ruled against the buyers who purported to reject the goods, but his decision was reversed by Wright J., whose judgment was affirmed both by the Court of Appeal and by the House of Lords. The c.i.f. contract in question was for the sale of staves of Russian timber which, though allowing a variation with respect to the lengths and breadths thereof, afforded no similar allowance in thickness, the latter being specified as at half an inch. It was held that the fact that the goods were fit for the particular purpose for which they were required was immaterial. The implied condition under section 14(1) (as it then was)[31] of the Sale of Goods Act, unless otherwise provided, is additional to the condition under section 13.

In a more recent case[32] the court had to construe a contract for the sale of 1,000 cases of Spanish apricot pulp of a certain description expressed to be "subject to approval of 25 cases to be shipped to London by first available steamer." The 25 cases, when they arrived, were not to the buyers' satisfac-

---

[26] [1919] 1 K. B. 198.
[27] *Ibid.* at p. 207.
[28] [1921] 2 K. B. 519.
[29] *Ibid.* at p. 524.
[30] [1933] A. C. 470.
[31] The section was redrafted and modified by s.3 of the Supply of Goods (Implied Terms) Act 1973, and the condition in s.14 *inter alia* is now independent of, and ceases to be dependent on the sale being by description.
[32] *John Bowron & Son Ltd.* v. *Rodema Canned Foods Ltd.* [1967] 1 Lloyd's Rep. 183.

tion and they proceeded to claim damages in an arbitration. The arbitrator found the contract to be one of sale by description, not sample, and the purpose of the words ''subject to approval of 25 cases'' was to enable the buyers to satisfy themselves that the goods conformed to the specification laid down in the contract before the bulk had been shipped to them. Widgery J. upheld the award rejecting the sellers' allegation that the contract became null and void on the buyers' disapproval of the preliminary shipment. He could not support their interpretation that the real purpose of the contract was to enable the sellers to send forward 25 cases of the particular kind of pulp available to them so that the buyers could then form their opinion as to whether or not to buy. The sellers were held to be in default for failure to send forward 25 cases of the contract description in all respects.

Whether the courts will, in future, adopt a more lenient view on the implied condition imposed by the first sentence of section 13 of the Act remains to be seen. There is a feeling in some circles that some of the authorities may have been excessively technical in this matter, and that a fresh examination might be warranted. This sentiment was first expressed by Lord Wilberforce in his speech in *Reardon Smith Line v. Hansen–Tangen*[33] where he opined that his preference would be ''to [first] ask whether a particular item in a description constitutes a substantial ingredient of the 'identity' of the thing sold, and only if it does, to treat it as a condition''.

Where the sale is also by sample (and not merely by description) the buyer, unless the contract restricts his freedom in any way, retains an unfettered right to reject the sample. He need not show good cause or reason, and approval of the sample may not obligate him to accept the balance. In *Wood Components of London v. Webster*,[34] a contract for the sale of 5,100 cubic feet of Bulgarian beech squares provided for a sample shipment of 500 cubic feet, with delivery of the balance to follow approval of the sample. Sellers L.J. found there was a concluded contract (by description) for the sample shipment, coupled with a firm offer or option for a further quantity to be accepted or exercised by the buyers approving the sample. Approval of the sample shipment in itself and for the purposes of its own sale did not, in his view, necessarily entail a commitment to accept the balance.

If the contract contains a provision as to the method of performance, it must be followed, since it will be deemed to form a part of the description of the goods and will usually be treated as a condition of the contract. Thus, where the sale was of beans in bags per steamship *Luzo* ''afloat,'' payment in London by cash against documents on arrival of steamship, but in fact, before the date of the contract the steamer had, without the knowledge of sellers or buyers, arrived and discharged the beans, and the buyers took up the documents, but then, having discovered the fact of the vessel's arrival and discharge of the goods, claimed to reject, Shearman J.[35] held that the

---

[33] [1976] 1 W.L.R. 989 at p. 998 (H.L.).
[34] [1959] 2 Lloyd's Rep. 200.
[35] *Benabu & Co. v. Produce Brokers Co. Ltd.* (1921) 37 T.L.R. 609, C.A., *ibid.*, at p. 857.

word "afloat" was used in reference to the goods and was a condition of the contract. The buyers were therefore entitled to reject and recover the price paid by them. So, too, where goods were sold "afloat per the SS. *Moreton Bay*, due London approximately June 8," McNair J. held that the whole phrase was part of the description of the goods.[36]

The quantity

47   The seller does not fulfil his contract if he ships a greater or smaller quantity of goods than he contracted to sell. Section 30 of the Sale of Goods Act 1893 (now section 30 of the Sale of Goods Act 1979) provides:

> "(1) Where the seller delivers to the buyer a quantity of goods less than he contracted to sell, the buyer may reject them, but if the buyer accepts the goods so delivered he must pay for them at the contract rate.
>
>   (2) Where the seller delivers to the buyer a quantity of goods larger than he contracted to sell, the buyer may accept the goods included in the contract and reject the rest, or he may reject the whole. If the buyer accepts the whole of the goods so delivered he must pay for them at the contract rate."

Subsection (3) of the 1893 Act (which is now subsection (4) of the 1979 Act) entitles the buyer to reject the contract goods when mixed with other goods. This subsection was considered in *Dawood Ltd. v. Heath Ltd., Dalal (London) (Third Party)*,[37] where the plaintiffs bought from the defendants 50 tons of galvanised steel sheets c.i.f. Port Louis, Mauritius. The sheets were to be "assorted equal tonnage per size" and were by the seller's invoice described to be "... assorted over 6, 7, 8, 9, and 10 feet long ..." The sellers, however, delivered 50 tons of sheets of 6-foot lengths. The buyers claimed to accept one-fifth of the sheets and reject four-fifths, and to recover four-fifths of the price as money paid on a consideration which had wholly failed. The sellers argued that section 30(3) of the 1893 Act could not be invoked because no part of the delivery was an assorted parcel within the contract. Moreover, they alleged that the provision as to equal weight for each size was a warranty and not a condition of the contract,[38] and, that if buyers were entitled to a remedy, it was in damages. McNair J., allowing the claim, held that the term "assorted equal tonnage per size" was made a part of the description of the contract and therefore a condition thereof. In his opinion section 30(3) of the 1893 Act could be invoked by the buyer. The seller delivered to the buyer one-fifth of the goods he contracted to sell mixed with goods of a different description, in the sense that no permission to ship the 6-foot lengths in excess of one-fifth of the total weight was included in the contract. By contrast, in *Gill & Duffus S.A. v. Berger & Co. Inc.*,[39] the

---

[36] *Macpherson Train & Co. Ltd. v. Howard Ross & Co. Ltd.* [1955] 1 Lloyd's Rep. 518.

[37] [1961] 2 Lloyd's Rep. 512.

[38] See as to distinction between conditions and warranties, *post*, § 316.

[39] [1983] 1 Lloyd's Rep. 622, reversing [1981] 1 Lloyd's Rep. 101.

majority of the Court of Appeal held that a conclusive certificate (as to quality and description) that covered 455 tonnes out of a 500 ton shipment of Argentine Bolita beans was ineffective, because by virtue of subsections (1) and (3) of the Act, the buyer could either reject the whole of the shipment (which he purported to do) or none of it. But this decision was reversed by the House of Lords which held that the buyer had wrongfully repudiated the contract, and the question did not arise except in the context of reducing his liability in damages, were he able to prove (which he was not) that the shipment consisted of non-conforming goods.[40]

By subsection (4) of section 30 (now subsection (5) of the 1979 Act), however, the provisions of the section are expressed to be "subject to any usage of trade, special agreement, or course of dealing between the parties," and it is not uncommon for the seller to protect himself by qualifying the specified contract quantity by the addition of terms such as "approximately," "more or less" or "about."[41]

Nevertheless, some slight elasticity is permitted on the *de minimis* principle, provided that the contract has been properly performed in the commercial sense. In *Harland & Wolff v. Burstall.*[42] sellers of 500 loads of timber for shipment at Quebec c.i.f. Belfast, shipped 470 loads. The ship and cargo were lost on the voyage. The documents were not tendered to the buyers but it was intended that the shipment should be applied to the contract. The buyers claimed damages for breach of the contract, and the question was whether the sellers had performed their obligations. Bigham J. held that they had not. He added that:

> "Of course, in carrying out a commercial contract such as this some slight elasticity is unavoidable; no one supposes that the delivery is to be within a cubic foot of the named quantity, but it must be substantially of the quantity named."[43]

48   In *Shipton, Anderson & Co. v. Weil Bros. & Co.*,[44] the contract was for the sale of a cargo of wheat "weight as per bill or bills of lading . . . say 4,500 tons, 2 per cent, more or less; seller has the option of shipping a further 8 per cent, more or less on contract quantity." The sellers tendered a cargo of wheat which weighed 55 lb, more than 4,950 tons, the limit of the quantity allowed by the contract. The buyers rejected the tender on the ground of excess, the value of which, at the contract price, was 4s. The contract price of 4,950 tons exceeded £40,000. The sellers made no claim for the 4s. Having sold the cargo after rejection at a loss, they claimed damages for non-acceptance. On a special case stated by arbitrators, Lush J., held that the

---

[40] [1984] 1 Lloyd's Rep. 227, *post*, § 325a.
[41] *e.g. Reuter v. Sala* (1879) 4 C.P.D. 239, "25 tons, more or less, Penang pepper"; *Payne and Routh v. Lillico & Sons* (1920) 36 T.L.R. 569, "4,000 tons of meal, 2 per cent more or less"; *Harland & Wolff v. Burstall* (1901) 6 Com. Cas. 113, "about 500 loads of timber"; and cases cited in the text below.
[42] (1901) 6 Com, Cas. 113.
[43] *Ibid.* at p. 116.
[44] [1912] 1 K.B. 574.

quantity in excess was trifling, and, as the price of the excess was not claimed, the sellers had substantially performed the contract. Consequently the buyers had no right to reject under section 30(2) of the Sale of Goods Act 1893.[45]

> "The question is whether there has been a substantial departure from the contract ... The right to reject is founded upon the hypothesis that the seller was not ready and willing to perform or had not performed his part of the contract. The tender of a wrong quantity evidences an unreadiness and unwillingness, but that, in my opinion, must mean an excess or deficiency in quantity which is capable of influencing the mind of the buyer. In my opinion, this excess is not. I agree that directly the excess becomes a matter of possible discussion between reasonable parties, the seller is bound to justify what he has done under the contract; but the doctrine of *de minimis* cannot, I think, be excluded merely because the statute refers to the tender of a smaller or larger quantity than the contract quantity as entitling a buyer to reject."[46]

He added that if the sellers had expressly or impliedly insisted upon payment of the 4s., the case would have been different.

This decision was followed by the Court of Appeal (Scrutton Freer and Slesser L.JJ.) in *E. A. Ronaasen and Son v. Arcos Ltd.*,[47] where it was pointed out that although the court will not heed a variation which is microscopic, the burden of showing that the breach comes within the *de minimis* rule is on the party seeking to excuse the breach.

Meaning of "cargo"

49   Where the sale is of a "cargo,"[48] the precise effect to be given to that word may be a question of some difficulty. The answer depends upon the construction of the contract and the particular circumstances of the case. No rule of general application can be formulated, but the usual meaning seems to be a full and complete cargo.

In *Kreuger v. Blanck*,[49] the defendant ordered from the plaintiffs in Sweden "a small cargo (of lathwood) of about the following lengths ... in all about sixty cubic fathoms" c.i.f. Bristol Channel. The plaintiffs were not able to procure a vessel of the exact size, and so chartered a vessel loaded with 83 fathoms. On arrival, the plaintiff's agent measured and set apart the amount of the defendant's order, and tendered to him a bill of lading for that quantity and a draft for acceptance; but the defendant declined to accept the same on the ground that the "cargo" was in excess of the order. It was held by Kelly

---

[45] Set out *ante.* § 47.
[46] [1912] 1 K.B. at p. 577.
[47] (1932) 37 Com. Cas. 291, affirmed [1933] A.C. 470 (H.L.).
[48] "'Cargo' is a word with different meanings. It may mean one thing in a charterparty, another in a policy, another in a contract of sale." *Per* Lord Bramwell, *Colonial Insurance Co. of New Zealand v. Adelaide Marine Insurance Co.* (1886) 12 App. Cas. 128 at p. 129.
[49] (1870) L.R. 5 Ex. 179.

C. B. and Cleasby B., with Martin B. dissenting, that "cargo" meant a whole cargo and not part of a cargo. That it was so treated in the correspondence between the parties, and that the plaintiff had not complied with the order. It was held furthermore that the plaintiff was not entitled to make a selection, and had part of the timber been lost or damaged in transit there would be nothing to show whether it was the defendant's (or other) timber that was affected. The defendant might also have to pay freight for the whole cargo before he could obtain possession of what was his own. Thus, the defendant had good grounds for insisting on a complete cargo for himself.

Ireland v. Livingston[50] shows that when the seller is a commission agent for the buyer, the use of the word "cargo" may not be given so stringent an effect. Moreover, Blackburn J. in that case said that "if necessary I should advise your Lordships to reconsider the decision of the Court of Exchequer in *Kreuger v. Blanck*," on the ground that the buyer does not suffer if the ship is larger than is required, and the superfluous space is used in a way consistent with his contract".[51]

50   In *Borrowman v. Drayton*[52] the sale was of "a cargo of from 2,500 to 3,000 barrels (seller's option)" of petroleum, to be shipped from New York. The sellers chartered a ship and loaded 3,000 barrels and took a bill of lading for this quantity; but, as this quantity did not constitute a full cargo, a further quantity of 300 barrels was shipped, marked with a different mark, under a separate bill of lading. Notice of shipment of 3,000 barrels was given to the buyer and the sellers were ready to deliver either the 3,000 or 2,750, the mean between 2,500 and 3,000 barrels; but the buyer refused to accept any. It was held by the Court of Appeal (Cockburn C.J., James and Mellish L.JJ., and Baggallay J.A.) that on the true construction of the contract "cargo" meant the entire quantity of goods loaded on the vessel, and the buyer was therefore not bound to accept part of a cargo.

> "Generally speaking." said Mellish L.J., delivering the judgment of the court. "the term 'cargo,' unless there is something in the context to give it a different signification, means the entire load of the ship which carries it, and it may fairly be assumed that when one man undertakes to sell and another to buy a cargo, the subject-matter of the contract is to be the entire load of the ship. And that such must have been the sense in which the term 'cargo' is used in this contract is materially strengthened by the agreement that the vessel shall proceed to a port of discharge to be determined, within certain limits, by the buyer, showing plainly that what was contemplated was that the vessel and its entire cargo were to be at his disposal. There are various reasons why a purchaser may wish to buy the whole quantity of goods loaded on board a particular vessel. Such a contract gives him the complete control of the vessel. It enables him to select the port of discharge, to appoint the place in the port at which the discharge is

---

[50] (1872) L.R. 5 H.L. 395.
[51] *Ibid.* at p. 410.
[52] (1876) 2 Ex.D. 15 (C.A.): followed in *Re Harrison and Micks, Lambert & Co.* [1917] 1 K.B. 755, Bailhache and Atkin JJ. ("the remainder" of the cargo "(more or less about) 5.400 quarters Manitoba wheat").

to take place, to be free from the inconvenience of other persons' goods being unloaded at the same time as his own, and from the competition arising from other persons' goods being ready for sale, at the same place, and at the same time, with his.''[53]

In *Paul Ltd. v. Pim & Co.*,[54] the contract was for the sale c.i.f. of ''the cargo of Galatz and/or Foxanian maize shipped in good condition ... per S.S. *Rijn*, consisting of about 2,813 French tons, or what steamer carries as per bill or bills of lading dated about March 8, 1921.'' After arrival of the steamer, the buyers discovered that in addition to the maize there were about 58 tons of tobacco which had been put there without the seller's knowledge and which were not mentioned in any bill of lading. The buyers claimed to reject the maize on the ground that they were entitled to a full and complete cargo of maize. Arbitrators found that the contract was for the sale of the cargo of maize actually shipped at the time of the contract, as comprised in the bill of lading, that the maize was in accordance with the contract, and that the buyers were not entitled to reject. Bailhache J. held that the arbitrators were right. In coming to that conclusion he mentioned three points of difference between that case and the case of *Borrowman v. Drayton* (*ante*): first, in the latter case, the cargo was a cargo to be loaded and not a cargo actually loaded in respect of which a bill of lading had been signed; secondly, the tobacco was of a different nature from the maize on board and there was no possibility of confusion; thirdly, the tobacco was put on board, not under any contract with the sellers but in fraud of the charterparty and of the sellers.

Where in the contract there is added to the word ''cargo'' a statement of a particular quantity of goods, then, unless the circumstances show that the intention was otherwise, the word ''cargo'' is nevertheless prima facie the ruling word, and the statement as to quantity is to be regarded as a mere estimate.

The transit

51   The transit contemplated by c.i.f. contracts is generally, but not necessarily, by sea alone. Frequently these contracts involve some land transit[55] as, for instance, contracts for the sale of cotton to be exported from the United States, which are usually carried out by means of through bills of lading from the interior. There, shipment generally takes place when the goods are put on the railroad and the seller receives from the railroad authorities a through bill of lading covering both the land and the sea transit. Similarly, goods may be shipped under a c.i.f. contract into the interior of the country, *e.g.* c.i.f. Leeds.[56] The rapid expansion in the use of containers has of course already

---

[53] 2 Ex.D. 15 at p. 19.
[54] [1922] 2 K.B. 360.
[55] For example, see *Burstall v. Grimsdale* (1906) 11 Com.Cas. 280, but *cf. Re An Arbitration between L. Sutro & Co. and Heilbut, Symons & Co.* [1917] 2 K.B. 348, *post*, §§ 72 *et seq.*
[56] As in *Johnson v. Taylor Bros. & Co.* [1920] A.C. 144.

contributed to a substantial increase in the volume of sales involving combined (sea-land or land-sea) transits and modes of transport.[57] But a contract using the term c.i.f. in connection with air transport is not a true c.i.f. contract (in view of the non negotiable nature of the airway bill)[58] as Graham J. correctly held in *Morton-Norwich Products Inc. v. Intercen Ltd.*[59] where goods were sent from Holland to purchasers in the United Kingdom "c.i.f. Gatwick".

Meaning of "shipment"

52   But if there is an express provision as to "shipment" in an English contract, "shipment" means the loading of the goods onto a ship; and evidence that by the custom of a particular trade it means loading into railway cars in the interior of the country is inadmissible, as such construction would be inconsistent with the express term of the contract.[60] Thus in *Mowbray, Robinson & Co. v. Rosser*,[61] where a contract was made in England through the American sellers' broker for the sale of American timber, "*shipment* to be made not later than the end of November next," and the English buyers refused to carry out the contract because (*inter alia*) the goods had not been shipped by the specified date, it was unsuccessfully contended by the sellers that by the custom of the trade in America "shipment" meant loading on railroad cars or loading on cars at the saw mills from which the timber comes. In an English contract, "shipment" means putting on board a ship, unless the sense is varied by other terms of the contract.

It has already been noted that, in the absence of a stipulation to the contrary, a c.i.f. contract can normally be performed in one of two alternative methods, and the seller has the option (or obligation) of either arranging for the actual shipment of the goods or of purchasing them afloat.

However, the contract may expressly or by necessary implication deny any such option by providing that it shall be performed by shipment only. In that case the seller who is prevented by lack of shipping or other facilities or by governmental prohibition from shipping need not prove that the contract could not be performed by purchasing goods afloat. If these events amount to a frustration of the contract because the seller has not undertaken an absolute obligation to perform or to pay damages in lieu thereof, the contract is thereby discharged. Accordingly, where a contract for the sale of Egyptian cotton

---

[57] See, *e.g. Lindon Tricotagefabrik v. White and Meacham* [1975] 1 Lloyd's Rep. 384 (C.A.) where the sale was c.i.f. buyer's warehouse at Ealing and the goods, which were shipped in a container, were not insured with respect to the inland transit in England.
[58] *Ante.*, § 3.
[59] [1976] F.S.R. 513.
[60] "To fall within the exception of repugnancy [the custom] must be such as, if expressed in the written contract, would make it insensible or inconsistent." *Per* Lord Campbell C. J., *Humphrey v. Dale* (1857) 7 E. & B. 266 at p. 275. "I accept and agree with [this test]." *Per* Lord Birkenhead L. C., *Palgrave, Brown & Sons Ltd. v. SS. Turid* [1922] 1 A.C. 397 at p. 406.
[61] (1922) 91 L.J.K.B. 524 (C.A.).

seed oil c.i.f. Rotterdam, provided, *inter alia*, that "should the shipment be delayed by . . . prohibition of export . . . or any other cause comprehended in the term *force majeure* other than war . . . the time of shipment shall be extended by two months," McNair J. rejected the contention of the buyers that, in order to enjoy the benefit of this stipulation, the sellers also had to prove that they could not purchase goods afloat that were not affected by a prohibition imposed by the Egyptian Government on the export of cotton seed oil.[62]

The judgment, which was affirmed by the House of Lords,[63] states:

> "In regard to the suggestion that the sellers have to show that they could not buy goods afloat, it seems to me that the use of the phrase 'the shipment,' coupled with the later phrase 'as soon as shippers announce their inability to ship,' in the third sentence of cl. 11B, points clearly to the conclusion that, in this particular contract, the parties are, in terms and designedly, providing protection for the sellers in a case where the first method of performing their obligation under the c.i.f. contract, namely, shipping by themselves or by their agents, is delayed. In my judgment, this clause will not work in any business sense if it were held that the sellers, in addition to proving that the contemplated shipment was delayed, had further to prove that they were unable to purchase goods afloat which were unaffected by the prohibition."[64]

53   In *Lewis Emanuel & Son Ltd. v. Sammut*[65] a contract for the sale of 1,000 half sacks of Maltese new spring crop potatoes, c.i.f. London, entered into on April 14, 1958, provided, *inter alia*, for "shipment on or before April 24th." The contract was not performed because the seller was unable to obtain space on the one and only vessel that called at Malta between April 14 and 24. An award by an umpire holding the seller responsible for damages was affirmed by Pearson J. The umpire had found that no usage or custom, as the seller alleged, existed by virtue of which an implied warranty that shipping space would be available within the shipment period stipulated was to be imported into the contract, and that, in the event of shipping not being available, the contract would be at an end. Pearson J. further held that, though there was nothing to prevent the application of the doctrine of frustration to the case of a c.i.f. contract for the sale of unascertained goods,[66] the contract in the case before him was not frustrated as a result of the seller's inability to obtain shipping space. However, the buyers' contention that no impossibility of performance was proven and that the contract could have been

---

[62] *J. H. Vantol Ltd. v. Fairclough Dodd & Jones Ltd.* [1955] 1 W.L.R. 642.
[63] *Fairclough Dodd & Jones Ltd. v. J. H. Vantol Ltd.* [1957] 1 W.L.R. 136.
[64] [1955] 2 All E.R. 516, at p. 520.
[65] [1959] 2 Lloyd's Rep. 629.
[66] Having reviewed a long line of authorities, Pearson J. concluded:
"In my view, there is nothing exceptional in principle as regards c.i.f. contracts for unascertained goods. But, of course, it may well be that, in view of the nature of these contracts, it would be more difficult to find a frustrating event than it would in the case of some other contracts for specifically ascertained goods and so on, but, to my mind, exactly the same principle of frustration applies; it is only that there may be greater difficulty in showing it in cases of that character" (at p. 640).

performed by purchasing goods afloat, also failed. Not because the word "shipment" excluded it,[67] but because the description of the goods was such that from a practical point of view, the contract could not have been performed unless potatoes of the contract description were present on the one ship which called at Malta between April 14 and 24.

54   However, there was no need to establish whether or not goods of the contract description were in fact present on that one ship. Because even if they were not, the contract would not be at an end by virtue of such impossibility.

> "Under a contract of this kind the seller has an obligation, and he undertakes the duty of finding or providing cargo, finding or providing shipping space, and providing a contract of insurance; that is the responsibility which he undertakes. If he is not sure of being able to provide cargo or shipping space or a policy of insurance, he can guard himself by some provision in the contract, that it is subject to shipping space being available, or such potatoes being available, or subject to a contract of insurance being procurable. But it seems to me that, if the buyers had been asked whether, in the event of the seller being unable to obtain shipping space, the contract would be off, the buyers would have said "Certainly not. That is the seller's duty and responsibility. It is his job to find shipping space. That is what he undertakes to do. That is what he is being paid for in this contract, among other things." As I say, it is a matter of impression, but that is my impression of the possible business effect of this contract."[68]

Where, therefore, the seller desires to protect himself against failure to ship (or some other impossibility to perform), he must so provide expressly, inserting in the contract an exception clause to this effect. Such a clause will normally be strictly construed, and, for this reason, should be drafted with the utmost caution and care. In *Hong Guan & Co. Ltd. v. R. Jumabhoy & Sons Ltd.*[69] the Judicial Committee of the Privy Council had occasion to consider the meaning of a clause "subject to *force majeure* and shipment" in a contract for the sale of 50 tons of Zanzibar cloves, December shipment, to the appellants in Singapore. The contract was not performed because, due to the early rain, shipments of Zanzibar cloves had fallen far below what had been anticipated. The respondents, who were the sellers under the contract, did however ship to Singapore during the month of December certain quantities of Zanzibar cloves, including one consignment of 50 tons, pursuant to some other contracts but those contracts included no similar exception clause. The buyers claimed damages for non-delivery. Their action failed before the trial judge and the Singapore Court of Appeal. It was there held that the contract was made subject to shipment, and that no shipment to the respond-

---

[67] "The answer [to that] may be this, that this is a sale of goods predominantly, and what it really means is that the seller will procure to be delivered to the buyers, through the mechanism of a c.i.f. contract, goods shipped in that period and it does not matter whether they are shipped by him or anybody else so long as they comply with all the requirements of the contract" (at p. 639).

[68] *Ibid.* at p. 642.

[69] [1960] A. C. 684.

ents of the goods contracted to be sold having taken place, the appellants had not defaulted. The Judicial Committee reversed these decisions. In advising that the appeal be allowed Lord Morris of Borth-y-Gest, who delivered their Lordships' decision, explained:

> "It must . . . be borne in mind that the clause now under consideration is not 'subject to shipment' but 'subject to force majeure and shipment.' There is, therefore, a double-barrelled condition in which there is a juxtaposition of *'force majeure'* and of 'shipment.' Having regard to this consideration their Lordships think that the clause in the contract should be construed as meaning that the contract was (a) conditional upon the sellers not being prevented by circumstances amounting to *force majeure* from carrying it out, and (b) conditional upon the sellers being able to procure the shipment in December, 1950, of cloves to the quantity and of the description referred to in the contract. So far as the clause deals with *force majeure* it appears to be designed to protect the respondents from liability in the event of their being prevented from performing the contract by circumstances beyond their control. It seems to their Lordships to be in consonance with this to construe the second branch of the condition as being designed to protect them from liability in the event of their being prevented from carrying out the contract through inability to procure the shipment. If the words were to be construed as covering a situation when shipment did not take place merely as the result of the arbitrary choice of the vendor, then there would be no contractual force in the document, which would merely give an option to the vendor."[70]

55   As the shipment pursuant to the other contracts there showed that shipment was not prevented by circumstances beyond the sellers' control, and, as the sellers could not excuse their non-performance by reference to their other commitments, to which, *vis-à-vis* the claimant buyers, they were not entitled to attach priority, the sellers were in breach of their contract.

In *Hollis Bros. & Co. Ltd. v. White Sea Timber Trust Ltd.,*[71] the parties had entered into a contract for the sale of parquet blocks, c.i.f., for shipment from a port in the Arctic Circle in North Russia, which was only open for shipping for about one month in the year. In respect of one parcel of the blocks there was an undershipment of blocks of a particular size. The contract contained a provision that:

> "In the event of under-shipment of any item buyers are to accept or pay for the quantity shipped, but have the right to claim compensation for such short shipment. . . ."

Another provision, however, stated that:

> "This contract is subject to sellers making necessary chartering arrangements for the expedition, and sold subject to shipment: any goods not shipped to be cancelled."

---

[70] *ibid.* at pp. 699, 700.
[71] [1936] 3 All E.R. 895.

Porter J. held, on a case stated by an arbitrator, that there was an option in the sellers to ship or not to ship and that the words "subject to shipment" meant "provided the sellers in fact ship." For this reason, the buyers' claim for short delivery could not succeed. Referring to this decision in the *Hong Guan* case, Lord Morris of Borth-y-Gest explained[72] that Porter J. ". . . held, however, that if the goods were shipped they had to be attributed to the contract, and that the sellers [had any goods been shipped] could not treat them as free goods unattributed to any contract."

56   In *Sociedad Iberica De Moltracion S.A. v. Tradax Export S.A.*[73] a clause in a c.i.f. contract for the sale of U.S. soya beans for shipment October 5 to 25, 1971 provided that "should shipment of the goods or any part thereof be prevented at any time during . . . contract period . . . by reason of strikes . . . at port or ports of loading . . . then shipper shall be entitled at the termination of such . . . strikes . . . to an extension of time for shipment . . . Shipper shall give notice by cable . . . if he intends to claim an extension of time for shipment." On October 25, 1971 the sellers sent a telex message to the buyers invoking the strike extension clause but the buyers alleged that the sellers were in default, *inter alia*, in specifying eight potential loading ports as being strikebound, and because the strikes were not of such a nature as to have totally prevented the sellers from shipping from any other U.S. port not being a West Coast port. Donaldson J., affirming a decision of an umpire, and of an arbitration appeal tribunal, rejected both allegations as a basis for liability to the buyers for breach of contract, and refused to infer an obligation on part of the sellers to ship from an alternative U.S. port which might have been possible in the circumstances. The words "should shipment . . . be prevented . . . by . . . strikes . . . at port or ports of loading" are intended to refer to the ports through which the seller intended to ship or through which he would in fact have shipped but for the occurrence of the strike. Therefore the fact that the strikes were not of such a magnitude as to have totally prevented the sellers shipping from any other U.S. port (not being a West Coast port) was not material, although any doubts on the construction of such clauses is to be resolved in favour of requiring performance.

The ship

57   If the contract specifies that shipment is to be in a particular class or type of vessel, the stipulation must be complied with. In the old case of *Ashmore & Son v. C. S. Cox & Co.*,[74] a requirement that shipment should be "by sailer or sailers" amounted to a condition of the contract that shipment should be on a sailing vessel. If there is no provision, or a neutral term such as "vessel"

---

[72] [1960] A.C. 684 at p. 698.
[73] [1978] 2 Lloyd's Rep. 545.
[74] [1899] 1 Q.B. 436.

is used, the seller satisfies his obligation by shipping on the kind of vessel by which similar goods are in practice shipped,[75] the test being whether the bill of lading by such class of ship, as the case may be, is the usual bill of lading in the trade.

So, for example, in the case of the sale of clover seeds to be shipped from Italy c.i.f. New York, the Supreme Court of Wisconsin held that the seller was in default, having shipped the goods on a tramp vessel that took 44 days to complete the passage, whereas it was the general custom among those engaged in the trade that the consignor would ship by vessel sailing direct from the port of exportation to the port of importation.[76]

Likewise, the contract may expressly (or by implication) confer a right to deliver on more than a single vessel. Where the quantity was large and a prolonged shipment period was stipulated, such an intention was inferred by Parker J. in *Pagnan and Fratelli v. Tradax Overseas S.A.*[77]

58   So, too, where the contract specifies the name of the vessel, it does more than merely identify the ship on which the goods are to be transported. It would, it is submitted, normally form part of the description of the goods, and any failure to comply therewith would give rise to a right of rejection notwithstanding the substitute vessel being otherwise acceptable.[78]

But where the seller nominates the carrying vessel, he generally can substitute another contractual vessel with a contractual cargo, provided shipment, or arrival at the contractual destination (as the case may be), within the contract time frame is unaffected thereby. However, once a firm nomination has been accepted by the buyer the substitution may have to be immediate, and the seller will be denied the ability to invoke a *force majeure* clause excusing his performance that did not exist (or of which he was unaware) at the time the nomination was withdrawn, and before a substitute vessel was named. This was held in *Coastal (Bermuda) Petroleum Ltd. v. Vit Vulcan Petroleum S.A. (The "Marine Star"),*[79] where the Court of Appeal, affirming a judgment of Saville J., held the c.i.f. sellers of a cargo of oil liable to their buyers. The sellers were unable to invoke a *force majeure* clause relieving them from their obligation to perform due to "impairment or interference with sellers' means of supply". The contract in question provided that the ships' nomination was to be given to the buyers latest at the time the vessel passes Gibraltar, with arrival at the Dutch Antilles between August 4 and 10, 1991. The sellers first nominated the *Marine Star* as the nominated vessel but later switched that vessel to perform another contract they had previously made

---

[75] *e.g.* shipment by steamer in the basic slag trade. *Ransom Ltd. v. Manufacture D'Engrais* (1922) 13 L1. L. Rep. 205.
[76] *Scaramelli & Co. v. Courteen Seed Co.*, 217 N.W. 298 (1928).
[77] [1980] 1 Lloyd's Rep. 665.
[78] See Lord Blackburn's speech in *Bowes v. Shand* (1877) 2 App. Cas. 455, 480, quoted *post,* § 60, and *The Manhattan*, 284 F. 310 (1922), where it was held that a purchaser of grain to be shipped in one ship could not be required to take it if it came in another.
[79] [1993] 1 Lloyd's Rep. 329.

with Exxon. At the time the sellers believed they would be able to perform their contract with the respondents with a different vessel, but this substitution became impossible due to shortage of supply of black sea oil of the contract specifications, and the sellers then attempted to invoke the force majuere clause to excuse their non performance. It was held that since the substitution of the *Marine Star* had nothing whatsoever to do with the *force majuere*, the sellers obligation remained intact. The sellers had no right to substitute their nominated vessel. The firm nomination of the *Marine Star*, "had the effect of locking the vessel into the contract, subject only to the right to substitute another contractual vessel with a contractual cargo in immediate replacement of the *Marine Star*.[80]

However, as illustrated by *Barry v. Slade*,[81] decided in the Supreme Court of New South Wales, the buyer may forgo his right of rejection where the name of the ship becomes part of the description of the goods, or in circumstances where no right of substition of a nominated vessel exists, if he does not base it on the contract of sale. There the plaintiffs imported goods from Vancouver for the defendants in Sydney under a c.i.f. contract that provided for payment by acceptance of a bill of exchange on sight of documents. The plaintiffs tendered their draft together with the documents and they were accepted by the defendants at 30 days. The draft, however, purported to be "against merchandise *per* S.S. *Makura*." The bill of lading did not name the ship by which the goods were to be carried, while the invoice described them as intended for shipment *per* S.S. *Makura*; the marine insurance covered the goods "on the *Makura* or other steamer"; and the war risk certificate definitely described them as shipped on the *Makura*. The draft was dishonoured on presentation and a few days later the goods arrived safely on the S.S. *Waimarino*. To an action on the bill of exchange the defendants pleaded:

(1) that the documents tendered represented the goods to be on the *Makura* whereas they were not, and that the said documents were of no use or value to the defendant;

(2) that there was a total failure of consideration inasmuch as the consideration for the acceptance of the bill was the delivery of documents entitling the defendant to receive goods *ex Makura*.

The Court held that, the action having been brought on the bill and not on the contract of sale, although the documents tendered to the defendants were not such as they were entitled to insist upon under the contract, yet, having accepted the bill upon the presentation of those documents, they were estopped from disputing their sufficiency. It was further held that, since the documents were such as would have entitled the defendants to obtain possession of the goods upon arrival, the fact that they did not get the consideration that they might have insisted upon did not constitute a total failure of consideration for the bill (of exchange) which they could not therefore dishonour.

---

[80] *Ibid. per* Hirst L. J. at p. 332.
[81] (1920) 20 S.R. (N.S.W.) 121.

The seller must also ensure that any provisions in the contract as to the stowage of the goods are complied with, failing which the buyer may reject the goods. For conditions such as "timber to be shipped under deck"[82] or "to be loaded on deck one third"[83] are part of the description of the goods.

The time and place of shipment

59   Stipulations in the contract of sale as to time and place of shipment are ordinarily conditions of the contract, not just collateral warranties or mere representations, and failure by the seller to comply with them entitles the buyer to refuse to accept the documents when presented. If no time for shipment is specified in the contract, the goods must be shipped within a reasonable time.[84]

By section 10 of the Sale of Goods Act 1979 (previously section 10 of the 1893 Act), it is enacted that:

> "(1) Unless a different intention appears from the terms of the contract stipulations as to time of payment are not of the essence of a contract of sale.
> (2) Whether any other stipulation as to time is of the essence of the contract depends on the terms of the contract."

But section 62(2) of the 1979 Act preserves the rules of the common law, including the law merchant, save in so far as they are inconsistent with the express provisions of the Act, and the common law and the law merchant, in the absence of express terms in the contract, looked rather at the nature of the contract and the character of the goods sold than at the terms of the contract for determination of the question whether time was of the essence.[85] In general, in mercantile contracts, as regards stipulations other than such as relate to time of payment,[86] time is of the essence of the contract.

In *Reuter v. Sala*,[87] where a contract for the sale of pepper required the name of vessel or vessels, marks and particulars to be declared within 60 days, Cotton L. J. said[88]:

> "It was argued that the rules of courts of equity are now to be regarded in all courts, and that equity enforced contracts though the time fixed therein for completion had passed. This was in the case of contracts such as purchases and sales of land, where, unless a contrary intention could be collected from the contract, the court presumed that time was not an essential condition. To apply this to

---

[82] *White Sea Timber Trust v. W. W. North* (1932) 148 L. T. 263.
[83] *Messers v. Morrison's Export Co.* [1939] 1 All E. R. 92.
[84] See *per* Scrutton J., *Landauer & Co. v. Craven & Speeding Bros.* [1912] 2 K. B. 94 at p. 105.
[85] *Per* McCardie J., *Hartley v. Hymans* [1920] 3 K. B. 475 at p. 483.
[86] But see *Toepfer v. Lenersan-Poortman N. V.; Toepfer v. Verheijdens Veervoeder Commissiehandel* [1978] 2 Lloyd's Rep. 555, aff'd [1980] 1 Lloyd's Rep. 143 (C. A.) discussed *post*, §271.
[87] (1879) 4 C. P. D. 239 (C. A.); and see *V. Berg and Sons v. Landauer* (1925) 42 T. L. R. 142.
[88] (1879) 4 C. P. D. at p. 249.

mercantile contracts would be dangerous and unreasonable. We must therefore hold that the time within which the pepper was to be declared was an essential condition of the contract, and in such a case the decisions in equity, on which reliance is placed, do not apply.''

60   In the well-known case of *Bowes v. Shand*,[89] where contracts of sale of rice to be shipped at Madras during March and/or April 1874, *per Rajah of Cochin*, were held not to have been satisfied by shipments in February, Lord Cairns L.C. said:[90]

> "It is a mercantile contract, and merchants are not in the habit of placing upon their contracts stipulations to which they do not attach some value and import- ance, and that alone might be a sufficient answer. But, if necessary, a further answer is obtained from two other considerations. It is quite obvious that mer- chants making contracts for the purchase of rice, contracts which oblige them to pay in a certain manner for the rice purchased, and to be ready with the funds for making that payment, may well be desirous both that the rice should be forthcoming to them not later than a certain time, and also that the rice shall not be forthcoming to them at a time earlier than it suits them to be ready with funds for its payment. . . . There is still another explanation . . . these contracts were made for the purpose of satisfying and fulfilling other contracts . . . made with other persons, and it is at least doubtful whether . . . a contract made in another form, or a contract made without this stipulation as to the shipment during these months, would have been a fulfilment of those other contracts which they desired to be in a position to fulfil."

And Lord Blackburn said[91]:

> "It was argued, or tried to be argued, on one point, that it was enough that it was rice, and that it was immaterial when it was shipped. As far as the subject- matter of the contract went, its being shipped at another and a different time being (it was said) only a breach of a stipulation which could be compensated for in damages. But I think that is quite untenable. I think, to adopt an illustration which was used a long time ago by Lord Abinger, and which always struck me as being a right one, that it is an utter fallacy, when an article is described, to say that it is anything but a warranty[92] or a condition precedent that it should be an article of that kind, and that another article might be substituted for it. As he said, if you contract to sell peas, you cannot oblige a party to take beans. If the description of the article tendered is different in any respect it is not the article bargained for, and the other party is not bound to take it. I think in this case what the parties bargained for was rice, shipped at *Madras* or the coast of *Madras*. Equally good rice might have been shipped a little to the north or a little to the south of the coast of *Madras* . . . and probably equally good rice might have been shipped in February as was shipped in March, or equally good rice might have been shipped in May as was shipped in April, and I dare say equally good rice might have been put aboard another ship as that which was put on board the *Rajah of Cochin*. But the parties have chosen, for reasons best

---

[89] (1877) 2 App. Cas. 455.
[90] *Ibid.* at p. 463.
[91] (1877) 2 App. Cas. at p. 480.
[92] The term ''warranty'' is here used as strictly equivalent to condition precedent, and not, as it is used in the Sale of Goods Act, to contrast it with a condition precedent.

known to themselves, to say: We bargain to take rice, shipped in this particular region, at that particular time, on board that particular ship, and before the defendants can be compelled to take anything in fulfilment of that contract it must be shown not merely that it is equally good, but that it is the same article as they have bargained for—otherwise they are not bound to take it.''

61   A stipulation as to time for shipment, therefore, forms part of the description of the goods sold, and as such, by section 13 of the Sale of Goods Act 1979 (previously section 13 of the Sale of Goods Act 1893),[93] is a condition of the contract. It is also an implied condition of the contract that the bill of lading shall be accurately dated with the date of shipment.[94] In any case where the bill of lading does not record the true date or period of shipment, whether fraudulently or innocently, the buyer therefore has the right to reject the goods[95] which may also be rejected though the documents have been accepted. But a stipulation as to time of shipment is more than part of the description of the goods; it is an independent condition precedent, as the following cases show:

In *Ashmore & Son v. C.S. Cox & Co.*[96] the contract was for the sale of 250 bales of Manila hemp c.i.f. shipment to be made from a port or ports in the Philippine Islands, by sailer or sailers, direct or indirect to London, between May 1 and July 31, 1898. Owing to war it was impracticable to ship hemp from the Philippines between the dates specified. On September 15 the sellers shipped hemp, which as regards quantity and quality was in accordance with the contract, on a steamer which was expected to arrive at the same time as the hemp would have arrived if shipped on a sailer within the specified dates. The sellers declared this hemp under the contract. The buyers refused to accept the declaration and claimed damages for breach of contract, and Lord Russell of Killowen C.J. held that they were right.

> ''No doubt,'' he said,[97] ''there are a number of cases, all turning upon the particular contract, in which the Courts have held that certain stipulations, which did not go to the essentials of the contract, are not conditions precedent. But those cases do not, in my judgment, apply to the dates of shipment in the present contract, and I am inclined to think also they do not apply to the provision that shipment is to be made by sailer or sailers, on this short ground, that in the present contract the parties have chosen, by the very terms in which the stipulation appears, to make those events conditions precedent. They have said that the buyers shall not be called upon to accept a shipment not in sailer or sailers, or not made between May 1 and July 31. I therefore hold that those stipulations are conditions precedent.''

62   In the case of *J. Aron & Co. v. Comptoir Wegimont*,[98] a contract of sale

---

[93] Set out *ante*, 45.
[94] *James Finlay & Co. Ltd. v. N. V. Kwik Hoo Tong H. M.* [1929] 1 K.B. 400 (C.A.).
[95] *Kwei Tek Chao v. British Traders & Shippers N. V. Haudelsmaatschapp J. J. Smits Import Export, Third Party* [1354] 1 All E.R. 779, *Post*, § 335.
[96] [1899] 1 Q.B. 436.
[97] *Ibid.* at p. 441.
[98] [1921] 3 K.B. 435.

of cocoa powder c.i.f. Antwerp provided for "shipment by steamer and/or steamers ... from U.S.A. ports during October 1919," and it contained a clause that "whatever the difference of the shipment may be in value from the grade, type or description specified, it is understood that any such question shall not ... entitle the buyers to reject the delivery or any part thereof, nor to refuse payment of the draft or drafts," but should be settled by arbitration. The goods were not shipped until November and the buyers rejected the documents when tendered. It was argued for the sellers that the date of shipment specified in the contract was part of the "description" of the goods and that therefore by virtue of the allowance clause in the contract, quoted above, the buyers were not entitled to reject. Holding for the buyers McCardie J. said:[99]

> "I agree that in one sense the time of shipment is part of the description of the goods. Indeed in *Bowes v. Shand*,[1] Lord Cairns said: 'That is part of the description of the subject-matter of what is sold.' So it is, I agree, in one sense, but in my humble view the express requirement of a contract that goods shall be shipped at a particular period is a good deal more than a mere description of the goods within section 13[2] of the Sale of Goods Act 1893; it is an express term of the contract independent of that which is generally known as the description of the goods. It is, I think, a condition precedent ... that the goods shall be shipped as required by the contract."

63   In *Thomas Borthwick (Glasgow) Ltd. v. Faure Fairclough Ltd.*[3] which arose as a special case stated by arbitrators, the construction of a c.i.f. contract providing for shipment in a vessel nominated by the shipping line (West African Conference Lines) for carrying cargoes coming forward in the contract period was considered. The contract was for bills of lading to be dated in February. No ship was nominated for February, but a ship was offered, and the proposal was to ship on it, sailing on March 21. This the buyer rejected, and the seller, although he might have served notice under the contract to substitute this ship, failed to do so. The issues were whether there was a trade custom, affecting the ports concerned, that the nominated ship for the "contract period" implied a two-month period and could supersede the clause stipulating February bills of lading, and whether the failure of the shipping line to nominate a ship for the contract period, taking it to mean February only, was an event of *force majeure*, within the meaning of a provision providing for relief of liability for failure to ship.

On both issues, the seller failed, and the undue eagerness of arbitrators to import custom into a contract so as effectively to contradict the express terms the parties had agreed to was specifically disapproved of. Donaldson J. rejected the argument that since the vessel in the case was nominated *for* February cargoes though not *to* load in that month there was no default. As

[99] *Ibid.* at p. 440.
[1] (1877) 2 App.Cas. 455, 468, *ante*, §60.
[2] Set out *ante*, §45.
[3] [1968] 1 Lloyd's Rep. 16.

for the contention that the *force majeure* clause applied this was dismissed on the following ground:

> "The sellers' inability to ship in February resulted from the failure of the Conference Lines to put in a vessel to load during that month. This failure was not caused by an unforeseen or unusual fact such as collision, storm, breakdown of machinery or the closing of the Suez Canal. So far as is known the Conference Lines simply decided not to provide a vessel to load cargo at Bathurst in February to carry it to Avonmouth. This is not, in my judgment, *force majeure*."[4]

64   In the Australian case of *Lubrano v. Gollin & Co. Pty. Ltd.*,[5] the plaintiff sold to the defendant 30 tons of tartaric acid, c.i.f. and e. plus war risk, shipment April, May, June direct steamer from Italy. The acid was shipped in four shipments, the first being made in June, the second in September and the last two in later months. The defendant company accepted and paid for the first two shipments, but refused to take delivery in respect of the last two. In an action for damages for refusing to accept delivery of the two last shipments, the plaintiff relied upon acceptance of the September shipment, and on a variety of other acts and admissions, for the purpose of proving that the defendants had waived strict compliance with the shipment dates stipulated in the contract. The court held that the subject-matter of the contract was tartaric acid of the kind specified as shipped direct from Italy in the months April, May and June. The defendants, therefore, were under no obligation to accept goods of a different description from those which they had agreed to purchase. It was further held that under the Statute of Frauds only a written instrument could vary the terms of the original bargain, and that, in the absence of such instrument, the plaintiff could not recover in the action.

However, if the parties assume that the goods will arrive on a certain date but the contract includes no express stipulation in respect thereof, as in *Piesse v. Tasmanian Orchardists & Producers Co-operative Association Ltd.*,[6] the Tasmania Supreme Court held that the buyer cannot refuse to accept the goods if the vessel was delayed through no fault of the seller. The relationship between the parties there was that of principal and agent. The contract was for supply of Scandinavian paper "c.i.f.e., Hobart, net cash against bills of lading or delivery order." The agent entered into a contract with a Sydney merchant on similar terms. There was a dislocation of shipping at the time, which was known to both parties, but it was nevertheless expected that the paper would arrive at Hobart in the month of February 1919. Because of a series of misfortunes, the vessel was delayed and did not arrive until August. The agent paid for the documents, but the buyer refused to accept them, alleging a breach of contract. It was held that the contract made by the agent with the Sydney merchant was in accordance with the contract between him and his principal; that he was not in any way negligent or in breach of his

---

[4] *Ibid.* at p. 28.
[5] (1921) 21 S.R.(N.S.W.) 300.
[6] (1919) 15 Tas.L.R. 67.

duty to use reasonable diligence, and that, there being no express provision as to the time of delivery, the buyers were not entitled to refuse to accept delivery by reason of the delay.

65   Where no date for shipment is specified, the seller is bound to forward the goods "within a reasonable time." In *Thomas Borthwick (Glasgow) Ltd. v. Bunge & Co. Ltd.*[7] the court affirmed a decision of the Board of Appeal of the Cattle Food Trade Association which ruled that a c.i.f. contract for the sale of Canadian soya bean meal providing for shipment "to be made *per Bristol City*, expected to load January 3/5, 1968, or substitute, direct or indirect, with or without transhipment . . ." did not contain a fixed shipping date. In this case, due to delay, the *Bristol City* only arrived at the loading port on January 20, and left without loading the contract goods, at which time the soya bean meal was loaded on a different vessel, not hitherto expected to load in a Canadian port during the January 3 to 5, 1968 period. On February 20, 1968 the sellers gave notice of appropriation to the buyers, but this was rejected by them on the grounds that it was not in conformity with the contract. As summarised by Browne J.[8] their contention was:

> ". . . that the sellers' contractual obligation was to ship the goods to which the contract related on the *Bristol City* . . . and that goods shipped on any ship other than the *Bristol City* could only be a good tender under the 'or substitute' provision if three conditions were fulfilled:
> (1) the option of substituting was exercised by the shipowners: the sellers had no option to substitute;
> (2) a different ship was substituted for the *Bristol City* on the shipowners schedule in the sense that the *Bristol City* was withdrawn . . . and replaced on that voyage by another ship;
> (3) the substituted ship was at the date of the substitution also expected to load on January 3 to January 5."

The Court rejected all of these contentions, holding that, although the primary obligation was to ship on the *Bristol City*, if that vessel was unavailable to carry the goods, any other vessel could be substituted therefore, and that, on this construction, no exact time for shipping the goods was fixed. Consequently, section 29(2) of the Sale of Goods Act 1893 applied, and the sellers discharged their contractual obligation by sending the goods within reasonable time.[9]

66   In *V. Berg and Sons v. Landauer*,[10] a mistake in the provisional invoice as

---

[7] [1969] 1 Lloyd's Rep. 17.
[8] *Ibid.* at p. 27.
[9] But see *Finnish Government (Ministry of Food) v. H. Ford & Co. Ltd.* (1921) 6 Ll.L.Rep. 188 (f.o.b. contract) *post*, §453, which was distinguished on the grounds that there the words "expected ready to load" were construed as applying to the substitutes as well as to the ships originally designated by name, while in the case under consideration the words "expected to load January 3/5" were construed as applying only to the *Bristol City* and not to any substitute vessel.
[10] (1925) 42 T.L.R. 142.

to the date of the bill of lading was held to constitute a breach of condition. The sale was of peas of the 1924 crop, "shipment as per bill of lading dated or to be dated February or March 1925." Clause 1 of the contract provided that "provisional invoice based on the bill of lading weight with the ship's name and date of bill or bills of lading shall be sent by shipper's house . . . to his buyer." The provisional invoice stated that the bill of lading was dated February 1, but when the latter document came to be presented, it was found that it was actually dated February 2. Rowlatt J. said that he thought it clear that the expression "date of bill of lading" included the date of the day as well as that of the month. The question was whether this provision was a warranty or a condition. All stipulations of this kind were inserted for the purpose of informing the buyer of all the circumstances affecting the goods to be tendered in fulfilment of the contract. They were designed to enable the buyer to know as accurately as the circumstances permitted exactly where he stood, and prima facie they were all to be regarded as conditions; and he could not hold that this stipulation came into any other category.

So, too, where the contract called for the bill of lading to be dated December 1909 and/or January 1910 the buyers were entitled to reject when a bill dated February 1910 was tendered regardless of the fact that the goods were actually shipped in January.[11] A provision in the contract that the "bill of lading was to be considered proof of the date of shipment in the absence of evidence to the contrary" did not assist the sellers because, as construed by Lawrence J., it only became applicable when the date of the bill of lading is in accordance with the contract requirements.

67   Where, however, the condition of shipment is held to be satisfied by the tender of a "received for shipment" bill of lading,[12] stipulations on the time of shipment may, likewise, be held to refer to the date on which the seller delivered the goods to the carrier rather than to the date on which they were actually loaded on board the vessel, as would normally be the case.[13] Thus, for example, in *Childs & Brothers v. Adolph Hirsch*[14] the court held that a c.i.f. contract calling for "September-October shipment" was satisfied where the seller delivered the goods to the shipping company on October 31, although they were not actually loaded until some time thereafter. It was the opinion of the court:

> "that under modern conditions, and in the absence of special circumstances showing a different intention of the parties, the words 'for September-October shipment' should be construed as meaning that the goods could be delivered on any day during the specified time to the steamship line for transportation."

---

[11] *Re An Arbitration between the General Trading Co. (Ltd.) and Van Stolk's Commissiehandel* (1911) 16 Com.Cas. 95.
[12] For example, *Stallman v. Francis A. Cundill & Co.*, 288, Fed. 643 (1922), and see generally *post*, § 141 *et seq.*
[13] *Suzuki & Co. v. Burgett & Newsam* (1922) 10 Ll. L.Rep. 223, discussed *post*, § 145.
[14] 202 N.Y.S. 226 (1923).

68   The importance of stipulations relating to the time and place of shipment in c.i.f. contracts, and the strictness with which they are construed, are not altered "by the fact that the buyer . . . chooses to accept documents relating to goods shipped out of time." This was stated by Donaldson J. in *Aruna Mills Ltd. v. Dhanrajmal Gobindramis*[15] where the buyers agreed to accept cotton shipped from Port Sudan c.i.f. Bombay on June 27, 1966, although the contract in question called for shipment by an earlier date, a date subsequently extended by agreement of the parties to be no further than May 31, 1966. The contract included a provision whereby the buyers agreed to bear and pay to the sellers the difference, if any, in or between the exchange rate prevailing on the date of the contract and on the date when the full price is paid. The price was stated in Indian rupees expressing a sterling equivalent of the weight unit of the cotton on the date of the contract. On June 6, 1966, the Indian rupee was devalued in relation to sterling and the dispute, which came to the court as a special case from an award by the Liverpool Cotton Association, requested the court to decide whether or not the buyers were entitled to claim as damages the difference between the original contract price and the enhanced price (resulting from payment after the devaluation date) that they paid under protest. Donaldson J. answered this question in the affirmative. The buyers, by accepting the goods, did not waive their right to damages for the breach, and if they could show that had the goods been shipped on or before May 31, 1966 the documents would in the ordinary course of events have been tendered to them on or before June 5, 1966, they were entitled to recover. Since the arbitrators had not made any finding on this point, the court remitted the award for such a finding to be made. Donaldson J. accepted the contention that there was (at the time) no special rule whereby losses resulting from changes in the valuation of currencies were always too remote to be recoverable in damages for breach. Because the parties in the present case actually contemplated devaluation of the Indian rupee between the date of the contract and the date of payment as a serious possibility, they must be assumed to have contemplated that late delivery was liable to result in the buyer suffering a loss by paying an enhanced price.

69   Normally the fixing of the exact shipping date within the time limits of the contract is for the c.i.f. seller to determine. Problems have sometimes arisen with respect to the exact meaning of extension of shipment or delivery clauses that are now inserted in many c.i.f. contracts as a precaution against strikes and other events preventing fulfilment. Such an example was the case in *European Grain & Shipping v. J. H. Rayner*,[16] where the c.i.f. buyer of a quantity of Indian groundnut extraction was held liable for wrongful repudiation. In this case shipment from India was to take place during March 1968. Owing to a strike at the port of Calcutta that broke out on March 20, and after the sellers had arranged to purchase groundnuts fulfilling the contract

---

[15] [1968] 1 Q.B. 655 at p. 665.
[16] [1970] 2 Lloyd's Rep. 239.

description in Calcutta and to ship them therefrom, the sellers on the basis of certain contractual stipulations claimed an extension which the buyers refused to give. It was the buyers' contention that no right to extension existed unless the sellers proved that on the outbreak of the strike they were unable to ship any branded Indian groundnut extractions from any Indian port or ports during the month of March. However, Mocatta J. refused so to hold construing the relevant strike and *force majeure* clauses in the contract as permitting extension on the facts in the case.

The controversies surrounding these clauses are seldom peculiar to c.i.f. contracts. They relate mostly to questions of interpretation and some of them are reviewed below.[17] In some cases, however, the contract may give the buyer the right to select the shipping date. For example, in *Alexandria Cotton & Trading Company (Sudan) Ltd. v. Cotton Company of Ethiopia Ltd.*[18] the meaning of a stipulation that shipment was to be effected "as from 1st June 1960. However, the buyers have the option to postpone the shipment until 1st June 1961 . . ." was considered. It was there construed by Roskill J. to mean that June 1, 1961, was the termination date of the contract by which time it should have been performed, and that no option to ship later than that date was afforded thereunder.

70   The seller must also comply with any requirement as to the port of shipment.

The extract from the judgment of Lord Blackburn in *Bowes v. Shand*, already quoted *ante*,[19] shows that the place of shipment specified in the contract is equally a condition thereof.[20]

Likewise, in *Filley v. Pope*,[21] the Supreme Court of the United States held that a contract for the sale of 500 tons of pig iron to be shipped from Glasgow "as soon as possible" was not satisfied by shipment from Leith. It appeared that the seller's iron works were about equally distant from Glasgow on the west coast of Scotland, and from Leith on the east, and that in the ordinary course of trade shipments were made indifferently from either. At the time of the sale, no vessel from Glasgow was immediately available, and the only ship by which prompt transportation was possible was about to leave Leith. The seller accordingly put the iron upon her, and it arrived at its destination earlier than it could possibly have done had it gone from Glasgow. The trial court held that Glasgow as the port of shipment was not a material provision of the contract, but the Supreme Court reversed this. It was there held that in a mercantile contract a statement descriptive of the subject matter, or of some material incident, such as the time or place of shipment, is ordinarily to be

---

[17] See *post*, § 71. See also *Bremer Handelsgesellschaft mbH v. Finagrain Compagnie Commerciale Agricole et Financière S.A.* [1981] 2 Lloyd's Rep. 259 (C.A.) reversing [1981] 1 Lloyd's Rep. 224, and further the cases cited *ante* at § 41, n. 5.

[18] [1963] 1 Lloyd's Rep. 576.

[19] At § 60.

[20] See also *Harper et al. v. Hochstim et al.*, 278 Fed. R. 102 (1921) (U.S.), *post*, § 221.

[21] 115 U.S. 213 (1885).

regarded as a condition precedent upon the failure or non-performance of which the party aggrieved may repudiate the entire contract. The following portions of the judgment delivered by Gray J. explain the decision.

> "The court has neither the means, nor the right to determine why the parties in their contract specified shipment from Glasgow, instead of using the more general phrase 'shipment from Scotland,' or merely 'shipment,' without naming any place; but it is bound to give effect to the terms which the parties have chosen for themselves. The term 'shipment from Glasgow' defines an act to be done by the sellers at the outset, and a condition precedent to any liability of the buyer. The sellers do not undertake to obtain shipment, nor does the buyer agree to accept iron shipped at any other port. The buyer takes the risk of delay in getting shipment from Glasgow, or of delay or disaster in prosecuting the voyage from Glasgow to New Orleans; but he does not take the risk of delay or of sea perils which may occur in the course of the different voyage from Leith to the same destination. One or two illustrations may help to make this clear. If the sellers had shipped the iron by the first opportunity from Glasgow, the buyer could not have refused to accept it, even if it could have been shipped sooner from Leith. Again, the buyer would have an insurable interest in the iron during the voyage, by reason of the title which would accrue to him under the contract on arrival and delivery, and of the profits that he might make in case of a rise in the market . . . but a policy of insurance upon the iron for a voyage from Glasgow would not cover a voyage from Leith."[22]

So too in *Continental Imes Ltd. v. H. E. Dibble*,[23] a c.i.f. contract for the sale of Chilean onions to be shipped from Valparaiso to Liverpool *per* the S.S. *Pont Audemer* was held to have been breached by the seller because the onions were trans-shipped in New York, and a variation (agreed to with respect to the name of the carrying vessel) still meant that the shipment was to be from Valparaiso (on the substitute vessel) and not from New York from where she sailed.

71   Many contracts, and particularly standard contracts, nowadays contain express provisions granting the seller (or the parties) the option to extend the shipment period on the occurrence of certain events for example, where the original date cannot be met because of a *force majeure* event. In such cases, and where the seller wishes to rely on the clause in question, he must carefully follow the terms stipulated and ensure compliance with all of its requirements. In *V. Berg & Son Ltd. v. Vanden Avenne-Izegem P.V.B.A.*[24] the sellers sold 1,000 tons of Chinese sweet potato slices c.i.f. Antwerp, shipment from China January/February 1973. The contract contained a *force majeure* clause that relieved the sellers from liability for delay in shipment provided they gave the buyers timely notice of the cause of delay. The clause further provided that "If after giving such notice an extension of the shipment period is required, then shippers shall give further notice not later than two days

---

[22] *Ibid.* at pp. 220, 221.
[23] [1952] 1 Lloyd's Rep. 220.
[24] [1977] 1 Lloyd's Rep. 499 (C.A.).

after the last day of the contract period of shipment stating the port or ports of loading from which the goods were intended to be shipped.'' On March 1, 1973 the sellers advised the buyers by telex that, owing to bad weather conditions, the sweet potatoes could not be loaded, and requested that the shipment date be extended to March 31. The buyers refused to grant the extension and declared the sellers in default. Donaldson J. held for the sellers.[25] In his view although the clause required the sellers to give both a warning notice and an operative notice, a single notice could (and, in the circumstances of this case, did), serve both purposes. The Court of Appeal (Lord Denning M.R., Roskill and Lawton L.JJ.) disagreed, and held that the sellers did not fulfil all the requirements of the clause in that their notice failed to specify the port or ports of loading, and was, therefore, insufficient as a notice.[26] The fact that the buyers did not complain or make any inquiry about the port of shipment did not necessarily mean that they had in any way estopped themselves from insisting on strict compliance with the contractual terms.

Similarly, in *Bremer Handelsgesellschaft Schaft mbH. v. Vanden Avenne-Izegem P.V.B.A.*[27] the House of Lords took the view that a notice specifying the intended ports of shipment, in a contract for the c.i.f. sale of U.S. soya bean meal, as ''the usual ports on the Lakes/East Coast/Gulf'' could not be regarded as a valid notice since it is the intention of the clause that the specific relevant port or ports be named. The port or ports which must be named by the seller in such a case apparently are those from which it was intended to ship in consequence of the *force majeure,* and not those from which it was originally intended to ship. But the House of Lords (in the latter case) determined that the buyers had waived their rights to challenge the validity of the notice (as to the multiple unspecified ports) because none of their communications took any objection to it.[28]

On the other hand, in *Alfred C. Toepfer v. Peter Cremer.*[29] the Court of

---

[25] [1976] 1 Lloyd's Rep. 348.

[26] Had the single notice given all the required information it would probably have sufficed: see *per* Lord Denning M. R. in *Tradax Export S.A. v. André Cie S.A.* [1976] 1 Lloyd's Rep. 416, at p. 422, describing such a single notification as a ''rolled up notice.'' The view has been expressed that the object of the provision is to put some limitation on the seller's choice of ports. It is inserted so that he cannot put forward a spurious claim for an extension, for example, by stating a strike bound port from which he never intended to ship. See also *Alfred C. Toepfer v. Peter Cremer* [1975] 2 Lloyd's Rep. 118 (C.A.). But in *Bremer Handelsgesellschaft mbH v. Vanden Avenne-Izegem P.V.B.A.* [1978] 2 Lloyd's Rep. 109 (H.L.) contrary views were expressed. Viscount Dilhorne (at p. 119) opined as follows:

"In my opinion the clause does not require the shipper to nominate the port or ports from which the goods were originally intended to be shipped but the port or ports from which it was intended to ship at the time of the giving of the notice when the *force majeure* was operating, the intention at the time of the notice not necessarily being that previously held."

[27] [1978] 2 Lloyd's Rep. 109.

[28] For additional cases in which the question of waiver and estoppel, in regard to extention of shipment notice terms in c.i.f. contracts, was considered, see *Bremer Handelsgesellschaft m.b.H. v. Westzuker G.m.b.H.* [1981] 1 Lloyd's Rep. 207 at pp. 212, 213; *Bremer Handelsgesellschaft m.b.H. v. Macprang Jr.* [1979] 1 Lloyd's Rep. 221, and *Cook Industries v. Tradax Export S.A.* [1985] 2 Lloyd's Rep. 454 at p. 461.

[29] [1975] 2 Lloyd's Rep. 118.

Appeal refused to permit a seller who had given a notice that did not specify the port or ports of shipment (and to which the buyer did not object) from taking advantage of this defect in order to advance the date of his default (in a rapidly rising market). The seller invoked the *force majeure* clause and gave the extension notice naming "Mississippi River Port(s)," and he would not be permitted to say it was a bad notice because the market price had risen. The validity of such notices, however, does not depend on the seller establishing that, but for the supervening event, he would have shipped in accordance with the contract, and it was for the buyer to show that it was not the event specified that prevented the fulfilment of the contract.[30]

The route

72   If the contract designates a particular route it must be followed. This was decided in *Re An Arbitration between L. Sutro & Co. and Heilbut, Symons & Co.*[31] the facts of which were as follows:

By a contract dated March 27, 1916 the appellants agreed to sell to the respondents 25 tons of plantation rubber c.i.f. "to be shipped . . . by vessel or vessels (steam or motor) from the East to New York direct and/or indirect, with liberty to call and/or tranship at other ports." The sellers made a declaration under the contract of 15 tons which were shipped under a through bill of lading. This stated that the goods were shipped at Singapore for New York via Seattle, from whence they would be sent by rail to New York. The buyers objected to this declaration on the ground that by the provisions of the contract the rubber was to be conveyed to New York by sea. The dispute was referred to arbitration under a clause in the contract. The arbitrators found that after the outbreak of the war great difficulty was experienced in obtaining shipping space from the East and that in consequence shipment to the eastern seaboard of the United States, which had before gone the whole distance to New York by water, began to be made by steamer to a port on the Pacific Coast for transmission by rail to destination; that this course was well known to those engaged in the trade as one of the usual routes for rubber sold under terms similar to those considered; that there was, at the date of the contract, such a course of business established as would make it within the contemplation of the parties that the rubber might come by this route; and that accordingly there was a good tender under the contract which the buyers should have accepted.

73   The Court of Appeal (Swinfen Eady L.J. and Bray J., Scrutton L.J. dissenting) held that the contract provided for a sea carriage to New York. Any contrary usage found by the arbitrators was therefore inconsistent with

---

[30] *Bremer Handelsgesellschaft mbH v. Vanden Avenne-Izegem P.V.B.A.* [1978] 2 Lloyd's Rep. 109 (H.L.).
[31] [1917] 2 K.B. 348.

the terms of the contract, and therefore was not applicable. The tender was not a good tender and the buyers were not bound to accept the same.

Swinfen Eady L.J. said:

"... where a particular method of conveyance is stipulated for, it is not permissible to inquire whether there is not some other usual method; and a finding that there is another usual method is irrelevant" (at p. 358).

Bray J. said:

"All these words [in the contract] point, in my opinion, quite clearly to the goods arriving by vessel and at a port of discharge. The destination is to be the port of New York. The custom is that they should go to Seattle and arrive by rail at New York. In my opinion the custom is quite inconsistent with the express terms of the written instrument. It was argued that after the words 'New York' there should be added the words 'by one of the usual routes.' That may be, but the usual route must be that of a vessel from the East to New York, and the place of arrival must be a port of discharge" (at p. 366).

Scrutton L.J.'s dissent was based on the observation that the words "port" and "vessels" in a standard printed form of contract, such as was before the court in this instance, could not be conclusive as they would certainly cover a mode of transport other than by water (for example, if the sale was for shipment c.i.f. to a land-borne point, say Birmingham). For this reason, he opined, no particular importance attached to those words, and the general rule applied. And what was the general rule? In his view it was as follows:

"Where there is a contract to carry from A to B if the exact route or method of carriage is not specified in the contract, the carriage must be by one of the usual routes and methods of carriage, at the option of the carrier. If the other party wishes to exclude some usual route or method of carriage, he can do so by inserting such a term into the contract, but in the absence of such a term the option of selecting a usual method of performance is with the person who has to perform. What is a usual route or method is a question of fact to be found by the arbitrators, and they have found as a fact that when the contract was entered into the route from the East by sea and rail from the Pacific seaboard was well known to those engaged in the trade as one of the usual routes for rubber sold on contracts in this form, and that there was such a course of business established as would make it within the contemplation of the parties to this contract that the goods might come by this route" (at p. 362).

Although the observation that, in the absence of a term designating the route, the usual or customary route is to be followed was questioned by some of their lordships in *Tsakiroglou & Co. Ltd. v. Noblee Thorl G.m.b.H.*,[32] who thought that shipment by any reasonable route would satisfy a c.i.f. contract, Viscount Simmonds doubted whether, if an appeal were lodged thereon, the *Sutro* decision would have stood. It was his opinion that Scrutton L. J. was

---

[32] [1962] A.C. 93, see *post*, §78.

probably correct inasmuch as the arbitrators found that the method of transport followed in the case had become a usage of the trade.[33]

74   In the absence of express terms, the route must be a reasonable route, *i.e.* in all probability, the customary or usual route. If there is no customary or usual route, then a practicable commercial route must be chosen, the question depending on the circumstances prevailing not on the date of the contract, but at the time of performance thereof.[34] In the absence of special considerations the contract is not frustrated merely because the route contemplated at the time the contract was concluded becomes unavailable, and performance is more costly to the seller. For, in such a case, the seller must ship by some alternative route which may be reasonable or practicable in the circumstances. What is reasonable or practicable will naturally depend on the facts of any given case, but the seller will, it is thought, be deemed to have satisfied his contract if he can show that he has, in the words of section 32(2) of the Sale of Goods Act 1979, made "such contract with the carrier . . . as may be reasonable having regard to the nature of the goods and the circumstances . . ." It is not necessary for this route to be the shortest geographical route, nor need it be the invariable route. When, therefore, there is more than one usual route, shipment by any usual route will perform the contract. And, if there is only one route at the time of performance, that may be taken if it is practicable and is not prejudicial to the condition of the goods or fundamentally alters the nature of the transaction.

75   In *Frenkel v. MacAndrews & Co. Ltd.*,[35] the House of Lords had to consider whether there was any deviation from route in the case of olive oil shipped at Malaga on board the *Cervantes* under two bills of lading, with destination in one case to Liverpool and in the other to Bradford. The respondents owned a fleet of cargo steamers including the *Cervantes* which were in the habit of going from Liverpool to the ports of Spain and Portugal and back. As in the present case, sometimes the ships called at Malaga on the outward journey before proceeding up the east coast of Spain, and in other cases on the return journey, the route being advertised at Malaga as either "via Levante" or "directo." The olive oil belonging to the appellant was lost in a storm between Malaga and Cartagena.

The Court of Appeal (Scrutton, Greer and Sankey L.JJ.) held that the *Cervantes* was proceeding on the agreed voyage and gave judgment for the respondents. This decision was upheld by the House of Lords. Lord Sumner, referring to the route "via Levante," said[36]:

> "This was shown to be a usual commercial route for the *Cervantes* to follow under the circumstances and to be the route which had been advertised for her

---

[33] *Ibid.* at p. 113.
[34] See *Tsakiroglou & Co. Ltd. v. Noblee Thorl GmbH* [1962] A.C. 93, considered *post*, § 78.
[35] [1929] A.C. 545.
[36] *Ibid.* at p. 561.

for this voyage some time beforehand, and it was one which I think was reasonable under the circumstances. I cannot see that it is the less a reasonable and usual commercial route, though the evidence referred only to the ships of the respondents' own line. Their prominent position in this trade, the number of ships they run, and the length of time that this kind of practice has been followed by them all go to prove this conclusion. The evidence further shows that these facts were well known to those of his employees to whom the plaintiff [the appellant] confided this part of his business, and the usual and reasonable commercial character of such a voyage was therefore strongly confirmed, since no objection was taken.''

Further consideration was given to the question of what is a usual and reasonable route by the House of Lords in *Reardon Smith Line Ltd. v. Black Sea and Baltic General Insurance Co. Ltd. (The Indian City).*[37] In that case, a vessel was chartered to proceed to Poti (on the Black Sea) and there load, and being so loaded, to proceed with all convenient speed to Istanbul and thence to Sparrows Point, U.S. The vessel made the voyage from Poti to Istanbul not by the shortest route, but via Constanza owing to the facilities there for obtaining oil cheaply. It was held that this constituted a usual and reasonable commercial route. Lord Wright, after referring to previous cases (including *Frenkel's* case[38]), said[39]:

"The cases cited were cases of liners or general traders, and it may be said that the same principles do not apply in the same sense to a chartered vessel, carrying a single cargo for a single shipper or consignee. But even in such cases it is obvious that there will be in general various considerations, commercial or navigational, which determine what sea route is usual and reasonable. Thus, in the old sailing-ship days, routes were chosen in order to make use of trade winds, and varied from season to season, and between the same termini there might be several usual routes. In modern times, in all long ocean voyages, the need to replenish bunkers (coal or oil) has to be considered. The doctrine of stages of the voyage, which enables a ship-owner to start with bunkers sufficient for the stage, so long as he fills up his bunkers at the next bunkering port, necessarily involves calling at that port, and perhaps later ports, in order to fulfil the recurring obligation to keep the vessel seaworthy in regard to bunkers. Thus to call at such ports has become an ordinary incident of the voyage. The need to do so may help to determine the general route ... A shipowner is entitled, within certain limits determined by what is reasonable, to be guided in his choice of bunkering ports by consideration of cheapness and convenience."

76   But the liberty of the shipowner is confined to following the ordinary sea track of the voyage from the port of shipment to the port of discharge. Where by the terms of the bill of lading liberty to call at any ports is granted, the condition usually refers to ports of call *substantially* within the course of the contemplated voyage. It does not give the shipowner a licence to interrupt the voyage by proceeding to go to any port in the world. Thus, when goods were shipped from Fiume to Dunkirk with liberty to call at any ports in any

---

[37] [1939] A.C. 562.
[38] [1929] A.C. 545.
[39] [1939] A.C. at p. 574.

order and the ship, instead of proceeding direct to Dunkirk, sailed for Glasgow, and was lost with her cargo off the mouth of the Clyde, the Court of Appeal held in *Leduc & Co. v. Ward & Ors.*,[40] that Glasgow being altogether out of the course of the voyage was not a port to which the ship was entitled to proceed under the contract. The vessel therefore was lost while deviating from the voyage contracted for, and the excepted perils clause in the bill of lading did not exonerate the shipowner from liability in respect of non-delivery of the goods.[41]

Whether or not the vessel must sail directly to the port of discharge, or may visit other ports en route may depend on the terms of the contract in question. This can, *e.g.* stipulate expressly that the shipment may be "direct or indirect".[42] Where no such term is included in the contract, the implication probably is, in the absence of special circumstances, that shipment need not be direct. However, where the parties expressly agree that shipment should be "direct", the term would usually have the character of a condition, and a breach thereof would entitle the buyer to reject upon arrival of the goods at their destination, even if the facts were known to the buyer on an earlier date and he did not waive his right of rejection. This was held by Hobhouse J. in *Bergerco U.S.A. v. Vegoil Ltd,*[43] upholding a trade arbitration award to the same effect.

The question as to what route must be followed in the case of a c.i.f. contract, and whether such a contract is discharged where the normal and customary route foreseen at the time of entering into the contract is no longer available at the time of performance, was the subject of extensive review in a number of disputes that arose from the closure of the Suez Canal on November 2, 1956.

77   In *Carapanoyoti & Co. Ltd. v. E. T. Green Ltd.,*[44] McNair J. held that the duty of the seller is to ship by a route that is usual and customary at the time of performance. But he further held that, if at the time of performance, the only available route makes performance substantially more expensive than was envisaged by the seller at the time of the agreement, the contract is frustrated. Such a development in his view imposed upon the seller an obligation fundamentally different from the one originally undertaken by him. In *Albert D. Gaon & Co. v. Société Interprofessionelle des Oléagineux Fluides Alimentaires*[45] Ashworth J., on somewhat similar facts, held that the contract was not frustrated. The obligation of the seller to ship via the Cape did not in his view entail "a thing radically different from that which was undertaken

---

[40] (1888) 20 Q.B.D. 475. See also *Glynn v. Margetson & Co.* [1893] A.C. 351.

[41] Such liability may include the buyer's loss of profit. See *Satef-Huttenes Alberns S.p.A. v. Paloma Tercera Shipping Co. S.A. (The "Pegase")* [1981] 1 Lloyd's Rep. 175. As to the seller's obligation not to interfere with the performance of the contract of carriage and to refrain from redirecting the vessel from the contractual route, see *post*, § 87.

[42] As is, *e.g.* provided by cl. 10 of GAFTA 28.

[43] [1984] 1 Lloyd's Rep. 440.

[44] [1959] 1 Q.B. 131.

[45] [1960] 2 Q.B. 334, affirmed [1960] 2 Q.B. 348 (C.A.).

by the contract.'' The question was finally settled by the House of Lords in *Tsakiroglou & Co. Ltd. v. Noblee Thorl G.m.b.H.*,[46] where *Carapanoyoti* was partially overruled. The House upheld the former part of this decision, but took exception to, and expressly disassociated itself from, the latter part. In *Carapanoyoti*, a contract dated September 6, 1956 for the sale of cottonseed cake for shipment from Port Sudan during October or November c.i.f. Belfast was considered. At the date of the contract the usual and customary route for the shipment of goods from Port Sudan to Belfast was via the Suez Canal, which on November 2, was closed to navigation. The sellers did not ship the goods and McNair J. held that their failure to do so was justified. In the course of his judgment, he said[47]:

> "In principle, it seems to me that where a contract expressly, or by necessary implication, provides that performance, or a particular part of the performance, is to be carried out in a customary manner, the performance must be carried out in a manner which is customary at the time when the performance is called for. This is particularly so in the case of forward contracts like many c.i.f. contracts which call for performance at some future date, when one bears in mind that in mercantile matters custom and usage are subject to rapid change: see the speech of Lord Wright in *Reardon Smith Line Ltd. v. Black Sea and Baltic General Insurance Co. Ltd.*[48] For example, in times of strained international relations the customary form of bills of lading may change by the universal acceptance of a particular form of war-risk protection. Can it be said that the seller is bound to tender the form of bill of lading which was customary at the date of the contract when, by the time when performance has arrived, that form has been supplanted by another customary form? I think not. . . .
>
> In my opinion, as a matter of principle, the sellers' obligation under a contract such as this where no route is specified is not confined to shipping by a route which was a usual and customary route at the date of the sale contract, but is to ship by a route usual and customary at the time of performance."

78   In *Tsakiroglou & Co. Ltd. v. Noblee Thorl G.m.b.H.*,[49] which by the consent of the parties was a combined appeal on the *Gaon* dispute also,[50] the appellants agreed to sell to the respondents 300 tons of Sudanese groundnuts at £50 per 1,000 kilos, including bags, c.i.f. Hamburg, shipment during November/December 1956. No goods were shipped by the appellants, who contended that the contract was frustrated as a result of the closure of the Suez. The plea was, *inter alia*, based on a clause in their contract providing that "In case of prohibition of import or export, blockade or war, epidemic or strike, and in all cases of *force majeure* preventing the shipment within the time fixed, or the delivery, the period allowed for shipment or delivery shall be extended by not exceeding two months. After that, if the case of *force majeure* be still operating, the contract shall be cancelled." Their lordships held, affirming the decision of the Court of Appeal, that the contract was not

---

[46] [1962] A.C. 93.
[47] [1959] 1 Q.B. at p. 145.
[48] [1939] A.C. 562. *Ante*, §75.
[49] [1962] A.C. 93.
[50] *Ante*, n. 45.

terminated by the closure of the Suez Canal and that a term that shipment should be through the Canal, namely via the route contemplated by the seller at the time the contract was entered into, was not to be implied into the contract. The contract could be performed by shipment via the Cape of Good Hope which would make it more costly, but that this change in the method of performance was not such a fundamental change from that undertaken under the contract to say that it was frustrated. Furthermore, the exception clause did not apply in the circumstances, because "shipment," *viz.,* placing the goods on board a vessel for the right destination, was not prevented.

79   Viscount Simonds said:

> "I turn now to what was the main argument for the appellants: that the contract was frustrated by the closure of the Canal from November 2, 1956, till April 1957. Were it not for the decision of McNair J. in *Green's* case[51] I should not have thought this contention arguable and I must say with the greatest respect to that learned judge that I cannot think he has given full weight to the decisions old and new of this House upon the doctrine of frustration. He correctly held upon the authority of *Reardon Smith Line Ltd. v. Black Sea and Baltic General Insurance Co. Ltd.*[52] that 'where a contract, expressly or by necessary implication, provides that performance, or a particular part of the performance, is to be carried out in the customary manner, the performance must be carried out in a manner which is customary at the time when the performance is called for.' But he concluded[53] that the continued availability of the Suez route was a fundamental assumption at the time when the contract was made, and that to impose upon the sellers the obligation to ship by an emergency route via the Cape would be to impose upon them a fundamentally different obligation which neither party could at the time when the contract was performed have dreamed that the sellers would be required to perform. Your lordships will observe how similar this line of argument is to that which supports the implication of a term that the route should be via Suez and no other. I can see no justification for it. We are concerned with a c.i.f. contract for the sale of goods, not a contract of affreightment, though part of the sellers' obligation will be to procure a contract of affreightment.[54] There is no evidence that the buyers attached any importance to the route.

---

[51] [1959] 1 Q.B. 131, *ante,* § 77.
[52] [1939] A.C. 562.
[53] [1959] 1 Q.B. 131 at p. 149.
[54] But in *Ocean Tramp Tankers Corporation v. V/O Sovfracht, The Eugenia* [1964] 2 Q.B. 226 Lord Denning M.R. observed that:
"I know that a contract of affreightment is different from a contract for the sale of goods, but I should find it strange if, in the case of a ship loaded with cargo, the contract of affreightment was frustrated by the closure of the Canal and the contract of sale was not" (at p. 241). The decision overruled *Société Franco Tunisienne D'Armement v. Sidermar S.p.A. (The Massalia)* [1961] 2 Q.B. 278 where it was decided that the closure of the Canal frustrated the charterparty. *The Eugenia* was followed in *Palmeo Shipping Inc. v. Continental Ore Corp. (The "Captain George K")* [1970] 2 Lloyd's Rep. 21. However since the question is one of applying the principles of the doctrine of frustration to the facts of individual cases, there is no determination that a prolongation of a voyage can never produce frustration of a charterpary. With regard to the aforecited observation of Lord Denning, Mocatta J., it is submitted correctly, noted in *The Captain George K* that there was force in the contention that the position which might obtain under a c.i.f. contract in respect of cargo was, strictly speaking, irrelevant when the matter under consideration was a charterparty. Adding to what was said in the *Tsakiroglou* case (where shipment had never taken

They were content that the nuts should be shipped at any date in November or December. There was no evidence, and I suppose could not be, that the nuts would deteriorate as a result of a longer voyage and a double-crossing of the Equator, nor any evidence that the market was seasonable. In a word, there was no evidence that the buyers cared by what route or, within reasonable limits, when the nuts arrived. What, then, of the sellers? I recall the well-known passage in the speech of Lord Atkinson in *Johnson v. Taylor Bros. & Co. Ltd.*[55] where he states the obligations of the vendor of goods under a c.i.f. contract, and ask which of these obligations is (to use McNair J.'s words) 'fundamentally' altered by a change of route. Clearly the contract of affreightment will be different and so may be the terms of insurance. In both these respects the sellers may be put to greater cost: their profit may be reduced or even disappear. But it hardly needs reasserting that an increase of expense is not a ground of frustration.... Reluctant as I am to differ from a judge so experienced in commercial law as McNair J., I am glad to find that my view is shared by Ashworth J.[56] and all the members of the Court of Appeal'' (at pp. 114, 115).

80   While Lord Radcliffe observed:

"This is a sale of goods on c.i.f. terms. Such a sale involves a variety of obligations, both those written out in the contract itself and those supplied by implication of law for the business efficacy of the transaction. The only sector of these obligations that is relevant for the purpose of this case is the vendors' duty 'to procure a contract of affreightment under which the goods will be delivered at the destination contemplated by the contract' (see *Biddell Brothers v. E. Clemens Horst Co.*,[57] per Hamilton J.). Even within this sector, however, there are gaps which the law has to fill in: for instance, what form of contract of affreightment will meet the needs of the transaction, and what route or routes are permissible for the carrying vessel selected? In the present case nothing turns on the form of the bill of lading, which is not in evidence: everything turns on the question of route. The written contract makes no condition about this, its only stipulation being that shipment is to be from a West African port, by which we are asked to assume that the parties in fact meant Port Sudan. So the voyage was to begin at Port Sudan and to end at Hamburg. The primary duty under this part of the contract was to dispatch the groundnuts by sea from one port to the destination of the other.

"At the date when the contract was entered into the usual and normal route for the shipment of Sudanese groundnuts from Port Sudan to Hamburg was via the Suez Canal. It would be unusual and rare for any substantial parcel of Sudanese groundnuts from Port Sudan to Europe to be shipped via the Cape at any time when the Suez Canal was open. The Suez Canal was blocked on November 2, 1956, and remained blocked until April, 1957. Nevertheless, during the months of November/December, 1956, the period in which the vendors had to ship under the contract, it was feasible for them to transport the goods via the Cape of Good Hope. It would have involved a voyage of some 11,137 miles as against 4,386

---

place so that the seller was not in a position to discharge his obligations by tendering documents to the buyer) Mocatta J. said: "Here the Canal was not closed until 32 days after the completion of loading. Had the cargo been sold c.i.f. the seller could have presented the appropriate documents to the buyer and demanded and recovered payment whether the charter was frustrated or not, just as he could, had the vessel and her cargo been at the bottom of the sea" (at p. 31).

[55] [1920] A.C. 144 at p. 155; *ante*, § 8.
[56] In *Albert D. Gaon & Co. v. Société Interprofessionelle des Oléagineux Fluides Alimentaires* [1960] 2 Q.B. 334.
[57] [1911] 1 K.B. 214 at p. 220; *ante*, § 6.

miles by way of Suez, and would have meant a rise in freight rate of 25 per cent. (and in the last two weeks of December, 100 per cent.) above that ruling when the sale contract was made. These differences did not, however, in the opinion of the board of appeal of the Incorporated Oil Seed Association who state the case, render transport by the Cape route commercially or fundamentally different from transport by way of the Suez Canal.

81   "Now in these circumstances were the appellants under obligation to procure a bill of lading for the transport of the goods by the Cape route, the Suez Canal not being available? That depends on how their obligation is defined. It is said on their behalf that the duty of shipment is a duty to ship by the 'customary or usual route,' a route which can be ascertained as that followed by settled and established practice (see Kennedy, *C.I.F. Contracts* (1st ed.), p. 39). Failing express provision on the point by the terms of the contract, that is, in my opinion, a correct general statement of what the law would imply; but I do not accept the further proposition which the appellants' argument requires, namely that, given the existence of such a route at the date of the contract, the whole of the vendor's obligation with regard to shipment is contained in this phrase, 'the customary or usual route.' Putting aside exceptional cases in which there never has become established any customary route at all from one port to the other, we have to consider the case in which, while there has been a customary route at or before the date of the sale, that route is not available at the time when the vendor is ready to ship. The appellants say that, since the whole obligation consists in shipping by the customary or usual route, the contract would in that event become unenforceable, either because its terms had become impossible of performance or because it was avoided by frustration. In this context the two alternatives would amount to the same thing. I think, however, that the vendor's obligation has to be determined in the light of matters as they stand at the date of shipment, and it may be proper for him to take a course in those circumstances which it would not have been proper for him to take at the date of the contract.

"In my opinion there is no magic in the introduction of the formula 'customary or usual route' to describe the term implied by law. It is only appropriate because it is in ordinary circumstances the test of what it is reasonable to impose upon the vendor in order to round out the imperfect form of the contract into something which, as mercantile men, the parties may be presumed to have intended. The corpus of commercial law has been built up largely by this process of supplying from the common usage of the trade what is the unexpressed intention of the parties. It is necessary first to ascertain what is the commercial nature or purpose of the adventure that is the subject of the contract; that ascertained, it has next to be asked what within this scope are the essential terms which, so far as not expressed, must be implied in order to make the contract efficacious as a business instrument. The natural way to answer this question is to find out what is the usual thing in the same line of business. Various adjectives or phrases are employed to describe the point of reference. I can quote the following from judicial decisions: recognised, current, customary, accustomed, usual, ordinary, proper, common, in accordance with custom or practice or usage, a matter of commercial notoriety: and, of course, reasonable. I put 'reasonable' last because I think that the other phrases are at bottom merely instances of what it is reasonable to imply having regard to the nature and purpose of the contract. The basic proposition is therefore that laid down by Brett M. R. in *Sanders v. MacLean*[58]: 'The stipulations which are inferred in mercantile contracts are always that the party will do what is mercantilely reasonable.'

---

[58] (1883) 11 Q.B.D. 327 at p. 337; *post*, § 242.

82   ''Applying that proposition to the present case, I do not think that it is enough for the appellants to point out that the usual and customary route for the transport of groundnuts from Port Sudan to Hamburg was via the Suez Canal, and that at the date of the sale contract both parties contemplated that shipment would be by that route. This contract was a sale of goods, which involved dispatching the goods from Port Sudan to Hamburg; but, of course, the transport was not the whole but only one of the incidents of the contract, in which particular incident neither vendors nor buyers were directly implicated. There was nothing to prevent the vendors from dispatching the goods as contracted, unless they were impliedly bound as a term of the contract to use no other route than that of the Suez Canal. I do not see why that term should be implied and, if it is not implied, the true question seems to me to be, since shipment was due to be made by some route during November/December, whether it was a reasonable action for a mercantile man to perform his contract by putting the goods on board a ship going round the Cape of Good Hope and obtaining a bill of lading on this basis. A man may habitually leave his house by the front door to keep his appointments; but, if the front door is stuck, he would hardly be excused for not leaving by the back. The question, therefore, is what is the reasonable mercantile method of performing the contract at a time when the Suez Canal is closed, not at a time when it is open. To such a question the test of 'the usual and customary route' is *ex hypothesi* inapplicable.

''On the facts found by the special case I think that the answer is inevitable. The voyage would be a much longer one in terms of miles; but length reflects itself in such matters as time of arrival, condition of goods, increase of freight rates. A change of route may, moreover, augment the sheer hazard of the transport. There is nothing in the circumstances of the commercial adventure represented by the appellants' contract which suggests that these changes would have been material. Time was plainly elastic. Not only did the vendors have the option of choosing any date within a two-month period for shipment, but also there was a wide margin within which there might be variations of the speed capacity of the carrying vessel or vessels selected. There was no stipulated date for arrival at Hamburg. Nothing appears to suggest that the Cape voyage would be prejudicial to the condition of the goods or would involve special packing or stowing, nor does there seem to have been any seasonal market to be considered. With all these facts before them, as well as the measure of freight surcharge that would fall to the vendors' account, the board of appeal made their finding that performance by shipping on the Cape route was not 'commercially or fundamentally different' from shipping via the Suez Canal. We have no material which would make it possible for us to differ from that conclusion'' (at pp. 120–123).

83   Some of their lordships entertained certain reservations with respect to Scrutton L.J.'s opinion in *Re L. Sutro & Co. and Heilbut, Symons & Co.*[59] already quoted (*ante,* § 73), Lord Guest, for example, observed:

''In regard to the question of whether the usual or customary route must be followed reliance was placed on an *obiter dictum* of Scrutton L.J. in *In re L. Sutro & Co. and Heilbut, Symons & Co.*: 'Where there is a contract to carry from A to B. . . .' The first part of the quotation is clearly dealing with a contract of affreightment where the carrier has the option of selecting a usual route. In the second part of the quotation I am not clear whether the learned Lord Justice is dealing with a c.i.f. contract or a contract of affreightment. I am not at all

[59] [1917] 2 K.B. 348 at p. 362.

satisfied that this dictum . . . is justification for implying into every c.i.f. contract an obligation on the seller to obtain a contract of affreightment by the usual and customary route. As Harman L.J. in the Court of Appeal[60] said: 'Why it should be necessary to imply such words as "by the usual and customary route," I do not see.' In my opinion, all that the seller has to do is to procure a reasonable contract of affreightment" (at pp. 132, 133).

This, however, is not to say that a c.i.f. contract for the shipment of goods can never be the subject of frustration by virtue of an impossibility to follow the usual or customary route. Where such a route is the only possible or available route and no alternative route exists, the contract might well be regarded as frustrated. For example, a c.i.f. contract in respect of goods to be shipped from a Black Sea port to the Mediterranean may be at an end if the Dardanelles were rendered impassable and such event was unforeseen at the time the contract was concluded. The import of the decision is that the duty to ship is to be read in the light of the circumstances prevailing at the time of performance and not at the time when the contract was concluded. Although the question was considered and determined by reference to the doctrine of frustration, it is in full harmony with the underlying notion of the c.i.f. contract that imposes upon the seller the risk of any rise in the cost of transportation that occurs after the contract is concluded.

When there is no direct means of shipment from the place where the goods are to be shipped to the destination contemplated by the contract, it is necessary to tranship the goods in the course of transit. Commercial practice as to transhipment appears to vary and the question in a particular case whether the seller has fulfilled his obligation to procure a contract of affreightment (i) on shipment, and (ii) of such a character that, on transfer to the buyer, it gives the buyer a right to sue the shipowner, if necessary, in respect of the entire transit, may involve some difficulty and is discussed in the succeeding chapter.[61]

The destination

84   Finally, the shipment must be on a vessel bound for the contractual destination. The seller is under a duty to procure the shipment of the goods under such a bill of lading as will, subject to the permissible exceptions therein contained, ensure their delivery at the destination specified in the contract of sale.[62]

---

[60] [1960] 2 Q.B. 318 at p. 369.
[61] At § 147, *post.*
[62] See, *e.g. G.H. Renton & Co. Ltd. v. Palmyra Trading Corporation of Panama* [1956] 1 Q.B. 462 (McNair J. and C.A.); [1957] A.C. 149; timber was shipped to London or Hull at Canadian ports under bills of lading which provided, *inter alia,* that in the event of strikes the master might discharge the cargo ". . . at . . . any . . . safe and convenient port." Owing to strikes at London and Hull the ship discharged at Hamburg. The cargo owners claimed damages for breach of contract, but the House of Lords, affirming the decision of the Court of Appeal where McNair J. was reversed agreed with the defendant shipowners that by discharging at Hamburg due

In *Lecky & Co. Ltd. v. Ogilvy, Gillanders & Co.*,[63] the contract was for the sale of sugar bags by the defendants to the plaintiffs, shipment from Calcutta c.i.f. Tripoli. It was the intention of the parties that the goods be shipped to Tripoli in Africa (Libya). Because of some blunder by the shipping company, and due to no negligence of the defendants, the bags were in fact shipped to Tripoli in Syria, and the goods were delivered in that port. The Court of Appeal (Smith, Rigby and Collins L.JJ.), affirming Mathew J., held that the action for non-delivery of the goods must succeed. The defendants failed to perform their contract by delivering a bill of lading under which the goods were not shipped to the contractual destination.

In *S.I.A.T. di Del Ferro v. Tradax Overseas S.A.*,[64] some 5,000 tonnes of Brazilian soya bean meal were sold c.i.f. Venice. The sellers tendered four sets of different documents in respect of the contract. Three sets were rejected by the buyers, one because the bills of lading referred to Ancona or Ravenna as the destination, and the other two sets because the port of discharge was described "as per charterparty," and no charterparty was presented. It was held that the buyers were entitled to reject all three sets. In the course of his judgment Megaw L.J. said with respect to the Ancona or Ravenna bills of lading[65]:

> "I find it impossible to think that it could be seriously argued that a buyer whose contract was c.i.f. Venice was not entitled to reject those documents as they then stood. To my mind, it is inconceivable that he should be required by law to accept them and pay for them and take his chance of what might befall, with a remedy merely of a potential claim for damages against the seller. I would reject out of hand the suggestion that a buyer who refused to accept such a bill of lading under such a contract would himself be liable for a breach of contract towards the seller."

In reaching a similar conclusion with respect to the other two sets of documents (which an arbitration award noted were in a form "not unusual" in the trade in question) his honour described them as likewise "fatally defective" since:

> ". . . they failed to comply with a requirement of the contract which can properly be described as fundamental to a c.i.f. contract. It may be—it is not necessary to decide this—that a tender of documents would not be invalid if the bill of lading, showing the port of discharge 'As Per Charter Party,' were to be accompanied by the charterparty, or an acceptable copy of it, which showed that the contract of carriage unequivocally required delivery of the bill of lading cargo at the port of discharge named in the contract of sale. But in the absence of such inclusion among the documents, the buyer does not get that which he is entitled to require:

---

delivery under the bills of lading had been effected. Art. III, r. 8. of the Schedule to the Carriage of Goods by Sea Act 1924, which invalidated any clause which relieved the carrier from the liabilities under the Act, is inapplicable when the carrier is empowered to deviate in the event of an occurrence of an emergency over which he has no control.

[63] (1897) 3 Com. Cas. 29.
[64] [1980] 1 Lloyd's Rep. 53.
[65] *Ibid.* at p. 63.

a document which evidences a contract of carriage to the port of discharge specified in the contract of sale. Even if the charterparty had been tendered in this
case, it would not have filled the gap: for by its terms it did not show a contract
of carriage with discharge of the goods at Venice. Venice was, in the charterparty, merely one of two ports to which the charterer could . . . order the
vessel to go 'on signing bills of lading,' The very fact that the bills of lading,
when signed, merely said 'port of discharge as per charterparty,' would cause
the prudent buyer, not only to realise that he did not have the assurance to which
he was entitled, but, affirmatively, to suppose that orders as to the port of discharge had not been given when the bill of lading was signed, as required by the
charterparty contract.''[66]

When the documents were rejected, the sellers attempted to cure the
defects by having the master of the vessel alter the bills of lading in question
by substituting in each case "Venezia" for the defective words. The court
held that this could not cure the pre-existing defect as the buyers had no
reason to suppose that there had been merely clerical errors which were being
belatedly corrected. The sellers could not oblige the buyers to treat the documents as proper and acceptable on re-presentation. The alterations showed a
variation of the original contract of carriage at some unknown date.

> "But the buyers were entitled—and it was a matter of importance against the
> possibility of short delivery of, or damage to the goods—to have in the docu-
> ments proper evidence of a contract of carriage which covered the goods from
> the time they were shipped, as being goods which were, from that moment
> onwards, to be carried to Venice'' (*ibid.* at p. 64).

85   In *Acme Wood Flooring Co. v. Sutherland, Innes & Co.*,[67] the contractual
destination was a particular wharf. The goods were sold c.i.f. to buyer's
wharf, Victoria Docks, London. The bill of lading did not provide for delivery
at buyer's wharf. The goods were discharged in London elsewhere, and under
the "London Clause" in the bill of lading certain charges became payable
which would not have been payable if delivery had been made at the buyer's
wharf. The question was on whom these charges fell. It was held by Bruce
J. that they must fall on the sellers, since, if the shipping documents had
provided for delivery at the contractual destination, the "London Charges"
would not have been payable.

In *Sargant & Sons v. East Asiatic Co. Ltd.*,[68] the sale was of 100 tons of
block gambier c.i.f. London. The sellers declared 100 tons per S.S. *Selandia*,
which arrived in London and discharged some cargo there. As the sellers,
who were also the shipowners, had not received the bills of lading they gave
delivery orders to the buyers against payment for the goods. The delivery

---

[66] *Ibid.*
[67] (1904) 9 Com. Cas. 170.
[68] (1915) 85 L.J.K.B. 277. In the same case there was a second contract for the sale of pepper
c.i.f. London, where the bill of lading was forthcoming. The bill of lading provided for delivery
at Copenhagen, but was indorsed by the defendants, as shipowners, "to be delivered in London."
No exception was taken to it so indorsed, and it was treated as if it had originally been made
out for London.

orders were duly presented, lighters were sent for the goods, but delivery was refused by the ship's agents, and the *Selandia* sailed for Copenhagen carrying the goods in her. The block gambier was delivered at a later date to the buyers in London. It appeared, when the bills of lading came to hand, that the goods had been shipped under bills of lading making them deliverable at Copenhagen. The buyers recovered damages for loss resulting from the delay.

Thus, the seller is under a duty to provide documents so that the goods will be delivered at the precise point agreed upon between the parties. It has been held that where there is a contract to deliver to particular docks at a named port and the goods are sent in a ship that is too large to get into the dock, the buyer is entitled to reject the documents.[69]

86   Likewise, the Victoria Supreme Court held in *Alexander Cross & Sons Limited v. Hasell*[70] that under a contract for the sale of superphosphates to be shipped from Glasgow, price 70s. per ton c.i.f., destination Sydney and/ or Melbourne railway wharves, buyers' option, the seller had not performed his contract by tendering bills of lading which merely provided for delivery at wharves in Melbourne and not at railway wharves there. In this case, payment was to be by a confirmed credit in London, but because of the non-conformity above-mentioned the bank refused to accept the documents. The seller's action to recover the price failed, it being held that the delivery of shipping documents in strict accordance with the contract and credit was a condition precedent, and that as the bill of lading did not provide for the contractual destination of the goods, the buyer was entitled to avoid the contract. But where the contract of sale provides that the buyer shall be entitled to direct the vessel, *inter alia*, "to any safe port in United Kingdom of Great Britain and Ireland" the seller is not in default by tendering shipping documents that exclude certain ports which the vessel cannot safely approach.[71]

Where goods were sold c.i.f. the buyer's warehouse in Ealing, the contract is not fulfilled by misdelivery to the buyer's office from which they were stolen. The seller could not recover the price as goods "sold and delivered" because the consignment was never delivered at the contractual destination, and no insurance was tendered with respect to the inland transportation to Ealing.[72]

87   Some c.i.f. contracts now expressly place the risk of discharge of the goods on the buyer, so that the seller do not assume any responsibility in respect of inability to reach or unload at the contemplated destination. Where the con-

---

[69] *Marshall Knott & Barker Ltd. v. Arcos Ltd.* (1933) 44 Ll.L.R. 384.
[70] (1908) V.L.R. 194.
[71] *Re an Arbitration Between Goodbody and Co. and Balfour, Williamson and Co.* (1899) 82 L.T. 484, where the Court of Appeal held that a stipulation "Manchester excepted" in the shipping contract did not violate the contract of sale because the vessel on which the goods were loaded could not get to Manchester without dismantling at Runcorn Bridge, by virtue of which Manchester was to be considered as an unsafe port.
[72] *Lindon Tricotagefabrik v. White and Meacham* [1975] 1 Lloyd's Rep. 348 (C.A.).

tract so provides the buyer obviously cannot avoid the contract by pleading frustration for such inability,[73] but the position is generally identical even where the contract contains no such provisions. This type of risk (strike at port of destination, congestion, import embargo), which the carrier is generally not liable for, is generally also not insured against, and is certainly beyond the ambit of the type of insurance coverage that the c.i.f. seller must procure.[74] The risk must be viewed as normally falling on the buyer, unless a term to the contrary has been agreed or can be implied.

In *Congimex Companhia Geral De Commercio Impotadora E. Exportadora S.A.R.L. v. Tradax Export S.A.*,[75] four contracts for the sale of soya bean meal c.i.f. Lisbon were considered. Payment was to be in New York on delivered weights ascertained by weighing after discharge. Under Portuguese law, at the time the contracts were entered into, an import licence was necessary. This licence could not be obtained in view of a prohibition imposed in respect of private imports after the contracts were entered into but prior to some of the shipments that were still pending. The sellers tendered documents in respect of some of these shipments, but the buyers rejected them. The sellers declared the buyers to be in default of these shipments, and sued for the balance under the contracts, on the grounds that the buyers repeatedly stated they could not take delivery, and failed to open letters of credit as they were obliged to do in respect of some of the purchases. The buyers unsuccessfully argued that the contracts were frustrated. The Court of Appeal, affirming Staughton J., held that supervening illegality was only a defence if it arose by the proper law of the contract (which in the present case was English) or by the law of the place of performance and, in the case under consideration, the place of payment was New York, and payment by the buyer did not become illegal under New York law. In the course of his judgment Sir John Donaldson L.J. stated that c.i.f. contracts are not contracts "for the sale of goods at or guaranteed to arrive at the contractual destination" (at page 253). The fact that the contracts provided that price was to be related to delivered weights, which was to take place in Lisbon, did not alter this result. Discharge, in other words, was not part of the performance of a c.i.f. contract, and is something which is done by arrangement between the buyer and the shipowner after the c.i.f. contract has been fully performed.[76]

> "Whilst it is quite clear that the changes in the Portuguese import regulations made it impossible for either weighing or sampling to take place after importation, it is not found that either was prohibited if delivery at Lisbon was for the purpose of reshipment or transhipment to a non Portuguese destination ...

---

[73] [1981] 2 Lloyd's Rep. 687, aff'd [1983] 1 Lloyd's Rep. 250 (C.A.).
[74] See *post*, § 182.
[75] [1983] 1 Lloyd's Rep. 250 (C.A.).
[76] Sometimes c.i.f. contracts attempt to fix the contractual rate of discharge obligating the buyer to pay demmurage for failing to discharge at that rate, and for entitlement of despatch money if the rate is exceeded. These clauses are not to be construed as they would have been construed had they appeared in a charter party. See *Establissements Soules et cie v. Intertradax S.A.* [1991] 1 Lloyd's Rep. 378 (C.A. and Q.B.) where such a clause was considered.

Furthermore ... the fact that some minor part of performance becomes impossible does not necessarily frustrate the contract and it would also have been necessary to have obtained a finding that such impossibility as existed destroyed the
commercial basis of the contract".[77]

On the other hand, where the seller orders and redirects the vessel away
from its contractual destination it was held by Mocatta J. in *Peter Cremer v.
Brinkers' Groudstoffen B.V.*[78] that he was in breach, and that the buyer could
recover transshipment costs. The dispute there involved a sale of a parcel of
a bulk shipment of Indonesian copra c.i.f. Rotterdam. The seller time chartered the vessel, and the copra was afloat when the particular parcel was sold.
As a result of an alleged congestion at Rotterdam, the vessel was ordered to
discharge its entire cargo in Hamburg. Judgment for the buyers was given on
the narrow ground that, since the contract related to an unascertained quantity
of bulk copra, appropriation could only take place at Rotterdam where final
weighing was to occur. The seller, therefore, was in breach in not making
delivery, and settling final payment on Rotterdam weights. The judgment,
however, noted that there was much to be said for two additional general
propositions put forward for the plaintiff, namely: first, that there was an
implied term that a c.i.f. seller will not interfere with performance of the
contract of carriage he has procured for the buyer, such a term being not only
reasonable but also necessary to give business efficacy to the contract, and
secondly, that there was an implied term that would require the seller not
only to enable performance at the contractual destination but also to do his
best to prevent frustration of such performance.[79] As to the first of these
implied terms it was reiterated by the Court of Appeal in *Empressa Exportadora Azucar v. Industria Azucarera Nacional S.A.*[80] where the sellers, on
instructions from their Government, diverted a c. and f. shipment consisting
of a cargo of sugar from Chile to North Vietnam. Although the court held
that in so doing the sellers were in breach of the warranty that the buyer shall
have and enjoy quiet possession of the goods implied by section 12(2) of the
Sale of Goods Act 1979 (*post*, § 318), the judgment noted that even if section
12(2) did not apply there was much to be said for the proposition that there
must be an implied obligation "that a c.i.f. seller will not interfere with the
performance of the contract of carriage he has procured for his buyer" (*per*
Ackner L.J. at page 180). In other words the seller must do nothing to interfere with or prevent the performance of the contract of carriage under which
the cargo is to be carried pursuant to a c.i.f. or c. and f. contract:

"It would seem ... an absurdity if a buyer, who has never obtained the goods
the subject of the contract, by reason of the seller wrongfully interfereing with
the essential working of that contract by preventing the performance of the contract of carriage which he was under an obligation to arrange, nevertheless could

---

[77] *Ibid.* at p. 253.
[78] [1980] 2 Lloyd's Rep. 605.
[79] *Cf. Baxter, Fell & Co. Ltd. v. Galbraith & Grant Ltd.* (1941) 70 L1.L.Rep. 142 *post*, § 250.
[80] [1983] 2 Lloyd's Rep. 171.

not maintain a claim for breach of contract. Such an implication seems . . . alto-gether necessary for the business efficacy of the contract. The fact that there may be a remedy in tort is . . . irrelevant. The buyer stands in a special relationship to the seller, because of the contract which binds them together. That relationship is not extinguished by the negotiation of documents, so that thereafter the buyer is limited to the remedy which is appropriate were the seller an entire stranger''. (Ackner L.J. *Ibid.*).

Finally, it may be of interest to note that where a c.i.f. contract for the sale of La Plata oats and maize to "one safe port west coast of Italy" (that provided, *inter alia*, that the first or second port was "to be agreed between the sellers and buyers on the ship passing the Straits of Gibraltar") came up for consideration, the Court of Appeal decided the provision was not legally enforceable as it merely provided that the parties *may* agree on first or second port; not that they *must* so agree. No damages (not even nominal) could therefore be claimed for failure to comply with the stipulation. This was decided in *Mallozzi v. Carapelli S.p.A.*[81] (Megaw, Roskill and Goff L.JJ.) where the sellers directed the vessel to first go to Genoa, whereas the buyers desired that it first travel to Naples. Both ports were seriously congested, and the sellers interests (who had grain of their own on the vessel) conflicted with the interests of the buyers. Because of a provision in the contract the buyers were not liable to the sellers for any demurrage on account of delay in unloading at Naples, but the buyers' claim for damages, for breach of the above quoted provision, failed. Megaw L.J. for the Court of Appeal held that there was no breach by the sellers of any obligation in respect of negotiating as to the first or second port because there was no legally binding obligation to negotiate. In the course of his judgment he stated[82]:

> "There was a possibility, it was contended, that if the sellers had used reasonable efforts to negotiate, they would have realised that there was a possible solution, such as sending the vessel to some other port, neither Genoa or Naples, which would have been to the advantage of the sellers themselves, as well as of the buyers; as a result of their failure to negotiate, the sellers have thus deprived themselves (which for this purpose does not matter), and also the buyers (which for this purpose does matter), of a possible financial advantage. . . .
>
> "Accordingly, I would hold that the view that the learned Judge took in rela-tion to this second issue cannot now be supported because the dictum on which he properly relied has since been deprived of validity. It has to be held that there was here no breach by the sellers of any obligation in respect of negotiating as to the first or second port, because there was no legally binding obligation to negotiate."

88   Where the destination is not fixed by the contract, the buyer is under an obligation to nominate it, before he can complain that the seller has not performed his contract. And where he fails to make the nomination known to the seller by the earliest date on which the contract could have been per-

---

[81] [1976] 1 Lloyd's Rep. 407.
[82] *Ibid.* at p. 413.

formed, he has committed a breach of a condition precedent that entitles the seller to treat the contract as at an end.

Whether inability to import the goods to the intended destination is an event excusing the buyers' performance under a c.i.f. contract is discussed elsehwere.[83] Clearly the c.i.f. buyers' intention to transship the goods from their original c.i.f. port of discharge to some other (final) destination is generally of no concern to the seller. And where the buyer is prevented from so doing because of an import embargo at the (intended) final destination, he cannot successfully plead frustration or illegality as an excuse for non performance. Thus in *Congimex S.A.R.L. (Lisbon) v. Continental Grain Export Corp.*[84] under contracts for the sale of U.S. soya bean meal c.i.f. Rotterdam, the buyer was held in default for failure to take up the shipping documents, and could not plead impossibility or frustration on the grounds that the goods were purchased in order to be transshipped to Lisbon, and such importation had become illegal under Portuguese law. Whatever the situation in Portugal was (and whether or not the buyers' intention was known to the seller)[85] it did not affect the performance of the c.i.f. contracts in question since delivery could still have taken place in Rotterdam, and the goods resold to others there.

In a subsequent case, the same result was reached with respect to contracts for the sale of soya bean meal c.i.f. Lisbon.[86] The Court of Appeal noted that the buyer should have considered redirecting the goods to some other destination. In so far as Portuguese law made it illegal to weigh and sample the goods in Lisbon (as *per* the terms of the contract) the court held that, in the absence of proof this would have been impossible had the goods been delivered at Lisbon for reshipment or transshipment, no finding on frustration was permissible and moreover, that even if such a finding were made, it would not avail the buyers unless they could also show that this impossibility destroyed the commercial basis of the contract.

Time provisions

89 Where the contract stipulates a time limit for the nomination of the port of discharge by the buyer, problems have sometimes arisen with regard to the intended expiration date.

In *Carapanayoti & Co. Ltd. v. Comptoir Commercial André & Cie S.A.*[87],

---

[83] See *ante*, §87 and *post*, §111.
[84] [1979] 2 Lloyd's Rep. 346.
[85] The situation would be different where the final destination became a term of the contract. While c.i.f. contracts normally do not contain any guarantee for arrival at the contractual destination, there is obviously nothing to prevent parties from agreeing otherwise. However, it would appear wise to stipulate for this expressly, as the courts are rightly inclined to construe c.i.f. contracts as implying no guarantee of arrival at the contractual destination.
[86] *Congimex Companhia Geral de Comercia Importadora e Exportadora S.à.r.l. v. Tradax Export S.A.* [1983] 1 Lloyd's Rep. 250 (C.A.), affirming [1981] 2 Lloyd's Rep. 687, *ante*, §87.
[87] [1971] 1 Lloyd's Rep. 327.

the plaintiffs sold to the defendants 500 tons of Nigerian groundnuts c.i.f. a range of alternative United Kingdom, Northern Europe and Mediterranean ports, shipment February/March 1968. Clause 3 of the contract provided *inter alia* that "if the groundnuts are sold to two or more ports Northern range at Buyer's option, the port of destination shall be declared by the last Buyer to his Seller not later than 21 days before commencement of shipment period . . . ," while another condition (22) provided that "where an act has to be done on or before a given day such day shall be considered to have commenced at 10 a.m. and to have ended at 4 p.m. Monday to Friday inclusive." On December 11, 1967 the defendants contracted to sell a similar quantity of groundnuts under a contract containing similar terms except for price (which had greatly increased as a result of the devaluation of sterling that had occurred in the interval) to one Valensi of Marseilles. After a number of requests by the defendants to nominate the port of discharge, and subsequent to one invalid nomination of a Japanese port, Valensi, at 10.30 a.m. on January 11, 1968 (which was the 21st day before the commencement of the shipment period), declared Dunkirk as the port of destination. The defendants transmitted the nomination to the plaintiffs, who maintained that the nomination was too late. On a case stated to the court by the Board of Appeal of the Seed, Oil, Coke & General Produce Association (Inc.), Donaldson J. held that on the true construction of clauses 3 and 22 of the contract read in conjunction with each other, notice given after 10 a.m. and before 4 p.m. on the 21st day before the beginning of the shipment period, *i.e.* one given on January 11, complied with the requirements of the contract.

His lordship reviewed the various methods of reckoning time in commercial contracts and the different formulas used for the purpose. After admitting that "[t]ime provisions of the sort with which [he was] here concerned are notorious for giving rise to disputes and for stimulating nicely balanced arguments," he commented that "those who are engaged in the trade would be astonished and appalled to be told that in order to understand the meaning of the contract it was necessary to read and compare the judgments in 17 cases going back to the year 1808. . . ."[88] He found the contention advanced by the plaintiffs that condition 22 was irrelevant because notice did not have to be given on or before a given day but "not later than 21 days before the commencement of a period," unacceptable. It was his view that "[a] requirement that a notice be given not later than 21 days before the commencement of a period, which itself begins at the first moment of a day, necessarily involves the notice being given on or before a given day. The only problem [being] which day."[89] This day he held to be the 21st, and not the 22nd day before the beginning of the shipment period.

But the Court of Appeal disagreed with this conclusion and allowed the appeal, holding that (where an act was to be done "not later than 21 days before" the happening of an event) the day on which the event happened

[88] *Ibid* p. 331.
[89] *Ibid* p. 332.

must be excluded, and 21 clear days were to be counted backwards to arrive at the last day on which the act, namely, shipment, could be done.[90]

90   In *Tsakiroglou & Co. Ltd. v. Transgrains S.A.*,[91] the controversy arose under a contract for the sale of Sudanese groundnuts for shipment during November 1956 at a price of £51 10s. per 1,000 kilos landed weights c.i.f. basis freight rate Hamburg/Rotterdam. It was not disputed that this term meant that the buyers had the option of choosing either of these two places as the port of c.i.f. destination, or, alternatively, that the buyers were entitled to choose a usual Mediterranean port, either Marseilles or Genoa, and that if the buyers exercised their option to declare a Mediterranean port, then the price would be reduced on the basis of the freight to that place ruling at the time the contract was made. The buyers designated Marseilles as the port of destination, but did not do so until October 31, the last day before the one on which the sellers could have elected to ship. However, because of telegraphic and postal delays, the sellers only came to know of this nomination on November 5, whereupon they cancelled the contract. McNair J. upheld the decision of the Board of Appeal of the Incorporated Oil Seed Association that the sellers were justified in cancelling the contract and that the buyers were not entitled to recover any damages for non-performance. His honour declared himself in entire agreement with the Board's view:

> "That is was a necessary implication that the buyers should make known to the sellers the exercise of their option as to the port of c.i.f. destination within a reasonable time before the earliest date for shipment under the contract and that the buyers' failure to notify the sellers of the exercise of such option within a reasonable time as aforesaid was a breach of condition entitling the sellers to treat the contract as determined. . . ." (at p. 572).

As to the risk of telegraphic or postal delays, it was clearly to be borne by the buyers, since their duty is not merely to nominate the destination but to make that nomination known to the sellers, and a breakdown of communications does not excuse them from their failure to notify the sellers of the port that they had nominated.

In *Michel Verseux S.à.r.l. v. Schwarz & Co. (Grain) Ltd.; Schwarz & Co. (Grain) Ltd. v. R. & H. Hall Ltd.*,[92] 2,500 tons of French maize were sold, the terms being c.i.f. Dublin/Cork/Waterford at buyer's option to be shipped in two parcels of 1,250 tons each under bills of lading to be dated February 1969, and March 1969, respectively. Destination was to be declared by the buyers not later than 15 days prior to first day of shipment. The maize was resold on similar terms, and Dublin declared as the port of destination. The declarations were upset by strikes at Irish ports, including Dublin, and extensions in the times of shipment were granted by the sellers. After a series of

---

[90] [1972] 1 Lloyd's Rep. 139.
[91] [1958] 1 Lloyd's Rep. 562.
[92] [1971] 2 Lloyd's Rep. 39, affirming [1971] 1 Lloyd's Rep. 291.

telexes between the parties, the option of selecting the destination port was reinstated and shipments had to be made, the first between March 25 and April 15, and the balance in the second half of April. The question arose as to whether these telexes exchanged between the parties left the original provisions as to notification intact requiring the buyers to declare the port of destination 15 days prior to shipment, or whether the provision had been modified so as to place upon the buyers the duty to make the declaration whenever the sellers demanded it of them (in time for the maize to be shipped within the new dates). The latter being the correct interpretation, it was held by the Court of Appeal, affirming Donaldson J., that the buyers could succeed in an action for breach against the sellers who failed to ship any maize although the buyers redesignated Dublin as the port of discharge. The sellers took exception to this designation as not been given 15 days before the new shipping date. But the Court of Appeal agreed that the sellers defence failed. In the circumstances, it was impossible to accept the contention that the 15-day notice period had remained unaltered by the exchange of telexes, because *inter alia* the extended shipping date (March 25) was not agreed to until March 13, leaving less than 15 days between both dates.

Lastly, it should be noted that any inability to unload the goods at the agreed destination as would, *e.g.* arise from the sudden imposition of an import quota, is normally for the risk of the buyer in the case of c.i.f. contracts.[93]

The contract of affreightment

91   The duty of the seller in arranging for shipment is to enter into a contract of affreightment for the carriage by sea of the goods. A contract of affreightment is defined as a contract of carriage for reward which arises when a shipowner (or person having for the time being as against the shipowner the right to make such an agreement) agrees to carry goods by sea or to furnish a ship for the purpose of so carrying goods in return for a sum of money to be paid to him which is called the freight.[94]

When the agreement between the seller and the shipowner is for the carriage of a complete cargo or for the provision of a ship which is let or demised to the seller by the shipowner, the contract is generally contained in a charterparty. The seller will usually in addition take a bill or bills of lading as a receipt for the goods that have been shipped. Where, however, and this is in general the case in regard to c.i.f. contracts, the seller makes a contract for the shipment of a consignment of goods which compose only part of a general cargo, there will not be a charter-party to which the seller is a party. The seller will simply receive a bill of lading on shipment of the goods.

---

[93] *Warner Bros. & Co. Ltd. v. Israel*, 101 F. 2d 59 (1939). See also *ante*, § 88.
[94] As to the question whether the seller must prepay the freight or whether he enjoys the option of deducting it from the purchase price, see *post*, § 104.

The bill of lading

92   A bill of lading is a document which is signed by the shipowner or his agent (or sometimes by a charterer, where the vessel is under charter) acknowledging that goods have been shipped on board a particular vessel which is bound for a particular destination and stating the terms on which the goods so received are to be carried.

"It is a receipt for the goods," said Lord Bramwell in *Sewell v. Burdick*,[95] "stating the terms on which they were delivered to and received by the ship, and therefore excellent evidence of those terms, but it is not a contract. That has been made before the bill of lading was given. Take for instance goods shipped under a charterparty, and a bill of lading differing from a charterparty; as between shipowner and shipper at least the charterparty is binding."

Further consideration of the relationship between the contract of affreightment and the bill of lading was given by Lord Goddard C.J. in *The Ardennes*,[96] where there was an oral warranty given by the shipowners that was not included in the bill of lading.

In that case shippers were exporting mandarin oranges from Spain to England. The shipowners promised orally that the ship would arrive in London by November 30, 1947. This date was essential to the shippers as an import duty was being imposed from December 1. The ship did not arrive until December 5, and the shippers therefore sued for damages for delay. The shipowners pleaded a deviation clause in the bill of lading as a defence. Lord Goddard gave judgment in favour of the shippers. In the course of his judgment,[97] he said:

"It is, I think, well settled that a bill of lading is not in itself the contract between the shipowner and the shipper of goods, though it has been said to be excellent evidence of its terms: *Sewell v. Burdick*,[98] per Lord Bramwell and *Crooks v. Allen*.[99] The contract has come into existence before the bill of lading is signed; the latter is signed by one party only, and handed by him to the shipper usually after the goods have been put on board. No doubt if the shipper finds that the bill contains terms with which he is not content, or does not contain some term for which he has stipulated, he might, if there were time, demand his goods back; but he is not, in my opinion, for that reason, prevented from giving evidence that there was in fact a contract entered into before the bill of lading was signed different from that which is found in the bill of lading or containing some additional term. He is no party to the preparation of the bill of lading; nor does he sign it."

[95] (1884) 10 App.Cas. 74 at p. 105.
[96] *SS. Ardennes (Cargo Owners) v. SS. Ardennes (Owners)* [1951] 1 K.B. 55.
[97] *Ibid.* at p. 59.
[98] (1884) 10 App.Cas. 74 at p. 105.
[99] (1879) 5 Q.B.D. 38.

The terms of the contract of affreightment

93   The duty of the c.i.f. seller is to enter into such a contract of affreightment as will enable him to comply with the express terms of the contract of sale. In all other respects, the contract of affreightment that the seller has to obtain is one which is reasonable and usual in the trade at the time of shipment. This obligation is satisfied if the contract is in a form current in the trade or on the contemplated route. The seller is not called upon to procure a contract on more favourable terms than those usually contained in the ordinary bill of lading in use in the trade or on the route concerned. In any given case, the test to be applied is whether it is in accordance with the usage and practice in the trade to carry goods of the contractual description shipped from and to the places in the contract under a contract of carriage such as that in question.

In *Burstall v. Grimsdale*,[1] the contract was for the purchase of meal c.i.f. London from America. The bill of lading gave liberty to deviate. The buyers refused to take up the documents as the ship in fact deviated to Bremen. Kennedy J. held on the facts that the documents tendered were not necessarily inconsistent with the terms of the contract of sale and the buyers were not justified in their action.

> "If the effect of the clause in the bill of lading," he said,[2] is to make the calling at another port, such as at Bremen, out of the direct line to London, permissible, the question then is, was the adoption by the shippers under the through bill of lading of such a method of carriage by the Leyland Line—a well-known line of steamers—necessarily inconsistent with the terms of the sale contract and the American germ meal contract which it embodies? That appears to me to be eminently a question of fact or commercial usage, and upon the findings in the case it seems to me that there was no inconsistency. If I were trying this case as an action before a jury, the question I should have to ask the jury would be whether it is or not in accordance with the usage and practice in the trade to accept this method of carriage to London under a contract such as this, and is such custom or practice or usage well known and acted upon? I feel no doubt— in fact, it is found for me in the case—that that question would be answered, as it has been in this case, in the affirmative."

In *Shipton, Anderson & Co. v. Weston & Co.*,[3] where the contract of sale called for shipment from Atlantic or Canadian ports with option of calling at another port in the United Kingdom to Bristol and Avonmouth or Portishead, direct or indirect, sellers' option, and the vessel called at Glasgow, and then at Belfast before proceeding to Avonmouth, under liberties contained in the bill of lading "so wide that the ship might have called anywhere she liked and almost have gone round the world before she came to the port of discharge," Greer J. held that tender of the bill of lading was not a good tender under the contract.

---

[1] (1906) 11 Com. Cs. 280.
[2] *Ibid.* at p. 290.
[3] (1922) 10 Ll.L.Rep. 762.

94   In *Fischel & Co. v. Spencer*,[4] the contract was for the sale of Manila copra cakes to be shipped per steamer or steamers from port or ports in the Philippine Islands c.i.f. Rotterdam. The bill of lading procured by the sellers was in the usual form adopted by the four shipping companies that carried the bulk of the trade from the islands: it provided for transhipment from steamer to steamer, sailing vessels or lighters. On arrival at London, the goods were discharged into lighters and put upon a vessel for Amsterdam, where they were again put on board lighters and carried to Rotterdam. The buyer refused the tender of the bill of lading by reason that the goods had been transhipped. The court (Lord Hewart C.J., Bailhache and Salter J.J.), on a case stated by trade arbitrators, held that it was bound by a finding of fact in the case that where a seller desires to have power to tranship it is usual and customary for him to insert in the contract a clause authorising transhipment, and since the contract in question contained no such provision, the bill of lading was not a good tender. Where transshipment is permissible, there usually must be continuous documentary cover, and the buyer is not bound to accept a bill of lading that relieves the issuer from liability on discharge, and leaves him exposed till the cargo is received by a subsequent carrier.[5]

In the case of *Finska Cellulosaforeningen v. Westfield Paper Co. Ltd.*,[6] which concerned the sale of sulphite pulp from Finland, Viscount Caldecote C.J. held that the insertion in the bill of lading of a war risk clause giving the shipowners wide discretionary liberties did not prevent the bill of lading from being a good performance of the contract. In the course of his judgment,[7] he said:

> "The argument was pressed upon me that a bill of lading under a c.i.f. contract must be in a form which is reasonable and usual in the trade, and that this clause was neither the one nor the other. It was said on behalf of the defendants that the wide discretion given to the master to discharge the cargo at any convenient port or place in the conditions of war stated in the clause had the effect of making the bill of lading no longer one for the carriage of goods to Leith. I do not accept this contention. It is everyday practice to deal in bills of lading with war conditions, ... by inserting a clause not different in essence from that to which the defendants take exception. The insertion in a bill of lading of [such] a clause ... does not, in my opinion, prevent the bill of lading from being for the carriage of goods to a named port. Moreover, evidence was given to show that in this trade this identical clause, or one very like it, has been widely used since the outbreak of war in September, 1939. ... I accept the submission of counsel for the defendants that a bill of lading tendered under a c.i.f. contract must be, as in the case of the policy of insurance, in a form usual or current in the trade ... I find as a fact that the clause was a usual one, and current in the trade."

It was also decided in the above case that the time when the reasonableness of the terms of the bill of lading was to be considered was not the date of

---

[4] (1922) 12 Ll.L.Rep. 36.
[5] See *post*, § 97 and § 147.
[6] [1940] 4 All E.R. 473. For the facts of this case, see *post*, §102.
[7] *Ibid.* at p. 477.

the contract of sale, but the date of the procuring of the bill of lading. "It would be strange," said Viscount Caldecote,[8] "if, notwithstanding such circumstances, the sellers under a c.i.f. contract were to be obliged to produce a bill of lading in a form which it might be impossible to procure."

95   In the American case of *Madeirense De Brasil S/A v. Stulman-Emerick Lumber Co.*,[9] where naturally dried lumber was sold on c.i.f. terms, the Court of Appeals (Second Circuit) held that the seller was in default by shipping the lumber "on" instead of "below" deck. The court noted the seller's obligation to procure a contract of carriage "as may be reasonable, having regard to the nature of the goods and the other circumstances of the case," holding that this obligation was not discharged where under-deck carriage was not procured.

96   In the Australian case of *Plaimar Ltd. v. Waters Trading Co. Ltd.*,[10] the bills of lading for a consignment of Zanzibar clove oil to be shipped via Singapore c.i.f. Fremantle contained clauses exempting the shipowner from liability for loss or damage at the port of transhipment. The effect was to place the carrier in the position of a forwarding agent, the carriage of the goods after transhipment being governed by the terms of the bill of lading of the on-carrying ship. The goods disappeared in Singapore, and the seller brought an action for the purchase price. In his defence, the buyer, citing Lord Sumner's speech in *Hansson v. Hamel & Horley Ltd.*,[11] pleaded, *inter alia*, that this form of bill of lading did not satisfy the requirements of a c.i.f. contract. The court dismissed this allegation on the grounds that the evidence disclosed that the seller had no option in this instance, having utilised the only carrier available for shipment from Zanzibar. In the absence of an alternative, the seller could not be expected to obtain a more favourable bill of lading than was tendered by him and it was therefore a valid tender under the c.i.f. contract in question.

97   But in *Holland Colombo Trading Society Ltd. v. Segu Mohamed Khaja Alawdeen and Ors.*[12] the Judicial Committee of the Privy Council opined that a bill of lading containing a transhipment clause that did not provide for "continuous documentary cover" would be a bad tender under a c.i.f. contract.[13] The contract there considered was not a c.i.f. contract proper, as the seller was given the option to deliver either documents or the goods themselves once they had arrived. The goods were shipped from Rotterdam to Colombo under a bill of lading that purported to absolve the shipowner from any liability in respect of the goods if transhipped, from the time of tranship-

---

[8] *Ibid.* at p. 479.
[9] 147 F. 2d 399 (1945).
[10] (1945) 72 C.L.R. 304.
[11] [1922] A.C. 36, 46, quoted *post*, § 157.
[12] [1954] 2 Lloyd's Rep. 45.
[13] See more on this point, and on through bills of loding *post*, § 147.

ment. The vessel met with misfortune and caught fire near Genoa, from where the goods where transhipped on a different vessel. Though the goods did ultimately arrive safely in Colombo, the buyers refused to pay for them, *inter alia*, on the ground that the aforementioned bill of lading, which was the only one the buyers were ever offered (no additional document having been issued in respect of the goods upon transhipment), did not entitle them to enforce delivery from the ship in which they arrived as (they alleged) they had a right to receive under the contract. Their lordships did not deem it necessary to decide this question. The goods were discharged from the ship into the Colombo Customs House, and on the evidence it was clear that delivery could have been obtained by the buyers had they proceeded with an intention to perform the contract. Referring to the transhipment clause, Lord Asquith of Bishopstone, who delivered their lordships' judgment, said:

> "Their lordships repeat that this is not a c.i.f. contract. It was argued for the [seller] that even if it had been, there would have been a sufficient documentary tender to satisfy such a contract. Their lordships are not of that opinion. A bill of lading with a transhipment clause is not necessarily a bad tender under a c.i.f. contract: but it must in some way give 'continuous documentary cover' in respect of the goods over the whole transit (*Hansson v. Hamel & Horley Ltd.* [1922] 2 A.C. 36); and a bill of lading issued by a shipowner who by the transhipment terms in it disclaims all liability in respect of the goods in the event and as from the time of transhipment gives no such 'continuous' cover" (at p. 53).

Lord Sumner's speech in the *Hansson* case was also referred to in *Spillers Ltd. v. J. W. Mitchell Ltd.*[14] There, on a case stated by the Appeal Tribunal of the London Corn Trade Association, Branson J. held a bill of lading that contained a marginal note to the effect that "The deviation clause with its full stipulations is admitted as forming part and body of this bill of lading" a bad tender under a c.i.f. contract. The learned judge said:

> "... what may be the document which was referred to in this marginal note is one which could only be ascertained by calling evidence from the shipper and from the ship. They might agree; they might disagree; and the uncertainty which is introduced into this bill of lading by the presence of this provision in the margin is so great that, in my view, it is quite impossible to say that the bill is a good tender in pursuance of the contract" (at p. 91).

Benefits accruing under the contract of affreightment

98   The terms of the contract of sale may entitle the seller to make a profit on the carriage of goods sold. This may occur, for example, where there is a demurrage clause in the contract of sale. Demurrage may be defined as the sum agreed to be paid by the charterer to the shipowner as liquidated damages for delay beyond a stipulated or reasonable time for loading or unloading.[15]

---

[14] (1929) 33 Ll.L.Rep. 89.
[15] *Scrutton on Charterparties*, (19th ed.) Art. 153 p. 305 *et seq.*

"There is, however, no rule of law that the vendor in a c.i.f. contract may not secure for himself a profit under a demurrage clause contained in it. Neither is there any indisputable presumption of law that the parties to such a contract did not intend that he should receive such a profit. To use the words of Lord Blackburn in *Calcutta and Burmah Steam Navigation Co. v. De Mattos*,[16] in such contracts 'there is no rule of law . . . preventing the parties making any bargains they please.' "

These words are taken from the opinion of the Privy Council (given by Lord Atkinson) in *Houlder Bros. v. Commissioner of Public Works*,[17] where it was held that on the construction of the contract between the parties the sellers (who were the charterers) were entitled to recover from the buyer the full amount of demurrage stipulated in the contract and not merely an amount equal to the sum which they had been compelled to pay to the shipowner under the charterparties. It is, however, always a matter of construction of the contract whether a clause dealing with demurrage permits a seller to make a profit or merely entitles him to an indemnity to the extent of his actual expenses from the buyer.[18]

99   In *John George White v. James Leslie Williams*,[19] for example, the Judicial Committee of the Privy Council held that where two cargoes of coal were sold at specified prices for delivery c.i.f. Sydney with the stipulation that the "cost of stevedoring" at the port of discharge was to be for account of the purchaser, the sellers were nevertheless under a duty to account to the buyer for any contribution by the ship towards the cost of unloading. The charterparty which the sellers and the shipowners entered into in this case provided that the steamer would pay a shilling per ton towards the cost of discharge. It was held that the purchaser was entitled to claim the benefit of this stipulation and a corresponding reduction in the contract price was allowed. Their lordships opined that when the contract of sale stipulated that the purchaser was to pay the cost of stevedoring the expression should be read as meaning "so far as such cost is not provided by the ship in the way of tackle or steam or in money" (*per* Lord Mersey at page 819).

100   Conversely, the contract may be so construed or performed as to place upon the seller the onus of discharging the cost of demurrage. In *Tradax International S.A. v. R. Pagnan and Fratelli*,[20] the sellers sold to the buyers 11,500 tons of maize c.i.f. Genoa. The contract *inter alia* included a provision whereby the "ship (was) to discharge in accordance with the custom of the port, or according to the condition of bills of lading in force with regular

---

[16] (1863) 32 L.J.Q.B. 322 at p. 328.
[17] [1908] A.C. 276 at p. 291.
[18] See *Houlder Bros. v. Commr. of Public Works* [1908] A.C. 276; *Suzuki v. Companhia Mercantile Internacional* (1921) 8 Ll.L.Rep. 174; 9 Ll.L.Rep. 171 (C.A.); *French Govt. v. Sanday & Co.* (1923) 16 Ll.L.Rep. 238.
[19] [1912] A.C. 814.
[20] [1968] 1 Lloyd's Rep. 244.

Lines to the port of discharge. If documents are tendered which do not provide for discharging as above, or contain contrary stipulations, Seller to be responsible to Buyer for all extra expenses incurred thereby.'' By another provision it was agreed that "should the shipment, or any portion thereof, be included in a Bill of Lading for a larger quantity, payment shall be made against delivery order. . . .'' Sellers chartered a vessel to ship the maize, and, since the quantity carried was larger than the contract amount, availed themselves of the right to tender delivery orders to their purchasers. The chartered vessel arrived at Genoa but due to congestion of the port was unable to continue discharging her cargo for about nine weeks. The sellers became liable to pay about £16,000 demurrage to the vessel of which they sought to recover some £10,000 (their *pro rata* share of the maize) from the buyers. It was the sellers' contention that had they tendered bills of lading, the buyers would have been made liable to the shipowners for demurrage, and moreover that the parties could not have intended that liability should vary depending on which document was tendered. Donaldson J. rejected the claim. In his view, the clause in the contract imposed no obligation on either the sellers or the buyers to discharge the vessel within a specified time; that there was at no time any contract between the buyers and the shipowners, and that although the sellers' contention was eminently sensible, the facts in the case did not support their claim.

Bill of lading confined to goods sold

101   The bill of lading must comprise only the goods which are the subject of the sale. The buyer requires the bill of lading in order to receive the goods and also to be in a position to prosecute any claim against the shipowner arising out of the carriage, or to transfer these rights to a sub-purchaser. Obviously, difficulties would arise if the seller included in the bill of lading other goods than those destined to the particular c.i.f. buyer, and to adopt the language of A. T. Lawrence J.[21] the buyer under such a contract is not "buying a litigation" or compelled to take delivery of documents which may force a litigation upon him. There may, of course, be express agreement that negatives this.[22]

In the case of *Re Keighley, Maxted & Co. and Bryan, Durant & Co.*,[23] the contract was for the sale of "about 3,000 tons of wheat (10 per cent more or less) to be shipped by steamer" from India, payment to be made by cash in London within seven days from delivery of invoice in exchange for bill or bills of lading. The sellers had the option of shipping less or more than the

---

[21] 16 Com.Cas. 95 at p. 101. And see *per* Lord Sumner in *Hansson v. Hamel & Horley Ltd.* [1922] 2 A.C. 36 at p. 46, quoted *post*, §154.

[22] Sellers who deal in bulk shipments normally insist on the right to ship under a collective bill of lading in which case the c.i.f. contract is to be performed by tender of a ship's delivery order; see *post*, §135.

[23] (1894) 70 L.T. 155.

minimum and maximum quantity respectively. In the former case, the price of the quantity shipped short of the medium quantity was to be settled at the value at the date of appropriation; in the latter, the excess over the medium quantity was to remain for the sellers' account. The sellers shipped in fact 3,800 tons, and appropriated 3,000 tons of that shipment to the contract, sending the buyers an invoice for 3,000 tons. The bills of lading of the 3,800 tons were two for 1,750 tons each, and two for 150 tons each, and the sellers offered to deliver either all the bills of lading or two for 1,750 tons each, leaving 800 tons or 500 tons, as the case might be, balance of the cargo in the buyers' possession, but the property of the sellers. The buyers refused to accept the tender. It was held by the Court of Appeal (Lord Halsbury, Lopes and Davey L.JJ.) that as the contract, by the sellers' appropriation, had become one for 3,000 tons the buyers were entitled to delivery of a bill or bills of lading for that quantity, and, as the bills of lading did not correspond with that quantity, they were entitled to refuse the tender.

Likewise, the bill of lading must acknowledge the shipment to correspond in quantity to the quantity specified under the invoice. A bill of lading signed only for an unknown quantity of goods is a bad tender. So, where the seller tendered a bill of lading which, having stated the quantity shipped, contained the comment that "part of the cargo lost during loading by rafting," the buyer was entitled to refuse acceptance. In the words of Macnaghten J.:[24]

"Is such a document a bill of lading which the buyer under a c.i.f. contract is bound to accept? No authority precisely covering the point has been cited to me. I have come to the conclusion that it is not a proper bill of lading which a buyer under a c.i.f. contract is bound to accept as a sufficient bill of lading under the contract. It was pointed out ... on behalf of the sellers that this bill of lading contains what I suppose almost all bills of lading contain, a statement that although there is an acknowledgment of the shipment of a specified quantity of goods there is a qualification by the master of the ship that he does not know the quantity or condition or quality of the goods in question. And if I followed him [counsel for the sellers] aright every bill of lading is nothing more than an acknowledgment of the shipment of an unknown quantity of goods, the description of which may or may not be in accordance with the statement in the document. I think the argument [of counsel for the buyer] on that point is right. A bill of lading which the buyer is bound to accept must be a document acknowledging the shipment of a quantity of goods according with the quantity specified in the invoice and for which the seller demands payment. And if there is an invoice for a specified quantity and the bill of lading is for either an unknown quantity of goods or a quantity of goods substantially different from that in the invoice, a bill of lading would not be a proper bill of lading which the buyer would be compelled to accept."

Charterparty not normally to be tendered

102   The document to be tendered is one which represents the contract of affreightment. This is usually the bill of lading, and the charterparty is not

[24] *Libau Wood Co. v. H. Smith & Sons Ltd.* (1930) 37 Ll.L.Rep. 296 at p. 300.

normally required, despite the mention of it as one of the necessary shipping documents by Blackburn J. in *Ireland v. Livingston*.[25] It will be observed that all the other judicial definitions refer either to a contract of affreightment or simply to a bill of lading. There may be cases where the charterparty is required as an indispensable part of the contract of affreightment. Whether mention of the charterparty in the bill of lading necessitates its tender, would, it is thought, depend on the circumstances.

In *Finska Cellulosaforeningen v. Westfield Paper Co. Ltd.*,[26] the plaintiffs were woodpulp manufacturers in Finland who sold to the defendants a large quantity of sulphite pulp c.i.f. Leith. Some 253 tons were shipped on board the *Lapponia* under a bill of lading dated January 31, 1940, for carriage to Leith. The *Lapponia* sailed in February, but in May 1940 her cargo was discharged at Kotka in Finland. The buyers refused to take up the shipping documents, claiming that they were not in order. The bill of lading contained the clause ''All conditions and exceptions as per charterparty dated (blank).'' The buyers contended that a charterparty should have been tendered with the shipping documents. They also claimed that the bill of lading was defective in that it contained a current war risk clause which they alleged was not reasonable or usual in the trade.[27]

Viscount Caldecote C.J. found against the buyers on both these points. As to the charterparty, he found that the buyers well knew and understood what was intended by the clause in the bill of lading, and were well aware that shipments would take place, as in the past, in vessels chartered on the terms of the *''Baltpulp''* charter. He continued[28]:

> ''Counsel for the defendants put his case as high as to say that, in all cases of c.i.f. contracts, the charterparty must be tendered where it is a relevant document. As authority for that proposition, he referred to a passage from the judgment of Blackburn J. in *Ireland v. Livingston*,[29] '. . . for the balance a draft is drawn on the consignee which he is bound to accept (if the shipment be in conformity with his contract) on having handed to him the charterparty, bill of lading and policy of insurance.' It is to be observed that neither in the judgment of Hamilton J. in *Horst (E. Clemens) Co. v. Biddell Brothers*[30] nor in the judgment of Kennedy L. J. in that case in the Court of Appeal[31] is there any mention of the charterparty as one of the necessary documents to complete delivery in accordance with the agreement. Nor, again, in *Johnson v. Taylor Brothers & Co., Ltd.*,[32] where Lord Atkinson once more stated the sellers' duties under a c.i.f. contract, was there any mention of the charterparty as a necessary document to be produced by the seller, together with the invoices, bill of lading and policy of insurance, in order to entitle him to receive payment.

[25] (1872) L.R. 5 H.L. 395. Set out, *ante*, §5.
[26] [1940] 4 All E.R. 473.
[27] This is dealt with *ante*, §94.
[28] [1940] 4 All E.R. 473 at p. 476.
[29] (1872) L.R. 5 H.L. 395 at p. 406.
[30] [1912] A.C. 18.
[31] *Ibid.* at p. 934.
[32] [1920] A.C. 144 at pp. 155, 156.

"In the circumstances of this case at any rate, the tender of the bill of lading duly indorsed was, in my opinion, a sufficient compliance with the contract of sale to entitle the sellers to payment of the price of the goods. . . ."

Thus in the later case of *S.I.A.T Di Del Ferro v. Tradax Overseas S.A.*,[33] Donaldson J., whose judgment was upheld by the Court of Appeal, commented that:

"The mere fact that a bill of lading refers to a charterparty does not require production of that charter, if its terms are not incorporated into the bill of lading contract or do not affect the buyers' rights. Thus the bills of lading in the present case were claused 'Freight payable as per charterparty', but the [c.i.f.] sale contract provided that the sellers should settle the freight directly with the vessel. Nor need the charterparty be produced if the bill of lading refers to a known standard form and it is only the printed clauses of that form which are relevant, for example, 'Centrocon Arbitration Clause'. If the decision in *Firska Cellulosatoreningen v. Westfield Paper Co. Ltd* is correct, 'it is justified upon this ground.'"

It follows that where the charterparty is incorporated by reference into the bill of lading, it too (or a copy thereof), would, because of its effects on the terms of the contract of carriage, normally have to be tendered to the buyer as part of the shipping documents pursuant to a c.i.f. contract of sale.

Bill of lading issued on shipment

103   In the ordinary course of events, the bill of lading must be signed on shipment of the goods or within a reasonably short time thereafter. There may be exceptions in the case of through bills of lading, which are considered later.[34] Lord Sumner in the House of Lords in the case of *Hansson v. Hamel & Horley Ltd.*,[35] discussing the dictum of Scrutton J. in *Landauer & Co. v. Craven & Speeding Bros.*[36] that a bill of lading must be procured "on shipment," says:

"I do not understand this proposition as meaning that the bill of lading would be bad, unless it was signed contemporaneously with the actual placing of the goods on board. 'On shipment' is an expression of some latitude. Bills of lading are constantly signed after the loading is complete and, in some cases, after the ship has sailed. I do not think that they thereby necessarily cease to be procured 'on shipment,' nor do I suppose that the learned judge so intended his words. It may also be that the expression would be satisfied, even though some local carriage on inland waters, or by canal, or in an estuary by barge or otherwise, preceded the shipment on the ocean steamer, provided that the steamer's bill of

---

[33] [1978] 2 Lloyd's Rep. 470, affirmed [1980] 1 Lloyd's Rep. 53 (C.A.).
[34] See *post*, § 147.
[35] [1922] 2 A.C. 36 at p. 47. This case is discussed more fully, *post*, § 152.
[36] [1912] 2 K.B. 94.

lading covered that prior carriage by effectual words of contract. 'On shipment' is referable both to time and place.''

This principle was also applied by Wright J. in *Foreman and Ellams Ltd. v. Blackburn.*[37] In that case the plaintiffs sold to the defendant by a contract dated July 2, 1926 a quantity of New South Wales frozen furred rabbits, packed not earlier than May or later than July, c.i.f. Liverpool. Shipment was to be *per Suffolk* due to sail from Sydney during August to Liverpool. On August 17, the *Suffolk* sailed from Sydney to Liverpool, laden with rabbit skins. On November 25, the sellers tendered to the buyer the shipping documents, which included a bill of lading, and by the custom of the trade two freezing certificates. The bill of lading was dated August 17, and contained a deviation clause. The freezing certificates showed that the skins were shipped on June 25 and August 17.

The buyer inquired when the skins were actually shipped, and was informed by the sellers that the whole of the goods had been loaded direct in the *Suffolk* on June 25, the steamer then proceeded to Queensland ports and, having returned to Sydney, finally sailed for Liverpool on August 17. The buyer thereupon refused to take up the shipping documents and the sellers brought an action for damages for breach of contract.

The arbitrator found for the sellers, but his decision was reversed. Wright J. held that the word ''shipment'' in the contract referred to shipment in the future, and that the bill of lading stating ''shipment on the ss. *Suffolk* now lying in Sydney'' meant shipment during the then stay in Sydney, and was accordingly not in order. As to the promptitude with which the bill of lading should be issued after shipment, Wright J. said[38]

"... I consider that the bill of lading was not a good shipping document, and was not in proper regular form. It appears from the relevant documents that as regards some part at least of the goods the shipment had taken place not less than seven weeks before the date of the bill of lading, and that in itself was a fact which could properly lead to inquiry and call for explanation. It was also apparent and is not contested that in that interval of time the ship had proceeded from Sydney to a number of ports in North Queensland, and had then returned to Sydney, and that it was during her second stay in Sydney that the bill of lading was issued. It is true that, though a bill of lading must be issued on shipment, some latitude of time has been allowed."

Wright J. then referred to the words of Lord Sumner in *Hansson v. Hamel & Horley Ltd.*,[39] quoted above, and continued:

"In fact, I have never before known such a case as this. I am prepared, however, to hold, and I do hold, that a bill of lading is not regular if it is issued, though at the port of original loading, only seven weeks after the original loading of the cargo or some portion of it has taken place, after the vessel has left the port of

---

[37] [1928] 2 K.B. 60.
[38] *Ibid.* at p. 63.
[39] [1922] 2 A.C. 36.

loading and sailed some hundreds of miles to other ports, and has then come back to the original port of loading.''

The freight

104   The question whether, in the absence of an express stipulation, a c.i.f. contract imposes upon the seller the duty to prepay the freight or gives him an option to deduct the cost thereof from the invoice price does not appear to have been the subject of controversy in England. Dicta and observations made in the various decisions to which reference is made in the course of this work may be taken to lend support to either view. In the United States, on the other hand, this question was the subject of specific consideration in *Dixon Irmaos & Cia. Ltda. v. Chase National Bank of City of New York*,[40] where a judgment of the New York District Court ruling in favour of such an option was confirmed by the Circuit Court of Appeals. The court stated that "the tender of documents showing a deduction of freight from the invoices was not a deviation from the requirement of defendant's credits calling for c.i.f. shipment," and that the

> "seller has so long had the option of shipping either freight collect or freight prepaid that the cases recognise the option as part of the standard meaning of the term C.I.F., making no distinction between prepayment or shipping freight collect and crediting it on the invoice irrespective of whether the draft be time or sight . . .[41] if the buyer sells the documents before arrival of the goods, as frequently happens in C.I.F. transactions, whether freight was prepaid will be wholly immaterial to him" (at p. 763).

And the lower court stated: "The evidence establishes that there is no generally accepted custom or practice in the commercial world under a c.i.f. shipment as to the manner of payment of freight. It seems to be optional with the seller, whether he shall prepay it or deduct it from the invoice." In *Amco Transworld, Inc. v. M/V Bambi*,[42] the District Court of New Jersey likewise held with respect to a c. and f. contract, stating that such a contract permits either the seller to prepay the freight or the purchaser to deduct the actual freight charges from the purchase price. Statements supporting the proposition that a c.i.f. seller is, *inter alia*, required to *pay* the freight charges sufficient to carry the goods to their destination (which were cited to the court in

---

[40] 144 F. 2d 759 (1944), affirming 53 Fed.Sup. 933 (1943). See also *Warner Bros. & Co. Ltd. v. Israel*, 101 F. 2d 59 at p. 60 (1939).

[41] The court referred, *inter alia*, to Blackburn J.'s statement in *Ireland v. Livingston* (1872) L.R. 5 H.L. 395 at p. 406, quoted *ante*, § 5. See also *per* Lord Wellwood in *A. Delaurier & Co. v. J. W. Wyllie & Ors.* (1889) 17 R. (Ct. of Sess.) 167, where he said: "The meaning and effect of the expression c.i.f. simply is that the sellers undertake to insure for the purchaser and include in the invoice price the cost of the cargo, the insurance premium, and the full freight. From this they deduct the amount of freight to be paid at the port of discharge, and draw for the balance upon the consignee" (at p. 189).

[42] 257 F. Supp. 215 (1966).

the *Dixon* case) were construed as referring to the obligation to include the cost of freight in the quoted price but not as implying that he must also prepay it in fact.

It is submitted that the foregoing conclusion is sound, and, unless a reason can be shown by the buyer that he is likely to be prejudiced thereby,[43] the seller should be entitled to tender a freight collect bill of lading and receive the contract price less any amount payable to the shipowner on account of freight. Contracts governed by the Uniform Commercial Code, however, no longer afford this option. By the provisions of section 2–320(2)(b) of the Code, the seller is expressly instructed to "load the goods and obtain a receipt from the carrier (which may be contained in the bill of lading) showing that freight has been paid or provided for."

105   Contracts, however, sometimes contain specific stipulations with respect to the payment of freight, and in such cases they are normally binding on the parties thereto. In *Soproma S.p.A. v. Marine & Animal By-Products Corporation*[44] a c. and f. contract called for payment by an irrevocable letter of credit against tender of specified documents including "freight prepaid" clean bills of lading. The sellers tendered "freight collect" bills of lading which were rejected. On a case stated by the Board of Appeal of the London Cattle Food Trade Association, McNair J. held that the sellers could not succeed in their action for the price in view of their failure to tender the stipulated documents. The contention that the buyers usually do not take objection to bills of lading marked "freight collect" if either freight is deducted from the price or a freight receipt is tendered, could not be sustained at law because the documents would be mutually inconsistent.

106   In some cases, the contract may contain an express provision by which the freight is payable upon the discharge of the vessel at her destination. In *Modiano Bros. & Sons v. Bailey & Sons*,[45] where the contract so stipulated, Branson J. had to deal with the question whether the buyer who had paid the shipowner more in respect of freight than was deducted from the seller's invoice price was allowed to recover any such difference from the seller. Branson J. upheld an award stated by the Appeal Committee of the London Corn Trade Association which was in favour of the sellers. This dispute arose as a result of a complicated exchange provision in the bill of lading that the shipowner construed as a gold linked clause. Before the goods were discharged, the gold standard was abandoned by the United States. As a result,

---

[43] In the case of a sight draft, it is wholly immaterial to the buyer whether freight is prepaid or credit given on the invoice price. In the case of a time draft, the buyer may be deprived of the credit period as to the cost of freight and the possible loss to the buyer is the interest upon this sum for the period between arrival of the goods and the date the draft would fall due. This amount would normally be insignificant. Furthermore, if as noted in the *Dixon* case, the buyer sells the documents before arrival of the goods, which frequently happens, whether freight was paid or not would be wholly immaterial to him.
[44] [1966] 1 Lloyd's Rep. 367.
[45] (1933) 47 Ll.L.Rep. 134.

the shipowner claimed, and was paid under protest, the equivalent of £50 more in respect of freight than the amount which the parties contemplated. It was His Lordship's view that as between seller and buyer, once the shipping documents were taken up by the latter, the former was discharged from all further connection with the contract. The buyers were not to be considered as agents of the seller for the purposes of paying the freight and the fact that by the Bills of Lading Act 1855 the indorsement of a bill of lading did not discharge the original shipper from his liability to pay freight is immaterial to the question under consideration. Branson J. further held that the shipowner misconstrued the clause in the bill of lading and nothing in it entitled him to claim an amount exceeding the sterling equivalent of the sum contemplated by the parties. Consequently, any excess payment by the buyer was due to a mistake of law, and therefore (on that ground also) no money could be recovered back from the seller.

A similar provision to the one considered in the *Modiano* case formed the subject matter of a more recent dispute before Brandon J.[46] A c. and f. contract for the sale of Russian timber between Greek importers (the charterers) and Greek timber merchants (the cargo owners) stipulated that: "The freight is payable in cash upon arrival of the vessel." The charterers chartered the *Pantanassa* agreeing that freight was to be deemed to be earned "on shipment of the goods, ship lost or not lost." The *Pantanassa* ran aground en route to Athens and a salvage agreement was entered into. The issue which came to the court, as a special case from the appeal arbitrator under the salvage agreement, concerned the determination of the proportions in which the persons interested in the salvaged property were liable to contribute towards the salvage reward. Brandon J., reversing the arbitrators' decision, held that the freight element in the price of the cargo salved was at the risk of the charterers and not of the cargo owners. He rejected the charterers' interpretation that the provision as to payment of freight in the sales contract governed only the time at which this element of the price of the goods should be paid, *i.e.* on arrival, or, if the vessel did not arrive, when she would have arrived in the ordinary course. He then supported his conclusion by referring to the "usual position as regards such payment under c. and f. contracts where freight collect bills of lading are used." As to this aspect, the learned judge said as follows:

> "C. and f. contracts only differ from c.i.f. contracts in that the sellers are not required to insure the goods for the buyer. In the case of c.i.f. contracts, payment of the freight element in the price may be effected in one of two ways. The first way, is for the seller to prepay the freight and invoice the buyer for the full c.i.f. price, which is payable by the buyer against shipping documents. The second way is for the seller to leave the buyer to pay the freight on the delivery of the goods, invoicing him only for the c.i.f. price less freight. When the first method is used the seller provides freight prepaid bills of lading. When the second

---

[46] *The Pantanassa; Norsk Bjergningskompagni A/S v. Owners of the Steamship Pantanassa, her cargo and freight* [1970] 1 All E.R. 848.

method is used he provides what have conveniently been called freight collect bills of lading, *i.e.* bills of lading under which freight is payable by the receiver (who may be the buyer himself or a sub-buyer from the buyer) to the ship at the port of discharge. The distinction between the two methods was considered in *Soproma S.p.A. v. Marine and Animal By-Products Corpn.*[47]

"The classic description of a c.i.f. contract given by Blackburn J. in *Ireland v. Livingston*[48] relates to a contract under which freight collect bills of lading are used. It was clearly the view of Blackburn J. that, under such a contract, the buyer's obligation to pay freight was conditional on the arrival of the goods. This still seems to be the accepted view today: see British Shipping Laws, Vol. 5, *C.I.F. and F.O.B. Contracts* by D. M. Sassoon.[49] This passage follows statements made earlier in Kennedy on c.i.f. contracts.[50]

"The c. and f. contracts in the present case seem to me to have been contracts under which the second method of effecting payment of the freight element in the price, namely, by the use of freight collect bills of lading, was intended to be, and was in fact, used. On that basis, in the light of the usual position under such contracts, one would expect to find that the buyer's obligation to pay freight was conditional on the arrival of the goods. In fact the language used is to put it at its lowest, readily capable of having that effect and, that being so, I cannot see any reason for trying to construe it otherwise."

107   The risk as to any increase in the cost of freight is in the case of c.i.f. contracts to be borne by the seller. In *Blythe & Co.* v. *Richards, Turpin & Co.*[51] the sellers attempted to suspend a contract for the sale of Portuguese ore c.i.f. Manchester because the price of freight doubled as a result of conditions emanating from the First World War. Scrutton J. held that they were not entitled to rely on an exception clause which stated that "if war, or any other cause over which the sellers have no control, should prevent them from shipping or exporting . . . or delivering under normal conditions, the obligation to ship . . . under the . . . contract shall be . . . suspended during the continuance of such impediment . . ." It was his view that this exception did not apply if the only impediment was an increase in the price of freight which meant that the sellers would have had to perform their obligation at a loss to themselves.

In *Madeirense De Brasil S/A v. Stulman-Emerick Lumber Co.*[52] the Second Circuit Court of Appeals held that under a c. and f. contract for the sale of lumber the inclusion of a provision for payment for seller's account of freight charges of a specified amount was only an estimate of freight charges, and hence the seller was not entitled to a refund of additional (subsequently increased) freight which had been incurred and which was charged by the buyer against the purchase price.

In a more recent decision, the United States Court of Claims had to decide whether "war risk surcharges" imposed by carriers serving Vietnamese ports to cover:

---

[47] [1966] 1 Lloyd's Rep. 367.
[48] The paragraph cited is the one appearing, *ante*, § 5.
[49] (1968 ed.), Vol. 5, p. 127.
[50] (1st ed., 1924), p. 80, (2nd ed., 1928), p. 81 and (3rd ed., 1959), p. 82.
[51] (1916) 114 L.T. 753.
[52] 177 F. 2d 399 (1945).

The Shipment

(1) increased war risk premiums on hull insurance;
(2) crew bonuses for entering the Vietnamese war zone; and
(3) operating expenses during the delays caused by congestion in the port of Saigon, were for the account of a c.i.f. seller or buyer.[53]

The court characterised the seller's allegation "that war risk surcharges, being similar to war risk insurance,[54] should be borne by the buyer," as false. "War risk surcharges" said Durfee J., "are imposed by the carrier, and are not used to insure the goods, but to compensate for certain of the carrier's expenses. Since the seller, under a c. and f. contract, bears the cost of carrying the goods to the port of destination, it is clear that he, and not the buyer, should bear the burden of these surcharges.[55] Thus, despite what may be similarities between war risk surcharges and war risk insurance, their different functions dictate different allocations."

Yet, the parties are of course free to alter this general rule by express stipulation. In *D. I. Henry v. Wilhelm G. Claser*[56] a quantity of jute cuttings was sold c.i.f. Rotterdam under a written contract containing the provision "Cape surcharge buyer's account." This referred to a levy made by Conference vessels following the closure of the Suez Canal in June 1967. Part of the contract quantity however was supplied in chartered (non-conference) vessels, and the Court of Appeal, affirming a decision of the first instance upholding an arbitral award, held that, as the provision referred to payment which could only be made to a member of the conference, the seller could not recover surcharge in respect of the part of the contract goods shipped in chartered vessels. While it may seem odd that the buyers obligation should vary according to the vessel by which the goods went, the sellers had a clear advantage in shipping in non-conference vessels because of the special freight rates they enjoyed.

Other documents

108   Where by the terms of the contract of sale or by custom of the trade other documents are deliverable to the buyer, they must be obtained and tendered to the buyer; otherwise, the tender will not be a good one. Thus, for example, in *Re Reinhold & Co. and Hansloh*[57] the sale was of 1,000 tons of yellow La Plata maize in good condition: "with legalised Chamber of Commerce certificate as to shipment, sound, dry and fit for export," c.i.f. Hamburg. The

---

[53] *Continental Ore Corp.* v. *The United States*, 423 F. 2d 1248 (1970).
[54] As to this see *post*, § 185.
[55] In the case of *Tsakiroglou & Co. Ltd.* v. *Noblee & Thorl GmbH* [1962] A.C. 93, the House of Lords, in deciding that under a c.i.f. contract a longer route necessitated by the closing of the Suez Canal did not frustrate the contract, recognised that the resulting surcharges were the responsibility of the seller, *ante*, § 78.
[56] [1973] 1 Lloyd's Rep. 159, affirming [1972] 1 Lloyd's Rep. 392.
[57] (1896) 12 T.L.R. 422.

seller tendered two bills of lading to make up the 1,000 tons. Each described the maize as "marked and numbered as in the margin," that is, with an "F" on them. A certificate in the required form was obtained but did not state that the bags examined were those marked with an "F." The buyer refused to accept the documents on this ground, and the court (Pollock B. and Bruce J.), on a special case state, held that he was entitled to reject.

One of the most important documents that may now be required is an export licence.[58] Other documents are also often required, such as consular invoices or certificates as to origin and value, certificates of quality or of fitness or condition,[59] freezing certificates in, *e.g.* the frozen rabbit trade,[60] or phytopathological or health certificates of freedom from disease in the case of fruit or foodstuffs.[61]

109   Where the contract calls for the furnishing of one or more of such documents, the question whether their form must exactly conform to the contractual specification or whether the seller complies with his duty by furnishing documents which in the business sense satisfy the object that the document is designed to serve has sometimes been raised. In *John Martin of London Ltd. v. A. E. Taylor & Co. Ltd.*[62] the contract provided that the sellers would furnish the buyer, *inter alia* with "invoices . . . stating lodgement number and location of certificate of origin. . . ." The lodgement numbers were not given on the invoice, it having been left to the sellers' agents in London to advise the buyers of the numbers, after obtaining them from the customs authorities. Lord Goddard C. J. considered that the sellers satisfied their contract and that the absence of a lodgement number did not entitle the buyers to reject the goods. He indicated that stipulations of the type under consideration had to be construed in a business sense, and that if there is no adverse effect on the buyer and the object of the document is accomplished, strict compliance with the terms of the contract is not necessary. Since the obtaining of the necessary number was not in the control of the sellers in the sense that they had to get it from the customs authorities, he was of the view that the contractual wording was not obligatory but merely directory. However, where payment is arranged through a banker's letter of credit, normally not even the slightest deviation from the documents specified will be allowed and the doctrine of strict compliance usually applies.[63]

Where information is required to enable the seller to complete the necessary documents, and this information, to the knowledge of both parties, can only be supplied by the buyer a term that the buyer shall co-operate with the seller in making such information available is normally implied into the contract.[64]

---

[58] See *post*, 111 and 485 *et seq.*
[59] See *post*, 324.
[60] *Foreman & Ellams Ltd. v. Blackburn* [1928] 2 K.B. 60, *ante*, 103.
[61] *Yelo v. Machado* [1952] 1 Lloyd's Rep. 183.
[62] [1953] 2 Lloyd's Rep. 589.
[63] *Post*, § 612 *et seq.*
[64] *Kyprianou v. Cyprus Textiles Ltd.* [1958] 2 Lloyd's Rep. 60 (C.A.)

The invoice

110   It is the duty of the seller to tender to the buyer an invoice as one of the regular shipping documents. As Blackburn J. said in *Ireland v. Livingston*[65]:

> "The invoice is made out debiting the consignee with the agreed price (or the actual cost and commission, with the premiums of insurance, and the freight, as the case may be), and giving him credit for the amount of the freight which he will have to pay to the shipowner on actual delivery. . . ."

The invoice is a statement by the seller showing particulars of the goods shipped and the price to be paid. It is a representation by the seller of the goods which he is tendering under the contract, and it is regarded as evidence of the movement of the goods described therein. Frequently the buyer is sent a provisional invoice. This gives him advance information of the goods which are being destined to him, and is nothing more than an intimation of the way in which the seller intends to perform his contract.[66]

Licences

111   Subject to the terms of the contract, the procurement of any import licence which might be necessary is the obligation of the buyer and the procurement of any export licence the obligation of the seller under a c.i.f. contract. Whether these obligations are absolute or merely conditional, *i.e.* an obligation to use all reasonable diligence to obtain the necessary licence, probably depends on the terms of the contract. Where nothing is said in the contract the inference will normally be that an absolute obligation of the risk ie obtaining an import licence is with the buyer, whereas the seller has merely taken a conditional obligation to use all reasonable efforts to obtain the licence. Consequently, if the seller's efforts are to no avail, there is no default on his part and the contract is probably cancelled. In *Mitchell Cotts & Co. (Middle East) Ltd. v. Hairco Ltd.*[67] the defendants agreed to buy a quantity of goat hair from the plaintiff's branch in the Sudan. The terms were c.i.f. payment net cash after approval of the goods at the port of arrival. No mention was made as to who was to obtain an import licence under the Import of Goods (Control) Order 1940, and each party was under the impression that it was the duty of the other. When the goods arrived, the buyers had already accepted the shipping documents. But as there was no licence to import the goods, they were seized by the customs authorities and forfeited. The buyers refused to pay the price and contended that the duty to obtain the licence was on the sellers, and that approval of the goods was a condition

---

[65] (1872) L.R. 5 H.L. 395 at p. 406.
[66] *Per* Lord Wright in *Ross T. Smyth & Co. Ltd. v. T. D. Bailey, Son & Co.* [1940] 3 All E.R. 60 at p. 71.
[67] [1943] 2 All E.R. 552.

precedent to the obligation to pay. Held by the Court of Appeal (Scott, Mackinnon and Goddard L.JJ.) that the seller was entitled to recover the price.
The buyer could not avail himself of the condition of approving the goods
unless he could show that he was not in default in respect of his failure to
express approval or disapproval. It is the buyer's duty to take whatever steps
are necessary to obtain from the proper authority the right of making the
inspection of the goods upon which his expression of approval or disapproval
depended. Because the buyer made no effort at all to obtain the necessary
licence, the question of what would have been the consequences of an abort-
ive effort to get a licence was not considered.

112   In *Anglo-Russian Merchant Traders Ltd. v. Batt*[68] the sellers were held to
be excused from shipment by reason of inability to obtain an export licence.
The parties there contracted with knowledge of and in contemplation of an
existing prohibition of export, under which no shipment could be effected
without a licence from the British Government. The court held that the seller
did not undertake the liability for the consequences of an inability to obtain
the necessary licence but only to take all reasonable steps to obtain the
licence.[69] Where the contract contains the phrase "subject to granting of an
export licence" there is no doubt whatsoever that the seller merely undertakes
the conditional obligation to do his best to procure permission to export. The
only question, therefore, is whether or not he has in fact discharged that
duty.[70]

113   In *Ross T. Smyth & Co. Ltd. (Liverpool) v. W. N. Lindsay Ltd. Leith)*[71] the
sellers entered into a contract for the sale of 500 tons of Sicilian horse beans
for shipment from Sicilian port October and/or November 1951 at £31 15s.
per ton c.i.f. Glasgow. The contract provided that "should the fulfilment of
this contract be rendered impossible by prohibition of export . . . any unfulfilled part thereof to be cancelled." At the date of the contract, the export of
horse beans was permitted, but by an Italian regulation, dated October 20,
1951, as and from November 1, 1951, export was only allowed under a
specific licence. No shipments under the contract were made, and the buyers
declared the sellers in default. The dispute was referred to arbitration, wherein

---

[68] [1917] 2 K.B. 679.
[69] But the seller must make efforts to obtain a licence and show that it could not be obtained
on application or that it would have been useless for him to apply for one. See *J. W. Taylor &
Co. v. Landauer & Co.* (1940) 57 T.L.R. 47.
[70] See, *e.g. Société D'Avances Commerciales (London) Ltd. v. A. Beese & Co. (London) Ltd.*
[1952] 1 T.L.R 644. The seller having made one application which was not approved made no
further attempt to obtain licences, taking the view that any further steps would be useless. The
court held that he had failed in his duty to take all reasonable steps to obtain a licence. See also
Vidler & Co. (London) Ltd. v. R. Silcock & Sons Ltd. [1960] 1 Lloyd's Rep. 509, c.i.f. contract
not cancelled by virtue of prohibition to export except under a licence, notwithstanding exception
clause relating to export prohibition because sellers had not proved that any legitimate steps that
they might have taken to ship the goods were foredoomed to failure. As to the question of
licences, see further *post*, 485 *et seq.*
[71] [1953] 1 W.L.R. 1280.

it was held that the performance of the contract by the sellers had become impossible by reason of a change in the law of Italy. On a special case stated by the arbitration tribunal, Devlin J. held the sellers liable. The prohibition of export was not instantaneous but gave the sellers ten days in which to ship, and, in the absence of a finding that during that period the sellers had exercised diligence or that shipment would have been impossible notwith-standing, they were not to be excused from performing the contract. The award therefore could not be sustained.

So, too, a c.i.f. seller who can ship from one or other of a number of ports in various countries cannot normally escape liability because an export prohibition prevents him from shipping from the particular place from which he has purchased the goods he has resold and from which he intends and makes arrangements to ship.[72] But the situation may of course be otherwise if the contract contains an exception clause excusing performance in the event the prohibition (or a strike or other intervening impossibility) prevents ship-ment.[73]

114 In *K. C. Sethia (1944) Ltd. v. Partabmull Rameshwar*[74] the Court of Appeal dismissed an appeal from a decision of Lord Goddard C.J. upholding an award of the Committee of the London Jute Association. There four contracts for the sale of Indian jute c.i.f. Genoa by October 1948 were construed to contain no implied term that they would be cancelled if the seller was unable to obtain the necessary export licence. It appeared that the Indian Government had introduced a quota system for regulating the export of jute under which the shippers were required to choose a certain year as their "basic year" and were allocated a quota in regard to the countries to which they had shipped in their basic year. The sellers chose 1946 as their basic year. But as they had made no shipments to Italy in that year no quota was allotted to them for shipment to Italy. They were therefore unable to perform the contracts in question. The court held that, although both parties knew that the contracts could only be out of the sellers' quota, the question whether the quota would suffice for the purpose depended on matters concerning the conduct of the sellers' business which were peculiarly within their own knowledge and con-trol (they chose the basic year and they knew what other contracts had to be satisfied out of their quota). An implied provision that the contracts were subject to quota or that the sellers merely undertook to use their best endeav-ours to obtain a quota was not to be read into the contracts since this would be inadequate to secure their business efficacy. Consequently, the buyers were entitled to damages. The decision was affirmed by the House of Lords.[75] Subsequent decisions that opined on the question of allocation of supplies under a quota system (imposed after the conclusion of the contract), pro-

---

[72] See *Warnico A.G. v. Fritz Mauthner* [1978] 1 Lloyd's Rep. 151 (C.A.), more fully discussed *ante*, § 41.
[73] See cases discussed *ante*, § 71.
[74] [1950] W.N. 5.
[75] [1951] 2 All E.R. 352.

nounced that in such circumstances, what "the trade would consider to be proper and reasonable—whether the basis of appropriation is pro-rata,[76] chronological order of contracts or some other basis"[77] would be the correct criteria by which to determine whether or not the seller was in breach, and whether he could invoke any *force majeure* defence in respect of any unfulfilled quantity resulting therefrom. However under English law, the seller cannot (as the law presently stands) apportion or allocate scarce goods to non contractual as well as to contractual claimants, and to the extent he does so he incurs liability to contractual claimants for short delivery.[78]

115   Many contracts nowadays contain specific stipulations relating to the consequences which are deemed to flow in the case of export or import prohibitions, normally providing for a fixed extension of the shipment period, after which, if the impossibility persists, the contract is to be cancelled.[79] In *Malik Co. v. Central European Trading Agency Ltd.; Central European Trading Agency Ltd. v. Industrie Chimiche Italia Centrale S.p.A.*,[80] the sale of Sudanese sesame seed c.i.f. Ancona was considered. Shipment was to be made from the Sudan in January/February 1970. The sellers who had exported other products from the Sudan, but not sesame seeds (till then) were unaware until about the third week in February 1970, *i.e.* only two weeks or less from the end of the shipping period, that an export licence was required. At that time an application was made and refused (without reason). Thereafter the buyers agreed to extend the shipping period until March 31; and again to April 30. The sellers, however, were unable to reverse the decision and obtain the necessary licence, and ultimately they declared the contract cancelled in accordance with a clause permitting cancellation in the event of an export prohibition. The matter was referred to arbitration wherein a finding was made that the single late application for the licence "did not constitute the exercise of due diligence to obtain a licence since, within the remaining period available before the time of shipment lapsed, there would be inadequate opportunity to appeal against any rejection . . . of such application and to effect shipment if such an appeal was granted." A further finding was to the effect that "No evidence was produced by [the sellers] to establish that if an application had been made in November or December 1969 it would nevertheless have been refused." On the basis of these two findings, Kerr J.

---

[76] Subject to *de minimis*, see, *e.g. Bremer Handelsgesellschaft mbH v. Vanden Avennelzegem P.V.B.A.* [1978] 2 Lloyd's Rep. 109 (H.L.); *Bremer Handelsgesellschaft mbH v. Continental Grain Co.* [1983] 1 Lloyd's Rep. 269 (Mustill J. and C.A.) holding *inter alia* that the question of the appropriate method of distribution was one of fact, to be determined (where applicable) by the arbitrators.

[77] *Per* Donaldson J. in *Intertradax S.A. v. Lesieur-Tourteaux S.A.R.L.* [1977] 2 Lloyd's Rep. 146 at p. 155.

[78] See *Pan Commerce S.A. v. Veecheema B.V.* [1982] 1 Lloyd's Rep. 645. The situation in the U.S. under the UCC is different and the seller can allocate to contractual as well as non-contractual clients.

[79] See, *e.g. Walton (Grain & Shipping) Ltd. v. British Italian Trading Co. Ltd.* [1959] 1 Lloyd's Rep. 223.

[80] [1974] 2 Lloyd's Rep. 279.

held that the sellers could not invoke the cancellation clause and were liable for breach. As there was, or may have been, a causal connection between the failure to apply earlier and the denial of the licence, there was no fallacy in the findings and it was immaterial that the shipping period was in fact extended. And the fact that the sellers had acted in accordance with the normal local practice in Sudan was not necessarily "the same as using one's best endeavours."[81]

But the fact that the contract expressly exempts the seller from performance in the event of an export prohibition may be construed as placing on the buyer an absolute obligation to obtain a permit for import. Staughton J. so held in *Congimex Companhia Geral de Comercia Importadora e Exportadora S.a.r.l. v. Tradax Export S.A.*,[82] concerning import controls in Portugal in 1975 which the buyer contended amounted to a frustration of a c.i.f. contract (incorporating GAFTA terms) and providing for modification of price related to delivered weight. Whether such a (juxtaposing) inference is normally called for is doubtful, but the result is in accord with the general rule governing c.i.f. contracts that, in the absence of stipulations to the contrary, the c.i.f. contract is performed on shipment and tender of the documents, and that what happens thereafter is normally of no concern of the seller. Thus on appeal (where Staughton J.'s judgment was upheld),[83] the Court of Appeal noted that:

> "Since the supervening illegality did not arise by the proper law of the contract (which was English) or by the law of the place of performance (payment was to be in New York), the Portuguese prohibition on payment did not avail the buyers. Moreover, had this been a classic c.i.f. contract the only aspect which would have been affected by Portuguese law was the performance of the contract of affreightment. However, there were no findings that that contract could only be performed by importation of goods to Portugal. Indeed, there were findings that the buyers should have considered redirecting the goods to France."

And while the change in the Portuguese import regulations made it impossible for either weighing or sampling to take place after importation, there was no finding that either was prohibited if delivery at Lisbon was for the purpose of reshipment or transhipment to a non-Portuguese destination. Such a finding was a prerequisite to any conclusion that the contract was frustrated upon the basis of illegality by the law of the place of performance. Moreover, even if some minor aspect of performance became impossible that would not necessarily frustrate the contract as it would be necessary to establish that the impossibility destroyed the commercial basis of the contract. Thus, Donaldson L.J. stated for the court:

> "[F]rustrated expectations and intentions of one party to a contract do not necessarily or indeed usually lead to the frustration of that contract and . . . the Board's

---

[81] *Ibid.* at p. 283.
[82] [1981] 2 Lloyd's Rep. 687 at p. 693.
[83] [1983] 1 Lloyd's Rep. 250 (C.A.).

findings that the buyers should have considered reselling the goods impliedly
negatives this submission [of frustration].''[84]

A party must, of course, prove the existence or occurrence of the supervening event, and what efforts he made to overcome it. The seller therefore may
be required to show whether and what steps he has taken to obtain an alternative source of supply.[85]

Also, difficulties of interpretation have sometimes arisen in relation to the
meaning of extension clauses (where shipment was to be stretched over several months in consignments of specified quantity or weight) as to whether
the notice of extension applies to the entire contract, or only in respect of the
separate consignments affected.[86]

Moreover, such clauses may only provide whose duty it is to obtain the
licence, and not the actual scope of the duty. Thus in *Coloniale Import-Export
v. Loumidis Sons*[87] a contract for the sale of Brazilian coffee c.i.f. Piraeus
was considered. The contract contained a clause imposing the duty to obtain
any import licence on the buyers. This they were unable to do, despite timely
and repeated efforts. The court decided (Lloyd J.) that the sellers claim for
damages failed, and that the buyers could rely on the *force majeure* provision
of the contract. The only obligation that could be implied was the obligation
of the buyers to do their best endeavours to obtain a licence. The contract, in
other words, did not contain an absolute warranty to assume the risk of a
licence being denied.[88]

Where there is no immediate and absolute prohibition, and preban export
commitments up to a certain date can be honoured, arbitrators have sometimes regarded the question as to whether the seller was or was not justified
in relying on the relevant exemption clause as one of fact and not of law. In
Overseas Buyers Ltd. v. Granadex S.A.[89] it was held that it was not misconduct on the part of aribitrators to reach a wrong conclusion of fact in such
circumstances. The arbitrators decision that the seller, in that case, had used
his best endeavours to ship the goods but was unsuccessful would not be
upset, although there was a loophole in the export prohibition there imposed
by the Indian Government in respect of the contract goods (groundnuts)
which may have provided a basis for performance.[90]

Finally, it should be noted that a serious problem may arise for sellers in
string transactions who attempt to excuse their non performance *vis-à-vis*
their buyers in reliance on a prohibition of export that barred (and excused)

---

[84] *Ibid.* at p. 253.
[85] See, *e.g. P. J. Van Der Zijden Wildhandel N.V. v. Tucker & Cross Ltd.* [1975] 2 Lloyd's Rep.
240, and the discussion *ante.* § 41 on purchase of goods afloat.
[86] See, *e.g. Bremer Handelsgesellschaft mbH v. Archer Daniels Midland International* S. A.
[1981] 2 Lloyd's Rep. 483. See Further *post*, § 366.
[87] [1978] 2 Lloyd's Rep. 560.
[88] See further on this aspect *post*, § 501.
[89] [1980] 2 Lloyd's Rep. 608.
[90] See also the cases mentioned *ante*, § 41, n. 5 for the effect of a loophole on an export
prohibition.

delivery to them. For, in order to enjoy the benefit of an exemption that an export embargo may have conferred on their suppliers, the sellers must show that a string in fact existed between their buyers and their suppliers, namely, the shipper or party from whom they (the sellers) had contracted to buy. Where it is impossible to say with certainty who were to be the intended shippers of the goods to be appropriated to the contract in respect of which the export prohibition is alleged, the sellers may well be unable to establish that the particular shipment was subject to the embargo. The sellers might thus find themselves in the unenviable position of being caught between two stools. Their suppliers would not be liable to them, but they would be liable to their buyers.[91] Where proof of a string is required by the buyer, he must, however, ask for it in time, and may be deprived of his right to take advantage of the sellers' non performance, if the time lapse makes records unlikely to be available, as was the case in *Andre et cie v. Cook Industries Inc.*[92], where the matter was first raised by the c.i.f. buyer 11 years after the event.

[The next paragraph is 131.]

---

[91] *Vanden Avenne – Izegern P.V.B.A. v. Finigrain S.A.* [1985] 2 Lloyd's Rep. 99.
[92] [1987] 2 Lloyd's Rep. 457 (C.A.).

CHAPTER 3

THE BILL OF LADING

131 As has been seen in the preceding chapter, it is the duty of the seller under a c.i.f. contract to ship the goods and to procure the necessary shipping documents for tender to the buyer. Unless the contract otherwise provides, a bill of lading is always required.[1] The bill of lading enables the buyer or his agent to obtain actual delivery of the goods on their arrival at the port of destination. But the bill of lading has greater significance than that. Possession of the bill of lading is equivalent to possession of the goods,[2] and delivery of the bill of lading to the buyer or to a third party may (if so intended) be effective to pass the property in the goods to such person. The bill of lading is a document of title[3] enabling the holder to obtain credit from banks before the arrival of the goods, for the transfer of the bill of lading can operate as a pledge of the goods themselves. In addition, it is by virtue of the bill of lading that the buyer or his assignee can obtain redress against the carrier for any breach of its terms and of the contract of carriage that it evidences. In other words the bill of lading creates a privity between its holder and the carrier as if the contract was made between them.

Definition

132 A bill of lading is a document which is signed by the carrier or his agent acknowledging that goods have been shipped on board a particular vessel bound for a particular destination and stating the terms on which the goods so received are to be carried.[4]

The contract of affreightment is the contract of carriage and the bill of lading is the receipt for the goods stating the terms on which they are to be carried. Before dealing with the characteristics of a bill of lading it is proposed to distinguish it from a mate's receipt and a delivery order, which are both common documents in shipping transactions and sometimes required under the contract of sale.

---

[1] *Ante.* § 1.
[2] See *e.g.* Lord Wright in *Official Assignee of Madras v. Mercantile Bank of India* [1935] A.C. 53 at p. 59. See *post.* § 165.
[3] As defined in s.1(4) of the Factors Act 1889.
[4] *Sewell v. Burdick* (1884) 10 App. Cas. 74 at p. 105. See *ante.* § 92.

113

Mate's receipt

133   When the shipper delivers the goods on to the quay for shipment, and the goods are received by an agent of the carrier for shipment that agent gives the shipper a receipt known as a mate's receipt. When the goods are shipped on board the vessel, it then becomes the duty of the master of the vessel to deliver the signed bills of lading to the shipper in exchange for the mate's receipt. During this time, the mate's receipt may have been used by the shipper and delivered to some third party (*e.g.* as security for an advance), but a mate's receipt is not normally a document of title to the goods.

The mate's receipt was considered in the Privy Council in the case of *Nippon Yusen Kaisha v. Ramjiban Serowgee*,[5] where Lord Wright explained its characteristics and function in the following terms[6]:

> "The mate's receipt is not a document of title to the goods shipped. Its transfer does not pass property in the goods, nor is its possession equivalent to possession of the goods. It is not conclusive, and its statements do not bind the shipowner as do the statements in a bill of lading signed with the master's authority. It is, however, prima facie evidence of the quantity and condition of the goods received, and prima facie it is the recipient or possessor who is entitled to have the bill of lading issued to him. But if the mate's receipt acknowledges receipt from a shipper other than the person who actually receives the mate's receipt, and, in particular, if the property is in that shipper, and the shipper has contracted for the freight, the shipowner will prima facie be entitled, and indeed bound, to deliver the bill of lading to that person."

Where a bill of lading is given without delivering up the mate's receipt, it is usual for the carrier to protect himself by taking an indemnity from the person to whom the bill of lading is issued. This indemnity will (absent fraud or bankruptcy) hold him harmless from any claim made by the actual holder of the mate's receipt. The more modern practice, dispensing altogether with mate's receipts, whereby the shipper delivers his goods to a forwarding agent at the docks for him to arrange for shipment with loading brokers, is fully described by Devlin J. in *Heskell v. Continental Express Ltd.*[7]

134   The foregoing notwithstanding, mate's receipts may be treated as documents of title in particular trades as a result of an established custom. For example, the Malaysia Federal Court (Appellate Jurisdiction) so held in *Wah Tat Bank Ltd. and Oversea-Chinese Banking Corporation Ltd. v. Chan Cheng Kum and Hua Siang Steamship Co. Ltd., Tiang Seng Chan (Singapore) Ltd., and Others (Third Parties)*,[8] and found that there was a local custom to treat mate's receipts as documents of title in the Singapore-Sarawak trade. Chief Justice Wee Chong Jin, in a considered judgment tracing the recognition of

---

[5] [1938] A.C. 429.
[6] *Ibid* at p. 445.
[7] [1950] 1 All E.R. 1033 at p. 1037, See *post*, § 468.
[8] [1967] 2 Lloyd's Rep. 437.

bills of lading as documents of title at common law, stated eight different reasons leading to this finding. The most important of these was the fact that since 1927 bills of lading were seldom used in this trade, the mate's receipt being the only shipping document issued by the carrier. In the circumstances of the case, the charterer was found liable for wrongful conversion of the goods. These were on arrival released to the shipper (against an indemnity), and not to the consignee under the mate's receipt (a bank advancing money to the shipper) who had the exclusive right of issuing instructions as to whom the goods were to be delivered. The Privy Council affirmed the decision against the charterers, who, as bailees, were held liable for conversion because the cargo had been delivered to third parties without authority.[9] The Judicial Committee further advised that a custom contrary to the general principle holding that a mate's receipt is not a document of title may indeed be established with regard to particular trades. Although it was unnecessary to do so in the present case because of the finding in favour of the consignee-bank on the grounds of conversion, the Committee indicated that they would generally have been prepared to recognise the local custom and regard the bank as a pledgee by virtue of possession of the mate's receipt. Nevertheless, there was one factor which would have prevented their so holding in the present case in respect of the particular documents, because, unlike some others being used in the trade, the mate's receipt in this case was expressly marked "not negotiable." This notation, the Committee found, might have had many meanings but was sufficient to prevent the relevant receipts from being documents of title, despite the local custom upon which the bank might have otherwise relied.

Delivery order

135   Where the buyer is receiving only part of a parcel of goods shipped under a single bill of lading, it will not be appropriate or practicable to transfer to him the bill of lading in respect of the whole parcel. In such a case the contract would normally provide that the seller should perform his obligations by delivering to the buyer a delivery order for the part sold rather than a bill of lading. A delivery order may be issued by and be binding on the carrier or it may be an order addressed to a person in possession of the goods ordering him to deliver them to the holder. It will be a good tender, as the following cases show, when it is an order binding on the carrier or addressed to some person in possession of the goods who has attorned to the buyer by accepting the order. Even then a delivery order is not as valuable as a bill of lading, for it is not a negotiable instrument, and where it does not enable the buyer to bring an action against the carrier for any loss or damage to the goods it is a bad tender under a c.i.f. contract.

In *Comptoir d'Achat et de Vente du Boerenbond Belge S/A. v. Luis de*

---

[9] *Kum and Ano. v. Wah Tat Bank Ltd. and Ano.* [1971] 1 Lloyd's Rep. 439 (P.C.).

Ridder Limitada (The Julia),[10] the view was expressed by the House of Lords that a delivery order to be a good tender under a c.i.f. contract (which permitted performance by tender of a delivery order in place of a bill of lading) would have to be addressed to someone in possession of the goods and accepted by him. In the course of his judgment Lord Normand said[11]:

> "But I think that if the words 'delivery order' had had to be construed without the aid of the previous course of dealing, it would have been held to mean a document addressed to and accepted by one in physical possession of the goods. The sellers would then have been found to tender a document which was in fact the legal equivalent of the goods."

Lord Normand went on to say that the effect of the course of dealing was to release the sellers from that obligation, but not, however, so as to impose on the buyer any duty to accept it as a document of title. Since in this case the seller tendered a delivery order that was not binding on the carrier, the contract was not a c.i.f. contract but one on arrival terms, and the seller bore the risk of their non arrival at the contractual destination.

136   In *Colin & Shields v. W. Weddel & Co.,*[12] there was a contract for the sale of ox-hides for shipment from Rio Grande, c. and f. Liverpool, payment cash against shipping documents, such documents to be invoice, bills of lading and/or ship's delivery order (the latter to be countersigned by banker, shipbroker, captain, or mate, if so required), and the policy or certificate of insurance. The goods were shipped by mistake under a bill of lading to Manchester. They were there unloaded and eventually brought to Liverpool by dumb barge via the Ship Canal. The sellers then tendered to the buyers as part of the shipping documents a document described as a ship's company's release addressed to the master porter of the hide berth in the North Carriers Dock, Liverpool, which referred to the bill of lading (to Manchester) and instructed the porter to deliver the goods to the buyers.

The buyers rejected this document, but the arbitrators found the tender to be good. The buyers contested this finding, and Sellers J. held that the buyers were entitled to reject. In the course of his judgment he said[13]:

> "No bill of lading, original or fresh, even existed for the carriage of the goods to Liverpool, and, in my opinion, the sellers failed fundamentally to perform their contractual obligation by never having such a document. The delivery order tendered to the buyers did not overcome the omission. The contract provided that the documents should consist of bills of lading and/or ship's delivery order. A ship's delivery order must mean either a delivery order by the ship or to the ship. As provision is made for it to be countersigned, if required by the buyers, not only by a banker and the shipbroker, but also by the captain or mate, the contract would appear to contemplate a delivery order by the sellers to the ship

---

[10] [1949] A.C. 293.
[11] *Ibid.* at p. 322.
[12] [1952] 1 All E.R. 1021.
[13] *Ibid.* at p. 1023.

requesting the ship to deliver to the buyers the goods shipped under the bill of lading. Such an order would entitle the buyers to receive the goods from the ship in the same way as would a bill of lading, and it would have to be given and presented while the goods were in the ship's possession.

"*The Julia*[14] was a case concerning a contract very different from this, with terms that are not to be found here and with a course of business controlling the performance, but I think it gives support for the view that a ship's delivery order means an order on the ship. But, whether that is so or not, or whether or not, on the true construction of this contract, a delivery order on the ship is required (if there is to be a substitute for a bill of lading), the delivery order must, at least, be to someone who holds the goods and who could attorn to the buyers."

His lordship then cited the passage from Lord Normand's judgment, set out above,[15] and continued:

"On October 15, when the documents were tendered, the goods were in transit from Manchester to Liverpool. The master porter, to whom the delivery order was addressed, was not in possession of the goods, and, if they had never arrived and had been received by him, the delivery order, so far as I can see, would have been worthless. It gave no rights to the buyers against the shipowner under the bill of lading or otherwise. Rio Grande Bill of Lading No. 7 is referred to, but that bill of lading did not provide for carriage to Liverpool. There was no attempt at a physical delivery of the goods and the delivery order was in no sense a symbolic delivery, or a legal equivalent, of the goods. In my opinion, it was not a document which complied with the requirements of the contract."

This judgment was approved in the Court of Appeal where the appeal of the sellers was dismissed.[16]

137   In the subsequent case of *Warren Import Gesellschaft Krohn & Co. v. Internationale Graanhandel Thegra N.V.*[17] Kerr J. had to construe the meaning of the term "ship's delivery order" in a c.i.f. standard form of contract (GAFTA 100). The seller there tendered delivery orders addressed to the agents of the charterers who were an associated company of the sellers, and had been authorised to sign bills of lading, and to issue delivery orders. The buyers refused to accept the documents tendered as ship's delivery orders. After noting that it was of utmost importance to bear in mind that the words were used in the context of a c.i.f. contract, Kerr J. explained[18]:

"It is trite law that it is a fundamental feature of this type of contract, since it required the buyer to pay the price against documents . . . that he should so far as possible obtain control over the goods by means of the documents . . . where a c.i.f. contract entitles the seller to tender delivery orders instead of bills of lading, so as to enable him to split cargoes . . . the contract should prima facie be so construed that these objects, although they cannot be attained in full, are

---

[14] *Comptoir d'Achat, etc. v. Luis de Ridder Ltda. (The Julia)* [1949] A.C. 293.
[15] *Ante*, §95.
[16] [1952] 2 All E.R. 337.
[17] [1975] 1 Lloyd's Rep. 146.
[18] At pp. 153 *et seq.*

nevertheless attained so far as possible. I therefore consider that an option to tender delivery orders instead of bills of lading in a c.i.f. contract should prima facie be interpreted as intended to confer upon the buyer control over the goods covered by the delivery order, even though falling short of ownership, and also some right against the person in possession of the goods, even though falling short of the rights conferred by the transfer of bills of lading.

"These objects can in practice be achieved in two main ways so as to overcome, so far as possible, the shortcomings of delivery orders in comparison with bills of lading, *viz*, they are non-transferable documents of title and that they are a mere transfer of the goods and will not transfer contractual rights against the carrier. First, these objects can be achieved by the person in possession being ordered by the sellers to deliver the goods to the buyer and the latter thereupon attorning to the buyer. Secondly, they can be achieved by a direct undertaking by the person in possession to deliver the goods to the buyer or to his order. In either event the person in possession could of course effect the attornment or give the undertaking through a duly authorised agent. Both these objects can be achieved by means of documents which are described as 'delivery orders,' albeit in some cases loosely. On the other hand, a document which is not addressed to or issued by a person who is then in possession of the goods, or which does not contain an undertaking by the person in possession of the goods to hold the goods for, or to deliver them to, the buyer or his order, would fail to achieve an essential object of a c.i.f. contract even though it can also be described as a 'delivery order.' Prima facie, therefore, in the absence of language evidencing a contrary intention, the latter class of documents should be held to be an insufficient tender under a c.i.f. contract.

"The foregoing summarises what would appear to me to be the correct approach in principle in the absence of authority. But when one then turns to the two leading authorities in which this problem has been considered one can see that they in fact adopt precisely the same approach, and their effect is, in my view, correctly summarised in Vol. 5 of British Shipping Laws on C.I.F. and F.O.B. Contracts . . .

" . . . it then inevitably follows in my judgment that the delivery orders tendered in the present case fall far short of what was required. . . . They must fail in two respects. First, they are addressed to persons who are not in possession of the goods. If the goods never reached the addressees, then these documents were obviously worthless as the basis of any claim against the addressees. Secondly, they contain no undertaking by anyone that the goods will be delivered to the buyers, but merely an instruction to the addressees to deliver them to the order of the sellers, Mr. Pollock sought to overcome both, or at any rate the latter, of these difficulties by relying on the fact that the delivery orders stated that all terms and conditions of the underlying bill of lading were to apply. He submitted that this clearly showed that the shipowners were holding themselves responsible for delivery in the same way as if the buyers were in possession of the bills of lading. It may be, depending upon the facts in relation to which this issue might arise, that this would be the outcome if and when this question had to be decided between the buyers and the shipowners. But in my view the short answer to this argument is that if the buyers were held to be compelled to accept these documents on this basis then they would merely be put in the position of having to part with their money at the risk of buying litigation, whereas the object of a provision such as cl. 13 in a c.i.f. contract is precisely the contrary: to place the buyers in as strong and clear-cut a position of control over the goods vis-à-vis the shipowners as possible, albeit only on the basis of holding delivery orders and not bills of lading.''

The buyers were thus justified in their refusal to accept the delivery orders which the sellers tendered, and the sellers' action failed. At the same time Kerr J. refused to accept a finding of the arbitral tribunal (the matter had reached the court by means of a case stated procedure) according to which a ship's delivery order has a special trade meaning in terms of the type of goods sold under GAFTA (grain and food trade association) contracts. The arbitrators found that this meaning precluded the right to tender documents not issued by the Owner or Master of the carrying vessel or their agents, at a time when the goods are on board ship and that only documents by the terms of which the Owner or Master expressly undertake to deliver the goods to the holder or his order were allowed under the contract. Since the finding was not in relation to a particular trade (but in relation to the use of a form of contract), and not confined to a particular locality, his Lordship (at page 152) considered the finding lacking the requirements of certainty and reliability "which must exist as a basis for the establishment of a trade usage capable of affecting contractual relations."

138   In *Margarine Union G.m.b.H. v. Cambay Prince SS. Co.*[19] delivery orders which (though not permitted under the contract in question) were nevertheless accepted by the c.i.f. buyer were considered. The question before the court was whether the buyer could succeed in a claim against the carrier whose negligence in failing to fumigate the vessel caused damage to a consignment of copra. It was there held that no such action could be maintained by the buyer. The delivery orders which were in the present instance issued by the sub-charterer conferred no property right to the copra in question, and under English law (as it then stood) such a right was a precondition of the claimant's action in tort against the carrier. That the risk in the copra had, pursuant to the c.i.f. contract in question, passed to the purchasers at the time of their taking up the documents was held to be immaterial. In the opinion of Roskill J. this factor made no difference as to whether a duty of care on the part of the carrier towards the purchasers could be established and enforced. However in the subsequent case of *Schiffahrt und Kohlen G.m.b.H. v. Chelsea Maritime Ltd. (The Irene's Success)*[20] Lloyd J. refused to follow *Margarine Union,* and expressed the view that it should probably have been decided differently in light of later judicial pronouncements. Those recognised a duty of care where sufficient relationship or proximity existed (even if the claimant did not have the property or right of possession in the goods) and in the absence of any policy considerations to the contrary. In Lloyd J.'s view a c.i.f. contract pursuant to which the risk of loss or damage in the goods had been transferred to the buyer was sufficient to base an action against the carrier though the property had not passed by virtue of the seller's retention of the bills of lading. But this valiant effort was to no avail. Subsequently the House of Lords declared Lloyd J. to be wrong, and the *Margarine Union* decision to

---

[19] [1969] 1 Q.B. 219.
[20] [1981] 2 Lloyd's Rep. 635.

be right,[21] and the law had to be altered by means of the Carriage of Goods by Sea Act 1992 in order to permit an action against the carrier by the person who suffered the loss, even if he had no title or ownership in the goods.[22]

139   Where the delivery order is issued by the carrier and is held to incorporate the terms of any bills of lading issued in respect of the cargo in question. Kerr J. held that the holder of the order could recover against the shipowners for breach of contract. In *Cremer and Others v. General Carriers S.A.*[23] the first plaintiff bought a quantity of tapioca roots on c.i.f. terms from a shipper in Thailand reselling a portion thereof to the second plaintiffs, to whom ships' delivery orders incorporating the terms of the bills of lading were issued. Although the roots were not dry, a clean bill of lading was signed by the master. Kerr J. held that, on the facts, a contract in terms of the bills of lading came into effect between the shipowners and the second plaintiffs, notwithstanding that prior to delivery they were not owners of any part of the undivided bulk of the cargo, and that, accordingly, they had a cause of action against the shipowners for breach of the contract of carriage. The shipowners were estopped from relying on the pre-shipment condition of the goods by reason of the clean bills of lading which they had issued. It was further held, that the shipowners could not rely on the terms of the contract of sale between the first plaintiff and the shippers to show that the former would have been in breach of his c.i.f. contract (which in any event he would not have been in the case) if he had rejected a claused bill of lading.

Bill of lading necessary

140   As we have seen, the seller under a c.i.f. contract must generally procure a bill of lading for tender to the buyer. A delivery order or a ship's release usually will not suffice unless the contract expressly (or by implication) so provides. Neither document may satisfy the requirements (i) that the buyer is entitled to a bill of lading issued on shipment, and (ii) that he is entitled to a document which will give him a right of action against the carrier from the time the goods were shipped until the time when they were discharged.

In *Heilbut, Symons & Co. Ltd. v. Harvey & Co.*[24] some evidence was given that in the rubber trade, where a shipment under a bill of lading is split up and sold to two (or more) buyers, a practice has grown up whereby one of the buyers is given the bill of lading and the other buyer gets a ship's release, and, if he requires it, in addition a satisfactory guarantee to hold him harmless against any consequences arising from taking the delivery order. In the particular case, a ship's release was tendered without a guarantee, and Bailhache

[21] *Leigh and Sullivan Ltd. v. Aliakmon Shipping Co. Ltd.* (The "Aliakmon") [1986] 2 Lloyd's Rep. 1 at p. 11.
[22] See *post*, § 161.
[23] [1974] 1 W.L.R. 341.
[24] (1922) 12 Ll.L. Rep. 455.

J. held that it was not a good tender. He did not decide whether a ship's release with a guarantee would be a good tender, but it is conceived that on principle the same objection might prevail.

And, as illustrated by *Comptoir d'Achat et de Vende du Boereuboud Belge S/A v. Luis de Ridder Limitada (The Julia)*,[24a] where the contract permits the tendering of a document that does not confer on the buyer certain minimum c.i.f. attributes, it may lead to its not being construed as a c.i.f. contract at all, irrespective of its characterization as such by the parties themselves.

The form

141   The question arises as to what is meant by a bill of lading within a c.i.f. contract, and whether a receipt for goods not actually shipped but to be shipped at a future time, though otherwise in the form of an ordinary bill of lading, is a bill of lading within a c.i.f. contract. Bills of lading were in widespread use towards the close of the sixteenth century, and invariably acknowledged that the goods were actually shipped on board a particular vessel.[25] Commercial practice changed, however, and in the course of the nineteenth century it was quite common to issue bills of lading before the goods were actually shipped. Such bills, instead of reciting that the goods had been "shipped on board" a particular vessel, stated instead that they had been "received for shipment" to be put on board a particular vessel, or such other vessels as might be indicated. It became therefore a matter for the courts to decide how far tender of a "received for shipment" bill of lading was a proper performance of a c.i.f. contract.

142   In *The Marlborough Hill v. Alex. Cowan & Sons Ltd.*, in the Privy Council,[26] it was decided that a receipt for goods in the following form was a bill of lading for the purposes of the Admiralty Court Act 1861, s.6[27]:"'... received in apparent good order and condition from ... for shipment' ... by the sailing vessel called the *Marlborough Hill*, or by some other vessel owned or operated by the Commonwealth and Dominion Line, Ltd., Cunard Line, Australasian Service.'' It contained a provision to the effect that the ship-owner might substitute or tranship the whole or any portion of the goods by any other prior or subsequent vessel at the original port of shipment or at any

---

[24a] [1949] A.C. 293, *ante* § 17.
[25] See McCardie J. in *Diamond Alkali Export Corpn. v. Fl. Bourgeois* [1921] 3 K.B. 443 at p. 449.
[26] [1921] 1 A.C. 444 (P.C.) (Viscount Cave, Lords Dunedin, Moulton and Phillimore).
[27] Though this section has been repealed by subsequent legislation the material provisions of s.6 were as follows: "The High Court of Admiralty shall have jurisdiction over any claim by the owner, consignee or assignee of *any bill of lading* of any goods carried into any port in England or Wales in any ship, for any damage done to the goods or any part thereof by the negligence or misconduct of or for any breach of duty or breach of contract on the part of the owner, master, or crew of the ship, unless it is shown to the satisfaction on the court that at the time of the institution of the cause any owner or part owner of the ship is domiciled in England or Wales."

other place. It was signed by agents for the master of the *Marlborough Hill*, and admitted the obligation to carry and deliver.

The following extracts from the judgment sufficiently explain the grounds upon which the decision as to the effect of the document was based.[28]

"It is a matter of commercial notoriety . . . that shipping instruments which are called bills of lading, and known in the commercial world as such, are sometimes framed in the alternative form 'received for shipment' instead of 'shipped on board,' and further, with the alternative contract to carry or procure some other vessel (possibly with some limitations as to the choice of the other vessel) to carry, instead of the original ship. It is contended, however, that such shipping instruments, whatever they may be called in commerce or by men of business, are nevertheless not bills of lading within the Bills of Lading Act, 1855,[29] and it is said, therefore, not bills of lading within the meaning of the Admiralty Court Act, 1861.

"Their Lordships are not disposed to take so narrow a view of a commercial document. To take the first objection first. There can be no difference in principle between the owner, master or agent acknowledging that he has received the goods on the wharf, or allotted portion of quay, or his store-house awaiting shipment, and his acknowledging that the goods have been actually put over the ship's rail. The two forms of a bill of lading may well stand, as their Lordships understand that they stand, together. The older is still in the more appropriate language for whole cargoes delivered and taken on board in bulk; whereas 'received for shipment' is the proper phrase for the practical businesslike way of treating parcels of cargo to be placed on a general ship which will be lying alongside the wharf taking in cargo for several days, and whose proper stowage will require that certain bulkier or heavier parcels shall be placed on board first, while others, though they have arrived earlier, wait for the convenient place and time of stowage.

"Then as regards the obligation to carry either by the named ship or by some other vessel; it is a contract which both parties may well find it convenient to enter into and accept. The liberty to tranship is ancient and well established, and does not derogate from the nature of a bill of lading; and if the contract begins when the goods are received on the wharf, substitution does not differ in principle from transhipment.

"If this document is a bill of lading, it is a negotiable instrument. Money can be advanced upon it, and business can be done in the way in which maritime commerce has been carried on for at least half a century, throughout the civilised world. Both parties have agreed to call this a bill of lading; both, by its terms have entered into obligations and acquired rights such as are proper to a bill of lading. All the other incidents in its very detailed language are such as are proper to such a document."

The several clauses of the document similar to those usually contained in an ordinary bill of lading were then referred to.

"It should perhaps be added that it is evidently contemplated by the document that the shipper will assign his rights and that the assignee or holder of the bill of lading will present the document at the port of delivery, and that his receipt and not that of the shipper will be the discharge to the shipowner."

---

[28] [1921] 1 A.C. 451 at pp. 452–453.
[29] See *post*, § 161.

It was therefore held that the document was a bill of lading within the Admiralty Court Act 1861.

143   In *Weis & Co.* v. *Produce Brokers Co.*[30] the Court of Appeal (Bankes, Warrington and Scrutton L.JJ.) considered the case of shipments of China peas from the East under bills of lading describing the goods as "shipped or delivered for shipment." It is true that the buyers who claimed the right to reject did not object to the form of the bills, but contended, unsuccessfully, that the bills ought to have been marked with the date of actual shipment. The court did, however, consider the form of the bills, and in the course of his judgment Bankes L.J. said[31]:

> "There were two lots of peas and there were two bills of lading, and the bill of lading in respect of each of these two lots was in a form which we are told is quite usual in the trade—not universal but quite usual. It is the usual form adopted by the owners for this vessel, the *Polyphemus*, and it is a form which has come into use of recent years, and it states that the goods are shipped or delivered for shipment in apparent good order and condition. It has been recently held in a case[32] in the Privy Council to which our attention was called that, although in that somewhat unusual form, according to old notions, that is a perfectly good bill of lading within the meaning of the Bills of Lading Act."

Scrutton L.J.[33] was equally emphatic that the bills of lading were in an acceptable form:

> "Now anybody acquainted with the China trade and with shipping to a limited extent knows that the products of civilisation are carried into Chinese waters by ships all taking names out of the Odyssey or Iliad, and all belonging to the best-known line in those parts, and all carrying under a usual form of bill of lading; and I should be curious to see any leading official of the Produce Brokers' Association [the respondents] who would come and say to me that he did not know the *Polyphemus* was one of the well-known lines carrying under a well-known bill of lading, and that he had not seen dozens of these and had not known that the usual bill of lading for the line in which the *Polyphemus* runs, runs 'Shipped or received for shipment.'"

Indeed Scrutton L.J. goes so far as to explain why the bill of lading should be in that form, when he says[34]:

> "Now there is very good reason why it is framed in that way. The buyer is not the only person concerned in this contract. The ship and the shipper are also concerned in it. The ship wants to have a bill of lading beginning with the time delivered for shipment, because it wants the time delivered for shipment to be covered by the exceptions; and the exceptions throughout this bill of lading refer to matters which the ship wants. The shipper wants it in that form because he

[30] (1921) 7 Ll.L. Rep. 211.
[31] *Ibid.* at p. 212.
[32] *The Marlborough Hill v. Alex. Cowan & Sons Ltd.* [1921] 1 A.C. 444.
[33] 7 Ll.L. Rep. at p. 214.
[34] *Ibid.* at p. 215.

wants to be protected from the time he has given the goods into the hands of the ship for shipment.''

In a similar case that arose shortly afterwards relating to another part of the cargo in the same shipment. *United Baltic Corp. v. Burgett & Newsam*,[35] it was not admitted that the bills of lading were in a usual form in the trade but there was no express finding by the arbitrators on the point. In the Court of Appeal, Bankes L.J. (in a judgment with which Scrutton and Atkin L.JJ. concurred), repeated his words in *Weis & Co. v. Produce Brokers Co.*[36] which are quoted above, and added[37]:

"and when I remember what was said by counsel in that case in reference to these bills of lading and I find that the bill of lading itself is printed in the form which is apparently in common use, I think myself that it would only be a waste of money to send this case back for a finding on that point; and I consider that I am justified in treating this bill of lading as I have said as being the usual form in this particular trade."

144   Contemporaneously with these last two decisions in the Court of Appeal, but apparently independently of them, came the decision of McCardie J. in *Diamond Alkali Export Corp. v. Fl. Bourgeois*.[38] The question was there considered whether a bill in the "received for shipment" form, was, in the absence of any finding that it was usual or customary in the trade, a good tender under a c.i.f. contract.

The sellers of soda ash to be shipped from American seaboard c.i.f. Gothenburg tendered, and the buyer rejected, a document purporting to be a bill of lading, in a similar form, namely: "Received in apparent good order and condition from . . . to be transported by the S.S. *Anglia* . . . or failing shipment by the said steamer in and upon a following steamer, 280 bags Dense Soda, . . ." The buyer objected that the document was not a bill of lading at all and was not such a bill of lading as was required by the c.i.f. contract. McCardie J. held that it was not a bill of lading within the contemplation of a c.i.f. contract. He considered that the phrase "bill of lading" as used with respect to a c.i.f. contract meant a bill of lading in the established sense, that is to say, a document which acknowledged *actual shipment* on board the particular vessel, and that, as by the document in question the buyer was left in doubt as to actual shipment and the actual ship, it was not a document which he was bound to accept. With regard to the opinion of the Privy Council in the *Marlborough Hill* case,[39] he said[40]:

"I wish to point out first that the actual decision in the *Marlborough Hill* case

---

[35] (1921) 8 Ll.L. Rep. 190. See also *Suzuki & Co. v. Burgett & Newsam* (1922) 10 Ll.L. Rep. 223.
[36] (1921) 7 Ll.L. Rep. 211 at p. 212.
[37] (1921) 8 Ll.L. Rep. 190 at p. 191.
[38] [1921] 3 K.B. 443.
[39] *Ante*, § 142.
[40] [1921] 3 K.B. 443 at p. 452.

was merely that the bill of lading there in question (which closely resembles the one now before me) fell within section 6 of the Admiralty Court Act 1861. It may be that the phrase 'bill of lading' in that section permits of a broad interpretation. I point out next that there is no express statement in the *Marlborough Hill* case that the document there in question actually fell within the Bills of Lading Act 1855.[41] In the third place it seems to me to be clear that the Board did not consider the nature and effect of an ordinary c.i.f. contract or the decisions thereon in relation to the question before them. The case of *Bowes v. Shand*[42] moreover was not even cited to the Board. Lord Phillimore, in reading the advice of the Privy Council, said[43]: 'There can be no difference in principle between the owner, master, or agent acknowledging that he has received the goods on his wharf, or allotted portion of quay, or his storehouse awaiting shipment, and his acknowledging that the goods have actually been put over the ship's rail.' With the deepest respect I venture to think that there is a profound difference between the two, both from a legal and business point of view. Those differences seem to me clear. I need not state them. If the view of the Privy Council is carried to its logical conclusion, a mere receipt for goods at a dock warehouse for future shipment might well be called a bill of lading. Again the Board say[44]: 'Then as regards the obligation to carry either by the named ship or by some other vessel: it is a contract which both parties may well find it convenient to enter into and accept. The liberty to tranship is ancient and well established, and does not derogate from the nature of a bill of lading, and if the contract begins when the goods are received on the wharf, substitution does not differ in principle from transhipment.' I do not pause to analyse these words. I only say that in my humble view substitution and the right of transhipment are distinct things, and rest on different principles. The passage last cited can, I think, have no application at all to a c.i.f. contract which provides for a specific date of shipment. It will suffice if I say two things. First, that in my view the *Marlborough Hill* case does not apply to a c.i.f. contract such as that now before me. Secondly, that grounds for challenging the dicta of the Privy Council will be found in Art. 22, and the notes and cases there cited, in *Scrutton on Charterparties* (10th ed.),[45] as to what are called 'through bills of lading,' in the lucid article in the *Law Quarterly Review* of October 1889, Vol. V, p. 424, by Mr. Bateson, K. C.; and of July 1890, Vol. VI, p. 289, by the late Mr. Carver, and in *Carver on Carriage* (6th ed.), notes to Section 107.[46] I do not doubt that the document before me is a 'shipping document' within the U.S.A. Harter Act, 1893.[47] I feel bound to hold, however, that it is not a bill of lading within the c.i.f. contract of sale made between the present parties.''

But is not the question one of fact rather than of law? Is not the test to be applied whether it is or is not the usage or practice in the trade concerned to accept a bill of lading in the particular form in question and is such usage or practice well known and acted upon?[48]

---

[41] *Sed quaere*. See the passage cited *ante*, § 142 in reference to the Bills of Lading Act.

[42] (1877) 2 App. Cas. 455. See *ante*, § 60.

[43] *Ante*, §142.

[44] *Ibid*.

[45] See now 19th ed.

[46] See now, Carver, *Carriage by Sea* (13th ed.) Vol. 2, (*British Shipping Laws*), para. 1613 at p. 1127.

[47] And the United States Carriage of Goods by Sea Act 1936.

[48] Applying the language of Kennedy J. in *Burstall v. Grimsdale* (1906) 11 Com.Cas. 280 at p. 290, cited *ante*, §93. See, *e.g. Meyer v. Aune* [1939] 3 All E.R. 168, *post*, §155.

145   The present position therefore seems to be that until the decision of McCardie J. in *Diamond Alkali Export Corp. v. Fl. Bourgeois* has been reviewed, except in trades where a bill of lading in the form under consideration has become usual, and, therefore, it is submitted, is undoubtedly a good tender, the validity of a tender of a bill of lading in that form is questionable. The true view, it is submitted, is that in each case it is a question of fact whether the form of the bill of lading tendered is a form usual in the trade; if it is not, the buyer is not bound to accept it. But where the contract specifies a date for shipment, it means actual shipment, and the seller does not perform his obligation by producing a document which shows that the goods were "received for shipment" on the contract date.

In *Suzuki & Co. v. Burgett & Newsam*,[49] the contract was for a December/January shipment. The bill of lading describing the goods as "shipped or received for shipment" was dated January 31, but it was proved that the goods were not actually shipped until February. The buyers, who had taken up the documents and paid the price, were held to be entitled, on discovery of the true shipment date, to recover the price paid.

Where, however, the seller inserts in his contract the term that the bill of lading is to be considered proof of date of shipment in the absence of evidence to the contrary, he throws the burden of proving the contrary on the buyer.[50] On the other hand, the date shown in the bill of lading may, by the terms of the contract of sale, be made conclusive evidence of the date of shipment.[51]

False dating

146   The false dating of a bill of lading is bound to lead to legal complications, even if it is not the result of a forgery, as was the case in *Kwei Tek Chao v. British Traders and Shippers Ltd.*[52] In *Panchaud Frères S. A. v. Etablissements General Grain Company*,[53] Panchaud, the sellers, sold a quantity of Brazilian maize to the General Grain Company under a contract based on Form 77 of the London Corn Trade Association. The contract was c.i.f. Antwerp; it provided for shipment from a Brazilian port in June/July 1965, and contained the provision that "the bill of lading ... be dated when the goods are actually on board." It further provided that "the bill of lading [was] to be considered proof of date of shipment in the absence of evidence to the contrary." The shipping documents had to include a certificate of quality which had to be issued by a Brazilian superintendent company. The sellers sent the buyers by telex a notice of appropriation stating that "bill of

---

[49] (1922) 10 L.I.L. Rep. 223. The American practice on this question seems to be different; see the decisions mentioned *ante,* in §67.
[50] As in *Dewar & Webb v. Joseph Rank Ltd.* (1923) 14 Ll.L. Rep. 393 (C.A.).
[51] See *James Finlay & Co. Ltd. v. N. V. Kwik Hoo Tong H. M.* [1929] 1 K.B. 400 (C.A.).
[52] [1954] 2 Q.B. 459. See *post,* §335.
[53] [1969] 2 Lloyd's Rep. 109.

lading date: on or about July 31, 1965.'' When the shipping documents were tendered, the bill of lading bore the date of July 31, 1965 but the certificate of quality contained the remark "loaded on August 10 to 12, 1965" which was 10 to 12 days later. The buyers accepted the documents but then rejected the goods, first on the ground that the bags were unmarked, but later on the ground that the bill of lading contained a false date. The matter went to arbitration and the arbitration appeal tribunal held that the buyers had waived their right to rely on the irregularity in the date of the bill of lading because they could not be deemed to be unaware of the contents of the certificate of quality which formed part of the shipping documents. The arbitration appeal tribunal, however, stated a case for the decision of the court, and Roskill J. held that the arbitration appeal tribunal was wrong and, following the *Kwei Tek Chao* case, that the false dating of the bill of lading entitled the buyers to reject the goods and reclaim the price and that they had not waived that right.

But his decision was reversed by the Court of Appeal.[54] Lord Denning M.R., in the leading judgment, said that it was well settled that if a buyer gave one ground for rejection, he was not confined to that ground alone. The fact that the buyers in the present case first rejected on the ground of insufficient markings of the bags and then changed over to the ground of the falsely dated bill of lading, was therefore not fatal to their claim. But, added Lord Denning,[55] this rule is subject to the qualification that a man may by his conduct preclude himself from setting up a later ground. This, in his Lordship's view, was not a case of waiver but of estoppel by conduct. While waiver occurred when a man, with knowledge of a breach, did an unequivocal act which showed that he had elected to affirm the contract as still existing, instead of disaffirming it, the basis of the estoppel by conduct doctrine was that a man had so conducted himself that it would be unfair or unjust to allow him to depart from a particular state of affairs which another had taken to be settled or correct. The present case was one of estoppel by conduct. By taking up the documents and paying for them, the buyers in his judgment were precluded afterwards from complaining of the late shipment or of the defect in the bill of lading.[56] That the Court of Appeal was aware of the difficulty is clear. Laxity in the dating of bills of lading is a most undesirable practice and should not be condoned by the courts. Consequently, the ruling of Roskill J. has been preferred by some to the ruling of the Court of Appeal in this case.[57] As stated by Winn L.J.[58]:

---

[54] [1970] 1 Lloyd's Rep. 53.
[55] *Ibid.* at p. 56.
[56] But, as pointed out by Roskill J., "If one looks at the two documents (bill of lading and certificate of quality) together can it be properly said that the certificate makes it more probable than not that the bill of lading date is false? Why should it not equally be the case that the certificate contains an erroneous statement?" [1969] 2 Lloyd's Rep. 109 at p. 125.
[57] See, *e.g.* comment in [1970] J.B.L. 41.
[58] [1970] 1 Lloyd's Rep. 53 at p. 59.

"What one has here is something perhaps in our law not yet wholly developed as a separate doctrine—which is more in the nature of a requirement of fair conduct—a criterion of what is fair conduct between the parties. There may be an inchoate doctrine stemming from the manifest convenience of consistency in pragmatic affairs negativing any liberty to blow hot and cold in commercial conduct."

The buyers may, moreover, lose the opportunity to reject the misdated bill of lading because they are unaware (as will often be the case) of the fact, and of the breach, when accepting the same, and where the misdating involves no fraud on part of the sellers. Having so lost the opportunity to exercise the remedy of rejection, they may be confined to recovering their financial loss, if any, suffered by reason of the breach as was the case in *Proctor & Gamble Philippine Manufacturing Corporation v. Kurt A Becher G.M.b.H. & Co. K.G.*.[59] There it was decided that the buyers were entitled to no damages since they had received goods that conformed to the contract in all respects including as to the date of the shipment, although the bill of lading was misdated, a breach that would have entitled them to reject it had they been aware of the fact at the time the documents were tendered. The effect of the decision was to deprive the buyers who had suffered a substantial loss (due to a falling market) from recovery, notwithstanding the fact that they had expressed concern as to whether the goods were actually shipped during the contractual period (which they were), and a notice that the goods would be rejected by them upon arrival because the bill of lading was misdated, and a suggestion that the goods would be resold (which they were) "without prejudice" in order to avoid further costs and expenses. One wonders whether the result would have been different had the concern, first expressed by the buyers related to the date of the bill of lading (rather than to the contractual shipment period), and why (except for the fact that they were attempting to benefit from a technicality)[60] the notice, and resale "without prejudice", was ineffective to assist their claim.

Through bills of lading

147   As has been seen, it is in the ordinary way the duty of the seller to procure a bill of lading on shipment of the goods that will give the buyer a right of action against the carrier in respect of any loss or damage to the goods during transit. This is a simple matter where the whole of the carriage is being undertaken in a single ship, or by a single ship-owner, but complications arise where the carriage involves transhipment from one shipping line to another, or from coast-wise to ocean-going vessels, or which is partly by sea and partly by rail or truck. In such cases where the carriage is to be under-

---

[59] [1988] 2 Lloyd's Rep. 21 (C.A.) reviewed in detail *post*, 337.
[60] As c.i.f. buyers were able to do in *The Kastellon* [1978] 2 Lloyd's Rep. 203, notwithstanding the regrets there expressed by Donaldson J. (as he then was) as to the result.

taken by two or more carriers the ordinary bill of lading issued by the first carrier may not deal with the whole carriage. In order to procure carriage of the goods to the final destination, a further bill or bills will be required. This would be commercially inconvenient, for what the parties wish to have is a single bill of lading which can be obtained on shipment and which is then available for transmission to the buyer or to a bank for the purposes of finance.

In order to meet this practical necessity for a single document, the practice grew up of issuing what is termed a through bill of lading. Through bills of lading can take various forms. The first carrier or the agent of the ocean-going steamer may sign a through bill of lading undertaking to carry the goods to their ultimate destination by himself and other carriers. The carrier then signs as agent on behalf of the other carriers, who may or may not be named in the bill, and he often makes it clear that he signs as agent for the carriers severally and not jointly. Another method is for the carrier receiving the goods to undertake to carry them to the port of transhipment and there to arrange for the goods to be forwarded to the ultimate destination. This the carrier generally agrees to do as agent for the shipper without incurring liability whatsoever and not as carrier. The only obligation undertaken by the carrier is that he will arrange to include a term in the second contract of carriage that delivery at the ultimate destination shall only he given on presentation of the original bill of lading. In the latter case, the carrier does not bind himself to contract with the on-carriers on any particular terms. The method once employed in trade from the Philippine Islands is described in the cases below, more particularly in *N. V. Arnold Otto Meyer v. Aune*.[61]

148 Such through bills of lading may in theory be subject to numerous legal defects. Questions may arise as to the agency of the first shipowner for other carriers. It may be difficult to prove that the on-carriers have actually received the goods. It was even questioned whether a through bill came within the Bills of Lading Act 1855, so as to transfer the benefit of the contract of carriage to an assignee of the bill of lading.[62] In practice, however, any fears expressed were not justified, largely because it is in the interests of many carriers to uphold the bill of lading.[63] In the event of there being no binding contract with the on-carriers, such carriers may be held liable at common law, where applicable, as carriers or in tort for negligence. It would therefore seem that they would be anxious to uphold the through bill of lading in order to obtain the benefit of exclusion clauses.

The law relating to through bills of lading is expressed in the cases reviewed below, and from these it would seem to be the rule that a through bill of lading is to be issued whenever it is usual and customary in the particu-

---

[61] [1939] 3 All E. R. 168. See *post* § 155.
[62] See more fully article by H. D. Bateson in *Law Quarterly Review* (1889), Vol. V, p. 424.
[63] See Scrutton L. J. in *Brandt v. Liverpool, Brazil and River Plate Steam Navigation* Co. [1924] 1 K.B. 575.

lar trade to do so. Through bills of lading must normally be issued on shipment, but this requirement may, it seems, be subject to a custom in the trade that the bill shall be issued on transhipment.

149   The first case, *Cox, McEuen & Co. v. Malcolm & Co.*,[64] is retained for the sake of completeness, but it appears to be of little usefulness in the face of the later cases, and particularly Lord Sumner's own remarks in *Hansson v. Hamel & Horley Ltd.*[65]

In *Cox, McEuen & Co. v. Malcolm & Co.*,[66] the contract was for the sale, c.i.f., of 500 bales of Manila hemp to be shipped from a recognised shipping port or ports in the Philippine Islands or from Hong Kong or Singapore, by steamer or steamers, direct or indirect, to London between August 1 and September 30, 1909 both inclusive, declaration to be made with due dispatch not later than 60 days from bill of lading. The sellers shipped 500 bales of Manila hemp from Manila to Hong Kong within the contract time, taking bills of lading to the order of themselves. On October 23, the hemp was transhipped at Hong Kong, fresh bills of lading being taken for carriage to London. The last-mentioned bills of lading were in due course presented to the buyers, but the buyers refused to take them up on the grounds that the goods had not been shipped to London directly or indirectly between August 1 and September 30, 1909 and that the date of the Hong Kong bills of lading was conclusive as fixing October 23, as the date of the actual shipment of the goods. An arbitration took place and the matter came before Hamilton J. on a special case stated by the arbitrator. The arbitrator found that it was usual that hemp from the Philippine Islands destined for London should be transhipped at Hong Kong, and that it was usual, but not in his opinion essential, that such hemp should be shipped from the Philippine Islands on through bills of lading, and he awarded that the sellers had fulfilled the contract. Hamilton J. upheld the award.

> "In my opinion," he said,[67] "the contract does not require, in order that a shipment may be made from Manila indirect to London, that there shall be a through bill of lading, or a bill of lading stating on its face that the shipment to the intermediate port is for the purpose of transhipment by the carrier to a London steamer. The goods were shipped indirect to London when the person entitled to the control of them, namely, the shipper and holder of the bill of lading, intended, when he shipped them at Manila, to tranship them at Hong Kong for delivery in London and in fact carried out that intention, which is the case here. There may be very good reasons for preferring that the bill of lading should be a through bill of lading, and that the Manila bill of lading should state that the goods were to be transhipped, and so preclude the shipper from having an opportunity of taking delivery of the goods at Hong Kong and diverting or detaining them, but if that is desired it must be the subject of express stipulation."

---

[64] [1912] 2 K.B. 107n.
[65] [1922] 2 A.C. 36.
[66] (1910), reported [1912] 2 K.B. 107n.
[67] *Ibid.* at p. 110.

150   In *Landauer & Co. v. Craven & Speeding Bros.*,[68] the contract was in the same form and the material facts were similar, but the arbitrator had found that by mercantile custom a seller c.i.f. must obtain on shipment a through contract of affreightment to the ultimate destination. This finding enabled Scrutton J. to distinguish the case from that just cited, but on the general question he differed from Hamilton J. In the course of his judgment he said[69]:

> "If when he [the seller] ships goods sold c.i.f. London he has no contract for carriage to London, but only an intention to make one, he cannot forward this and tender an intention to the buyer; and in cases where the buyer is near at hand this may delay him in selling and getting his money, for the buyer frequently wants, not to take delivery of the goods, but to sell them afloat to other people; and but for the decision of Hamilton J. I should have thought that the seller c.i.f. must ship his goods under a contract for conveyance to the port of destination which can be transferred, not under a contract for part of the way and an intention to make another, which cannot be transferred and which, as in this case, may not become effective for three months. I should have been disposed to read the words of this contract 'shipment at the port in one or more steamers which are going to London direct or indirect,' or at any rate 'shipment to London, that is, under a contract to carry to London either direct by the same steamer or indirect by transhipment to another steamer,' in other words, under a through bill of lading, which both arbitrators find is the usual method of forwarding."

151   There was another point taken in the case by the buyers, namely, that the documents tendered included only the bill of lading from Hong Kong and not the bill of lading from Manila to Hong Kong. As to this, the learned judge, after stating that the point could have been put but was not taken in the case of *Cox, McEuen & Co. v. Malcolm & Co.*,[70] and that it was a good point, said[71]:

> "The buyer wants the bill of lading for two purposes— first, to take delivery, for which purpose the Hong Kong bill will suffice; secondly, to claim on the shipowner for any breach of the contract of affreightment. As Blackburn J. said in *Ireland v. Livingston*,[72] 'Should the goods not be delivered in consequence of a peril of the sea, he is not called upon to pay the freight, and he will recover the amount of his interest in the goods under the policy. If the non-delivery is in consequence of some misconduct on the part of the master or mariners, not covered by the policy, he will recover it from the shipowner.' He therefore wants a policy and contract of affreightment covering the whole adventure. Supposing in this case the transhipment had been at Hamburg, would it have been enough to tender the bill of lading from Hamburg to London? If the transfer of the bill of lading from Manila to Hong Kong is necessary to enable the buyer to sue the shipowner, it should have been tendered; if being spent its endorsement will not

[68] [1912] 2 K.B. 94.
[69] *Ibid*. at p. 105.
[70] *Ubi supra*. Lord Sumner, however, says, in *Hansson v. Hamel & Horley Ltd.* [1922] 2 A.C. 36 at p. 49, that the form of the arbitrator's question prevented the buyers from raising this question in *Cox, McEwen & Co. v. Malcolm & Co*.
[71] [1912] 2 K.B. 94 at p. 106.
[72] (1872) L.R. 5 H.L. 395 at p. 407.

have that effect, this is another argument in favour of the tender of one contract of affreightment for the whole voyage.''

Through bills of lading were considered by the House of Lords in the case of *Hansson v. Hamel & Horley Ltd.*[73] It was there decided that the seller did not fulfil his obligations to tender a through bill of lading by tendering a bill of lading issued by the ocean-going carrier 13 days after the original shipment. Although this bill purported to be a through bill, in fact it was not as it did not cover the first voyage in the local vessel before transhipment.

152   In *Hansson v. Hamel & Horley Ltd.*,[73] the plaintiff, a Swedish merchant, sold to the defendants, an English company, on c.i.f. terms 600 tons of Norwegian cod guano to be shipped from Norway to Japan during March/April 1920. The guano was shipped in different parcels on a local steamer within the contract period at more than one Norwegian port. There was no direct connection between the ports of shipment and Japan, and therefore the shipment was made to Hamburg, where it was intended to tranship into a Japanese steamer for carriage directly to Japan. The seller arranged with the agent of the Japanese steamer at Hamburg that the latter should issue through bills of lading in respect of the goods as soon as they came into his possession. Accordingly, on May 5, that is, after the expiration of the time allowed for shipment and thirteen days after the date of the local bill of lading, the agent at Hamburg issued to the seller so-called through bills of lading showing that the goods had been transhipped at Hamburg. The bills of lading were in the following form: The document was headed ''Through Bill of Lading,'' and contained in the margin ''from Braatvag (the original port of shipment in Norway) to Yokohama'' and ''shipped from Braatvag according to bill of lading on April 22, 1920'' and began thus: ''Shipped in apparent good order and condition by Messrs. Hamel & Horley Ltd., on board the steamship *Kiev* (the local steamer) lying in or off the port of Braatvag and bound for Hamburg for transhipment into the Osaka Shosen Kaisha's Steamship *Atlas Maru* . . . 1,500 bags cod guano . . . to be delivered . . . at the port of Yokohama . . . unto order.'' The seller tendered to the buyers shipping documents which included these bills of lading. However, the buyers declined to pay on the ground that the bills were not in order and did not cover the whole transit from Norway to Japan, but only the transit between Hamburg and Japan.

Bailhache J.[74] held that the seller had made two contracts which together covered the whole voyage from Norway to Japan, and, secondly, where, as in that case, a voyage was not continuous and it was the practice to issue the through bill of lading at the port of transhipment, a seller under a c.i.f. contract fulfilled his obligation if he forwarded the bill of lading to the buyer within a reasonable time after its issue at the port of transhipment. He accordingly gave judgment for the seller.

[73] [1922] 2 A.C. 36.
[74] (1920) 26 Com. Cas. 107.

153   The Court of Appeal (Bankes, Warrington and Atkin L.JJ.) reversed this decision on the ground that the bills of lading were not such documents as the buyers were bound to accept under a c.i.f. contract, since they were not issued on shipment or within the time allowed for shipment. The court did not decide, though it doubted, whether in other respects the bills of lading issued at Hamburg constituted good through bills of lading for tender to the buyers under the contract.

> "These goods," said Bankes L.J.,[75] "were shipped at the port of shipment within the contract time, but the question is whether the seller did procure a contract of affreightment on shipment. What is meant by the expression 'contract of affreightment'? In my opinion to satisfy the requirements with reference to a contract of affreightment the seller must bring into existence a contract embodied in a form capable of being transferred to the buyer and which when transferred will give the buyer two rights (a) a right to receive the goods, and (b) a right against the shipowner who carries the goods should the goods be damaged or not delivered. If this is a correct view of what is meant in this case and in other cases by a contract of affreightment, no such contract ever came into existence on shipment or within the period fixed by the contract for shipment."

Atkin L.J. added the following observations on commercial practice in cases of transhipment[76]:

> "C.i.f. contracts can be, and are, properly carried out in accordance with commercial practice by transhipment, and the Courts are not in the least likely to interfere with that commercial practice. The objection here is that the practice adopted does not conform to that which is necessary and can well be adopted for the purpose of strictly carrying out the terms of a c.i.f. contract. The actual practice proved by the witnesses as applicable to such a case as this does not appear to have been adopted in this particular case. It is undoubtedly of the essence of such a contract as this that the buyer should be put as soon as reasonably possible in possession of the documents that represent the goods, for the obvious reason that he desires to dispose of them in the ordinary course of commerce as soon as he can. The practice as proved appears to me to be this: the owner of the ocean going ship who has to perform the greater part of the transit will, on a proper contract having been made with him at or before the time of shipment, either allow the master of the local vessel to sign a through bill of lading or will authorise his accredited agent at the port of loading to sign a through bill of lading; or if he is not able to do that will as soon as he receives the bill of lading for the goods in the local ship issue his through bill of lading ... but in this case nothing of the kind was done. The owner of the ocean going vessel refused to issue a through bill of lading until the goods had actually arrived at Hamburg, and that, it appears to me, must cause a delay which was not contemplated by the contract."

The decision of the Court of Appeal was affirmed in the House of Lords.[77] It was there clearly laid down that the seller under a c.i.f. contract has to cover

---

[75] (1920) 26 Com. Cas. at p. 239.
[76] *Ibid.* at p. 246.
[77] Lords Buckmaster Atkinson Sumner, Wrenbury and Carson [1922] 2 A.C. 36.

the buyer by procuring and tendering documents which will be available for his protection from shipment to destination. The ocean bill of lading afforded no protection to the buyer in the interval of thirteen days which elapsed between the dates of the local bill of lading and the ocean bill of lading. It was further held that a bill of lading issued thirteen days after original shipment at another port was not procured "on shipment."

Lord Sumner, who delivered the principal judgment, in the course of it[78] said:

"These documents have to be handled by banks, they have to be taken up or rejected promptly and without any opportunity for prolonged inquiry, they have to be such as can be re-tendered to sub-purchasers, and it is essential that they should so conform to the accustomed shipping documents as to be reasonably and readily fit to pass current in commerce. I am quite sure that, under the circumstances of this case, this ocean bill of lading, does not satisfy these conditions. It bears notice of its insufficiency and ambiguity on its face: for, though called a through bill of lading, it is not really so. It is the contract of the subsequent carrier only, without any complementary promises to bind the prior carriers in the through transit ... the buyer was plainly left with a considerable *lacuna* in the documentary cover to which the contract entitled him.

"The point is also put in a slightly different way, which equally relates especially to bills of lading. Scrutton J. points out in *Landauer & Co. v. Craven & Speeding Bros*[79] that in a sale of goods c.f. and i., the contract of affreightment must be procured on shipment.' Of course this is practicable and common even when a through bill of lading is necessary, containing provision for transhipment at an intermediate port from a local to an ocean steamer not in the same ownership. I do not understand this proposition as meaning that the bill of lading would be bad. unless it was signed contemporaneously with the actual placing of the goods on board. 'On shipment' is an expression of some latitude. Bills of lading are constantly signed after the loading is complete, and, in some cases, after the ship has sailed. I do not think that they thereby necessarily cease to be procured 'on shipment,' nor do I suppose that the learned judge so intended his words. It may also be that the expression would be satisfied, even though some local carriage on inland waters, or by canal, or in an estuary by barge or otherwise, preceded the shipment on the ocean steamer provided that the steamer's bill of lading covered that prior carriage by effectual words of contract. "On shipment" is referable both to time and place. In principle, however, and subject to what I have said, I accept this opinion of so great an authority, and I am quite sure that a bill of lading only issued thirteen days after the original shipment, at another port in another country many hundreds of miles away, is not duly procured "on shipment." Indeed the ocean bill of lading was not procured as part of this c.f. and i. shipment at all, and "on shipment" does not at any rate mean on re-shipment or on transhipment."

Lord Sumner explained his decision in *Cox, McEuen & Co. v. Malcolm & Co.*[80] on the ground that the issue there was limited by the findings and questions stated by the arbitrator, and did not turn on any question of the shipping documents required by c.i.f. terms in general.

---

[78] *bid* at p. 46.
[79] [1912] 2 K.B. 94, *ante*
[80] *Ante* § 149.

155   In *N. V. Arnold Otto Meyer v. Aune.*[81] the question arose as to whether certain bills of lading were good tender under contracts of sale of copra c.i.f. from the Philippine Islands. The board of appeal of the London Copra Association found as a fact that it was customary to ship transit cargo in coastal vessels from outports in the Phillipine Islands to a central port under through bills of lading and by the coastal steamer providing for transhipment into an ocean steamer at a central port. Ocean steamer bills of lading were then issued against surrender of the coastwise through bills of lading. The ocean bills were dated in accordance with the through bills of lading and statements were inserted upon them to show the port of origin and the name of the coastal vessel. The original coastwise bills were never forwarded to the final destination, nor were they tendered as part of the shipping documents. The ocean bills, on the other hand, were regularly accepted and negotiated by banks financing such shipments. The board of appeal found that the bills of lading tendered under the contracts were in a form usual in the trade and were good tenders and should have been accepted by the buyers.

Branson J. upheld the award on this point and stated:[82]

"Cases such as *Hansson v. Hamel & Horley Ltd.*[83] and *Landauer & Co. v. Craven & Speeding Bros.*[84] have laid down as a matter of law the essential characteristics which a bill of lading must possess if it is to be good tender under a c.i.f. contract. It must have been procured on shipment or not long afterwards, it must cover the contract goods, and none other, from shipment to the port of destination, and it must show shipment within the contract time. Here, say the buyers, the bills of lading tendered possess none of these characteristics. They were procured long after shipment at the coastal ports. They cover in two cases goods other than the contract goods, and they do not cover the goods from shipment to port of destination, and so are not good tender. The answer made on behalf of the sellers is that the appeal board has found as a fact that the bills of lading tendered under all the contracts were in the form usual in the trade, and were good tender, and should have been accepted as such by the buyers . . .

The buyers contend that the documents produced do not conform to the custom stated. For example, they say that the coastal bills of lading in this case are not "through bills of lading." No doubt that is true as a matter of legal description, but the board had before them the very documents which they so describe, and those documents are described in the same way on the ocean bills of lading given in exchange for them, showing that persons engaged in this trade regard coastal bills in this form as "through" bills.

The only argument left to the buyers on this point is that the custom found by the appeal board is invalid as being contrary to the law laid down in *Hansson v. Hamel & Horley Ltd.* In my opinion this argument is misconceived. The characteristics generally required by the common law to exist in a bill of lading, if it is to be good tender under a c.i.f. contract, are so required because, and only because, it is the general custom of merchants that such a bill shall possess those characteristics. If, in any particular trade, there is a custom that bills of lading should have other characteristics in addition to, or in substitution for, those gen-

---

[81] [1939] 3 All E.R. 168.
[82] *Ibid* at p. 172.
[83] [1922] 2 A.C. 36.
[84] [1912] 2 K.B. 94.

erally required by the custom of merchants, then, in that trade, bills of lading, to
be good tender, need only conform to that custom.''

156   *In Plaimar Ltd. v. Waters Trading Co. Ltd.*,[85] which has already been
noted, the High Court of Australia held that the seller complied with his
obligations under a c.i.f. contract by tendering a bill of lading that discharged
the carrier from any responsibility with respect of transhipment at Singapore
where, owing to the state of war then prevailing, the goods did in fact disappear. The seller had utilised the only carrier available at the port of shipment,
and could not be expected to obtain a more advantageous bill of lading if the
circumstances precluded him from exercising any such option. The circumstances under which the *Plaimar* dispute arose are therefore distinguishable
from those considered, by the Judicial Committee of the Privy Council in
*Holland Colombo Trading Society Ltd. v. Segu Mohamed Khaja Alawdeen &
Ors.*[86] where, following the *Hansson* case, their lordships advised that a transhipment clause which relieved the carrier from liability with respect to the
goods upon transhipment was repugnant to a c.i.f. contract. Where, however,
the bill of lading is tendered after safe arrival of the goods at their port of
destination, McNair J. opined that, if the bill were otherwise unobjectionable,
he would not consider it a bad tender merely because it contained a liberty
(excluding shipowners' liability in the event of transhipment) not in fact exercised.[87]

157   A new type of bill of lading, known as the combined transport document
or bill of lading,[88] has evolved as a result of the container revolution and the
intermodal transport system it gave rise to. The practice has grown for banks
to accept such documents as security, and as a valid tender in letter of credit
transactions. The document (if no contrary marking or notation appears
thereon) is (except where traffic by air may be involved) considered negotiable (by usage) and the fact that it may be issued by someone other than the
sea carrier does not appear to have given rise to any particular difficulties till
now. Whether a c.i.f. seller may tender such a document in performance of
his contract (absent agreement thereon) is unsettled and unclear. However,
the fact that the document usually does not establish privity with the shipowner could be construed as curtailing the rights of the c.i.f. buyer and (it is
thought) may be a valid ground for rejecting the same.

In addition to the combined transport bill of lading, the emergence of fast
container ships (whose arrival at the port of destination often precedes the
postal delivery of the bill of lading to the consignee) has given rise to new
types of documents that are not documents of title and cannot be negotiated.
Such documents are usually described as sea waybills and resemble the air

---

[85] (1945) 72 C.L.R. 304, see *ante*, 96.
[86] [1954] 2 Lloyd's Rep. 45, discussed *ante* 97.
[87] In *Soproma S.p.A. v. Marine & Animal By-Products Corporation* [1966] 1 Lloyd's Rep. 367.
[88] See ICC publication No. 298 on the Uniform Rules for a Combined Transport Document.

consignment note.[89] While the Carriage of Goods by Sea Act 1971 is by section 1(6)(b) made applicable (with minor exceptions) to waybills that incorporate its provisions,[90] and while the Carriage of Goods by Sea Act 1992, enables the consignee named in a sea waybill, or any other person to whom the carrier is duly instructed to deliver the goods under the terms of the sea waybill, to sue on the contract of carriage, the waybills lack of negotiability disqualifies it from being a document that can be tendered under a classic c.i.f. contract.[91]

The contents

158   The shipowner who carried goods by sea as part of a general cargo was at common law in the position of a common carrier and was virtually an insurer for the safe delivery of those goods. Shipowners limited their liability by entering into contracts of affreightment with shippers that exempted them from responsibility in certain events, the terms of such exemptions being set out in the bills of lading. The position became generally unsatisfactory as shipowners refused to carry except on their own terms, which were not always reasonable. Recommendations were accordingly made by the International Conference on Maritime Law at Brussels in 1922 that legislation should be passed by the countries concerned preventing shipowners from insisting upon unreasonable conditions. Most countries have passed Acts embodying the rules proposed (known as the Hague Rules), and in this country the Carriage of Goods by Sea Act 1924, was passed. In 1968, an amendment to the Hague Rules, known as the Visby Protocol, was agreed upon. At the time of writing, this 1968 Protocol has not received universal international recognition, but the UK is one of the major maritime powers to have adopted its provisions in the Carriage of Goods by Sea Act 1971. The Hague Rules were completely rewritten in 1978 in a new treaty (known as the Hamburg Rules) that incorporates the provisions of the Visby Protocol. The Hamburg Rules introduced several major changes in the regime governing the carriage of goods by sea but the new Rules have not been ratified by any of the major maritime powers and are unlikely to replace existing law in the foreseable future. The Hamburg Rules drastically alter the somewhat privileged position of the sea carrier (in comparison to other international carriers) and for this reason strong shipowner resistance to their adoption has developed in many countries.[92]

---

[89] *Ante*, §3.

[90] There is some doubt whether s.1(6)(b) similarly refers to combined transport bills of lading, since they usually evidence much more than contracts for the "carriage of goods by sea."

[91] See *post*, §161a for more on waybills.

[92] See generally with respect to the Hamburg Rules: *The Hamburg Rules on the Carriage of Goods by Sea* (S. Mankabady ed.), published for The British Institute of International and Comparative Law, Sijthoff-Leyden/Boston, 1978.

The Carriage of Goods by Sea Act 1971

159   This Act provides, in broad outline, that the Hague Rules (as amended by the Visby Protocol) shall *inter alia* apply to the carriage of goods by sea in ships carrying goods from Great Britain or Northern Ireland to any other port whether in or outside Great Britain or Northern Ireland, or to any port in Great Britain or Northern Ireland.

All bills of lading are to be read subject to these provisions, but the carrier, although he may not further limit his responsibility, may always accept increased liability as part of the terms of the contract of affreightment. After receiving the goods, the carrier is to issue a bill of lading showing the leading marks of the packages and their number, quantity or weight, but no sanction need attach for failure to include such particulars in the document. After the goods have been loaded, the shipper is entitled to a "shipped" bill of lading, or to have such other document of title (*i.e.* a "received for shipment" bill of lading) noted with the particulars of shipment.

Assignment

160   It has long been the position for the holder of a bill of lading to be able to pass the property in the goods to an assignee by endorsement and delivery thereof. It was established in the leading case of *Lickbarrow v. Mason*[93] that:

> "By the custom of merchant bills of lading for the delivery of goods to the order of the shipper or his assigns are, after the shipment, and before the voyage performed, negotiable and transferable by the shipper's endorsement and delivery, or transmitting of the same to any other person; and that by such indorsement and delivery or transmission the property in such goods is transferred to such other person."

To this statement, which was the finding of the special jury in the above case; two qualifications must be made. The property passes in the goods not by the mere assignment and delivery of the bill of lading, but by the contract between the assignor and assignee by which it is intended that the property should pass.[94] Further, the bill of lading is a living instrument and effective to pass the property even after the goods have been lost or landed, and, in the latter case, so long as complete delivery and possession has not been given to some person having the right thereto.[95]

The passing of property by such an assignment did not, however, by itself confer upon the assignee any rights in connection with the contract of carriage; he could not sue upon the contract of carriage nor was he

---

[93] (1787) 2 T.R. 63; Smith's *Leading Cases* (13th ed.), Vol. 1, p. 731.
[94] *Sewell v. Burdick* (1884) 10 A.C. 74.
[95] *Barber v. Meyerstein* (1870) L.R. 4 H.L. 317.

liable under it. His remedy, in the case of the goods being lost or damaged, lay against the assignor. The courts did, however, assist an assignee who presented a bill of lading to the shipowner and paid the freight, for it has been held that delivery and acceptance of the goods in such circumstances generally constitute acts from which a contract can be inferred that the goods shall be delivered in accordance with the terms of the bill of lading.[96]

More recently, the same principle was applied to an action based on a ship's delivery order incorporating bill of lading terms and authorising delivery of a part of a cargo to the holder or to his order. In *Cremer and Others v. General Carriers S.A.*[97] Kerr J. dismissed the allegation that as the buyers did not become the owners of any part of a bulk cargo until their portion of the cargo had been identified and segregated, they could not succeed in an action for breach of the contract of carriage against the shipowners. In his view, a contract in terms of the bills of lading had (on the facts before him) come into effect between the shipowners and the buyers, notwithstanding that prior to delivery they were not owners of any part of an undivided bulk of cargo a portion of which they had purchased on c.i.f. terms from a shipper in Thailand. But this is normally only true[98] if there is a contract with the carrier, *i.e.* if the delivery order is issued by the owner (or in the appropriate cases, charterer) of the vessel or on his behalf and incorporates the terms of the bill of lading, though presumably such incorporation could be implied. The principle has no application where the delivery order is issued by the seller or an agent of the seller, for such a document confers no rights against the carrier. And, absent an attornment by the latter, no right of action against him can be sustained.[99]

Actions against the carrier

161   In 1855, the Bills of Lading Act was passed in order to enable the assignee to sue in all respects as if he was the shipper of the goods. The effect of the Act was to assign the contract of affreightment to the assignee of the bill of lading who takes the property. However, where property passed prior to the indorsement and delivery of the bill of lading, or independently from it, the 1855 Act did not confer on the holder of the bill any right of action against the carrier. Such situations could arise in the context of c.i.f. sales as was the case in *Enichem Anic S.P.A. and Others v. Ampelos Shipping Co. Ltd. (The*

---

[96] *Stindt v. Roberts* (1848) 5 D. & L. 460; *Allen v. Coltart & Co.* (1883) 11 Q.B.D. 782; *Brandt v. Liverpool, Brazil and River Plate Steam Navigation Co.* [1924] 1 K. B. 575. See further, past § 165a.

[97] [1974] 1 W.L.R. 341.

[98] See passage from Kerr J.'s judgment in *Warren Import Geselleschaft Krohn & Co. v. International Graanhandel Thega N.V.* [1975] 1 Lloyd's Rep. 146 at p. 155, quoted *ante* § 137.

[99] And see further, *post* § 162.

"Delphini")[1] where there was a short delivery of a cargo of crude oil, sold on c.i.f. terms, in circumstances under which the bills of lading had not been delivered to the buyer at the time the cargo was discharged. The Court of Appeal denied the c.i.f. buyer's right to press a claim against the carrier on the basis of the 1855 Act, because, by the time the bill of lading was transferred to him, it was already spent. In other words the bill of lading ceased to be effective as a transferable document of title once the cargo was actually delivered. Its transfer, therefore, was not intended to have, and did not have, any part in the transfer of property. As a result of this, and other decisions, an express legislative amendment was required, and this was done by means of repealing the 1855 Act, and the enactment of the Carriage of Goods by Sea Act 1992.

Section 1 of the repealed statute, provided:

> "Every consignee of goods named in a bill of lading, and every endorsee of a bill of lading, to whom the property in the goods therein mentioned shall pass upon or by reason of such consignment or endorsement, shall have transferred to and vested in him all rights of suit, and be subject to the same liabilities in respect of such goods as if the contract contained in the bill of lading had been made with himself."

From what has already been said, it is clear that the requirements of the foregoing provision were, in the case of a c.i.f. contract, satisfied though the goods may have been lost before the tender of the documents to the buyer has taken place.

161a   However as noted, the 1855 Act was repealed and replaced (in respect of Scotland also) by the Carriage of Goods by Sea Act 1992, as of September 16, 1992.

The new Act solves several problems that the older Act gave rise to. In addition, it is designed to reflect and accommodate the newer and more modern shipping practices, including laying the foundations for the possible future use in international trade of Electronic Data Interchange (EDI), if in due course this becomes technically possible. Thus, section 1(5) of the Act empowers the Secretary of State to make provision by regulation for information given by means other than in writing to be of equivalent force and effect to that contained in documents.

The main innovations contained in the new Act are as follows: in the first place it is provided by section 2(4) that any lawful holder of a bill of lading may enforce the carriage contract against the carrier irrespective of the passing of title to the goods. The provision solves the "privity" problem, and follows the American practice embodied in the Federal Bills of Lading Act 1916 (The Pomerene Act), and the similar position in France and other Civil Law countries, where the principle is derived from the concept of contracting for the benefit of a third party. The new provision is designed to overcome

---

[1] [1990] 1 Lloyd's Rep. 252.

difficulties of the sort exemplified in *The Aramis*,[2] *The Aliakamon*,[3] or *The Delphini*.[4]

The new provision will also obviate the need to resort to the near fiction which English courts were required to adopt whenever pledgees of the bill of lading, such as banks, wished to enforce the contract of carriage. The "implied contract" fiction created in *Brandt v. Liverpool, Brazil and River Plate Steam Navigation Co. Ltd.*[5] removed certain difficulties encountered by pledgees (as described in greater detail *post*, § 165 but could be of no assistance in circumstances which precluded resort to the implied contract construction. In the *Brandt* case the bank paid the outstanding freight, so an implied contract could be inferred. However, the mere presentation of the bill of lading on discharge could not create such an implied contract. This was decided by the Court of Appeal in the *Aramis*[6] where freight had been prepaid, and there was nothing from which to imply a contract with the carrier. Moreover, the right of recovery against the carrier is not to be affected by whether the claimant has suffered a loss himself or not. Under section 2(4) of the new Act he will be able to recover damages for the benefit of the person who has suffered the actual loss.

The second innovation of the new Act (section 2(1)(b)) enables the consignee named in a sea waybill (which is not a negotiable document of title), or any other person to whom the carrier is duly instructed to deliver the goods under the terms of the sea waybill, to sue on the contract of carriage without prejudice to the rights of the original shipper. Sea waybills, which have come into increasing use of late have been defined by the Economic Commission for Europe as "a non negotiable document which evidences a contract for the carriage of goods, by sea and the taking over or landing of goods by the carrier, and by which the carrier undertakes to deliver the goods to the consignee named in the document".[7] Sea waybills thus resemble ship delivery orders (used to segregate portions of bulk cargos sold to different consignees and covered by section 2(1)(c) of the 1992 Act which, it is thought, merely codifies, but does not alter, pre existing law), but have come into use in lieu of bills of lading in many trades. Sea waybills perform two out of the three basic functions of the bill of lading, namely, they are both a receipt and evidence of the contract of carriage (though not necessarily subject to the liability limitations provisions of the 1971 Carriage of Goods by Sea Act, and the International Conventions underlying it)[8] but they are not and never

---

[2] [1989] 1 Lloyd's Rep. 213, *post*, § 165a.
[3] [1986] 2 Lloyd's Rep. 1 (H.L.), *post*, § 162.
[4] [1990] 1 Lloyd's Rep. 252, 270 (C.A.), *ante*, § 161.
[5] [1924] 1 K.B. 575, *ante* § 160.
[6] [1989] 1 Lloyd's Rep. 213, discussed *post*, § 165a.
[7] See Tetly "Waybills: Modern Contract of Carriage of Goods by Sea" [1983] 14 J.M.L.C. 501.
[8] The Hague, or Hague-Visby Rules only apply to bills of lading. The Rules must therefore be effectively incorporated into the sea waybill for them to be binding on the carrier who may otherwise contract out of them. See *The European Enterprise* [1989] 2 Lloyd's Rep. 185. For the purposes of effective incorporation it may be necessary to state that the document "is to be

can be negotiable, and could not pass rights of suit, under the Bills of Lading Act, 1855. The new Act remedies this situation, and may also pave the way to EDI transmission in future.

The question whether a sea waybill is a good substitute for the bill of lading within the context of a c.i.f. contract is, however, an entirely different matter. The answer, it is thought, must be in the negative so long as the contract of sale does not expressly allow such substitution, and the Incoterms 1990 definition[9] that allows for the provision of a sea waybill must, it is thought, be qualified to mean "where the contract between the parties so permits".[10] But assume the contract does permit this, could not the buyer argue that under a c.i.f. contract he is entitled to obtain not just a document that would bind the carrier (as provided for in section 2(1)(b) of the 1992 Act), but also a negotiable document of title? And could he not invoke the reasoning in *The Julia*[11] (*ante*, § 17) to demonstrate that the substitution destroys the the c.i.f. character of the transaction, and cannot be reconciled with its basic characteristics? The answer to this question must await future developments on which it would perhaps be better not to speculate. Suffice it to note that the sea waybill is not a document representing the goods which the buyer can transfer to third parties, with qualities similar to a bill of lading, and this may well result in a negative answer to the above question.[12]

It should perhaps be recalled that there is no equivalent to the c.i.f. term in airborne trade and where the carriage is to be by plane (*ante*, § 3), the reason being that air carriers have traditionally and adamantly refused to issue negotiable documents. So that while the advantages of the sea waybill might well outweigh its disadvantages, and although section 2(1)(b) of the 1992 Act is designed to facilitate their use in international trade, more may well be required in future (such as the adoption of new or different trade terms in substition for the classic c.i.f. term)[13] for them to be in a position to provide a viable alternative in the context of traditional documentary sales in general, and of trade in commodities in particular.

---

regarded as a bill of lading" *per* Steyn J., *ibid.* at p. 189, overruling Lloyd J. in *The Vescscroom* [1982] 1 Lloyd's Rep. 301 at 304. Under the 1992 Act this position is maintained. Bills of lading continue to enjoy certain advantages over sea waybills. This is because s. 5(5) of the Act provides for its application "without prejudice" to the Hague-Visby Rules (as embodied under the Carriage of Goods by Sea Act, 1971). Art. III.4 of the Hague-Visby Rules stipulates that in the absence of transfer, a bill of lading will only be prima facie evidence of receipt for shipment. S. 4 of the 1992 Act turns the bill of lading to a conclusive document *vis-à-vis* the carrier, but maintains the old position in so far as waybills are concerned.

[9] A.8, *ante*, § 24.

[10] Para. 15 of the Introduction to Incoterms 1990 in fact makes this clear. It states that the "obligation of the seller to provide a bill of lading under c.i.f. must necessarily be retained. However . . . they (the parties) may specifically agree to relieve the seller from the obligation to provide a bill of lading . . ."

[11] *Comptoir d'Achat et de Vente du Boerebond Belge S.A. v. Louis de Ridder Limitada* [1949] A.C. 293.

[12] See *Soproma S.A. v. Marine & Animal By-Products Corp.* [1966] 1 Lloyd's Rep. 367, *post*, § 162.

[13] Indeed Incoterms 1990 proposed two such new terms, *i.e.* CPT (Carriage Paid To), and CIP (Carriage and Insurance paid to) respectively.

The third innovation of the 1992 Act is a recognition of the ability to endorse a bill of lading, and pass the contractual rights against the carrier, even after delivery of the goods has been made and title transferred, provided the endorsement is effected in pursuance of arrangements made prior to the delivery of the goods or their rejection.

The last relevant provision of the 1992 Act requiring mention here is contained in section 3(1). It states that a holder of a bill of lading who seeks to enforce his rights against the carrier will be under the same liabilities as the original party to the bill of lading contract. Otherwise the mere holder is under none of the obligations of the contract contained in the bill. In other words, whoever wishes to benefit from the right of suit against the carrier is to be burdened with the attendant liabilities. As far as bulk shipments are concerned, the consignee will obviously only have potential exposure for liabilities arising from his portion or share of the bulk.

Prior to the passage of the 1992 Act, difficult questions as to the passage of property determined the rights to sue the carrier as the preceding and following paragraphs show.

162   Due to the particular nature of the c.i.f. contract which is performed by the delivery of documents including a bill of lading, the question whether any property can pass in goods which no longer exist is supposedly purely academic. Where the contract provides that any deficiencies in weight are for the account of the seller, or that he guarantees the condition of the goods on arrival, the buyer's right to sue the ship under the bill of lading for non-delivery or damage to the goods was normally unaffected.[14] If the price had already been adjusted to take account of the actual condition of the goods on arrival, or if the buyer has already been indemnified by the seller, he normally held any sum recovered from the carrier as trustee for the seller. The converse, however, was not true. The seller or original shipper could recover for loss or damage to the goods only to the extent that he had title or possession in the goods. Where the property and right to possession passed to the buyer (as will usually be the case in c.i.f. contracts), the seller was unable to recover from the carrier (anything but nominal damages) unless the buyer would never have had any available remedy against the carrier because, for example, no bill of lading was ever issued in respect of the goods. For some time it was thought on the authority of *Dunlop v. Lambert*[15] that there might be cases where the seller could plead a special contractual relationship with the carrier and recover, albeit the loss of all proprietary interest in the goods by endorsement of the bill of lading,[16] but in *The Albazero*[17] the House of Lords unanim-

---

[14] *The Arpad* (1933) 46 Ll.L.Rep. 115 at pp. 117, 118; *R and W. Paul Ltd. v. National Steamship Co. Ltd.* (1937) 43 Com. Cas. 68; *per* Sellers J. in *Ministry of Food v. Australian Wheat Board* [1952] 1 Lloyd's Rep. 297 at p. 311.

[15] (1839) Cl. & F. 600.

[16] See *per* McNair J. in *Gardano and Giampieri v. Greek Petroleum George Mamidakis & Co.* [1962] 1 W.L.R. 40 at pp. 53, 54; *Steamship Den of Airlie Co. Ltd. v. Mitsui Co. Ltd. and British Oil and Cake Mills Ltd.* (1911–12) 17 Com. Cas. 116, Bray J. and C.A.

[17] [1977] A.C. 774.

ously rejected this view, holding that in circumstances where a bill of lading had been issued the carrier was no longer obligated to the original shipper or the consignor. If, therefore, the action against the carrier is time barred because of the terms of the bill of lading, the seller was unable to sue under a charterparty with the carrier that was not subject to a similar prescription and his recovery was to be limited to nominal damages only.

On the other hand in *The Charlotte*,[18] the Court of Appeal (Lord Alverstone C.J., Farwell and Kennedy L.JJ.) decided that an action against the wrong-doing shipowner was maintainable in the name of a seller under a c.i.f. contract in respect of damage caused by collision. In this case the sellers sent the documents to the buyers, reserving, however, the right over them until the buyers stated whether they elected to accept the enclosed bills or to pay cash less discount. On the day on which the goods were damaged, the buyers sent the sellers a cheque in payment for the goods the proceeds of which were received by the sellers. The buyers brought an action against the ship to which the sellers were subsequently added as co-plaintiffs. In the meantime, the underwriters paid the buyers as for a total loss. Bargrave Dean J. held that as the plaintiffs had not suffered any damage they had no right of action under which they could recover from the ship.

But the judgment was reversed and the appeal allowed. The fact that the buyers' cheque was cashed was held to be no bar to the action, and the sellers were not thereby deprived of their right to say that the cargo, when lost, was their property. The shipowner therefore must pay them the damage sustained, though the benefit of the right of action probably accrued to the insurer.

However normally (contracts for insurance excepted, on the grounds that the original party to the contract is to be treated in law as having procured the policy for the benefit of all persons who have or may acquire an interest in the goods before they are lost or damaged) where the plaintiff has lost all proprietary interest in the goods, he could not recover in an action for breach of contract. As noted (*ante*, § 161a) it required specific legislative intervention by means of the Carriage of Goods by Sea Act 1992, to permit an action against the carrier, where the holder of the bill of lading had no title in the goods. But whether the new Act would assist in cases like *The Albazero*[19] where a decision of the Court of Appeal was reversed is less clear, because of the particular circumstances of that case. In *The Albazero*, the consignee, who had lost his right to sue the carrier by virtue of the limitation period contained in the bill of lading endorsed to him was a subsidiary (but a separate legal entity) of the consignor. The property in the goods (a cargo of oil) had been transferred to the consignee pursuant to a c.i.f. contract prior to an accident which resulted in a total loss of the shipment owing to a breach by the defendant carrier. The consignor (the plaintiff in the action) had chartered the vessel from the defendants. Brandon J., and the Court of Appeal permitted an action by the consignor against the carrier on the grounds that a special

---

[18] [1908] P. 206.
[19] [1977] A.C. 774.

contract (the charterparty) existed between the parties, and that the carrier who had entered into a contract with the plaintiff and received payment from him for the carriage could not be permitted to defeat the consignor's action on the grounds that he had lost all interest in the cargo. The House of Lords disagreed.[20] Lord Diplock, who delivered the main judgment, explained that no exception from the general rule could be admitted where it was contemplated that the carrier would enter into separate contracts of carriage (the bill of lading) with whomsoever might become the owner of goods carried pursuant to the original contract (the charterparty). Thus a c.i.f. seller would not in the ordinary course of events be in a position to sue the carrier for the benefit of his buyer. This is also the case in circumstances where the action was time barred, even under the new Act, unless (a most unlikely event) the buyer reendorsed the bill of lading to the seller and the action was not time barred, and, provided further, that such reendorsement is within the ambit of section 2(2) of the Act that is designed to prevent trading in claims. For under section 2(2) the endorsement must be affected in pursuance of arrangements made prior to delivery of the goods or because of their rejection.

On the other hand in *Leigh & Sullivan Ltd. v. Aliakmon Shipping Co. Ltd. (The Aliakmon)*[21] Staughton J. held that buyers of Korean steel coils c. and f. free out Immingham could maintain an action against the shipowner (who was liable for damaging the goods) although the property in the goods had revested in the sellers. The bill of lading was delivered to the buyers but, because the buyers had difficulty in reselling the goods and arranging for their payment, it was decided that the goods should be held "to the order of" or "at the disposal of" the sellers. But the bill of lading was not re-endorsed or delivered to the sellers. It was forwarded to agents at Immingham, so that the right of suit was not retransferred to the sellers, and, accordingly, the buyers action against the shipowner succeeded. However, this decision was reversed both by the Court of Appeal,[22] as well as by the House of Lords.[23] In order to enable a person to claim in negligence for loss or damage it was necessary to have ownership or at least a possessory title to the property when the loss or damage occured, and it was not enough for him to have had only contractual rights in relation to such property. The transfer of risk was insufficient to support a claim against the carrier. What the buyers should have done was to make it a term of their contract with the sellers that they (the sellers) would either exercise the right of suit against the carrier for the buyer's account, or assign such right to the sellers. As this was not done, the claim could not succeed. This hardship has, however, now been remedied by the provisions of section 2(1) of the Carriage of Goods by Sea Act 1992 (*ante*, § 161a) with the result that today Staughton J.'s decision could not be faulted.

---

[20] Overruling McNair J. in *Gardano and Giampieri v. Greek Petroleum George Mamidakis & Co.* [1962] 1 W.L.R. 40.
[21] [1983] 1 Lloyd's Rep. 203.
[22] [1985] 1 Lloyd's Rep. 199.
[23] [1986] 2 Lloyd's Rep. 1.

Since the efficacy of the bill of lading in transferring property and the right of suit depend upon endorsement, under English law the c.i.f. seller must tender a bill which can validly be endorsed to the buyer. Accordingly, McNair J. held in *Soproma S.p.A. v. Marine & Animal By-Products Corporation*[24] that bills of lading straight consigned to a bank, and not to its order blank endorsed, may be regarded as a bad tender by the buyer under a c.i.f. contract governed by English law.

163   Where the contract permitted the seller to tender a delivery order or ship's release, the provisions of the old Act (now repealed) generally did not apply. In such a case (as well as where the c.i.f. seller is held to reserve the property in the goods by means of retention of the bill of lading and damage for which the carrier is liable occurs before title has passed), the c.i.f. buyer was seriously prejudiced when he sought to recover from the carrier for damage to the goods while unable to show a legal or possessory title at the time of damage. As already noted,[25] the option of satisfying c.i.f. contracts by substituting for bills of lading documents such as these is sometimes granted in order to facilitate trading in small parcels (out of larger bulk quantities covered by bills of lading). Where such parcels cannot be segregated from the bulk prior to discharge at the c.i.f. destination, the buyer was usually barred not only from pressing a claim based on breach of the contract of carriage, there being no privity (such as would be founded on a bill of lading),[26] but also from suing the shipowner in tort (there being no legal or possessory title). Such was the case (prior to the repeal of the old, and the enactment of the new, Act), in *Margarine Union v. Cambay Prince SS. Co.*[27] where it was held that the fact that the risk passed to the buyer upon taking up of the delivery order pursuant to the c.i.f. contract in question did not alter the situation "The truth" as there stated by Roskill J., being:

> "that English law does not recognise and never has recognised a duty of care on a shipowner to anyone who was not the owner of the goods at the time when the tort was committed. In the vast majority of cases the point is not of practical importance, for the plaintiff will be the bill of lading holder, and as such has his rights in contract, including the rights to sue for antecedent tort which are given to him by virtue of the Bills of Lading Act 1855. . . ."

Yet there are (in what has been described as "freak" circumstances) cases in which this question is of utmost significance.

---

[24] [1966] 1 Lloyd's Rep. 367.

[25] *Ante*, § 135.

[26] Where the delivery order is issued by the shipowner and incorporates the terms of the bill of lading the situation may be different. In such a case the c.i.f. buyer, if he can show a contract with the carrier in terms of the bill of lading, can sue the carrier so far as concerns the portion of the bulk which has been delivered to him. See *Cremer and Others v. General Carriers S.A.* [1974] W.L.R. 341, where the shipowners were estopped from relying on a pre-shipment defect of the goods (a portion of a cargo) by reason of issuing (in respect of the entire cargo) clean bills of lading, the terms of which were incorporated in delivery orders issued to the plaintiffs, *ante*, §§ 139 and 160.

[27] [1969] 1 Q.B. 219.

164   In the *Margarine Union* dispute the damage was caused by failure of the carrier to fumigate the vessel's holds prior to departure, and the court refused to extend the duty of care, or the principle of foreseeability of damage likely to be suffered, to any c.i.f. buyer who might buy the goods while afloat. In the later case of *Karlshamns Olje Fabrikery v. Eastport Navigation Corp. ("The Elafi")*[28] 6,000 tons of Philippine copra, c.i.f. Karlshamn, were bought by the plaintiff under four identical contracts. The contracts permitted a quantity tolerance of five per cent, more or less at sellers' option. The vessel loaded a much larger cargo of copra, part of which was covered by 12 bills of lading. In the event more cargo had been loaded than was shown in the bills of lading, and after part of it was unloaded at Hamburg, the remainder (which was in excess of the contract quantity) was destined to the claimants at Karlshamn who had meanwhile further purchased 500 tons of the excess quantity from a third party to whom it was sold. Upon discharge of the vessel in Karlshamn, 825 tons of copra were damaged through water that entered the ship's holds. A total quantity of 6,997 tons was removed from the ship, all of which was delivered to the claimants in a single lot without separation of the portions covered by the individual bills of lading, or of the 500 ton portion acquired from the third party. The claimants did not purport to exercise their right to reject goods in excess of the contract tolerance margin. The carrier argued that no action (against him) could lie because no property in the copra could pass until the goods were discharged at Karlshamn, whereas in the claimants view (which prevailed) all the cargo remaining after discharge at Hamburg belonged to them, and their claim therefore must be recognised. In discussing the difficult issues raised in this case several passages from Mustill J.'s decision are pertinent. After stating the general principles that apply to appropriation and the transfer of property in English sales law, he said[29]:

"It is convenient to approach the present case in stages. . . . First, what would have been the position if the entire cargo had been sold to the claimants under a single contract? Here, since the contract was on c.i.f. terms, it is very probable that the property would have passed to the claimants when the shipping documents were negotiated, for the cargo was ascertained and appropriated from the outset, and the general rule is that under a c.i.f. contract the property passes with the documents. The only cause for uncertainty is the fact that the claimants had a right to reject goods in excess of the stipulated quantity, so that it would not be possible to know during the voyage whether any individual portion of cargo might not ultimately revert to the vendors. I believe, however, that in such a situation the property in the entire cargo would pass conditionally to the claimants, subject to a retransfer of any excess if the claimants so elected, and that this would be sufficient to found a claim in tort in respect of all such cargo as the claimants chose to accept. Next there is the situation which would exist if (say) half of the cargo was sold to each of two buyers. Here it would be clear that no property would pass until the goods had been discharged, and a physical separation effected between the goods delivered under each contract; notwith-

[28] [1981] 2 Lloyd's Rep. 679.
[29] At pp. 683 *et seq.*

standing that the contract was on c.i.f. terms. . . . The absence of any ascertainment would mean that s. 16 (of the Sale of Goods Act) prevented the property from passing; hence there could be no claim in tort: *Margarine Union GmbH v. Cambay Prince Steamship Co. Ltd.*

"The next step is to see what the position would have been if the whole of the cargo had been sold to the claimants, under four rather than one contract of sale. . . . Where there are multiple contracts of sale in the hands of different buyers, in relation to an undivided bulk, there are only two possible solutions. English law [holds] that the property does not pass until the goods are not only physically separated, but separated in a way which enables an individual buyer to say that a particular portion has become his property. . . . There is, however, no need to impose this solution on a case where there are parallel contracts between the parties, together comprising the whole of the bulk. . . . I am unable to envisage a situation in which it would make the least practical difference whether or not the purchaser of an entire cargo from the same seller under a series of contracts for homogeneous goods is able to identify which ton or bag of the whole relates to which contract."

The judge then went on to ask whether the fact that part of the cargo devolved along a different chain of title, that is, via the third party, made any difference, and answered the question in the negative. What was required was the claimants ability to say "those are my goods," and not to identify their source. However the question of appropriation (which might have arisen in the event of shortage instead of surplus) was less straightforward. In such a case the question whether the claimants could sue the carrier or the third party for non-delivery would arise. If appropriation was necessary in that event (as a precondition for the transfer of property), the same principle would govern the dispute in the present case.

But under English law, property in an undivided bulk can pass before appropriation although it normally would not. The question was one of intent. This case therefore was an exception. There was ascertainment during the voyage since, as is usual under a c.i.f. contract, property is intended to pass upon negotiation of the shipping documents. True this would have no affect until the goods were ascertained but that happened upon discharge of the balance of the cargo at Hamburg. So the claimants were (because of the unusual circumstances) able to succeed in their claim in tort but would not have been able to achieve the same result on a claim in contract based on the bills of lading because they had bills of lading covering only 6,000 tonnes of cargo, and hence, could not show how much, if any, of the damaged cargo was carried and delivered under the bills, and thus unable to show that they had suffered any loss by virtue of the breach of contract. The situation would of course have been different under the new Carriage of Goods by Sea Act 1992, that now permits an action in contract also.

On the other hand, in *Schiffahrt und Kohlen G.m.b.H. v. Chelsea Maritime Ltd, (The "Irene's Success")*[30] Lloyd J. took a somewhat different view. He held (as is subsequently appeared, wrongly) that the claimants, who were the

---

[30] [1981] 2 Lloyd's Rep. 635.

c.i.f. buyers of a cargo of coal, were able to sue in tort although they could not sue in contract, because they were never the holders of the bill of lading, and although they did not own the coal when the damage occurred. Lloyd J. refused to follow *Margarine Union* which, he opined, would have probably been decided differently in light of the subsequent judgment of the House of Lords in *Anns v. Merton London Borough Council*,[31] where Lord Wilberforce said (at page 751) that an action in tort depended on a duty of care arising from a "sufficient relationship or proximity or neighbourhood" pursuant to which carelessness "may be likely to cause damage," coupled with the absence of any considerations "that would negative, reduce or limit the scope of that duty or the class of person to whom it is owed or the damages to which a breach of it may give rise."

It was Lloyd J.'s opinion that[32]:

> ". . . sufficient relationship of proximity between the plaintiffs as c.i.f. buyers and the defendants as ocean carriers [existed], such that defendants ought reasonably to have contemplated that carelessness on their part in carrying the goods would be likely to cause damage to plaintiffs."

Nor did he see any argument of policy against such a conclusion. In his view (*ibid.* at page 637) ". . . it would require a much stronger argument of policy (than that the bill of lading's limitations and exceptions might not apply) for the duty of care in the present case, arising out of so close a relationship as that which exists between a carrier and a c.i.f. buyer, to be excluded." It is significant that Lloyd J. in *The Irene's Success* focused on the question of the transfer of risk in the goods pursuant to the c.i.f. contract, and not on the location of property or the right of possession which the earlier decisions (denying the buyer's right of action in tort against the carrier) emphasised. But Lloyd J. was not right nor followed. In a subsequent case, the House of Lords declared him wrong, and the *Margarine Union* decision right.[33] To remedy this situation the law had to amended, and with the enactment of the Carriage of Goods by Sea Act 1992, it was.[34]

Thus, while the benefits conferred by the Bills of Lading Act 1855, clearly depended on the existence of a bill of lading or a contract with the claimant incorporating its terms (except in *Brandt v. Liverpool* circumstances),[35] the intervention of the legislature was required in order to enable the c.i.f. buyer to claim against the carrier where no property, but only risk, had passed. Clearly where the carrier is liable, his liability extends beyond liability for

---

[31] [1978] A.C. 728.
[32] [1981] 2 Lloyd's Rep. 635. Lloyd J., however, refrained from considering the problem of potential double liability (to the seller as well as the buyer) that the carrier may incur under his ruling.
[33] *Leigh and Sillivan Ltd. v. Aliakmon Shipping Co. Ltd. (The "Aliakmon")* [1986] 2 Lloyd's Rep. 1 at p. 11.
[34] See *ante*, cf 161a.
[35] [1924] 1 K.B. 575. See also *Compania Portorafti Commerciale S.A. v. Ultramar Panama line, (The Captain Gregos (No. 2)* [1990] 2 Lloyd's Rep. 395.

physical loss or damage, and he may also have to indemnify the claimant for any expenses incurred through his negligence or other wrongdoing. An interesting question arose in *The "City of Columbo,"*[36] where the issue was whether a c.i.f. importer was entitled to recover customs duties from the carrier in respect of goods not delivered. Fifty bales of merchandise were shipped on the "City of Columbo" which was owned and operated by the defendants, under a bill of lading with c.i.f. invoice value for delivery to the plaintiffs at Montreal. Pursuant to a notice that the goods would be ready for unloading, the plaintiff importers effected an entry by bill of sight and made the payment necessary under Canada's Customs Act.

The cargo was unloaded without being checked by the defendant's agents. The bales were then sorted, but 34 of them were missing. The plaintiffs perfected the required entry in respect of the whole shipment of bales and the defendants paid for the invoice value of the bales not delivered.

The importers brought an action against the carrier claiming the customs duty they had paid in respect of the bales. Rather than claim for a refund of the customs duty from the customs authorities, they proceeded on the basis that it was the defendants' responsibility to make a report for the refund of import duties under Canadian customs law. The defendants made no such report. No refund could be obtained from the Customs authorities if the goods were imported into Canada, but could be obtained if they were not imported.

The Canada Federal Court (Trial Division) held for the plaintiffs. The Canada Federal Court of Appeal affirmed. Chief Justice Jackett, for the Court, indicated that the undelivered goods were included by the defendants in the manifest delivered to Customs with the result that, in the absence of proof to the contrary, they were deemed to have landed in Canada. The defendants, in effect, advised the plaintiffs that the goods were on the vessel which was approaching Canada and which subsequently discharged cargo in Montreal. The defendants at no time advised the plaintiffs that the goods were not imported into Canada, nor did they supply them with proof that they were not imported into Canada. The Chief Justice took the position that "in a case where a carrier fails to deliver goods in accordance with a contract of carriage, the consignee is entitled to be compensated for the loss directly attributable to non-delivery and that, in an appropriate case, the compensation may include not only the value of the goods not delivered but also other loss directly attributable to non-delivery."

Under the circumstances, it could not be said that the plaintiffs should have prosecuted a refund claim for the customs duty. Thus, the Court held that the plaintiffs were entitled to be indemnified by the defendants for the loss arising from having paid the duty. The Chief Justice stated:

"As it seems to me, the loss suffered by the respondent through payment of the duties is directly attributable to the fact that the appellants included the

---

[36] [1978] 2 Lloyd's Rep. 587 (Can. Ct.).

undelivered goods in their manifest, and served the usual notice on the respondent, whether or not the goods were actually imported into Canada, and that circumstances never arose that should have caused the respondent to minimise its loss by obtaining refund of the duties'' (at p. 592).

The benefits conferred by the Bills of Lading Act 1855 therefore depended on the existence of a bill of lading or a contract with the claimant incorporating its terms. Actions in tort on the other hand depended on the ability to prove ownership or at least a right of possession which preassumed a document of attornment binding the carrier.

By section 2 of the Bills of Lading Act (now repealed) the right of the owner to claim freight against the shipper was expressly preserved. Intermediate assignees, however, did not (nor do they now) continue to have any liability on the contract once they have assigned the bill to a fresh party.[37]

The 1855 Act, gave no definition of a bill of lading, and therefore there was some doubt whether the Act applied to a ''received for shipment'' bill of lading. It appeared logical to suppose, however, that any bill of lading recognised by mercantile custom as effective to pass the property fell within the Bills of Lading Act 1855.[38] As to ''combined transport bills of lading or documents'' issued in connection with intermodal carriage (*ante*, § 157) those probably were not bills of lading within the meaning of the Act, because even if their negotiability and efficacy as documents of title (by means of which property may be transferred) was not open to question by virtue of custom, it is doubtful whether their holders can bring direct suit against the underlying carrier(s) rather than against their issuers, normally, freight forwarders. While sec. 4 of the 1992 Act expressly refers to received for shipment bills of lading, the precise nature of the document is probably of far less significance now, because ''property'' and ''privity'' tests no longer determine rights against the carrier.

It must be noted, however that the Bills of Lading Act did not apply to indorsees who acquired not the general property in the goods, but only a special property, as, for instance, a pledge.[39] A pledgee, such as a bank, would therefore be able to hold the documents as a pledge without making himself liable under the contract of carriage. But of course he would have to pay the freight should he wish to realise his security and obtain actual delivery of the goods, in which case he could sue even under the old Act. Under the new 1992 Act, a pledgee is expressly given the right of suit (section 5(2)), and the consignee named in a sea waybill is likewise able to sue on the contract of carriage without prejudice to the rights of the original shipper (section 2(1)(b)).

---

[37] See *Smurthwaite v. Wilkins* (1862) 11 C.B. (N.S.) 842.
[38] See *The Marlborough Hill v. Alex. Cowan & Sons Ltd.* [1921] 1 A.C. 444 (P.C.) *ante*, § 142; *Scrutton on Charterparties* (18th ed.), p. 377; but see *Maclachlan on Merchant Shipping* (7th ed.), p. 321.
[39] See *Sewell v. Burdick* (1884) 10 A.C. 74.

Banker's pledge

165   The transfer of a bill of lading to a third party will pass such property in the goods as the parties intend, and where shipping documents are handed to a bank as security for an advance, the intention will frequently be to pledge the goods with the bank. In such a case, the bank obtains in addition to any property rights in the goods, also the right to their possession.[40]

Where a bank has become the pledgee of the goods, and the pledgor has defaulted, the bank is left with its remedy of selling the goods on its own account to satisfy the pledgor's debt. It is unusual for banks to deal themselves in goods in this way, and in many cases it would be difficult for them to do so in specialised markets. The practice has grown up whereby the banks release the bills of lading to the pledgor in order that he may use his standing and expert knowledge of the markets to deal with the goods on behalf of the bank. The bank therefore redelivers the documents to the pledgor who obtains custody of them and signs a document known as a letter of hypothecation or a trust receipt whereby the pledgor agrees to hold the goods and the proceeds of sale as trustee for the bank. In such a case the bank does not abandon its rights as pledgee.[41]

Such a procedure may be very necessary as a practical matter, but it has obvious dangers in the case of a dishonest pledgor, for the pledgor by the letter of hypothecation may be consituted a mercantile agent so as to be able to pass a good title to a bona fide purchaser.[42]

Where the bank wishes to obtain physical possession of the goods, it will have to present the bill of lading to the master of the vessel. As has been seen, the bank being a pledgee did not have assigned to it the contract of carriage under the Bills of Lading Act, 1855. Where, however, the bank payed the freight and accepted the goods, there was to be implied a contract between the bank and the shipowner to deliver the goods on the terms contained in the bill of lading.[43]

165   Where, however, no contract could be implied, the right of suit against the carrier would fail, a situation which has now been remedied by the Carriage of Goods by Sea Act 1992. Thus, in *The Aramis*[44] the Court of Appeal decided that the mere presentation of the bill of lading on discharge could not create an implied contract with the carrier. The facts of the case were as follows: By two bills of lading the carrier acknowledged shipment on board of two parcels forming part of a bulk cargo of Argentine Linseed Expellers. The bills of lading acknowledgment was qualified by the words ''weight

---

[40] See *Official Assigneee of Madras v. Mercantile Bank of India* [1935] A.C. 53 (P.C.) (*per* Lord Wright).
[41] *North Western Bank v. Poynter, Son and Macdonalds* [1895] A.C. 56.
[42] *Lloyds Bank Ltd. v. Bank of America* [1938] 2 K.B. 147 (C.A.).
[43] *Brandt v. Liverpool, Brazil and River Plate Navigation Co.* [1924] 1 K.B. 575 (C.A.).
[44] [1989] 1 Lloyd's Rep. 213 (C.A.). See also *Mitsui & Co. Ltd. v. Novorossiysk Shipping Co. (The Gudermes)* [1992] 1 Lloyd's Rep. 311, reversing [1991] 1 Lloyd's Rep. 456.

unknown''. The bills of lading were endorsed in blank by the shippers, and were presented to the ship's agents at Rotterdam by firms of forwarding agents acting for the plaintiffs. The plaintiffs contended that no goods were delivered against the first bill, and that only 11,500 kilos (out of 255,000 kilos the second parcel was said to weigh) were delivered against the second bill of lading. The plaintiffs claimed damages for non-delivery and short delivery but their action (which succeeded before Evans J.) was rejected by the Court of Appeal. The fact that it may be just and reasonable for a c.i.f. buyer of an individual part of a bulk cargo, to whom a bill of lading in respect of the contract quantity of that particular cargo has been transferred and endorsed, to have sufficient property in the goods to sue the carrier was considered immaterial. The real test, based on the decision of the House of Lords in *Sewell v. Burdick*,[45] was the intention on which the endorsement of the bill of lading was made. When property does not pass, because, *e.g.* the goods were unascertained, no contractual rights or liabilities against the carrier can be transferred. Section 1 of the Bills of Lading Act 1855 (then in force) was inoperative where property in the goods had not passed. The only other ground on which the action could succeed was the implied contract doctrine for which *Brandt v. Liverpool brazil and River Plate Steam Navigation Co.*[46] is the best known authority. However, as Bingham L. J.'s judgment makes clear, *Brandt* did not lack ancestors nor progeny. The gist of all these decisions, however, was and is that whether a contract (between the bill of lading holder and the carrier) is to be implied is a question of fact, and that a contract will only be implied where it is necessary to do so. Thus where the carrier, who has a lien on cargo for unpaid freight or demurrage or other charges, makes or agrees to make delivery of the cargo to the bill of lading holder who presents it, and seeks or obtains delivery by agreeing to pay the said charges a contract is generally to be implied. Such were the facts in the *Brandt* decision. And the parties may show an intention to adopt and perform the bill of lading contract in other ways also. But the mere fact that an endorsee of the bill of lading, entitled as holder thereof to demand delivery from the carrier, does so, and that the carrier, bound by his contract with the shipper to deliver goods to any party presenting the bill of lading, duly makes such deliveries is insufficient to imply a contract between the bill of lading holder (to whom the property has not passed) and the carrier, and any action by them for non-delivery or short delivery could not succeed. If the mere offer to take delivery, and the absence of any right by the carrier to refuse or impose conditions on such delivery, were to be regarded as creating an implied contract then in truth there was no need for the 1855 Act because it is impossible to imagine circumstances in which a bill of lading holder could obtain goods without becoming party to the bill of lading contract. At any rate in this particular case it was impossible to imply a contract between the plaintiffs and the defendants. The presentation of the bill of lading coupled

---

[45] (1884) 10 App. Cas. 74.
[46] [1924] 1 K.B. 578 (C.A.).

with part delivery was entirely consistent with the performance of obligations and rights of the parties under their existing contractual arrangements with others, and there was no evidence of the performance of any act which was explicable only on the basis that the terms of the bill of lading governed their relationship *inter se*. On these grounds the appeal was allowed without dissent. The undesirable result was, however, shortly thereafter remedied by means of the Carriage of Goods by Sea Act 1992.[47]

166   However, if the contract of carriage is discharged prior to the pledge of the documents with the bank there is a question whether the endorsement of a bill of lading will be effective to transfer the property therein to the bank. But the issue is open, for as held by Diplock L.J. in *Barclays Bank Ltd. v. Commissioners of Customs and Excise*,[48] it was never judicially decided, though *Barber v. Meyerstein*[49] does seem to lend the proposition some measure of support. In the former case, the buyer of a consignment of goods shipped from Rotterdam c.i.f. Cardiff deposited the bills of lading with the plaintiff bank some time after arrival of the goods at their destination in order to secure an advance which the bank had made on an overdraft. The defendants there recovered a judgment against the buyers for arrears of purchase tax and attempted to seize and take possession of the goods which had remained in a dockside warehouse into which they were placed by the shipowners. Upon presentation of the bills of lading by the bank the shipowner issued delivery orders to the warehouse against which delivery of the goods could be obtained. The defendants unsuccessfully alleged that the contract of carriage was performed and that as soon as that happened, and the bill of lading was in the hands of the person entitled to the property and possession of the goods, and was in a form which would entitle him to claim delivery from the shipowner, it ceased to be a document of title by delivery and endorsement of which the property in the goods could be transferred. Diplock L.J. found that when the bill of lading was pledged with the bank, the contract of carriage was not yet performed. The goods were in the constructive possession of the shipowner, and were being held in the physical possession of the warehouse on their behalf and to their order. The shipowner, therefore, was under no obligation to surrender constructive possession or the goods except on production of the bill of lading.

[The next paragraph is 181.]

---

[47] *Ante.*, § 161.
[48] [1963] 1 Lloyd's Rep. 81.
[49] (1866) L.R. 2 C.P. 38, 661; (1870) L.R. 4 H.L. 317.

CHAPTER 4

INSURANCE

181   As has already been seen, it is essential that goods shipped under a c.i.f. contract shall be covered by insurance against loss, and a policy of insurance or such certificate or other document of insurance as may be substituted for it by the contract of sale must be tendered by the seller to the buyer as one of the shipping documents. It is by virtue of this document of insurance that the buyer, in the event of the goods being lost or damaged, is entitled to recover the amount of his loss from the underwriters.

The duty of the seller

182   The duty of the seller is to procure such insurance cover as is required by the express provisions of the contract of sale, and to tender to the buyer such insurance document as the contract prescribes.

In the absence of any special provisions in the contract of sale, the duty of a seller under a c.i.f. contract,[1] with regard to insurance, is to effect at his own cost with reputable insurers a valid policy of marine insurance which shall be available for the benefit of the buyer, covering the transit contemplated by the contract, of the kind and on the terms current in the trade (with reference to the particular goods in question, the type of vessel, the route contemplated, the port of destination and any other considerations that may affect the risk), and in an amount representing the reasonable value of the goods.[2] Failure to procure an insurance in these terms, namely, failure to provide the required protection, and tender the necessary cover, will place the goods at the risk of the seller, and he will be unable to sue for the price. So, for example, in *Lindon Tricotagefabrik v. White and Meacham*[3] Danish pullovers were sold to an English firm, the terms being c.i.f. the buyer's warehouse at Ealing. The goods were misdelivered to the buyers' office and left outside it. Before collection could take place for the goods to be delivered

---

[1] See judgments cited in Chap. 1, *ante*, from *Biddell Bros. v. E. Clemens Horst Co.* [1911] 1 K.B. 214 at p. 220; *ibid.* at p. 956; [1912] A.C. 18; *C. Groom Ltd. v. Barber* [1915] 1 K.B. 316 at p. 324; *Johnson v. Taylor Bros. & Co. Ltd.* [1920] A.C. 144 at pp. 149, 156.
[2] In the cotton trade the ordinary insurance policy to be taken out under a c.i.f. contract may have to include "country damage," *i.e.* certain pre-shipment risks: see *Reinhart Co. v. J. Hoyle & Sons Ltd.* [1961] 1 Lloyd's Rep. 346.
[3] [1975] 1 Lloyd's Rep. 384 (C.A.).

to the correct address, they were stolen. The goods were only insured as part of a container load from port to port, and no cover with respect to the inland transit (port to Ealing warehouse) was procured. The sellers sued for the price claiming the goods as sold and delivered but their action failed. The sellers did not tender, as they ought to have done, a proper policy of insurance so their tender (if it be such) was defective. It is not necessary that the insurance be taken out for the immediate benefit of the buyer. A policy taken out to the order of the seller and later assigned to the buyer is valid and effective for all purposes under a c.i.f. contract.

Having procured such an insurance, it is the duty of the seller to tender to the buyer a policy of insurance in respect of the goods. It is to be noted, however, that this is no longer the general modern practice. The shippers, if they are merchants conducting substantial export business, will usually have a floating or open policy of insurance under which they will make declarations to the insurers in respect of particular c.i.f. shipments to be covered. In these circumstances it will not be possible for the seller to tender to the buyer a separate policy of insurance in respect of each shipment, and the contract of sale will, in these circumstances, generally provide that the buyer shall accept a "policy and/or certificate and/or letters of insurance." In the absence, however, of an express term of this nature the seller may have to tender an actual policy of insurance, and where the expression "shipping documents" is used the inference used to be (but possibly no longer is) that one of them is a policy proper.[4] It is therefore proposed to consider first the obligations of the seller as to insurance where no express terms are mentioned.

The terms of the policy

183   Hamilton J. stated that the policy of insurance required is one "upon the terms current in the trade,"[5] and Scrutton J. expressed the obligation in like manner when he described the necessary insurance as "the ordinary contract of insurance of the goods on that voyage."[6] Whether the policy of insurance complies with these requirements is a question of fact to be determined according to whether it is or is not the usage and practice in the trade to accept such a policy under such a contract of sale as that under which it is tendered.[7] The test will involve such considerations as the character of the goods, the nature of the vessel and the route of the transit. A question arose as to what was the usual form of insurance in the frozen meat trade in the following circumstances:

---

[4] See *per* Lord Sumner in *Yangtsze Insurance Association v. Lukmanzee* [1918] A.C. 585 at p. 589.
[5] In *Biddell Bros. v. E. Clemens Horst Co.* [1911] 1 K.B. 214 at p. 220.
[6] In *Arnhold Karberg & Co. v. Blythe* [1915] 2 K.B. 379 at p. 388.
[7] *Tamvaco v. Lucas* (1862) 3 B. & S. 89. *Cf. per* Kennedy J., *Burstall v. Grimsdale* (1906) 11 Com. Cas. 280 at p. 290.

In *Borthwick v. Bank of New Zealand*,[8] the plaintiff carried on business in London and was a purchaser of frozen meat c.i.f. London from sellers in New Zealand. In order that the sellers might draw on the buyer for the price as soon as the consignments were shipped, the buyer instructed the Dunedin branch of the defendant bank to establish a confirmed credit in favour of the seller upon terms contained in a letter of credit which provided (*inter alia*) that "the drafts" (*i.e.* bills of exchange) "are to be accompanied by shipping documents (*i.e.* bills of lading, invoice and insurance policy)." The bank negotiated a draft which was accepted by the buyer, who did not examine the documents. The policy of insurance was found to contain a clause "to pay a total loss by total loss of vessel only." A partial loss of the consignment took place and the buyer could not recover under the policy from the underwriters. As the sellers were in liquidation, the buyer sued the bank for breach of contract in negotiating a draft which was not accompanied by a proper insurance policy.

Evidence was given that it was the regular practice and invariable course of business in the New Zealand frozen meat trade to include in the shipping documents an "all risks"[9] insurance policy. In the course of his judgment Mathew J. said[10]:

> "In my opinion my judgment in this case must be for the plaintiff. The letter of credit states the terms on which the defendants were to negotiate and the plaintiff was to accept the drafts and I have no doubt that the letter is a contract in the fullest sense of the word. Under that contract, when a shipment was made and a draft was brought to the defendants for them to negotiate, their first consideration ought to be whether the draft was such as the plaintiffs would accept, and, therefore the representative of the bank should examine the documents attached to the draft in order to see whether they were those stipulated for in the letter of credit. If that precaution were taken, the documents should consist of proper bills of lading and invoices and a policy of insurance, and the object of the stipulations in the letter of credit being to protect the plaintiff, the policy should be an all risks policy, which, on the evidence, I am satisfied is the ordinary policy in business of this kind."

184   In *Plaimar Ltd. v. Waters Trading Co. Ltd.*,[11] the policy tendered contained an exception in respect of loss at the port of transhipment. This provided that unless the goods are loaded on the on-carrying vessel within a specified period of time, 15 days, the cover expires and does not reattach until reloading commences. The goods disappeared in the port of transhipment, Singapore, and the buyer refused to accept the documents tendered by the seller. The High Court of Australia held that he had no right to decline acceptance on the following grounds: that the policy tendered by the seller was a usual policy, that no marine insurance could be obtained at the time of the

---

[8] (1900) 6 Com. Cas. 1.
[9] As to "all risks" policies, see *post*, § 190.
[10] (1900) 6 Com. Cas. at p. 4.
[11] (1945) 72 C.L.R. 304 (Australia).

transaction covering the goods for more than 15 days pending transhipment or reloading, and that the seller shipped the goods by the only route available. In the circumstances, the buyer could not therefore demand a more favourable insurance cover.

According to the International Chamber of Commerce definition of the c.i.f. term, the c.i.f. seller (in the absence of express agreement on this matters) satisfies his obligation by procuring (and tendering to the buyer) a Minimum marine cover, with an underwriter of good repute.[12] Any special risks, namely, theft, pilferage, leakage, breakage, chipping, sweat, contact with other cargoes, etc., unless peculiar to any particular trade in respect of which a usage requiring cover thereof may be implied, are excepted. Consequently, it is advisable for the parties to expressly specify in their contract the extent (and terms) of the cover desired. By so providing, unnecessary disputes in connection with the extent and scope of insurance to be provided will be avoided. In the absence of such agreement, the c.i.f. seller may (absent any custom or usage to the contrary) satisfy his obligation in regard to insurance by procuring (and tendering) the most limited protection against marine risks.

"Free of capture and seizure"

185   The customary insurance will be found generally to exclude war risks; in other words, the policy of insurance is not improper because it contains the "f.c. and s." clause.[13] Such a question arose in respect of the jute trade in the case of *C. Groom Ltd. v. Barber.*[14] where Atkin J. approved a finding of the Appeal Committee of the United Kingdom Jute Goods Association that the tender of a policy containing the "f.c. and s." clause satisfied the seller's obligations in that trade.

The facts were that the defendant sold on June 8, 1914 to the plaintiffs on the terms of the United Kingdom Jute Goods Association 100 bales of hessian cloth for shipment from Calcutta between June 1 and July 15, to London upon c.i.f. terms. There was an express provision "war risk for buyer's account." On July 15, the goods were shipped in the *City of Winchester*, which was captured on August 6, by a German cruiser and subsequently sunk. The seller did not effect a war risks policy, and tendered the usual form of Lloyd's policy containing the "free from capture and seizure" (f.c. and s.) clause. The buyers refused to pay for the goods and the matter was referred to arbitration, the buyers contending that the seller should have insured against war risks. They also contended they were not bound to accept docu-

---

[12] *Ante*, § 24.
[13] "Warranted free of capture, seizure and detention, and the consequences thereof" or similar words.
[14] [1915] 1 K.B. 316. And see *Re Weis & Co. & Crédit Colonial et Commercial, Antwerp* [1916] 1 K.B. 346, cited in the text, *post*, § 201.

ments in respect of goods which were lost at the time of tender.[15] The umpire found in favour of the seller. On appeal to the London Local Appeal Committee of the Jute Goods Association, the committee decided as a question of fact that the insurance policy referred to in the contract was by the custom of the trade a policy which contained the free from capture and seizure clause, that the tender of such a policy was a sufficient tender within the meaning of the contract, and that there was no custom of the trade and it had never been the practice for a seller to effect any war risk insurance for buyer's account, and that the tender of a war risk policy had never in practice been made by merchants or others doing business in jute goods.

In giving judgment for the seller, Atkin J., dealing with the question of insurance said[16]:

> "In a contract on c.i.f. terms the seller has, as stated by Hamilton J. in *Biddell Bros. v. E. Clemens Horst Co.*,[17] to arrange for an insurance on the terms current in the trade which would be available for the buyer. I am satisfied that at the time this contract was made the terms current in the trade were terms which excluded war risk; in other words that the policy would contain the f.c. and s. clause, and therefore, apart from the special terms of this contract, a policy in such terms would be in order. The finding of the appeal committee in that respect makes the matter quite certain. But in this contract there are the words 'war risk for buyer's account.' It was said that that meant the seller was bound to take out a policy covering war risk but was entitled to charge the buyer with the expense of it. That would mean that at all times, even in times of peace, a war risk policy must be taken out at the expense of the buyer. I am satisfied that no seller or buyer contemplated such a thing, and if the buyer were charged with the expense of such a policy, he would, in ordinary times of peace, be the very first person to object. To my mind these words mean that war risk is the buyer's concern, and if he wants to cover war risk he must get it done."

186   War risks were again considered in the case of *Oulu Osakayetio v. Laver*,[18] which arose at the time of the Spanish civil war. The seller, the plaintiff, in Finland sold timber in October 1938 to the defendants c.i.f. Hull. The timber was to be shipped during November. The insurance was to include war risks, and it was provided that any increase in the premium for war risks insurance over the rate ruling on September 26, 1935, was to be for the buyers' account. By November 1938 the ruling rate had risen from 3d. to 2s. 6d. per £100, except for Spanish and Greek steamships, where the premium was at the discretion of the underwriters. The seller chartered a Spanish ship and owing to the Spanish civil war had to pay a premium of £5 per £100 for war risks insurance. There was no evidence that any other vessel was suitable. The seller claimed from the buyers the difference between 3d. and £5 per cent, in respect of the insurance.

The Court of Appeal (Slesser, Luxmoore and Goddard L.JJ.) held that,

---

[15] This aspect of the case is dealt with separately, *post*, § 252.
[16] [1915] 1 K.B. at p. 321.
[17] [1911] 1 K.B. 214 at p. 220.
[18] [1940] 1 K.B. 750.

though the seller was free to charter any ship he liked, he could on the true construction of the contract only recover the increase in the ruling or market rate of the premium for war risks. The seller therefore was only entitled to the difference between 3d. and 2s. 6d. per cent.

187   In *Re an Arbitration between Comptoir Commercial Anversois and Power, Son and Co.*,[19] eight contracts of sale made in June and July 1914 provided for shipment during August and part of September of that year of wheat from an Atlantic or Canadian port at seller's option to Rotterdam and Antwerp. The wheat was sold f.o.b. including freight and insurance, and the contracts provided that the sellers were to furnish marine insurance for 2 per cent over and above the invoice price free of war risk. Payment was to be effected in cash on presentation of bill or bills of lading and/or delivery order. The contract further contained the following clauses:

> (1) "In the event of war, should sellers not have received from buyers approved English and/or American policies . . . for approximate invoice amount covering war risk three days prior to shipment, sellers shall have the right, if they think fit, and are able, to cover war risk for account and risk of buyers."
> (2)"In case of prohibition of export, *force majeure*, blockade, or hostilities preventing shipment, this contract or any unfulfilled part thereof shall be at an end."

At the beginning of August, the sellers cabled the buyers that they could not effect insurance against war risks. They further stated that the absence of such a cover would prevent them from selling exchange, *i.e.* raising money on the documents in New York. Consequently, they requested payment in New York. This the buyers refused to do and the sellers then purported to cancel the contracts. The dispute was referred to arbitration in London and the arbitrators found in favour of the sellers. The arbitrators held (i) that the business of exporting grain from America was based upon the sale of exchange in America; (ii) that the sale of wheat could not be carried out unless such exchange was available; (iii) that it was an implied term of the contracts that the sellers should be able to sell exchange; (iv) that the buyers were aware of this usage when the contracts were made; (v) that in the absence of a policy against war risk the sellers were unable to sell exchange on Rotterdam or Antwerp throughout the entire shipping period; (vi) that the sellers were unable to procure such a cover; (vii) that the commercial purpose of the adventure so far as the sellers were concerned became frustrated by the impossibility in the circumstances prevailing of their being able to sell or negotiate exchange, and, finally, that shipment was prevented by hostilities within the meaning of the prohibition clause.

188   On appeal from a judgment of Bailhache J., Bankes, Warrington and Scrutton L.JJ. held the sellers liable on the following grounds: First, that "ship-

---

[19] [1920] 1 K.B. 868.

ment,'' which refers to the putting of the goods on board, and not to the wider question of fulfilment of the contract, which consisted partly only of putting goods on board, was not prevented by hostilities within the meaning of the exception in the contract. ''Preventing'' there meant physical or legal prevention and not inability to sell exchange. Secondly, that no term should be implied in the contracts providing for dissolution thereof on the ground of frustration merely because the sellers were unable to sell exchange. Referring to the war risk clause in the contract, Scrutton L.J. observed:

> "There is no doubt that, if war breaks out, failure to obtain war risk insurance may be important for both parties. The seller under such a contract usually takes the bill of lading to his own order to keep a proprietary hold on the goods till he is paid, or has a security for payment satisfactory to him; he, therefore, may want war risk insurance to cover his proprietary interest, as, of course, may the buyer. Now it is important to notice that the parties have thought of this, and have expressed certain terms about it. They have contemplated a war; they have provided that, if the buyer does not provide war risk insurance, the seller may insure, if he can, on buyer's account. But though they have contemplated inability to effect war risk insurance they have said nothing about the effect of that inability on the contract. This may be because they did not think about it; it may be because they could not agree what the effect should be; but why should the court assume that there is a term which they must have contemplated, rather than a failure on their part to think about or agree on the matter? And if they have not expressed a term about the effect on the contract of inability to get war risk insurance, which they have mentioned, can the court infer what they would have agreed about a matter they have not mentioned and a more remote result, failure to sell exchange because of failure to obtain war risk insurance?''[20]

189   The common form of Lloyd's policy, which is set out in the First Schedule to the Marine Insurance Act 1906, had for a long time included a free of capture and seizure clause.[21] This clause (as well as the other standard marine insurance forms) was amended from time to time by the Institute of London Underwriters, and was not the cause of any serious dissatisfaction for many years. Subsequently, however, the standard Lloyd's Marine forms and terms of cargo insurance policies were rewritten in an effort to put into plain and modern English many of the antiquated phrases. The policies have also been adapted to meet changing circumstances. New policy forms and clauses were prepared by the London market, and were ready for use as from January 1, 1982 to be fully in use by March 1983. The initiative to issue the new policy forms and clauses was a response to criticism levelled at the old forms by (including others) the United Nations Conference on Trade and Development (UNCTAD) that had issued several reports *inter alia* calling for a revision of the antiquated standard or model forms. While the new policies and terms of cargo policies clearly have a different look to them, little of substance has really changed, and the principles applied by the courts to the old forms will

---

[20] At p. 901.
[21] See the judgment of Atkin L. J. in *Britain SS. Co. v. R. (The Petersham)* [1919] 2 K.B. 670 at p. 692.

most probably continue to be relevant. The new forms of marine policies, like the old, exclude war risks from the scope of cover which in order to be obtained must be purchased separately.

As is apparent from the cases above referred to, however, it is not uncommon for c.i.f. contracts to include specific stipulations to the effect that war risk, if available, will be obtained, and charged to the buyer's account. Indeed, the practice now even has the sanction of law under the United States Uniform Commercial Code. Section 2–320(2)(c) of the Code provides that the c.i.f. seller shall, *inter alia*, obtain "... insurance, including any war risk insurance, of a kind and on terms then current at the port of shipment in the usual amount, in the currency of the contract ... but the seller may add to the price the amount of the premium for any such war risk insurance." The justification for this allowance and the reason for exonerating the seller from assuming the risk of including in the c.i.f. price the cost of any war insurance is that it often fluctuates rapidly, and, as already noted, is normally beyond the scope of the seller's duty.

Meaning of "all risks[22]"

190   There may be special stipulations in the contract of sale with regard to the perils to be insured against, or the *quantum* of damage to be covered, and in such case the seller must exactly comply with them. One of the commonest stipulations is for insurance against as it used to be, and is even today often, described, as "all risks." The meaning of this expression is a matter of construction which may vary with the context. In a contract of sale, it may have a wider meaning than it would receive in a policy of insurance.

In *Yuill & Co. Ltd. v. Scott-Robson*,[23] the sale was of cattle at Buenos Aires c.i.f. to Durban to be insured against "all risks." The seller delivered to the buyers an ordinary Lloyd's policy, to which were attached certain clauses, headed "All Risks, Live Stock," which included the following: "To cover mortality, jettison, washing overboard, and risks of every kind from time of arrival at wharf and until delivered to consignees, but free of all claim for particular average and depreciation in respect of animals which walk ashore. . . ." The policy also contained the clause, "warranted free of capture, seizure and detention, and the consequences thereof." On the voyage, foot and mouth disease broke out among the cattle, and in consequence the steamer was not allowed by the authorities at Durban to land cattle, and on that account a number of beasts had to be slaughtered on board, whereby the buyers suffered considerable loss, which they failed to recover from the underwriters. The buyers thereupon sued the seller, and the question in the action was whether the policy complied with requirement of an "all risks" policy in the contract. It was held by Channell J., whose decision was

---

[22] This form of policy is today known as Policy "A".
[23] [1907] 1 K.B. 685; [1908] 1 K.B. 270 (C.A.).

affirmed by the Court of Appeal (Lord Alverstone C.J., Buckley and Kennedy L.JJ.), that the policy tendered did not comply with the terms of the contract. In his judgment Channell J. says[24]:

> "A great deal of evidence has been given by gentlemen of experience in the insurance world to the effect that the warranty against capture, seizure and detention [the f.c. and s. clause] is always inserted in a policy against all risks, unless special instructions to the contrary are given, and it is obviously a convenient business practice, and probably well known to all who are conversant with the business of insurance. We are not, however, dealing in this action with a contract of insurance, but with a contract for the sale of bullocks for shipment, at a price including cost, freight and insurance, one provision of the contract being that the bullocks were to be insured by the defendant [the seller] on the voyage to Durban 'against all risks.' In my opinion the contract contemplates insurance against all risks whatever as between buyer and seller, and the case is not to be determined by the meaning of the expression 'against all risks' as between insurance brokers and underwriters. No doubt the evidence clearly shows that an insurance broker would expect a policy against all risks to contain the warranty against capture, seizure and detention, but the question as between buyer and seller of goods is a very different one indeed, and I very much doubt the admissibility of evidence given on behalf of the defendant. I think that in the present case the expression covers insurance against a risk so obvious to parties buying and selling live cattle for shipment as that of the cattle being prevented from landing at their destination by reason of the apprehension of the authorities of the importation of disease. Such a prohibition is very usual, and the risk would naturally be present to the minds of persons in the position of the plaintiffs and the defendant."

191   This case was commented upon by Scrutton L.J. in *Upjohn v. Hitchens*[25] (a case concerning a tenant's duty to insure under a lease) when he observed[26]:

> "At Lloyd's there is a form of policy f.p.a. [free of particular average] and another known as an 'all risks policy.'[27] The policy f.p.a. insures against total loss only. In every 'all risks policy' there has been inserted for years the f.c. and s. clause, so that the policy does not insure against risks due to the acts of hostile Governments. If an insurance against those risks was desired a policy against the risks excepted by the f.c. and s. clause had to be effected. There are also policies which are wider than 'all risks' policies and really cover 'against all risks.' This practice was well known in insurance circles, and in *Yuill & Co. v. Scott-Robson*[28] it was sought to be imported into a contract for the sale of cattle. There two people, not in the Lloyd's circle, made a contract for the sale of cattle for shipment from Buenos Aires to Durban, the seller to insure the cattle 'against all risks.' The contract did not speak of an 'all risks policy' or use any technical terms. It was contended, and evidence was given in support of the contention, that the contract had imported into it the insurance practice at Lloyd's as to all risks policies. The contention failed, the court holding that this practice could not be incorporated into a contract for the sale of goods."

---

[24] *Ibid.* at p. 687.
[25] [1918] 2 K.B. 48.
[26] *Ibid.* at p. 60.
[27] This is no longer the case. The f.p.a. policy is today known as policy "C", whereas the all risks policy is known as "A", *ante*, §189.
[28] [1907] 1 K.B. 685; [1908] 1 K.B. 270 (C.A.).

There was a further ambiguity in the expression "all risks" because it could be taken to apply to the extent of damage to the goods in respect of which the buyer could recover as distinguished from the various causes of the damage.

192   In *Vincentelli & Co. v. John Rowlett & Co.*,[29] where a contract for the sale of citrons c.i.f. Antwerp contained the term "Insurance to be effected by us (sellers) all risks," the citrons were damaged by reason of improper stowage on deck, against which the policy effected by the sellers afforded no protection. Hamilton J. held, upon the construction of the contract, in view of the evidence, that the word "risk" was used to describe the *quantum* of loss in respect of the accident producing the loss, and that the sellers satisfied their obligation by procuring an insurance to cover all risks in the sense of the entire *quantum* of loss, although it did not protect the buyer against all causes of accident.

> "... the question," said Hamilton J.,[30] "turns upon what is meant by the word 'risks' in the contract. In the expression 'insurance to be effected by us all risks,' it seems to me to be equally consistent with the meaning of the word 'risk' in ordinary language that it may be intended to describe the *quantum* of loss in respect of the accident against which the insurer is to give an indemnity, or to express the cause of the accident producing loss against which the assured is to have protection. I do not think that it does violence to language to speak of a man being insured 'all risks,' meaning thereby that he receives a full indemnity instead of a partial indemnity, or to say that he is insured 'all risks,' meaning thereby that whatever damage may happen he is to receive an indemnity measured in some way or other. It is quite familiar to those connected with insurance business, and I do not think that it is disputed by counsel in this case, that the word 'risk' is used in both these senses, and as an illustration of that well-known fact, I may refer to the discussion before Walton J. in *Schloss v. Stevens.*"[31]

193   In the same case of *Vincentelli & Co. v. John Rowlett & Co.*,[32] a point was raised in argument on behalf of the sellers that, under such a contract as appeared in that case, all that the seller need procure is contractual protection against all risks, partly under the contract of carriage, and partly under the contract of insurance, and that it is sufficient if, under the one or the other, there is a cause of action for all kinds of damage. It was not necessary to decide the point, and Hamilton J. refrained from expressing any opinion on the question, which he regarded as "novel and difficult," although he said that he did not think the proposition was supported by the authorities. It is submitted, however, that if the contract calls for insurance against "all risks," the buyer is entitled to the protection expressed in a policy.

Where the "all risks" insurance for which the contract calls is taken to refer, as it normally will, to the causes of the damage, the seller will satisfy

---

[29] (1911) 16 Com. Cas. 310.
[30] *Ibid.* at p. 317.
[31] [1906] 2 K.B. 665.
[32] (1911) 16 Com. Cas. 310.

his obligation by providing cover against accidental causes only. And, unless the seller warrants the quality or condition of the goods on arrival,[33] the buyer must usually suffer any loss or damage caused by inherent vice or nature of the subject-matter insured.[34]

"There are, of course, limits to 'all risks' . . . the expression does not cover inherent vice or mere wear and tear. . . . It covers a risk not a certainty," said Lord Sumner in a leading case.[35] The principle that damage due to inherent vice is excluded from an 'all risks' policy also applies to damage caused as a result of the insufficiency in their packing.[36] Similarly an "all risks" cover normally does not afford protection against losses that do not arise from damage to the subject matter insured as, *e.g.* losses caused by delay, loss of profits, etc. But while a certainty is always excluded from insurance certain types of inherent vice may be made the subject matter of insurance.[37]

And of course the policy will not provide protection if the goods sold were damaged or defective and were never exposed to any risk. Thus, *e.g.* in *Fuerst Day Lawson Ltd. v. Orion Insurance Co. Ltd.*,[38] 495 drums of essential oils were purchased by the plaintiffs from an Indonesian firm under a c. and f. contract. When the ship arrived, the drums were found to contain water and not oil. The court found that there had been no substitution of the drums once they were loaded on board the vessel. The plaintiffs therefore failed to prove that the oils they purchased had ever been loaded, or that the drums from their outset did not contain water with a thin film of oil for deception purposes, and their action against the underwriters failed.

The seller must comply with any particular stipulation in the contract of sale relating to insurance. In *Oranje Ltd. v. Sargant & Sons*,[39] the sellers of a quantity of clove stems from Zanzibar sold c.i.f. Rotterdam contracted to cover by insurance particular average over 5 per cent, but they effected insurance free of particular average. Damage having been sustained over 5 per cent, they were held liable subject to no limitation to the amount recoverable in similar circumstances from an underwriter.

The amount

194   The amount for which the goods must be covered is the reasonable value of the goods.[40] What is the reasonable value is a question of fact. The value

---

[33] As to this question generally, see *post*, §319.

[34] *Schloss v. Stevens* [1906] 2 K.B. 665; *British & Foreign Mar. Ins. Co. v. Gaunt* [1921] A.C. 41 at pp. 46, 47.

[35] *British and Foreign Marine Insurance Co. v. Gaunt* [1921] A.C. 41 at p. 57.

[36] *F. L. Berk & Co. Ltd, v. Style* [1956] 1 Q.B. 180.

[37] See *Soya G.m.b.H. Kommanditgesellschaft v. White* [1982] 1 Lloyd's Rep. 136 (C.A.) where a c.i.f. shipment of Indonesian soya beans was damaged as a result of spontaneous combustion due to moisture (inherent vice) and was, under the particular language of the policy, held covered.

[38] [1980] 1 Lloyd's Rep. 656.

[39] (1924) 20 Ll.L.Rep. 329; 21 *ibid.* 58.

[40] *Tamvaco v. Lucas* (1861) 31 L.J.Q.B. 296; *Johnson v. Taylor Bros. & Co. Ltd.* [1920] A.C. 144 at p. 149.

is the value at the place of shipment, and not the value at the destination of the goods, a matter on which the seller is necessarily often ignorant. Most probably, it nowadays also covers a reasonable amount of anticipated profit and the costs of forwarding charges (freight, customs duties, etc.) also. According to "Incoterms,"[41] the seller must include the cost of freight in the insurance and must, moreover, obtain cover to the extent of the c.i.f. value plus 10 per cent.[42] Against this, it may be argued that if the goods arrive, the buyer gets the value of the freight in the increased value of the goods; whereas, if they are lost in the transit, no freight is payable.[43] In the absence of a special stipulation, it was once said that the cost price of the goods would be a proper measure of value[44]; and it is questionable whether there can be any obligation on the seller to cover a rise in value of the goods between the date of the contract and the time of shipment.[45] If the buyer desires to cover increased value or his anticipated profit, he would be well advised to stipulate in the contract for such increased insurance, or effect additional insurance on his own account. So contracts of sale c.i.f. frequently provide for insurance in excess of the invoice price, *e.g.* "gross invoice amount plus (a specified) per cent.," or "insurance (a specified) per cent. over net invoice amount to be effected by sellers for account of buyers."

195   In *Plaimar Ltd. v. Waters Trading Co. Ltd.,*[46] the High Court of Australia had to consider, *inter alia*, whether the stipulation that insurance was to be in an amount which did "not exceed the [c.i.f.] value plus 10 per cent" indicated that insurance was for the benefit of the seller and not of the buyer, and implied that the contract, though designated as a c.i.f. contract, was in fact a destination contract under which the seller undertook any risk of loss in transit. The court refused to place this interpretation on the clause, and held that the failure to fix the maximum amount for which insurance was required did not alter the nature of the transaction. The intention of the clause was to set the limit of the amount of insurance but, subject to that limit, to

---

[41] International Chamber of Commerce definition of the c.i.f. term, *ante*, § 24.
[42] See *ante*, §24, see also Eisemann, *Die Incoterms in Handel und Verkehr*, p. 134 (Vienna, 1963).
[43] But where the contract of affreightment fixes the time for the payment of freight and it is paid or becomes due before delivery of the goods takes place, it may be that it will not be recoverable from the shipowner though the goods be lost. This rule seems to be peculiar to English law, for as stated by Lord Inglis in the Scottish case of *Watson v. Shankland* (1871) 10 M. 142 (Ct. of Sess.), "All the nations of the trading world, with the exception of England, concur in holding that an advance of freight by the charterers for ship's disbursements at the port of loading ... is, in the event of the loss of the ship and cargo, recoverable" (at p. 153). Similarly in *Allison v. Bristol Marine Insurance* (1876) 1 App. Cas. 209 at p. 253 Lord Selborne described it to be "the peculiar rule of English mercantile law, that an advance on account of freight to be earned ... is, in the absence of any stipulation to the contrary, an irrevocable payment at the risk of the shipper of the goods." The subject is more fully discussed in Carver's *Carriage by Sea* (13th ed.) Vol. 2 (*British Shipping Laws*), para. 1691 *et seq.*
[44] See, *e.g. Harland & Wolff v. Burstall* (1901) 6 Com. Cas. 113 at p. 117.
[45] The point was raised, but not decided, in *Manbre Saccharine Co. Ltd. v. Corn Products Co. Ltd.* [1919] 1 K.B. 198.
[46] (1945) 72 C.L.R. 304 at p. 313.

have the seller under the same obligations of effecting a reasonable insurance with respect to amount as to any other terms.

196   *In Tamvaco v. Lucas,*[47] there was a contract for the sale of a cargo of wheat afloat c.i.f. any safe port in the United Kingdom. The seller tendered to the buyer with other shipping documents a provisional invoice that estimated the cargo of wheat, calculated at 50s. a quarter, at £4,626, including the freight at £1,001 10s. The policy of insurance tendered valued the cargo at £3,600. The buyers, claimed to be entitled to reject the tender because the policy was of an insufficient amount. The Exchequer Chamber held, affirming the judgment of the Court of Queen's Bench, that it was not a question of law, but a question of fact whether, in all the circumstances, the policy was a sufficient document within the meaning of the contract; that the freight formed no part of the value to be insured; and that a deficiency of £24 10s. in the value insured after deduction of the freight from £4,626 was not so great as to justify the buyer in refusing the documents on the ground of inadequate insurance.

197   "... it is said on the part of the plaintiffs," said Cockburn C.J. in his judgment,[48] "that at all events the insurance was not to cover the freight, but only the value of the cargo, as compounded of the cost of the cargo at the place of shipment, the shipping of it, and the commissions and other charges which would be incidental to the shipping of the cargo, and also the premiums of insurance, and if the £1,001 10s. were therefore deducted, as that amount ought to be, from the sum total, that there would only remain uncovered by the policy a comparatively insignificant sum of £24 10s. The first question is, whether that is a correct view of the matter, and whether the freight ought to be deducted, as not meant to be included in the policy of insurance and covered by it. I think that is the correct view, and when we are dealing with a policy of insurance as one of the shipping documents that are to be delivered by the seller to the buyer in order to protect the buyer, that freight is not a matter that ought to be included in the terms of such an agreement, so as to be covered by the policy of insurance. . . .

"Then comes the question, whether the deficiency of £24 10s, is a matter that could fairly be objected to on the delivery of such a shipping document as this. On that part of the case, as it is presented to us, I think that our decision ought to be in favour of the plaintiffs. The contract provides for the payment by the buyers on the delivery of the shipping documents. By that I understand the ordinary and usual shipping documents, as they are understood in contracts of this nature by members of the mercantile community. The policy of insurance is undoubtedly one of these; and if the policy, instead of being such as is contemplated as an ordinary and usual shipping document, turns out substantially a defective one, and such as would not afford the buyer a reasonable protection and indemnity against risk, which he is entitled to under the terms of such a contract, and the shipping documents were accordingly rejected, and the performance of the contract resisted on that ground, I am far from saying that it would not be a sufficient ground to justify a buyer in refusing to fulfil the terms of the contract of purchase and sale. But it becomes a very different question whether the present small and comparatively insignificant deficiency may be made a mere

[47]   (1861) 30 L.J.Q.B. 234; 31 L.J.Q.B. 296.
[48]   (1861) 30 L.J.Q.B. at p. 238.

pretext for a departure from the contract, when substantial and bona fide protection is afforded to the buyers by means of the policy.''

Crompton J. said[49]:

''. . . the terms of the contract relate to the policy on the shipment—that the insurance must cover the value of the goods, and the cost of the insurance, as at the port of loading, but does not include the freight or profit at the port of discharge. The buyer buys what the seller sells, and puts himself, in effect, in his shoes. If the first man buys from the original shipper, I think he puts himself in his shoes as it were, and takes the policy from him—supposing the policy is a right policy with regard to the first shipper—and it is not determined by the supposed value of the goods that the buyer thinks them worth when they come to England. That being so, the only question would be one of fact—is this a document fairly to be taken as a shipping document, accompanying the rest of the papers, and a fair bona fide policy?''

while Blackburn J. added[50]:

''. . . I quite agree with what has fallen from the other members of the court, that the policy of insurance was not to include the freight, which was never at the risk of the defendants; for if the ship had gone down they could not have been called upon to pay this freight, and, therefore, to say that they were entitled to a policy, which in the event of the ship going down, would enable them to recover the value of the freight, which they had not paid for, would be, in my opinion, an argument *ad absurdum*. . . .''

Although the obligation to insure was there limited to the cost price of the goods in the absence of any other stipulation in the contract, it is doubtful whether this principle still prevails. Under modern conditions, the seller must generally procure a policy which (in the very least) covers the cost of forwarding charges and some element of reasonable profit. And of course there is no objection for the c.i.f. contract to provide expressly for the precise amount to be covered.

198   In *Loders & Nucoline Ltd. v. The Bank of New Zealand*,[51] there was a contract of sale of copra from Australasia at £27 5s. a ton c.i.f. London, made in writing on a form issued by the London Copra Association. The contract provided that the insurance to be taken out by the buyers should be at the contract price plus 5 per cent on the net shipping weight, and to include a ''warehouse to warehouse'' clause, the freight being payable on arrival. The goods were shipped on the *Clan MacWilliam*, which took fire at the Tonga Islands and became a total loss. The sellers tendered policies of insurance which were taken out on the total cost of the goods less the freight payable. There was a special provision whereby the policies included the freight in

---

[49] *Ibid.* at p. 241.
[50] *Ibid.* at p. 243.
[51] (1929) 33 Ll.L.Rep. 70.

the value of the goods after the freight became due, but this did not operate as the goods never arrived. The buyers refused to accept the policies of insurance. The sellers contended that even if they should have tendered to the buyers policies including the freight, the buyers had suffered no damage because the underwriters would in law have been entitled to reopen the valuation and recover the value of the freight which had never been on risk.

Wright J. found that policies ought to have been policies on the goods valued at the contract price, namely, £27 5s. per ton. As to the contention of the sellers that the buyers had suffered no damage, he held that the policy would have been a valued policy and that it was of primary importance in the law of marine insurance that the valuation in a policy should be treated as binding and conclusive. It is provided by section 27(3) of the Marine Insurance Act 1906, that in the absence of fraud the value fixed by the policy is conclusive of the insurable value, as between insurer and assured. That was also the law before the Marine Insurance Act. Wright J. then proceeded[52]:

> "In this particular case a policy on goods valued at the contract price including freight no doubt may involve a possible profit to the buyer if he obtains possession of the documents and is entitled to recover on the policy without having paid the freight, but that, I think, is merely an ordinary incident in business life. It has been pointed out many times that, though the purpose of marine insurance is to give an indemnity, the effect of a valuation may be to give much less than an indemnity. It may be that, though the insured has not had to pay the freight but has had to take the documents and therefore make a profit on the insurance to the extent of the freight, he may yet be a very heavy loser indeed, notwithstanding the profit that he has got through collecting the whole insured value under those circumstances, because the market may have risen to such an extent that he is a very heavy loser. It is an ordinary business risk, and in my opinion it is quite legitimate within the ordinary principles of marine insurance law that goods under a c.i.f. contract should be valued as this contract provides—a contract of a very well-known trade association—and I see nothing objectionable in any sense in this valuation."

Notice of shipment

199   Since the buyer under a c.i.f. contract may wish to take out at his own cost additional insurance, either to cover risks not covered by an insurance "on terms current in the trade," or to cover increased value, it would seem not unreasonable that he should be entitled to receive from the seller timely notice of shipment.[53] It seems to be settled, however, that he is not entitled to receive any such notice, unless he has expressly stipulated for it in the contract or unless there are risks not covered by the seller against which it is usual for the buyer to insure. The Sale of Goods Act 1893, s.32(3), (now section 32 of the Sale of Goods Act 1979) provided:

---

[52] *Ibid.* at p. 76.
[53] Where goods are forwarded by and agent to his principal it may be the agent's duty to insure. See *Smith v. Lascelles* (1788) 2 Term Rep. 187.

"Unless otherwise agreed, where goods are sent by the seller to the buyer by a route involving sea transit, under circumstances in which it is usual to insure, the seller must give such notice to the buyer as may enable him to insure them during their sea transit, and, if the seller fails to do so, the goods shall be deemed to be at his risk during such sea transit."

200   In the case of *Wimble v. Rosenberg*,[54] where the Court of Appeal (Vaughan Williams and Buckley L.JJ., Hamilton L.J. dissenting) held, reversing Bailhache J., that the subsection applied to f.o.b. contracts, it seems to have been conceded that it would not generally apply to c.i.f. contracts, and in the later case of *Law & Bonar Ltd. v. British American Tobacco Co. Ltd.*[55] Rowlatt J. definitely so held.[56] In that case the contract, which was made before the outbreak of the First World War, was for the sale of Calcutta hessian at a price c.i.f. Smyrna to be shipped from Calcutta in time to arrive at Smyrna by September 1914. The goods were duly shipped on the British steamer *City of Winchester*, the bill of lading being dated July 20, 1914 and an insurance was effected "f.c. and s." On August 6, two days after the declaration of war between Great Britain and Germany, the vessel was captured by a German cruiser and subsequently sunk. No notification of the shipment had been made to the buyers, and the goods were not covered against war risks. The buyers refused to take up the documents, resting their refusal in part upon the contention that it was the sellers' duty to notify them at the earliest possible moment of the name of the steamer by which the goods had been shipped and they had failed to do so. In his judgment, Rowlatt J. said[57] with regard to the subsection referred to:

"It clearly does not apply to a c.i.f. contract in times when no one contemplates war, and when, therefore, war is not being usually insured against. It does not apply because the contract c.i.f. provides for all the insurance that is contemplated or usual and the seller is to effect it. That was the nature of this contract when made. It dealt exhaustively and expressly with all the insurance that was in view. But now it is said that, on war becoming imminent, another form of insurance emerged and the contract ceased to be one which dealt exhaustively with the question of insurance and a new obligation arose for the seller. I cannot agree. This subsection annexes a term to the contract, and the question whether it is applicable or not falls to be decided as at the time when the contract is made. I say nothing as to whether the subsection could apply to a contract c.i.f. made at a time when insurances other than those to be provided by the seller— *e.g.* against war risks—are usual. That point does not arise."

201   In the case of *Re Weis & Co. & Crédit Colonial et Commercial (Antwerp)*,[58] sellers of bean oil to be shipped from the East c.i.f. to Antwerp under a contract made in June 1914 declared in July a portion of the goods

[54] [1913] 1 K.B. 279; [1913] 3 K.B. 743 (C.A.); followed in *Northern Steel & Hardware Co. v. John Batt & Co. (London) Ltd.* (1917) 33 T.L.R. 516 (C.A.); see *post*, §§662 *et seq.*
[55] [1916] 2 K.B. 605.
[56] Where the contract is c. and f. the subsection probably applies.
[57] *Ibid.* at p. 608.
[58] [1916] 1 K.B. 346.

shipped on the British steamer *Glenearn* in May. On the outbreak of war on
August 4, the *Glenearn* was seized by the Germans while at sea and taken
to Hamburg. The sellers tendered the documents, including a policy containing the f.c. and s. clause, on August 18, and the buyers refused to take
them up. Bailhache J. held that it was sufficient for the sellers to procure a
policy containing the f.c and s. clause. The buyers, in fact, had notice of the
shipment in July and, therefore, had the opportunity, if they had been so
minded, to cover themselves against war risks.

In practice, however, the absence of any obligation to give notice of shipment to the buyer probably causes little difficulty. A buyer who desires to
obtain additional protection to cover his interest may be able to do so by
means of a floating policy or open cover, followed by a declaration. But in
many contracts at the present time express provision is inserted requiring a
declaration of shipment, such as, for example, "the name of the vessel, marks
and full particulars to be declared to the buyer with due dispatch." A declaration then usually becomes a condition of the contract and its breach would
give the buyer a right to rescind the contract.[59]

Whether or not the seller can then cure a defective declaration by a subsequent notice, depends largely on the terms of the contract and the circumstances of the case. In *Aure v. Van Cauwenberghe & Fils*,[60] where the seller
made three consecutive declarations, each one being defective in one respect
or another, the Court of Appeal (Greer, Slesser and Clauson L.JJ.) held that
the third declaration, being itself invalid, could not be cured by importing
into it details from the second invalid declaration. In that case a contract for
the sale of 100 tons of palm kernels of a particular quality c.i.f. Marseilles
inter alia provided that "particulars of the kernels, namely, quantity, port of
shipment and ship's name, must be duly declared." It further provided that
"declarations made on cable advices shall be subject to the errors of the
cable companies only." Two of the seller's declarations were made subject
to telegraphic "or other errors," a qualification which he was not entitled
under the contract to add, while the third declaration omitted to mention the
port of shipment. Slesser L.J. said[61]:

> ". . . two declarations were defective in that, though they stated the port of ship-
> ment the ship's name was stated with reserve, and therefore did not comply with
> the requirements of cl. 8 [of the contract]. The third declaration was defective in
> that, while it stated the ship's name clearly and without reserve, it omitted to
> state the port of shipment, so that the declaration, therefore, taken by itself, was
> bad. I agree with the appellent to this extent, that, on the first declaration being
> bad, and therefore being no declaration, it may well be that he was entitled to

---

[59] See *Reuter v. Sala* (1879) 4 C.P.D. 246 (C.A.), *ante*, §59. See also cases dealing with terms
concerning the seller's duty to serve notice of shipment and name of vessel for purposes of
appropriation, *post* §§279 *et seq.*, whose principles it is thought would apply, *mutatis mutandis*,
if the object of the term was insurance, and delay or error frustrated the buyer from obtaining
additional cover that he may have required.
[60] [1938] 2 All E. R. 300.
[61] At p. 304.

submit a second valid declaration, but that he never did. It is now argued that he may cure the defect of the third declaration, which is the only declaration on which he can now really intend to rely, and which omits, as I have said, the port of shipment, by obtaining the port of shipment from the second invalid declaration, and by reading it into the third. Like Greer L.J., I wish to express no concluded opinion as to whether or not there may be circumstances in which it is proper to gather a declaration from one or more documents, or from documents and an oral declaration. I am clear that in this case the obligation duly to declare must require in the 'duly declare' the particulars required in cl. 8—namely, both the port of shipment and the ship's name must be supplied, and in no single declaration which has been produced are both those requirements satisfied.''

Insurance confined to goods sold

202   Just as the bill of lading must be confined to goods which are the subject-matter of the sale, so the insurance must cover only the goods mentioned in the bills of lading and invoices[62]; otherwise, the buyer would be only one of those interested in the insurance, and the rights on the policy might become so involved that neither the policy nor the goods insured by it could be safely dealt with.[63]

> ''These documents have to be handled by banks, they have to be taken up or rejected promptly and without any opportunity for prolonged inquiry, they have to be such as can be retendered to sub-purchasers, and it is essential that they should so conform to the accustomed shipping documents as to be reasonably and readily fit to pass current in commerce.''[64]

In *Hickox v. Adams*,[65] sellers at New York of 1,000 quarters of wheat c.i.f. Bristol by mistake shipped a cargo of 2,000 quarters to a third party, Kruger & Co., at Bristol, and forwarded them a bill of lading and a policy of insurance for the entire quantity shipped, and drew upon them for the price. When the mistake was discovered, and while the goods were still afloat, the sellers told the buyers of it, and that Kruger & Co. would deliver to them (the buyers) 1,000 quarters of wheat and present a draft for the price. The buyers refused to accept. It was held (Lord Cairns L.C., Lord Coleridge C.J., and Mellish L.J.) that assuming that Kruger & Co. had been willing to hand over the policy to the buyers, the latter would not have been in the same position as if they had had a separate policy, and their refusal was justified.

As has been already explained, a modern c.i.f. contract will probably provide for a certificate in place of a policy of insurance, the convenience of a separate policy being sacrificed to the expediency of an open or floating policy.

---

[62] See *Manbre Saccharine Co. Ltd. v. Corn Products Co. Ltd.* [1919] 1 K.B. 198; see *post*, § 208.

[63] See *per* Turner L.J., *Ralli v. Universal Marine Ins. Co.* (1862) 6 L.T. 34 at p. 37; *per* McCardie J., *Manbre Saccharine Co. v. Corn Products Co.* [1919] 1 K.B. 198 at p. 205.

[64] *Per* Lord Sumner. *Hansson v. Hamel & Horley Ltd.* [1922] 2 A.C. 36 at p. 46.

[65] (1876) 34 L.T. 404.

Must cover entire transit

203   The insurance must cover the whole transit contemplated; otherwise the buyer will not receive the protection he has contracted to get. The buyer "wants a policy covering the whole adventure."[66]

In *Belgian Grain and Produce Co.* v. *Cox & Co. Ltd.*[67] the sale was of Japanese green peas to be shipped from Japan c.i.f. to Marseilles, direct or indirect, with or without transhipments, buyers to furnish an irrevocable letter of credit in favour of the sellers. The defendant bank, on the buyer's instructions, open a documentary credit in favour of the sellers against surrender of the documents on the arrival of the steamer. In due course, the sellers tendered the documents to the defendants, but they refused to pay on the ground that whereas the policy covered the peas on the S.S. *Kassado Maru* and S.S. *Koyei Maru*, the peas arrived in the *SS. Saigon Maru*. The facts were that the peas were loaded on the *Koyei Maru*, and were transhipped into the *Kassado Maru* and thereafter transhipped into the *Saigon Maru* under rights reserved by the bill of lading. The policy of insurance, however, contained the clause "including all liberties as per contract of affreightment," and the Court of Appeal (Bankes, Warrington and Scrutton L.JJ.) held that the clause in the policy included the rights reserved by the bill of lading, and the policy was therefore sufficient.

204   In *Lascelles & Co. Ltd v. George Wills & Co. Ltd.*[68] a New South Wales decision, the court had to consider, *inter alia*, whether a certificate of insurance that contained no indication of the terms of the cover was a valid tender. The contract was for sale of goods shipped from New York c.i.f. and e. Sydney. The vessel called at several ports in New Zealand as well as Melbourne before arrival at Sydney. The buyer, who refused to accept a draft for the price, alleged that he committed no breach because, in addition to some other reasons, the certificate did not permit any deviation such as was undertaken by the vessel in the present instance, which, he argued, would have been sufficient to vitiate any claim under the policy. The argument failed. The court held that the defendant had agreed by the contract to accept a certificate of insurance in lieu of an actual policy and the plaintiffs, having given an express guarantee that the cover represented by the certificate covered the goods on the actual voyage between New York and Sydney, were entitled to their claim.

"Warehouse to warehouse" clause

205   Under the old standard Lloyd's policy, the insurance only covered the goods against the perils of the sea. The insurance therefore started when the

---

[66] *Per* Scrutton J., *Landauer & Co.* v. *Craven & Speeding Bros.* [1912] 2 K.B. 94 at p. 105; but see *Plaimar Ltd.* v. *Waters Trading Co. Ltd.* (1945) 72 C.L.R. 304 (Australia), *ante*, 184.
[67] [1919] W.N. 308 (C.A.).
[68] (1921) 21 S.R. (N.S.W.) 773.

goods were loaded on board ship and the risk ceased the moment the goods were landed. This cover was inadequate to protect the goods during their movement on shore before loading at the port of departure and after landing at the port of arrival. It therefore became customary for a clause to be inserted in Lloyd's policies covering the goods from the time they left the warehouse of the consignor until their arrival at the warehouse of the consignee. This is known as the "warehouse to warehouse" clause. So common is this that it was held as early as 1900 that insurance on the "usual Lloyd's conditions" included the "warehouse to warehouse" clause.

In the case of *Ide and Christie v. Chalmers and White*,[69] the plaintiffs sold to the defendants 250 bales of jute to be shipped from Calcutta to Dundee. The contract was on the printed form issued by the London Jute Association and provided that the goods should be insured on "usual Lloyd's conditions." Insurances were effected which covered the goods until delivered to any wharf or warehouse within the limits of the port. While the jute was lying in a shed on the wharf at Dundee, a fire occurred and the jute was damaged. The buyers claimed that the goods not being covered were not properly insured, and Kennedy J. upheld this contention. He found that the "warehouse to warehouse" clause was a usual and customary clause obtained at Lloyd's without any special terms in this class of business, and that under such a Lloyd's clause the goods would be covered until they reached the warehouse of the consignee and not, as in this case, merely any wharf or warehouse within the limits of the port.[70]

The form of "warehouse to warehouse" clause varies from time to time, the current clause being one which covers the goods from the time the goods leave the warehouse at the place named in the policy for commencement of the transit until delivery to final warehouse at the destination named in the policy, provided that in no case shall the period of cover after completion of discharge overside of the ship extend beyond 60 days.

Insurable interest

206   Where the goods are damaged before shipment, the c.i.f. buyer may sue on the policy, provided it has been assigned to him, although he has no insurable interest in the goods at the time. This was held in *J. Aron and Co. (Incorporated) v. Miall*,[71] where a quantity of cocoa, which was covered from the time of leaving its original warehouse in the African interior until delivery at a warehouse in Boston, was ultimately resold to the plaintiffs under a c.i.f. contract. The cocoa was in fact damaged before shipment, and the under-

---

[69] (1900) 5 Com. Cas. 212.
[70] See also *John Martin of London Ltd. v. Russell* [1960] 1 Lloyd's Rep. 554, where Pearson J. held that goods damaged in a transit shed at Liverpool were at the time insured under a "warehouse to warehouse" cover, since the shed was not deemed to be a "final warehouse," delivery to which would have terminated the cover.
[71] (1928) 34 Com. Cas. 18.

writers declined a claim under the policy on the ground that at the time when the goods were damaged the plaintiffs had no insurable interest in them. The Court of Appeal (Scrutton, Greer and Sankey L.JJ.), affirming a decision by Roche J., held that by assignment of the policy, the assignee became entitled to sue on any claim of the assignor, whether or not he had an interest in the subject-matter insured at the time of the loss. The plaintiffs therefore were entitled to recover. The question as to whether the proceeds or any part thereof are to be held for the benefit of the assignor is to be determined as between the assignee and the assignor, and was of no concern to the underwriter.

The c.i.f. seller, on the other hand, having no insurable interest in the goods subsequent to their shipment, was denied a right to claim under a special policy issued pursuant to an open cover by the United States Court of Appeals for the Fifth Circuit in *York-Shipley Inc. v. Atlantic Mutual Insurance Co. et al.*[72] There a boiler was damaged while in transit from Miami to Guatemala. The sellers held an open cargo policy issued by the respondent company covering all their international shipments and permitting them to issue special policies when selling on terms which require them to obtain insurance for the benefit of customers abroad. The sellers who sold the boiler in question (and one other boiler that was not damaged) on c.i.f. terms issued such a special policy in the instant case. But their right to sue on this policy was denied. The court stated that once the sellers:

> "put the boilers in the possession of the carrier in Miami, [They] no longer had any interest in them. Indeed, [they were] prohibited from tendering the goods instead of the appropriate documents. [They] therefore [had] no insurable interest in the cargo and, consequently, ... no standing to sue ... *York-Shipley* has no interest in the outcome of this suit, other than that of an unsecured creditor of its foreign customer. Such an interest is insufficient to meet the requisites of standing."

Insurance is always required

207   The insurance must be contained in a policy capable of being assigned to the buyer, unless it is otherwise provided by the contract of sale,[73] and the policy must be tendered to the buyer with the other documents on presentation.[74] Failure to include marine insurance among the c.i.f. documents tendered to the buyer is fatal to a claim of performance of the contract, and the buyer may refuse to accept the goods even though they have arrived safely at their destination before presentation of the documents. Thus, in *Orient Co. Ltd. v. Brekke and Howlid*,[75] goods were shipped under a c.i.f. contract at

---

[72] 474 F. 2d 8 (1973).

[73] See, *e.g. Burstall* v. *Grimsdale* (1906) 11 Com.Cas. 280.

[74] See *Ireland* v. *Livingston* (1872) L.R. 5 H.L. 395 at p. 406; *Biddell Bros.* v. *E. Clemens Horst Co.* [1911] 1 K.B. 214 at p. 220; and *post*, Chap. 5, § 261.

[75] [1913] 1 K.B. 531.

Bordeaux for Hull, and a bill of lading and an invoice were sent to the buyers, but no insurance of the goods from Bordeaux to Hull was ever effected. The goods arrived safely at Hull, but the buyers refused to accept them. The sellers sued for the price, and the buyers set up the defence that, no insurance having been effected, the contract had not been fulfilled. Lush and Rowlatt JJ. held that the sellers, having failed to fulfil an essential condition of the contract by not effecting an insurance, were not in a position to sue for non-acceptance.

In *Denbigh, Cowan & Co. v. Atcherley & Co.*,[76] by a contract expressed to be c.i.f., sellers sold to buyers tapioca to be shipped at Java for Liverpool "to be taken on c.i.f. terms . . . payment cash (before delivery, if required) against documents or *delivery order.*" When the tapioca arrived, the sellers tendered to the buyers a delivery order, but no insurance policy. The buyers refused to take delivery on the ground that there was no insurance policy. The sellers, on the other hand, contended that under the contract they had an option of treating the contract either as a c.i.f. contract or as an "arrival" contract, that is, of either indorsing the usual shipping documents, or, in the first instance, a delivery order only. It was held by the Court of Appeal (Bankes, Scrutton and Atkin L.JJ.), on the construction of the contract, that the buyers were entitled to receive either all the documents under a c.i.f. contract or a delivery order "in lieu of one of those documents necessary for giving possession of the goods," *i.e.* the bill of lading, and that consequently the buyers were justified in refusing to take delivery without a policy of insurance.[77]

208 In *Manbre Saccharine Co. Ltd. v. Corn Products Co. Ltd.*,[78] the sellers, instead of tendering a policy of insurance, wrote to the buyers stating that they held them covered by insurance "for the amount of £4,322 in accordance with the terms of policy of insurance in our possession *re* shipment ex S.S. *Algonquin.*" The insurance covered a quantity of goods in addition to the goods which were the subject-matter of the sale. The sellers contended that by this letter they had discharged their obligations. They argued that a seller's duty under a c.i.f. contract had been modified by recent practice amongst business men; but an attempt to prove a general custom modifying the seller's obligation to tender a policy was abandoned, and they failed to show any usage or practice between the parties themselves involving the buyers in an obligation to accept the letter in place of an actual policy of insurance. In the course of his judgment, McCardie J. said[79]:

> "It was suggested on behalf of the plaintiffs that the letter amounted either to an equitable assignment of the insurance moneys to the extent of £4,322 or to a declaration of trust to such amount in respect of these moneys. Even if this suggestion be well founded, yet there is a wide difference between an actual

---

[76] (1921) 90 L.J.K.B. 836 (C.A.). See *ante*, § 12 Compoe *The Julia* [1949] A.C. 293 *Ante*, § 17.
[77] See also *Harper et al.* v. *Hochstim et al.* 278 Fed. R. 102 (1921) (US), *post*, § 221.
[78] [1919] 1 K.B. 198.
[79] *Ibid.* at p. 205.

policy of insurance transferable to the defendants as contemplated by section 50, sub. s.3 of the Marine Insurance Act 1906,[80] and such a letter as that of the defendants here. The plaintiffs, I hold, were clearly entitled to a policy and not to a mere assertion by the defendants that a policy existed and that the defendants would hold the plaintiffs covered.''

209   In *Wilson, Holgate & Co. v. Belgian Grain and Produce Co. Ltd.*,[81] where the sellers instructed their brokers to insure the goods sold for the amount of the contract price, and the brokers wrote to the buyers stating that they had effected the insurance for that amount and enclosed the broker's cover note therefor, evidence was tendered on behalf of the sellers that a custom had arisen according to which the seller might tender a broker's note instead of a policy, but Bailhache J. held that the proof of the alleged custom was insufficient. He said[82]:

> "The only question I have to decide is whether or not there was an effective legal tender of the shipping documents by the plaintiffs which the defendants were bound to accept. It has been settled, at any rate since Blackburn J. delivered his well-known judgment in *Ireland v. Livingston*[83] about 47 years ago, and it had apparently been settled even earlier, that under a c.i.f. contract for the sale of goods the documents which the seller is bound to tender to the buyer are a bill of lading, an invoice and a policy of insurance, and it is well understood that under a contract of that kind these are the documents which the seller is required to tender.''

He then referred to the evidence of witnesses who had stated that it was the common practice now for sellers to tender, instead of a policy of insurance, a broker's cover note or a certificate of insurance, and continued:

> "A certificate of insurance is generally, but not always used in a case where the goods which are the subject-matter of the sale are insured by an open or a floating policy, which covers other goods as well as the particular goods in question, and is for a larger amount than if it covered these goods only. One of the witnesses, Mr. Matheson, says that the certificate of insurance is also used to take the place of a broker's cover note. It must be borne in mind that, in dealing with certificates of insurance, I am not referring to American certificates of insurance which stand on a different footing and are equivalent to policies, being accepted in this country as policies.[84] I am now dealing only with brokers' cover notes and certificates of insurance as issued by brokers in this country. The plaintiffs' witnesses have stated that these brokers' cover notes and certificates of insurance are constantly accepted by buyers in place of policies of insurance. . . . These witnesses, however, could give no instance in which there has been any contest as to the validity of a tender of a cover note or certificate, still less did they give any instance in which on a buyer's demand for and insistence upon a policy being resisted, he has given way. On the contrary, these witnesses were all very careful to explain that they were not prepared to say that the buyer was bound to take a cover note

---

[80] "A marine policy may be assigned by endorsement thereon or in other customary manner."
[81] [1920] 2 K.B. 1.
[82] *Ibid.* at p. 7.
[83] (1872) L.R. 5 H.L. 395, at p. 406, *ante.* § 5.
[84] But see, as to this, *post*, §210.

or certificate of insurance instead of a policy of insurance. All that they could say was that so far as they knew these cover notes and certificates were constantly taken and never refused. The true position appears to me to be this: the seller must be prepared to deliver and if required to do so must deliver a policy of insurance, but in order to facilitate business, particularly during the war when there was a shortage of clerks and a superabundance of business, commercial men have resorted to this practice of not insisting upon their strict right to a policy, and have been taking these cover notes and certificates of insurance.

"I am not satisfied that since *Ireland v. Livingston* was decided any custom has arisen which obviates the necessity for a tender by the seller of a policy of insurance if the buyer requires it. There are of course obvious differences between the buyer's position under a policy of insurance and his position under a broker's cover note or a certificate of insurance, I will mention only one or two of these. On a policy of insurance which deals with the buyer's own contractual goods and with those of nobody else, the buyer has a direct right of action on the policy against the underwriters. On a broker's cover note he has apparently no right of action against anybody, even, I am inclined to think, where the cover note is indorsed. The broker I should suppose is liable to his own principal. Moreover a right of action against a broker even if it exists is a very different right from that of an action against underwriters. The same observation applies to a certificate of insurance. So far as the broker's cover note is concerned, and, possibly also, so far as a certificate of insurance is concerned, the buyer might also be faced with a further serious difficulty arising from the assertion by the broker of his general lien for his charges against the person who instructed him to take up the policies, and on whose behalf he issued his cover note or his certificate of insurance. These are some of the practical differences between a policy of insurance on the one hand and a cover note or a certificate of insurance on the other. In my judgment it has not been proved that under a c.i.f. contract the buyer is bound to take any other document than a policy of insurance. He has, as I understand it, a legal right to require a policy, and a policy which relates to the goods which are the subject-matter of his own contract of sale and to no other goods."

Certificates of insurance

210   Where the certificate of insurance is merely a statement of fact that there is an insurance policy in existence, there is no doubt from the cases already discussed, that such a certificate cannot be a good tender under a c.i.f. contract unless the contract specifically so provides. The practice has grown up, however, of issuing a certificate which is something more than a bare statement of fact. Indeed, this practice is now expressly sanctioned by American law. By section 2–320(2)(c) of the Uniform Commercial Code, the c.i.f. seller is authorised to obtain a policy "or certificate of insurance, including any war risk insurance, of a kind and on terms then current at the port of shipment in the usual amount, in the currency of the contract, shown to cover the same goods covered by the bill of lading and providing for payment of loss to the order of the buyer or for the account of whom it may concern. . . ." The certificate herein referred to is a document which is expressed to convey rights to the holder, a common form being "This certificate represents and takes the place of the policy and conveys all the rights of the original policy holder as fully as if the property was covered by a special policy direct to the holder of this certificate.'' When these certificates are sent to the United Kingdom, there is very often a provision that they shall be stamped as if there were a policy of insurance.

A certificate in this form is usually not a complete policy, and it must be read in conjunction with the policy of insurance to which it refers. The underwriters may be sued on these certificates,[85] even by an assignee,[86] and such certificates probably constitute a good tender under a c.i.f. contract nowadays. It is to be noted, however, that in all the cases referred to later, the certificates were rejected as a good tender, and Scrutton L.J. remarked in *Koskas v. Standard Marine Insurance Co. Ltd.,*[87] that he regarded that case as ''a justification of the ruling of the English law that a certificate of insurance cannot be tendered as a policy of insurance to satisfy a c.i.f. contract.''

211   In *Diamond Alkali Export Corporation v. Fl. Bourgeoise,*[88] the sellers of soda ash to be shipped from American seaboard c.i.f. Gothenburg tendered with other documents a certificate of insurance issued by an American insurance corporation, the substantive words of which were as follows:

"This is to certify that on the 8th of November, 1920, this Company insured under policy No. 2,319 for D. A. Horan $5,790 on 280 bags 58 per cent. dense soda ash N.L. & Y. Test, valued at sum insured. Shipped on board of the S.S. *Anglia* and/or other steamer or steamers at and from Philadelphia to Gothenburg. And it is hereby understood and agreed that, in case of loss, such loss is payable to the order of the assured on surrender of this certificate. This certificate represents and takes the place of the policy and conveys all the rights of the original policy holder ... as fully as if the property was covered by a special policy direct to the holder of his certificate. ..."

The buyers contended that the tender of this certificate was not a good tender under a c.i.f. contract, and McCardie J. upheld their contention. In the course of his judgment he said[89]:

"In all the cases a 'policy of insurance' is mentioned as an essential document. The law is settled and established. I may point out that in *Burstall v. Grimsdale*[90] it was expressly provided by the contract that a certificate of insurance might be an alternative for an actual policy. I ventured in *Manbre Saccharine Co. v. Corn Products Co.*[91] to discuss the relevant authorities, including the lucid judgment of Atkin J. in *C. Groom Ltd. v. Barber*[92]—a judgment which I have again most carefully read. It seems plain that a mere written statement by the sellers that

[85] *Koskas v. Standard Marine Insurance Co. Ltd.* (1927) 32 Com. Cas. 160.
[86] *De Monchy v. Phoenix Insurance Co. of Hartford* (1928) 33 Com. Cas. 197.
[87] (1927) 32 Com. Cas. 160.
[88] [1921] 3 K.B. 443.
[89] *Ibid.* at p. 454.
[90] (1906) 11 Com.Cas. 280.
[91] [1919] 1 K.B. 198, *ante,* § 208.
[92] [1915] 1 K.B. 316, *post,* § 252.

they hold the buyers covered by insurance in respect of a specified policy of insurance is not itself a policy of insurance within a c.i.f. contract: see the *Manbre Saccharine Case*. It seems plain also that a broker's cover note or an ordinary certificate of insurance are not adequate agreements within such a contract: see Bailhache J. in *Wilson, Holgate & Co. v. Belgian Grain and Produce Co.*[93]

"Does the present document fulfil the seller's contractual duty? In *Wilson, Holgate & Co.'s Case* Bailhache J. said: 'It must be borne in mind that, in dealing with certificates of insurance, I am not referring to American certificates of insurance which stand on a different footing and are equivalent to policies, being accepted in this country as policies.' It will be observed that Bailhache J. used the word 'accepted,' he does not say that buyers are 'bound to accept' them. . . . I assume that this document (which is not stamped) was given under a floating policy issued by the insurance company to D. A. Horan. Now the certificate is not a policy. It does not purport to be a policy. This is conceded by Mr. Hastings in his able argument for the sellers. It is a certificate that a policy was issued to D. A. Horan, and it incorporates the terms of that policy. Those terms I do not know, nor is there anything before me to indicate that the buyers knew them. The certificate does not show whether that policy was in a recognised or usual form or not. The certificate does not therefore contain all the terms of the insurance. Those terms have to be sought for in two documents—namely, the original policy and the certificate. But even if this document is not a policy yet the sellers say it is 'equivalent to a policy.' In connection with that phrase it is well to quote from another part of the judgment of Bailhache J. in *Wilson, Holgate & Co.'s Case*. He there says: 'He'—the buyer—'cannot be compelled to take a document which is something like that which he has agreed to take. He is entitled to have a document of the very kind which he has agreed to take, or at least one which does not differ from it in any material respect.' This leads me to ask whether the document before me differs in any material respect from a policy of insurance. To begin with, I do not see how the buyer here could know whether the document he got was of a proper character (one he was bound to accept) unless he saw the original policy, and examined its conditions, whether usual or otherwise. In the next place I feel that a certificate of insurance falls within a legal classification, if any, different to that of a policy of insurance. The latter is a well-known document with clearly defined features. It comes within definite, established and statutory legal rights. A certificate, however, is an ambiguous thing; it is unclassified and undefined by law; it is not even mentioned by *Arnould on Marine Insurance*.[94] No rules have been laid upon it. Would the buyer sue upon the certificate or upon the original policy plus a certificate? If he sued simply on the certificate he could put in a part only of the contract, for the other term of the contract—namely, the conditions of the actual policy—would be contained in a document not in his control and to the possession of which he is not entitled. Thirdly, I point out that before the buyer could sue at all he would have to show that he was the assignee of the certificate: see Arnould (9th ed.), ss. 175–177.[95] In what way can he become the assignee? It is vital to remember the provisions of the Marine Insurance Act, 1906. Now the relevant statutory provision is section 50(3), which says: 'A marine policy may be assigned by endorsement thereon or in other customary manner.' This subsection, however, only applies, as far as I can see, to that which is an actual marine policy. Section 90, the interpretation clause, says: 'In this Act unless the context or subject matter otherwise requires,—"policy" means a marine policy.' The Act contains

---

[93] [1920] 2 K.B. 1 at p. 7, *ante*, § 209.
[94] *British Shipping Laws.*
[95] See now 16th ed., ss. 253–255.

no reference, express or implied, to a certificate of insurance. Section 22 says: 'Subject to the provisions of any statute, a contract of marine insurance is inadmissible in evidence unless it is embodied in a marine policy in accordance with this Act.' If, as is admitted, this document be a certificate only and not a policy, it therefore seems not even to be admissible in evidence before me. If the certificate does not fall within the Marine Insurance Act it appears to be only assignable if at all by writing in accordance with the provisions of the Judicature Act 1873, s. 25(6). The certificate may have less legal effect than a slip, as to which see Arnould, s. 34,[96] and the Marine Insurance Act, 1906, s. 21.

"I mention these considerations briefly. Time does not permit to discuss them further and to develop their significance, or to emphasise the points arising under sections 91–95 of the Stamp Act, 1891. In my view the Act of 1906 deals with marine policies only. It does not, I think, cover other documents although they may be said to be the 'business equivalent' of policies. I do not think that the Act of 1906 covers the document now before me. In my humble view a document of insurance is not a good tender in England under an ordinary c.i.f. contract unless it be an actual policy and unless it falls within the provisions of the Marine Insurance Act, 1906, as to assignment and otherwise. . . . It may well be that this decision is disturbing to business men. It is my duty, however, to state my view of the law without regard to mere questions of convenience. I desire to add four remarks:

(1) That there is no finding or evidence before me of any course of dealing between the parties.

(2) That there is no finding or evidence before me of any custom or rights of a buyer under a c.i.f. contract. If any such custom or usage be asserted, then the point can be dealt with in some future action in the Commercial Court. Whether such an assertion can be proved may well be a question of doubt in view of the matters appearing in the *Manbre Saccharine Case*[97]: see, too, *Wilson v. Holgate & Co.'s Case*,[98] where Bailhache J. said: 'I am not satisfied that since *Ireland v. Livingston* was decided any custom has arisen which obviates the necessity for a tender by the seller of a policy of insurance if the buyer requires it.'

(3) It may [well be] that legislation is needed to enlarge the operation of . . . the Marine Insurance Act, 1906.

(4) It may well be also that the greater part of the difficulties indicated in this judgment can be easily, promptly and effectively met by the insertion of appropriate clauses in c.i.f. contracts.''

212   In *Donald H. Scott & Co. Ltd. v. Barclays Bank Ltd.*[99] a Dutch firm bought from an English firm a quantity of ship's plates c.i.f. Rotterdam. Payment was to be made by the buyers opening a banker's credit in favour of the sellers in London. The buyers opened a credit with Barclays Bank in London, and the latter notified the sellers that they were prepared to honour the sellers' drafts upon terms specified, which included the requirement that the sellers should present "an *approved insurance policy* covering a shipment including war risk." The sellers tendered an American certificate of insurance. It was a certificate of the Firemen's Fund Insurance Company, and was stated on

---

[96] 16th ed.
[97] [1919] 1 K.B. 198 at p. 216, *ante*, § 208.
[98] [1920] 2 K.B. 1 at p. 8, *ante*, § 209.
[99] [1923] 2 K.B. 1 (C.A.).

the face of it to represent and take the place of the policy. It was expressed to be "subject to the full terms of the policy in respect of being free from claim in respect of capture, seizure, detention or the consequence of hostilities. . . ." "This certificate is hereby extended to cover war risk in accordance with the terms, valuations and conditions of open policy and war risk indorsement attached hereto" . . . "shipped on board S.S. *Capulin* and/ or subsequent steamers (as per conditions of policy)." The bank declined to honour the drafts against this certificate, and for their refusal to do so the sellers brought an action for damages. Sankey J. held that the certificate amounted to an approved insurance policy within the meaning of the contract between the sellers and the bank, but his decision was reversed by the Court of Appeal (Bankes, Scrutton and Atkin L.JJ.), where it was held that a certificate of insurance which did not state the terms of the insurance was not an approved policy within the terms of the credit. The court approved the decisions in *Wilson, Holgate & Co. v. Belgian Grain and Produce Co. Ltd. (ante),* and *Diamond Alkali Export Corporation v. Fl. Bourgeois (ante).* With regard, however, to Bailhache J.'s statement in the former case that American certificates of insurance are equivalent to policies, and are accepted in this country as policies, very guarded opinions were expressed. Bankes L.J. said[1]:

> "What form of American certificate the learned judge had in mind at the time he made that statement I do not know. It may be that he had in mind a form of certificate which contains all the essential terms which are required to constitute a good policy of marine insurance according to English law; if he had it may well be that such a document as that is the exact equivalent of a policy of insurance expressed according to English form. I myself express no opinion upon it, but I think that the learned judge's view must not be accepted as a view which covers American certificates of insurance in whatever form they are expressed."

With regard to the certificate in question, he said[2]:

> "Now all that is indicated by that certificate is that a policy has been issued, but what the terms of that policy are, what the risks covered are, what the conditions of the policy with reference to shipment are, it is impossible to ascertain. Those things can only be ascertained by the production of some document which did not accompany the certificate and as to the terms of which the bank must be and remain perfectly ignorant."

He approved and applied the language of McCardie J. in *Diamond Alkali Export Corporation v. Fl. Bourgeois*:

> ". . . I do not see how the buyer here could know whether the document he got was of a proper character (one he was bound to accept) unless he saw the original policy and examined its conditions, whether usual or otherwise";

but he reserved his opinion on the question discussed by McCardie J. in the

---

[1] (1923) 28 Com.Cas. 253 (C.A.) at p. 257.
[2] *Ibid.* at p. 258.

extract from his judgment above set out, whether the certificate complied with the English law in reference to marine policies.

213   Scrutton L.J. said[3]:

> "Now the point on which I propose to decide this case is whether Messrs. Scott tendered an approved insurance policy. I take the meaning of that to be the same as the meaning which has been given to 'approved bill,' which has substantially been defined by Lord Ellenborough in *Hodgson v. Davies*[4] as a bill to which no reasonable commercial objection can be taken, and which therefore ought to be approved. I take 'approved policy' to have the same reasonable meaning; that the policy tendered must be one to which no reasonable commercial objection can be taken and which therefore ought to be approved.
>
> Now what was tendered in this case was a document called an American certificate. I am not deciding that all American certificates are a bad tender."

He then referred to the terms of the certificate, and continued:

> "The result is that when this document is tendered to the bank they cannot tell by reading it what are the terms of insurance which they are offered. In my view they have a right to see a document or documents which contain the terms of the insurance which is offered to them as security for the loss of the goods, and if the document tendered to them does not show them what the terms of that insurance are, they are from a commercial point of view reasonable in refusing to approve it or accept it as a policy. . . . I am not deciding that a certificate which does show all the terms of the insurance and which can be sued on in the United States is a bad tender."

214   Atkin L.J. stated that an "approved policy means a policy such that no reasonable objection could be taken to it by commercial men," and proceeded to say[5]:

> ". . . upon that footing it appears to me that it is in every sense a reasonable objection to a document which comes masquerading as a policy to say, 'This is not a policy at all and does not purport to be one; it purports to certify that a policy has been issued.' That is a good objection to such a document; and then you have the further fact that the so-called policy does not contain on the face of it the terms of the actual contract of insurance. It does not contain the risks against which the insuring company purport to insure the assured, and indeed it contains no means of ascertaining what terms of insurance are except by reference to a document which is not produced and is not within the convenient reference of the person to whom the certificate is produced. Even if the terms were within easy reference I am far from saying that that in itself would prevent the objection from being a valid one. But as it is, inasmuch as a bank who do rely upon the policy of insurance to cover them against loss in case they have no recourse against the customer who has asked them to give the credit have no

---

[3] *Ibid.* at p. 261.
[4] (1810) 2 Camp. 530. In *Ralli v. Universal Marine Ins. Co.* (1862) 31 L.J.Ch. 313, the expression was "policies of insurance effected with approved underwriters, but for whose solvency the sellers are not to be responsible."
[5] Com. Cas. at p. 264.

means of ascertaining to what extent they really are covered by the policy, it seems to me to be a perfectly valid and reasonable objection. I agree therefore that upon that ground the documents were rightly rejected.''

215   In *Malmberg v. H. J. Evans & Co.*[6] the document tendered by the Swedish seller purported to be a Swedish policy of insurance. It did not specify the risks insured against, but it purported to insure ''against all and every risk for which the said Insurance Company shall be liable pursuant to the maritime laws in force, the conditions and clauses of its policy of insurance, and the rules of the said insurance company,'' and a marginal note stated that ''to conform with the Revenue laws of Great Britain, in order to collect a claim under this policy it must be stamped within ten days after its receipt in the United Kingdom.'' Bailhache J. decided that the document tendered was not an effective policy, because it did not set out the risks insured against and there was nothing in the course of dealing between the parties to prevent the buyers taking exception to it. ''Anyone looking at this policy could not find out without a great deal of research as to the maritime laws of Sweden and an examination of all sorts of documents what the risks undertaken by the insurers really were.'' But the Court of Appeal declined to consider the question of the validity of the document as a policy in view of an admission in the court below that the document would not have been a valid policy apart from special circumstances created by the course of dealing between the parties. Scrutton L.J., however, in the course of his judgment, said[7]:

> ''A course of business is growing up, has grown up in some countries, I think partly with regard to America and as appears in this case with regard to Sweden, by which mercantile men, instead of passing on the policy, desire to pass on a document which is a certificate that there is a policy, the policy not being handed over. That is the American form. It is quite easy for them, if they will only take the trouble, to insert in their contracts when referring to shipping documents, 'policy to be a certificate,' or some other such words as meet the case; but they do not do it.''

And later, after expressly reserving for future consideration the question whether the document in the form presented in that case was or was not a good tender as a policy apart from commercial usage or custom, he said[8]:

> ''It is quite obvious at once on looking at the form of the document in *Scott v. Barclays Bank*,[9] which is a decision of this court, that this Fylgia document is a very different document from the American certificate which was tendered in that case. The American certificate was simply a statement: 'This is to certify that there is a policy': conditions not stated. This is a document professing to be a policy, which the certificate did no profess to be . . . I am not deciding anything as to what I should do with this policy if there was not an admission; but it

---

[6] (1924) 29 Com. Cas. 235; 30 Com. Cas. 107 (C.A.).
[7] 30 Com. Cas. at p. 112.
[8] *Ibid* at p. 113.
[9] *Ante*, § 212.

seems to me quite obvious that a thing does not necessarily cease to be a policy because it incorporates another document which is not produced. I take it a Lloyd's policy incorporating Institute clauses, without setting them out in full, would not cease to be a policy because you did not see on the face of the policy what the Institute clauses were.''

216   In *John Martin of London Ltd. v. A. E. Taylor & Co. Ltd.*,[10] a contract for the sale of 2,250 cases of minced meat loaf shipped from Australia c.i.f. London gave the seller the option of tendering "Insurance policy/certificate and/or indemnity in lieu thereof.'' The seller tendered a document in the following terms:

> "We confirm that the above goods are covered against 'marine and war risks' and that we hold the relative insurance policy for 10 per cent. above the value of our invoice to you. We therefore indemnify you from any consequences which may arise due to your accepting these documents without a policy of insurance.''

Lord Goddard C.J. was satisfied that the tender of this document, which was designed to enable the sellers to ship goods to a variety of consignees under one single cover without having to go to the trouble of issuing a great number of separate policies, complied with the terms of the contract. With reference to the obligation to tender an insurance policy under a c.i.f. contract which includes no particular stipulation, the learned judge said as follows:

> "... no one denies that had this been an ordinary c.i.f. contract without this special clause the cases make it perfectly clear that the sellers would have had to tender a policy of insurance which insured these goods only.[11] There is no question about that. . . . As I say, therefore, if this had been an ordinary c.i.f. contract—by which I mean if the terms had simply been 'c.i.f.'—there is no doubt that a proper policy would have had to be tendered and that any documents which might be said, in some respects, to be as good as a policy, or in substitution for a policy, would have been a bad tender. But one knows that business men who carry on business in a certain way, using certain methods, and then find that those methods are not in accordance with the strict law as laid down by the courts, very soon find ways of getting round or avoiding the decisions which have been given by altering their contracts. That is not only a perfectly legitimate thing to do, but it is the way that the law merchant to some extent has been raised. The law has always followed the mercantile practice because it has to follow it before it can incorporate it into the law merchant, and if the direct application of the law merchant at any particular time is found inconvenient by business men, they alter their documents so that the particular decision no longer applies to them'' (at p. 593).

In *Forbex Corporation v. Madesr*,[12] the High Court of Barbados followed both *Donald H. Scott & Co. Ltd. v. Barclay's Bank Limited* and *Wilson, Holgate & Co. v. Belgian Grain and Produce Co. Ltd.* On March 13, 1969 the defendants ordered a quantity of upholstery materials from the plaintiff,

---

[10] [1953] 2 Lloyd's Rep. 589.
[11] *Ante*, §§ 202 *et seq.*
[12] (1976) 27 W.I.R. 49.

an American company doing business in New York. On April 18, 1969 the plaintiff acknowledged receipt of the order and advised that shipment would be made at the earliest possible time. On May 16, 1969 the plaintiff advised the defendants in writing that the order had been shipped stating that the following documents were enclosed: a commercial invoice, the amount of invoice, a bill of lading, an insurance certificate and a consular notice. The insurance certificate was not in fact enclosed but the letter contained instructions as to the documents to be sent to the consignors in the event that a claim had to be made in respect of any loss or damage to the goods in transit. There was also on the face of the invoice a notation—"This shipment is insured under our Marine and War Risk Open Policy No. 509 with the Great American Insurance Company against all risks of physical loss or damage from any external cause irrespective of percentage including war, strikes, riots and civil commotions at an insured value of c.i.f. plus 10 per cent." The insurance certificate did not reach the defendants until September 1970. The issue was whether the notation on the invoice together with the instructions contained in the letter of May 16, 1969 constituted a sufficient compliance with the seller's stipulations under a c.i.f. contract. The Court held it did not. Following the two above cited cases, Douglas C.J. said:

> "In my view they were under obligation in terms of the c.i.f. contract between the parties to forward proof of insurance coverage, whether by way of a policy, or where the custom of the trade permits it, by way of a certificate of insurance. In my view also, the plaintiffs not having included any proof of insurance among the documents despatched in connection with the shipment of the goods, they were under an obligation to send a policy or a certificate to the defendants within a reasonable time. Counsel for the plaintiffs contends that the supply of the certificate in September 1970 sufficiently satisfies the plaintiff's obligations. I cannot agree. It seems to me that a delay of 16 months in the despatch of documents in connection with c.i.f. contract is quite unreasonable."[13]

It should be noted that under "Incoterms" (*ante* § 24) the seller is only required to procure insurance which grants the buyer (or any other) person having on insurable interest in the goods "a direct right of claim against the insurer by providing a policy or *other* evidence of insurance cover."

Where the seller is able to tender a certificate of insurance, he does not discharge his obligation by tendering a broker's cover note that is generally no more than a certificate that a contract of insurance on unspecified terms has been effected. A cover note is not the same as a certificate of insurance, and the buyer can, of course, reject the tender thereof, and treat the breach as a default.[14]

---

[13] *Ibid.* at p. 51.
[14] See *Promos S.A. v. European Grain & Shipping Ltd.* [1979] 1 Lloyd's Rep. 375. The c.i.f. term was in that case subsequently varied to an ex warehouse sale but many of the observations including those relating to the inadmissibility of cover notes and defective certificates are pertinent.

217   Where the sale is on c. and f. terms, however, and the seller agrees to procure insurance for the buyer, it has long been held that the contract may be satisfied by the tender of an insurance certificate. This was decided in *Muller, MacLean & Co. v. Leslie & Anderson*,[15] where the defendants, buyers under a c. and f. contract, requested the plaintiffs—sellers, a New York firm, to procure insurance. They then refused to take up the documents, *inter alia* on the ground that a policy instead of a certificate of insurance should have been tendered. Roche J. dismissed this contention and said: "Whatever the rule may be with regard to a c.i.f. contract, I know of no such rule in connection with the contract for cost and freight only" (at page 330).

Whether foreign policy may be tendered

218   In *Malmberg v. H. J. Evans & Co.*[16] Bailhache J. held that a policy which was valid in other respects could not be rejected by an English buyer under a c.i.f. contract, merely because it was issued in the country in which the seller carried on business and was not issued in England.

> "I should not be prepared to hold," he said,[17] "and I do not think it is the law, that any objection can be taken to this policy on the ground that it is policy of a Swedish company. It seems to me that inasmuch as we under our c.i.f. contracts as sellers always provide an English policy, we are bound when we are buyers to accept as a policy to which no objection can be taken a policy issued by a company or underwriters in the country from which the goods come and in which the sellers carry on business."

The question, however, was left undecided by the Court of Appeal. In a later case,[18] the point was taken that a Swiss policy was not an insurance "with Lloyd's and for Companies," but the court expressed no opinion upon it. Whether an English c.i.f. buyer can nowadays complain if the policy tendered is foreign, is however doubtful. But the insurer must be reputable, and the policy should be denominated in the currency of the contract of sale. To avoid doubts on this matter the parties are well advised to include specific insurance provisions in their contract. Indeed, most standard contracts now include provisions relating to the kind or type of insurance the seller is required to procure. Thus, *e.g. in Promos S.A. v. European Grain & Shipping Ltd.*,[19] the following provision appeared:

> "Insurance: Insurance on W.A. terms (Institute Cargo Clauses) with average payable, with 3 per cent. franchise or better terms, including the risks of War Strikes Riots Civil Commotion and usual Warehouse to Warehouse clause to be

---

[15] (1921) 8 Ll.L.Rep. 328.

[16] (1924) 29 Com. Cas. 235.

[17] 29 Com. Cas. at p. 238.

[18] *A.C. Harper & Co. Ltd. v. Mackechnie & Co.* [1925] 2 K.B. 423.

[19] [1979] 1 Lloyd's Rep. 375.

effected at Seller's option with first class underwriters and/or Companies who are domiciled in the United Kingdom, or who for the purpose of any legal proceedings accept a British domicile and provide an address for service of process in London . . . Claims to be paid in the United Kingdom in the currency of the contract. Seller shall give all Policies and/or Certificates and/or Letters of Insurance provided for in this contract. duly stamped . . . for not less than 2 per cent. over the invoice amount.''

219   *Summary*. The conclusion from the cases cited appears to be that:

(1) there is as yet no general acknowledgment by the English courts that obviates the necessity for tender of a policy by the seller;

(2) a broker's cover note or a document called a certificate of insurance which does not contain all the terms of the insurance will not suffice as tender, unless the buyer has contracted to accepted it[20];

(3) whether a certificate of insurance that contains all the terms of the insurance will suffice remains undecided, but, under modern conditions it probably suffices provided the insurer can be sued upon it[21];

(4) it is doubtful whether a document purporting to be a policy that does not state the risks insured against, but incorporates them by reference to another document not included in the documents presented or not conveniently available, can be a good tender;

(5) the English buyer is not entitled to require the foreign seller to tender an English policy in the absence of special stipulation to that effect in the contract.

Effect of statements in certificate

220   When a certificate of insurance is tendered by the seller and accepted by the buyer in lieu of a policy, there is an implied warranty by the seller, that the assertions in the certificate are true and that he will procure the production of the policy referred to in the certificate. It was so held by Roche J. in *A. C. Harper & Co. v. Mackechnie & Co.*[22] In that case, a certificate of insurance was tendered to and accepted by the buyers as signed by the brokers, who certified that ''on March 2, 1922, we have insured with Lloyd's and/or companies the following merchandise below described, shipped or to be shipped per str. and/or strs.'' The certificate related to a policy to be issued by a company who had issued a slip on the same date covering the goods. The slip was afterwards cancelled and no policy was issued, the insurance brokers having transferred their business to other companies. On April 24, a month after the goods had been shipped, new slips were issued to the insurance brokers and a policy of insurance effected on the goods by two Swiss companies. A loss having occurred, a claim was made, but the companies refused to pay on the ground of

---

[20] *Ibid.*

[21] It is thought to be sufficient if custom or the contract allows it. *Phoenix Insurance Co. of Hartford v. De Monchy* (1929) 35 Com. Cas. 67.

[22] [1925] 2 K.B. 423.

non-disclosure of the fact that the vessel had sailed. The buyers brought an action against the sellers to recover their loss. It was held by Roche J. that the sellers in handing over the certificate warranted by implication that the statements in it were true and that they would produce or procure the production of the policy referred to in the certificate, and he gave judgment against them.

Buyer's right of action

221   It is the duty of the seller to procure insurance cover which shall be available for the benefit of the buyer. The ordinary Lloyd's policy and other common forms of marine insurance policies contain words stating that the insurance is made not only by the person effecting it, but also in the name of "all and every other person or persons to whom the same doth, may or shall appertain in part or at all." The effect of these words has long been recognised to give a right of action to any person having an insurable interest, provided that such person can prove that he was one whom those effecting the policy had in contemplation at the time.[23] If the buyer to whom a policy is delivered cannot bring himself within these provisions, he must be able to bring an action on the policy as an assignee.[24]

In *Harper et al. v. Hochstim et al.*,[25] the United States Second Circuit Court of Appeals had to consider the question whether a provision in a contract, (for 30,000 Shantung weasels with tails to be shipped from China per steamer direct or indirect c.i.f. to New York) to the effect that if "the goods are damaged while in transit, the buyer agrees to accept in settlement thereof the same percentage of allowance as the seller may secure from the insurers by way of settlement or recovery" entitled the sellers to perform by tendering the goods in New York instead of shipping them from China. The sellers never shipped the weasels. Instead they obtained part thereof in New York which they purported to tender in performance of their contract. The buyer, however, refused acceptance on the ground that he was entitled to delivery of documents representing goods shipped from China. The court held that the contract was a c.i.f. contract and that the buyer was under no obligation to accept an alternative method of performance. Referring to this Insurance provision, Hough J. said:

> "It cannot be doubted that it is only when parts of a written agreement are so radically repugnant that "there is no rational interpretation that will render them effective and accordant that any part must perish." . . . Applying this rule, it must be admitted that for the seller under a c.i.f. contract to insure in his own name is an apparent departure from the theory of such a sale; for the goods are the buyer's from and after delivery of the documents, yet it is perfectly possible for the seller or any one else to act as buyer's agent and validly insure for his

---

[23] See *Boston Fruit Co. v. British and Foreign Marine Ins. Co.* [1906] A.C. 336.

[24] See *J. Aron & Co. (Inc.) v. Miall* (1928) 34 Com.Cas. 18, *ante*, §206.

[25] 278 Fed. R. 102 (1921).

principal's benefit ..., and the whole of this agreement may be consistently regarded as containing an authorisation from buyer to seller to get the insurance and in case of loss settle for the buyer with the underwriters ... it is matter of common knowledge, insurance for "account of whom it may concern" was known to be procurable, and it might run to seller, yet inure to buyer. There is no radical repugnancy here presented, and the reconcilement above suggested is far less difficult than in many reported cases. ..." (at p. 104).

Seller's right of action

222   Even though the policy is in the normal case of a c.i.f. contract taken out for the benefit of, and is debited to, the buyer, "if when the goods come to hand it is found that they are not in accordance with the contract and therefore are rightly rejected, or if for some reason good or bad the buyer refuses to accept the bill, then if there is a claim under the policy the seller may use that policy and sue upon it, although the buyer has been originally debited with it."[26] The plaintiff in the decision from which this quotation is taken was the successor in title of merchants in India who had sold a quantity of hides to purchasers in Bulgaria. The contract was treated as one c.i.f. Bourgas. In view of the uncertainty of the First World War, the plaintiffs took out a war risks policy on behalf of and at the cost of the buyer. The hides were requisitioned by the Austrian Government subsequent to their arrival in Trieste, from whence they were to be transhipped to Bourgas. The action was brought by the seller against the underwriters, who defended it on the ground that inasmuch as the policy was issued pursuant to a c.i.f. contract the seller had no interest in the policy and was not the real person to sue. As above noted, Bailhache J. rejected this argument, but the action nevertheless failed on the merits, it being held that the requisition and sale of the hides by the Austrian Government were not within the terms of the cover provided by the war risks policy.

Policy must be Valid

223   The policy must be a valid policy; otherwise it will not be available for the benefit of the buyer.[27] In *Cantiere Meccanico Brindisino v. Constant*,[28] where it was argued for the seller that there was no implication of a warranty as to the policy being valid, the contract was for the sale of a floating dock at a price including cost of towage from Avonmouth to Brindisi, cost of insurance, and all fittings, etc., necessary for the voyage, and it contained the

---

[26] *Per* Bailhache J. in *Fooks v. Smith* (1924) 30 Com. Cas. 97 at p. 101.
[27] *Biddell Bros. v. E. Clemens Horst Co.* [1911] 1 K.B. 214 at p. 220; *ibid*, at p. 956; *Johnson v. Taylor Bros. & Co. Ltd.* [1920] A.C. 144 at p. 156. See further, as to validity at the time of presentation of documents, *post*, § 247.
[28] (1912) 17 Com.Cas. 182; affirmed on appeal, *ibid.* 332, but the dictum of Scrutton J. was not referred to.

clause "before the dock leaves, vendors agree to hand to purchasers Lloyd's policies of insurance for £16,500. This insurance will be duly indorsed over to them and they shall receive the full benefit of such policies." Insurances were effected against the usual risks, "seaworthiness admitted." The underwriters set up the defence to a claim on the policies that the policies were void on the ground of concealment of a material fact, *viz.*, that the dock was sent on the voyage without necessary additional strengthening. Scrutton J. held, on the facts, that the defence failed, but he said that if he had set the policies aside he should have found that the contract was a contract to give valid policies, that the contract had been broken and that the seller would have been liable in damages for the amount which the buyers failed to recover from the underwriters.

So the seller does not satisfy his obligation by procuring a p.p.i.[29] or honour policy[30] which are wager policies. Such a policy cannot be put in suit and the buyer may properly object to it on that ground.[31]

The question of the validity of the documents is further considered in the next chapter (*post*, § 247).

Solvency of insurers

224   Whether the c.i.f. seller contracts that at the time of tender of the documents the insurers will be solvent does not appear to have been discussed in any reported case. That he contracts to procure an insurance with responsible insurers is clear; but, so far as can be found no case has arisen for legal discussion where between the time of issue of the policy and presentment of it to the buyer the insurers have failed. In some cases, of which examples have been mentioned,[32] the contracts have stipulated that the seller is not to be responsible for the solvency of underwriters. It may be said that the seller who tenders a policy of insurance with insurers who have failed subsequently to its issue does not fulfil his bargain that "at the date of the tender the documents must be valid and *effective* documents."[33] But probably the true

---

[29] Policy proof of interest.

[30] As to commercial practice regarding honour policies, see Hamilton J. in *Strass v. Spillers & Bakers Ltd.* [1911] 2 K.B. 759 at p. 768. The facts are set out *post*, § 226.

[31] The Marine Insurance Act 1906, s.4, is as follows:

   "(1) Every contract of marine insurance by way of gaming or wagering is void.

   (2) A contract of marine insurance is deemed to be a gaming or wagering contract—

   (*a*) Where the assured has not an insurable interest as defined by this Act, and the contract is entered into with no expectation of acquiring such an interest; or

   (*b*) Where the policy is made 'interest or no interest,' or 'without further proof of interest than the policy itself,' or 'without benefit of salvage to the insurer,' or subject to any other like term:

Provided that, where there is no possibility of salvage, a policy may be effected without benefit of salvage to the insurer."

[32] *Ante*, §213, n. 2.

[33] *Per* Swinten Eady L. J., *Arnhold Karberg & Co. v. Blythe, Green, Jourdain & Co.* [1916] 1 K.B. at p. 508; and see Chap. 5, §§247, 248.

view is that while he contracts that the contract of insurance shall be effective in the sense of being capable of enforcement, he does not guarantee that at the time of tender, or at any time, the full measure of indemnity granted by the policy shall be recoverable.

Right to excess insurance

225   Questions have arisen as to who is entitled to receive, in case of loss, any excess insurance effected by the seller.

In *Ralli v. Universal Marine Insurance Co.*[34] sellers shipped a cargo of wheat from Odessa to England, valued at £7,000, and effected two policies of insurance, for £4,000 and £3,000 respectively. The cargo fell in value and it was sold afloat for £5,358 including freight and insurance, payment to be in exchange for bills of lading and policies of insurance effected with approved underwriters. The sellers endorsed on the policy for £3,000: "We transfer this policy to (the buyer) to the extent of £1,700." The shipping documents with the policies were duly delivered to the buyer. The ship and cargo having been lost, the buyer claimed and received the £4,000 on the first policy, but of the £3,000 insured by the second policy, the sellers objected to his claim to receive more than £1,700 and claimed the remaining £1,300 for themselves, and brought action against the insurance company and the buyer, claiming to be entitled to receive that amount, which the insurance company then brought into court. Knight Bruce and Turner L.J., reversing the decision of Wood V.-C.,[35] held that the whole of the £3,000 belonged to the buyer on the ground that on the construction of the contract the sale was of the wheat as already insured by the sellers.[36]

A similar question arose in the case of *Landauer v. Asser*[37] in a different form. There a contract of sale c.i.f. contained the clause "Insurance 5 per cent. over net invoice amount to be effected by sellers for account of buyers." The sellers then effected a policy of insurance for a larger amount than 5 per cent. over the net invoice amount and delivered the policy with the other documents to the buyers against payment of the price. A loss having occurred, the underwriters were prepared to pay the buyers the whole of the amount insured, but the sellers objected. The question for decision was whether the buyers, as regards the amount received by them in excess of their loss, were trustees for the sellers. The court (Alverstone L.C.J. Kennedy and Ridley

---

[34] (1862) 31 L. J. (N.S.) Ch. 313.
[35] *Ibid.* p. 207.
[36] *Arnould on Marine Insurance*, commenting on this case (4th ed.), p. 308), said:
"The defendants (the underwriters) had paid the full amount into court in the first instance; if they had not adopted this course and the judgment of the learned Vice-Chancellor against the vendee's claim had been affirmed, it is difficult to understand upon what principle at law the *vendor* would have based his claim to the balance";
cited with approval by Kennedy J. in *Landauer v. Asser* [1905] 2 K.B. 184 at p. 195. Later editions repeat the comment in somewhat different language.
[37] [1905] 2 K.B. 184.

J.J.) held that the buyers were entitled to retain the whole amount received by them. The basis of the decision was that the sellers had no interest in the subject-matter of the insurance at the time of the loss and could not make any valid claim against the underwriters. However no opinion was expressed as to whether the buyers could require the underwriters (who were not parties to the proceedings) to pay them the excess of their loss as a matter of legal right.

226   In *Strass v. Spillers & Bakers Ltd.*,[38] the defendants bought a cargo of wheat at a price "including freight and insurance" under a contract containing the clause "Seller to give policies of insurance (free of war risk) for 2 per cent over the invoice amount, and any amount over this to be for seller's account in case of total loss only." In order to fulfil the contract, the seller bought the wheat from a person to whom the plaintiff had sold it, the contracts throughout being in the same form and containing the last-mentioned clause. The plaintiff delivered to his buyer a policy for 2 per cent over the invoice amount, and this policy was delivered to the defendants. The plaintiff, before selling the cargo, had taken out an honour policy on increased value of the wheat for his own benefit, and that policy he retained in his own possession. A loss occurred, and the insurers paid the defendants the full amount under the policy which had been delivered to them. The plaintiff then sent the increased value policy to the defendants, requesting them to collect from the insurers the amount payable thereunder. The defendants did so, and upon being paid the amount by the insurers they claimed to retain it on the ground that under the contract of sale the plaintiff was bound to hand over all policies effected on the wheat at the time when he entered into the contract of sale. In an action by the plaintiff to recover the amount as money had and received to his use, Hamilton J. held that the contract was made in view of insurances to be thereafter effected, and not, as was the case in *Ralli v. Universal Marine Insurance Co.*,[39] so as to affect policies already effected; that the increased value policy was an independent honour policy effected by the plaintiff for his own benefit, and that the defendants were not entitled to it under the contract.

In *Karinjee Jivanjee & Co. v. W. F. Malcolm & Co.*,[40] the sellers insured for the invoice price together with an extra insurance of £444. Two days after the documents were taken up by the buyers, news of the loss of the cargo arrived. The buyers having obtained the full insurance moneys, claimed to retain them, including the excess insurance. The sellers, having regard to a provision in the contract that "should the goods or any portion thereof not arrive . . . this contract to be void for any such portion," claimed the benefit of the documents and the full amounts of the insurance. It was their contention that the effect of the clause was to require rescission of the contract and

---

[38] [1911] 2 K.B. 759.
[39] See *ante*, § 225.
[40] (1926) 25 Ll.L Rep. 28, *ante*, § 13.

restoration of the parties to the position they occupied before performance of the contract. Roche J., affirming the decision of the umpire in an arbitration, decided against the sellers' contention, holding that the clause in question did not affect the position where, as in that case, the contract had been performed, *i.e.* by tender of the documents and payment. The buyers accordingly were entitled to retain the excess insurance.

[The next paragraph is 241.]

CHAPTER 5

TENDER AND PAYMENT

Tender

241   The seller having procured the necessary documents, namely, a bill of lading and the required insurance cover, and/or any other documents required by custom or by the terms of the contract, is (unless otherwise agreed, as for example would be the case where payment was to be by an irrevocable credit, see *post*, § 612) under an obligation to send them forward to the buyer, accompanied by an invoice showing the amount due from the buyer, within a reasonable time.

242   *Time of tender.* The seller must make every reasonable effort to send the documents forward as soon as possible after he has destined the goods shipped to the buyer.

In *Barber v. Taylor*,[1] where the seller was to deliver to the buyer a bill of lading for 150 bales of cotton which had been bought on the buyer's orders, the court held that the seller was bound to deliver the bill of lading within a reasonable time after its receipt, without reference to the arrival or unloading of the cargo, and that, there having been an unreasonable delay in delivering the bill of lading, the buyer was entitled to reject the cotton.

Brett M. R. in *Sanders v. Maclean*[2] said:

> ". . . merchants never could have contemplated that after a cargo had been destined to a purchaser or consignee the shipper should keep the bill of lading as long as he pleased. Therefore some stipulation with regard to this must be implied. The stipulations which are inferred in mercantile contracts are always that a party will do what is mercantilely reasonable. What, then, is the contract duty which is to be imposed by implication on the seller of goods at sea with regard to the bill of lading? I quite agree that he has no right to keep the bill of lading in his pocket, and when it is said that he should do what is reasonable, it is obvious the reasonable thing is he should make every reasonable exertion to send forward the bill of lading as soon as possible after he has destined the cargo to the particular vendee or consignee. If that be so, the question whether he has used such reasonable exertion will depend upon the particular circumstances of each case. If there is a perishable cargo or one upon which heavy charges must surely be incurred the reasonable thing for him to do is to make even a greater

---

[1] (1839) 9 L.J.Ex. 21. And see *Borrowman v. Free* (1878) 4 Q.B.D. 500.
[2] (1883) 11 Q.B.D. 327 at p. 337.

exertion than he would in the case of another cargo. That is one of the circumstances to be considered. Another circumstance would be from whence is the shipment? How near is the consignor to the ship so as to enable him to get possession of the bill of lading?''

The seller, said Scutton J. in *Landauer & Co. v. Craven & Speeding Bros.*, ''must, as soon as possible after he has sent forward the cargo, send forward the documents to the vendee or consignee.''[3] He is bound to tender the documents to the buyer ''within a reasonable time after shipment,'' said Lord Birkenhead, and ''with all reasonable dispatch,'' said Lord Atkinson, in *Johnson v. Taylor Bros. & Co. Ltd.*[4]

243   Accordingly, when in *C. Sharpe & Co. v. Nosawa & Co.*[5] the damages had to be assessed in an action for non-fulfilment by sellers of a c.i.f. contract for the sale of goods to be shipped in June from Japan to London, and it was proved that the documents relating to the last possible shipment in June would, if sent forward with reasonable dispatch, have reached London on July 21, Atkin J. measured the damages by the difference between the contract price and the price about July 21. ''The contract is performed in fact, and the date of its performance is the date when the documents would come forward, the vendor making every reasonable effort to forward them.''[6]

For the buyer, by getting the documents into his hands at the earliest possible moment, ''obtains the privilege and absolute power of profitably dealing with the goods days or weeks, or, perhaps, in the case of shipments from a distant port, months, before the arrival of the goods themselves. This is, indeed, the essential and peculiar advantage which the buyer of imported goods intends to gain under the c.i.f contract. . . .''[7]

But there is no condition implied in the contract that the seller shall deliver the documents to the buyer in sufficient time to enable the buyer to send on the bill of lading to meet the arrival of the ship, or in time to reach the place of discharge before charges on the goods are incurred there. ''It is . . . equally impossible, to my mind,'' said Brett M.R. in *Sanders v. Maclean*,[8] to say that even a stipulation[9] ought to be implied in the contract that the bill of lading should be delivered so that it may arrive before or at the time of the arrival of the ship or before charges are incurred.''

The contract however may of course expressly provide otherwise. Where it does, the seller must tender documents that comply with the stipulation, and which (as such provisions normally state) will permit the buyer to obtain delivery of the goods on the vessel's arrival. In such a case, any delay in tendering the requisite documents will generally be construed as a breach of

---

[3] [1912] 2 K.B. 94 at p. 105.
[4] [1920] A.C. 144 at pp. 149, 156.
[5] [1917] 2 K.B. 814; and see *post*, § p. 302 where this case is dealt with fully.
[6] *Ibid.* at p. 819.
[7] *Per* Kennedy L.J., *Biddell Bros. v. E. Clements Horst Co.* [1911] 1 K.B. 934 at p. 958.
[8] (1883) 11 Q.B.D. 327 at p. 337.
[9] Meaning a warranty as distinct from a condition.

a condition entitling the buyer to terminate the contract by reason of the seller's default. In *Toepfer v. Lenersan-Poortman N.V.; Toepfer v. Verheijdens Veervoeder Commissiehandel*[10] the dispute arose out of a contract for the sale of rapeseed c.i.f. Rotterdam with payment of cash against documents on arrival of the vessel or 20 days after the date of the bills of lading "whichever should be earlier." The bills of lading were dated December 11, but did not reach the buyers until February 7. The cargo itself which had to be transhipped (because the original vessel on which it had been loaded had grounded) did not arrive until April. It was held that the buyers were entitled to reject the bills due to the delay in tender. On the other hand in *Cereal-mangimi S.p.A. v. Toepfer (The Eurometal)*[11] where the contract provided for payment in exchange for shipping documents but allowed the seller to claim payment against providing "other documents" entitling the buyers to obtain delivery "if shipping documents have not been sighted at time of vessel's arrival," the buyers were held liable for failure to pay on arrival of the vessel. Although documents had not been signed at the time, the buyers had waived their rights to treat the non-production of alternate documents as a breach by not insisting upon them. Lloyd J. held that although there was no fixed time for tendering the shipping documents, payment was due when the vessel arrived at which time the sellers (but for the waiver) were obliged to tender alternative documents. In other words, under such a stipulation the seller can tender documents as late as the date of payment. If he has not shipped the goods he must buy goods afloat and tender the documents at any time up to the moment at which tender was required, and a failure to do so is (as aforesaid) a repudiation which entitles the buyer to terminate the contract.[12] The buyers' obligation to pay and the sellers' obligation to present the documents within the stipulated time are thus correlative.

244   *Place of tender.*The place of tender of the shipping documents is, unless the contract otherwise provides, *the buyer's* place of business or residence. Atkin J. in *Stein, Forbes & Co. v. County Tailoring Co.,*[13] where payment was to be "net cash against documents on arrival of the steamer," expressed doubt whether there was an obligation on the seller to tender them at the buyer's office in the absence of any express stipulation to that effect, or some trade usage or course of business between the parties importing such a stipulation. He cited section 29(1) of the Sale of Goods Act 1893 (in substance unchanged by the 1979 Act), as apparently providing the contrary, which reads as follows:

> "Whether it is for the buyer to take possession of the goods or for the seller to send them to the buyer is a question depending in each case on the contract,

---

[10] [1980] 1 Lloyd's Rep. 143 (C.A.), affirming [1978] 2 Lloyd's Rep. 555.
[11] [1981] 1 Lloyd's Rep. 337.
[12] *Tricerri Ltd. v. Crosfields & Calthrop Ltd. and Oth.* [1958] 1 Lloyd's Rep. 236.
[13] (1916) 115 L.T. 215.

express or implied, between the parties, Apart from any such contract, express or implied, the place of delivery is the seller's place of business, if he have one, and if not, his residence: Provided that, if the contract be for the sale of specific goods, which to the knowledge of the parties when the contract is made are in some other place, then that place is the place of delivery.''

245   But it is a little difficult to see what the alternative is. The authorities[14] show that the seller is under an obligation to send forward and tender the documents to the buyer. To do this, he may transmit them by mail direct to the buyer, or he may transmit them to his agent for presentation, or he may deliver the documents to a banker for collection, leaving the banker to forward the documents to his agent at the place of payment for collection of the price. In the latter cases, the seller's agent or the banker's agent may merely notify the buyer that the documents are ready, leaving the buyer to call and take them up, or he may actually seek out and present the documents to the buyer. In these circumstances, if any defined obligation is to be implied in the contract, it is suggested that practical convenience supports the implication of an obligation to tender at the buyer's place of business or residence. It is suggested that either there is an implied contract ''for the seller to send them to the buyer,'' or the section of the Act quoted has no reference to the tender of documents under a c.i.f. contract. This apparently is taken for granted in the United States, where the Court of Appeals of New York once stated in connection with a contract which was designated as a c.i.f. contract but which was in fact on arrival terms that[15] ''The invoice, receipt for freight, bills of lading, and other documents were not forwarded by the seller to the purchaser as required under a c.i.f. contract. . . .''[16] Similarly Lord Atkinson has stated[17] that the result of the cases,[18] which were the same authorities as were considered by Atkin J. in *Stein, Forbes & Co. v. County Tailoring Co.*,[19] establishes ''that if no place be named in the c.i.f. contract for the tender of the shipping documents, they must prima facie be tendered at the residence or place of business of the buyer.'' But examination of the cases referred to does not reveal any direct decision to the effect stated.

On the contrary, there is at least one authority which appears to state just the reverse. In *Rein v. Stein*[20] the Court of Appeal held that where goods were sold by an English merchant to a German consignee, c.i.f. Hamburg, and the contract provided for ''cash against bills of lading,'' no stipulation

---

[14] *Ireland v. Livingstone* (1871) L.R. 5 H.L. 395, 406; *Biddell Bros. v. E. Clemens Horst Co.* [1911] 1 K.B. 934, 962; [1912] A.C. 18; *C. Sharpe & Co. v. Nosawa & Co.* [1917] 2 K.B. 814 (a decision of Atkin J.).

[15] *Cundil v. A. W. Milhauser Corporation*, 257 N.Y. 416 at p. 420 (1931).

[16] The Uniform Commercial Code expressly so provides. Under s.2–320(2)(e) the seller must ''forward and tender with commercial promptness all the documents in due form and with any endorsement necessary to perfect the buyer's rights.''

[17] *Johnson v. Taylor Bros. & Co. Ltd.* [1920] A.C. 144 at p. 156. See *ante,* § 8.

[18] *Ante,* § 8.

[19] (1916) 115 L.T. 215.

[20] [1892] 1 Q.B. 753.

being included as to the place of tender or payment, the inference was that payment was to be made at the seller's place of business. Kay L.J. said:

> "Prima facie, in commercial transactions, when cash is to be paid by one person to another, that means that it is to be paid at the place where the person who is to receive the money resides or carries on business. I therefore think that 'cash' must mean cash to be paid in England" (at p. 758).

246   Whether any distinction can or ought to be drawn between the place where the price is to be offered is doubtful. In view of the conflicting authorities, the question of the place of tender of the documents may perhaps be regarded as open and unsettled, though, as suggested, the normal inference would be in favour of the buyer's place of business. This apparently is now also accepted by the courts, as the following passage from Brandon J.'s judgment in *The Albazero*,[21] indicates: "I fully accept the proposition that, under the ordinary c.i.f. contract, where the delivery of the shipping documents is to be made only against payment, it is an implied term of the contract, in the absence of any express terms relating to the matter, that the documents should be tendered at the place of business or residence of the buyer."[22] The prima facie presumption mentioned by Kay L.J. should therefore probably be considered as rebutted and inapplicable in the case of c.i.f. contracts. Indeed, since it is the buyer's duty to take up the documents when they are presented, it is a little difficult to see how the rule could be otherwise, though where payment is arranged through a banker's letter of credit to be opened or confirmed in the seller's place of business or in the country of origin, which is the normal practice under modern conditions,[23] the contract is obviously performed by the tender of the documents to the bank at that place.

Demand or tender of delivery of documents must be made at a reasonable hour, which is a question of fact, and unless so made may be treated as ineffectual.[24]

Valid documents must be tendered

247   The documents must be valid and effective at the time of the tender. The tender of documents, originally valid, but which before tender have become invalid is not a good tender. Reference has already been made to the case of *Cantiere Meccanico Brindisino v. Constant*,[25] where the validity of policies of insurance on a floating dock effected by the seller was challenged by the

---

[21] [1974] 2 All E.R. 906 at p. 928. This judgment was overruled by the House of Lords in [1977] A.C. 774 but on a different point, *ante*, § 162.
[22] See to a similar effect *Chattanooga Tufters Co. v. Chenille Corp. of S.A.* [1974] 2 S.A. 10, where the place of tender under the c.i.f. contract in question was found to be Johannesburg, the respondent's principal place of business.
[23] As to the principles that govern letters of credit, see *post*, § 612 *et seq.*
[24] Sale of Goods Act 1979, s.29(5).
[25] (1912) 17 Com. Cas. 182; C.A. 332; see *ante*, § 223.

underwriters on the ground of concealment of the fact that the dock required extra strengthening, and Scrutton J., while refusing to set aside the policies, said that if he had set them aside he would have found that there was a contract on the part of the seller to give valid policies and the contract would have been broken. The law on the point has been clearly laid down in the following cases:

In *Arnold Karberg & Co. v. Blythe*[26] there were two contracts for the sale of beans to be shipped from Chinese ports to Naples and Rotterdam respectively, each of which provided that payment was to be made net cash in London on arrival of the goods at the port of discharge in exchange for bills of lading and policies of insurance, but payment was to be made in no case later than three months from the date of the bills of lading or upon posting of the vessel at Lloyd's as a total loss. The beans were shipped on German vessels in July 1914 and, on the outbreak of war between Great Britain and Germany on August 4, 1914 these vessels entered ports of refuge in the East, where they remained. At the expiration of three months from the date of the bills of lading, the sellers tendered to the buyers the documents, which included in one case a German bill of lading and an English policy of insurance, and in the other case a German bill of lading and a German policy of insurance. The buyers in each case refused to accept the tender and pay for the goods. It was argued on their behalf that the contract of affreightment was rendered void on the outbreak of war, or, if it was not, to become party to it would involve trading with the enemy, and that the tender of documents representing such contracts was therefore bad. The same argument was applied to the policy in the second case. The substantial argument for the sellers was that in a c.i.f. contract it was immaterial that the contract of affreightment became void on the outbreak of war; that after the sellers ship the goods and obtain contracts of affreightment and insurance, the goods and the contracts are at the buyer's risk; that it makes no difference if the parties contracting to carry subsequently become alien enemies so that the contracts are void, or otherwise become inoperative, unenforceable, or useless; the risk is the buyer's, and they must insure against war risk.

248   Scrutton J., before whom the issue came on a special case stated by arbitrators, on the question as to "what condition and validity of these documents were required to make them a good tender," held that on August 4, the contracts of affreightment and the German policy of insurance became void except as regards claims then accrued, if any, which, however, could not be enforced during the war; that when the sellers tendered the documents, they tendered documents which had been contracts, but which were then, by considerations of public policy, void and unenforceable as regards any obligations of performance which would, but for the war, have been carried out after August 4.

---

[26] [1915] 2 K.B. 379; C. A. [1916] 1 K.B. 495.

". . . I cannot believe," he said,[27] "that contracts which are illegal and void can be regarded as good tenders and available for the benefit of the buyer. It is clearly not essential that if the goods do not arrive, the buyer should have a good claim on one of the contracts, but I think it is essential that each contract should be one into which he can legally enter as a contracting party, and when the legal relations of the seller under the contract of affreightment tendered have become void, and it is illegal for the buyer to enter into any similar legal relations with the shipowner or insurer, I cannot hold that such documents are good tender, or that the buyer can be required to pay against them."

The decision was affirmed by the Court of Appeal (Swinfen-Eady, Bankes and Warrington L.JJ.). Swinfen-Eady L.J. in the course of his judgment said[28]:

"The point is upon whom the loss is to fall where documents which were originally valid have become invalid before they were tendered. In my opinion, although there is no direct authority on the point, the decisions which have been given as to the effect of c.i.f. contracts, and the language which is used in those cases, make it reasonably clear what the obligation of the seller is . . . In my opinion the cases dealing with c.i.f. contracts have all proceeded upon the footing that upon delivery of the shipping documents the purchaser will obtain a right either to the goods or, if the goods are lost or damaged, to such claims in respect of the goods as the shipping documents may entitle him, not necessarily covering every loss or damage, but they were to be effective documents; and I think that the language used by the judges in dealing with c.i.f. contracts is only consistent with the view that the documents tendered are to be effective shipping documents, and that where the bill of lading has become avoided by war it is not a sufficient compliance with the contract to tender it . . . that at the date of the tender the documents must be valid and effective documents."

Bankes L. J. said[29]:

"What is the meaning of the buyer's contract . . . that he is to pay in exchange for a bill of lading? In my opinion it means what it says, that in exchange for the price he is to receive a bill of lading which is still a subsisting contract of affreightment of the goods to the port of destination, and a policy or policies of insurance which is, or are still, a subsisting contract, or subsisting contracts of insurance. It is said that this construction, which seems to me so obviously the natural construction, ignores the fact that in a contract of this kind certain risks fall upon the buyer. For instance, in the present case all war risks fell upon the buyer, as the parties have agreed that the seller shall be under no obligation to obtain policies covering war risks.[30] I agree also that the condition of the goods at the time of the tender of the shipping documents is not material, nor is the value of the documents at the time of tender material. In all such matters the risk is on the buyer. He may be obliged to pay for goods although they may be at the bottom of the sea, or although through some unforeseen circumstance they may never arrive, or although they may have been lost owing to some cause not

---

[27] [1915] 2 K.B. at p. 392.
[28] [1916] 1 K.B. at pp. 504, 506, 508.
[29] *Ibid.* at p. 509.
[30] Normally, war risks, independently of express agreement, fall upon the buyer. See *ante*, § 185.

covered by the agreed form of policy. All these risks, however, are risks affecting the goods. In effect the contention of the appellants appears to me to be a contention that one of the risks undertaken by the buyer is a risk affecting his contract, and not the goods the subject-matter of the contract. I cannot agree with this view. It appears to me that the question of the construction of the contract must depend upon the language used, and not upon any such considerations as these. In the present case it is not disputed that the outbreak of war dissolved the contract of affreightment, and that so far as any further prosecution of the voyage was concerned the bill of lading was no longer an effective document. Under those circumstances, in my opinion that bill of lading was not a bill of lading within the meaning of the contract in respect of which the [buyer][31] was under an obligation to pay cash in exchange.''

And Warrington L.J. said[32]:

"Is the obligation of the seller which he has to fulfil performed by delivering what he has purported to deliver in the present case—a document which does not entitle the buyer to obtain delivery of the goods because the contract of affreightment has ceased to be effective? In my opinion quite plainly not. In order to perform his contract he has to deliver documents by virtue of which the buyer may, if the goods are in existence, obtain delivery of them, and by virtue of which, if the shipowner has not fulfilled his obligation imposed by the contract of affreightment he, the buyer, may have such remedies as the contract of affreightment would give him. Neither of those conditions is fulfilled by the delivery of a document evidencing a contract which has been dissolved by the outbreak of war, and the further performance of which has become impossible.''

249   In *Duncan Fox & Co.* v. *Schrempft & Bonke*,[33] English sellers sold in 1914 to English buyers about 300 barrels Chilean honey June and/or July shipment c.i.f. Hamburg, payment net cash in Liverpool in exchange for shipping documents. The honey was shipped in June on a German steamer, *Menes*, for Hamburg. A clause was indorsed on the bill of lading providing that all questions thereunder were to be governed by German law and to be decided at Hamburg. War between Great Britain and Germany broke out on August 4, and on August 5 a proclamation was issued directed against British subjects trading with the enemy, and on the same day the shipping documents were tendered to the buyers, who refused to accept them. The *Menes* had not then arrived at Hamburg but had put into a neutral port for refuge. It was held by the Court of Appeal, approving Atkin J., that the buyers were entitled to refuse the tender because by accepting the documents they would be carrying out a contract in violation of the proclamation.

On the other hand in *Re Weis & Co. Ltd. & Crédit Colonial et Commercial, Antwerp*,[34] performance of the contract involved no illegality, and the tender was upheld. There a contract was entered into before the war between an English company and Belgian buyers for the sale of bean oil to be shipped

---

[31] "Seller" erroneously in the report.
[32] [1916] 1 K.B. at p. 514.
[33] [1915] 1 K.B. 365; aff'd. [1915] 3 K.B. 355 (C.A.).
[34] [1916] 1 K.B. 346.

from an Eastern port c.i.f. to Antwerp. Some of the goods were shipped on a British steamer which, on the outbreak of war, was seized by the Germans on the high seas and taken to Hamburg. At a subsequent date the shipping documents were tendered to and rejected by the buyers. Bailhache J. held that the tender was a good tender, since there was no illegality as between the sellers and the buyers in tendering documents calling for delivery at Antwerp (which was not then in the possession of the Germans), and the inability of the buyers to get the goods owing to the seizure of the steamer by the Germans did not affect the validity of the tender; it was a war risk against which the buyers could have protected themselves by insurance.

250   In *Baxter, Fell & Co. Ltd. v. Galbraith & Grant Ltd.*[35] the sellers had sold to the buyers in June 1939, a quantity of Continental mildsteel rods, c and f. Bombay, payment cash against documents. Part of the order was shipped at Antwerp in August in the German steamship *Rauenfels*. On August 25, the ship, having sailed, was diverted to Bremen on the orders of the German Government. On August 28, the sellers tendered in London to the buyers bills of lading for the rods already shipped. The buyers contended that the tender was a bad one. Atkinson J. held that the tender was ineffective as the bills of lading were no longer valid and effective at the time of tender. By the sailing to Bremen under the orders of the German Government in the state of imminent war that then existed the contracts of affreightment had been frustrated.[36] The tender was therefore one which the buyers were not bound to accept.

In *Hindley & Co. v. East Indian Produce*[37] Kerr J. permitted an action for return of the purchase price and for damages for breach by a c. and f. buyer of a quantity of jute that was never shipped. The buyers there objected to the presentation of a bill of lading which on its face purported to cover the contract goods. When the carrying vessel arrived at Bremen, the port of destination, no jute was found on board because it had never been shipped. The sellers (who had purchased the jute from a third party) argued that they had performed their contract by delivery of the required documents but their defence failed. The court held that the sellers were in breach because no goods had been shipped, and because the bill of lading which was tendered was not a "proper" one, as it contained untrue and inaccurate material statements whereas they were under a duty to present a "proper" bill of lading.

In *Empresa Exportadora de Azucar v. Industria Azucarera Nacional S.A. (The Playa Larga and Marble Islands)*[38] Cuban sellers of sugar (on the instruction of the Cuban government following the overthrow of the Allende regime in Chile) diverted various ships carrying cargoes destined to Chilean buyers. The documents in respect of one of the cargoes had (on the date of

---

[35] (1941) 70 L1.L. Rep. 142.
[36] See also *ante*, § 87.
[37] [1973] 2 Lloyd's Rep. 515, more fully discussed *ante*, § 26.
[38] [1983] 2 Lloyd's Rep. 171 (C.A.).

the diversion) been tendered to a banker who paid the sellers pursuant to a letter of credit. However, the quality of the sugar diverted was below the minimum stipulated in the contract and in the letter of credit authorisation. It was therefore held by the Court of Appeal (Stephenson and Ackner, L.JJ and Sir Sebag Shaw) that the buyers had every right to reject the documents and had effectively done so. But the court further noted that even if this were not the case "the circumstances in which the change of destination was made resulted in the documents being defective at the moment of tender. They related to a contract of carriage to a destination which was not the one named in the contract of sale, and they were false in that they purported to represent a contract which had in fact been privately varied."[39] The buyers therefore were entitled to the return of the price because the consideration for its payment had wholly failed.

In the same case Mustill J. (whose decision was upheld by the Court of Appeal) said as follows[40]:

> "It seems to me that at the moment of tender the documents were [in]effective[41] in two respects:
> (1) they related to a contract of carriage to a destination which was not the one named in the contract of sale;
> (2) they were false in that they purported to represent a contract which had privately been varied . . . documents which confer only a speculative right of action of this kind are not, in my judgment, 'valid and effective' within the principles laid down in the cases previously reviewed. . . ."

Finally it should be noted that where the contract contains a clause that requires the buyer to take up the documents "notwithstanding contradictions, errors or omissions" in them (provided the seller "guarantees performance"), the clause protects the seller against technical inconsistencies between the documents and the sale contract but is generally ineffective to cure major breaches (*e.g.* a discrepancy between the contractual port of shipment and the one stated in the documents). The buyer may therefore reject the documents,[42] or if payment has already been made, recover the price and sue for damages.

251   On the foregoing principles, a tender of a forged or fraudulent bill of lading would be a bad tender. But a banker who, having discounted the seller's bill of exchange drawn upon the buyer, presents it to the buyer for acceptance or payment, with the shipping documents attached, does not by English law warrant or represent to the buyer the genuineness of the bill of lading, and if the bill of lading be a forged one, he is under no liability to the buyer to refund the price paid by him.[43] And where payment is to be through a letter

---

[39] *Ibid.* at p. 184, *per* Ackner L. J.
[40] *Sub. Nom.* [1982] Com. L. R. 171 at p. 178.
[41] In the report, erroneously "effective."
[42] *S.I.A.T. Di Del Ferro v. Tradax Overseas S.A.* [1980] 1 Lloyd's Rep. 53 (C.A.).
[43] *Guaranty Trust Co. of New York v. Hannay* [1918] 2 K.B. 623 (C.A.), following *Leather* v. *Simpson* (1871) L.R. 11 Eq. 398.

of credit, the bank is not liable (unless it was negligent in examining the documents) if it subsequently appears that the bill of lading (or some other document) was forged.[44] The bank may moreover be under an obligation to pay though the bill of lading is fraudulent (*e.g.* because of a false dating) provided the beneficiary of the credit was not privy to the fraud, and the security value of the bill of lading is not negated by it.[45]

252   *Goods lost before tender.* It is immaterial that at the time of tender the goods shipped have been damaged or lost in transit. The seller fulfils his obligation by delivering to the buyer the shipping documents, ordinarily the bill of lading, invoice and insurance policy. It is contemplated that the buyer will obtain an indemnity in respect of the damage or loss under one or the other documents, though whether he is actually able to do so depends upon the terms of the bill of lading and the policy, and the circumstances of the damage or loss. In *C. Groom Ltd. v. Barber*,[46] where, as is commonly the case, there was no appropriation of the goods by the seller to the particular buyer until the tender of the documents, and before that time the goods had been lost, it was unsuccessfully argued on behalf of the buyer that the seller could not recover where there was no appropriation of specific goods to the contract so as to pass the property before tender, and before the goods were lost. Atkin J., in rejecting this argument, said[47]:

"... The contract of the seller is performed by delivering to the buyer within a reasonable time from the agreed date of shipment the documents, ordinarily the bill of lading, the invoice, and the policy of insurance, which will entitle the buyer to obtain on arrival of the ship delivery of goods shipped in accordance with the contract, or in case of loss will entitle him to recover on the policy the value of the goods if lost by a peril agreed in the contract to be covered, and in any case will give him any rightful claim against the ship in respect of any misdelivery or wrongful treatment of the goods. It therefore becomes immaterial whether before the date of the tender of the documents the property in the goods was the seller's or buyer's or some third person's. The seller must be in a position to pass the property in the goods by the bill of lading if the goods are in existence, but he need not have appropriated the particular goods in the particular bill of lading to the particular buyer until the moment of tender, nor need he have obtained any right to deal with the bill of lading until the moment of tender. If it were otherwise the shipper of goods in bulk, or of goods intended for several contracts, or the intermediate seller who may be the last of a chain of purchasers from an original shipper, might find it impossible to enforce a contract on c.i.f. terms. The seller's obligation cannot depend upon whether the goods are lost or not, and if when there is no loss the property has to pass to the buyer before delivery of the documents, at what stage of the transaction must it pass? Unless it be at the time of shipment I can see no reason for fixing upon any other time than on delivery of the documents, and if it be the law that a tender of documents is ineffectual unless in fact at the moment of shipment the property actually

[44] *Singh (Grain) & Co. Ltd. v. Banque de l'indochine* [1974] 2 All E.R. 754 (P.C.).
[45] *United City Merchants v. Royal Bank of Canada* [1982] 2 W.L.R. 1039 (H.L.).
[46] [1915] 1 K.B. 316.
[47] *Ibid.* at p. 324.

passed to the ultimate buyer, it appears to me that business operations would be very seriously embarrassed.''

253   It makes no difference to the legal position if the fact be that the seller at the time of the tender of the documents knows that the goods have been lost. In *Manbre Saccharine Co. v. Corn Products Co.*,[48] there were contracts for the sale of starch and syrup c.i.f. London. On March 12, 1917 the S.S. *Algonquin*, carrying a portion of the goods, was sunk by submarine or mine. The sellers, with knowledge of the loss, tendered the documents to the buyers on March 14. It was held that the seller's knowledge of the loss was immaterial.

> ''If,'' said McCardie J.[49] ''the vendor fulfils his contract by shipping the appropriate goods in the appropriate manner under a proper contract of carriage, and if he also obtains the proper documents for tender to the purchaser, I am unable to see how the rights or duties of either party are affected by the loss of ship or goods, or by knowledge of such loss by the vendor, prior to the actual tender of the documents. If the ship be lost prior to tender but without the knowledge of the seller, it was, I assume, always clear that he could make an effective proffer of the documents to the buyer. In my opinion it is also clear that he can make an effective tender even though he possess at the time of tender actual knowledge of the loss of the ship or goods. For the purchaser in case of loss will get the documents he bargained for; and if the policy be that required by the contract, and if the loss be covered thereby, he will secure the insurance moneys. The contingency of loss is within and not outside the contemplation of the parties to a c.i.f. contract.''

The buyer, therefore, where the proper documents are tendered to him, is ''obliged to pay for goods although they may be at the bottom of the sea, or through some unforeseen circumstances they may never arrive, or although they may have been lost owing to some cause not covered by the agreed form of policy'',[50] and whether the seller was or was not aware of loss at the time of tender is immaterial. It is doubtful whether a different result would have been obtained even if there was no appropriation prior to the loss. Is the position different if the loss or damage occured prior to the time the contract was made? This question does not appear to have been judicially considered until now, and perhaps a distinction can be drawn between this situation, and the appropriation of lost or damaged goods generally.[51]

In *M. Golodetz & Co. Inc. v. Czarnikow-Rionda Co. Inc. (The Galatia)*[52] a c. and f. contract for the sale of sugar provided for payment against ''clean'' bills of lading. After part of the consignment was loaded, a fire broke out damaging 200 tonnes of the sugar which had to be discharged. There were two bills of lading. One for the damaged 200 tonnes which had attached to it a type-written note stating that fact. The other bill of lading covered the

[48] [1919] 1 K.B. 198.
[49] *Ibid.* at p. 203.
[50] *Per* Bankes L.J., *Arnhold Karberg & Co. v. Blythe, Green, Jourdain & Co.* [1916] 1 K.B. 495 at p. 510.
[51] See Feltham, ''The Appropriation to a C.I.F. Contract of Goods lost or Damaged at Sea'' [1975] J.B.L. 273.
[52] [1980] 1 W.L.R. 495.

remainder of the shipment. The buyers accepted the latter bill but rejected the former. The Court of Appeal held they had acted wrongfully, and that the sellers were also entitled to the price of the sugar which had been damaged and discharged. The bill of lading was "clean" because the apparent good order and condition of the goods *on shipment* was not qualified, and there was no evidence that it was not a document which would have ordinarily been accepted in the trade as being an appropriate document.

254 *All documents to be tendered.* All the documents required by the contract must be tendered. The omission of any one of them places the buyer in the position to reject, even though the goods have already arrived in safety.

> "The invoice is made out debiting the consignee with the agreed price ... and giving him credit for the amount of the freight which he will have to pay to the shipowner on actual delivery, and for the balance a draft is drawn on the consignee which he is bound to accept (if the shipment be in conformity with his contract) on having handed to him the charterparty, bill of lading, and policy of insurance."[53]

This final duty of the seller is necessary in order that the buyer "may know what freight he has to pay and obtain delivery of the goods, if they arrive, or recover for their loss if they are lost on the voyage."[54] Thus "... a tender of delivery entitling the vendor to payment of the price must, in the absence of contractual stipulation to the contrary, be a tender of possession. How is such a tender to be made of goods afloat under a c.i.f. contract? By tender of the bill of lading, accompanied in case the goods have been lost in transit by the policy of insurance."[55]

255 Mention has already been made in the earlier chapters of cases where the failure or alleged failure of the seller to fulfil his obligation to tender the proper documents called for by the contract had led to the buyer's rejection and refusal to pay the price.

The fact that the documents have been altered does not entitle the buyers to reject them without inquiry, and if it is manifest that the alterations were made before execution, then the documents must be accepted.

---

[53] *Per* Blackburn J., *Ireland v. Livingston* (1872) L. R. 5 H. L. 395 at p. 406. A charterparty is not normally required see *ante*, § 102.

[54] *Per* Hamilton J., *Biddell Bros. v. E. Clemens Horst Co.* [1911] 1 K.B. 214 at p. 220.

[55] *Per* Kennedy L.J., *ibid.*, at p. 956. In *Landauer & Co. v. Craven & Speeding Bros.* [1912] 2 K.B. 94, Scrutton J., referring to this, said (at p. 107):

> "I am unable to follow this *obiter dictum*. At time of tender the goods are generally at sea, and nobody on land knows whether they are afloat or at the bottom, and, in my view, the buyer is entitled to require the policy in his shipping documents, whether it is known that there has been a loss or not."

But as was pointed out by Lush and Rowlatt JJ. in *Orient Co. Ltd. v. Brekke* [1913] 1 K.B. 531 at pp. 535, 537, where the limited view of Kennedy L.J.'s words was unsuccessfully sought to be used to justify sellers' failure to effect a policy of insurance on the ground that the goods had in fact arrived in safety, Kennedy L.J. was referring not to an ascertained past fact, but to a present risk, when he used the words, "in case the goods have been lost."

In the case of *Re Salomon and Naudszus*[56] buyers rejected the documents on the ground that two of them appeared on their face to have been altered. The contract was for the sale of wheat c.i.f. Hamburg, payment net cash against documents to consist of bills of lading, policy of insurance and certificate of inspection. The sellers in due course tendered the three documents, two of which, the bill of lading and certificate of inspection, contained erasures and alterations, the third, a certificate of insurance, being unaltered. The buyers refused to accept by reason of the alterations. It appeared that the two documents had been altered before execution to correct a mistake as to the holds in the ship in which the wheat was stowed, and that, as altered, they conformed with the certificate of insurance and with the facts. The Committee of the London Corn Trade Association found "that the documents were a fit and proper tender under the contract and ought to have been accepted by the buyers."

256   On a special case stated for the opinion of the court, Darling and Phillimore JJ. differed and therefore the appeal was dismissed. Darling J. held that the tender ought to have been accepted as the buyers were put on inquiry, and since one of the altered documents agreed with the unaltered one, they ought to have concluded that the altered documents were altered before execution and agreed with the facts. Phillimore J. was of the opinion that the tender was not a good one. To the question whether the buyer is "to be compelled to take documents which may be good and probably are good, but which quite conceivably may be worthless, or, in the alternative, to incur the liability to an action if it turns out that he has rejected documents which in fact are quite good," he answered: "I do not think that is a duty which is imposed upon a man of business; and I think it is still less so in a case of this kind, because a purchaser is entitled to require not merely what conveyancers call a good holding title, but a good marketable title—language which my brother Day paraphrased in his judgment (*Bernays v. Winter* (1898) unreported[57]) to which I was a party, by the use of the words 'perfect document.' ... In this class of cases a man requires a good marketable title. He is probably dealing largely on borrowed money, and he is possibly buying to sell again. In either case he requires not only documents that would satisfy him, but documents which he can compel others to take as being satisfactory."[58] The judgment of Phillimore J., however, having been withdrawn, the judgment of Darling J. stood as the judgment of the court.

257   *Bills of lading in sets.* It has long been common practice for bills of lading to be drawn in sets, usually of three parts, but sometimes of more. These were dispatched for safety by different routes to the buyer. The first part used

---

[56] (1899) 81 L.T. 325.
[57] In that case, it appears that the court held tender of bills of lading which had been altered *after arrival* to be a bad tender.
[58] 81 L.T. at p. 329. The buyer is not "buying a litigation," *ante*, § 101. The documents must be such as to be "readily fit to pass current in commerce," *ante*, § 141.

to come by fast passenger steamer. Now it comes by air. Often the seller or shipper kept a part himself. Each part was as effective as another, being expressed to be "of even tenor" with the rest, and each part was equally effectual to pass the property. Any bill could be presented to the master of the vessel for delivery of the goods, but "the one being accomplished, the others to stand void"—as the usual term in the bills runs—as soon as one is acted upon, the others are of no effect. This system presents an opportunity for fraud, which has been criticised,[59] but still prevails in many cases. It is however frequent now for a set to consist of only two bills. On occasion there is even only one.

In *Barber v. Meyerstein*,[60] it was decided in the House of Lords that the endorsement and transfer, with intent to pass the property of one bill of lading out of a set of three, passes the property in the goods which the bill of lading represents and that any subsequent endorsement of any other of the set is ineffective for that purpose. In *Glyn, Mills & Co. v. E. & W. India Dock Co.*,[61] the House of Lords, while confirming the law as laid down in *Barber v. Meyerstein (ante)* with regard to passing of property by bills of lading, decided that the holder of the first bill of lading could not sue the shipowner or master who had innocently delivered the goods to the holder of a subsequently endorsed bill of the set.

258   In *Sanders v. Maclean*,[62] an attempt was made by buyers to maintain an objection to presentation of two only out of a set of three bills of lading, though it appeared that the third had never been dealt with. In that case, the sale was of 2,000 tons of iron rails, c.i.f. Philadelphia, payment to be made in cash in London in exchange for bills of lading and policies of insurance of each cargo or shipment. The rails were shipped at Sevastopol for Philadelphia on account of the sellers. Three bills of lading were signed by the master, of which the shipper kept one, which he did not deal with. The other two were sent to the sellers, who tendered them to the buyers. The latter refused to accept them or pay for the rails on the ground that one of the bills of lading was outstanding. The Court of Appeal (Brett M. R., Bowen and Cotton L.JJ.) held that as the third bill of lading had not been dealt with, the other two bills were effectual to pass the property and the tender was good; that if the seller endorses and parts with one of the set of bills to another person before the tender of the others, such tender is not in compliance with the contract, since the bills of lading tendered would not be effectual to pass the property; but in refusing to accept the tender, the buyer does so at the risk of investigation showing that the bills tendered were effectual to pass the property.

Per Lord Blackburn in *Glyn, Mills & Co. v. & W. India Dock Co.* (1882) 7 App-Cas. 591 at p. 605.
(1870) L.R. 4 H.L. 317.
(1882) 7 App.Cas. 591.
(1883) 11 Q.B.D. 327. The well-known passage from Bowen L.J.'s judgment in this case, stating the law as to indorsement and delivery of bills of lading, is set out, *ante*, § 3.

"The bill of lading," said Bowen L.J.,[63] ". . . may be regarded as a key of the warehouse where the goods are. Can a person who has contracted to pay on delivery of the keys of the warehouse refuse to accept the keys tendered to him on the ground that there is still a third key in the hands of the vendor which, if fraudulently used, might defeat the vendee's power of taking possession? I think business could not be and is not carried on upon any such principle."

259   In *Cederberg v. Borries, Craig & Co.*[64] the contract stipulated that the buyers should accept bills "on receipt of and in exchange for *all* the shipping documents." The word "all" had been inserted in ink in a printed form of contract at the buyer's request. The sellers were unable to supply more than three out of five parts of the bill of lading. The buyers received and disposed of the cargo, but, in an action for the price, contended that they were not liable to pay for the goods until every part of the bill of lading was delivered up to them, though they admitted that in face of *Sanders v. Maclean* (ante) in the absence of the word "all" they could not have insisted on tender of more than one part of the bill of lading. Grove J., after telling the jury—with apparent justification—that it was a very melancholy action, directed them to consider whether the word "all" had altered the buyer's rights, whether the words "shipping documents" had a wide or a strict technical sense. Did they mean every single piece of paper, (*i.e.* invoice, manifest and bills of lading, etc.), or only such as are usually handed over? Had the plaintiffs tendered all the customary documents? The result was verdict and judgment for the plaintiffs.

But where the contract calls for tender of a full set of bills of lading the buyer has been held entitled to reject the tender if the requirement is not fulfilled. This was decided in *Donald H. Scott & Co. Ltd. v. Barclays Bank Ltd.*,[65] where, by the terms of a sale of steel plates c.i.f. Rotterdam, the buyers were to open a credit in London, and their bank in London notified the sellers that they would honour the sellers' drafts against a full set of clean bills of lading. The sellers tendered only two out of three bills of lading, offering an indemnity or an undertaking to produce the third, and the bank was held to be entitled to reject the tender.

The foregoing decision was rendered in 1923 and no doubt reflected the position at that time. Since then, however, commercial practice has probably developed to the extent of recognising an adequate indemnity for a missing part of a "full set of bills of lading" as a valid tender. An American decision to this effect, *Dixon, Irmaos & Cia Ltd. v. Chase National Bank of City of New York*[66] was given in 1944, on the grounds that custom among New York banks issuing letters of credit was to accept in lieu of a missing part of a full set of bills of lading a guarantee by a responsible New York bank. Section 2–323 of the Uniform Commercial Code now provides that where in the case

---

[63] (1883) 11 Q.B.D. at p. 343.
[64] (1885) 2 T.L.R. 201.
[65] [1923] 2 K.B. 1 (C.A.).
[66] 144 F.2d 759 (1944).

of a c.i.f., c. and f. or f.o.b. contract for the purchase of goods from abroad "a bill of lading has been issued in a set of parts . . . only one part of the bill of lading need be tendered. Even if the agreement expressly requires a full set."

260   *Withdrawal of rejected tender.* A tender not in accordance with the contract and rejected by the buyer may be withdrawn by the seller. The seller may afterwards, within the contract time, make another tender according to the contract which the buyer will be bound to accept.

In *Borrowman v. Free*,[67] sellers tendered a cargo of maize that was rejected by the buyers as not being in accordance with the contract. Later, but within the contract time, the sellers tendered another cargo which was in accordance with the contract. It was held that the second tender was good. So too where the contract provides (i) for the seller to give the buyer a declaration or notice of shipment (see *ante*, § 199) and (ii) that a valid declaration cannot be withdrawn except with the buyers' consent, and the buyers reject the first notice as being invalid and stale, the seller is free to make a fresh declaration and tender of different goods (within the time permitted by the contract). Donaldson J. said in a case concerning such provisions that "the buyers cannot both maintain that it [the first declaration] is a valid declaration of shipment that cannot be withdrawn without their consent and an invalid one because it was sent to them out of time."[68] Moreover "a valid declaration of shipment only appropriates goods to a contract, and so modifies the rights and obligations of the parties to that contract, if it is applied to that contract by a valid notice. Any attempt to apply it by a stale notice is as ineffective as the tender of goods without the shipping documents. Such a tender leaves the seller free to make a fresh tender of different goods with the shipping documents."[69]

A similar question arose in *Hindley v. General Fibre Co.*,[70] where there was a contract dated July 27, 1939 for the sale by the defendants to the plaintiffs of 250 bales of jute to be shipped from Calcutta to Hamburg, Antwerp, Rotterdam or Bremen in September and October 1939. The particular port of destination was to be declared by the buyers to the sellers. When war broke out, it became illegal to ship to German ports. By letter dated September 11, the buyers declared Bremen as the port of destination but this declaration was not accepted by the sellers, who regarded the contract as cancelled. The buyers then declared the port of destination to be Antwerp, but the sellers refused to ship the goods.

The Appeal Committee of the Jute Association found in favour of the buyers, and this award was upheld by Atkinson J., who said[71]:

---

[67] (1878) 4 Q.B.D. 500 (C.A.).
[68] *Gertreide Import Gesellschaft m.b.H. v. Itoh & Co. (America) Inc.* [1979] 1 Lloyd's Rep. 592 at p. 594.
[69] *Ibid.*
[70] [1940] 2 K.B. 517.
[71] *Ibid.* at p. 532.

"... one arrives at the conclusion that when war broke out the buyers lost their right to declare Bremen or Hamburg but the contract did not come to an end as there still remained a legal way in which it could be performed; that the duty then resting upon them was to declare a legal port, that is either Rotterdam or Antwerp, and that when they made the declaration nominating Bremen, they did something they were not entitled to do. The declaration of Bremen could only become a term of the contract if it imposed a contractual duty on the sellers, but it was a nullity; it imposed no duty and it in no way became a part of the contract completing its last term. In my opinion that was a declaration they were not entitled to make and it had no more effect than if they had declared Timbuctoo. It being a bad declaration, in my view they were entitled to withdraw it and make the declaration which was made."

Payment

261   The seller having tendered the proper documents, it becomes the buyer's duty to accept and pay in accordance with the terms of the contract. The delivery contemplated by a c.i.f. contract being a delivery of the documents representing the goods, and not of the goods themselves, possession of the bill of lading places the goods at the disposal of the buyer, and the buyer is not (unless otherwise agreed) entitled to postpone payment until the goods have arrived or he has had an opportunity of examining them to ascertain whether they are in accord with the contract. This was finally settled in the leading case of *Biddell Bros. v. E. Clemens Horst Co.*,[72] when the effect of sections 28 and 34 of the Sale of Goods Act 1893 upon c.i.f. contracts was considered.

Those sections which remain unchanged by the 1979 Act are as follows:

"28. Unless otherwise agreed, delivery of the goods and payment of the price are concurrent conditions, that is to say, the seller must be ready and willing to give possession of the goods to the buyer in exchange for the price, and the buyer must be ready and willing to pay the price in exchange for possession of the goods."

* * *

"34.—(1) Where goods are delivered to the buyer, which he has not previously examined, he is not deemed to have accepted them unless and until he has had a reasonable opportunity of examining them for the purpose of ascertaining whether they are in conformity with the contract.

(2) Unless otherwise agreed, when the seller tenders delivery of goods to the buyer, he is bound, on request, to afford the buyer a reasonable opportunity of examining the goods for the purpose of ascertaining whether they are in conformity with the contract."

---

[72] [1911] 1 K.B. 214; C.A., *ibid.* at p. 934; [1912] A.C. 18. In *Elliott & Co. v. Caudor Manufacturing Co.* (1920) 3 Ll.L.Rep. 105, evidence of a custom at Tunis that the buyer should have a reasonable time after arrival of the vessel for taking up the documents was rejected as inconsistent with a c.i.f. contract.

The buyers under a contract for the sale of hops "c.i.f. to London, Liverpool or Hull. Terms net cash," declined to pay for the hops except against delivery and examination of the bales. Hamilton J. (later Lord Summer)[73] held that under a c.i.f. contract the buyer is bound to pay in exchange for the documents even where there is no express term in the contract that payment is to be made "against documents," that either a c.i.f. contract is an agreement "otherwise" within section 28 or possession must be deemed to be given when the goods are put on board and the documents are tendered. The Court of Appeal (Vaughan Williams and Farwell L.JJ., Kennedy L.J. dissenting) held that the rule of law, now embodied in section 34(1), is that the buyer is entitled to inspect before payment and that the right cannot be taken away except by express or implied terms of the contract, which, in their view, did not exist in that case.

Kennedy L.J., whose dissenting judgment subsequently was adopted in the House of Lords, was of opinion that "net cash" is equivalent to "net cash against documents." Tender of goods afloat, he said, is made by tender of the shipping documents, and the bill of lading, being a symbol of the goods, gives the buyer constructive possession.

262   Kennedy L.J. said:[74]

> "The application of the principles and rules of the common law, now embodied in the Sale of Goods Act 1893, to the business transaction embodied in the c.i.f. contract appears to me to be decisive of the issue between these parties. Let us see, step by step, how according to those principles and rules the transaction specified in such a c.i.f. contract as that before us is and, I think, must be carried out in order to fulfil its terms.
>
> "At the port of shipment—in this case San Francisco—the vendor ships the goods intended for the purchaser under the contract. Under the Sale of Goods Act 1893, s. 18,[75] by such shipment the goods are appropriated by the vendor to the fulfilment of the contract, and by virtue of section 32,[76] the delivery of the goods to the carrier—whether named by the purchaser or not—for the purpose of transmission to the purchaser is prima facie to be deemed to be a delivery of the goods to the purchaser. Two further legal results arise out of the shipment. The goods are at the risk of the purchaser, against which he has protected himself by the stipulation in his c.i.f. contract that the vendor shall, at his own cost, provide him with a proper policy of marine insurance intended to protect the buyer's interest, and available for his use, if the goods should be lost in transit,[77] and the property in the goods has passed to the purchaser, either conditionally

---

[73] *Ante*, § 6.

[74] [1911] 1 K.B. at p. 955.

[75] s. 18, r. 5, is set out *post*, § 278.

[76] s. 32(1) was (and remains) as follows: "Where, in pursuance of a contract of sale, the seller is authorised or required to send the goods to the buyer, delivery of the goods to a carrier, whether named by the buyer or not, for the purpose of transmission to the buyer is prima facie deemed to be a delivery of the goods to the buyer."

[77] This statement was not intended to convey the idea that the right of the buyer to receive a policy of insurance was limited to the case where the goods are lost in transit. See *ante*, § 254. The seller is bound to hand to the buyer a policy of insurance in all cases, unless he is excused from so doing by the terms of the contract. See *ante*, § 207.

or unconditionally. It passes conditionally where the bill of lading for the goods, for the purpose of better securing payment of the price, is made out in favour of the vendor or his agent or representative: see the judgments of Bramwell L.J. and Cotton L.J. in *Mirabita v. Imperial Ottoman Bank.*[78] It passes unconditionally where the bill of lading is made out in favour of the purchaser or his agent or representative, as consignee. But the vendor, in the absence of special agreement, is not yet in a position to demand payment from the purchaser; his delivery of the goods to the carrier is, according to the express terms of s.32, only 'prima facie deemed to be a delivery of the goods to the buyer'; and under s.28 of the Sale of Goods Act 1893, as under the common law (an exposition of which will be found in the judgments of the members of the Exchequer Chamber in the old case of *Startup v. Macdonald*[79]), a tender of delivery entitling the vendor to payment of the price must, in the absence of contractual stipulation to the contrary, be a tender of possession. How is such a tender to be made of goods afloat under a c.i.f. contract? By tender of the bill of lading, accompanied in case the goods have been lost in transit[80] by the policy of insurance. The bill of lading in law and in fact represents the goods. Possession of the bill of lading places the goods at the disposal of the purchaser. . . . The meaning of 'delivery' under the Sale of Goods Act is defined by s.62 to be 'voluntary transfer of possession from one person to another.' Such delivery . . . may be either actual or constructive; see Chalmers' Sale of Goods Act 1893 (7th ed.) p. 140[81]; and, as Bowen L.J. has pronounced,[82] in the case of seaborne goods, the delivery of the bill of lading operates as a symbolical delivery of goods.''

263   The seller is (in the absence of a term fixing the exact time) bound to tender the documents within a reasonable time and there is a corresponding obligation on the buyer to pay against tender. If the buyer were not bound to pay against tender, the seller must either hand the documents to the buyer without payment, which is unreasonable, or retain them, and land and warehouse the goods himself and by so doing incur charges beyond those which alone he has agreed by the contract to pay, *viz.*, the freight and premium of insurance. Moreover, if the buyers' contention were right, and the goods were lost in transit, the buyers need not pay. What then is the necessity of insurance? The buyers' contention involved the proposition that the sellers were bound to deliver the goods themselves in this country, which would be inconsistent with a c.i.f. contract.

With regard to section 34, Kennedy L.J. was of opinion that a c.i.f. contract constitutes an agreement ''otherwise'' within section 34(2); and as to section 34(1) he said that it was not suggested that the buyer by paying becomes precluded from rejecting the goods if, after their arrival, they are found not to be in accordance with the contract.

264   In the earlier case of *Polenghi v. Dried Milk Co. Ltd.*,[83] where milk powder was sold by sample c.i.f. London, payment to be made ''in cash in London

[78] (1878) 3 Ex.D. 164, discussed *post*, § 558.
[79] (1843) 6 Man. & G. 593.
[80] See *ante*, § 254, n. 55.
[81] Now 15th ed.
[82] *Sanders v. Maclean* (1883) 11 Q.B.D. 327 at p. 341, cited *ante*, § 3.
[83] (1904) 10 Com. Cas. 42.

on *arrival* of powders against shipping or railway documents,'' Kennedy J. had likewise held that the buyer was not entitled to insist on having an opportunity of comparing the bulk with the sample under section 15(2)(b) of the Sale of Goods Act 1893,[84] before paying the price. He said[85] that under the terms of the contract:

> "The sellers must (1) show that the goods are arrived goods and (2) produce the shipping documents. Payment on delivery is excluded by express stipulation, which provides for payment on arrival. The plain meaning of the contract is that, on those two conditions being fulfilled, payment is to be made. If the goods do not answer the description, the buyer has a right to reject, which right is not impaired by the express condition in the contract that 'payment is to be made . . . in London on the arrival of the powders against shipping or railway documents.'''

265 *Buyer must pay if he accepts bill of lading.* If the buyer accepts the bill of lading he must pay the price. By section 19(3) of the Sale of Goods Act 1893 (and 1979), it is enacted that:

> "Where the seller of goods draws on the buyer for the price, and transmits the bill of exchange and bill of lading to the buyer together to secure acceptance or payment of the bill of exchange, the buyer is bound to return the bill of lading if he does not honour the bill of exchange, and if he wrongfully retains the bill of lading the property in the goods does not pass to him."

The reason for this rule has been very plainly stated, by Lord Cairns in the House of Lords in *Shepherd v. Harrison,*[86] and this decision is the foundation of the section. He said:

> "I hold it to be perfectly clear that when a cargo comes in this way, protected by a bill of lading and a bill of exchange, it is the duty of those to whom the bill of lading and the bill of exchange are transmitted in a letter, either 'to approbate or to reprobate' entirely and completely, then and there. If they accept the cargo and the bill of lading, and accept the bill of exchange drawn against the cargo, the object of those who shipped the goods is obtained. They have got the bill of exchange in return for the cargo; they discount or use it as they think proper; and they are virtually paid for the goods. But if, on the other hand, the persons to whom the bill of lading is sent do not refuse *in toto* the consignment of the goods, but keep the bill of lading, but do not accept the bill of exchange, then the agents of the foreign shippers have neither the goods nor the money to deal with; if they had repudiated the transaction *in toto* the agents of the shippers might have dealt with some other house and raised money on the goods."

In a later case Kennedy J. said:

---

[84] The subsection provides, in both the 1893 and 1979 Acts, that in the case of a contract of sale by sample, there is an implied condition that the buyer shall have a reasonable opportunity of comparing the bulk with the sample.
[85] 10 Com. Cas. 42 at p. 47.
[86] (1871) L.R. 5 H.L. 116 at pp. 132, 133.

". . . a person who takes shipping documents which are offered to him upon the condition of his fulfilling . . . a contractual obligation—namely, to pay for them by accepting a bill drawn upon him . . . cannot keep the goods with one hand and also refuse the terms upon which they are put in his possession with the other."[87]

On another occasion, Pickford J. said:

". . . the buyer of goods on a c.i.f. contract must accept the draft against shipping documents and then make a claim for damages for breach of contract; if he is going to reject the goods he ought not to take the shipping documents."[88]

266   Where, therefore, the defendants refused to accept a bill of exchange on account of the non-conformity of the goods, Key J. held that they had no right to retain the bill of lading which they claimed to have as security for part of the freight.[89] The plaintiffs were entitled to damages for having been kept out of possession of their goods, the measure of which was the value of the cargo after making a deduction for freight.

267   But by section 25(2) of the Sale of Goods Act 1893[90] it was provided:

"Where a person having bought or agreed to buy goods obtains, with the consent of the seller,[91] possession of the goods or the documents of title to the goods,[92] the delivery or transfer by that person, or by a mercantile agent[93] acting for him, of the goods or documents of title, under any sale, pledge, or other disposition thereof, to any person receiving the same in good faith[94] and without notice of any lien or other right of the original seller in respect of the goods, shall have the same effect as if the person making the delivery or transfer were a mercantile

---

[87] *Barton, Thompson & Co. v. Vigers Bros.*, (1906) 19 Com. Cas. 175 at p. 177.
[88] *Jordeson & Co. v. London Hardwood Co.* (1913) 19 Com. Cas. 161 at p. 164.
[89] *Rew v. Payne, Douthwaite & Co.* (1885) 53 L.T. 932.
[90] See now s.25(1) of the Sale of Goods Act 1979. *Cf.* s.9 of the Factors Act 1889, which is practically identical with this section.
[91] "Consent of the seller" means that which the law regards as consent. It includes the case where possession has been obtained under a contract defeasible on the grounds of fraud; but it excludes the case where possession has been obtained in circumstances amounting to larceny by a trick. See *Cahn & Mayer v. Pockett's Bristol Channel Steam Packet Co. Ltd.* [1898] 2 Q.B. 61; C.A. [1899] 1 Q.B. 643; *Oppenheimer v. Frazer & Wyatt* [1907] 1 K.B. 519; 2 K.B. 50 (C.A.); *Whitehorn Bros. v. Davison* [1911] 1 K.B. 463 (C.A.); *Folkes v. King* [1923] 1 K.B. 282 (C.A.); *Pearson v. Rose & Young Ltd.* [1951] 1 K.B. 275 (C.A.).
[92] "Documents of title" includes "any bill of lading, dock warrant, warehousekeeper's certificate, and warrant or order for the delivery of goods, and any other document used in the ordinary course of business as proof of the possession or control of goods, or authorising or purporting to authorise, either by indorsement or by delivery, the possessor of the document to transfer or receive goods thereby represented." Sale of Goods Act 1979, s.61(1); Factors Act 1889, s.1(4).
[93] "Mercantile agent" means "a mercantile agent having in the customary course of his business as such agent authority either to sell goods or to consign goods for the purpose of sale, or to buy goods, or to raise money on the security of goods." Sale of Goods Act 1979, s.26; Factors Act 1889, s.1(1).
[94] "A thing is deemed to be done "in good faith" within the meaning of this Act when it is in fact done honestly, whether it be done negligently or not": Sale of Goods Act 1979, s.61(3).

agent[95] in possession of the goods or documents of title with the consent of the owner.''[96]

The effect of this provision, in relation to the matter under consideration, is that if the buyer having obtained in ordinary course the bill of lading and a draft for his acceptance disposes of the bill of lading without accepting the draft, to a third party who takes it in good faith and without notice, the third party obtains a good title and the right of the unpaid original seller to resume possession and control is gone. If possession of the bill of lading has been obtained in circumstances amounting to larceny by a trick, it is otherwise.

In *Cahn & Mayer v. Pockett's Bristol Channel Steam Packet Co. Ltd.*,[97] where the buyer took and parted with the bill of lading but did not accept the bill of exchange, it was held that the sellers' right of stoppage *in transitu*[98] was defeated. The facts of that case were that Steinmann & Co., of Liverpool, sold certain copper to Pintscher, a merchant of Altona, to be delivered c.i.f. at Rotterdam, payment to by "30 days acceptance from date of bill of lading." The copper was shipped and the sellers forwarded to Pintscher the bill of lading and a bill of exchange for his acceptance. In the meantime, Pintscher resold the copper to Cahn & Mayer. When the documents arrived, Pintscher was insolvent. He thereupon handed the bill of lading to his bankers for delivery to Cahn & Mayer in pursuance of his contract of resale and against payment of the price, which was to be placed to the credit of his account, which was then overdrawn, at his bankers, and this was done, Cahn & Mayer acting in good faith and without notice of the rights of Steinmann & Co. Pintscher never accepted the draft. Before the copper arrived at Rotterdam, Steinmann & Co., having learnt that Pintscher was insolvent, gave notice to stop *in transitu*, which they were able to do upon giving the shipowners an indemnity. Cahn & Mayer, as indorsees of the bill of lading, then sued the shipowners for damages for non-delivery of the copper. Mathew J. gave judgment for the defendants on the grounds (i) that as Pintscher, not having accepted the bill of exchange, was bound to return the bill of lading, the property in the goods did not pass to him by virtue of section 19(3) of the Act,[99] and he could transfer no title to Cahn & Mayer; (ii) that as Pintscher did not accept the bill of exchange he was never in possession of the bill of lading "with the consent of the seller" within the meaning of section 25(2) of the Act.[1]

---

[95] See *ante*, n. 93.
[96] See the Factors Act 1889, s.2.
[97] [1898] 2 Q.B. 61; C.A. [1899] 1 Q.B. 643.
[98] By s.39(1) of the Sale of Goods Act 1893 (now s.39(1) of the Sale of Goods Act 1979), notwithstanding that the property in the goods may have passed to the buyer, the unpaid seller of goods, as such, has by implication of law . . ., in case of the insolvency of the buyer, a right of stopping the goods *in transitu* after he has parted with the possession of them. As to the right of stoppage generally, see § 349.
[99] Set out, *post*, § 281.
[1] Set out, *ante*.

268   The Court of Appeal (A. L. Smith, Collins and Romer L.JJ.) reversed this decision. They held that section 19(3) of the Act was not a relevant provision because it is addressed not to the original obtaining of possession, but to the duty of the recipient after he has got it, which assumes custody with assent; that Pintscher obtained possession of the bill of lading with the consent of the sellers within the meaning of section 25 of the Act; that it was immaterial whether the consent was afterwards withdrawn; that having once got possession by consent, Pintscher's subsequent disposition of the bill of lading was effectual notwithstanding that the consent no longer subsisted; and that the right to stop *in transitu* had therefore gone.

269   In the course of his judgment Collins L.J. said[2]:

> "The Factors Act 1889, which is thus referred to, and as to part of it in terms again enacted, in the Sale of Goods Act, is the last of a series of statutes whereby the Legislature has gradually enlarged the powers of persons in the actual possession of goods or documents of title, but without property therein, to pass the property in the goods to bona fide purchasers. Possession of, not property in, the thing disposed of is the cardinal fact. From the point of view of the bona fide purchaser the ostensible authority based on the fact of possession is the same whether there is property in the thing or authority to deal with it in the person in possession at the time of the dissposition or not. But the Legislature has not carried the rights of a purchaser under these Acts so far as to make the sale equivalent to a sale in market overt. The purchaser must accept the risk of his vendor having found or stolen the goods, or documents, or otherwise got possession of them without the consent of the owner. But, if a mercantile agent, or one of the persons whose disposition is made as effectual as that of a mercantile agent, has obtained possession by consent of the owner, even though it were under a contract voidable as fraudulent (see *Baines v. Swainson*[3]; *Sheppard v. Union Bank of London*[4]), he is able to pass a good title to a bona fide purchaser. However fraudulent the person in actual custody may have been in obtaining the possession, provided it did not amount to larceny by a trick, and however grossly he may abuse confidence reposed in him, or violate the mandate under which he got possession, he can by this disposition give a good title to the purchaser. See the distinction between possession obtained by a trick and possession under a contract voidable for fraud noted by Blackburn J. in *Cole v. North Western Bank.*[5] These considerations seem to me decisive of the crucial question in this case. By sending the bill of lading and the bill of exchange direct to Pintscher, Steinmann & Co. constituted him bailee of both of them. It seems impossible to say that there was any wrongful taking by Pintscher. There was no trick which would have negatived a bailment. If he became criminally responsible for his subsequent dealing with the bill of lading, it must have been as bailee, which presupposes a taking by consent. The circumstances of the obtaining possession would not have supported an indictment for larceny, and the subsequent abuse of his opportunity could not alter the character of the original taking. He might conceivably have fully intended to accept the draft and forward it by the first

[2] [1899] 1 Q.B. at p. 658. And see *per cur. Oppenheimer v. Frazer & Wyatt* [1907] 2 K.B. 50 (C.A.).
[3] (1863) 4 B. & S. 270.
[4] (1862) 7 H. & N. 661.
[5] (1875) L. R. 10 C. P. 354 at p. 373.

post. If he had disposed of the bill of lading, while he remained in this attitude of mind, and subsequently accepted the draft, and forwarded it, and became insolvent before the transitus of the goods was over, could Steinmann & Co. have stopped them effectually on the ground that Pintscher had not obtained possession of the bill of lading with their consent? If not, it could only be because the original taking was with their consent. The possession, *i.e.* the actual custody, was obtained once for all when the bill of lading was placed in Pintscher's hand, and no subsequent changes in his intention with regard to the draft could change the character of this completed act. It would in my opinion defeat the purpose of the Act, and work a public mischief, if a vendor who had himself placed the bill of lading in the hands of his purchaser were entitled as against a bona fide sub-purchaser from the latter to enter into nice questions as to the intention with which the original purchaser took the document of title into his possession."

The misfortune of Steinmann & Co. in that case would have been avoided if they had adopted the safer practice of sending the bill of lading to their own agents instead of sending it to Pintscher direct.

270   *Time for payment.* The buyer must be prepared to pay or accept the draft, as the case may be, according to the terms of the contract of sale within a reasonable time after the shipping documents are tendered to him. What is a reasonable time is a question of fact depending on the circumstances. In ordinary cases, it is conceived that payment or acceptance must come promptly after tender. Business could hardly be conducted otherwise. The ship may be arriving or have arrived, and landing and other charges may be accruing when the documents are tendered. It is a matter of importance for the seller that he should know one way or the other without delay whether the buyer is going to take up the documents.

The case of *Ryan v. Ridley & Co.*[6] is an authority for the proposition that where the sale is of perishable articles, the buyer must be practically ready with his money. In that case, the sale was of a cargo of Newfoundland codfish per the *Margaret* "sailed on October 9 to Lisbon for orders to be delivered at Bari," c.i.f. "payment to be made by cash in London in exchange for bill of lading and policy of insurance." The *Margaret* arrived at Lisbon on October 24, and shortly afterwards the seller tendered the shipping documents and requested payment in exchange. Payment not having been made by the buyers on November 1, the seller sold the cargo a day or two later and then sued the buyers for the loss of that sale. Kennedy J. held that they were entitled to resell and recover their loss. He held that "cash against documents" meant that when the documents were tendered, the cash must, in a practical and business sense, be ready. It did not mean that ". . . if the seller walks into the buyer's office and offers the documents, the buyer will have committed a breach of contract because he does not at once tender money or a cheque in payment. That would not be business. The clause means that the payment against the documents must be made within a reasonable time from their presentation; *e.g.* if the buyer says: 'You shall have a cheque tomorrow

---

[6] (1902) 8 Com. Cas. 105.

morning,' that would, I think, ordinarily be sufficient. Or even a greater delay might not be unreasonable if it would not affect the interests of the parties. If ever there was a case in which the nature of the cargo demanded promptitude, that of the cargo in the present case did.''[7]

271   *Payment against documents.* In *Toepfer v. Lenersan-Poortman N.V.; Toepfer v. Verheijdens Veervoeder Commissiehandel*[8] contracts for the resale of Canadian rape-seed c.i.f. Rotterdam/Europort provided for "payment: net cast against documents and/or delivery order on arrival of the vessel at port of discharge but not later than 20 days after date of bill of lading. . . ." Bills of lading were issued upon shipment on December 11, 1974 but the carrying vessel grounded and suffered serious damage, and the cargo, which had to be transhipped, did not arrive in Europe till April 1975. Because of certain unconnected difficulties the shipping documents were not delivered to the sub-purchasers until February 7, 1975 at which time they rejected them. The sellers claimed that the buyers were in default since they had done all they could to send the documents forward as soon as they could, that the delay in their presentation caused no harm to the buyers because the vessel was at all material times undergoing repairs, and that the buyers suffered no loss by virtue of the late presentation. Donaldson J.,[9] on a case stated, disagreed with the arbitration tribunal and found for the buyers. In his view (which was affirmed by the Court of Appeal) the obligations imposed by the "payment against document" clause were mutual, and defined not the latest or earliest date for payment but *the* date. The clause was binding on both parties and was a "condition," and not a mere warranty of the contract. The casualty could not alter the nature of the obligation of the seller or of the status of the clause with regard to the presentation of the documents as a condition of the contract. In arriving at this conclusion the judge noted that merchants sought certainty in their contracts, particularly in documentary transactions involving banks. "If," said Donaldson J:

> "the paying bank has to take account of the general mercantile obligation of a c.i.f. seller, it will be in real difficulty. It can know little of the relevant facts. Furthermore, unless it has a direct line to the House of Lords, it will not know whether the duty is to make every reasonable exertion to send forward the bill of lading as soon as possible after he has destined the cargo to the particular vendee or consignee [*per* Brett M. R. in *Sanders v. Maclean* (1883) 11 Q.B.D. 327 at p. 337 and to a similar effect *per* Mr. Justice Scrutton, in *Landauer & Co. v. Craven & Speeding Bros.* [1912] 2 K.B. 94 at p. 105] or within all reasonable despatch [*per* Lord Atkinson *in Johnson v. Taylor Bros. & Co. Ltd.* [1920] A.C. 144, 156] or within a reasonable time after shipment [*ibid. per* Lord Birkenhead at p. 149].''[10]

---

[7] (1902) 8 Com.Cas. at p. 107.
[8] [1980] 1 Lloyd's Rep. 143 (C.A.), affirming [1978] 2 Lloyd's Rep. 555.
[9] [1978] 2 Lloyd's Rep. 555.
[10] [1978] 2 Lloyd's Rep. 555 at p. 558.

The buyers were thus entitled to treat the breach as a repudiation of the contract. The learned judge further opined, on the more general question of time of performance, that a breach of a term as to the date of shipment under a c.i.f. commodity contract will *always* entitle the buyer to rescind "in the absence of waiver or estoppel or some wholly unusual surrounding circumstance" notwithstanding that, on the particular facts, the date of shipment was commercially immaterial. The reason being that commodities are commonly dealt in by reference to a description which includes the date of shipment, and which, thus, has a vital impact upon market value and price. This decision was upheld by the Court of Appeal. On the other hand, the buyer may of course waive strict compliance with the condition on timely presentation of the documents in which case he cannot later treat the untimely production of the documents as a breach of a condition.[11] The fact that the buyer was ignorant of his rights to insist on immediate provision of the documents was immaterial and his later attempt to justify failure to pay on this ground and attempt to cure his default thereby was thus doomed. The buyer may thus become liable for breach of contract if he has no other valid defence to the claim.

272   *Currency of account and of payment.* Problems sometimes arise as a result of ambiguous terms with respect to currency provisions in international sales contracts. Ordinarily, where the contract provides for payment in a specified currency, any change in exchange rates in that currency will not affect the obligation of the buyer. A devaluation of that currency will harm the seller, while an appreciation thereof would inure to his benefit. Consequently, parties to contracts sometimes stipulate as to the effects of a change in currency rates on the payment provisions of their contracts in order to guard against the risks of currency fluctuations. Mention has already been made of the term "c.i.f. and e." which is sometimes held to refer to the seller's specific agreement to assume the risk of currency conversion.[12] This however appears to be the position even absent any such or similar designation.

For this reason, where a different result is desired, any stipulation attempting to place the risk of variation in exchange rates (between the time of conclusion of the contract and the time of payment) should be as unambiguous as possible.

In *Woodhouse A.C. Israel Cocoa Ltd. S.A.* v. *Nigerian Produce Marketing Co. Ltd.*,[13] English buyers bought cocoa from Nigerian sellers. From 1963

---

[11] See, *e.g. Cerealmangimi S.p.A.* v. *Toepfer ("The Eurometal")* [1981] 1 Lloyd's Rep. 337. Contract contained clause requiring "payment in cash ... in exchange for shipping documents. ... If shipping documents have not been sighted at time of vessel's arrival, ... sellers shall provide other documents ... entitling buyers to claim delivery of the goods ... and payment must be made in exchange for same." In this case, the buyers were held in default, and liable for damages for failure to make payment on arrival of vessel. Although documents had not been sighted, buyers waived their right to treat non-production of alternate documents as a breach of condition by not insisting upon them.

[12] *Ante*, § 21.

[13] [1971] 2 Q.B. 23, aff'd. [1972] A.C. 741 (H.L.).

onwards, the contracts which called for delivery c.i.f. Liverpool provided for payment in Nigerian pounds in Lagos against presentation and in exchange for shipping documents. Fearing devaluation of sterling, the English buyers tried to get the sellers to vary the contracts. After certain negotiations, the Nigerian sellers wrote to the buyers on September 30, 1967, confirming that payment could be made in sterling, and in Lagos. On November 18, 1967, sterling was devalued by 14 per cent. The Nigerian pound was not devalued. Thereupon the buyers claimed that payment should be made in sterling whereas the Nigerian sellers claimed that the buyers had to provide enough sterling to cover the contract number of Nigerian pounds. The House of Lords concurred with the judgment of the Court of Appeal which found for the sellers, and reversed a decision by Roskill J. who (feeling bound by an arbitration award) held that the sellers were bound to accept payment as if the contract price was expressed to be in sterling. The basis of the decision is a distinction between the money of account and the money of payment. As explained by Lord Denning M.R. in the Court of Appeal[14]:

> "At the heart of this case lies the difference between the *money of account* and the *money of payment*. It is this: the *money of account* is the currency in which an obligation is measured. It tells the debtor how much he has to pay. The *money of payment* is the currency in which the obligation is to be discharged. It tells the debtor by what means he is to pay."

The opinion states the interpretation of the exchange of letters between the parties to be a matter of law for the court to decide unless a special case was stated in such a way as not to leave to the court a particular point of construction. Therefore, the court was not bound by the Umpire's findings. It was free to decide that by the letter of September 30, 1967 (in which the sellers informed the buyers that for all contracts then open they were at liberty to make payment in sterling provided payment was made in Lagos and buyer bore all transfer charges) did not alter the money of account, *i.e.* Nigerian pounds, but varied the contracts only in respect of the money of payment. Consequently, after sterling devalued, the buyers still had to pay the stipulated number of Nigerian pounds but could do so by providing enough pounds sterling to acquire these Nigerian pounds. It will be seen that the decision is based on the interpretation of the contract and the surrounding circumstances, and that whilst in the arbitration the matter was construed one way, the court took a different view. In refusing to hold that by the letter of September 30 the sellers represented to the buyers that the money of account had been altered, the court held that the buyers' understanding of the letter was in fact irrelevant.

A similar problem arose in *W. J. Alan & Co. Ltd. v. El Nasr Export and Import Co.*[15] There sellers of coffee with a business in Kenya agreed to sell to the buyers, an Egyptian state trading corporation, two lots of 250 tons of coffee f.o.b. Mombasa. The price stated was "shs. 262/- . . . per cwt. . . . "

---

[14] [1971] 2 Q.B. at p. 54.
[15] [1972] 2 Q.B. 189 (C.A.).

and payment was to be through a confirmed irrevocable letter of credit to be opened one month prior to shipment. The buyers resold the coffee to sub-buyers who opened an irrevocable letter of credit in Madrid in sterling, which letter the buyers later transferred up to an amount of £131,000 in favour of the sellers. The letter of credit was expressed in terms of payment in sterling and did not conform with the contracts in a number of respects. The sellers however accepted the confirmation of the letter of credit in those terms and presented documents including invoices expressed in sterling. When the final 221 tons under the second contract had been loaded, the sellers prepared an invoice dated November 18, again expressed in sterling. Sterling however was devalued on the same day and before the documents were presented. By November 21, it was known that Kenya would not follow this devaluation. The sellers claimed that Kenya shillings were the currency of account and that the buyers had not discharged their obligations to pay the price by tendering 262s. sterling per cwt. and that they were liable to pay such additional sum as would bring the price up to 262 Kenya shillings at the new rate. The buyers claimed that their obligation had been discharged because the currency of account was sterling, and even if it was not because the sellers had by their conduct in relation to the letter of credit agreed to vary or had waived the payment terms by accepting sterling.

The Court of Appeal (Lord Denning M.R., Megaw and Stephenson L.JJ.) agreed with Orr J. in the court of first instance that the currency of account was Kenya shillings, the decisive factor being the expression of the price in "shs.," an abbreviation appropriate to Kenya shillings but not to shillings in sterling currency. However, the appeal was allowed because the sellers by accepting payment (under a sterling letter of credit) had irrevocably waived their right to be paid in Kenya currency, or accepted a variation in the sale contract so that when the whole price had been paid under the letter of credit, the buyers had discharged their whole contractual obligation and could not be required to pay more. One method of avoiding this type of risk would be through a forward purchase of the relevant currency, but for that a forward market for that currency would have to exist and that, as was the situation in the *Israel Cocoa* case, is not always a certainty.

273 *Payment of duties.* Subject to the terms of the contract, payment of import duties on goods imported under a c.i.f. contract forms no part of the seller's obligation, and if the seller should have to pay them, because tender is made after arrival of the goods, he can recover the amount from the buyer. In the case of *American Commerce Co. Ltd. v. Frederick Boehm Ltd.*[16] the sale was of saccharine to be shipped from New York to a British port at the price of 220s. per lb. c.i.f. "duty paid." Between the date of the contract and tender, the import duty on saccharine imported into Great Britain was increased, and the sellers were obliged to pay the increased duty. They sought to recover the amount of the increase from the buyers. Bray J. held that the words "duty

---

[16] (1919) 35 T.L.R. 224.

paid'' did not constitute an agreement that the sellers should pay the amount of the increase after the date of the contract, and there was therefore ''an agreement to the contrary'' within section 10(1) of the Finance Act 1901, and the sellers were entitled to recover the amount in accordance with the provisions of the section.

Conversely, export duties in the absence of agreement to the contrary,[17] are payable by the seller under a c.i.f. contract, since they are an expense necessarily incurred before he can fulfil his obligation to ship the goods.

The passing of the property

274   The passing of the property is a matter of great significance in c.i.f. contracts and will carry serious consequences for the parties, *e.g.* in the event of the insolvency of the buyer or seller, the loss or destruction of the goods where the loss is not covered by insurance, and the liability to capture and seizure on the outbreak of war. As a general rule in a contract for the sale of goods, the property and the risk pass at the same time,[18] but this is not the usual case in a c.i.f. contract. Under a c.i.f. contract, the buyer is in effect the insurer, as of the time of shipment. The transfer to him of the bill of lading and the policy of insurance giving him the right of action in respect of loss or damage to the goods has the effect of placing the goods at his risk on and after shipment.[19] But the property in the goods may not, and generally does not, pass on shipment. It very often will not pass until tender and payment. The moment at which the property passes is entirely a question of intention to be gathered from the terms of the contract, the conduct of the parties and the circumstances of the case.[20] In the absence of expressed inten-

---

[17] *Produce Brokers New Company (1924) Ltd. v. British Italian Trading Co. Ltd.* [1952] 1 Lloyd's Rep. 379, where the contract provided that ''any variation in export duties or taxes'' to be for buyers' account.

[18] s.20, Sale of Goods Act 1893 (now s.20 of the Sale of Goods Act 1979), following the rule in *Martineau v. Kitching* (1872) L.R. 7 Q.B. 436. Discussed in *The Parchim* [1918] A.C. 159 at p. 168 (P.C.).

[19] *Tregelles v. Sewell* (1862) 7 H. & N. 574, *ante*, 14 *per* Kennedy L.J., *Biddell Bros. v. E. Clemens Horst Co.* [1911] 1 K.B. 934, *ante*, 262; *C. Groom Ltd. v. Barber* [1915] 1 K.B. 316, *per* Atkin J., *ante*, 252. The parties may, however, stipulate for an earlier transfer of risk. In *Reinhart Co. v. J. Hoyle & Sons Ltd.* [1961] 1 Lloyd's Rep. 346, the Court of Appeal (Sellers and Willmer L.JJ.; Donovan L. J. dissenting) considered a c. and f. contract for the sale of cotton. The parties had for many years transacted business on c.i.f. terms under contracts which provided that cover against certain preshipment risks (known as country damage) would be effected by the sellers for the benefit of the buyers, and that the buyers would only be entitled to hold the sellers liable for any damage suffered to which the cover did not extend. The parties then changed their terms of trade to c. and f., and the question arose as to whether the buyers were under the obligations previously assumed by the sellers, namely, to issue cover against country damage, or whether this being a c. and f. contract and the damage having originated prior to delivery to the ship, it should be considered to be for the sellers' account. The majority of the Court of Appeal held that the relevant provision in the contract had been unaltered; that it now placed upon the buyers the duty to effect an appropriate insurance against country damage, and that they could not therefore recover any loss on account thereof from the sellers, because the loss arose from their own breach of duty to provide the necessary insurance cover.

[20] s.17(2), Sale of Goods Act 1979.

tion in the contract, the Sale of Goods Act (1893 as well as the 1979 version) lays down a number of rules which are now discussed, to be applied in order to infer, or, as has been said, to create the intention as to when the property passes.

275   *Unascertained goods.* Whenever goods are sold by description which is usual in c.i.f. contracts, the goods will generally be unascertained and the seller is free to deliver to the buyer any parcel of goods corresponding with the description. The property cannot in any event pass until the goods become ascertained, for the Sale of Goods Act 1979, s.16, provides that:

> "Where there is a contract for the sale of unascertained goods no property in the goods is transferred to the buyer unless and until the goods are ascertained."

The goods become ascertained when they are identified in accordance with the agreement after the time a contract of sale is made.[21] Thus no property can pass whatever the intention of the parties until the goods are ascertained.

The question whether it was possible under a contract for the sale of goods for the property to pass in equity before the goods were ascertained was raised and considered at length in the case of *Re Wait*,[22] but the Court of Appeal (Lord Hanworth M. R. and Atkin L.J., Sargant L.J. dissenting) decided that it could not.

By a c.i.f. contract of November 20, 1925, Wait bought from a London merchant 1,000 tons of Western White wheat *ex Challenger* expected to load at Oregon in December. By a c.i.f. contract of November 21, Wait sold 500 tons of this cargo to sub-purchasers. The wheat was shipped at Oregon on December 21, and a bill of lading for 1,000 tons forwarded to Wait, who received it on January 4, 1926. The purchase-money was due on February 6 (30 days after sight) and on February 5, the sub-purchasers, although they had never received any bill of lading, warrant, delivery order or any document of title representing the goods, and although the 500 tons were never appropriated, gave Wait their cheque for the price of the 500 tons less half the freight payable at destination. Wait, having paid this cheque into his bank and hypothecated the bill of lading for the 1,000 tons, became a bankrupt before the ship arrived. The trustee in bankruptcy redeemed the bill of lading and claimed to be entitled to retain the entire 1,000 tons, leaving the sub-purchasers their remedy in damages provable in the bankruptcy. The sub-purchasers claimed specific performance of the 500 tons under section 52 of the Sale of Goods Act 1893, alternatively for the return of the price paid, alternatively for a declaration that they had a beneficial interest in the arrived wheat to the extent of 500 tons and a charge upon the whole 1,000 tons to secure the repayment of the price. The Court of Appeal disallowed the claim of the sub-purchasers, holding:

---

[21] *Per* Lord Atkin, *Re Wait* [1927] 1 Ch. 606.
[22] [1927] 1 Ch. 606.

(1) that the 500 tons were not specific or ascertained goods in respect of which specific performance of the contract of sale would be ordered; and

(2) that there never was any such appropriation or identification of or any such obligation to deliver a particular 500 tons, so as to effect an equitable assignment giving the sub-purchasers a beneficial interest therein or a lien in respect thereof.

276   This case raised the broad issue whether there could be any equitable assignment of the goods under a contract of sale or in other words whether there was any passing of the property in equity, notwithstanding the provisions of the Sale of Goods Act 1893, s. 16 (now the Sale of Goods Act 1979, s. 16). The decision of the majority of the court proceeded on the ground that specific performance was only rarely ordered in the case of sale of goods and in any event specific performance would not be ordered in respect of unascertained goods. It was held that there could be no equitable assignment as the goods to be assigned were not properly identified, and it was not possible to say which 500 tons out of the whole cargo had been assigned. Atkin L.J., however, went further and considered the general question of the passing of the property in equity under a contract for the sale of goods, and in the course of his judgment he said[23]:

> "Without deciding the point, I think that much may be said for the proposition that an agreement for the sale of goods does not import any agreement to transfer property other than in accordance with the terms of the Code,[24] that is, the intention of the parties to be derived from the terms of the contract, the conduct of the parties and the circumstances of the case, and unless a different intention appears, from the rules set out in s.18. The Code was passed at a time when the principles of equity and equitable remedies were recognised and given effect to in all our Courts, and the particular equitable remedy of specific performance is specially referred to in s.52. The total sum of legal relations (meaning by the word 'legal' existing in equity as well as in common law) arising out of the contract for the sale of goods may well be regarded as defined by the Code. It would have been futile in a code intended for commercial men to have created an elaborate structure of rules dealing with rights at law, if at the same time it was intended to leave, subsisting with the legal rights, equitable rights inconsistent with, more extensive, and coming into existence earlier than the rights so carefully set out in the various sections of the Code."

Atkin L.J. then went on to emphasise that there was nothing to prevent equitable rights coming into existence "dehors" the contract of sale. This decision of the majority of the court was severely criticised at the time by Sir Frederick Pollock,[25] but since then the issue does not seem to have been judicially raised in any way.

---

[23] *Ibid.* at p. 635.
[24] The Sale of Goods Act 1893.
[25] (1927) 47 L.Q.R. 293.

It should however be noted that, as Mustill J. more recently held,[26] goods may be ascertained (for the purposes of section 16) where there are parallel contracts between the parties encompassing the *whole* of a consignment of unascertained goods passing from a seller to a buyer or from different sellers to the buyer. In such a case property may pass even in the absence of appropriation.

277 *Specific or ascertained goods.* Where the subject-matter of the contract are specific goods, that is to say goods identified and agreed upon at the time the contract is made,[27] or else are ascertained goods,[28] then, as has been stated, the general principle is that the property is transferred at the time when the parties intend it to pass. This principle is embodied in the Sale of Goods Act 1979, s.17, which provides as follows:

(1) Where there is a contract for the sale of specific or ascertained goods the property in them is transferred to the buyer at such time as the parties to the contract intend it to be transferred.
(2) For the purpose of ascertaining the intention of the parties regard shall be had to the terms of the contract, the conduct of the parties, and the circumstances of the case.

This rule is easy to state, but it is difficult to apply to cases where the parties have never had any intention at all in their own minds as to when the property should pass. This difficulty is to a large extent removed by the rules laid down in section 18 which are to apply unless a different intention appears. Rules 1–4 relate to specific goods. Applying Rules 1–4 to a c.i.f. contract, prima facie, subject to the terms of the contract, the property in specific or ascertained goods does not pass before the goods are shipped, since, though the goods are ascertained and agreed upon, not only is shipment a condition of the contract to be performed by the seller,[29] but two out of the three instruments which evidence title to a c.i.f. contract, namely, the bill of lading and insurance policy, cannot normally be properly filled out and issued until shipment arrangements have been completed. Whether the property then passes depends upon whether the seller has reserved the right of disposal.[30]

278 *Appropriation.* In the case of unascertained goods, the property cannot pass until the goods have been appropriated to the contract. Rule 5 of section 18 of the Sale of Goods Act 1979, which is subject always to the intention of the parties, provides as follows:

(1) Where there is a contract for the sale of unascertained or future goods

---

[26] *Karlshamns Olje Fabriker v. Eastport Navigation Corp. (The Elafi)* [1981] 2 Lloyd's Rep. 679 (see *ante*, § 164 where the case is more fully considered).
[27] *Ante*, § 275.
[28] See Sale of Goods Act 1979, s.61.
[29] s.18, r. 2.
[30] See *post*, § 281.

by description, and goods of that description and in a deliverable state are unconditionally appropriated to the contract, either by the seller with the assent of the buyer, or by the buyer with the assent of the seller, the property in the goods thereupon passes to the buyer. Such assent may be express or implied, and may be given either before or after the appropriation is made:

(2) Where, in pursuance of the contract, the seller delivers the goods to the buyer or to a carrier or other bailee or custodier (whether named by the buyer or not) for the purpose of transmission to the buyer, and does not reserve the right of disposal, he is deemed to have unconditionally appropriated the goods to the contract.

Appropriation is the act whereby the goods are attached to the contract. It does not necessarily pass the property to the buyer, but it obliges the seller to deliver to the buyer the particular goods that have been appropriated to the contract. It is to be distinguished from a mere desire or intention that a particular parcel of goods shall go to satisfy the contract. Thus, for a seller to ship goods of the contract description on board the ship named in the contract to his own order does not appropriate the goods to the contract. As Scrutton L. J. explained in *Produce Brokers Co. v. Olympia Oil and Cake Co.*[31]

> "The mere shipment of the cargo does not appropriate it to the contract; that is to say, a man who has sold a cargo, supposing that the original seller to him had shipped a cargo at the Oriental port during the named period, would not by that fact alone be bound to deliver it under this contract, and you would consequently expect, if you were familiar with commercial transactions, that there might be some provisions by which the seller was either bound to or might during the voyage or at the time of shipment appropriate the cargo to the contract, not in the sense of passing the property in the cargo, but in the sense of binding himself to deliver that cargo against that contract."

Until the goods are appropriated, they remain at the disposal of the seller and he may do as he wishes with his own property. He is free to dispose of the goods in a manner inconsistent with his obligations under the contract, even though it makes a breach of contract with the buyer inevitable.

Appropriation consists of some act in the nature of an election, done usually by the seller, irrevocably binding himself to deliver a particular parcel of goods to the buyer, and this act might well be the dispatching of goods addressed to the buyer, or the taking of a bill of lading to the buyer's order. As will have been seen from Section 18 Rule 5 above, the appropriation takes place with the assent, express or implied, of the buyer, but this assent is generally inferred from the terms of the contract or the practices of the trade.[32]

The act of appropriation does not, however, by itself alone pass the prop-

---

[31] [1917] 1 K.B. 320 (C.A.) at p. 329.
[32] *Per* Lord Wright in *Ross T. Smyth & Co. Ltd. v. T. D. Bailey, Son & Co.* [1940] 3 All E.R. 60 (H.L.) at p. 66.

erty in the goods to the buyer.[33] The property will only pass provided it is so intended by the parties, or where there has been under Rule 5 an appropriation which is unconditional. In practice, however, the appropriation is sometimes conditional by reason of the fact that the seller has reserved the right of disposal, which is discussed below.[34]

Rule 5, in other words, creates a rebuttable presumption on the transfer of property and it does not make appropriation a precondition of the passing of property where the goods are ascertained. In c.i.f. contracts, the intention is usually that property passes on the transfer of the shipping documents.[35]

However, where the transaction involves portions of bulk cargoes sold to different purchasers, very difficult problems relating to ascertainment and appropriation may arise as there usually can be no physical identification of each separate contract or portion until discharge and (in the usual case of c.i.f. contracts) actual delivery thereof at the port of destination. In such cases, and since so much of English sales (and other) law still depends on the location of property at any given moment, the ordinary rights and obligations arising from c.i.f. contracts may have to yield, and give way to unexpected results.[36] As noted above, the situation was somewhat ameliorated by means of the Carriage of Goods by Sea Act 1992, which was required to negate the result of some of the decisions.

As to the possibility of the c.i.f. seller of unascertained goods appropriating lost or damaged goods to the contract, this, as previously explained (*ante*, § 252), is possible, and the courts have rejected attempts to modify transactions on this basis even where, it is thought, the seller knows of the loss or damage before the appropriation. For only in this way could a c.i.f. seller perform his contractual obligations by the tender of documents representing goods previously shipped by a third party. But the situation may well be different if the loss or damage occured prior to the time the sales contract was made, and certainly, it is thought, where the seller was aware of this fact at such time.

279   *Notice of appropriation.* It is usual in the case of c.i.f. contracts for the goods to be appropriated to the contract by a notice of appropriation which is sent by the seller to the buyer. It is generally required by the contract that such notice shall be delivered within a specified time after shipment, containing details of the name of the ship, the date of the bills of lading, and the exact quantity loaded.[37] This enables the buyer to pass on this essential information to his sub-purchasers as soon as possible.[38] The significance of

---

[33] *Ibid.*

[34] *Post*, § 281.

[35] See *e.g. Karlshamns Olie Fabriker v. Eastport Navigation Corp. (The Elafi)* [1982] 1 All E. R. 208, *ante*, § 164 (buyer able to sue carrier in tort though goods unappropriated).

[36] See *ante*, § 161a and § 162.

[37] For examples, see, *inter alia, Dalgety v. Bradfield* (1930) 35 Com. Cas. 213; *Compagnie continental d'Importation v. Handelsvertretung der U.S.S.R. in Deutschland* (1928) 138 L.T. 663 (C.A.).

[38] For a case of delay, see *André v. Vantol* [1952] 2 Lloyd's Rep. 282.

the date of the bill of lading is that the buyer can satisfy himself that the goods have been shipped within the time specified in the contract.[39]

Where the contract requires the seller to furnish such notice, the requirement usually constitutes an essential step in the seller's performance of his contractual obligations. His failure to comply with it (*e.g.* by serious delay) thus entitles the buyer to reject the documents, and rescind the contract: *Société Italo-Belge Pour le Commerce et l'Industrie v. Palm and Vegetable Oils (Malaysia) Sdn. Bhd. (The "Post Chaser")*,[40] where Goff J. said in the course of his judgment concerning the sale of Malayan palm oil c.i.f. Rotterdam:[41]

> "[T]he requirement of 'declaration of ship' in the present form of contract constitutes an essential step in the seller's performance of his contractual obligations. It is, moreover, an important step; because, once such a declaration is made, the buyer can then appropriate goods from the ship so declared in performance of his obligations to a particular sub-buyer to whom he has already agreed to sell goods of the same contractual description . . . In my judgment, the circumstances of the present case indicate strongly that precise compliance is required in relation to the stipulation as to the time for the declaration of ship in the mercantile contract now before this Court. It is true that the time for compliance is not fixed; but the requirement that the declaration should be made 'as soon as possible after vessel's sailing' indicates that speedy declarations are regarded as important."

Failure to provide the requisite notice of appropriation on time is thus a default for which the buyer may claim damages as of the last date on which the notice could have been given under the contract, and a late notice is therefore an ineffective notice which the buyer is normally entitled to reject.[42] The buyer is right in declaring a default as soon as the relevant notice period has expired if the breach is one that might be remedied retrospectively, *e.g.* as a result of an extension clause that may permit the seller to delay transmittal of the required notice. Where the notice of appropriation is subject to such extension (because of an unforseen supervening event) the seller must provide it by the end of the extended period and failure to do so is a default and the aforegoing principles likewise apply.[43]

The giving of a notice of appropriation cannot (unless the contract other-

[39] See Scrutton L.J. in *C. C. d'Importation* (*ante*) at p. 667.
[40] [1981] 2 Lloyd's Rep. 695.
[41] *Ibid.* at p. 700.
[42] *Bunge G.m.b.H. v. C.C.V. Landbouwberland G.A.* [1978] 2 Lloyd's Rep. 217, aff'd. by C.A. in [1980] 1 Lloyd's Rep. 458. See also *Bunge S.A. v. Schleswig-Holsteinische Landwirtschaftliche Hauptgenossenschaft Enigeter G.m.b.H.* [1978] 1 Lloyd's Rep. 480. But *cf. Bremer Handelsgesellschaft m.b.H. v. Vanden Avenne-Izegem P.V.B.A.* [1978] 2 Lloyd's Rep. 109, where the House of Lords differed with the view of the court of Appeal, and held that in the contract (GAFTA 100) and circumstances there considered a delay in transmitting a notice extending the period in which the notice of appropriation was due (that had to be furnished by the seller without delay) did not result in the loss of the right of extension of the time of performance and cancellation of the contract in question, since the term was not to be construed as a condition.
[43] *Bunge A.G. v. Fuga A.G.* [1980] 2 Lloyd's Rep. 513 where the seller (in a rapidly rising market) unsuccessfully attempted to advance the date of the breach (for the purpose of assessing damages) by alleging that the extension initially claimed by him was bad and invalid.

wise provides[44]) be revoked by the seller, even if the seller has by mistake declared the wrong ship.

In *Grain Union S.A. Antwerp v. Hans Larsen A.S. Aalborg*,[45] the appellants sold to the respondents a quantity of maize to be shipped to the buyers at Copenhagen from certain Danube or Black Sea ports. By one of the conditions of the contract, notice of appropriation with ship's name, date of bill of lading, and approximate quantity loaded, was to be mailed to the buyers within three days, or telegraphed within seven days from the date of the bill of lading, and a valid notice of appropriation once given was not to be withdrawn. The sellers received information that a cargo to fulfil the contract had been loaded in the *Triton* and a clerk employed by the sellers sent a notice of appropriation to the buyers by telegram stating erroneously that the goods were shipped in the *Iris*. This was corrected later by the sellers, but the buyers refused to accept the cargo on the ground that the notice giving the name of the *Iris* was a valid notice of appropriation within the meaning of the contract and could not be withdrawn.

Branson J. (affirming the award of the Appeal Committee of the London Corn Trade Association) held that the buyers were entitled to reject. In the course of his judgment he said[46]:

"Unless it can be shown that that was not a valid notice of appropriation it seems to me that the Appeal Committee were perfectly right. It is suggested that it was not a valid notice of appropriation, because, as Mr. Willink [counsel for the appellants] contends, in order to be a valid notice of appropriation, there must in fact have been an appropriation and the notice must represent what that appropriation in fact was. He says that appropriation is a thing which takes place in the mind of the individual who has to appropriate, and that a notice of it, in order to be valid, must correctly reproduce the effect upon the mind of him who has appropriated. I do not think this contract means that at all. It seems to me that a notice which contains all the essentials, the ship's name, the date of the bill of lading, and the approximate quantity of the goods on board, if all those three elements are in conformity with the contract, is a valid notice of appropriation."

In *Waren Import Gesellschaft Krohn & Co. v. Alfred C. Toepfer (The Vladimir Ilich)*,[47] the sellers of a quantity of Thai tapioca chips-pellets, c.i.f. Hamburg, telexed an appropriation notice describing the name of the vessel as "Vladimir (or better name)." The buyers rejected the notice as non-contractual advising the sellers that, in accordance with their information, no steamer by that name loaded at the relevant time in Bangkok. The sellers then telexed the buyers that the correct name of the vessel was Vladimir Ilich. Apart from that, the appropriation notice was in compliance with the contract terms. Donaldson J. dismissed the buyer's defence and said:

---

[44] Many c.i.f. contracts now provide for the right to correct errors.
[45] (1933) 38 Com.Cas. 260.
[46] *Ibid.* at p. 266.
[47] [1975] 1 Lloyd's Rep. 322.

"It is important to remember that an appropriation is a matter of contract, not of performance. That comes later. Accordingly, validity depends upon form and timing and not upon substance or factual accuracy. The appropriation was made within the proper time and was not defective in form. At first sight it might be thought that to specify the "Vladimir (or better name)" deprived the appropriation of its essential certainty, but it appears that the addition of those words [or better name] has been accepted in the trade for over 40 years. . . . They have been held to have no further effect than the limited right to correct errors in transmission. . . ."[48] Accordingly, the . . . appropriation was valid." (at p. 329).

Nor were the buyers successful in their alternative argument that they could accept the appropriation as an anticipatory breach on the grounds that the sellers could not perform since the goods had been shipped on the *Vladimir Ilich* and not on the *Vladimir*. That argument failed for a variety of reasons including the inability of the buyers to have it both ways.

However in *Kleinjan & Holst N.V. v. Bremer Handelsgesellschaft m.b.H.*,[49] the sale was of sugarbeet pulp pellets c.i.f. Rotterdam. It was provided that "notice of appropriation" stating the vessel's name would be despatched but that such notice would be "open to correction of any errors occurring in transmission." The appropriation notice named the wrong vessels and the seller subsequently sought to correct the error. Cooke J. held that the error was not one occurring in transmission, and that the correction was of no effect. In principle he thought the buyer could reject[50] but since the buyer there accepted the goods, the breach was reduced from a breach of condition to a breach of warranty and his remedy was confined to damages resulting from the breach, namely, the difference between the contract price, and the market price of similar goods at the time the documents were tendered.[51]

It should be noted that although the buyer must promptly decide on whether or not to accept a non-contractual notice of appropriation (*e.g.* in respect of a late shipment) he does not waive his rights by failing to act instantaneously. Thus, when a notice of appropriation which was for late shipment was put forward (i) the recipient of that notice was at least entitled to see whether his sub-buyers wished to accept or not, and (ii) to consider whether he himself wished to accept or not, and two days delay could not produce any particular result, and could not be regarded as an affirmation of the contract by the buyers.[52] Nor can the fact that the buyer has (in an instalment contract) accepted untimely notices of appropriation and late shipments

---

[48] See, *e.g. Aure v. Van Cauwenberghe & Fils* [1938] 2 All E.R. 300.
[49] [1972] 2 Lloyd's Rep. 11.
[50] In *Vargas Pena Apezteguiaŷ Cia Saic v. Peter Cremer G.m.b.H.* [1987] 1 Lloyd's Rep. 394 Saville J. opined that the views expressed by Cooke J. as to the unqualified right of a c.i.f. buyer to reject for failure to be presented with the proper documents were open to question, and in *Proctor & Gamble Philippine Manufacturing Corp. v. Kurt A. Becher G.m.b.H. & Co. K.G.* [1988] 2 Lloyd's Rep. 21 (*post*, § 337) the Court of Appeal concurred with his views. However, the outcome of the case was not open to challenge because, under the facts, Cooke J. only awarded damages for breach of warranty.
[51] See *post*, Chap. 6.
[52] *Bremer Handelsgesellschaft m.b.H. v. Deutsche-Conti Handelsgesellschaft m.b.H.* [1981] 2 Lloyd's Rep. 112, affirmed in [1983] 2 Lloyd' Rep. 45 (C.A.).

in respect of certain deliveries be treated as an indication that the contractual right was being abandoned for the future.[53]

Nevertheless the fact that the appropriation notice includes details which were not expressly required by the contract in question and/or that some of the information included in the notice turns out to be erroneous is not of itself, without evidence or reason to suppose that the error has caused any harm, to be considered as a repudiation or a fundamental breach of contract.[54] In some cases of string transactions between buyers and sellers who are under common ownership, but possess distinct legal entities, difficulties have sometimes arisen as to compliance with the time the appropriation notice was given from the "seller" to the "buyer."[55] The terms of the particular term or clause in question will of course determine the period within which the notice of appropriation must be provided by the different sellers (to their respective buyers). But where the contract provides that:

> "Notice of Appropriation stating the vessel's name and approximate weight shipped, shall, within
>   (i) 10 consecutive days if shipped from the US Gulf and/or US and/or Canadian Atlantic ports,
>   (ii) 14 consecutive days if shipped from any other port, from the date of the Bills of lading be despatched by or on behalf of the shipper to the first buyer ... and by or on behalf of each subsequent seller to his buyers ... but if notice of appropriation is received by a subsequent seller after the period ... his notice of appropriation shall be deemed to be in time if despatched (1) on the same calendar day, if received not later than 16.00 hours on any business day (2) not later than the next business day, if received after 16.00 or on a non-business day,"

and the notice to a particular buyer (in the string transaction) is dispatched more than 10 (or 14) days after the date of the bill of lading, it is for the sellers to prove, on the balance of probabilities, that every seller in the string despatched his notice of appropriation in time for the notice to be valid. A seller, in other words, cannot (under the terms of the said clause) validate a late notice *vis-à-vis* his buyer by despatching it promptly.[56]

280 Effect of appropriation on ability to claim benefit of exemption clause in case of partial performance

Difficult problems as to the effect of the appropriation of goods to a particular c.i.f. contract have sometimes arisen in situations where the contract could not be performed in full because of *e.g.* an export embargo that is subsequently lifted in part. Does the *ex post facto* appropriation in part performance of the particular contract (in such circumstances) indicate that per-

[53] *Finagrain S.A. Geneva v. P. Kruse Hamburg* [1976] 2 Lloyd' Rep. 508 (C.A.).
[54] *Bremer Handelsgesellschaft m.b.H. v. Toepfer* [1980] 2 Lloyd's Rep. 43 (C.A.).
[55] *Ibid.*
[56] *Tradax Export S.A. v. André & Cie S.A.* [1977] 2 Lloyd's Rep. 485 (C.A.).

formance of the balance of the contract was also prevented by the embargo, or must the seller further show that a general justification for non-performance (from alternative sources of supply) obtained. Such a question arose in *Bremer Handelsgesellschaft m.b.H. v. Continental Grain*[57] where the sellers were held liable to the buyers for the non-delivery of the balance of a June instalment of soya bean meal. The soya became subject to an export embargo (which however was subject to certain loop-holes) and the embargo was subsequently lifted to the extent of 40 per cent of pre-existing commitments. The seller appropriated a quantity of soya bean meal in fulfilment of 40 per cent of the contract and in reliance thereon attempted to invoke an exemption clause in respect of the balance. The issue before the court was whether the tracing of a chain of appropriations (in a string transaction) leads inevitably to the identification of the relevant ''shipper'' who could establish an excuse based on the export embargo. The Court of Appeal, affirming Mustill J., answered this question in the negative.[58] The court held that while the appropriations may point to the relevant ''shipper,''[59] this is not necessarily the position in every case. Here the seller retained the freedom to appropriate to the contract goods either shipped by himself or goods appropriated to him by pre-sellers and the contrary inference was drawn by the court. The fact that *ex post facto* the seller achieved part fulfilment by means of goods derived from one source, cannot demonstrate conclusively that if there had been no supervening export embargo he would have made complete fulfilment with goods from the self same source. There is no commercial logic in treating subsequent performance as conclusive, since, if it were the test, the seller could pick and choose which contracts he decided to perform, on the basis of those that were most favourable to him. Subsequent performance may be useful evidence, depending on the particular facts of a given case, but it cannot be said that it necessarily follows that he who shipped after the embargo should necessarily have shipped if there had been no such event.

281   *Reservation of right of disposal.* The property in unascertained goods cannot pass until the goods are appropriated to the contract. Whether the effect of such appropriation is there and then to vest the property in the goods in the buyer depends in substance upon the form in which the bill of lading is taken. If by the bill of lading delivery is to be to the buyer or his agent, it would appear that the property passes to the buyer immediately on shipment, unless the seller retains the bill of lading as security for the price, in which case the property vests on tender of the price; if by the bill of lading the goods are deliverable to the seller or his agent, the principles stated in the judgments of Bramwell and Cotton L.JJ. in *Mirabita v. Imperial Ottoman*

---

[57] [1983] 1 Lloyd's Rep. 269 (C.A.).
[58] A similar conclusion was reached in *Deutsche Conti Handelgesellschaft M.B.H. v. Bremer Handelsgesellschaft M.B.H.* [1984] 1 Lloyd's Rep 447.
[59] As was, *e.g.* the case in *Tradax Export S.A. v. Cook Industries Inc.* [1982] 1 Lloyd's Rep. 385 (C.A.).

Bank[60] and enacted in section 19(1) and (2) of the Act of 1893 and 1979 may apply.

This section provides as follows:

(1) Where there is a contract for the sale of specific goods or where goods are subsequently appropriated to the contract, the seller may, by the terms of the contract or appropriation, reserve the right of disposal of the goods until certain conditions are fulfilled. In such case, notwithstanding the delivery of the goods to the buyer, or to a carrier or other bailee or custodier for the purpose of transmission to the buyer, the property in the goods does not pass to the buyer until the conditions imposed by the seller are fulfilled.

(2) Where goods are shipped, and by the bill of lading the goods are deliverable to the order of the seller or his agent, the seller is prima facie deemed to reserve the right of disposal.

(3) Where the seller of goods draws on the buyer for the price, and transmits the bill of exchange and bill of lading to the buyer together to secure acceptance of payment of the bill of exchange, the buyer is bound to return the bill of lading if he does not honour the bill of exchange, and if he wrongfully retains the bill of lading the property in the goods does not pass to him.

The effect of taking the bill of lading to the order of the seller may be to withhold the goods from the contract and then there is in fact no appropriation. There may, however, be an appropriation which is conditional upon a subsequent event, *i.e.* the tender of the price, in which case the property passes when the condition has been fulfilled.

As stated by Scrutton J. in one case[61]:

"... where the seller by taking the bills of lading in his own name or to his own order has reserved the jus disponendi or power of dealing with the goods, the property does not pass on shipment, but is vested in the vendor until he receives payment from the buyer in exchange for the documents of title. If the seller has taken the bill of lading in the purchaser's name but retains it as security for the price, the property appears to vest on the buyer's tendering the price."

And in *Eastwood & Holt v. Studer*, Roche J. said[62]:

"... although, as Lord Parker said in *The Parchim*[63] ... the presumption of the reservation of a right of disposal that is derived from the retention of documents until payment is made is a presumption which may be rebutted, yet the general and natural conclusion from the retention of documents is that the right of disposal of the goods is thereby retained."

---

[60] (1878) 3 Ex.D. 164 (C.A.), *post*, 558 *et seq.*
[61] *Arnhold Karberg & Co. v. Blythe, Green, Jourdain & Co.* [1915] 2 K.B. 379 at p. 387. The passage refers to Scrutton J.'s summation of the effect of the judgments in *Mirabita v. Imperial Ottoman Bank* (1878) 3 Ex.D. 164, *post*, 558.
[62] (1926) 31 Com. Cas. 251 at p. 255.
[63] [1918] A.C. 157 (P.C.), *post*, § 569.

282   Where the seller discounts the bill of exchange drawn upon the buyer with a banker and delivers him the bill of lading as security, the general property remains in the seller until the bill of exchange is accepted by the buyer when the property passes.

In *The Prinz Adalbert*,[64] a Prize case, American sellers shipped lubricating oil in a German steamer and consigned it to a Hamburg firm, two bills of lading being taken to the seller's order at Hamburg. The bills were indorsed in blank and attached to two drafts drawn by the sellers on the Hamburg firm and discounted with an American bank which forwarded the documents to Germany. One draft was accepted by the Hamburg firm on August 1, 1914 the other was stated to have been accepted on August 10. In the meantime the First World War broke out, and on August 5 the steamer was captured by the British. The sellers, on August 18, claimed the oil in the Prize Court as their property. The Privy Council held that it was the sellers' intention that the property should pass on acceptance of the drafts, that therefore the property in the first consignment passed to the German firm on August 1. As regards the second consignment, the sellers were held not to have proved that they were the owners on August 18.

In the course of expressing the opinion of the court, Lord Sumner said[65]:

> "... the delivery of an indorsed bill of lading, made out to the shipper's order while the goods are afloat, is equivalent to delivery of the goods themselves, and is effectual to transfer ownership if made with that intention. The bill of lading is the symbol of the goods. Apart from specific formalities or similar prescriptions of municipal law, which are not now material, such intention is a question of fact. The usual course of dealing in the export of merchandise and the interest of the parties concerned in it suffice for the necessary inference in the absence of evidence to the contrary. When a shipper takes his draft, not as yet accepted, but accompanied by a bill of lading, indorsed in this way, and discounts it with a banker, he makes himself liable on the instrument as drawer, and he further makes the goods, which the bill of lading represents, security for its payment. If, in turn, the discounting banker surrenders the bill of lading to the acceptor against his acceptance, the inference is that he is satisfied to part with his security in consideration of getting this further party's liability on the bill, and that in so doing he acts with the permission and by the mandate of the shipper and drawer. Possession of the indorsed bill of lading enables the acceptor to get possession of the goods on the ship's arrival. If the shipper, being then owner of the goods, authorises and directs the banker, to whom he is himself liable and whose interest it is to continue to hold the bill of lading till the draft is accepted, to surrender the bill of lading against acceptance of the draft, it is natural to infer that he intends to transfer the ownership when this is done, but intends also to remain the owner until this has been done. Particular arrangements made between shipper and consignee may modify or rebut these inferences, but in the absence of evidence to the contrary, and apart from rules which arise only out of a state of war existing or imminent at the beginning of the transaction,[66] the general law

---

[64] [1917] A.C. 586 (P.C.).
[65] *Ibid.* at p. 589.
[66] In the case of war, the following principles apply: (a) Neutral property going to be delivered to an enemy is subject to seizure even if the property in the goods has not passed to the enemy at the time of seizure unless the contract was made in time of peace and without any contempla-

infers under these circumstances that the ownership in the goods is transferred when the draft drawn against them is accepted.''

283   On the same principles, in the earlier case of *The Miramichi*,[67] where the buyers refused to accept the bill of exchange or take up the documents, the property was held not to have passed. There, by a contract made in June 1914, American merchants sold wheat c.i.f. to a German firm of Colmar, payment by "check against documents." The sellers bought the wheat for implementing the contract from one Fox, who shipped it at Galveston, Texas, in July 1914, taking the bill of lading to the order of one Davis or his or their assigns. It was indorsed generally, and the sellers, having paid Fox, obtained it but did not indorse it in favour of the buyers. They drew a bill of exchange on the buyers and discounted it with bankers, depositing with the latter the bill of lading and insurance certificates to be delivered to the buyers against payment of the bill, and on the same day they sent an invoice to the buyers with full particulars of the shipment, draft and documents. The goods were shipped in the *Miramichi*, a British ship bound for Rotterdam, but which on the outbreak of war was directed by its owners to proceed to a British port, and the cargo was seized on September 1. On September 3, the buyers refused to accept the documents. It was held by Sir S. Evans P., in the Prize Court, that the sellers had reserved the right to disposal, and the wheat belonged to the sellers and the bankers.

> "In my opinion," said the President,[68] "the result of the many decisions from *Wait v. Baker*[69] up to *Ogg v. Shuter*,[70] *Mirabita v. Ottoman Bank*,[71] and thence up to the Sale of Goods Act 1893; and of the provisions of the Sale of Goods Act 1893, itself, following closely on these matters the judgment of Cotton L.J. in *Mirabita v. Ottoman Bank*; and of the decision subsequent to the Act, *e.g.* *Dupont v. British South Africa Co.*,[72] *Ryan v. Ridley*[73] and *Biddell v. E. Clemens Horst*,[74] is that, in the circumstances of the present case, the goods had not at

---

tion of war. (b) Enemy property cannot pass to a neutral while it is *in transitu* so as to protect it from capture. But the latter rule does not apply in the following three classes of cases:

> "(1) Where the goods were shipped upon a vessel chartered by the purchaser and payment was made and all documents handed over before the vessel sailed, the contract being f.o.b., payment to be made against documents at the port of loading;
>
> (2) where the goods were shipped on a general ship, not chartered by the purchaser, under a contract f.o.b. including freight and insurance, payment against documents at the port of loading, or c.i.f with the same provision as to payment, and payment was made and the documents handed over before the vessel sailed . . .;
>
> (3) where the same conditions existed, but payment was not made and the documents not handed over till after the ship sailed, because of the accidents of business, and not because there was any intention to reserve the right of disposition. . . ."

Per Lord Sterndale P. in *The Dirigo. The Hallingdal, and Other Ships* [1919] P. 204 at p. 220.

[67] [1915] P. 71.
[68] *Ibid* at p. 78.
[69] (1848) 2 Ex. 1, *post*, §§ 555 *et seq.*
[70] (1875) 1 C.P.D. 47, *post*, § 557.
[71] (1878) 3 Ex. D. 164, *post*, §§ 558 *et seq.*
[72] (1901) 18 T.L.R. 24, *ante*, § 15.
[73] (1902) 8 Com. Cas. 105, *ante*, § 270.
[74] [1911] 1 K.B. 214; *ibid.* 934; [1912] A.C. 18, *ante*, § 261

the time of seizure passed to the buyers; but that the sellers had reserved a right of disposal or a jus disponendi over them, and that the goods still remained their property and would so remain until the shipping documents had been tendered to and taken over by the buyers, and the bill of exchange for the price had been paid.''

284   The case of *Stein, Forbes & Co. v. County Tailoring Co.*[75] affords, perhaps, a useful example of the application of the principles stated to an ordinary c.i.f. contract. There buyers of sheepskins c.i.f. Liverpool, "payment net cash against documents on arrival of the steamer," refused to take up the documents. The sellers sued, not for damages but for the price, which they could only recover if the property had passed to the buyers. They contended unsuccessfully that the property passed to the buyers on shipment or on tender of the documents and that they were entitled to the price. Atkin J. said:[76]

"At what time property passes under a contract of sale depends upon the intention of the parties . . . The Act provides certain rules for ascertaining the intention of the parties unless a different intention appears. Counsel for the plaintiff's contends that, as soon as the goods are unconditionally appropriated to the contract and the seller holds the documents at the disposal of the buyer, the property passes. The value of that proposition depends on the meaning of 'unconditionally.' I doubt whether goods are appropriated unconditionally if the seller does not mean the buyer to have them unless he pays for them. But it seems to me impossible to lay down a general rule applicable to all c.i.f. contracts. The overruling question is 'Does the intention of the parties appear in the course of the making and the fulfilment of the contract?'' . . . In the present case the goods were shipped at New York, on behalf of the plaintiffs and the bill of lading was taken to the order of the banking firm which financed the transaction for the plaintiffs. On arrival of the ship the plaintiffs had to take up the bill of lading from the bankers, and, as the defendants would not take up the documents, the plaintiffs had to take delivery of the goods from the ship. It seems quite plain that the seller or his banker reserved the jus disponendi. It was said that the property passed to the buyer on shipment, and the seller only received his unpaid seller's lien. That view seems to me inconsistent with section 19 of the Sale of Goods Act 1893,''[77] and with every business probability.

"Then it is said that, whatever the original intention may be, at any rate the property passes when there is appropriation of specific goods, as by the invoice in this case and a tender or willingness to tender. It would be a remarkable intention in a commercial man to keep the property on shipment in order to secure payment, but yet in taking the necessary steps to procure payment by appropriation and tender to part with the property before payment is in fact made, I think that in such cases the ordinary inference to be drawn is that the seller does not intend to part with the property except against payment. It seems to me that this view is confirmed by the provision of section 19, subsection 3, of the Act.''

---

[75] (1916) 86 L.J.K.B. 448.
[76] *Ibid.* at pp. 448, 449.
[77] (Now s. 19 of the Sale of Goods Act 1979) set out *ante*, § 281.

285   In *The Glenroy*,[78] the Judicial Committee of the Privy Council dismissed the appeal of H.M. Procurator-General from a decision of the Prize Court. The Judicial Committee held that there was nothing that differentiated the facts in question from an ordinary c.i.f. contract, and that, accordingly, the buyers having refused to accept the draft or take up the documents, the property had not passed to them.

The facts were that Mitsui, a Japanese corporation, had branches in Hamburg and London as well as at Otaru in Japan. In July 1939 the Otaru branch sold to the Hamburg branch a cargo of beans c.i.f. Hamburg, payment to be made by a three months' sight draft against a letter of credit on a bank. An irrevocable letter of credit was duly issued by the Hamburg branch of the Yokohama Specie Bank authorising Mitsui (Otaru) to draw on the London branch of the bank at three months for account of Mitsui (Hamburg). Bills of lading to be drawn in triplicate were to be made out to the order of the bank, and the invoices and insurance, in triplicate, were to be in the bank's name or in that of the shipper and blank indorsed. Two sets of documents were to be sent to the bank at Hamburg and one set, with drafts on London attached, was to be delivered to the bank in London against acceptance of the drafts.

On July 31, the goods were shipped in Japan on the M.V. *Glenroy*, a British vessel, and bills of lading were taken out for delivery in Hamburg unto order of the bank. The three sets of documents were delivered as arranged, the bill being drawn by the Japanese company on August 7. The set sent to London was received on September 13, and owing to the outbreak of war the draft was not accepted nor the documents taken up. On September 13 Mitsui (Hamburg) cancelled the contract unconditionally. Meanwhile the *Glenroy* had been diverted to Liverpool, where she arrived on October 17, and there on November 2, the goods were seized as prize. The Crown claimed that the goods were enemy property or contraband of war and as such liable to condemnation. One of the issues was whether under the contract, assuming that Mitsui in Japan and Mitsui in Germany were two separate entities, the property had passed to the German company so as to become enemy property.

286   Lord Porter, giving the judgment of the Privy Council, explained that this was prima facie a typical c.i.f. contract and in the ordinary way the property did not pass until the documents were taken up and paid for. He then continued[79]:

> "The appellant [the Crown] agrees that in the ordinary case the property in the goods does not pass, but he says that this is not an ordinary case. So far as subs.(2) [of section 19, Sale of Goods Act 1893] is concerned, he says that normally the bank to whose order the goods are deliverable is the seller's, not the buyer's agent, but that in the present case the bank was the buyer's agent.

---

[78] *Part cargo ex M.V. Glenroy. H.M. Procurator-General v. M.C. Spencer, Controller of Mitsui & Co. Ltd.* [1945] A.C. 124.
[79] *Ibid.* at p. 135.

Further, he says that in any case the intention to reserve the right of disposal is only a prima facie one and can be disproved by other circumstances. The facts on which he relied for this disproof were:

(1) That the sellers had obtained a letter of credit from the bank undertaking, if certain conditions were fulfilled (which, in fact, were fulfilled), that the drafts would be honoured on presentation at its house in London;

(2) that under the letter of credit two copies of the documents were to be sent to the Hamburg branch of the bank without any conditions being imposed on that bank to withhold delivery in case the draft sent to London was not accepted;

(3) that the draft must be negotiated through a branch of the same bank;

(4) that the relationship of the parties was such that security for payment was immaterial: the profit would go in any case to one or the other; and

(5) that the invoice described the goods as shipped 'by order and for account of Mitsui (Hamburg).'

"For the purpose of this argument it must, of course, be assumed that the two companies are separate entities, capable of contracting with one another and so organised that the property may pass from the one to the other. It *had* passed, said the Crown, because the sellers had no interest in retaining it: they had negotiated a bill of exchange and received payment, and not only was acceptance and payment to be made by their subsidiary, but they had received a letter of credit from the bank undertaking that it should be honoured: they were no longer interested in the goods: they had been paid in full.

"This argument, in their Lordships' view, neglects the liability of the sellers as drawers of the bill of exchange: the bank might fail, or some such event might come to pass as in fact occurred in the present case: the sellers were still interested, and not only in theory but in fact were very much interested in the final disposal of the goods. Nor do their Lordships think that the provision in the letter of credit that two of the sets of documents were to go to the bank at Hamburg is a circumstance from which an inference as to change of property can be drawn. From a letter sent on August 7, 1939, by the Otaru branch of the bank to its Hamburg branch it is plain that the bills of exchange had been drawn on the London office in pursuance of the letter of credit emanating from the Hamburg branch, and that branch from the start was aware that the drafts would be attached to the documents sent to London. The most obvious inference is that the two sets of documents sent to Hamburg were in duplicate for safety's sake, and they may well have been transmitted to Germany so that the goods might be released at the earliest moment at which it was known that the bill had been honoured in London without waiting for the transmission of the bills of lading thence. In any case, the issue of a set of three bills of lading is usual, and no inference can, in their Lordships' opinion, be drawn from the mere fact that for convenience sake two are dispatched to a destination where they may be required ... In their Lordships' view the property had not passed to the Hamburg company."

287   Similarly, where the plaintiffs refused to tender the shipping documents to the defendants, suspecting their financial position because a 90-day draft drawn in respect of a previous consignment was dishonoured, Roskill J. held in *Cheetham & Co. Ltd. v. Thornham Spinning Co. Ltd.*[80] that the property in the goods did not pass. The contract was for the sale of American cotton c.i.f. Manchester, payment cash in exchange for documents on arrival of vessel. After the cotton was unloaded, the parties agreed that the bales should

---

[80] [1964] 2 Lloyd's Rep. 17.

be sent to the defendants' warehouse in order to save quay rent and other expenses. The defendants went into voluntary liquidation and a dispute arose between the sellers, who claimed that the cotton remained their property, and the liquidator. The liquidator contended that the property in the cotton had passed to the buyers and that the sellers were entitled to no more than their dividend as unsecured creditors in the winding up. But Roskill J. held in favour of the sellers. According to section 17 of the Sale of Goods Act the passage of property depends on the intention of the parties, and the fact that the sellers at no time allowed the buyers to obtain the shipping documents, which they presumably returned to the carrier for the purpose of receiving the shipment, evinced an intention to retain the property.

288   In *Ginzberg & Others v. Barrow Haematite Steel Co. Ltd. and McKellar*,[81] the question arose as to whether the plaintiffs who had enabled the defendants to obtain delivery of the goods from the ship by means of a delivery order had parted with the property therein before the condition of payment was met. There the plaintiffs sold to the first defendants 10,000 long tons of manganese ore, c.i.f. Birkenhead payment against clean bills of lading. The ore was shipped from India in a ship chartered by the plaintiffs. As a result of delays experienced in obtaining release of the signed bills of lading, the ship arrived at her port of destination before the bills were available. In order to accommodate the buyers who urged the sellers to expedite delivery, the latter obtained the agreement of the shipowner to issue a delivery order which they tendered to the defendants together with a provisional invoice for the goods. The first defendants then obtained delivery of the ore but they failed to remit the price. A few weeks thereafter, the second defendant was appointed receiver of the buyers undertaking by the trustees of certain secured creditors, whereupon the plaintiffs sent notice to the defendants claiming the goods as owners, and warning them not to part with the possession thereof. Since the receiver failed to acknowledge the claim, an action to recover the goods, or their value, was commenced. The question before the court was whether the property in the goods passed to the defendants when the goods were delivered by the ship pursuant to the delivery order in accordance with the plaintiffs' instructions. McNair J. answered this question in the negative. He noted that:

> "It [was] well settled law that in the case of an ordinary c.i.f. contract for the sale of unascertained goods, the seller fulfils the contract by transferring the bills of lading and the policies to the buyer together with an invoice, but as a general rule he does so only against payment of the price less the freight, if any, payable at destination which the buyer has to pay, and normally no property passes to the buyer until he has paid the price so reduced . . . This case raises the interesting and, I believe, novel question whether, when, as is not uncommon in these days when . . . the bills of lading do not reach the sellers until after the ship with the goods has arrived at the port of destination, the practice of tendering to the

---

[81] [1966] 1 Lloyd's Rep. 343.

buyer a delivery order on the ship coupled with an invoice requiring payment for the goods has any different effect." (at p. 348.)

In the opinion of McNair J. the terms of the contract had not been varied by the substitution of a different method of delivery and a different method of payment as the defendants in this case contended. He rejected the submission that payment had ceased to be a condition upon which the passage of property depended, and had become a mere concurrent obligation to delivery; for no evidence of any intention or agreement to vary the terms of the contract was produced. He therefore concluded that:

"... the true inference from the facts and the documents in the present case is that the plaintiffs intended merely to expedite the delivery for the benefit of the defendants (albeit they were not themselves in a position to tender bills of lading) without in any way departing from the fundamental principles of their c.i.f. contract the implementation of which would safeguard them against losing the property in the goods until payment was made. It was at most merely an alteration in the mechanics of delivery. Furthermore, in so far as the question is one of actual intention as distinct from inferred intention, it may be relevant to state that there was evidence ... that the plaintiffs make it a rule never to sell on credit." (at p. 353.)

289   The authoritative statements which have been quoted of the principles upon which the court acts in determining the question as to when property passes in a sale of goods to be shipped, amplifying the terms of the Sale of Goods Act, afford a working guide for determination of the question in relation to c.i.f. contracts. No good purpose, it is thought, would be served by the citation of decisions on particular contracts and facts which rarely present substantial similarity.[82] The recital of decisions on different sets of facts tends rather to obscure than to elucidate the principles. Moreover, as Atkin J. has pointed out in *C. Groom Ltd. v. Barber*,[83] it is generally immaterial in whom the property in goods sold c.i.f. was before tender, whether it was in the seller or in the buyer or in a third party, since the seller's obligation is to deliver the documents to the buyer within a reasonable time after shipment and possession of the documents gives the buyer the right to obtain delivery of the goods, and in the case of loss or damage or misdelivery to recover therefore, in a proper case, under the policy of insurance or the contract of carriage. There is no doubt whatsoever that a reservation of the property in the goods until payment does not destroy the nature of a c.i.f. contract. Indeed, the seller "need not have appropriated the particular goods in the particular bill of lading to the particular buyer until the moment of tender nor need he have obtained any right to deal with the bill of lading until the moment of tender. If it were otherwise, the shipper of goods in bulk, or of

---

[82] American and other foreign cases on this topic are reviewed by Crawford, "Analysis and Operation of a C.I.F. Contract," in *The Tulane Law Review*, Vol. 29, p. 396 at pp. 400 *et seq.* (1955).
[83] [1915] 1 K.B. 316, *ante*, § 252.

goods intended for several contracts, or the intermediate seller who may be the last of a chain of purchasers from an original shipper, might find it impossible to enforce a contract on c.i.f. terms.''[84]

However, the foregoing notwithstanding, the problem (and the precise time of the transfer of property) may be of great import in specific cases. It may *inter alia* be of importance in relation to claims against third parties (*ante*, §§ 163 *et seq.*), the warranty imported by section 2(2) of the Fertilisers and Feeding Stuffs Act 1926 (*post*, §§ 406 *et seq*), the rights in case of insolvency and the seller's right to claim the price of the goods as distinct from damages for breach. For, if it is held that the seller has reserved his right of disposal, a default by the buyer in refusing to accept tender of the documents would be a bar to recovery of the price, and his remedy would sound in damages for breach only.[85] The latter difficulty is compounded in the case of f.o.b. contracts, and it is therefore proposed to defer a further discussion of this problem for consideration in connection therewith.[86] Suffice it to say here that where the documents are presented against a letter of credit in the country of origin and collection is completed immediately, as is the normal occurrence under present conditions, the difficulty above mentioned is overcome and many of the problems experienced in the past no longer arise.

[The next paragraph is 301.]

---

[84] *Ibid.* at p. 324.
[85] *Post*, § 353.
[86] *Post*, §§ 569 *et seq.*

CHAPTER 6

REMEDIES

301 It would be outside the scope of this book to attempt to deal fully with the subject of legal remedies for breaches of contract of sale, in regard to which the reader is referred to the well-known textbooks on the Sale of Goods and Damages. It is intended in this chapter to make some reference, in summary form, to the remedies available to buyer and seller, but in the main to direct attention to certain kinds of questions which commonly present themselves in regard to c.i.f. contracts.

Breach of contract by the seller

302 *Failure to ship or to tender valid documents.* In the event of breach of contract by the seller in failing or refusing to ship the goods or to tender valid documents, the buyer has his remedy in an action for damages for non-delivery.

In the absence of a contrary agreement between the parties,[1] the right of the buyer to damages in respect of such breach is set out in section 51(2) and (3) of the Sale of Goods Act 1979, which read as follows:

> "(2) The measure of damages is the estimated loss directly and naturally resulting, in the ordinary course of events, from the seller's breach of contract.
> (3) Where there is an available market for the goods in question the measure of damages is prima facie to be ascertained by the difference between the contract price and the market or current price[2] of the goods at the time or times when they ought to have been delivered, or (if no time was fixed) then at the time of the refusal to deliver."

The time or times when the goods ought to be delivered in a c.i.f. contract means the time or times when the documents (which represent the goods) would have been tendered to the buyer, if the seller had shipped at the agreed

---

[1] Parties are free to depart from the rule on damages stipulated in the Act. See *per* Lord Wilberforce in *Bremer Handelsgesellschaft m.b. H. v. Vanden Avenne-Izegem P.V.B.A.* [1978] 2 Lloyd's Rep. 109 at p. 117.
[2] As to market price, see *per* James L. J., *Dunkirk Colliery Co. v. Lever* (1878) 9 Ch. D. 20 at p. 25 (C.A.); *Wertheim v. Chicoutimi Pulp Co.* [1911] A.C. 301 at p. 316 (P.C.); *Weiss & Co. v. Sagarmull* (1923) 15 Ll.L. Rep. 134 (no market price: price in contract of resale taken into account).

time and sent the documents to the buyer with all reasonable diligence[3] after shipment.[4] If the contract provides for an extension of the shipping period, then the date for assessment of the damages may be not the last day for performance, or the last day on which the seller could comply with his obligation, but the day after that, particularly if the contract provides for the buyer to enter the market once default has occurred and purchase similar goods, as the latter right cannot be exercised till the later date.[5] The date when the goods would have reached the contractual destination is not the criterion. This was so held by Atkin J., in *C. Sharpe & Co. v. Nosawa & Co.*,[6] in reference to subsection (3) of section 51 above; and, though McCardie J. in a later case[7] seems, perhaps, to have entertained some doubt as to the correctness of the decision, it is submitted that it is only the logical application to section 51(3) of the accepted principle that the delivery intended by a c.i.f. contract is constructive delivery by tender of the shipping documents.

The facts of the case in *Sharpe v. Nosawa* illustrate the application of the principle in the ordinary case. Japanese peas were sold c.i.f. London to be shipped in June. They were not shipped. Shipping documents relating to the last possible shipment in June, in accordance with the course of business between the parties, would have reached London by Trans-Siberian Railway on July 21. The goods, if shipped, would have arrived on August 30. During the month of August the price of Japanese peas in London rose considerably. The sellers admitted that there had been a breach of the contract of sale, but contended that they were only liable for the difference between the contract price and the market price of peas in July. The buyers contended that they were entitled to the market price in August.

303   Atkin J. held that the time for performance of the contract was the time when the documents should have been tendered, namely, on July 21, and he dealt with the question of damages in the following way[8]:

> "What, then, is the remedy of the buyer? His remedies are specified in section 51 of the Sale of Goods Act 1893. His right is to place himself as nearly as possible in that position in which he would have been if the contract had been fulfilled.
>
> "In this case there is first the question: Could the buyers have gone into the

---

[3] See *ante*, § 242.

[4] In a contract for unascertained goods a defective tender of documents may on occasion be cured by a re-tender of comforming documents within the performance period.

[5] See *Alfred C. Toepfer v. Peter Cremer* [1975] 2 Lloyd's Rep. 118 (C.A.) where the shipment period was extended by two months due to a *force majeure* event. The market rose rapidly in that period which ended on July 10, but, by July 11, had again fallen sharply. It was held that the date of default was July 10, and not July 11, but this was considered a wrong decision by the House of Lords in *Bremer Handelsgesellschaft m.b.H. v. Vanden Avenne-Izegem P.V.B.A.* [1978] 2 Lloyd's Rep. 109.

[6] [1917] 2 K.B. 814.

[7] *Produce Brokers Co. v. Weis & Co.* (1918) 87 L.J. K.B. 472, where, having regard to the special terms of the contract, McCardie J. assessed the damages as at the date when a provisional invoice should have been given to the buyers.

[8] [1917] 2 K.B. at p. 819.

market at the time when the contract ought to have been performed and have bought goods c.i.f. June shipment? If so, the difference of price would be the measure of damages. I am not satisfied that they could have bought 93 tons of Japanese peas c.i.f. June shipment, although there was some evidence that they could have bought smaller parcels. The damages are to be assessed on the basis of reasonable conduct on the part of the purchaser. In the circumstances of this case the reasonable thing for a merchant to do who could not buy goods coming forward would be to go into the market and buy goods on the spot. In that way he would put himself as nearly as may be in the position as if the contract had been fulfilled, and would have got control of an equivalent amount of goods. It is true that he may incur further expense by reason of having to take up goods at once, the cost of warehousing, insuring, etc., but that would be part of his damages. It has been suggested that he might and ought to wait until the goods would have arrived. That, in my view, puts him into a different position. If the contract had been performed he would have had control of the goods at the time when the documents would have arrived. If he awaits the arrival of the goods, inasmuch as that may not happen for weeks or months, he is in the meantime subjecting the vendor to the risk of fluctuations in the market not contemplated by the parties and not reasonable. The reasonable course was for the plaintiffs to go into the market and buy goods. There is no doubt that they could have bought Japanese peas on the spot in July.''

304   In *Ströms Bruks Aktie Bolag v. John & Peter Hutchison*,[9] however, the House of Lords held that where failure to deliver to the buyer under a c.i.f. contract is caused by a breach of the contract of carriage, the seller may recoup from the carrier the damages paid to the buyer. These damages in the very least equal the cost of replacing the goods at their destination at the time when they ought to have arrived, less the value of the goods at the port of shipment and the freight and insurance. In this case, the appellants in Sweden entered into a charterparty with the respondents by which the latter agreed to carry 900/1,000 tons of wood pulp to Cardiff in two consignments, one in May and the second in August/September. The charterparty was entered into pursuant to a contract of sale c.i.f. Cardiff ''Time of delivery—in two cargoes, first open water, and August–September 1900.'' The first cargo, consisting of 500 tons, was shipped and accepted by the purchasers. But the respondents wholly failed to fulfil their contract with regard to the second shipment. The appellants therefore were unable to complete their contract with their purchaser (alternative tonnage being unavailable in Sweden), who bought against them 367 tons in several parcels in Manchester, Liverpool and London. Having paid their purchasers, the appellants sought to recover the amount paid by them from the respondents. The respondents argued that the terms of the sale did not correspond or coincide with the term of their contract inasmuch as their contract could have been performed by shipment on September 30, whereas the sale contract required delivery in Cardiff by that date. They argued moreover that since no damages were proven in respect of storage, insurance, or diminution in the value of the goods left on the hands of the appellants, only nominal damages were due. But the House of Lords held

---

[9] [1905] A. C. 515.

that even assuming this was a correct construction of the respective contracts and that the dates of delivery thereunder did not exactly coincide, in view of the inability to secure alternative tonnage the measure of damages for which the respondents were liable to the appellants was the cost of replacing the goods at their place of destination at the time when they ought to have arrived, less their value in Sweden and the freight and insurance.

305   In some American decisions, damages have been measured by the difference between the contract and market price at the place of shipment at the time of breach, no account being given to the destination value as, for example, was held by the Court of Appeal of New York in *Seaver v. Lindsay Light Co.*[10] The action was for breach of a contract by an American seller who failed to deliver goods which were to be shipped from Chicago c.i.f. London Dock. The measure of damages was held to equal the difference between the contract and market price of the goods in Chicago and not the cost of replacing them in London. The court expressly overruled the Illinois decision of *Staackman, Horschitz & Co. v. Cary,*[11] which held that in the case of a breach of contract for the sale of linseed cake to be shipped from Chicago c.i.f. Antwerp the measure of damages for non-delivery should be determined as the difference between the value of the goods and the contract price at Antwerp on the date on which the goods should have arrived. The latter case appears to have been based on the erroneous presupposition that the place of delivery under a c.i.f. contract is the destination of the goods.

306   Some American decisions appear to have considered the problem entirely from the rather dogmatic viewpoint of the transfer of property in the goods, denying the buyer any recovery based on the market price of the goods at the destination contemplated on the sole ground that under a c.i.f. contract the transfer of property and risk occurs at the point of shipment. This, it is submitted, is too narrow an approach to adopt where the question at issue is the measure of damages, in which case the point of delivery under the contract is by no means the exclusive governing consideration. It will be recalled that even the Sale of Goods Act[12] in setting out the guidelines for determining the measure of damages refers only to the time, but not to the place, of delivery.

Indeed, in *Scaramelli & Co. v. Courteen Seed Co.,*[13] the Supreme Court of Wisconsin agreed that

---

[10] 233 N.Y. 273 (1922). See to a similar effect *S. B. Penick & Co. v. Helvetia Commercial Co. Inc.* 212 App. Div. 519; 209 N.Y. Supp. 202 (1925), damages for breach of a contract for the sale of insect flowers to be shipped from Trieste c.i.f. New York are to be computed by reference to the difference between the contract price and the market price at Trieste. In allowing the appeal the Appellate Division stated "we are of the opinion that the trial justice erroneously held that damages should be measured by the market price at New York."
[11] 197 Ill.App. 601 (1916).
[12] s. 51(3) set out *ante*, § 303.
[13] 217 N.W. 298 (1928).

"under a c.i.f. contract, the place where title passes is not controlling with reference to what market the buyer's damages shall be determined. In this case it is perfectly apparent, and must have been in contemplation of the parties, that, in the event of the failure of the seller to perform, the buyer would be compelled to resort to the markets of this country to supply the goods. It would have been physically impossible for the buyer, after the seller's default, to have purchased goods in Italy and transported them to this country in time to meet its needs" (at p. 301).

307 In *Garnac Grain Co. Inc. v. H. M. F. Faure and Fairclough Ltd.*,[14] the Court of Appeal (Sellers, Danckwerts and Diplock L.JJ.) awarded damages on the difference between the contract price and the destination market price of the goods at the time when the shipping documents would have been tendered had the contract been performed. This was a sale of lard to be shipped from America c.i.f. Bromborough/Purfleet December 1963/January 1964 at buyer's call. It was argued that the buyers accepted an anticipatory breach on January 17, but the court refused to assess damages as of that date.[15] First because rescission was not proved and, secondly, because (even if it had been proved) there was no failure to take reasonable steps to mitigate the loss. Sellers L.J., referring to the judgment of Atkin J. in *C. Sharpe & Co. v. Nosawa & Co.*,[16] said:

"The last day for shipment was the end of January 1964, and there was evidence that the shipping documents would take three or four days to arrive in England. The judge was entitled therefore to fix February 4 as the date on which to assess the damages. . . ." (at p. 675).

Whereas, Diplock L.J. added:

"Had it been possible to buy on the market between January 28 and February 4, 1964, 15,000 tons of North American prime steam lard for shipment in January 1964, c.i.f. Bromborough/Purfleet, it may well be that the measure of damages would be based upon the price at which such a shipment could have been bought at some time between those dates. But it is clear on the evidence that North American lard was not at that time available in anything like the contract quantity. It is indeed by no means clear whether given small parcels were available and, in any event, I do not think that the buyers were under any duty to see if they could buy piecemeal small parcels of lard which they would not have been obliged to accept if they had been tendered . . . under the contract" (at p. 687).

These judgments were upheld by the House of Lords, where the appellants' contention that no assessment could properly be made on the basis of the difference between the contract price and the market price on February 4, 1964 because there was then no market in the United Kingdom for 15,000 tons of lard for immediate delivery, and the evidence did not reveal any other

---

[14] [1966] 1 Q.B. 650.
[15] *Post*, § 314.
[16] *Ante*, § 302.

basis for assessing damages, failed.[17] Where there is no available market, it is the buyer's duty to act reasonably in mitigating the damage.

308 In *Lesters Leather & Skin Co. Ltd. v. Home & Overseas Brokers*,[18] there was a sale of 10,000 snakeskins from India "c.i.f. a United Kingdom port." On arrival at Liverpool, the snakeskins were rejected by the buyers as unmerchantable. The buyers bought a small quantity of dressed skins that were available, and they could at considerable inconvenience and delay have sent out to India to buy replacements for the rest of the consignment. When the buyers brought an action for damages for loss of profit, it was held that they were entitled to recover. If there had been any skins in any United Kingdom port, it would have been the duty of the buyers to purchase them, but they were not bound to send out to India. The result might have been different, Lord Goddard C.J. indicated, if a fresh consignment could have been obtained in a very short time, *e.g.* if it had been a shipment of wine from Bordeaux.

This case shows that, where there is no readily available market in which the buyer can obtain substitute goods to satisfy his sub-purchasers, the seller may be liable for the buyer's loss of profit.[19] He may also be liable for damages that the buyers must pay in respect of failure to fulfil sub-contracts.[20] The seller will be liable for such loss as was reasonably foreseeable at the time of the sale as the probable consequences of the breach.[21] The same may be true where the seller knows of the buyer's intention to resell (so that the contract is interpreted to include a term regarding resale), and the market price of the goods has fallen by the time of the failure to deliver. In such a case loss of profit, as well as any damages which the buyer may be liable for on breach of the contract of resale, may be recovered.[22] On the other hand, the existence of an available market does not require the buyer to enter the market on the relevant date. He may wait if he so chooses; and if the market turns in his favour, the liability of the seller is not diminished.[23] But where, after a breach of contract by non-delivery, or after the rejected delivery of defective goods, the selfsame goods become the subject matter of a contract of purchase and sale between the selfsame parties (not as an independent or disconnected transaction, but as part of a continuous

---

[17] *Garnac Grain Co. Inc. v. H. M. F. Faure and Fairclough Ltd.* [1968] A.C. 1130.

[18] (1948) 82 Ll.L.Rep. 202 (C.A.).

[19] See also *Marshall, Knott & Barker Ltd. v. Arcos Ltd.* (1933) 44 Ll.L.Rep. 384. In *Coastal (Bermuda) Petroleum Ltd. v. VTT Vulcan Petroleum S.A. (No. 2) (The Marine Star)* [1994] 2 Lloyd's Rep. 629 (C.A.), loss of profit to the c.i.f. buyer was denied because of the existance of an "available market".

[20] *Grébert-Borgnis v. Nugent* (1885) 15 Q.B.D. 85; *Hammond v. Bussey* (1887) 20 Q.B.D. 79.

[21] *Hadley v. Baxendale* (1854) 9 Exch. 341, as explained in *Victoria Laundry (Windsor) Ltd. v. Newman Ltd.* [1949] 2 K.B. 528 (C.A.); *Trans Trust S.P.R.L. v. Danubian Trading Co. Ltd.* [1952] 2 Q.B. 297 (C.A.).

[22] *Re R. and H. Hall Ltd. and W. H. Pim (Junior) of Co.'s Arbitration* [1928] All.E.R. 763 (H.L.). See however the *Coastal (Bermuda)* case, *ibid.* n. 19 where the Court of Appeal appears to have opined that the contemplation of the parties was only relevant where no available market (for the contract goods) exists.

[23] *Cf. A.K.A.S. Jamal v. Moolla Dawood, Sons & Co.* [1916] 1 A.C. 175, and *Campbell Mostyn (Provisions) Ltd. v. Barnett Trading Company* [1954] 1 Lloyd's Rep. 65.

course of dealing between them) at a price lower than the then prevailing market price so that the buyers have in effect suffered no loss, they cannot claim an additional sum by way of damages on the original breach. This was so held in *R. Pagnan & Fratelli v. Corbisa Industrial Agropacuaria Ltda.*,[24] where c.i.f. buyers purchased from their sellers goods previously rightfully rejected by them at a substantial discount from the contract price, and thereafter attempted to collect damages based on the difference in market price also. Their action failed. In such circumstances. the prima facie rule for ascertaining the measure of damages in section 51(3) cannot apply. The claim is for a fictitious loss, and to allow it would, in the words of Salmon L.J.[25] "be contrary alike to justice, common sense and authority." And where the buyer waives compliance with the date of performance advising the seller that he will take late delivery but the seller further fails to supply within the extended period, the date of default is the original (not the extended) delivery date. Such an extension was construed as an option which the buyer gave the seller, but, since the seller did not take advantage of it, damages must be assessed with reference to the earlier date.[26]

Loss of profit may also determine the amount of damages where a resale is contemplated by the parties. This was held by the House of Lords in *Rand H. Hall Ltd. and W. H. Pim(Jr.) & Co.'s Arbitration*[27] where sellers sold an unspecified cargo of Australian wheat on c.i.f. London terms. The contract provided that notice of appropriation of a specific cargo in a specific ship should be given within a specified time, and also contained express provisions as to what should be done if the cargo should be sold one or more times before arrival at destination. Both parties knew that such a resale was a strong possibility, but the buyers did not give the sellers an express notification of an intention to resell. The market rose, and on November 21 1925 the buyers resold the cargo at an enhanced price to a sub-buyer, who subsequently resold, the market having risen further, at a still higher price. On February 10, 1926 the sellers gave the buyers notice of appropriation of a specific cargo to the contract, and the buyers immediately gave a similar notice to the sub-buyers. The market then fell, and on March 22, 1926 when the nominated vessel arrived, the sellers failed to tender documents and to deliver. The dispute as to the proper measure of damages was decided in favour of the buyers who were awarded damages for loss of profit on the individual resale, and for the amount which they would be liable for their breach of contract of resale, because such damages must reasonably be supposed to have been in the contemplation of the parties at the time the contract was made. Loss of profit will, however, not cover unusual or extravagant amounts, even if embodied in the resale contract.[28] However, the parties may expressly exclude the right to claim loss of profits, even if a resale was within

[24] [1970] 1 W.L.R. 1306 (C.A.).
[25] *Ibid.* at p. 1316.
[26] *Toepfer v. Schwarze* [1980] 1 Lloyd's Rep. 385 (C.A.). See also *E. J. M. Mertens & Co. P.V.B.A. v. Veevoeder Import Export Vimex B.V.* [1979] 2 Lloyd's Rep. 372.
[27] [1928] All E.R. 763.
[28] See *per* Viscount Dunedin, *ibid.* at p.767, and *Coastal International Trading Ltd. v. Maroil A.G.* [1988] 1 Lloyd's Rep.

their contemplation, and limit the damages for breach to the difference between the contract and the market price as was the case in *C. Czarnikow Ltd. v. Bunge of Co. Ltd.*[29] There parties to a c.i.f. contract (FOSFA 80) that included a default clause providing, *inter alia*, that "... the damages awarded against the defaulter shall be limited to the difference between the contract price and the market price on the day of default" were unable to agree as to its meaning, and the buyer (who was the plaintiff) argued that in light of the contemplation of a resale, and the fact the day of default would not arrive until the expiry of the period permitted to serve a declaration of shipment notice, he was entitled to damages for loss of profits or liabilities arising from sub sales. Saville J., affirmed a trade arbitration award, denying such entitlement in light of the default provision above quoted.

309   Finally, the construction of terms providing for damages to be paid on the "value of the goods" at the date of default, which are found in some standard c.i.f. terms of contract, should be noted. In *R. Pagnan & Filli v. Lorico (Lebanese Organisation for International Commerce) (The Caloric)*[30] Lloyd J. had to determine the meaning of such a term in a contract for the sale of 8,500 tonnes of Argentine maize c.i.f. Beirut. Because of disorders at Beirut (resulting from the Lebanese civil war) the vessel could not unload, and the sellers rather than continue incurring demurrage charges (at a rate of $1,000 per day above the rate they could charge the buyers) ordered the vessel to Genoa, where the cargo was sold. The buyers who were anxious to obtain delivery were unable to recover more than $1 (nominal damages) because it was determined that the value of the goods on the date of default was less than their contract price. Lloyd J. refused to upset an award by arbitrators since the contractual term, in his view, did not mean to refer to other goods of the contract description but to the contract goods themselves (on board the *Carloric*) which, because of the demurrage rate and the situation at Beirut, were of no commercial value.

310   *Devaluation.* Losses resulting from revaluation of currencies were once considered to be too remote to be recoverable as having no causal connection with the breach, or because the loss was not within the contemplation of the parties. This rule is probably now superseded by virtue of the decision of the House of Lords in *Miliangos v. George Frank (Textiles)*[31] where as a result of the continuing instability of sterling (and other currencies) it was held that English Courts may render judgments in foreign currency (*post,* § 705). However, even before the rule was changed, it was subject to certain exceptions. Thus, where a c.i.f. contract between two Indian nationals for the sale of Sudan cotton c.i.f. Bombay at a price of Rs. 393.68 per quintal provided for a variation in price, should the prevailing rate of exchange of the rupee vary between the date of the contract and the date when the price was paid,

---

[29] [1987] 1 Lloyd's Rep. 202 (The full name of this case is somewhat longer).
[30] [1981] 2 Lloyd's Rep. 675.
[31] [1976] A.C. 443.

the buyers succeeded in establishing a right for damages based on the devaluation of the rupee. This was decided in *Aruna Mills Ltd. v. Dhanrajmal
Gobindram,*[32] a special case on an award of the Liverpool Cotton Association.
There, the sellers, who were in breach through late shipment, failed in
defeating a claim for damages based on devaluation of the Indian rupee as a
result of which the buyers had to pay an enhanced price for the goods when
they actually arrived. Donaldson J., after reviewing the authorities on
remoteness of loss, concluded that in the present case.

> "the parties actually contemplated the possibility of revaluation during the period
> between the date of the contract and the date of payment for the goods as being
> a sufficiently serious possibility or real danger to justify their making expres
> provision for that eventuality. In the circumstances they must be assumed to have
> contemplated that late delivery was "liable to result" . . . in the buyers suffering
> a loss by payment of an enhanced price."[33]

He dismissed the allegation that whatever may be the general rule, (this was
prior to the decision in *Miliangos v. George Frank (Textiles) Ltd.* [1976]
A.C.443) there was a special rule that "losses resulting from revaluation of
currencies were always too remote in law to be recoverable." As to the causal
connection between the late shipment and delivery, and the fact that payment
was made after the date of the devaluation, the learned judge held that such
a connection existed if the buyers could show that the documents (against
which the price was payable under the contract) would have in the ordinary
course of events and in the absence of a default, been tendered to the buyers
on or before the date of devaluation which was but six days after the final
shipping date fixed by the contract.

311   *Liquidated damages.* Although the courts would not enforce a clause in a
contract providing for the payment of a penalty or a fine in the event of a
breach, it has been held[34] that a provision that in calculating damages under
a c.i.f. contract "The invoicing price in the case of the seller's default shall
include a penalty of not less than 2 per cent nor more than 10 per cent over
the estimated market value" is enforceable. Such a provision is to be construed as a genuine pre-estimate of damages, since the prima facie measure
of damages under the Sale of Goods Act does not necessarily provide
adequate and full compensation to the innocent party in every case. McNair
J. said:

> "It was suggested that, as illustrations of those additional heads of damage
> [which are not necessarily covered by measuring damages with reference to the
> difference in market prices], there might be loss of the brokerage fee or some
> expenses in the making of the contract which had become abortive by reason of
> the default, or it might [the fixed penalty] reflect the additional loss which may

---

[32] [1968] 1 Q.B. 655.
[33] *Ibid.* at p. 668.
[34] *Robert Stewart & Sons Ltd v. Carapanayoti & Co. Ltd.* [1962] 1 W.L.R. 34.

be expected to occur if goods which have been rejected are thrown on the market, when, although there is an available market price for goods of that description and quality and condition, that market price may not be the price which the rejected goods may in fact command'' (at p. 39).

312 *Delay in shipment or tender.* Similarly, when the documents have been accepted by the buyer after delay in shipment constituting a breach of contract by the seller, prima facie the measure of damages is the difference between the c.i.f. value of the goods on the date when, if the goods had been shipped at the agreed time, the documents sent forward with reasonable dispatch would have reached the buyer.[35] If the goods were shipped at the agreed time and the breach of contract was delay in sending forward the documents, the prima facie measure of damages would be the difference between the c.i.f. value of the goods at the date of actual tender of the documents and their c.i.f. value at the time when the documents should have been tendered. In other words, in either case, the measure of damages is the difference between the selling value of the documents at the time of tender and the selling value which they would have had at the time when they would have been tendered if there had been no delay.[36]

313 *Anticipatory breach.* If, however, the seller has repudiated the contract before the time has arrived for tendering the documents, the buyer may either accept the repudiation as an immediate breach or hold the seller to the contract until the time for tender arrives. In the well-known words of Cockburn C.J.[37]:

"The promisee, if he pleases, may treat the notice of intention as inoperative, and await the time when the contract is to be executed, and then hold the other party responsible for all the consequences of non-performance: but in that case he keeps the contract alive for the benefit of the other party as well as his own: he remains subject to all his own obligations and liabilities under it. and enables the other party not only to complete the contract, if so advised, notwithstanding his previous repudiation of it, but also to take advantage of any supervening circumstances which would justify him in declining to complete it.[38]

"On the other hand, the promisee may, if he thinks proper, treat the repudiation of the other party as a wrongful putting an end to the contract, and may at once bring his action as on a breach of it; and in such action he will be entitled to such damages as would have arisen from the non-performance of the contract

[35] The prima facie rule is that the damage is the difference between the value of the article contracted for when it ought to have been and when it actually was delivered: *Elbinger v. Armstrong* (1874) L.R. 9 Q.B. at p. 477.
[36] In this connection, it is helpful to bear in mind the expression used by Scrutton J. in *Arnhold Karberg & Co. v. Blythe* [1915] 2 K.B. 379 at p. 388 that a.c.i.f. sale is not a sale of goods, but rather a sale of documents, as to which see *ante*, § p. 26.
[37] *Frost v. Knight* (1872) L.R. 7 Ex. 111 at p. 112.
[38] In other words the mere commission of a repudiatory breach does not bring the contract to an end. It merely provides the other party with a right of election to treat the contract as terminated if he wishes to do so. If, and so long as, he does not opt for termination, all contractual obligations remain alive, and the defaulting party may still be entitled to sue for breach by the other party. See *C.S. State Trading Corporation of India v. M. Goldetz Ltd.* [1989] 2 Lloyd's Rep. 277 (C.A).

at the appointed time, subject, however, to abatement in respect of any circumstances which may have afforded him the means of mitigating his loss.''

This is a correct statement of the principle to be applied in assessing damages for anticipatory breach. The rule in subsection (3) of section 51 of the Act, that if no time for delivery is fixed, then the measure of damages is to be ascertained by the difference between the contract price and the market or current price at the time of refusal to deliver, does not apply where the breach is an anticipatory breach.[39]

314   The acceptance by the buyer of an anticipatory breach does not afford him the right to have the damages assessed with reference to the date of such acceptance. If the market subsequently falls so that by the time the documents should have been tendered (or the goods delivered) their price does not exceed the contract price, the buyer cannot claim anything but nominal damages. This was so held in *Melachrino and Anr. v. Nickoll and Knight*,[40] where Bailhache J. dismissed the buyers' allegation that damages should be assessed with reference to the market price ruling on the date on which the anticipatory breach was accepted. The learned judge was of the opinion that the date on which the shipment would have arrived in England had the contract been performed was the proper date for assessing damages. Any loss suffered by the buyer who has acted reasonably in the performance of his duty to go into the market with a view of mitigating his damages in such a case is, however, recoverable.

If the property in the goods has passed to the buyer[41] and he is entitled to actual possession and delivery of the documents, he may, instead of bringing an action for damages for non-delivery, maintain an action against the seller for detention or conversion.[42] A third person to whom the seller in such circumstances has resold the goods may be liable for conversion, but his liability is very much limited by section 24 of the Sale of Goods Act 1979. This section contains substantially the same provisions as the Factors Act 1889, and protects the third party who purchases in good faith from the seller remaining in possession.

315   *Specific performance.* By the Sale of Goods Act 1979, s.52, the court is empowered to order specific performance of a contract to deliver goods ''in

---

[39] *Millett v. Van Heek & Co.* [1921] 2 K.B. 369 (C.A.); *Garnac Grain Co. Inc. v. H.M.F. Faure & Fairclough & Ors.* [1968] A.C. 1130; *Tai Hing Cotton Mill Ltd. v. Kamsing Knitting Factory* [1978] 2 W.L.R. 62.
[40] [1920] 1 K.B. 693.
[41] See *ante*, § 274 as to property passing.
[42] See *Empresa Exportadora de Azucar v. Industria Azucarera Nacional S.A. (The Playa Larga and Marble Islands)* [1983] 2 Lloyd's Rep. 171 (C.A.) where such an action succeeded in respect of one cargo but denied in respect of another, as documents relating to the latter cargo were validly rejected by the buyer prior to the date of the alleged conversion (diversion of ship carrying Cuban sugar on orders of Cuban authorities, seller being an instrumentality of these authorities), and, thus, had no rights to the possession of the cargo at the time.

any action for breach of contract to deliver specific or ascertained goods.'' ''Specific goods'' means ''goods identified and agreed upon at the time a contract of sale is made'' (section 61). ''Ascertained'' probably means identified in accordance with the agreement after the contract of sale is made.[43] This section makes the award of specific performance a matter for the discretion of the court. In the case of *Re Wait*,[44] where this topic received consideration, Lord Hanworth M.R. expressed the view[45] that the operation of this section remains limited and has not altered the law. Specific performance would therefore only be granted on equitable grounds where damages were not a sufficient remedy. Atkin L.J., however, in the same case reserved the question whether this section does not give the buyer a larger remedy than he possessed in equity.[46] In practice, specific performance is refused where damages are an adequate remedy.[47] As the common form of c.i.f. contract is for the sale of unascertained goods, the remedy of specific performance is in any event rarely available. However, there may be circumstances where, *e.g.* the seller is the only source of supply available to the buyer, and the sole means by which the buyer is able to continue his business, where the remedy of specific performance (or an injunction restraining the seller from withholding the supplies which is tantamount to it) may be granted even in the case of unascertained goods, because damages would be an insufficient remedy.[48] So too, the issue may arise in a situation where the c.i.f. seller decides to sell the goods that were destined to one buyer to another person at a profit. Can the original c.i.f. buyer claim in respect of restitution of the profits so gained by the seller? Clearly the original buyer would have no property rights in the goods, but there is, it is thought, sufficient causal connection to support a claim for restitution under such circumstances, provided the plaintiff will not be unjustly enriched by the multiplicity of remedies, it being immaterial whether the contract was or was not rescinded by him.[49]

316 *Distinction between conditions and warranties.* If the seller ships the goods and tenders the documents to the buyer but has not complied with all the terms, express or implied, of the contract, the question will arise whether such non-compliance is a breach giving rise to the right to reject the documents and/or the goods, and to treat the contract as repudiated, or is a breach for which the remedy lies in an action for damages only. Great assistance was originally given by the Sale of Goods Act 1893, which declared certain terms of the contract of sale to be conditions,[50] but there are still problems

---

[43] *Per* Atkin L. J., *Re Wait* [1927] 1 Ch. at p. 630.
[44] [1927] 1 Ch. 606. *Ante*, § 275.
[45] *Ibid.* at p. 617.
[46] *Ibid.* at p. 630; see also Wright J. in *Behnke v. Bede Shipping Co. Ltd.* [1927] 1 K.B. 649 at p. 660.
[47] *e.g. Cohen v. Roche* [1927] 1 K.B. 169.
[48] See *Sky Petroleum Ltd. v. V.I.P. Petroleum Ltd.* [1974] 1 W.L.R. 576.
[49] Friedman ''Restitution of Profits gained by Party in Breach of Contract'' (1988) L.Q.R. 383, reporting on a successful claim under a c.i.f. contract for restitution of profits in Israel.
[50] See *ante* chap. 2.

for the courts.[51] The question whether any term in the contract contained is to be construed as a condition or as a collateral warranty only (or as an intermediate or innominate term, *post*, § 317, depends upon the intention of the parties which may be expressed or which may have to be inferred from the contract and the circumstances legally admissible in evidence with reference to which the contract is to be construed.[52]

The matter was put in the following way by Bowen L.J.[53]:

"There is no way of deciding that question except by looking at the contract in the light of the surrounding circumstances, and then making up one's mind whether the intention of the parties, as gathered from the instrument itself, will best be carried out by treating the promise as a warranty sounding only in damages, or as a condition precedent by the failure to perform which the other party is relieved of his liability. In order to decide this question of construction, one of the first things you would look to is, to what extent the accuracy of the statement—the truth of what is promised—would be likely to affect the substance and foundation of the adventure; ... not the effect of the breach which has in fact taken place, but the effect likely to be produced on the foundation of the adventure by any such breach of that portion of the contract."

To qualify as a condition the parties must therefore:

"have agreed, whether by express words or by implication of law, that *any* failure by one party to perform a primary obligation, irrespective of the gravity of the event that has in fact resulted from the breach, shall entitle the other party to elect to put an end to all primary obligations of both parties remaining unperformed. . . ."[54]

"The task of the court is to look at the contract in the light of the surrounding circumstances and make up its mind whether the intention of the parties is best carried out by treating the terms as a condition or a warranty".[55]

---

[51] *e.g. T. & J. Harrison v. Knowles and Foster* [1917] 2 K.B. 606. More recent developments in the law of contract introduced concepts such as the "fundamental term" which are not mentioned in the Act but which have, nonetheless, to be harmonised with its provisions. It is not here proposed to deal with these developments which are not peculiar to c.i.f. or f.o.b. transactions, and the reader is referred to Lord Devlin's article on "The Treatment of Breach of Contract" in [1966] Camb, L.J., p. 192, where the subject is reviewed in detail. In essence the principle of the fundamental term doctrine postulated that where a party violates a fundamental term of the agreement, the entire basis of the contract is removed, and the other party can sue for repudiation, so that the right of the offending party to rely on any term which relieves or diminishes his liability, in particular—in this context—terms which provide that some or all of the implied conditions and warranties are excluded, will be denied. The doctrine of fundamental breach was developed in *Suisse Atlantique Société d'Armement Maritime S.A. v. N.V. Rotterdamsche Kolen Centrale* [1967] 1 A.C. 361, and explained in *Photo Production Ltd. v. Securicor Transport Ltd.* [1980] A.C. 827.
[52] *Per* Parke B., *Graves v. Legg* (1854) 9 Ex. 709 at p. 716; cited by Blackburn J. in *Betini v. Gye* (1876) 1 Q.B.D. 183 at p. 186 and followed in *Luis de Ridder Ltda. v. André & Cie S.A. (Lausanne)* [1941] 1 All E.R. 380.
[53] In *Bentsen v. Taylor, Sons & Co.* [1893] 2 Q.B. 274 at p. 281, referring to a charter-party. See, *e.g. Schuler A.G. v. Wickman Machine Tools Sales Ltd.* [1974] A.C. 235 (H.L.).
[54] *Per* Lord Diplock in *Photo Production Ltd. v. Securicor Transport Ltd.* [1980] A.C. 827 at p. 84SE.
[55] *Per* Bingham J. in *Michael I. Warde v. Feedex International Inc.* [1983] 2 Lloyd's Rep. 289 at p. 298.

Section 11(3) of the Sale of Goods Act 1979, provides that:

> "Whether a stipulation in a contract of sale is a condition, the breach of which
> may give rise to a right to treat the contract as repudiated, or a warranty, the
> breach of which may give rise to a claim for damages but not to a right to
> reject the goods and treat the contract as repudiated, depends in each case on the
> construction of the contract; a stipulation may be a condition, though called a
> warranty in the contract."

And, likewise of course, a stipulation may be a warranty (the breach of which
is remediable by damages but does not affect the validity of other obligations)
though called a condition. The guiding principle is that contracts are to be
construed according to the intention of the parties, and that to this intention
(which will in part, but not exclusively, be collected from their words) all
technical forms of expression must give way.

So, for example, in *Tradax Export S.A. v. European Grain & Shipping
Ltd.*[56] Bingham J. determined that the term "maximum 7.5% fibre" in a c.i.f.
contract for the sale of soya bean meal was a condition of the contract. The
issue came to the court in the form of a special case submitted by an arbitration appeal board that found the term to be a warranty (albeit forming part
of the description of the goods), a breach of which gave rise to a claim for
damages (or to a price adjustment or allowance) but not to a right of rejection.
Nevertheless, and as aforesaid, Bingham J. held otherwise, and in the course
of his judgment said that the question had to be determined by construing
"the whole of the . . . contract between the parties in a reasonable and commercial way, against the background of the trade in which the contract was
made, in order to ascertain the intentions of the parties. . . . In carrying out
its own task the court will attach weight to the construction put upon the
contract by trade arbitrators. The specific object of the construction here is
to ascertain whether the words [employed] were words of description used
to identify the goods which were to be the subject of the contract . . . or
whether they were words relating to quality only . . . the task of construction
should not be conducted in a mechanical, legalistic, old fashioned or narrow
way. . . . The inclusion of a maximum fibre percentage meant that while any
percentage below that specified was acceptable any percentage above it by
more than a de minimus amount was not."[57] Nevertheless "the courts should
not be too ready to interpret contractual clauses as conditions",[58] though in
suitable cases, "the court should not be reluctant, if the intentions of the
parties . . . so indicate, to hold that an obligation has the force of a condition,
and that indeed they should usually do so in the case of time clauses in
merchantible contracts".[59] Thus, *e.g.* a provision that the seller was to give
the c.i.f. buyer "minimum two working days" advance notice of the vessels'

---

[56] [1983] 2 Lloyd's Rep. 100.
[57] *Ibid.* at pp. 104, 105.
[58] *Per* Lord Wilbeforce in *Bunge Corp. v. Tradax Export S.A.* [1981] 2 Lloyd's Rep. 1 at p. 6.
For details of this case see *post*, § 444.
[59] *Ibid.*

arrival at the designated port of loading, was held to be condition, entitling the buyer to terminate the contract forthwith if he so wished.[60] On the other hand there was no breach by the c.i.f. seller where the term was "Delivery Feb. 15/March 15 basis Rotterdam," and the discharge was fixed at "River Tees", with notice given on March 16. Webster J. affirmed a trade arbitration award that business common sense required the construction of the term to mean that if the discharge port was not Rotterdam there would be an adjustment of freight, and the notice was not too late.[61] If another port was nominated, delivery was to be sooner or later than March 15, depending on whether the port was closer to, or further from, the vessel's last port of loading than Rotterdam. The buyers thus were not entitled to reject, and the sellers claim for damages for wrongful rejection succeeded.

317   *Innominate or intermediate terms.* Finally, there may be contractual stipulations that are neither conditions nor pure warranties but of an intermediate or innominate nature.[62] In stipulations of this type, the seriousness or severity of the breach will determine whether the contract is at an end, and whether the buyer is entitled to consider himself as discharged, or whether an action for breach is the correct, and only, remedy. In *Cehave M. V. v. Bremer Handelsgesellschaft m.b.H. (The "Hansa Nord")*[63] the Court of Appeal (Lord Denning M.R., Roskill and Ormrod L.JJ.) had to consider the nature of a stipulation in a contract for the sale of U.S. citrus pulp pellets c.i.f. Rotterdam providing for "shipment to be made in good condition." The circumstances of the case were somewhat unusual. The buyers who had agreed to pay some £100,000 equivalent for the pulp which arrived partially damaged rejected it on the ground that it was not shipped in good condition. Subsequently (with both buyers and sellers disclaiming ownership) the buyers were able to repurchase the very same pulp for some £29,903 by means of an intermediary in Rotterdam who had acquired the pulp for their benefit. They used the pulp for the original purpose (manufacture of cattle food) for which they had sought to acquire it in the first place, and there was no proof that they had suffered any loss. In the sellers' view the buyers were not entitled to reject, but both a trade arbitration and the lower court held for the buyers on the ground that the sellers had committed a breach of a condition that entitled the buyers to treat the contract as repudiated. The Court of Appeal disagreed. In its view section 61(2) of the 1893 Sale of goods Act which saved the rules of the Common Law, save insofar as they are inconsistent with the express provisions of the Act, did not exclude the possibility of a term being neither a pure condition or warranty but a *tertium quid*. Lord Denning M.R. in an exhaustive review of earlier authorities explained the task of the court thus:

[60] *Nova Petroleum International Establishment v. Tricon Trading Ltd.* [1989] 1 Lloyd's Rep. 312.
[61] *P. & O. Oil Trading Ltd. v. Scanoil AB* [1985] 1 Lloyd's Rep. 389.
[62] See *Hong Kong Fir Shipping Co. Ltd. v. Kawasaki Kisen Kaisha Ltd.* [1962] 2 Q.B. 26.
[63] [1975] 2 Lloyd's Rep. 445.

"First see whether the stipulation, on its true construction, is a condition strictly so called, that is a stipulation such that, for breach of it, the other party is entitled to treat himself as discharged. Second, if it is not such a condition, then look to the extent of the actual breach which has taken place. If it is such as to go to the root of the contract, the other party is entitled to treat himself as discharged but, otherwise, not. To this may be added an anticipatory breach. If the one party, before the day on which he is due to perform his part, shows by his words or conduct that he will not perform it in a vital respect when the day comes, the other party is entitled to treat himself as discharged."

Applying these principles to the facts before it, the Court decided that the "condition" there stipulated was not a "condition" strictly so called, and that a breach thereof gave no right to reject unless it went to the root of the contract which it did not do in the circumstances of the case before it. The Court further held that the goods were "merchantable" in a commercial sense, and that there was no breach of the implied condition as to merchantable quality set out in section 14(2) of the Sale of Goods Act 1893. Therefore, the buyers were not entitled to reject the goods, but could only claim damages for the difference in value between the damaged and sound goods on arrival at Rotterdam, and the case was remitted to the arbitral tribunal to determine the amount of damages recoverable.

The view that the doctrine of innominate terms is applicable to contracts for the sale of goods (albeit the uncertainty it creates) was subsequently endorsed by the House of Lords in *Bremer Handelsgesellschaft m.b.H. v. Vanden Avenne-Izegem P.V.B.A.*[64] where the question of the timing of a notice from a c.i.f. seller to buyer, concerning cancellation of the contract resulting from an export prohibition, was considered. The clause was silent as to when the notice was to be served, and the buyer maintained that it had to be given "without delay," and that breach of this duty was a breach of a condition precedent and a repudiation of the contract by the seller. The House of Lords disagreed, as the following passage from Lord Wilberforce's speech, shows:

"In my opinion the clause may vary appropriately and should be regarded as . . . an intermediate term: to do so would recognise that while in many, possibly most, instances breach of it can adequately be sanctioned by damages, cases may exist in which, in fairness to the buyer, it would be proper to treat the cancellation as not having effect. On the other hand, always so to treat it may often be unfair to the seller, and unnecessarily rigid."[65]

318   Illustrations have been given in Chapter 2, *ante*, and elsewhere of stipulations in c.i.f. contracts that have been held to be conditions, that is to say, entitling the buyer on breach to reject. But there may be breaches which are purely technical, and for which, therefore, no remedy would in effect be available. For example, where a contract for the sale of Bombay castor oil

[64] [1978] 2 Lloyd's Rep. 109.
[65] *Ibid* at p. 113. And see further on intermediate or innominate terms *post*, § 693.

c.i.f. London provided for the sellers to make a declaration of shipment within 10 days from the date of the bill of lading by cable, telegram or telex, and such declaration was made by letter which was received in the buyers' office (though they seem to have been unaware of it) six days after shipment, it was held[66] that the buyers had suffered no prejudice from the fact that a letter rather than a cable was used for the purpose of giving notice of appropriation. Consequently, the breach did not discharge the buyer from performance under the contract. Donaldson J. summarised the position by stating[67]:

"... it is perfectly open to parties to provide by their contract that breach of any particular term either shall or shall not have the characteristic that the other party is thenceforward discharged from any further obligation to perform the contract. That expression of the parties' intention may be express or it may be implicit in the contract as a whole. Again, the nature of a particular term of a contract, viewed in the context of the business with which the contract is contained, may be such that one can say that any breach of that term must have the effect of discharging the other party from further performance, or alternatively, one may be able to say that no breach of that term could be of such a nature as to discharge the other party from further performance. The last possibility is that there is a term of the contract, a breach of which may or may not discharge the other party from further performance, according to the nature and circumstance of the breach."

Apart from express stipulations, there are, or may be, in the particular circumstances prescribed by the Sale of Goods Act, the well-known implied conditions that the seller has or will (at the time when property is to pass) have a right to sell the goods[68] that the goods shall correspond with the description,[69] that they shall be reasonably fit for their ordinary purpose or for a particular purpose for which they have been bought, if the buyer makes

---

[66] *Daulatram Rameshwarlall v. European Grain & Shipping Ltd.* [1971] 1 Lloyd's Rep. 368.

[67] *Ibid.* at p. 372.

[68] s.12(1) of the 1979 Act. There is also an implied warranty (previously a condition) that the buyer will be free to enjoy quiet possession and shall be free from interference by the owner or third parties except as otherwise disclosed at the time of the sale (previously a condition). As to the application of this implied term (on enjoying quiet possession) to c.i.f. contracts see *Empresa Exportadora de Azucar v. Industria Azucarera Nacional S.A. (The Playa Larga and Marble Islands)* [1983] 2 Lloyd's Rep. 171 (C.A.), holding that there could be a breach of the implied term even if there is no impediment of free enjoyment of the goods in existence at the time of delivery. In that case c. and f. sellers (for political reasons emanating from a change of government in the buyers country) diverted (on the instructions of their government) a ship carrying a cargo which had already been paid for (against transfer of the documents) by the buyers. The sellers' contention that since delivery was complete the implied term could not extend beyond the time of performance of the contract was rejected. Ackner L.J., who delivered the judgment of the court, stated that there were three stages of delivery in a c.i.f. contract, and, citing *Kwei Tek Chao v. British Traders and Shippers Ltd.* [1954] 2 Q.B. 459 (*post*, § 335, opined that transfer of the shipping documents normally only passed conditional property in the goods and that the term applied so long as title had not passed unconditionally. The court further held that even if this submission was erroneous and the term implied by the Act was inapplicable in the circumstances "there was much to be said for the proposition that there must be an implied obligation that a c.i.f. seller will not interfere with the performance of the contract of carriage he has procured for his buyer." (at p. 180).

[69] s.13 of the 1979 Act.

such particular purpose known to the seller),[70] that they are of merchantable quality,[71] and, in the case of a contract for sale by sample, that the bulk shall correspond with the sample in quality, that the buyer shall have a reasonable opportunity of comparing the bulk with the sample, and that the goods shall be free from any defect, rendering them unmerchantable, which would not be apparent on reasonable examination of the sample.[72]

The Supply of Goods (Implied Terms) Act. By the Supply of Goods (Implied Terms) Act 1973 and thereafter by section 6(3) of the Unfair Contract Terms Act 1977 the foregoing implied terms, which could have been varied by agreement between the parties, became mandatory in respect of domestic transactions involving the ordinary consumer, and subject to a reasonableness test in respect of non consumers. In other words, contracting out of sections 12–15 of the Sale of Goods Act has been curtailed (and prohibited where the buyer is an ordinary consumer) except in respect of contracts for the international sale of goods where freedom of contract has been maintained. Hence, the application of the rule against contracting out of the aforementioned implied terms would be negligible to most export sales. Nevertheless, where a c.i.f. (or f.o.b.) contract is concluded between two residents of the United Kingdom (*e.g.* a manufacturer selling to an exporter for the purpose of resale by the latter to a foreign client) the implied terms of sections 12–15 of the Sale of Goods Act may be mandatory as far as the first two parties are concerned (provided the exporter is considered an ordinary consumer or, if not, where the expulcutory provision is regarded as unreasonable by the court) but subject to variation by agreement in the context of the contract between the last two parties. Moreover the Act prohibits evasion of these mandatory provisions through agreement on subjecting the contract to a foreign legal system by means of a choice of law or jurisdiction clause.

319   *Deterioration of goods in transit.* The question as to whether there is, and, if so, to what extent, an implied term in the contract by which the seller warrants that the goods shall be reasonably fit for travel and arrival at their destination in a condition which enables the buyer to use them for the purpose for which he intended to apply them was the subject of controversy in *Mash & Murrell Ltd. v. Joseph I. Emanuel Ltd.*[73] There 2,000 bags of Cyprus spring potatoes were sold c. and f. Liverpool, net cash against first presentation of documents, and upon arrival at Liverpool were found to be wholly unfit for human consumption. The buyers alleged, as stated by Diplock J., "that there is an implied warranty in a c.i.f. or c. and f. contract, as this was, that the goods should be fit to stand the voyage from Cyprus to Liverpool on

---

[70] s.14(3) of the 1979 Act.
[71] s.14(2) of the 1979 Act.
[72] s.15 2(a) of the 1979 Act.
[73] [1961] 1 W.L.R. 862, reversed by C.A. in [1962] 1 W.L.R. 16 on factual, not legal, grounds, see *post*, 322.

which the . . . [vessel] was about to embark, a normal voyage from Cyprus to Liverpool, and should arrive sound and fit for human consumption after arrival."[74] Diplock J. upheld this contention, which in his opinion was no more than an application of the principles set forth in section 14(1) and (2) of the Sale of Goods Act 1893 (as they were then drafted) to c.i.f. contracts. In other words, he was of the opinion that there was an implied term in the contract that the condition of the goods when shipped would be such that upon arrival at their destination they would be suitable for the ordinary purpose for which such goods are intended to be used and of merchantable quality.[75] In support of his judgment, he referred to a passage from the judgment of McCardie J. in *Evangelinos v. Leslie & Anderson*,[76] where the conclusion of an umpire to the effect that in the contract in question (a sale of tinned salmon shipped from Japan c.i.f. Port Said and found unfit for human consumption upon arrival) was confirmed:

> "the sellers were under an obligation to ship the goods in such a condition as would enable the goods to arrive at their destination on a normal voyage, and under normal conditions, in merchantable condition."

Diplock J. confessed that he did not consider that he was laying down any novel principle of law:

> "I have," he said, "so far travelled through my legal life under the impression, shared by a number of other judges who have sat in this court, that when goods are sold under a contract such as a c.i.f. contract, or f.o.b. contract, which involves transit before use, there is an implied warranty not merely that they shall be merchantable at the time they are put on the vessel, but that they shall be in such a state that they can endure the normal journey and be in a merchantable condition upon arrival" (at p. 865).

320   Except for *Evangelinos v. Leslie & Anderson*, Diplock J. cited no further authority in support of this proposition.[77] But, *Evangelinos v. Leslie & Ander-*

---

[74] *Ibid.* at p. 866.

[75] Suitability and merchantability are, however, two entirely distinct warranties: see *post*, 325. For an action to succeed under the old version of s.14(1), it was necessary to show that the buyer expressly or by implication made known to the seller, the particular purpose for which the goods were required "so as to show that the buyer relied on the seller's skill and judgment." For an action to succeed under the old version of s.11(2), it was necessary to show that the goods when tendered were of no use for any purpose for which goods which comply with the description under which they were sold would normally be used, and hence were not saleable under that description: *H. Kendall & Sons v. William Lillco and Sons Ltd. and Others* [1969] 2 A.C. 31 (H.L.). The new version of these provisions introduced by s.3 of the 1973 Act modifies the foregoing requirements to some extent. As to s.14(1), the buyer no longer has to show that he relied on the seller's skill or judgment. This is now implied by law *unless* the seller can establish no reliance. As to s.14(2), the changed wording, does not require that the sale be by description in order for the condition of merchantability to apply.

[76] (1920) 4 Ll.L.Rep. 17 at p. 18.

[77] See, *e.g. Broome v. Pardess Co-operative Society* [1939] 3 All E.R. 978, f.o.b. contract, reversed on the grounds of an express stipulation to the contrary in [1940] All E.R. 603 (C.A.). See also McNair J.'s statement in *Gardano and Giampieri v. Greek Petroleum George Mamidakis & Co.* [1962] 1 W.L.R. 40 to the effect that:

son can perhaps be distinguished on the grounds that the implication there was not assumed to exist as a matter of law, but was based upon a finding of fact by the umpire that such a term was contemplated by the parties. In actual fact, an Australian decision, *Bowden Brothers & Co. Ltd. v. R. Little (Trading as Robert Little & Co.),*[78] held that no such condition could be implied in the c.i.f. contract there considered, but was not followed by Diplock J. on the grounds that it was rendered prior to the enactment of the Sale of Goods Act in New South Wales (where the action in that case originated), and before section 14(1) (old version) of the Act was explained as extending considerably the provisions of the earlier common law in *Manchester Liners Ltd. v. Rea Ltd.,*[79] and *Cammell Laird v. Manganese Bronze and Brass Co. Ltd.*[80]

321   In the *Bowden* case, the action was brought in respect of a sale of 450 tons of Japanese onions c.i.f. Sydney. The onions shipped were merchantable at the port of shipment, Kobe, but on arriving at Sydney were found to have become rotten and unfit during the voyage. The High Court of Australia held that a c.i.f. contract is normally performed by putting on board ship, at the dates specified, onions of the kind and quality contracted for, and that thereafter the risk in the goods was wholly upon the purchaser. Griffith C.J. said:

> "It cannot be implied, from the mere fact of a sale of goods to be shipped abroad, that the vendor enters into any warranty except that the goods shall be merchantable. The facts of the particular case may justify the implication of warranties of various effect. For instance, the circumstances might justify the implication of an absolute warranty that the goods shall be reasonably fit to undergo the risks of the particular voyage, or they might justify the implication of a warranty that the goods shall apparently be in that condition. Other warranties that might be implied from the circumstances are that the goods should be such in quality and condition as a reasonably prudent man, determined to make a shipment at that time, would ship on his own behalf, or that the vendors will take reasonable care that the goods when shipped shall be fit for shipment, or that they shall be as fit as is practicable with respect to such goods under the particular circumstances. But which, if any, of these or any other warranties that may be suggested is the one which ought to be implied must depend upon the extent to which the buyer is shown by the facts to have trusted to the judgment and skill of the vendor" (at pp. 1380, 1381).

While Isaacs J. said:

> "It was urged, however, on behalf of the purchaser that the mere fact that the contract stated that the onions were to be shipped to Sydney, and that the sellers

---

"Nor do I think it clear at all on this contract that the charterers' obligation as to the condition of the kerosene were in any way limited, as they normally are in a c.i.f. contract, to shipping goods of the contract description in a condition in which they would normally arrive by the ordinary course of ocean transit in the same condition." (at p. 53).

[78] (1907) 4 C.L.R. 1364.

[79] [1922] 2 A.C. 74.

[80] [1934] A.C. 402.

knew that the onions were to be shipped to Sydney, was sufficient to establish in law the further implied condition that the goods should be reasonably fit for the purpose of the voyage so as to arrive in Sydney in merchantable condition, except for the necessary and inevitable deterioration caused by the voyage[81] ... It was put on behalf of the purchaser that the implied condition referred to necessarily arose as a matter of law.

"In my judgment that is not a sound position. The mere fact that in the written document itself the fact and dates of shipment are referred to does not conclude the matter, because that is common to all c.i.f. contracts, and, unless such an implied condition exists in every contract of the character, the position contended for cannot be maintained ... The suggested implied condition of reasonable fitness for the purpose must arise, if at all, on facts showing that the purchaser not only made known to the seller the particular purpose for which the onions were required, but also did this so as to show he was relying on the seller's skill and judgment" (at pp. 1391, 1392).

322   The views set forth in the *Bowden* case also seem to reflect the position adopted by the United States courts, where the weight of authority appears to be against any such implied condition. There the normal inference, which is of course always subject to contrary stipulation, is that

"Where goods of a perishable nature are ordered from a distance, a warranty may be implied that they are properly packed and fit for shipment, but not that they will remain sound for any particular or definite length of time. The implied warranty extends only to the condition of the goods when they leave the seller's possession, and he is not liable for any deterioration resulting from the transit."[82]

Moreover, section 33 of the Sale of Goods Act, which was not cited in *Mash & Murrell Ltd. v. Joseph I. Emanuel Ltd.*, and was not considered by Diplock J. postulates that:

"Where the seller of goods agrees to deliver them at his own risk at a place other than that where they are sold, the buyer must nevertheless (unless otherwise agreed) take any risk of deterioration in the goods necessarily incident to the course of transit."

This principle on first sight appears to be the exact reverse of the rule stated by Diplock J., since it applies to cases where the transit is at the risk of the seller, and should therefore *a fortiori* apply to cases, like c.i.f. sales, where the transit is at the risk of the buyer. This apparent inconsistency may, however, be reconciled by distinguishing between two different types of inevitable deterioration. The first, to which the Act probably refers, is a deterioration which all goods of the kind called for by the contract would necessarily suffer during transit. The second, which Diplock J. probably considered, is a deterioration caused by the inferior quality of the particular goods which were delivered pursuant to the contract of sale. As stated by the learned judge,[83] in the case of c. and f. or c.i.f. sales it was only the:

---

[81] This exception probably refers to the provision of s. 33 of the Act, see *post*, §322.
[82] *American Jurisprudence*, Vol. 46, para. 350, p. 535.
[83] [1961] 1 W.L.R. 862 at p. 871.

"extraordinary deterioration of the goods due to abnormal conditions experienced during transit for which the buyer takes the risk. A necessary and inevitable deterioration during transit which will render them unmerchantable on arrival is normally one for which the seller is liable."

Though Diplock J.'s judgment was reversed by the Court of Appeal,[84] the court, regretfully, refrained from commenting on the substance of his decision, the appeal being allowed on the ground that the facts did not permit the inference drawn by him. It was the Court of Appeal's view that:

"even assuming that the alleged warranty was implied in the contract ... the proper inference on the facts proved and on the balance of probabilities was that the potatoes remained unventilated ... [and] the voyage, was, therefore, not a normal voyage. ..."[85]

323   Diplock J.'s judgment in the *Mash & Murrell* case was briefly considered by Winn J. in *Cordova Land Co. Ltd. v. Victor Brothers Inc.*,[86] where the learned judge suggested that its application be restricted to the sale of perishable goods. There the English buyer of a quantity of skins shipped from Boston c.i.f. Hull, which arrived in a damaged condition, sought leave to serve notice of a writ out of the jurisdiction on the American seller.[87] The buyer cited the *Mash & Murrell* decision in support of his contention that by tendering defective skins in Hull a breach of contract was committed in England. Winn J. refused to grant the permission sought, and in so deciding offered the following comments[88]:

"I do not think that passage in the judgment of Diplock J. founds "a good arguable case" that the vendors in the present matter, the present transactions, entered into a warranty to be performed in Hull that the goods on arrival there would there and then be of the contract description and quality. It seems to me, whilst obviously this topic will call for some further consideration in some future case, that there is a real distinction between the obligation undertaken by a vendor who ships goods such as skins, which though plainly vulnerable to some extent to deterioration in transit are not nearly so vulnerable as potatoes; the latter may, *inter alia*, mature and ferment."

324   Thus, the question perhaps still remains open of whether any term (apart of course from express terms)[89] which extends beyond the adequate packing of the goods,[90] as invoked by Diplock J., is to be imported into the normal

---

[84] [1962] 1 W.L.R 16. The case is more fully reported in [1961] 2 Lloyd's Rep. 326.
[85] *Ibid.*
[86] [1966] 1 W.L.R. 793.
[87] As to this topic generally, see *post*, §390.
[88] [1966] 1 W.L.R. 793 at p. 796.
[89] See, *e.g. Oleificio Zucchi S.p.A. v. Northern Sales Ltd.* [1965] 2 Lloyd's Rep. 496, where a c.i.f. contract for the sale of Canadian rape seed screenings c.i.f. Genoa provided that a price allowance was due if the goods arrived "sea or otherwise damaged."
[90] See, *e.g. George Wills & Sons Ltd. v. Thomas Brown & Sons and Ors.* (1922) 12 Ll.L.Rep. 292, where a cargo of herrings shipped to Australia f.o.b. London arrived in unsound condition due to inadequate packing.

c.i.f. contract. For, unless the seller knowingly or carelessly tenders defective or inferior goods, in which case different considerations may apply,[91] a term cannot be implied, save where it is both reasonable and necessary, and necessary in the sense that the parties must have intended such a stipulation to exist when they entered into their contract.[92] Indeed Diplock J. (after becoming a Lord Justice) himself acknowledged that the rule in the *Mash & Murrell* case was formulated by him "with incautious wideness."[93] Its application, he explained, depended on the particular circumstances of the case. In *Mash & Murrell*, the description of the goods was generic and the purpose for which the buyer required them was communicated to the seller in reliance on his skill and judgment.

In order to avoid any doubts on the matter, an express stipulation relating to inevitable deterioration would not be superfluous. Indeed, the point is sometimes covered by the "latent defect" clauses that are inserted in most standard contracts and which generally provide that "the goods are not warranted free from defect, rendering same unmerchantable, which would not be apparent on reasonable examination."[94] Such a clause, however, falls short of relieving the seller from liability, in appropriate circumstances, arising from the amended section 14(3) of the Sale of Goods Act,[95] because suitability and merchantability are two distinct factors.[96]

Finally, it should be mentioned that there may be cases where the carrier could be held liable for deterioration. Where deterioration is caused by improper stowage or improper care or handling of the goods the carrier would usually be in breach. But the carrier is not required to do more and could not, for example, be made liable for the sellers shipping overripe apples although he had engaged an expert to examine the cargo.[97]

325   *Certificate of quality.* On the other hand, the buyer may insert a provision in the contract requiring the issuance of a certificate of quality in order to ensure that the goods, *e.g.* are of the contract description, quality, and quantity, before he parts with the contract price. Such provisions are fairly common, but, unless drafted in very clear language, they will not normally be construed as making the certificate conclusive as to the goods being in accordance with the contract. In *Rolimpex Centrala Handlu Zagranicznego*

---

[91] See Sassoon. "Deterioration of Goods in Transit" [1962] *J.B.L.* 352.

[92] *Per* Mackinnon L.J. in *Broome v. Pardess Co-operative Society* [1940] 1 All E.R. 603.

[93] *Teheran Europe Co. v. S. T. Betton Ltd.* [1968] 2 Q.B. 545 at p. 560.

[94] Query: the effect of such a clause in cases where the defect is discoverable by scientific analysis only: see *per* Megaw J. in *Lindsay & Co. Ltd. v. European Grain & Shipping Agency Ltd.* [1962] 2 Lloyd's Rep. 387 at p. 395, judgment reversed by C.A. in [1963] 1 Lloyd's Rep. 437.

[95] Old s.14(1).

[96] The difference between the two is that merchantability (now defined in s. 14(6) of the 1979 Act) means that the thing sold is reasonably fit for the general purpose for which it is manufactured and sold, whereas suitability is designed to meet a specific purpose made known to the seller.

[97] *The Hoyanger* [1979] 2 Lloyd's Rep. 79 (Can. Ct.).

v. Haji E. Dossa & Sons Ltd., [98] the plaintiffs agreed to buy from the defendants a quantity of cotton seed extraction meal f.o.b. Karachi. The contract provided *inter alia* that surveyors would be engaged to analyse samples at the port of loading and that an "Analysis Certificate . . . stating that the goods are sound merchantable, from fresh production not rancid, free from foreign odour materials . . . and are fit for animal consumption" would be issued. The surveyors issued certificates stating that to the best of their knowledge and belief the cotton seed met all of the foregoing tests. But on arrival it appeared that the merchandise was mouldy and unsuitable for animal consumption. Donaldson J. held that it would not necessarily be commercially unrealistic to enter into a contract making the certificate conclusive as alleged by the defendants. But he nevertheless upheld the claim of the buyers on the grounds that such a provision must be drafted with care if that result is intended, and found that, in the present case, the contract failed to so provide. The plaintiffs' claim, therefore, succeeded, and they were entitled to an allowance in the contract price on the grounds of breach in shipping non-conforming goods. In a similar vein in *Commercial Banking Co. of Sydney Ltd. v. Jalsard Pty. Ltd.* [99] the Judicial Committee of the Privy Council held, allowing an appeal from the Supreme Court of Australia, that where the contract called for a certificate of inspection this did not mean a document certifying the condition and quality of the goods inspected (which could not have been discovered by visual inspection but only through physical testing) but merely that they had been inspected. If a particular method of inspection was desired then that should have been expressly stated. This was an action by the buyer against a bank which had opened a letter of credit for payment to the seller against documents including a "Certificate of Inspection." Such a certificate was issued by surveyors who had supervised the packaging of the goods and the quantity and external condition thereof but as they conducted no tests were unable to know that they were of defective quality. The Council in addition advised that it was a well-known principle in relation to commercial credits that if instructions given by the customer were ambiguous or capable of covering more than one kind of document, the banker was not in default if he acted upon a reasonable meaning of the ambiguous expression or accepted any kind of document which fairly fell within the wide description used.

Many standard contracts now provide for the "conclusiveness" of the inspection certificate issued (normally at the port of shipment)[1] with the con-

---

[98] [1971] 1 Lloyd's Rep. 380.

[99] [1973] A.C. 279.

[1] As to a case where a conclusive (or final) certificate of quality was to be given at the port of discharge, see *Gill & Duffus S.A., v. Berger & Co* [1984] 1 Lloyd's Rep. 227 (H.L.) reversing [1983] 1 Lloyd's Rep. 227. In *Cefetra B.V. v. Alfred C. Toepfer International G.m.b.H.* [1994] 1 Lloyd's Rep. 93, discussed *post* § 325a, the sellers' duty to share the costs of surveyors appointed at the port of discharge (as per an express clause in the c.i.f. contract – GAFTA 100 – in question) was disputed, because of the tender by them of a final quality certificate issued on shipment that was permitted under another clause in the contract. The sellers were held liable to participate in the survey costs, and an arbitration board of appeal decision in their favour was reversed by Colman J., on the ground the first clause was not vitiated.

sequent result that the buyer is barred from raising claims against the description or quality (or other factors attested to in the certificate) when the breach is undetected by the certifier and is only discovered upon arrival. Disputes thus often arise as to the exact scope of the certification, and as to whether the terms thereof were fully complied with or not. For example in *N.V. Bunge v. Compangnie Noga D'Importation et D'exportation S.A. (The "Bow Cedar")*[2] a shipment of Brazilian crude groundnut oil became admixed during shipment with soya bean oil. The seller relied on a surveyor's certificate that was provided and which was, by the terms of the contract in question, to be "final and conclusive." Lloyd J. (upholding an arbitration award in favour of the buyers) held that the certificate failed to certify the commodity in question and merely described the chemical analysis of the product, and that, even if this was not the case, the wording of the clause in question indicated that the matters to be covered by the certificate were moisture and impurities, and not the commodity itself. Although the presence of the soya bean oil did not affect the quality of the groundnut oil (which was excellent) the goods were not the contract goods and the buyer could recover damages amounting to the difference in value of sound ground-nut oil and the price realised by the oil as delivered. Clearly, a false or fraudulent certificate or one that does not comply with the terms required is entirely ineffective.[3] But an error or mistake innocently made by the certifier even when later admitted by him to be a mistake was held not to invalidate the conclusiveness of the certificate, and remained binding as between the seller and buyer.[4] The buyer's remedy in such a case is to sue the negligent certifier.[5] And where the buyer avails himself of a right to supervise the shipment, and his representative fails to detect an apparent breach in description or quality of the goods, he may likewise be entitled to nominal damages only, since if his representative had acted reasonably the breach could have been rectified.[6]

Where the certificate discloses a breach, the question may arise as to whether the breach is a breach of a condition (that goes to the root of the contract) or a breach of a warranty (that can be satisfied by a price

---

[2] [1980] 2 Lloyd's Rep. 601

[3] See, *e.g. Kollerich and Cie S.A. v. The State Trading Corp. of India* [1980] 2 Lloyd's Rep. 32 (C.A.). The company designated to inspect and certify delegated the assignment to another company who prepared the certificate and had the original appointed company sign it. Held, the certificate falsely indicated the provenance and was invalid.

[4] *Alfred C. Toepfer v. Continental Grain Co.* [1979] 1 Lloyd's Rep. 11 (C.A.).

[5] See, *e.g. International Petroleum Refining and Supply Sociedad Ltda. v. Caleb & Son Ltd and Oth. (The "Busiris")* [1980] 1 Lloyd's Rep. 569 (C.A.). However the certifiers hability may be limited by his contract.

[6] *Toepfer v. Warnico A. G.*[1978] 2 Lloyd's Rep. 569 where 2,400 tonnes of fine ground soya bean meal f.o.b. Hamburg were sold. The buyers appointed a superintendent to supervise the loading, but the supervisor did not notice that the meal was coarse ground (rather than fine ground) until after 1,900 tonnes had been loaded. It was held that the supervisor had no authority to waive the terms of the contract of sale but since it should have been apparent that the wrong type of meal was loaded the buyer's failure to protest the breach was tantamount to a failure to mitigate damages and only nominal damages (for a $12,500 loss) could be recovered.

adjustment), or a breach of an innominate term in which case the severity of the breach will determine the appropriate remedy.[7]

325a In some cases the certificate is to be given after discharge of the goods at the port of destination. How does this affect the parties obligations under a c.i.f. contract? This issue was at the heart of the judgment in *Gill & Duffus S.A. v. Berger & Co. Inc.*[8] where the House of Lords reversed a decision by the Court of Appeal[9] which in turn was preceded by five other decisions, a procedure that lasted seven and a half years, and one that was described by Lord Diplock as a "disgrace to the judicial system" Lord Diplock, who declared the judgment in the case, answered this question as follows:

> "a certificate by GSC as to the quality of the goods at port of discharge under the certification clause in the contract is not, and is indeed incapable of being, included among shipping documents which a buyer (should be *seller*) is required to tender to his seller (should be *buyer*) in return for payment of the price under a contract of sale in ordinary c.i.f. terms". (at p. 230).

The question in this case was whether the buyer or the seller was guilty of a breach when the entire 500 ton shipment of Argentine Bolita beans was to be the subject of an inspection in Le Havre, but only 445 tonnes were in fact inspected, because the balance of 55 tonnes was carried to Rotterdam and arrived back at Le Havre 13 days later. Meanwhile, the buyer rejected the documents, and payment under a letter of credit was refused on two separate occasions. The first time when the documents presented did not include any certificate of inspection, and the second time when a certificate relating to 445 tonnes (instead of 500) was presented. On these facts the question arose as to whether the c.i.f. buyers were entitled to reject, or whether they were guilty of a wrongful repudiation as contended by the sellers. It was their Lordships view that the termination of the contract by the seller:

> "had the consequence in law that all primary obligations of the parties under the contract which had not yet been performed were terminated. This termination did not prejudice the right of the party so electing to claim damages from the party in repudiatory breach for any loss sustained in consequence of the non-performance by the latter of his primary obligation under the contract, *future as well as past*. Nor did the termination deprive the party in repudiatory breach of the right to claim, or to set off, damages for any *past* non-performance by the other party of that other party's own primary obligations, due to be performed before the contract was rescinded. In the instant case these latter obligations included a primary obligation, to be performed by the sellers at the time of shipment, and thus before the date of termination of the contract, albeit that the

---

[7] See *Tradax Internacional S.A. v. Goldschmidt S. A.* [1977] 2 Lloyd's Rep. 604 where it was decided that the buyer was not entitled to reject where the certificate disclosed an insignificant impurity (of 0.10 per cent.) over the tolerance permitted by the contract.

[8] [1984] 1 Lloyd's Rep. 227.

[9] [1983] 1 Lloyd's Rep. 622.

right of disposal of the goods was reserved by the sellers until payment by the buyers for the shipping documents upon presentation'' (at p. 230).[10]

However there was no support for a finding that non-conforming goods were sent, even though the inspection certificate tendered did not cover the entire contract quantity. In passing Lord Diplock mentioned that:

> "in the case of a c.i.f. contract it is difficult to see how, without fraud on his part, the seller could ship beans but nevertheless be in a position to tender shipping documents conforming to those called for by a c.i.f. contract to sell peas" (at pp. 230, 231).

Since the buyers refusal to pay for the documents, described by his Lordship, as "a legal characteristic of a c.i.f. contract so well established by English law as to be beyond the realm of controversy", constituted a fundamental breach of the contract, the sellers were entitled to treat the contract as repudiated, and were relieved from their obligation to deliver to the buyers any of the goods that were the subject-matter of the contract. In their Lordships view, therefore, the absence of the inspection certificate notwithstanding, the sellers were entitled to payment upon presentation of the usual c.i.f. documents, *i.e.* invoice, bill of lading, and the insurance policy or certificate, and could rightfully treat the buyers failure to pay as a wrongful repudiation. The buyer could not then subsequently show that the actual goods shipped under the conforming documents did not in fact conform to the contract. In so holding, the judgment overturns what had been thought to be the *ratio decidendi* of the decision of the High Court of Australia in *Henry Dean and Sons (Sydney) Ltd. v. O'Day Proprietary Ltd.*[11] by pronouncing that "what was expressed to be the ratio decidendi of those judgments (the majority view) was not the law of England" (at pages 231, 232). What the buyers could, in such a case, do, was to reduce the amount of damages they became liable for (the difference between the contract price and the market price of the documents representing the goods) because the actual goods did not conform to their description or quality as represented by the documents. The certification clause in the contract was, thus, held to be relevant only to the measure damages to which the sellers were entitled, and the conclusiveness of the certificate would be limited to those characteristics of the contract goods "that would be apparent on reasonable examination of the sample" (at page 233). However, had the sellers committed a repudiatory breach, *e.g.* by failing to ship conforming goods, the buyers would probably have prevailed. This is because the buyer may refuse to pay against conforming documents because *before* such refusal, the sellers had committed a repudiatory breach. In such a case the buyer himself would be entitled to rescind even

---

[10] Of course if the buyers had paid they would still have been entitled to reject the goods if upon arrival and examination they were found to be non-conforming. See *Kwai Tek Chao v. British Traders & Shippers Ltd.* (*post*, §335).

[11] (1927) 39 C.L.R. 330.

though, at the time of the refusal, he gave a different ground for it, or no ground at all.[12] Likewise where no goods were shipped, or where the seller has ordered the ship to go to some other destination than the contractual c.i.f. destination, the seller cannot demand payment on tendering conforming documents.[13] And of course where the seller is guilty of fraud, and he tenders false documents, even if they appear on their face to be in order, the buyer is similarly justified in refusing to pay or in rejecting the documents.

326   *Fitness for purpose.* Where a term was imported under the old section 14(1) of the Act (the amended version as to fitness for purpose is found in section 14(3) of the Act of 1979) the question also sometimes arose as to whether the goods became unmerchantable (which, as already stated, is a separately implied term under section 14(2) of the Act) merely because they were unsuited for the purpose for which they had been ordered. The answer to this question appears to have been the subject of two different schools of judicial thinking. According to one view, goods were "unmerchantable" where no reasonable person in the buyer's position would have agreed to buy them had he known their defect. In contrast, the more recent current of authority on this point seems to have been to the effect that:

> "... if goods are sold under a description which they fulfil, and if goods under that description are reasonably capable in ordinary use of several purposes, they are of merchantable quality within section 14(2) of the [Sale of Goods] Act if they are reasonably capable of being used for any one or more of such purposes even if unfit for use for that one of those purposes which the particular buyer intended."[14]

In *Phoenix Distributors Ltd. v. L. B. Clarke (London) Ltd., Cullen Allen & Co. (Third Parties)*,[15] the sellers sold to the buyers a quantity of potatoes, f.a.s. Belfast, for delivery in Poland. When the potatoes arrived in Poland, the Polish authorities refused to allow them to enter the country because they were diseased. The sellers sued for the price, but the buyers refused to pay, alleging that it was an express term of the contract or else a collateral warranty that the potatoes would be suitable for use in Poland. The buyers also pleaded that the goods were unfit for the purpose under the Sale of Goods Act 1893, section 14(1), and were not of merchantable quality under section 14(2) of that Act. McNair J. held that all the defences failed, and that the buyers were liable to pay the price. The buyers had not proved that there was an express term or collateral warranty as to suitability for use in Poland. Further, they had not shown that they had relied on the sellers' skill and judgment so as to bring (old) section 14(1) of the Act into operation. Finally,

---

[12] *Taylor v. Oakes Roncoroni & Co. Ltd.* [1922] 38 T.L.R. 517, *British and Bennington Ltd. v. North Western Cacher Tea Co. Ltd.* [1923] A.C. 48. *post*, § 339.
[13] *Ante*, §26.
[14] *Per* Lord Wright in *Canada Atlantic Grain Export Company (Inc.) v. Eilers and Ors.* (1929) 35 Ll.L. Rep. 206 at p. 213.
[15] [1966] 2 Lloyd's Rep. 285.

the potatoes could have been sold elsewhere under the description under which they were sold. Accordingly they were of merchantable quality, and no breach of (old) section 14(2) had been committed.

In an effort to clarify this somewhat confusing situation old section 14 of the 1893 Act was entirely redrafted by the Supply of Goods (Implied Terms) Act 1973. Under the redraft, now incorporated in the 1979 Act, the several implied conditions are separated and "merchantability" which is defined as fitness "for the purpose or purposes for which goods [of the kind bought] are commonly bought as it is reasonable to expect having regard to any description applied to them,"[16] is clearly made separate and distinct from fitness for purpose. The burden of proof requirements have been altered and the buyer no longer has to show that he had relied on the seller's skill and judgment which is presumed *unless* the seller shows to the contrary. The sale has only got to be in the course of business and not, as before, in respect of goods which it is in the course of the seller's business to supply. And unless the particular purpose for which the goods are required is expressly made known to the seller, there is only an implied condition that they should be reasonably fit for the purpose for which such goods are commonly sold. However, (apart from the broad statement originating from section 7(2) of the Supply of Goods (Implied Terms) Act 1973) the statute does not contain any exhaustive definition of "merchantable quality," and, as Lord Reid pointed out in *Brown v. Craiks*,[17] "Judicial observations can never be regarded as complete definitions: they must be read in the light of the facts and issues raised in the particular case. I do not think it is possible to frame, except in the vaguest terms, a definition of "merchantable quality" which can apply to every kind of case." What is clear is that the words "merchantable quality" in the Act are used in a "commercial" sense, and do not have some other "statutory" sense as some arbitral tribunals had assumed.[18] The test to be applied in light of the serious repercussions (namely, rejection in the case of breach) was most recently reviewed by the Court of Appeal in *The Hansa Nord* case.[19]

For a claim to succeed on the ground that the goods are unsuitable for a particular purpose for which they were required, the buyer therefore must bring himself within the provisions of section 14(3) of the Act. A failure to do so is probably fatal to the claim and cannot be cured by invoking section 14(2) and showing that the goods were not of merchantable quality for that particular purpose. And, conversely, there may of course be circumstances where a claim will succeed under section 14(3) but fail under section 14(2) of the Act.[20]

---

[16] See the Sale of Goods Act 1979.
[17] [1970] 1 W.L.R. 752 at p. 754.
[18] See *per* Lord Denning M.R. in *Cehave M.V. v. Bremer Handelsgesellschaft m.b.H.* (*The Hansa Nord*) [1975] 2 Lloyd's Rep. 445 at pp. 451–452.
[19] See n. 18.
[20] See *Ashington Piggeries Ltd, and Fur Farm Supplies Ltd. v. Christopher Hill Ltd. and Oth.* [1971] 1 Lloyd's Rep. 245 (H.L.).

327   Finally, where a breach of warranty of quality is alleged, the burden of proving the cause of the deterioration is on the buyer. He does not discharge it merely by pointing out that the loss occurred during what appeared to be a normal transit, thus purporting to shift the onus of demonstrating that it was caused by some extraordinary or abnormal circumstance unto the seller. Indeed, where the buyer alleges that the deterioration was due to one of a number of causes, his burden becomes correspondingly greater because he must show that all the causes which might have induced the deterioration are the responsibility of the seller.[21]

Where, however, the unmerchantable quality of the goods is due not to any deterioration caused during the transit but to some original latent defect in them which is in no way aggravated by their movement thereafter (for example, a poisonous content in food) the seller obviously assumes liability therefore. In the absence of a stipulation to the contrary, the goods are in such a case unmerchantable upon shipment, and the question as to who bears the risk of deterioration in transit under a c.i.f. contract is irrelevant. Presumably Havers J. had this in mind when he stated in *Hardwick Game Farm v. Suffolk Agricultural and Poultry Producers' Association Ltd.*[22] that:

> "It is clear that in all the contracts the goods were sold by description and the sellers . . . were sellers who dealt in goods of that description.[23] There was, therefore, in each contract an implied condition under section 14(2) of the Sale of Goods Act 1893, that the goods should be of merchantable quality. As the goods were in each case c.i.f. London, the condition required that the goods should remain of merchantable quality from the time of shipment in Brazil throughout normal transit to the destination London and for a reasonable time thereafter for disposal." (at p. 270).

328   The maxim *caveat emptor* is, as was held in *Jones v. Just*,[23a] inapplicable in such a case. There the defendant sold to the plaintiff a quantity of Manila hemp to be shipped from Singapore c.i.f. Liverpool. The hemp was examined upon arrival and was found to have been damaged by salt water. It appeared that the wetting occurred while the hemp was on its way from Manila to Singapore, where it was unpacked and dried and repacked and shipped. The defendant was not cognisant of these facts, since he had acquired them from suppliers in Singapore. In an action for breach of contract the defendant unsuccessfully pleaded the maxim of *caveat emptor vis-à-vis* the plaintiff. Blackburn J., whose judgment was affirmed by the Court of Queen's Bench, allowed the claim and assessed damages on the difference between what the hemp was worth when it arrived and what it would have realised had the seller shipped hemp of the contract quality.

---

[21] *Cf. A. R. Kemp Ltd. & Oth. v. Tolland* [1956] 2 Lloyd's Rep. 681.

[22] [1964] 2 Lloyd's Rep. 227; statement unaffected by decision of C.A. in [1966] 1 All E.R. 309, reversing Havers J., and considered more fully *post*, §409.

[23] Since the passage of the Supply of Goods (Implied Terms) Act 1973 these are no longer prerequisites to the application of the implied condition of merchantable quality.

[23a] (1868) L.R. 3 Q.B. 197.

Mellor J., delivering judgment for the Court of Queen's Bench, stated:

> "On the argument before us, it was contended that the contract was performed on the part of the defendant by the shipping at Singapore of an article which answered the description of 'Manila hemp,' although at that time it was so damaged as to have become unmerchantable. It was said that there being no fraud on the part of the vendor, and both parties being equally ignorant of the past history and actual condition of the article contracted for, and neither of them having had the opportunity of inspecting it, it was the duty of the vendees to have stipulated for a merchantable article if that was what they intended to contract for. In other words, it was said that the maxim, caveat emptor, applied in such a case, in the same way as on a sale of a specific article by a person not being the manufacturer or producer, even though the defect was latent and not discoverable upon examination.
>
> "We are of the opinion that there is a great distinction between the present case and the sale of goods in esse. . . . We are aware of no case in which the maxim, caveat emptor, has been applied where there has been no opportunity of inspection, or where that opportunity had not been waived." (at pp. 201–204).

329 *Waiver of conditions.* But the buyer may not be able to take advantage of the breach of a condition to be performed by the seller. In the first place he may have waived it.[24] A party may waive a condition which is for his benefit, the essence of waiver being that the party entitled to complain of a breach of condition has led the other party to believe that he is not intending to treat the contract as at an end, but to regard the breach as a breach of warranty only,[25] and by section 11(1)(a) of the 1893 Act (now largely contained in section 11(2) of the 1979 Act) it was enacted that:

> "Where a contract of sale is subject to any condition to be fulfilled by the seller, the buyer may waive the condition, or may elect to treat the breach of such condition as a breach of warranty, and not as a ground for treating the contract as repudiated."[26]

So, *e.g.* in *Heinjin Holst v. Bremer*,[27] where a quantity of sugarbeet pulp pellets was sold for shipment c.i.f. Rotterdam in February or March 1971 under a contract providing that notice of appropriation "stating the vessel's name and the approximate weight shipped shall be dispatched and open to correction of any errors occurring in transmission," it was held that the notice of appropriation which named the wrong vessel was not one occurring in

---

[24] *e.g.* where buyers retained documents which they knew they were entitled to reject, from September 22 to October 3. *Shipton, Anderson & Co. v. Weston & Co.* (1922) 10 Ll.L.Rep. 762.
[25] *Bentsen v. Taylor* [1893] 2 Q.B. 274 (C.A.) at p. 284.
[26] The concept of "fundamental term," *ante*, § 316, n. 51, was introduced into the law of sales primarily in order to limit the application of exception clauses to which the buyer assented and which were designed to protect the seller against his failure to deliver goods which answer the contract description. Where the concept has been applied the effect has been to preserve the buyer's right to treat the contract as repudiated, the exception clause notwithstanding.
[27] [1972] 2 Lloyd's Rep. 11.

transmission but that since the buyer accepted the pellets the breach was reduced from a breach of condition to a breach of warranty.

330   Waiver normally operates as an estoppel, but, to sustain the latter defence, the court must be satisfied (i) that the party who was said to be estopped had made an unequivocal representation to the other party that he did not intend to enforce his strict legal rights, and (ii) that the representee had so acted or omitted to act in reliance upon the representation that it would be wrong to permit the representor to go back upon it.[28]

In *Bremer Handelsgesellschaft m.b.H. v. C. Mackprang Jr.*,[29] Lord Denning M.R. stated the principle in the following words:

> "... If a buyer who is entitled to reject goods or documents on the ground of a defect in the[m] ... so conducts himself as to lead the seller reasonably to believe that he is not going to rely on any such defect—whether he knows of it or not— then he cannot afterwards set up the defect as a ground for rejecting the goods or documents when it would be unfair and unjust to allow him to do so." (at p. 226).

Both conditions must be present for the doctrine to apply. If the seller does not suffer any prejudice from the buyer's conduct he cannot rely on it. In *Société Italo-Belge Pour le Commerce et l'Industrie v. Palm and Vegetable Oils (Malaysia) Sdn. Bhd. (The Post Chaser)*,[30] the sellers failed to make a "declaration of ship" as soon as possible in accordance with a c.i.f. contract incorporating the rules of the Federation of Oils, Seeds and Fats Association Ltd. (FOSFA). Although there was a sufficient representation that the buyers would complete the contract which would amount to a waiver, there was no detriment to the sellers and thus the doctrine of estoppel could not be applied. Observed Goff J.:

> "[T]he sellers ... presented the documents on the same day as the buyers made their representation; and within two days the documents were rejected. Now on these simple facts, although it is plain that the sellers did actively rely on the buyers' representation, and did conduct their affairs in reliance on it, by pre-senting the documents, I cannot see anything which would render it inequitable for the buyers thereafter to enforce their legal right to reject the documents. In particular, having regard to the very short time which elapsed between the date of the representation and the date of presentation of the documents on the one hand, and the date of rejection on the other hand, I cannot see that, in the absence of any evidence that the sellers' position had been prejudiced by reason of their action in reliance on the representation, it is possible to infer that they suffered any such prejudice. In these circumstances, a necessary element for the applica-tion of the doctrine of equitable estoppel is lacking; and I decide this point in favour of the buyers." (at p. 695).

Moreover, if the waiver is induced by misrepresentation (or is not granted

---

[28] *Peter Cremer v. Granaria B.V.; Granaria B.V. v. C. Schwarze* [1981] 2 Lloyd's Rep. 583.
[29] [1979] 1 Lloyd's Rep. 221.
[30] [1981] 2 Lloyd's Rep. 695.

freely) it is invalid, and the buyer will be restored to his original rights. Thus, *e.g.* where a c.i.f. seller induced the buyer to agree to take 40 per cent of the contract amount in fulfilment of the contract, and abandon any claim to the remaining 60 per cent on the basis of misrepresenting United States law as requiring such an undertaking, the Court of Appeal, affirming Ackner J., held that the agreement was based on a misrepresentation, and thus not binding on the buyer, and rescindable by him.[31] The buyer's claim for damages under section 2(1) of the Misrepresentation Act, 1967 (which prima facie treats the victim of an innocent misrepresentation as a victim of a fraudulent misrepresentation) was sustained.

Secondly, section 11(4) of the 1979 Act provides that:

> "Where a contract of sale is not severable[32] and the buyer has accepted[33] the goods, or part of them the breach of condition to be fulfilled by the seller can only be treated as a breach of warranty, and not as a ground for rejecting the goods and treating the contract as repudiated, unless there is an express or implied term of the contract to that effect."

Thirdly, performance of a condition (or of the entire contract) may be excused by reason of impossibility in law, such as where performance becomes illegal, or in fact.[34]

Decisions concerning the denial of export licences in c.i.f. contracts (*ante,* § 111) are illustrations of this type of excuse even if directed against nationals of a particular country only. Thus, *e.g.* in *Empresa Exportadora de Azucar v. Industria Azucarera Nacional S.A. (The Playa Larga and Marble Islands)*[35] contracts for the sale of sugar by a Cuban State agency to Chilean buyers on c.i.f. terms were considered. Subsequent to the overthrow of the Allende government in Chile, the Cuban government adopted certain anti-Chilean measures which terminated commercial relations between Cuba and Chile thus rendering performance of the unshipped balance of the contracts illegal.

The Court of Appeal did not consider these measures repugnant to British ideas of international morality as to require English courts to ignore them,

---

[31] See *André & Cie S.A. v. Ets Michel Blanc & Fils* [1979] 2 Lloyd's Rep. 427 (C.A.) affirming [1977] 2 Lloyd's Rep. 166. A misrepresentation of foreign law is a misrepresentation of a fact, but Lord Denning M.R. opined that the time had come for the long standing distinction between misrepresentations of "law" and of "fact" to be abolished.

[32] An illustration of a severable contract is one for delivery of goods by instalments where the price is payable separately. See, as to this, *post*, §352.

[33] As to acceptance, see *post*, §332.

[34] s.11(6) of the Sale of Goods Act 1979, provides that: "Nothing in this section affects a condition or warranty, whose fulfilment is excused by law by reason of impossibility or otherwise." Two cases of impossibility are dealt with in ss.6, 7 of the Act, *viz*: s.6. "Where there is a contract for the sale of specific goods, and the goods without the knowledge of the seller have perished at the time when the contract is made, the contract is void"; and s.7, "Where there is an agreement to sell specific goods, and subsequently the goods, without any fault on the part of the seller or buyer, perish before the risk passes to the buyer, the agreement is avoided." The words "or otherwise" in s.11(6) are sufficient to cover the fourth ground stated in the text. See also Law Reform (Frustrated Contracts) Act 1943, and *ante*, § 252.

[35] [1983] 2 Lloyd's Rep. 171 (C.A.).

and did not preclude the sellers (whom the court refused to identify with the Government) from relying on them. The sellers were thus relieved from liability with respect to the unshipped balance of the sugar as that portion of the contract was frustrated. But to excuse performance (under English law) the illegality must arise under the proper law of contract or the law of the place of performance.

Fourthly, the buyer may, by his own acts, excuse the seller from fulfilling the condition by (i) preventing its performance,[36] (ii) rendering himself unable to perform his own part, or (iii) refusing to perform his own part.[37]

If for any reason the buyer is not entitled to reject the documents and treat the contract as repudiated, his remedy lies in damages for breach (section 53 of the Act).

However, if the goods on arrival are found not to be in accordance with the contract, the buyer who has paid against the documents,[38] may reject the goods and recover the price and damages.[39]

331   Where, however, as Devlin J. put it in one case,[40] the:

"goods are rejected in a c.i.f. contract for some reason that has nothing to do with quality—the shipment date was wrong, or documents were not in order, or something of that sort . . . and then the buyer goes out into the market to buy goods of the contract quality, it is open to the seller to go to him and say: 'Well, then, I tender you these goods. These goods are of the contract quality. You are looking for goods of the contract quality. You rightly rejected them on a basis that had nothing to do with their quality. If you are looking, therefore, for goods to make good your loss, here they are, and I can supply cheaper than you would be able to buy them at the market rate outside.' If the seller does that, that is a matter which must be taken into consideration in arriving at what is the proper sum of damages to award to the buyer. It may or may not be conclusive, but it has to be taken into consideration in answering the question of whether or not the buyer has acted reasonably, as it is his duty to do, in mitigating damage."

However, no such circumstances existed in the case under consideration for as Devlin J. subsequently stated[41]:

"But I think it is quite plain that there is no room for considerations of that sort in the circumstances of this case. . . . In the first place, there is no finding at all [by the arbitrator] that the seller, after rejection, offered the goods to the buyer, and nothing to suggest that the buyer was aware that the seller would have been

---

[36] If performance of a condition precedent has been made impossible by the neglect or default of the other party, "it is equal to performance." *Per* Ashurst J., *Hotham v. East India Co.* (1787) 1 T.R. at p. 645. *E.g. Mackay v. Dick* (1881) 6 A.C. 251; dist. in *Colley v. Overseas Exporters* [1921] 3 K.B. 302.
[37] *e.g. Braithwaite v. Foreign Hardwood Co.*, and other cases cited, *post*, § 338 n. 82.
[38] See *ante*, § 261.
[39] See *Heilbutt v. Hickson* (1872) L.R. 7 C.P. 438, *post*, § 642 n. 25. For example, as in *Molling v. Dean, post*, § 631.
[40] *Heaven & Kesterton Ltd. v. Etablissements François Albiac et Cie* [1956] 2 Lloyd's Rep. 316 at p. 321.
[41] *Ibid*

willing to have parted with the goods at the contract price, or at any other price, after rejection. But more formidable than that is the fact . . . that this was not a case of rejection simply because there was a defect in documents, or the shipment date was not complied with. These two grounds are both found in the case; but, in addition to that, it is plain from the case that the goods themselves were not up to the contract quality. Whether the buyer rejected them on that ground is not quite clear . . . because it is not clear whether he ever inspected the goods.

"What makes it quite plain that the goods were not up to contract quality is the finding . . . that the buyer would be adequately compensated by an allowance of £1 per standard. . . . Of course, that is tantamount to depriving a buyer of his right to reject altogether, and saying that, notwithstanding that he is properly rejecting, he is to be put in precisely the same position as if he had taken up the goods, and as if his only remedy was to be compensated for the damage on the basis of defective quality.

"That seems to me to be manifestly wrong in law."

332 *Time and place of rejection.* Where the seller's breach gives rise to a right of repudiation (because of delivery of non-conforming documents or goods) the buyer must exercise his right of rejection within reasonable time; otherwise he may be held to have accepted the tender, in which case his remedy sounds in damages only. Whether the buyer acted in time is a question of fact to be determined on the circumstances of each particular case.[42] Once the buyer has discharged this burden and proved what, on its face, amounts to a clear and unequivocal rejection,[43] it is for the seller to prove, if he can, that the apparent effect of the buyers' conduct is destroyed by other conduct having a different and inconsistent effect and not for the buyers to establish the negative case that they did nothing subsequently to disentitle themselves from asserting their right of rejection.[44] The relevant sections of the Sale of Goods Act 1979 are sections 34 and 35. By section 34 it is provided:

"(1) Where goods are delivered to the buyer, and he has not previously examined them, he is not deemed to have accepted them until he has had a reasonable opportunity of examining them for the purpose of ascertaining whether they are in conformity with the contract. (2) Unless otherwise agreed, when the seller tenders delivery of goods to the buyer, he is bound on request to afford the buyer a reasonable opportunity of examining the goods for the purpose of ascertaining whether they are in conformity with the contract."[45]

By section 35 it is provided:

"The buyer is deemed to have accepted the goods when he intimates to the seller

---

[42] See, *e.g. Manifatture Tessile Laniera Wooltex v. J. B. Ashley Ltd.* [1979] 2 Lloyd's Rep. 28 (C.A.) where it was held the buyers had not lost their right of rejection.

[43] The situation is different if the buyer says one thing and does another so as to cast doubt on the bona fides of the rejection (see, *e.g. Chapman v. Morton* (1843) 11 M. & W. 534). Likewise the buyer may act in a manner that creates an estoppel against him, or enter into a new agreement with the seller in which he consents to withdraw his right of rejection.

[44] *Tradax & Export S. A. v. European Grain & Shipping* [1983] 2 Lloyd's Rep. 100, reversing an arbitration award on this point.

[45] This subsection was considered in *Biddell Bros. v. E. Clements Horst Co.* [1911] 1 K. B. 214 (C. A.); *ibid.* 934; [1912] A. C. 18. See *ante*, § 261.

that he has accepted them, or (except where section 34 of this Act otherwise provides[46]) when the goods have been delivered to him and he does any act in relation to them which is inconsistent with the ownership of the seller,[47] or when after the lapse of a reasonable time he retains the goods without intimating to the seller that he has rejected them."[48]

Questions sometimes arise under c.i.f. contracts in relation to these provisions as to the place where and the time when the buyer c.i.f. must make his examination of the goods, if he is to be entitled to reject, as well as with regard to the circumstances which constitute an act in relation to the goods "which is inconsistent with the ownership of the seller" within the meaning of section 35.[49]

Prima facie the place of examination is in the case of c.i.f. contracts the place of destination. In the absence of unusual circumstances, there is no rule requiring examination at the port of shipment, where, subject to the tender of the appropriate documents, delivery is normally said to take place.[50] Delivery for the purposes of these sections means actual delivery of the goods, and not of the documents representing them.[51]

333   In the case of *Hardy & Co. (London) Ltd. v. Hillerns and Fowler*,[52] there was a sale of Rosario and/or Santa Fe wheat shipped by steamer from a port or ports in the Argentine c.i.f. Hull. The steamer arrived at Hull on March 18, and reported on March 20. On March 21, the buyers, without having examined the wheat, resold a substantial part of it and forwarded it to sub-purchasers. On March 23, the buyers, having examined samples of the wheat, rejected it as not being Rosario or Sante Fe wheat. It was in fact Entre Rios wheat. The sellers disputed the right to reject and the dispute went to arbitration. The arbitrators held that the notice of rejection was given with reasonable promptitude, and the buyers were entitled to reject. It was held by Greer J. and the Court of Appeal (Bankes, Atkin and Younger L.JJ.) that the buyers by reselling a part of the wheat without examination and sending it to their sub-purchasers had done an act "inconsistent with the ownership of the seller," and, therefore, had lost the right of rejection. The buyers unsuccessfully argued that, though section 35 of the Sale of Goods Act 1893 provides that the buyer is deemed to have accepted the goods in certain circumstances, that must be read subject to section 34(1),[53] and he is not to be deemed to

---

[46] The words in brackets were added by s.4(2) of the Misrepresentation Act 1967. This amendment resolves many of the difficulties to which the Sale of Goods Act gave rise in the past. See *post*, §§ 333, 334.
[47] See *Hardy & Co. (London) Ltd. v. Hillerns & Fowler* [1923] 2 K. B. 490 (C. A.).
[48] See *Heilbutt v. Hickson* (1872) L. R. 7 C. P. 438, where the cases were reviewed.
[49] See *ante*, n. 46.
[50] The cases discussing the proper place of examination are reviewed in connection with f.o.b. contracts *post*, §§ 629 *et seq.*
[51] *Schmoll Fils & Co. Inc. v. Scrive Bros. & Co.* (1924) 19 Ll.L. Rep. 118.
[52] [1923] 1 K.B. 658:[1923] 2 K.B. 490 (C.A.).
[53] Quoted *ante*, §§334. This was subsequently provided for by s.4(2) of the Misrepresentation Act 1967, see *post*, §332.

have accepted the goods unless he has had reasonable time for examining them, which it was said had not expired at the date of rejection. But it was held that the true construction of sections 34(1) and 35 was that by section 35 one of the acts upon the happening of which "the buyer is deemed to have accepted goods" is intimation to the seller that he has accepted them; that such an intimation may be made before there has been a reasonable opportunity of examining them, and if such intimation is given, section 35 operates and the buyer is deemed to have accepted the goods; that similarly when goods have been delivered to the buyer and he does an act in relation to them inconsistent with the ownership of the seller, section 35 can operate before a reasonable opportunity of examining them has expired.

Atkin L.J. considered the position of the buyer under a c.i.f. contract after delivery of the documents (but before the right to reject the goods is exercised) when he said, in the course of his judgment:[54]

> "If the goods were not in accordance with the contract, the property would not in fact pass to the purchasers upon taking up the documents, if they had not at that time an opportunity of knowing whether or not the goods were in accordance with the contract,[55] or it might be that the property passed conditionally, subject to its reverting to the sellers when the persons who had taken up the documents had exercised their undoubted right to reject. There was no doubt that, after delivery was taken under the documents, there was a period during which the buyers could hold the possession, and hold the possession in a position which was neutral as to the rights of property, and as long as they retained the possession on that footing the buyers quite plainly had the right to reject. But if they transferred the possession after it had in fact been handed to them, in circumstances inconsistent either with the goods remaining at that time the property of the sellers, or inconsistent with the goods being eventually restored to the sellers, the buyers did an act which was inconsistent with the ownership of the sellers."

In the later case of *E. & S. Ruben Ltd. v. Faire Bros.*,[56] the plaintiffs sold to the defendants a quantity of rubber material. The material was intended for resale to a shoe manufacturer and the plaintiffs agreed with the defendants to deliver the material direct to the sub-purchaser. The sub-purchaser rejected the material, and in turn the defendants claimed to be entitled to reject as against the plaintiffs. Hilbery J. held that the defendants were not entitled to reject. In asking the plaintiffs to deliver on their behalf, the defendants were constructively taking delivery at the plaintiff's premises and were doing an act in relation to the goods which was "inconsistent with the ownership of the sellers" within the meaning of section 35 of the Sale of Goods Act 1893.

334   In order to remedy this unsatisfactory situation, section 4(2) of the Misrep-

---

[54] (1923) 39 T.L.R. 547 (C.A.) at p. 549. *Cf.* the report [1923] 2 K.B. at p. 499.
[55] In *Kwei Tek Chas v. British Traders and Shippers Ltd.* [1954] 2 Q.B. 759 Devlin J. rejected this view that property does not pass in the circumstances described opting for the alternative suggested by Atkin L. J. *post*, §337.
[56] [1949] 1 K.B. 254.

resentation Act 1967 incorporated an amendment to section 35 of the Sale of Goods Act. The amendment (now incorporated in section 35 of the Sale of Goods Act 1979) provides that a buyer is not deemed to have accepted goods which have been delivered to him, even if he has done an act in relation to them inconsistent with the ownership of the seller, unless he has had a reasonable opportunity to examine them. In other words, the very argument the buyers advanced in the *Hardy v. Hillerns* case (*ante*) was subsequently adopted by Parliament. The Law Reform Committee in recommending this change noted that section 35 of the Sale of Goods Act was not in harmony with modern trading conditions in which goods are often sold in sealed containers.[57] The amendment thus reconciled the provisions of sections 34 and 35 of the Act, and assures the logical sequence of events: examination precedes acceptance or rejection and, in the normal course of events, the buyer need not make a decision before inspection of the goods is possible and has taken place. It should be borne in mind, however, that no rejection can take place unless the buyer can put the goods at the seller's disposal. Accordingly, if the buyer resells and delivers goods to a sub-buyer, before he has had a reasonable opportunity of examining them, his right of rejection depends on whether his sub-buyer is in turn prepared to reject or to agree to rescission of the sub-sale. And of course the buyer may still elect to waive the condition and decide to treat it as a breach of warranty.

Rights of rejection in a c.i.f. contract[58]

335   The rights of rejection in a c.i.f. contract were considered by Devlin J. in *Kwei Tek Chao v. British Traders and Shippers Ltd.*[59]

The sellers, who carried on business in London, agreed in August 1951 to sell to the buyers in Hong Kong a chemical known as Rongalite C, c.i.f. Hong Kong, with payment by confirmed letter of credit against the sellers' draft accompanied by on-board bills of lading and shippers' documents. The date of shipment was agreed to be on or before October 31.

Before the date of shipment the buyers had instructed the Mercantile Bank of India to open a letter of credit, and had pledged the goods to them in advance as security for the price. The buyers had also contracted to resell the goods to sub-purchasers. The goods themselves were on quay at Antwerp by October 31, but were not loaded until November 3. The bills of lading were signed by the shipowners bearing the words "Received for shipment and since shipped 31st October." Some time during the next three days the words "received for shipment and since" were deleted by some person with the knowledge of the shipping agents, but not of the sellers and in circumstances for which the sellers could not be held to blame.

---

[57]   Tenth Report (*Innocent Misrepresentation*) Cmnd. 1782 (1962), p. 8.
[58]   See Treitel, "Rights of rejection under c.i.f. sales" [1986] L.M.C.L.Q. 565.
[59]   [1954] 2 Q.B. 459.

336   On November 19, the documents arrived in Hong Kong and were presented by the Mercantile Bank to the buyers who accepted them. Towards the end of November the sub-purchasers discovered that the goods had not been shipped on time. They informed the buyers accordingly, and requested cancellation of the sub-sale. The goods arrived in Hong Kong on December 17 and the buyers then took delivery on behalf of the Mercantile Bank, who retained the go-down warrants as security.

By this time the market in Hong Kong for Rongalite C had fallen seriously and the buyers were obliged to accept the repudiation of the sub-purchasers. The buyers brought an action against the sellers alleging that there was a condition of the contract that genuine and accurate documents should be tendered and claiming the return of the price and, alternatively, damages. The sellers contended that any breach of contract had been waived by the buyers in accepting the goods.

Devlin J. (as he then was) found that the buyers were entitled to damages, and that the true measure of damage was the difference between the contract price and the value or market price of the goods at the time of delivery of the goods. In other words the measure of damage is not calculated by refrence to the date of the breach but the date when the buyers could, acting with reasonable diligence, and after they knew of their rights, have resold the goods on the market (if there was one) and obtained the best price they could far them. Dealing with the right of rejection, he said[60]:

> "There is not, in my judgment, one right to reject; there are two rights to reject. A right to reject is, after all, only a particular form of a right to rescind the contract. Wherever there is a breach of condition there is a right to rescind the contract, and if there are successive breaches of different conditions committed one after the other, each time there is a breach there is a right to rescind in respect of that breach. . . .
>
> "If there is a late shipment, as there was in this case, the date of the shipment being part of the description of the goods, the seller has not put on board goods which conform to the contract description, and therefore he has broken that obligation. He has also made it impossible to send forward a bill of lading which at once conforms with the contract and states accurately the date of shipment. Thus the same act can cause two breaches to two independent obligations."

His lordship went on to consider the duty of the buyers in respect of each breach, and continued[61]:

> "Having a right to reject the documents separately from a right to reject the goods, it is obvious that as a matter of business very different considerations will govern the buyer's mind as he applies himself to one or other of those questions.

---

[60] *Ibid.* at p. 480.

[61] *Ibid.* at p. 482. The principle of two rights of rejection applies when documents have been accepted. This will not prejudice the right to reject the goods subsequently. But the *reverse* is not true. If the buyer accepts the goods (that have arrived before the documents) he cannot thereafter reject the goods on the ground that the documents were defective. See *Enichem Anic S.p.A. and Oth. V. Ampelps shipping Co. Ltd. (The "Delphini")* [1990] 1 Lloyd's Rep. 252 (C.A.).

When he has to make up his mind whether he accepts the documents, he has not
parted with any money. If he parts with his money and then has to consider
whether to reject the goods, wholly different conditions would operate. In the
interval he may have had dealings with the goods; he may have pledged them to
his bank, he may have agreed to re-sell the specific goods, and the position may
have been entirely altered. . . .

"If I might call the breach of the term to deliver correct documents breach A,
and the failure to ship goods on the contract date as breach B, it seems to me
that the right to damages for breach A vests when the breach is committed, that
the measure is then determined as being the proper measure required to put the
buyer in as good a position as he would have been in if the breach had not been
committed; and that when a separate breach, breach B, is committed the buyer
has a separate and independent right to elect upon that breach as to the way in
which he is going to deal with it, whether he treats it as a condition or as a
warranty, and that he cannot be fettered in the exercise of that right as he would
be if by his election he altered the measure of damage for breach A. That measure of damage must remain the same however the buyer elects to deal with
breach B."

337 The failure of the buyers to reject the goods on arrival did not therefore
prevent them from claiming damages for their loss of the right of rejection
of the documents, which amounted to the difference between the contract
price and the market price at the time of delivery of the goods themselves,
and not on the date of tender of the documents.[62] Because, at this later date,
the goods were virtually unsaleable, the buyers were entitled to damages
calculated on the basis of the difference between the contract price less the
salvage value, a very substantial amount. In other words, the "market price"
is the selling and not the buying price. And while ordinarily this would not
be a matter of importance, where there are no buyers (as was the situation in
this case) it could be a difference of considerable importance.

Although it was not necessary for the purposes of the decision, Devlin J.
went on to consider whether the pledging of the bill of lading before the
goods arrived amounted to an acceptance under section 35 of the Sale of
Goods Act 1893, and, having referred to the two points of view put forward
by Atkin L.J.,[63] he continued[64]:

"If there is no property in the goods how can the buyer pledge them? It would
provide a simple answer to the point had it arisen in this case, since there could
not be a pledge. I think the true view is that what the buyer obtains, when the
title under the documents is given to him, is the property in the goods, subject
to the condition that they revest if upon examination he finds them to be not in
accordance with the contract. That means that he gets only conditional property
in the goods, the condition being a condition subsequent. All his dealings with
the documents are dealings only with that conditional property in the goods. . . ."[65]

---

[62] Following *James Finlay & Co. Ltd. v. N. V. Kwik Hoo Tong H. M.* [1928] 2 K.B. 504; [1929]
1 K.B. 400 (C.A.).
[63] See *ante* § 333.
[64] [1954] 2 Q.B. 459 at p. 487.
[65] Devlin J. (as he then was) did not answer the question (that he himself posed) as to whether
the pledge may actually defeat the possibility of exercising the right of rejection on the ground

"So long as he [the buyer] is merely dealing with the documents he is not purporting to do anything more than pledge the conditional property which he has. Similarly, if he sells the documents of title, he sells the conditional property. But if, as was done in *Hardy & Co. (London) Ltd. v. Hillerns and Fowler*,[66] when the goods have been landed, he physically deals with the goods and delivers them to his sub-buyer, he is doing an act which is inconsistent with the seller's reversionary interest. The seller's reversionary interest entitles him, immediately upon the operation of the condition subsequent, that is, as soon as an opportunity for examination has been given, to have the goods physically returned to him in the place where the examination has taken place without their being despatched to third parties. The despatch to a third party is an act, therefore, which interferes with the reversionary interest. A pledge or a transfer of documents such as that which takes place on the ordinary string contract does not."

But when the buyer or his agent (*e.g.* a bank) takes up defective documents (*i.e.* documents that would have revealed a defect to a person reading them or to one that should have read them), and pays against them without objection, the right to reject the documents is lost. This loss (of the right to reject the documents) may also be the result of misdating the bill by the seller (or the carrier) and the question will then arise as to the proper measure of damages where the buyer has taken delivery of the goods relying on the accuracy of the bill of lading date that turns out to be false.[67] In *Procter & Gamble Philippine Manufacturing Corp. v. Kurt A. Becher G.m.b.H. & Co. H.K.*,[68] the Court of Appeal (Kerr, Groom–Johnson and Nicholls L.JJ., had to consider the right of c.i.f. buyers of copra expeller cake to damages under clause 6 of the G.A.F.T.A. 100 form of contract that provided, *inter alia*:

"Period of shipment . . . as per bill(s) of lading dated or to be dated . . .; the bills of lading to be dated when the goods are actually on board. Date of bill(s) shall be accepted as proof of date of shipment in the absence of evidence to the contrary."

The last shipment date under the contract in question was extended by agreement to February 29, 1984. Notice of appropriation (that was to be provided under another clause in the contract) showed shipment from the Philippines on January 31, and the bills of lading indicating the same shipment date were thereafter presented to the buyers. The sellers accepted that the contract goods had actually been loaded on February 6 and 10, and they were willing to suffer a deduction of 3.5 per cent in the price, but the buyers sought to recover the actual damages suffered, after first attempting to reject the goods on their arrival in Rotterdam (claiming repayment of the purchase price), and upon receiving a negative response from the sellers, suggesting

---

that the buyer "cannot by his own voluntary act in putting the condition subsequent into operation defeat the pledge".

[66] [1923] 2 K.B. 490 (C.A.). See *ante*, §333.
[67] See also *ante*, § 146.
[68] [1988] 2 Lloyd's Rep. 21, affirming Leggatt J. [1988] 1 Lloyd's Rep. 88, who allowed an appeal and reversed an arbitration decision.

that the goods be sold without prejudice to avoid further expenses. The issue then went to arbitration, and to the courts.

Kerr L. J. reviewed the earlier authorities in this field. He first noted *Bowes v. Shands*[69] in which the House of Lords held that a stipulation in a c.i.f. contract that goods be shipped during a particular period forms part of the description of the goods and is, accordingly, in the nature of a condition. In *Taylor & Sons Ltd. v. Bank of Athens*[70] the buyers claimed damages for late shipment but did not rely on the misdating of the bill of lading as in itself constituting a breach, and it was held they were only enbtitled to nominal damages, since the late shipment made no difference to the value of the goods. Thereafter, in *James Finlay & Co. Ltd. v. M. V. Kwik Hoo Tong Handel Maatschappij*[71] the buyers relied upon presentation of a misdated bill of lading as a breach which was separate from, and additional to, the breach of shipping the goods out of time, and it was held that the buyers were entitled to substantial damages based on the difference between the contract price and the market price of the goods realised after their arrival. *Kwei Tek Chao v. British Traders and Shippers Ltd*[72] took the *James Finlay* decision one step further by holding that the buyers' entitlement to substantial damages remained intact even though they had discovered the misdating of the bill of lading, and the late shipment, before the goods had arrived, because, having paid the price (upon presentation of the documents) they had no viable alternative but to deal with the goods in the best way possible in the circumstances. Finally in *Panchaud Frères S. A. v. Establissements General Grain Co.*[73] it was held that the buyers had waived their right to claim damages by accepting the misdated documents, and could not rely on the date of shipment to reject either the documents or the goods because they were estopped by their conduct from so doing. In the present case (*Procter & Gamble Philippine Manufacturing Corp. v. Kurt A. Becher G.m.b.H. & Co. K. G.*) while the bill of lading was misdated, the goods were actually shipped during the contractual period, and, as the sellers were not involved in the false dating, so that no action in fraud lay against them,[74] the buyers, having lost the opportunity to reject the documents (because they did not then know of the existence of the breach), were only entitled to recover the actual financial loss if any, they suffered. Because the buyers had suffered no financial loss (they received goods which conformed to the contract in all respects including as to the date of shipment) they were not entitled to any damages. Kerr L.J. (at pages 29–30) explained what he believed to be the true position based on the earlier authorities in the following language:

---

[69] (1877) 2 App. Cas. 755, *ante*, § 60
[70] (1922) 10 Ll.L. Rep. 88.
[71] [1929] 1 K.B. 400 (C.A.), affirming [1928] 2 K.B. 504.
[72] [1954] 2 Q.B. 759, *ante*, § 335.
[73] [1970] 1 Lloyd's Rep. 53, *ante* § 146.
[74] The result of the case would have been different had the sellers been guilty of fraud, because in cases of fraudulent misrepresentation the innocent party is entitled to be put in the same position as if the representation had not been made, see *per* Kerr L.J. at p.28 citing *Doyale v.*

"1. The presentation of the documents by sellers under a c.i.f. contract implies a guarantee or warranty—or whatever term one chooses to use—in the nature of a condition that the contents of the documents are true in all material respects. In relation to the dates of bills of lading this is an express obligation under clause 6 of G.A.F.T.A. 100. But the judgments in *James Finlay* show that the same result follows by implication from the mere act of tendering the documents under the contract.

"2. If the contents of the documents are untrue in any material respect, then the buyers can reject them and refuse to pay the price. No doubt . . . it may then be open to the sellers to make a second correct tender if they can. But in practice this will not often be possible.

"3. Ignoring all questions of waiver, which must depend upon the circumstances, if the buyers pay against documents which are untrue in any material respect, then the next question is whether they would have been entitled to reject the documents if their contents had been correct. If they could have done so, because there would then still have been some other material breach of the contract, as in *James Finlay*, *Kwei Tek Chao*, and *The Kastellon*[75] in relation to the date of shipment, then—but only then—will the buyers be entitled to the full measure of damages, *i.e.* generally the difference between the contract and market prices. The reason is that in that event this would be . . . the estimated loss directly and naturally resulting in the ordinary course of events . . . from the sellers' breach in presenting documents which contained untrue material statements".

Kerr L.J. then cited with approval parts of paragraphs 1763 to 1771 of Benjamin's, *Sale of Goods*,[76] on "Defects in the Documents Alone" wherein it is stated that where the goods are in all respects in accordance with the contract, but the seller tenders a defective document which the buyer accepts (even in ignorance of his right to reject it) "he" (the buyer) "should have no right to substantial damages." But his Lordship added that it did not necessarily follow that:

"in such a situation the buyers will never be able to recover substantial damages for the sellers' breach in presenting documents whose contents were incorrect in some material respect. For instance, a falsely dated bill of lading becomes effectively unmerchantable, in the sense of being non-negotiable (or, more accurately, non-transferrable) once its true date is known. Its presentation by the sellers was a breach of contract even if the goods shipped were in fact shipped during the contractual shipment period, as in the present case. In such circumstances it may well be possible for the buyers to show that they suffered a loss as a result of this breach. Thus, they may have found themselves 'locked in' on a falling market by holding a non-transferrable bill of lading, when they might otherwise have been able to sell the goods afloat, albeit already at substantially less than their original

---

Olby (Ironmongers) Ltd. [1969] 2 Q.B. 158, and *Saunders v. Edwards* [1987] 1 W.L.R. 1116 at p. 1121.
[75] [1978] Lloyd's Rep. 203 where the bill of lading was misdated on a falling market. Shipment had taken place a few days out of time, without any material effect on the time of arrival of the cargo or its value, and the buyers were awarded full damages because the sellers were unable to come within a force majuere exception on which they sought to rely to justify the delay. Donaldson J. (as he then was) expressed regret about this result since the claim was based on a mere technicality.
[76] (3rd ed., 1987).

contract price. Alternatively, they might be able to show that if the bill of lading has been correctly dated they could have used it to fulfil a previously concluded sub-sale caused by a notice of appropriation with which they were now unable to comply''.

Therefore, there may well be situations where c.i.f. buyers might be able to put forward claims for substantial damages for a mere defect in the documents alone, but such was not the situation before the court in the case under consideration. The result therefore was to affirm Legatt J.'s decision, that reversed the arbitration award in favour of the buyers, whose claim for anything, but nominal damages, failed. In light of the foregoing statement of the law, Cooke J.'s observation in *Kliejan & Holst N.G. Rotterdam v. Bremer Handelgeselschaft M.b.H.*[77] in which he expressed the view that the buyer is always entitled to damages where the seller has broken a condition of the contract by failing to tender proper documents, and the buyer has not, rescinded, is open to serious question. Cooke J. stated that "the reasons why the buyers have not rescinded are immaterial. Whether they have been misled or have elected not to rescind with full knowledge of the facts the position is the same, namely, that if they had rescinded, they would not have had to pay a price (*viz.* the contract price) in excess of the market price of the goods at the time of the breach''. Already in *Vargas Pena Apeztegnia Y Cia SIAC v. Peter Cremer G.m.b.H.*[78] (an f.o.b. case) Saville J. disagreed with this exposition that in his view mistated the law, because he said that if the buyers knew of the breach, and the parties have entered into a special agreement then the taking of the goods would be without prejudice to the buyers right of rejection (as were the facts in the *Klienjan case*):

> "there is no causal connection between the breach and the loss of the right to reject. The buyers know that they may reject it if they wish to do so—the breach does not cause them to accept the documents. In such a case to award damages where the documents have been accepted on the basis of the difference between the contract and the market prices at the date of the breach is to award damages that simply do not flow from the breach''.

The proper measure of damages in such circumstances is the difference between the value of the goods as warranted, and their value in fact. And if there is no difference between the two, as was the case in *Vargas*, no damages can be recovered despite the loss resulting from a fall in the market price occuring subsequent to the sale. The buyers in the *Vargas* case were unwise to act as they did. They advised the sellers that they were in breach for sending Paraguay cottonseed expeller which showed a content of fat in excess of the agreed percentage, but accepted the documents, and resold the cargo, albeit after notifying the sellers of their non-acceptance, and of their intention (in the absence of any satisfactory reply from the sellers) of reselling with

---

[77] [1972] 2 Lloyd's Rep. 11, at pp. 21–22.
[78] [1987] 1 Lloyd's Rep. 394.

the aim of "protecting the cargo". This resale was considered an acceptance by them (as no special no prejudice agreement was shown to exist), resulting in the loss of the right to reject, and a trade arbitration award entitling them to substantial damages was reversed.

338   *Rejection on wrong ground.* If the buyer rejects the documents on an insufficient ground he is not thereby precluded from subsequently supporting the rejection on other and valid grounds.[79]

> "It is a long established rule of law that a contracting party who, after he has become entitled to refuse performance of his contractual obligations, gives a wrong reason for his refusal, does not thereby deprive himself of a justification which in fact existed, whether he was aware of it or not."[80]

But the buyer may by his conduct preclude himself from setting up a different ground. In such a case the doctrine of "estoppel by conduct" may be invoked, and the buyer will be deemed to have waived his remedy.[81] So, *e.g.* buyers of maize were held to have been estopped from rejecting goods on the grounds that the bill of lading contained a false date, because they had earlier accepted the documents and claimed rejection on the wrong ground—*i.e.* that the packing of the maize was defective.[82] Where the buyer wrongfully repudiates the contract, so as to waive the performance of the conditions still performable or dispense the other party from performing his obligations any further, is he released from liability by proving that if he had not repudiated the contract, but called for its performance, the other party would have been unable or unwilling to fulfil his obligations, *e.g.* that goods would have been tendered which the buyer would have been justified in rejecting? In English law the answer to this question is negative. In other words the buyer *cannot* set up such a defence. Where the buyer wrongfully repudiates, the seller is entitled to recover substantial damages, even though the buyer establishes that defective goods would have been tendered.[83] The premise for this supposition is well stated by Lord Mansfield in the following passage:

> "Take it on the reason of the thing. The party must show he was ready; but if the other stops him on the ground of an intention not to perform his part, it is not necessary for the first to go farther, and do a nugatory act."[84]

---

[79] See *Sanders v. Maclean* (1883) 11 Q.B.D. 327, *per* Brett M.R. at p. 333; *Manbre Saccharine Co. v. Corn Products Co.* [1919] 1 K.B. 198, *per* McCardie J. at p. 204; *Taylor v. Oakes* (1922) 38 T.L.R. 349, *per* Greer J. at p. 351; C.A. 38 T.L.R. 517; *Hansson v. Hamel & Horley Ltd.* [1922] 2 A.C. 36 at p. 42, *per* Lord Sumner.
[80] *Per* Greer J., *Taylor v. Oakes* (1922) 38 T.L.R. 349.
[81] *Ante*, §329.
[82] See *Panchaud Frères S.A. v. Etablissement General Grain Co.* [1970] 1 Lloyd's Rep. 53 (C.A.), reversing [1969] 2 Lloyd's Rep. 109, more fully discussed *ante*, §146.
[83] See *Braithwaite v. Foreign Hardwood Co.* [1905] 2 K.B. 543 (C.A.); applied in *Taylor v. Oakes* (1922) 38 T.L.R. 349 and discussed in *British & Beningtons Ltd. v. N. W. Cachar Tea Co. Ltd.* [1923] A.C. 48; *Continental Contractors Ltd. v. Medway Co. Ltd.* (1925) 23 Ll.L. Rep. 56, 124 (C.A.).
[84] *Jones v. Barkley* (1781) 2 Doug. 684 at p. 694.

More recently the principle was reiterated by the House of Lords in *Gill & Duffus S.A. v. Berger & Co. S.A.*[85] All the buyer can do, in such circumstances, is to reduce his liability for damages due on account of his wrongful repudiation from the difference between the contract price, and the market price obtainable for the documents.

339   In *Braithwaite v. Foreign Hardwood Co.,*[86] the contract was for the sale of rosewood deliverable in instalments and to be paid for by cash against bill of lading. Before arrival of the first shipment the buyers repudiated the contract on the ground of breach by the seller of an alleged collateral agreement not to supply anyone else in the trade. On its arrival the seller offered the bill of lading to the buyers, and the buyers again refused, and the seller resold. The second shipment was treated in the same way. The buyers subsequently discovered that part of the first shipment was of a somewhat inferior quality. In an action for non-acceptance the buyers contended (i) that the collateral agreement had been made and broken, (ii) that they were entitled to repudiate on the ground that the first shipment was not according to contract. Kennedy J. held that the collateral agreement never existed, that the repudiation was wrongful and that it was accepted by the seller as final. He also held that the first shipment was not according to contract and would have entitled the buyers to repudiate had they not already wrongfully repudiated. It was held by the Court of Appeal (Collins M.R., Mathew and Cozens-Hardy L.JJ.) that, assuming the seller by offering the cargo after repudiation had elected to keep the contract alive, he was excused from performance of the obligation to prove that the first shipment was not of inferior quality by the act of the buyer which absolved him from performance of conditions of the contract.

This case, as reported, is "not quite easy to understand,"[87] and it has been sometimes supposed to be inconsistent with the rule of law that a man who puts forward a bad reason for refusing to perform his contract is not liable in damages if there exist in fact grounds which in law justify his refusal. But Greer J., in the case of *Taylor v. Oakes,*[88] discussing the decision in this aspect, expressed the opinion, which was approved in the Court of Appeal (Bankes, Scrutton and Atkin L.JJ.), that the decision merely meant that a buyer cannot justify his refusal of an offer to deliver goods under the contract by proving that, if he had not refused, the goods when delivered would not have been according to the contract.

> "It does not decide that if wrong goods or wrong documents of title are actually presented for acceptance to the buyer, and refused by him without knowledge of their defects for an untenable reason, he, the buyer, is liable for damages for his justifiable refusal because he gave a wrong reason for it."[89]

---

[85] [1984] 1 Lloyd's Rep. 227, *ante,* § 325a.
[86] [1905] 2 K.B. 543.
[87] *Per* Lord Sumner, in *British & Beningtons'* case (*post* § 340) at p. 70.
[88] (1922) 38 T.L.R. 349 (C.A.) *ibid.* 517.
[89] 38T.L.R. 351.

340 In *British & Beningtons Ltd. v. N. W. Cachar Tea Co.*,[90] where, on the somewhat peculiar facts of the case, it was held that buyers having wrongfully repudiated contracts for delivery of teas in London, the sellers were not bound to prove that they were ready and willing at the date of repudiation to deliver the teas in London, Lord Sumner said, with regard to *Braithwaite's* case, as follows[91]:

> "I do not think that the case, as reported, lays it down that a buyer, who has repudiated a contract for a given reason which fails him, has, therefore, no other opportunity of defence either as to the whole or as to part, but must fail utterly. If he had repudiated, giving no reason at all, I suppose all reasons and all defences in the action, partial or complete, would be open to him. His motives certainly are immaterial, and I do not see why his reasons should be crucial. What he says is of course very material upon the question whether he means to repudiate at all, and, if so, how far, and how much, and on the question in what respects he waives the performance of conditions still performable in futuro or dispenses the opposite party from performing his own obligations any further; but I do not see how the fact, that the buyers have wrongly said 'we treat this contract as being at an end, owing to your unreasonable delay in the performance of it' obliges them, when that reason fails, to pay in full, if, at the very time of this repudiation, the sellers had become wholly and finally disabled from performing essential terms of the contract altogether. *Braithwaite's* case says nothing, which affects the regular consequences, when it appears that at the time of breach the plaintiff is already completely disabled from doing his part at all."

And in *Scammell* v. *Ouston*[92] Lord Wright added:

> "As Lord Sumner pointed out in *British & Beningtons Ltd. v. N. W. Cachar Tea Co.*[93] If a party repudiated a contract giving no reasons at all, all reasons and all defences in the action, partial or complete, would be open to him. Equally would this be so, I think, if he gave reasons which he could not substantiate."

341 It was sometimes thought that a contrary view was expressed by the High Court in Australia[94] in a case where the seller tendered documents purporting to relate to goods of the contract description which the buyer wrongfully refused to pay against on presentation. It was generally thought that the decision there was to the effect that the buyer was not thereby debarred from recovery for non-delivery if the seller actually shipped non-conforming goods. The majority of the court (Knox C.J., Higgins and Starke JJ.; Isaacs and Powers JJ. dissenting) disagreed with the seller's contention that since the buyer was not willing and ready to perform, inasmuch as he insisted, as a condition of payment, on having inspection of the goods, his right of claim was forfeited. Knox C.J. said:

---

[90] [1923] A.C. 48.
[91] *Ibid.* at p. 71. See the remarks of Scrutton L.J. in *Continental Contractors Ltd. v. Medway Co.* (1925) 23 Ll.L.Rep. 56, 124 at p. 132, where he discusses Lord Sumner's observations in this case.
[92] [1941] A.C. 251 at p. 268.
[93] [1923] A.C. 48 at p. 71.
[94] *Henry Dean & Sons (Sydney) Ltd. v. P. O'Day Pty. Ltd.* (1927) 39 C.L.R. 330.

"A purchaser who refuses to pay on presentation of documents purporting to relate to goods of the contract description no doubt takes the risk that the description contained in the documents may prove to be correct, but in the present case the risk taken was justified by the result" (at p. 338).

But Isaacs J. expressed the following dissenting opinion:

"It [the dispute] ultimately raises no question but this: Is the buyer of goods c.i.f. who on tender of proper shipping documents persistently refuses to receive them and pay the stipulated price except on inspection of the goods, or other proof of their compliance with the contract, entitled to recover damages from the seller because it is afterwards discovered that the goods shipped were not in accordance with the contract? However great the failure of the vendor to perform his primary duty, the question I have stated, must, in my opinion, be answered in the negative" (at p. 339).[95]

In *Gill & Duffus S. A. v. Berger Co. S. A.* the House of Lords explained that the majority view in that case was a wrong exposition of English Law, and that in any event all that was said was in the nature of an *obiter dictum*.[96] It is now clear, therefore, that a c.i.f. buyer cannot reject conforming documents by reference to the defective nature of the goods represented by the documents. He is, subject to the qualifications earlier noted in paragraph 26, obliged to accept the documents, and if his supposition of the seller's breach is correct, await the arrival of the goods and then reject them. As already noted, in such a case, the seller will not be in a position to argue that the market value of the goods on the date the documents were accepted is the measure of damages, which will be calculated by reference to the later date.[97]

Where the question of whether the buyer is justified in repudiating is referred to settlement by an arbitrator or by a court before the contract is entirely performed, damages are to be assessed with reference to the date on which the decision of the arbitrator or the court is made. The buyer therefore is under no duty to enter the market and purchase against the seller at any prior time. Thus, where goods were sold by description and sample for delivery in instalments, and shipments were by agreement suspended pending a

---

[95] This view was also adopted by the Madras High Court of Judicature in somewhat similar circumstances in *Gulamali Abdul Hussain & Co. v. Mohamed Yousuf and Bro. & Anor. [1953] 1 Mad.L.J.R. 504 at p. 507*, where the court said:

"... in a c.i.f. contract, the purchaser is bound to accept the documents which represent the goods and honour the draft and is not entitled to raise at that stage any question as to whether the goods are in accordance with the contract or not. If, after taking delivery of the goods, it is found that they are not in accordance with the contract, then of course the purchaser has a right to reject the goods and to pursue his remedies against the seller. Therefore, the plea that the goods were not in accordance with the contract, though open to consideration in the counter-claim of the appellants, is not admissible as a defence to the action of the plaintiffs for damages for wrongful refusal to accept the documents and to honour the drafts. The contention of the defendants that they were not bound to honour the [drafts] because the goods were not in accordance with the contracts must accordingly be overruled."

[96] [1984] 1 Lloyd's Rep. 227 at p. 231, *ante*, § 325a.

[97] *kwei Tek Chao v. British Traders and Shippers Ltd.* [1954] 2 Q.B. 459, *ante*, § 335.

decision of an arbitrator on whether the quality of the instalment first shipped was in accordance with the contract, the buyer was able to recover loss of profit on the quantity that would otherwise have been delivered up to the date of the award which confirmed the seller's fault. But damages in respect of the undelivered balance thereafter were not allowed. The market had fallen, and the buyer could have acquired similar goods at no loss to himself.[98]

Breach of contract by buyer

342 Under a contract for the sale of goods c.i.f., the duties of the buyer are first of all to accept the documents representing the goods, and secondly to pay for the goods in accordance with the terms of the contract.[99] The buyer may, however comit an anticipatory breach, which, if accepted by the seller, will amount to a repudiation by the buyer. Such acceptance does not require any communication to the buyer but may be by conduct, e.g., by selling the goods to a third party.[1]

343 *Non-payment.* Where the property has passed to the buyer[2] and there is a failure on the part of the buyer to pay for the goods, the seller has an action against him for the price, for it is provided by the Sale of Goods Act 1979, s.49(1), that:

> "Where, under a contract of sale, the property in the goods has passed to the buyer, and he wrongfully neglects or refuses to pay for the goods according to the terms of the contract, the seller may maintain an action against him for the price of the goods."

It is, however, provided by subsection (2) that:

> "Where, under a contract of sale, the price is payable on a day certain irrespective of delivery and the buyer wrongfully neglects or refuses to pay such price, the seller may maintain an action for the price, although the property in the goods has not passed and the goods have not been appropriated to the contract."

But this provision does not avail the seller under an ordinary c.i.f. contract because the ordinary express or implied stipulation that payment is to be

---

[98] *Per* Lord Parker C.J. in *Goodall Young & Co. Ltd. & Anor. v. N. C. Boost, S. A.* [1959] 2 Lloyd's Rep. 674.
[99] In cases where the seller charters the vessel, the contract may, in addition, provide for the buyer to pay demurrage expenses in the event of unloading at the port of destination being delayed. But where the contract states that demurrage "at the rates indicated in the charterparty" shall be for the buyer's account and the relevant charterparty contains no provision for demurrage (because it is a "time" and not a "voyage" charter) the seller cannot recover for the delay involved. *Mallozzi v. Carapelli S.p.A.* [1976] 1 Lloyd's Rep. 407 (C. A.).
[1] *Vitol S. A. v. Norelf Ltd. (The "Santa Clara")* [1993] 2 Lloyd's Rep. 301.
[2] See *ante*, § 274.

against tender of the documents, *e.g.* "net cash against documents," or "net cash," makes the price *not* "payable on a day certain irrespective of delivery." The point was raised and decided in *Stein, Forbes & Co. v. County Tailoring Co.,*[3] where payment was to be by "cash against documents on arrival of the steamer," and the buyers who rejected the documents were sued for the price. Atkin J. held that in such a contract the price was payable expressly against delivery, *i.e.* of the documents, and not on a day certain irrespective of delivery.

Under present conditions, however, payment will frequently be by means of a confirmed and irrevocable documentary letter of credit. When this form of payment is adopted the risk that the price will not be paid upon tender of the stipulated documents is substantially eliminated. In brief the transaction may be described as follows: The buyer instructs his bankers to open a documentary credit in favour of the seller. The bank thereunder promises the seller to pay him the price of the goods, or to accept a draft for the like amount, against the tender of specified documents including normally the bill of lading, insurance policy and invoice. When the seller tenders these documents to the bank payment must be made. The bank obtains from the buyer reimbursement of the amount paid. The documents constitute the security of the bank for any advance.

344   The principles which apply to documentary letters of credit are discussed in detail in relation to f.o.b. contracts.[4] They govern c.i.f. contracts also. Suffice it here to mention some of the most important aspects of this method of payment. First, where the credit is irrevocable, the bank is under an absolute obligation to pay the seller against tender of the stipulated documents and once the credit has been established no instructions flowing between the buyer and the bank can revoke it.[5] In other words, the irrevocable credit is independent of the contract of sale for the finance of which it was opened. The bank cannot, save in the case of forgery or fraud, resile from payment even where it is informed that there has been a breach of performance of the contract of sale. On the other hand the bank is under a duty to adhere strictly to its mandate, and its right of reimbursement depends on its accepting a faultless tender from the seller. Secondly, the arrangement of an irrevocable letter of credit is of mutual advantage to both parties. If the seller has failed to tender the stipulated documents (which the bank has rightly rejected) within the time limits of the contract he cannot cure the default, after the expiration of the currency of the credit, by presenting the correct documents to the buyer.[6] Only if

---

[3] (1917) 86 L.J.Q.B. 448. And see *per* Roche J., *Muller, Maclean & Co. v. Leslie & Anderson* (1921) 8 Ll.L. Rep. 328, dismissing the contention that the rule laid down in *Stein's* case was based on the terms of the contract there considered, *i.e.* that payment was to be made on arrival.
[4] *Post*, 612 *et seq.*
[5] *Urquhart Lindsay v. Eastern Bank* [1922] 1 K.B. 318.
[6] See *Soproma S.p.A.v. Marine & Animal By-Products Corporation* [1966] 1 Lloyd's Rep. 367.

the bank has failed to pay for reasons of insolvency, might the seller have a direct claim for the price against the buyer in such a case. Thirdly, where no date for the opening of the credit is provided, the credit must be established before the earliest shipping date on which the seller can lawfully ship the goods in compliance with the contract. Any failure by the buyer to furnish the credit in time is a breach not of a separate collateral obligation but of a condition precedent to the contract which releases the seller from his obligation to perform.[7]

Similar rules appertain to the furnishing of a bank guarantee by the buyer that the documents will be taken up upon presentation as some c.i.f. contracts stipulate. In *Sinason–Teicher Inter-American Grain Corp. v. Oilcakes & Oil-seeds Trading Co. Ltd.*,[8] an American corporation agreed to sell a British company a quantity of Canada feed barley for shipment during October/November 1952, c.i.f. Antwerp/Hamburg range buyer's option. Payment was to be net cash in London on first presentation of documents but the buyers were to issue a guarantee through their London bank that the documents would be taken up on first presentation.

The contract did not expressly provide when the buyers were to furnish this guarantee. At the beginning of September the sellers began calling for the guarantee and when, by September 10, it had not been given, they purported to cancel the contract. On September 10, the buyers' London bank sent to the sellers a form of letter of credit, substantially in the terms of the guarantee required by the sellers, which the sellers refused to accept. On September 16, the buyers accepted the repudiation, but claimed that the cancellation was wrongful. On a case stated by an arbitral tribunal it was said: "In so far as it is a question of fact we find, and in so far as it is a matter of law we hold, that the buyers' obligation was to provide a bank guarantee within a reasonable time before October 1, 1952 and that such reasonable time had not arrived by September 10, 1952." The tribunal further found that even if the obligation was simply to provide the guarantee within a reasonable time, the guarantee was provided within that time. The sellers contended that the guarantee had not been given within a reasonable time, and asked for the case to be remitted for a finding on that point. But they failed. It was held by Devlin J., whose judgment was affirmed by the Court of Appeal, that as the contract was silent as to the time when the guarantee should be issued, the buyers' obligation in law was to provide it within a reasonable time before the first date for shipment, *viz.* October 1, 1952; accordingly there was no error of law in the award.

---

[7] *Pavia & Co. S.p.A.v. Thurmann-Nielsen* [1952] 2 Q.B. 84 (C.A.). *Transpetrol Ltd.v. Transol Oweproducten B.v.* [1989] 1 Lloyds' Rep. 309, where the c.i.f. buyers' failed to comply with their obligation to open the credit within one working day after sellers' nomination of vessel, that was to be given at least three working days prior to loading.

[8] [1954] 1 W.L.R. 935; [1954] 1 W.L.R. 1394 (C.A.).

345   *Non-acceptance.* Where the buyer wrongfully fails to accept the documents,[9] the seller has a right of action for damages for non-acceptance only in accordance with section 50 of the Sale of Goods Act:

> "(1) Where the buyer wrongfully neglects or refuses to accept and pay for the goods, the seller may maintain an action against him for damages for non-acceptance.
> (2) The measure of damages is the estimated loss directly and naturally resulting, in the ordinary course of events, from the buyer's breach of contract.
> (3) Where there is an available market[10] for the goods in question the measure of damages is prima facie to be ascertained by the difference between the contract price and the market or current price at the time or times when the goods ought to have been accepted,[11] or (if no time was fixed for acceptance) then at the time of the refusal to accept."

Although the application of this provision to c.i.f. contracts would probably fix the seller's damages as the difference between the contract price and the value of the documents at the date of the buyer's default, a New York court[12] has held that the seller's damages equal the difference between the contract price and the value of the goods on their arrival at their destination. This seems to be equally true in England even where the documents are to be tendered at a place other from that to which the goods are destined. In *Muller Maclean & Co. v. Leslie & Anderson*,[13] goods were shipped from New York to Calcutta. The buyer was a London merchant and payment should have been in London. The buyer refused to take up the documents. Upon suit by the seller, Roche J. held that the price was not recoverable, only damages, which were awarded on the basis of the difference in the market price of the goods in Calcutta, and not in London where at all material times the market price did not change. It is submitted that this result is sound so long as the seller has not acted unreasonably and has not unduly delayed the resale of the documents. That any such delay is to be disregarded seems entirely clear. Where therefore the seller delays the resale of the goods any rise or fall in their market price is for his own account. On the other hand, the buyer must pay damages to the full value of the difference between the market and contract price at the relevant date. Whether the seller has in fact been able to cut his losses or even realise a profit on the goods by reselling them at a later date is of no concern to the buyer and does not mitigate his liability.[14]

On the other hand, where the contract determines the amount of damages

---

[9] As to justifiable excuse by virtue of illegality see, *e.g. Duncan Fox & Co. v. Schrempft & Bonke* [1915] 1 K.B. 365; [1915] 3 K.B. 355, *ante*, §249 and *Arnhold Karberg & Co. v. Blythe, Green, Jourdain & Co.* [1916] 1 K.B. 495, *ante*, §247.
[10] See *ante*, §302, n. 2.
[11] See *ante*. §302. The remarks there with regard to the damages recoverable by the buyer against the seller apply *mutatis mutandis*.
[12] *Ruttonjee v. France*, 205 N.Y. App. Div. 354; 199 N.Y.S. 523 (1923).
[13] (1921) 8 Ll.L. Rep. 328.
[14] *Cf. John Martin of London Ltd. v. A. E. Taylor* [1953] 2 Lloyd's Rep. 589 at pp. 594, 595.

as not exceeding the difference between the contract price and the market
price on the date of default, a c. and f. seller was denied the right to recover
the entire amount paid by him for the cancellation of a charterparty (which
he had assumed in contemplation of performance) by virtue of the unjustified
repudiation of the contract. The court awarded damages on the freight rate
market difference (some $300,000 less) on the respective dates, and not on
the actual penalty paid by the seller for the cancellation of the charterparty.[15]
The seller, however, was permitted to recover damages for the full contract
quantity (10 per cent more than the mean quantity), and not merely for the
mean quantity, because that was the quantity which the sellers would have
elected to ship, and which the buyers would have had to accept had the
contract been performed.[16]

While in *Vitol S.A. v. Phibro Energy A.G. (''The Mathraki'')*[17] where the
c.i.f. buyers wrongfully repudiated the contract (alleging the sellers had failed
to give them the required minimum three working days' notice of nomination
together with vessel's demurrage rates in time), the sellers (who accepted
such repudiation) were held entitled to recover the amount payable to the
shipowner (by virtue of the delay caused by a resale) as damages, regardless
of whether the vessel would have been discharging or on demurrage, during
the period in question, had the contract been performed.

346   *Anticipatory breach.* Where the buyer commits an anticipatory breach,
which the seller accepts,[18] and resells the contract goods at a price lower
than the contract price (and such price is greater or equal to the available
market price), the seller will receive the difference in price as damages
as per section 51(3) of the Sale of Goods Act. In *Vitol S.A. v. Norlef Ltd.
(the ''Santa Clara'')*[19] the question arose as to the form the acceptance (of
the anticipatory breach) must take. There, the defendants sold the plaintiffs
a specific cargo of propane, to be loaded aboard the Santa Clara at Huston,
on c.i.f. terms. The price agreed was U.S.$400 per ton, and payment was
to be made 30 days after the bill of loading date. While the propane was
being loaded, the plaintiffs sent the defendants a telex stating they were
advised the vessel was unlikely to complete loading within the agreed
contractual period, and advised repudiation of the contract in light of this
alleged breach. No further communication took place between the parties
at that stage, nor was there any further attempt to perform the contract.
Instead, the defendants sold the cargo a few days after receipt of the
telex, but, because of a substantial fall in the market price of propane,
they only succeeded in obtaining U.S.$170 per ton. The defendants were
then awarded U.S.$1 million in damages (as the difference between the

---

[15] *Toprak Mahsulleri Ofisi v. Fingrain Compagnie Commerciale Agricole et Financière S.A.*
[1979] 2 Lloyd's Rep. 98 (C.A.).
[16] *Ibid.*
[17] [1990] 2 Lloyd's Rep. 84.
[18] *Ibid.* § 313, as to acceptance of an anticipatory breach.
[19] [1993] 2 Lloyd's Rep. 301.

contract price and the resale price) in a trade arbitration. The award was appealed and sought to be set aside with leave of the court, but the attempt failed. It was contended, on the part of the defendants, that there was no verbal or written acceptance of the anticipatory breach which they maintained was a precondition of acceptance of the repudiation. The court did not share this view, and affirmed the arbitration award. Phillips J. held that acceptance of a repudiation could be indicated by acts, and not only by words. Nor was there any reason why the act in question could not be one which, but for the fact that it was a response to an anticipatory breach, would itself be a breach of contract. In other words where the innocent party proceeds to take action (*e.g.* the failure to tender a bill of lading, or the resale in the case under consideration) that is incompatible with his own continued performance of the contract, it may be quite clear that he is responding to the repudiation by treating the contract as at an end. The case is thus authority for the proposition that the mere failure to perform (or continue to perform) contractual obligations can constitute acceptance of an anticipatory breach.

347 *Other rights.* In addition, the seller c.i.f. has the ordinary rights of the unpaid seller against the goods. He is an "unpaid seller"[20] if the whole[21] of the price is due[22] but has not been paid or tendered, or if he has received as conditional payment a bill of exchange or other negotiable instrument and the condition has not been fulfilled by reason of dishonour or otherwise, *e.g.* insolvency[23]; and the expression includes persons in a position analogous to that of an unpaid seller,[24] as, for example, an agent of the seller to whom the bill of lading has been endorsed,[25] a consignor or agent who has himself paid or is directly responsible for the price,[26] a principal consigning goods to a factor,[27] a surety for the buyer who has paid the seller,[28] and also a person who has contracted to buy goods and resells them without having any property in them.[29] If the buyer becomes insolvent, the fact that the bill of exchange has not yet matured does not divest the unpaid seller of his rights as such.[30] Nor does the existence of an unsettled account current between

---

[20] See Sale of Goods Act 1979, s.38.
[21] "The whole of the price" is the price of all goods where the contract is an entire contract. If the contract is severable, the price can also be apportioned, and in that case it would be the apportioned price of that part of the goods which has not been paid for.
[22] The price must be due. "There can be no lien without an immediate right of action for debt." *Per* Lord Ellenborough, *Raitt v. Mitchell* (1815) 4 Camp. 146 at p. 150.
[23] As in *Valpy v. Oakley* (1851) 16 Q.B. 941. Payment by bill or other negotiable instrument is prima facie only conditional on it being met at maturity, and the burden of proving that the instrument was taken as absolute payment rests upon those who allege it.
[24] s.38(2) of the Act.
[25] *Ibid.* See Chap. 1, § 27.
[26] *Ibid.*
[27] *Newsome v. Thornton* (1805) 6 East 17.
[28] *Imperial Bank v. London & St. Katherine's Docks Co.* (1877) 5 Ch.D. 195.
[29] *Jenkyns v. Usborne* (1844) 7 M. & G. 678.
[30] *Gunn v. Bolckow, Vaughan & Co.* (1875) L.R. 10 Ch. 491 at p. 501.

seller and buyer prevent the seller from being an unpaid seller,[31] unless, it seems, there is an ascertained balance against him.[32]

His rights against the goods are, summarily stated, as follows[33]:

348   (1) *Withholding delivery.* Where the property in the goods has not passed to the buyer, he can withhold delivery by retaining the bill of lading, if the price is due and unpaid or the buyer becomes insolvent, in addition to his other remedies.

349   (2) *Lien.* In the exceptional case where the property has passed but he has reserved the right of disposal of the goods, *e.g.* by taking the bill of lading to his own order, he has a lien on the goods.

350   (3) *Stoppage in transitu.* In the case of insolvency of the buyer, when the property has passed and the seller has departed with possession but the buyer is not yet in actual possession of the goods, the seller has the right of stopping the goods *in transitu* and retaining them until payment.

The right of withholding delivery is the ordinary remedy of the unpaid seller, because, as already stated, in the ordinary case the seller c.i.f. reserves a right of disposal by taking the bill of lading to his own order, and the property in the goods does not pass until payment or tender of the price. The right of lien does not strictly arise until the seller has parted with the property in the goods, and the right of stoppage *in transitu* does not arise until he has parted with both property and possession, and then only in the case of insolvency of the buyer.[34]

351   (4) *Resale.* The effect of the exercise by the unpaid seller of any one of the rights mentioned is not to rescind the sale, but even if this were not so where he resells the goods the buyer acquires a good title as against the original buyer.

It was once thought[35] that by reselling in such circumstances, the seller affirms the contract and resells in order to secure the price.[36] Thus any deposit paid must be credited to the original purchaser, who will also be entitled to any profit on resale.[37] However, in *R. V. Ward Ltd. v. Bignall,*[38] the Court of Appeal (Sellers, Diplock and Russell L.JJ.) rejected this interpretation. It was

---

[31] *Wood v. Jones* (1825) 7 D. & R. 126 (a case for stoppage *in transitu*).

[32] *Vertue v. Jewell* (1814) 4 Camp. 31.

[33] See s.39(2) of the Act as to withholding delivery; ss.41–43 as to lien; ss.44–46 as to stoppage in transit; s.47 as to resale, etc., by the buyer; s.48 as to resale by the seller. It would be outside the scope of this book to discuss these remedies in detail.

[34] *Post,* 708 *et seq.*

[35] See *Gallagher v. Shilcock* [1949] 2 K.B. 765.

[36] The interpretation was based on the fact that s. 48(4) of the Sale of Goods Act expressly provides for rescission in the event the seller reserves a right of resale, whereas s. 48(3) contains no express stipulation regarding rescission.

[37] *Gallagher v. Shilcock* [1949] 2 K.B. 765.

[38] [1967] 1 Q.B. 534.

held that whenever an unpaid seller resells under section 48 of the Act the original contract of sale is rescinded. As Sellers L.J. explained[39]:

> "If the unpaid seller resells the goods, he puts it out of his power to perform his obligation under the original contract, that is, to deliver the contractual goods to the buyer. . . . If [the buyer] fails [to pay the price], the seller in possession of the goods may treat the bargain as rescinded and sell the goods. The suit for damages becomes comparable to a claim for damages for non-acceptance of the goods where the property never has passed."

Similarly, where the seller expressly reserves a right of resale in case the buyer should default, and on the buyer defaulting resells, the original contract is thereby rescinded without prejudice to any claim by the seller for damages[40]; and in such case the seller is entitled to any profit arising from the resale.

Instalment shipments

352 C.i.f. contracts are frequently performed by several shipments, and in such cases questions arise which require special consideration:

353 *Delivery by instalments.* The contract of sale may provide expressly for shipment by instalments. Even where there is no express provision the circumstances of the contract may involve the implication that shipment is to be by instalments.[41] In many cases of contracts to supply a quantity of goods to be delivered within a fixed period, the whole quantity cannot, from the nature of the case, be delivered on one vessel or at one time.[42] Further, an agreement to accept delivery by instalments may be inferred from acceptance and payment of a shipment of part of the goods without objection that com-

---

[39] *Ibid.* at p. 544.
[40] s. 48(4) of the Act.
[41] See, *e.g. Pagnan and Fratelli v. Tradax Overseas S.A.* [1980] 1 Lloyd's Rep. 665, where a sale of some 10,000 tonnes of Brazilian soya meal was considered. The seller served notices of appropriation in respect of shipments on two separate vessels, and the buyers rejected the documents relating to the second shipment. It was decided that the buyers were in default. The contract terms (relating to the shipment of feeding stuffs in bulk) implied that more than one vessel might be used in fulfilment of the contract, and that even small parcels might constitute the subject matter of separate shipments. But even absent the specific wording of the contract the result would be the same. For as Parker J. noted:
> "when considering whether a single delivery or part delivery can be made by the seller, it is legitimate to consider the quantity involved and the shipment period. It would not, I would suppose, be contended that a contractor who agreed to sell three million pairs of boots to the Army, delivery January/June was obliged to make a single delivery. In the present case the quantity was, in the trade, large and the shipment period some six weeks, both circumstances indicating a common intention that more than one vessel might be used" (at p. 672).
[42] *Colonial Ins. Co. of New Zealand v. Adelaide Ins. Co.* (1886) 12 App.Cas. 128 at p. 138 (P.C.).

plete delivery was not made.[43] But unless shipment by instalments has been expressly or impliedly agreed between parties, the buyer is not bound to accept[44] or entitled to demand[45] shipment by instalments.

In contracts for delivery by instalment, the buyer who accepts and pays for one shipment is not thereby precluded from rejecting another shipment if it is not in conformity with the contract. Thus, in *Brandt v. Lawrence*,[46] there was a contract for the sale of 4,500 quarters of Russian oats (10 per cent more or less) at a price including freight and insurance to London "shipment by steamer or steamers" during February. Payment was to be cash against shipping documents.[47] The seller shipped on one steamer 1,139 quarters against the contract. The buyers refused to accept them. The seller afterwards shipped on another steamer the balance of the contract quantity. The jury found that the shipment on the first steamer was made in time, while that on the second steamer was made too late. It was held by Mellish and James L.JJ. and Baggallay J., affirming the judgment of Lord Coleridge C.J., that the words "by steamer or steamers" showed an intention that the shipment should be made in different parcels and that the buyer was bound to accept them as they arrived if they were shipped in time and was not entitled to wait to see if the whole quantity was shipped in time. The buyer, therefore, was bound to accept the quantity shipped on the first steamer, but not the shipment on the second steamer. It must not be taken that the case of *Brandt v. Lawrence* necessarily laid down any judicial interpretation of the words "per vessel or vessels" in a contract which would otherwise be entire and indivisible. The contract must be considered as a whole in deciding whether a delivery by instalments was contemplated by the parties. This was the view expressed by Cotton L.J. in *Reuter v. Sala*,[48] although Brett L.J. in his dissenting judgment does not appear to agree.

354   In *Tarling v. O'Riordan*,[49] where a retail dealer in Cork ordered from a wholesale clothier in London a quantity of ready-made clothing consisting of various particulars, and one bale of goods in accordance with the contract was sent by the seller and accepted by the buyer, and a second bale sent ten days later was rejected by the buyer as part of the goods contained in it were not in accordance with the contract, the Court of Appeal in Ireland held that the inference was that the goods were to be delivered in different parcels and that acceptance of the first bale did not preclude him for rejecting the second bale.

---

[43] *Cf. Tarling v. O'Riordan* (1878) 2 L.R.Ir. 82 at p. 86 (C.A.).
[44] s.31(1) of the Act.
[45] *Kingdom v. Cox* (1848) 5 C.B. 522 at p. 526, *per* Wilde C.J., "If a man contracts to buy 150 quarters of wheat, he is not at liberty to call for a small portion without being prepared to receive the whole quantity."
[46] (1876) 1 Q.B.D. 344.
[47] The term as to payment appears from the judgment of Cotton L.J. in *Reuter v. Sala* (1879) 4 C.P.D. 239 at p. 250, and not from the report.
[48] *Ibid.* at p. 250.
[49] (1878) 2 L.R.Ir. 82.

"The Defendant here," said Morris C.J.,[50] "accepted the first bale, and used it finding it was correct; at the time he so accepted it he could not contemplate that the remaining goods would not be sent also correctly. In my opinion the Defendant was only bound to pay for the bale that was correct and accepted by him in part performance of his contract, and was not bound to pay for any portion of the second bale which he was not bound to accept."

These words of Morris C.J. were approved by the Court of Appeal (Cozens–Hardy M. R., Farwell and Kennedy L.JJ.) in *Jackson v. Rotax Motor & Cycle Co.*[51] where there was a contract for a specified variety of motor horns to be delivered "as required." The court drew the inference that it was intended by the parties that there should be deliveries by instalments. The fact, therefore, that the buyers had accepted the first delivery did not prevent them from rejecting later deliveries on the ground that the goods in the later deliveries were unmerchantable.

355 Further, breach of an instalment contract as regards one or more of the instalments by the seller or by the buyer is not necessarily breach of a condition precedent to the liability of the other party to accept or deliver the remaining instalments.[52] The question of instalment contracts was considered by the Court of Appeal in *Reuter v. Sala*.[53] The argument was as to the effect of a declaration of a single shipment under a contract, which might or might not have entitled the seller to deliver by instalments. In the course of his judgment Thesiger L.J. referring to an instalment contract, said[54]:

"... each delivery of coal was really like a delivery under a separate contract, to be paid for separately, and in respect of the non-delivery of which the parties might well be assumed to have contemplated a payment in damages rather than a rescission of the whole contract."

The principle, as stated by Brett L.J. in the same case[55] is that:

"... where in a mercantile contract of purchase and sale of goods to be delivered and accepted the terms of the contract allow the delivery to be by successive deliveries, the failure of the seller or buyer to fulfil his part in any one or more of those deliveries does not absolve the other party from the duty of tendering or accepting in the case of other subsequent deliveries, although the contract was for the purchase and sale of a specified quantity of goods, and although the failure of the party suing as to one or more deliveries was incurable in the sense that he never could fulfil his undertaking to accept or deliver the whole of the specified quantity. The reasons given are that such a breach by the party suing is a breach of only a part of the consideration moving from him; that such a breach can be compensated in damages without any necessity for annulling the

---

[50] 2 L.R.Ir. at p. 89.
[51] [1910] 2 K.B. 937 (C.A.).
[52] s.31(2) of the Act, *post*, § 355.
[53] (1879) 4 C.P.D. 239.
[54] *Ibid.* at p. 246.
[55] *Ibid.* at p. 256: approved by Farwell L.J., *Jackson v. Rotax Motor & Cycle Co.* [1910] 2 K.B. at p. 947 (C.A.).

whole contract; that the construction of such contracts is that it is not a condition precedent to the obligation to tender or accept a part; that the other party should have been or should be always ready, and willing and able to accept or tender the whole. A consideration of the mercantile consequences of otherwise construing such contracts seems to me to fortify the one construction and to condemn the other.''

356   But a mere partial breach of an instalment contract may justify the other party in repudiating the unfulfilled part of the contract. Whether it has this effect depends upon the circumstances of the case. By section 31(2) of the Sale of Goods Act 1979 it is provided that:

> ''Where there is a contract for the sale of goods to be delivered by stated instalments, which are to be separately paid for, and the seller makes defective deliveries[56] in respect of one or more instalments, or the buyer neglects or refuses to take delivery of or pay for one or more instalments, it is a question in each case depending on the terms of the contract and the circumstances of the case whether the breach of contract is a repudiation of the whole contract or whether it is a severable breach giving rise to a claim for compensation[57] but not to a right to treat the whole contract as repudiated.''

It is to be observed that this section does not apply to all instalment contracts. It only applies to those where the goods are to be delivered by stated instalments to be separately paid for. This section is, however, declaratory of the common law and the same principle may apply even if the contract does not fall within the words of the statute.

357   It is not easy, nor would it be appropriate here to attempt, to reconcile some of the decisions in which it has been held that refusal to deliver, accept, or pay for a particular instalment justified treatment of the contract as repudiated with other decisions in which the contrary has been held.[58] It is comparatively easy to state the principles to be applied. The difficulty arises in their application. These are, first, that the breach must be a breach going to the root of the contract,[59] and, secondly, that each case must be judged on its own merits. As regards the first principle:

---

[56] This expression is presumed to cover failure to make a delivery. See *Coddington v. Paleologo* (1867) L.R. 2 Ex. 193; *Bergheim v. Blaenavon Iron & Steel Co.* (1875) L.R. 10 Q.B. 319.
[57] This expression covers the price of an instalment as well as damages. *Per* Farwell L.J., *Workman, Clark & Co. v. Lloyd Brazileirro* [1908] 1 K.B. 968 at p. 979.
[58] See, on the one hand, *Withers v. Reynolds* (1831) 2 B. & Ad. 882; *Hoare v. Rennie* (1859) 29 L.J.Ex. 73; *Honck v. Muller* (1881) 7 Q.B.D. 92 (C.A.); and, on the other hand, *Jonassohn v. Young* (1863) 32 L.J.Q.B. 385; *Simpson v. Crippen* (1872) L.R. 8 Q.B. 14; *Freeth v. Burr* (1874) L.R. 9 C.P. 208; *Munro & Co. v. Meyer* [1930] 2 K.B. 312; *Maple Flock Co. Ltd. v. Universal Furniture Products (Wembley) Ltd.* [1934] 1 K.B. 148.
[59] *Mersey Steel & Iron Co. v. Naylor, Benzon & Co.* (1884) 9 App.Cas. 434, where 5,000 tons of steel were to be delivered by instalments, and non-payment of one instalment, under mistaken advice, was held not to justify treatment of the contract as repudiated; *per* Lord Blackburn at p. 443; and see *per* Jessel M. R. in C.A., 9 Q.B.D. at p. 657; *Rhymney Rail Co. v. Brecon Rail. Co.* (1900) 69 L.J. Ch. 813; *Cornwall v. Henson* [1900] 2 Ch. 298 at p. 300, *per* Collins L.J.

"... in cases of this sort," said Lord Coleridge C.J.,[60] "where the question is whether the one party is set free by the action of the other, the real matter for consideration is whether the acts or conduct of the one do or do not amount to an intimation of an intention to abandon and altogether to refuse performance of the contract. I say this in order to explain the ground upon which I think the decisions in these cases must rest. There has been some conflict amongst them. But I think it may be taken that the fair result of them is ... whether the acts and conduct of the party evince an intention no longer to be bound by the contract. Now, non-payment, on the one hand, or non-delivery on the other, may amount to such an act, or may be evidence for a jury of an intention wholly to abandon the contract and set the other party free."

In *Mersey Steel & Iron Co. v. Naylor. Benzon & Co.*, Lord Blackburn said[61]:

"The rule of law ... is that where there is a contract in which there are two parties, each side having to do something (it is so laid down in the notes to *Pordage v. Cole*[62]), if you see that the failure to perform one part of it goes to the root of the contract, it is a good defence to say 'I am not going on to perform my part of it when that which is the root of the contract goes to the foundation of the whole and the substantial consideration for my performance is defeated by your misconduct.'"

And, in the words of Lord Selborne in the same case[63]:

"... you must look at the actual circumstances of the case in order to see whether one party to the contract is relieved from its future performance by the conduct of the other. You must examine what that conduct is, so as to see whether it amounts to a renunciation, to an absolute refusal to perform the contract, such as would amount to a rescission if he had the power to rescind, and whether the other party may accept it as a reason for not performing his part."

These principles were expressed in a practical way by Lord Hewart C.J. in *Maple Flock Co. Ltd. v. Universal Furniture Products (Wembley) Ltd.*,[64] when he said, referring to the authorities:

"We deduce that the main tests to be considered ... are, first, the ratio quantitatively which the breach bears to the contract as a whole, and secondly the degree of probability or improbability that such breach will be repeated."

358   Some illustrations of the application of these principles to c.i.f. contracts may be useful. In the case of *Millar's Karri & Jarrah Co. (1902) v. Weddel, Turner & Co.*,[65] there was a contract for the sale of 1,100 pieces of blue gum timber in two shipments c.i.f. to a safe port in the United Kingdom. The first

---

[60] *Freeth v. Burr* (1874) L.R. 9 C.P. 208 at p. 213; approved in the H.L. in *Mersey Steel & Iron Co. v. Naylor, Benzon & Co., ubi supra.*
[61] (1884) 9 App.Cas. at p. 443.
[62] 1 Wms. Saund 548 (1871 ed.).
[63] *Ibid.* at p. 438.
[64] [1934] 1 K.B. 148 at p. 157.
[65] (1908) 14 Com. Cas. 25.

shipment of 750 pieces was refused by the buyers on the ground (which was established in an arbitration which followed) that the wood did not accord with the contract, and they at the same time intimated that they would refuse to accept the second shipment on the ground that the first instalment was such a departure from the contract as to justify them in refusing to accept either parcel. The sellers, who had tendered the documents in respect of each shipment, denied the allegations and maintained that in any event the buyers were not entitled to say that they would not accept the second shipment before they saw it. Bigham and Walton JJ. held that the umpire in the arbitration was entitled to draw the inference from the defective delivery of the first instalment that the second instalment would also be bad, and that being so, there was no ground for disturbing his award that the buyers were entitled to treat the contract as repudiated.

> "... if the breach," said Bigham J.,[66] "is of such a kind, or takes place in such circumstances as reasonably to lead to the inference that similar breaches will be committed in relation to subsequent deliveries, the whole contract may there and then be regarded as repudiated and may be rescinded," whether the breach be in payment by the buyer or in delivery by the seller. And Walton J. pointed out that a party may be repudiating the contract "although he may be contending that he is performing the contract, and may be intending and expressing an intention to perform what is left of the contract."[67]

359   In *Robert A. Munro & Co. Ltd. v. Meyer,*[68] the plaintiffs, who were merchants dealing in cattle foods in London, sold to a merchant in Hamburg 1,500 tons of meat and bone meal, c.i.f. Hamburg, to be shipped in about equal weekly quantities at the rate of 125 tons monthly during 1928. After 611 tons had been delivered it was discovered by the defendant that all the meal so far delivered contained cocoa husks. The husks had been deliberately added by the manufacturers who were supplying the meal to the plaintiffs. It was done without the knowledge of the plaintiffs but it prevented the meal supplied from complying with the contract description. The defendant claimed under section 31(2) of the Sale of Goods Act 1893 to be entitled to refuse all further deliveries. Wright J. found in favour of the defendant and said,[69] in the course of his judgment:

> "No doubt the plaintiffs here had no intention to break the contract, but in my opinion in such a case as this, where there is a persistent breach, deliberate so far as the manufacturers are concerned, continuing for nearly one-half of the total contract quantity, the buyer, if he ascertains in time what the position is, ought to be entitled to say that he will not take the risk of having put upon him further deliveries of this character, and will not accept the position that he must always be watchful and analyse the goods that are delivered to see whether or not they answer to the contract. My conclusion is that in such circumstances the

---

[66] *Ibid.* at p. 29.
[67] 14 Com.Cas. at p. 31.
[68] [1930] 2 K. B. 312.
[69] *Ibid.* at p. 331.

intention of the seller must be judged from his acts and from the deliveries which he in fact makes, and that being so, where the breach is substantial and so serious as the breach in this case and has continued so persistently, the buyer is entitled to say that he has the right to treat the whole contract as repudiated.''

360   *Maple Flock Co. Ltd. v. Universal Furniture Products (Wembley) Ltd.*[70] was a case where the plaintiffs sold to the defendants 100 tons of rag-flock, to be delivered in three loads of $1\frac{1}{2}$ tons each per week as required, all flock to conform to Government standards, which permitted not more than thirty parts of chlorine in 100,000 parts of flock. The sixteenth load was analysed and was found to contain a contamination of 250 parts of chlorine. The defendants refused further deliveries and claimed to rescind the contract. The plaintiffs sued for breach of contract in that the defendants so refused. It was found at the trial that the plaintiffs' business was well conducted, and that the contamination was extraordinary. It was therefore held that the breach of the contract was not, within section 31(2) of the Sale of Goods Act 1893, a repudiation of the contract.

361   *"Each instalment a separate contract."* An instalment contract sometimes exhibits the attributes of a bundle of separate contracts in the sense that each instalment is virtually to be performed as a single contract. Nonetheless, as Lord Hewart C.J. declared in *Maple Flock Co. Ltd. v. Universal Furniture Products (Wembley) Ltd.*,[71] "a contract for the sale of goods by instalments is a single contract, and not a complex of as many contracts as there are instalments under it."

It is, however, a common practice for the contract to provide in a sale by instalments a term that each shipment is to constitute a separate contract. This term has received the attention of the courts on a number of occasions.

362   In *Robert A. Munro & Co. Ltd. v. Meyer*,[72] the facts of which have already been set out,[73] there was a provision in the contract that "each delivery or shipment shall be treated as a separate contract, and the failure to give or to take any delivery or shipment shall not cancel the contract as to future deliveries or shipments." This provision was dealt with by Wright J. in the following way:[74]

"That is a clause which is often found in contracts of this description and which is very difficult to construe, or at least to apply to all possible emergencies. It seems to me, however, that whatever effect it may have—and I am not going to attempt to exhaust the possibilities of this clause—it cannot be construed so as to defeat the rights of the buyer under s.31 of the Sale of Goods Act. The matter can be tested by a simple illustration. Suppose the seller in the middle of performing the contract said in terms that he would not in any circumstances make

---

[70] [1934] 1 K. B. 148.
[71] *Ibid.* at p. 154.
[72] [1930] 2 K.B. 312.
[73] *Ante,* § 358.
[74] [1930] 2 K.B. at p. 332.

any further deliveries, would the buyer then be bound to wait until each delivery became due, and then, if and when it was not delivered, and then only, be entitled to bring his action? In my opinion this clause could not operate so as to prevent the buyer in such circumstances from bringing his action, if he were so minded, so soon as the complete and positive refusal to fulfil the contract was expressed; but the rule under s.31, subs.2 of the Sale of Goods Act is only a method of giving effect to the same principle as would arise in the case of a definite and express refusal; because the acts of the seller in such a case are treated as being equivalent to declaring that he will not fulfil the contract.''

362   Such a provision was again adverted to in the case of *Ross T. Smyth & Co. Ltd. v. T. D. Bailey Son & Co.*[75] where the House of Lords had under consideration the construction of a c.i.f. contract. Lord Wright, expressing a view approved by the other members of the House, said:[76]

> "A clause that each delivery is to be treated as a separate contract is quite common in instalment contracts. Even in this contract, apart from the stamped clause, there is a provision that each shipment (for there may be more than one under the contract) is to be considered a separate contract. Such clauses are subsidiary clauses, which generally have effect upon questions of performance. There is still only one contract and one contract quantity, though, for certain purposes, in the way of performance, particular instalments or shipments and parcels may be treated in separation from the others.''

The precise significance of this term would not appear to have been exhaustively considered, but at any rate it is clear that it does not operate to defeat the right of the buyer under section 31(2) of the Sale of Goods Act 1893 (unchanged by the 1979 Act), entitling him to repudiate the contract and to refuse to accept future shipments.

363   In the more recent case of *Rosenthal & Sons Ltd v. Esmail*,[77] the House of Lords divided on whether a c.i.f. contract performed by shipment in one vessel but under separate bills of lading and providing that ''each shipment under the contract shall be deemed as a separate contract,'' was indivisible or severable. Lords Reid, Upjohn and Pearson considering the contract indivisible whereas in the opinion of Lord Hodson and Lord Guest the contract was severed as a result of the shipment under two separate bills of lading. The dispute in this case concerned a sale of grey cotton cloth by the respondent, a Hongkong exporter, to the appellants, a Manchester firm of cotton converters, c.i.f. Liverpool, February shipment. The entire contract, which embodied the ''separate contracts'' clause, was performed by shipment on the S.S. *Benrinees*. But because the goods were shipped under separate export quotas two bills of lading were issued in respect thereof, one relating to bales numbered 1–70, and the other to bales numbered 71–140. The supporting documents

---

[75] [1940] 3 All E.R. 60.
[76] *Ibid.* at p. 73.
[77] [1965] 1 W.L.R. 1117.

including the invoices, the insurance policies, certificates of value and origin were likewise separate.

365   The buyers took up the first bill of lading and paid for the goods covered thereunder but they rejected the other bill alleging inferior quality of the cotton. The parties agreed that all 140 bales were of the same quality. The question therefore arose as to whether the acceptance of bales numbered 1–70 precluded the buyer from exercising his right of rejection with respect to the balance of the goods in view of section 11(1)(c) of the Sale of Goods Act 1893 (section 11(4) of the 1979 Act). This provides that:

> "where a contract of sale is not severable, and the buyer has accepted the goods, or part thereof ... the breach of any condition to be fulfilled by the seller can only be treated as a breach of warranty, and not as a ground for rejecting the goods and treating the contract as repudiated, unless there be a term of the contract, express or implied, to that effect."

Although the appeal was ultimately dismissed on the ground that the defect in the goods was within the tolerances permitted under the contract by virtue of which the right of rejection was in any event foreclosed, the House of Lords went on to examine the more general question above noted. On this issue the House divided, the majority of their lordships holding that the contract was indivisible and that section 11(1) (c) was applicable. The division of the House discloses an interesting difference of opinion between its members. The two minority opinions appear to have proceeded on the assumption that the contract in question being a c.i.f. contract, and there being two bills of lading, it was incumbent upon the court to regard the contract as severable. Lord Guest said:

> "The duty of the seller in a c.i.f. contract is to procure a contract of affreightment on shipment (*Hansson v. Hamel & Horley Ltd.*[78]). It must have been contemplated by the parties that a bill of lading would be procured. If the sellers were entitled to procure two separate bills of lading without breach of contract—as I think they were—then by doing so two separate contracts were entered into. For my part, I would hold that there were in the circumstances two shipments and, therefore, two contracts" (at p. 1122).

366   The majority of their lordships, on the other hand, refused to concede that their view was inconsistent with the notion of a c.i.f. contract which could in their opinion be indivisible regardless of the fact that two separate bills of lading were issued. The question was one of fact to be determined on the circumstances of any particular case. The "separate contracts" clause affords the seller the option to treat the contract as indivisible or severable, and this option is exercised by the seller when he performs his contract. The seller clearly makes the contract severable if, as he is entitled, he ships the goods in several vessels. In the present case, the majority held that the facts evinced

---

[78] [1922] 2 A.C. 36 at p. 47, see *ante*, §152.

an intention to treat the contract as indivisible. Lord Pearson, with whose judgment Lords Reid and Upjohn concurred, explained:

">. . . by forwarding to the appellants two sets of documents the respondent was giving an apparent indication of an intention to divide the contract into two transactions. The documents tendered or offered to the appellants as buyers included two separate bills of lading. That fact in some other case might be highly important, or even conclusive, as evidence of severability of the contract, because the two separate bills of lading would enable, and might be said to invite, the buyers to sell the two lots of goods separately to different persons, sub-buyer A and sub-buyer B. In that event the buyers, having conditionally obtained the property in the goods by paying the price and taking the bills of lading (*Kwei Tek Chao v. British Traders and Shippers Ltd.*[79] *per* Devlin J.) would conditionally pass the property to the sub-buyers. Then, if sub-buyer A found his lot of goods, though defective, suitable for his purpose and accepted them, but sub-buyer B found his lot of goods defective and unsuitable for his purpose and rightly rejected them, what, then, is the position of the buyers in relation to the seller? They ought to be able to accept the one lot of goods and reject the other lot, and this they cannot do unless the contract is severable. However, on the particular facts of this case that point loses much of its force, because there had been a long course of dealing between the parties, and the respondent was likely to know that the appellants were buying the grey cloth for conversion and not for resale in the same state. When the respondent forwarded the separate bills of lading and other documents to the appellants, he would not reasonably be regarded as inviting them to resell the two lots of goods separately. The appellants had been told that there were two quotas, which accounted for the two sets of documents. On the particular facts of this case I do not think that the respondent's forwarding of the two sets of documents is conclusive to show that he was electing to divide the contract into two transactions, in other words to make the contract severable" (at p. 1131).

367   So too in *Cobec Brazilian Trading and Warehousing Corp. v. Alfred C. Toepfer*[80] the Court of Appeal, affirming Parker J., decided that a c.i.f. contract for the sale of Brazilian soya beans to two different destinations (Santander and Seville) was not a contract for delivery in two instalments. The subject-matter of the contract was a single quantity, a full cargo of 25.000 tonnes, 5 per cent more or less, to be shipped on a single vessel to two destinations in the quantity laid down respectively for each, with one tender of documents, albeit comprising bills of lading for both ports. The dispute arose because a portion of the cargo destined for Seville—5711 mt.— was shipped (on July 14) outside the shipment period (that ended on July 10), and the buyers rejected the entire shipment. The judgment was in their favour, and the sellers' appeal was dismissed. The sellers other contention that late shipment of part of the quantity, was not a sufficiently serious breach to entitle the buyers to also reject the documents relating to Satander likewise failed.

---

[79] [1954] 2 Q.B. 459 at p. 487, see *ante*, §335.
[80] [1983] 2 Lloyd's Rep. 386.

368   Finally, the difficulties that have sometimes arisen with respect to construing or interpreting the exact meaning of extension or cancellation clauses
(resulting from events excusing performance) and their effect on instalment
contracts should be noted. In such a case where the clause refers to "this
contract or any unfulfilled portion thereof"—does the intervening event
affect the remaining unfulfilled part of the contractual tonnage in totality, or
merely each of the several and separate instalments? The question is particularly relevant in circumstances where the intervening event excuses partial
but not total performance. For example, where an export licensing quota ban
that frees the seller of his obligation in relation to 60 per cent of his commitment is imposed, how is a notice by the seller claiming a cancellation based
thereon to be construed? Does it bring about the cancellation of 100 per cent
of the outstanding contract tonnage or does it refer only to a particular
monthly instalment? This issue was considered by the Court of Appeal in
Bremer Handelsgesellschaft m.b.H. v. Vanden Avenne–Izegem P.V.B.A.[81]
where 2,500 tonnes of U.S. soya bean meal were to be shipped to Rotterdam
c.i.f. in quantities of 500 tonnes per month (May to September 1973
inclusive) and where the view was expressed, following Lord Diplock's
decision in *Bahamas International v. Threadgold*,[82] that the court was not
entitled to adopt a construction (which it considered erroneous) merely
because both parties agreed to it. The court, in other words, could not shelter
behind the admission of a party, or the concurrence of both parties on a
question as to the true legal effect of a document. In the *Bremer* decision
both parties agreed to view the clause as applying merely to a single 500 ton
shipment, and not to the "unfulfilled portion" of the 2,500 tonnes. But the
majority of the Court of Appeal (Geoffrey Lane L.J. dissenting) disagreed.
In the course of his judgment Megaw L.J. said[83]:

> "It is so much of the unfulfilled portion as has been affected by the prohibition
> that is cancelled, and that only. The portion so affected—the portion that cannot
> be shipped as a result of the prohibition—may be the whole or it may be a part
> of a particular month's tonnage; or it may be the whole or part of the tonnage
> for more than one month."

The practical effect, as explained by Browne L.J. in the same case, is that
"if a total prohibition of exports came into force before the first instalment
was due to be shipped and remained in force throughout the contract period,
the whole contract would be 'affected' and cancelled. If, as here, price of the
tonnage for several months is 'affected' by the prohibition, that 'portion' is
cancelled. But if (for example) the prohibition in this case had been lifted on
August 1, the August and September instalments would not have been 'affected' and would not be cancelled."[84] While the House of Lords, in considering

---

[81] [1977] 2 Lloyd's Rep. 329.
[82] [1974] 1 W.L.R. 1514.
[83] [1977] 2 Lloyd's Rep. at pp. 335, 336.
[84] *Ibid.* p. 341.

an appeal on this decision,[85] expressed certain reservations on other portions of the judgment, the speeches of their Lordships appear to approve the decision on this point.

[The next paragraph is 381.]

---

[85] [1978] 2 Lloyd's Rep. 109.

CHAPTER 7

CONFLICT OF LAWS

Substantial changes relating to the issues considered hereunder (and in Chapter 14, *post*) have been introduced into English Law, as a result of the United kingdom's accession to various treaties and conventions resulting from its membership in the EEC and European Union. These changes that emanate from the Civil Jurisdiction and Judgments Act 1982 (that came into full force on January 1, 1987), as amended by the Civil Jurisdiction and Judgments Act 1991, as well as by the Contracts (Applicable Law) Act 1990, are described in detail in Dicey and Morris, *The Conflict of Laws*,[1] and the other well known authuorities on the subject. Since the High Court still has jurisdiction to entertain an action *in personam* against a defendant (other than a person domiciled or deemed to be domiciled in a State party to the 1968 Brussels or the 1988 Lugano Conventions or in Scotland or Northern Ireland) on the basis of the earlier principles (surveyed hereunder), and since the substantial principles for ascertaining the proper or "applicable law" of a c.i.f. contract under the Contracts (Applicable Law) Act 1990, for contracts entered into after April 1, 1991 do not appear to deviate significantly from the principles developed under pre-existing English Law, and especially since the earlier rules still apply in many non-European countries which had borrowed the Order 11, r. 1 of the Rules of the Supreme Court regime as a model for their own jurisdictional rules and followed, and continue to follow the Common Law for determining the proper law of contracts, it was felt that it would not be advisable to rewrite this chapter in light of the aforesaid changes or to describe them in addition to, or in lieu of, the preexisting text. The following description must therefore be read subject to the modifications introduced by the European legislation which will apply, in whole or in part, where the plaintiff brings an action in a United Kingdom Court, and the defendant is domiciled or deemed to be domiciled in a State party to the 1968 Brussels or the 1988 Lugano Conventions or in Scotland or in Northern Ireland. Where the Civil Jurisdiction and Judgment Act 1982 applies, service of a writ out of the jurisdiction is permissible *without* leave of the court, provided that *inter alia* no proceedings between the parties concerning the same cause of action are pending in the courts of any other part of the United Kingdom (*i.e.* Scotland or Northern Ireland) or in a court of any other party to the Conventions (embodied in the Acts) territory.

---

[1] (12th ed.)

Jurisdiction and process

381   It remains to consider (subject to the qualifications set forth in the preceed-
ing paragraph) the extent to which proceedings in the English courts can be
brought for breach of a c.i.f. contract where the party to be sued is outside
the jurisdiction. The original jurisdiction of the courts is founded either on
the actual presence of the defendant within the jurisdiction at the date of the
issue of the writ, or else upon the submission by the parties to the English
jurisdiction. In the latter case, if the defendant is not within the jurisdiction
when the time for service of the writ comes, there is power in the court to
order substituted service in accordance with the terms of the agreement
between the parties,[2] and outside the jurisdiction.[3]

382   *Service out of the jurisdiction.* There are, however, other occasions when
the courts are empowered to assume jurisdiction although the defendant is
resident abroad.[4] The rules relating to actions for breach of contract[5] are
contained in Order 11, r. 1(1)(d) and (e) of the Rules of the Supreme Court
which are modified and revised from time to time. The present Rules
(Amendment No. 2) 1983[6] which were revised to take account of the Civil
Jurisdiction and Judgments Act 1982 provide that service out of the jurisdiction of a writ of summons is permissible with the leave of the court, if:

> "(d) the claim is brought to enforce, rescind, dissolve, annul or otherwise affect
> a contract, or to recover damages or obtain other relief in respect of the breach
> of a contract, being (in either case) a contract which—
>> (i) was made within the jurisdiction, or
>> (ii) was made by or through an agent trading or residing within the jurisdic-
>> tion on behalf of a principal trading or residing out of the jurisdiction, or
>> (iii) is by its terms, or by implication, governed by English law, or
>> (iv) contains a term to the effect that the High Court shall have jurisdiction to
>> hear and determine any action in respect of the contract;
> (e) the claim is brought in respect of a breach committed within the jurisdiction
> of a contract made within or out of the jurisdiction, and irrespective of the fact,
> if such be the case, that the breach was preceded or accompanied by a breach
> committed out of the jurisdiction that rendered impossible the performance of so
> much of the contract as ought to have been performed within the jurisdiction;"

In addition the defendant may submit to the jurisdiction as *e.g.* where he files
a defence and does not contest the jurisdiction.

The plaintiff is not entitled to service out of the jurisdiction as of right. It
is a discretionary power exercised by the courts with care, and the applicant

---

[2] R.S.C., Ord. 10, r. 3
[3] Ord. 11, r. 1(1)(d)
[4] Set out in Ord. 11, r. 1.
[5] Actions in respect of torts, *e.g.* for frudulent misrepresentation are governed by R.S.C., Ord.
11, r. 1(1)(f) permitting the service of a writ out of the jurisdiction "if the claim is founded on
a tort and the damage was sustained or resulted from an act committed, within the jurisdiction."
[6] S.I. 1983 No. 1181.

must demonstrate that he has a "good arguable case" on the merits. The principles upon which the courts act are, first, to consider carefully whether a foreigner who owes no allegiance ought to be put to the inconvenience of defending his rights here, secondly, to resolve any doubt in favour of the foreigner, and, thirdly, to insist on a full and fair disclosure of all the material facts by the plaintiff.[7]

Referring to an earlier edition of the Rules, Winn J. stated the principle in his judgment in *Cordova Land Co. Ltd. v. Victor Brothers Inc.*[8]:

> "Th[e] Order, I think, clearly gives a discretion to the court to decide whether it is right in the particular case to serve or to give notice of the writ even though the conditions of the Order are satisfied. I refer to the words 'service of a writ, or notice of a writ, out of the jurisdiction is permissible with the leave of the court in the following cases.' I think it is a discretion of the court which should be exercised with extreme caution and with full regard in every case to the circumstances. Furthermore, it seems to me that where the country of origin of goods is a foreign country, and where the handling of them prior to shipment has in every sense of the word been conducted in that foreign country, and where the contract of shipment itself is one governed by the law of that foreign country, it would need a strong case, which I think is not this case, to satisfy the court that it would be right to take the action away from the American court and facilitate its conduct in this jurisdiction."

But the courts may feel less constrained in exercising their discretion in favour of the plaintiff where failure to permit litigation in England may result in depriving the plaintiff of a right because of a mandatory provision of law applicable in the defendant's domicile which the English courts do not feel bound to honour on the grounds of comity. This conclusion emerges from *Coast Lines Ltd. v. Hudig & Veder Chartering N.V.*[9] where a British ship was chartered in Rotterdam to Dutch charterers. The court decided the charter was governed by English law and permitted the service of a writ out of the jurisdiction because one of the terms of the charter would have been unenforceable in Holland. Comity, in the words of the court, does not demand that a party who wishes to have his dispute decided in accordance with the proper law of the contract, which does not offend the general public policy of maritime nations, should be precluded from having it so decided.

It is further provided by Order 11, r. 4(2) that:

> "No such leave shall be granted unless it shall be made sufficiently to appear to the Court that the case is a proper one for service out of the jurisdiction under this Order."

383 The meaning to be attached to this principle was considered by the House of Lords in the case of *Vitkovice Horni a Hutni Tezirstvo v. Korner.*[10] It was

---

[7] *The Hagen* [1908] P. 189. *Per* Farwell L.J. at p. 201.
[8] [1966] 1 W.L.R. 793 at pp. 796, 797.
[9] [1972] 2 Q.B. 34.
[10] [1951] A.C. 869.

there laid down that it was not necessary for the plaintiff to satisfy the court beyond all reasonable doubt of the facts to be established in order to confer jurisdiction upon the court under Order 11. It was sufficient to show that the case was a proper one for service out of the jurisdiction and this the plaintiff could do by showing that he had a good arguable case.

In a more recent case,[11] Megarry J., however, opined that the onus which the plaintiff must discharge in these circumstances consists of making it "sufficiently apparent" to the court that the case is a proper one for service out of the jurisdiction under Order 11. The case involved an action by an English resident suing a Portuguese company for damages in respect of an alleged breach of a contract of agency for the export to England of their wines and spirits. The plaintiff obtained leave *ex parte* for the writ to be issued for service out of the jurisdiction on the grounds that the contract was within the ambit of Order 11, r. 1(1)(f)(iii) (now rule 1(1)(d)(iii)), *i.e.* that it was "by its terms or by implication governed by English law." The defendant company managed to have the decision reversed. The court held that the contract was governed by Portuguese law as the legal system with which the agreement had its closest and most real connection.[12] In the course of his judgment, Megarry J. stated that in order to justify a service (or as the situation then was a notice) of a writ out of the jurisdiction the plaintiff ought to have established two things: first, that the contract was governed by English law, and, second, that England was the *forum conveniens*: "I think it is clear that the onus lies on counsel for the plaintiff to succeed on both limbs if the writ is to be sustained."[13]

If England is not the natural or appropriate forum, a stay will generally be ordered and jurisdiction will be declined.[14] The principles that should guide the courts as to declining jurisdiction (and ordering a stay of any permissible action under Order 11 of the Rules) were summarised by the Court of Appeal in *Trendtex Trading Corp. v. Credit Suisse*[15] and were as follows:

(1) The court must first consider whether there is another jurisdiction which is clearly more appropriate than England for the trial of the action. The burden of this is on the defendant.

(2) If the court concludes there is another clearly more appropriate jurisdiction, the burden remains on the defendant to show that trial in England will afford the plaintiff no real advantage, then a balance must be struck and the court must decide in its discretion whether justice demands a stay.

Where the proceedings fall within the Conventions embodied in the Civil Jurisdiction and Judgements Act 1982 different principles may apply.

---

[11] *Mauroux v. Sociedade Commercial Abel Pereira da Fonseca S.á.r.l.* [1972] 1 W.L.R. 962.
[12] *Post*, §399.
[13] *Ibid.* at p. 964.
[14] See *MacShannon v. Rockware Glass* [1978] A.C. 795 (H.L.).
[15] [1980] 3 All E.R. 721 at p. 734, folowed by Goff J. in *European Asian Bank A.G. v. The Punjab and Sind Bank* [1981] 2 Lloyd's Rep. 651, and aff'd by the Court of Appeal [1982] 2 Lloyd's Rep. 356.

384   *Choice of forum.* But where the parties have submitted their contract to the exclusive jurisdiction of a particular court, the discretion of the court (to permit or disallow proceedings) is in practice circumscribed; for the general policy of the English courts is to hold the parties to their bargain. Thus (i) if the court selected is English and the proposed defendant is outside the jurisdiction, leave to serve the proceedings out of the jurisdiction was stipulated under Order 11, r. 2 (now Ord. 11, r. 1(1)(d)(iv)); (ii) if there is a submission to the jurisdiction of a foreign court, but the plaintiff applies to the English court for leave to serve out of the jurisdiction under Order 11 (on the ground, *e.g.* that the contract was made in England) the English court will refuse *to serve out of jurisdiction unless* there are exceptional circumstances[16]; and (iii) if the court selected is a foreign court, and a plaintiff manages to invoke a jurisdiction of the English court (by service on the defendant in England) the defendant in the English proceedings may apply to the court for a stay of those proceedings which generally will be granted.[17] For the plaintiff to succeed in the latter case he must show "some good cause" why the English proceedings should continue, or a "strong case" why they should not be stayed. It is not merely a matter of the "balance of convenience."[18] In other words, current opinion is in favour of enforcing freely negotiated agreements in the sphere of international commerce with respect to the submission of disputes to an exclusive jurisdiction. Absent fraud, undue influence, overweening bargaining power, or some other exceptional circumstance, choice of forum clauses (ousting as well as conferring jurisdiction) will normally be given full effect.

385   *Place where contract is made.* An English court applies the rules of English domestic law for the purposes of determining the time and place at which a contract is made. In *Entores Ltd. v. Miles Far East Corp.,*[19] a c.i.f. sale of Japanese cathodes was not performed. The defendants were Dutch agents of an American firm and had transmitted their offer of sale to the plaintiffs in London by means of a telex communication. The plaintiffs made a counter-offer which was likewise dispatched and accepted by telex. The plaintiffs applied for leave to serve notice of a writ out of jurisdiction seeking to recover damages for breach of a contract "made within the jurisdiction."[20] The defendants alleged that the contract was made in Amsterdam and not in London. The Court of Appeal (Denning, Birkett and Parker L.JJ.) upheld

---

[16] See, *e.g. Mackender v. Feldia A.G. [1967] 2 Q.B. 590; Evans Marshall & Co. Ltd. v. Bertola S.A. [1973] 1 W. L. R. 349.*

[17] Compare *The Eleftheria* [1970]1 P. 97 with *Evans Marshall & Co. Ltd. v. Bertola S.A.* [1973] 1 W.L.R. 349 and *The Fehmarn* [1958] 1 W.L.R. 159 which has been severely criticised by scholars and judges alike.

[18] See Collins. "Choice of Forum and the Exercise of Judicial Discretion," 22 I.C.L.Q. 332 (1973) and the authorities there cited.

[19] [1955] 2 Q.B. 327 (C.A.).

[20] They alternatively claimed that the contract was by implication governed by English law and that jurisdiction could be assumed under Ord. 11, r. 1(1)(f)(iii) (now r. 1.(1)(d)(iii)) but this point was not considered by the court.

Donovan J. and permitted the service of the notice. The court noted that where a contract is made by post, acceptance is, under English law, complete as soon as it is mailed. That place therefore is also the place where the contract is made. But different principles apply where communications are virtually instantaneous as where contracts are concluded by telephone or telex. In such a case the contract is only complete when the acceptance is received by the offerer, and it is made at the place where it is received. In the present case acceptance of the original offer and confirmation of the counter-offer were made in London; leave, therefore, could properly be given for service out of the jurisdiction.[21]

386   *Place of breach.* It will be seen from Order 11, r. 1(1)(e) that in the case of a defendant domiciled abroad, the plaintiff must show that there has been a breach of the contract within the jurisdiction ''irrespective of the fact, if such be the case, that the breach was preceded or accompanied by a breach committed out of the jurisdiction that rendered impossible the performance of so much of the contract as ought to have been performed within the jurisdiction.''

As a matter of history, the rule originally provided that service out of the jurisdiction was allowed when the action was founded ''on any breach or alleged breach within the jurisdiction of any contract wherever made, which, according to the terms thereof, ought to be performed within the jurisdiction,''[22] whether in whole or in part,[23] unless the defendant was domiciled or ordinarily resident in Scotland or Ireland. In order, therefore, to commence suit in this country against a foreign seller it was necessary to show that the contract was such that the whole or part of it was expressly or by implication to be performed within the jurisdiction, and, secondly, that the action was for a breach within the jurisdiction. The decisions as to the application of the rule to c.i.f. contracts are obsolete, since the rule has been superseded, but they are worth mentioning, if only because they exhibit not uninteresting divergence of view as to many of the attributes of c.i.f. contracts.

387   In *Barrow v. Myers & Co.*,[24] a contract for the delivery of choice apples at New York c.i.f. for London was considered. The apples having arrived in bad order in London, and their condition not being due to any damage suffered during sea transit, Manisty and Mathew JJ. held that there was a breach in London. Matthew J. on the ground that, ''The objects which the plaintiffs sought to obtain by this contract was the delivery to themselves in London of a given quantity of apples of a certain quality. That being so, there was a contract which according to the terms thereof ought to be performed within

---

[21] See also *Brinkibon v. Stahag Stahl* [1982] 1 Lloyd's Rep. 217 (H.L.) Telex of acceptance sent to Austria where, therefore, the contract was made. Further, the contract was to be performed outside the jurisdiction and leave to serve a notice of the writ (as was possible under the old version of the Rules outside the jurisdiction would not be granted.
[22] Under the original Ord. 11, r. 1(e).
[23] *Rein v. Stein* [1892] 1 Q.B. 735, *ante*.
[24] (1888) 4 T.L.R. 441.

the jurisdiction,'' whereas Manisty J. spoke of a continuing breach which, by his own admission, was hardly an accurate expression. The decision is extremely difficult to justify. It was not followed in subsequent cases, and was in fact expressly overruled by the Court of Appeal in *Crozier, Stephens & Co. v. Auerbach.*[25]

In *Wancke v. Wingren*,[26] case of non-delivery, where the defendant in Sweden had sold wood c.i.f. to an English port, and failed to perform the main part of his contract, Day and A. L. Smith JJ. held that since all that the defendant had to do was to ship the goods at the Swedish port the breach occurred at the Swedish port where the seller failed to ship and not within the jurisdiction, and therefore the original Order 11, r. 1 (e) did not apply. It is interesting to observe that in that case it was argued, for the first time apparently, that there was a breach within the jurisdiction by failure of the seller to tender the shipping documents to the buyer in England, though the court did not deal with the argument in the judgments.

388   In *Hamlyn v. Griendtsveen*,[27] also a case of non-delivery, the sale was of 5,200 tons of moss litter to be shipped at Rotterdam c.i.f. London. No shipment was made. The buyers obtained leave from a judge in chambers to issue a writ for service on the Dutch sellers by notice, but the Divisional Court (Lord Coleridge C.J. and Fry L.J.) set aside the order, and their decision was affirmed by the Court of Appeal (Cotton and Lindley L.JJ.), on the ground that the plaintiffs had failed to show that the breach of contract occurred within the jurisdiction. No argument appears to have been presented to the court that the sellers' failure to tender the documents to the buyers in England constituted a breach of contract within the jurisdiction in respect of which the action might be instituted here.

Similarly, in *Parker v. Schuller*,[28] where the goods were sold to be shipped from Germany c.i.f. to Liverpool, and the seller made no shipment, the buyer alleged a breach within the jurisdiction by non-delivery of the goods at Liverpool. The judge in chambers, Farwell J., who heard the application under the original Order 11, r. 1 (e) *ex parte* in the first instance, and Lawrance J., who affirmed the order, held that non-delivery of the goods at Liverpool constituted a breach within the jurisdiction and gave the leave asked for. But a c.i.f. contract is not a contract to deliver goods in this country, and on this ground the order was set aside by the Court of Appeal (A. L. Smith M.R., Collins and Romer L.JJ.). The point was taken, however, in the Court of Appeal that there was a breach within the jurisdiction since the seller had failed to present any shipping documents; but the court declined to deal with a defence of the order appealed from other than that which was put forward in the writ of summons and affidavit.

---

[25] [1908] 2 K.B. 161, see *post*, §389.
[26] (1889) 58 L.J.Q.B. 519.
[27] (1890) 6 T.L.R. 225 (C.A.), *ibid.* at p. 274.
[28] (1901) 17 T.L.R. 299.

In *Rein v. Stein*,[29] an action to recover the price of goods sold by the plaintiff c.i.f. Hamburg, the Court of Appeal gave leave to service a writ on the German defendant, the grounds being that since payment was to be made in England that part of the contract was to be performed in England, and the failure to pay constituted a breach within the jurisdiction. No emphasis was placed on the fact that the goods were shipped from an English port.

389   *Crozier, Stephens & Co. v. Auerbach*[30] was a case of alleged defective delivery. On arrival of the goods sold in England the buyers alleged that they were not in accordance with the contract and obtained leave from Bigham J. to issue a writ of summons of which notice was to be served on the foreign seller out of jurisdiction. The Court of Appeal (Vaughan Williams and Farwell L.JJ.), however, set aside the order on the ground that, the contract being c.i.f., the alleged breach took place on shipment at Hamburg.

Referring to the arguments of counsel for the respondent, Vaughan Williams L.J. said:

> "Cases were cited to us for the proposition that under a c.i.f. contract the delivery must be a delivery on the ship at the port of departure, and it was said in answer that they were all cases in which the action was for non-delivery as distinguished from an action for delivering goods alleged not to be of contract quality. For myself, I cannot see that it makes any difference whether the action is for non-delivery or for delivering goods not according to the quality stipulated for in the contract; in either case the time and place of delivery are the time when and the place where the vendor delivers the goods on board ship. . . ." (at p. 165).

Commenting on *Barrow v. Myers & Co.*[31] the Lord Justice said[32]:

> "I have said that I do not understand that decision; I have no quarrel with the actual words of the judgment of Mathew J.; my difficulty is that the judgment does not accord with the facts of the case; it seems to overlook the fact that the contract was a c.i.f. contract; the learned judge speaks of the contract as if the place of delivery had not been on board ship at New York, but had been London. All I can say is that . . . if the judgment means that under such circumstances the breach would occur at the place of ultimate destination of the goods and not at the place of shipment under a c.i.f. contract, I say with deference, but without hesitation, that that case was wrongly decided."

Then in 1911 came the judgments in *Biddell Bros. v. E. Clemens Horst Co.*[33] which directed attention to the dual obligation of the seller c.i.f. to ship the goods and tender the documents against which the buyer is bound to make the agreed payment. Thereafter the practice developed in the case of these contracts of giving leave under the original Order 11, r. 1(e) where the

[29] [1892] 1 Q.B. 753.
[30] [1908] 2 K.B. 161.
[31] See *ante*, §387.
[32] [1908] 2 K.B. 161 at p. 166.
[33] [1911] 1 K.B. 214 (C.A.), *ibid.* 934; [1912] A.C. 18. See *ante*, §261.

cause of action alleged was non-delivery by failure to tender the documents to the buyer in this country.

390   In 1919 the decision of the House of Lords in *Johnson v. Taylor Bros. & Co. Ltd.*[34] changed the position. There the Swedish sellers of pig-iron c.i.f. Leeds or Manchester failed to make delivery, and the buyer applied for leave to serve notice of a writ of summons upon the seller in Sweden alleging breach of contract by failure to tender shipping documents. Lord Coleridge J. gave leave, and the Court of Appeal (Bankes, Warrington and Scrutton L. JJ.) affirmed his order. But the House of Lords (Lord Birkenhead L.C., Viscount Haldane, Lords Dunedin, Atkinson and Buckmaster) held that though there had been a breach within the jurisdiction by failure to tender the shipping documents, the substantial and effective breach was failure to ship the goods, and in such a case leave to serve notice of the writ out of the jurisdiction could not be granted. But if the sellers had shipped the goods sold and had failed to tender the shipping documents in England to the buyer, then a writ of summons for non-tender of the documents would have come within the original Order 11, r. 1(e).[35]

The practical effect of this decision was to compel English buyers complaining of non-delivery to sue the foreign seller in his own country; but this disadvantage was removed by the rules which came into force in 1933 (as is now provided by the language of Order 11, r.1(1)(e)) which extended the right of suit in this country against the foreign trader, thus nullifying the decision in *Johnson v. Taylor Bros. & Co. Ltd.*

The foregoing cases illustrate the types of claims in which attempt was made to sustain a plea on the ground that the contract was breached within the jurisdiction, a situation which is now governed by rule 1(1)(e) of Order 11. A more recent example of such an attempt was considered by Winn J.[36] on a plea to grant leave to serve notice of a writ (under an earlier version of the Rules) on an American corporation, the sellers of a quantity of skins shipped c.i.f. from Boston to Hull, having neither assets nor an agency in England. On arrival the skins were found to be badly damaged. The buyer sought leave to give notice of writs in America against both the seller and the shipowners. The claim against the seller was based on the allegation that a c.i.f. contract contains an implied warranty that the goods on discharge would be of the contract description and quality for which Diplock J.'s judgment in *Mash & Murrell Ltd. v. Joseph I. Emanuel Ltd.*[37] was cited in support. The claim against the shipowners was based on an alleged tort within the

---

[34] [1920] A.C. 144.
[35] *Per* Lord Atkinson, *ibid.* at p. 158. The possibility of performing the contract by means of purchasing goods afloat was not considered by their lordships; as to this alternative, see *ante*, §52. Commenting on this omission, *Scrutton on Charterparties* (19th ed.), p. 191, states: ''In holding that the seller breaks his contract by failing to ship the goods, did the House of Lords sufficiently distinguish between performance of the contract and the doing of something which is, or may be, a necessary step towards ability to perform the contract?''
[36] *Cordova Land Co. Ltd. v. Victor Brothers Inc.* [1966] 1 W.L.R. 793.
[37] [1962] 1 W.L.R. 16, *ante*, § 319.

jurisdiction consisting of a fraudulent misrepresentation which, it was contended, was committed by the issuance of clean bills of lading in respect of defective goods. Leave was denied in both actions. Winn J. being of the opinion that Order 11 applied to neither, and that even if it did America, and not England, was the *forum conveniens* for these actions and jurisdiction should therefore be denied as a matter of discretion also.[38] In so far as the claim against the seller was concerned, Winn J. refused to accept the statement in the *Mash & Murrell* case as authority for the proposition that every c.i.f. contract contains an implied warranty that the goods would not deteriorate in transit, and that where goods have so deteriorated delivery thereof at an English port constitutes a breach within the jurisdiction. As already noted,[39] Winn J. was of the opinion that the *Mash* case is best confined to the sale of perishable goods, and following *Crozier, Stephens & Co. v. Auerbach*[40] declined to accept the submission that the then Order 11, r. 1(1)(g) (now (e)), applied and that a breach of contract within the jurisdiction had occurred.

391   It may be of interest to note that the jurisdiction conferred by Order 11 extends beyond that conceded by English law to foreign courts, resulting in an undesirable lack of reciprocity which apparently is not cured by the Foreign Judgments (Reciprocal Enforcement) Act 1933. For despite the title and preamble of this Act, and though it does depart from the conditions which obtained at common law with respect to the enforcement of foreign judgments, it has been held that the only foreign judgments enforceable in England (prior to the enactment of the Civil Jurisdiction and Judgments Act 1982 which implemented a 1968 Convention designed to unify the rules on jurisdiction and enforcement of judgments in civil and commercial matters in member states of the European Economic Community now the European Union, which England joined) were those which came within the Act. In the case of actions *in personam*, section 4(2)(a) of the Act now provides the following exclusive list of grounds for recognising jurisdiction:

> "(i) if the judgment debtor, being a defendant in the original court, submitted to the jurisdiction of that court by voluntarily appearing in the proceedings; or
> (ii) if the judgment debtor was plaintiff in, or counter-claimed in, the proceedings in the original court; or
> (iii) if the judgment debtor being a defendant in the original court, had before the commencement of the proceedings agreed, in respect of the subject matter of the proceedings, to submit to the jurisdiction of that court or of the courts of the country of that court; or
> (iv) if the judgment debtor, being a defendant in the original court, was at the time when the proceedings were instituted resident in, or being a body corporate had its principle place of business in, the country of that court; or
> (v) if the judgment debtor, being a defendant in the original court, had an

---

[38] See *ante*, § 382.
[39] *Ante*, § 323.
[40] [1908] 2 K. B. 161, *ante*, § 389.

office or place of business in the country of that court and the proceedings in that court were in respect of a transaction effected through or at that office or place.''

The "original court" for the purposes of the foregoing provisions is the court in which the judgment was obtained. That the Act rejects the notion of reciprocity and comity of nations, and that it does not condone enforcement simply because the English courts may claim similar jurisdiction had the position of the two countries been reversed was established by Widgery J. in *Société Coopérative Sidmetal v. Titan International Ltd.*[41] in which the respondent, an English firm, sold to the plaintiffs, a Belgian company, a quantity of steel f.o.b. Liverpool. The sellers agreed to ship the steel to an Italian firm which had purchased it from the Belgian buyer. The Italian firm was not satisfied with the quality of the steel and brought proceedings in a Belgian court against the Belgian company which then joined the respondent to those proceedings and served him notice thereof in England. The respondent, however, failed to participate in the proceedings and did not submit to the jurisdiction of the Belgian court. Judgment having been given by the Belgian court against the respondent, the plaintiffs registered that judgment under the Foreign Judgments (Reciprocal Enforcement) Act 1933 in the Queen's Bench Division. But the court, having held that the Act was not based on reciprocity, set the registration aside on the grounds that the Belgian court had no jurisdiction in the circumstances of the case within the meaning of section 4 of the Act. The problems of enforcement (and indirectly of jurisdiction) in respect of civil and commercial judgments of an international character rendered by Courts of European Union's member countries are now governed by the Civil Jurisdiction and Judgments Act 1982,[42] as amended by the Civil Jurisdiction and Judgments Act 1990, insofar as the European Union members who have ratified the relevant Conventions are concerned. With respect to the latter, a judgment given by a court in a state party to the Brussels Convention or the Lugano Convention and which falls within their scope has, on registration (in the appropriate courts in the United Kingdom), the same force and effect as a judgment of the court in which it is registered, and proceedings for or with respect to its enforcement may be taken, as if the judgment had been originally given by the registering court.

392   *Service on agent.* Finally, it is to be observed that rule 2 of Order 10 enables a buyer or seller suing on a contract made within the jurisdiction with an agent resident or carrying on business within the jurisdiction on behalf of a foreign seller or buyer, as the case may be, to obtain leave to serve the writ of summons on the agent in England, without having to obtain

---

[41] [1966] 1 Q.B. 828.
[42] The Act gives effect to a Convention and Protocol signed pursuant to the Rome Treaty and has modified English law to some extent. See, *e.g. Tracomin S. A. v. Sudan Oil Seeds Co. Ltd.* [1983] 1 Lloyd's Rep. 560. This Act came into force in part on August 23, 1982.

an order for service out of the jurisdiction under Order 11. The terms of this rule are as follows:

> 2.—(1) Where the Court is satisfied on an *ex parte* application that—
>
> (a) a contract has been entered into within the jurisdiction with or through an agent who is either an individual residing or carrying on business within the jurisdiction or a body corporate having a registered office or a place of business within the jurisdiction, and
>
> (b) the principal for whom the agent was acting was at the time the contract was entered into and is at the time ·of the application neither such an individual nor such a body corporate, and
>
> (c) at the time of the application either the agent's authority has not been determined or he is still in business relations with his principal,
>
> the Court may authorise service of a writ beginning an action relating to the contract to be effected on the agent instead of the principal.
>
> (2) An order under this Rule authorising service of a writ on a defendant's agent must limit a time within which the defendant must acknowledge service.
>
> (3) Where an order is made under this Rule authorising service of a writ on a defendant's agent, a copy of the order and of the writ must be sent by post to the defendant at his address out of the jurisdiction.

It was laid down in the official memorandum as to the exercise of the power of service under this Rule (dated December 4, 1920) that leave to serve an agent should only be given with great caution. It ought not to be given when there was no difficulty in effecting service out of the jurisdiction in the ordinary way, merely because the defendant has contracted through an agent in this country. It is an important factor, continued the memorandum, whether the foreign firm have regular agents here doing large business for them, in which event it might be highly proper for the sake of convenience to allow service upon the agents, whereas if the action arises out of an isolated transaction carried out by a broker on one of the markets it would not be proper to order service on the broker. This still applies.[43]

Proper law of the contract

393   It has already been noted that by Rule 1(1)(d)(iii) of Order 11 an English court is empowered to summon a foreign defendant and permit service of a writ out of the jurisdiction where the contract "is by its terms or by implication governed by English law," that is to say, where what was once termed the proper, and is today known as the applicable law of the contract, is English.[44] However, the converse is not true. The fact that an English court has for one reason or another assumed jurisdiction over a certain dispute does not imply that its solution will be governed by English law. Since the proper

---

[43] See current *Supreme Court Practice*, Ord. 10, r. 2(2), Vol. 1, para. 10/2/2.

[44] The Rome Covention on the Law Applicable to Contractual Obligations, now embodied in the Contracts (Applicable Law) Act, 1990, that is applicable to any contract entered into after April 1, 1991, avoids the proper law terminolgy in favor of the contract's "applicable law."

law of the contract is the law which is applied in determining the obligations thereunder[45] and since the provisions of English and foreign law are often at variance,[46] the question as to which law governs a c.i.f. sale assumes a degree of importance far beyond the jurisdictional issue. "The legal principles which are to guide an English Court on the question of the proper law of the contract are now well settled." According to Lord Atkin who then continued[47]:

> "... It is the law which the parties intended to apply. Their intention will be ascertained by the intention expressed in the contract if any, which will be conclusive. If no intention be expressed the intention will be presumed by the Court from the terms of the contract and the relevant surrounding circumstances."

Generally speaking this will be the law of the country with which the contract is most closely connected. So that although the presumed intention of the parties test, has been discarded in favor of the objective connections of the transaction with a particular legal system test in the Contracts (Applicable Law Act 1990 (in the event the choice of the parties is not express or 'demonstrated with reasonable certainty'), the statutory change is more semantic than substantive. And it is generally presumed that that is the law of the country where performance is to be effected.

394   Although the proper or applicable law consists of a single legal system, particular aspects of the contract may be held to be governed by a different law. "In English law a transaction may be regulated in general by the law of one country although as to parts of that transaction which are to be performed in another country, the law of that other country may be the law applicable."[48] Accordingly, where the parties agree that their dispute should be settled by arbitration in London this generally implies that the proper law of the contract is English domestic law, but does not automatically exclude the application of all foreign law. As noted by Lord Dunedin, in a case[49] in which Scottish merchants agreed to buy from merchants in Hong Kong certain parcels of sugar to be shipped to Bombay c.i.f. from Java where the contract was made, such an agreement "... does not mean that everything

---

[45] The proprietary aspects (*i.e.* passing of property, right of stoppage, etc.) are governed by the *lex situs* see *post*, §406 *et seq.*

[46] However for an English court to apply foreign law, such foreign law must be pleaded and proven as a *fact* to the satisfaction of the court. In the absence of satisfactory evidence, foreign law will be presumed to be identical to English law which will be applied. But as to the provisions of Civil Evidence Act 1972 see *post*, §405.

[47] In *R. v. International Trustee for the Protection of Bondholders Atkiengesellschaft* [1937] A.C. 500 at p. 529.

[48] *Per* Lord Roche, *ibid* at p. 574, citing *Chatenay v. Brazilian Submarine Telegraph Co.* [1891] 1 Q.B. 79. Payment, however, is governed by the law where payment is to be made (or a letter of credit is payable) and not by the law of the country of the buyer. Consequently, it is no defence that due to foreign exchange restrictions in the buyer's country he was unable to perform. See *Congimex Companhia Geral de Comercia Importadora e Exportadora S.à.r.l. v. Tradax Export S.A.* [1981] 2 Lloyd's Rep. 687; *Congimex S.à.r.l. (Lisbon) v. Continental Grain Export Corp.* [1979] 2 Lloyd's Rep. 346.

[49] *N.V. Kwik Hoo Tong Handel Maatschappij v. James Finlay & Co.* [1927] A.C. 604.

that would have to be decided would necessarily be decided by English law. It means that the underlying law was the law of England.'' In this case, the respondents argued that since the contract was made out of the jurisdiction, between parties carrying on business out of the jurisdiction and (apart from payment which apparently was to be by a confirmed credit in London)[50] was to be performed out of the jurisdiction, leave to serve a writ out of the jurisdiction should be denied. The House of Lords, however, held that leave should be granted. The decision was based on the earlier version of Order 11, r. 1(e)(iii), now r. 1(1)(iii) which applied as a result of the provision for arbitration in London. The contract was deemed to be governed by English law.

It would be far beyond the scope of this work to even attempt to describe the methods by which the intention of the parties with respect to the applicable law of their contract is to be ascertained. On this question the reader is referred to the well known textbooks on the Conflict of Laws and Private International Law. All that is offered hereunder is a brief summary of some of the general principles which have from time to time been applied to c.i.f. sales.

395   *Express choice of law.* Since an express choice of law by the parties is normally honoured by the courts, the parties often insert a provision to the effect that any dispute between them shall be resolved in accordance with English law or that the contract shall be deemed to be an English contract or some other similar clause. Sometimes this effect is achieved indirectly by agreeing that an English arbitrator or court will have exclusive jurisdiction to hear any such disputes, in which case it is often, but not invariably,[51] presumed, in the words of the Latin maxim, that *qui elegit judicem elegit jus*,[52] and sometimes a combined provision relating to jurisdiction as well as the applicable law is stipulated, *e.g.* that any dispute arising under or in connection with the contract shall be submitted to the exclusive jurisdiction of the English courts (or to an arbitral tribunal situated in London) and that the law of England would apply to any such dispute.[53] However, there is no guarantee that any or all of these provisions will result in the application of English law since though the inference in these cases in favour of English law being the applicable law is strong it is not absolute. Thus, for example,

---

[50] See counsel's statement on p. 605.

[51] See *Compagnie d'Armement Maritime S.A. v. Compagnie Tunisienne de Navigation S.A.* [1971] A.C. 572.

[52] See *Tzortzis v. Monark Line A/B* [1968] 1 W.L.R. 406 (C.A.) quoting Lord Phillimore in the *Kwik Hoo Tong* case (*ibid.* n. 49 at p. 604) to the effect that where "The forum provided for the settlement of disputes is English . . . the contract is intended to be governed by English law."

[53] Arbitration provisions sometimes additionally stipulate that for the purpose of proceedings any party residing or carrying on business outside the United Kingdom shall be considered as ordinarily resident in the United Kingdom. The effect of such a provision on the jurisdiction of the court to make orders in respect of costs was considered in *Mavani v. Ralli Bros. Ltd.* [1973] 1 W.L.R. 468, and it was there decided that this clause did not oust the jurisdiction or limit the discretion of the court to order security for costs.

choice of law clauses were sometimes construed as intending to cover the formation of the contract only and not its performance, whereas choice of jurisdiction clauses did not necessarily preclude the court or arbitrator from determining that the contract should be governed by the private international law rules of the *lex fori* rather than by the provisions of its domestic law.[54] This latter option however is no longer possible because the doctrine of *renvoi* has been expressly abolished with respect to contracts in the UK, a change emanating from its membership in the European Union. Moreover, and as stated by the House of Lords in *Compagnie d'Armement Maritime S. A. v. Compagnie Tunisienne de Navigation S. A.*,[55] though choice of jurisdiction or arbitration clauses provide material for an inference as to the actual intention of the parties they are not to be regarded as providing an irresistible or conclusive inference as to that intention. In that case a charterparty stipulated for arbitration of disputes in London but also provided that the contract was, except for general average purposes, to be governed by the law of the flag of the vessels to be chartered. The Court of Appeal preferred the arbitration provision to the law of the flag provision as indicating the proper law

---

[54] See Sassoon, "Choice of Tribunal and the Proper Law of the Contract" [1964] *J.B.L.* 18. It should be noted that a provision to submit disputes to a foreign court does not exclude the jurisdiction of the English courts. The courts must, when such a provision exists, approach the matter with a strong bias in favour of holding the parties to their contract but may nevertheless decide to exercise its jurisdiction if it concludes that the inconvenience suffered by the plaintiff, were the action to be held abroad, would be greater than that of the defendant if the action were tried in England. An Australian decision illustrates the point. In *Lewis Construction Co. Pty. Ltd. v. M. Titchaner S. A.* [1966] V.R. 341, the plaintiff bought two cranes on c.i.f. terms from the defendant, a supplier of cranes incorporated under French law. After an exchange of cables the contract was concluded by the despatch of a cable by the plaintiff accepting the defendant's counter-offer. The contract contained a clause that in a case of litigation the Commercial Court of Lyons was the only competent court. After erection of the cranes in Melbourne an accident occurred due to an allegedly defective part. The plaintiff issued a writ claiming damages for breach of warranty and for negligence in supplying a defective crane. Service in France having been allowed by a Master, and a conditional appearance having been entered, the defendant applied before Hudson J. to have the service set aside. On the evidence concerning the making of the contract, his Honour held that the action was one brought in respect of the breach of a contract made within the jurisdiction: *Entores Ltd. v. Miles Far East Corporation* [1955] 2 Q.B. 327 (*ante*, §385). Counsel had also argued that there was jurisdiction on the grounds that the contract was (i) governed by Australian law and/or (ii) was breached within the jurisdiction.
  His Honour held that the clause referring all disputes to the French court showed an agreement that the law to regulate disputes was French law, and that this outweighed all other points of contact within Victoria: *N. V. Kwik Hoo Tong v. Finlay* [1927] A.C. 604.
  The argument based on allowing service where the breach of contract was committed within the jurisdiction, wherever the contract was made, was rejected on the ground that under a c.i.f. contract the seller's obligation is performed when he ships the goods and forwards an effective bill of lading and insurance policy, and if the goods shipped are not in accordance with contract the breach occurs at the place of shipment: *Crozier, Stephens & Co. v. Auerbach* [1908] 2 K.B. 161 (*ante*, §389).
  The contention that a tort had been committed within the jurisdiction was answered by *George Munro Ltd. v. American Cyanamid Corporation* [1944] K.B. 432.
  Hudson J. then discussed the significance of the clause referring all litigation to a French court on whether he should exercise his discretion in favour of the plaintiff and weighing the volume of evidence that each party would have to call, concluded that the inconvenience suffered by the plaintiff, were the action to be held in France, would be greater than that of the defendant if the action were tried in Australia. He therefore refused the motion with costs.
[55] [1971] A.C. 572.

but the House of Lords reversed this finding. Criticising the *Tzortzis*[56] decision and departing from the inflexible rule of *Kwik*[57] by a majority of three to one, the House, in the words of Lord Morris of Borth-y-Gest, stated:

> "An agreement to refer disputes to arbitration in a particular country may carry with it, and is capable of carrying with it, an implication or inference that the parties have further agreed that the law governing the contract (as well as the law governing the arbitration procedure)[58] is to be the law of that country. But ... there is no inflexible or conclusive rule to th[at] effect.... The circumstances that parties agree that any differences are to be settled by arbitration in a certain country may and very likely will lead to an inference that they intend the law of that country to apply. But it is not a necessary inference or an inevitable one though it will often be the reasonable and sensible one. Before drawing it, all the relevant circumstances are to be considered."[59]

Finally, the discretion of the parties is to some extent limited. A choice of law must be exercised bona fide and not merely for the purpose of evading some foreign law by which the performance of the contract may, for example, be illegal, while a choice of jurisdiction (though, as a result of the New York arbitration Convention, generally no longer of an arbitral tribunal)[60] may not be enforced through stay of proceedings before a competent English court on the grounds of the court refusing to exercise its discretion in this regard. Though the court will not readily or lightly use this discretion and disregard the contractual provisions the parties cannot, by agreement to submit all disputes exclusively to a foreign jurisdiction, oust the court's discretion which may be exercised where the circumstances justify the same.[61]

396   *Regazzoni v. K.C. Sethia (1944) Ltd.*[62] furnishes an apt illustration of the former exception. The parties, in that case an English seller and a Swiss buyer, agreed that their contract should be governed by English law. The contract was for the sale of a large quantity of jute bags c.i.f. Genoa. The jute was to have originated in India and it was destined for South Africa. The Government of India prohibited the direct or indirect exportation of certain specified goods, including jute bags, to the Union of South Africa because of political differences which had arisen between both Governments. Both parties intended, as the court found, to infringe the prohibition of Indian

---

[56] *Ibid.* n. 52.
[57] *Ibid.* n. 49.
[58] The law governing the arbitration, *i.e.* the procedural law of the arbitration will invariably be the *lex fori*. The distinction between the law governing the arbitration and that governing the contract is important and is well brought out in *James Miller & Partners Ltd. v. Whitworth Street Estates (Manchester) Ltd.* [1970] A.C. 572, a decision of the House of Lords.
[59] [1971] A.C. 572 at pp. 588–590.
[60] s. 1 of the Arbitration Act 1975.
[61] See *The Atlantic Star* [1974] A.C. 436 (H.L.), and *post*, §398.
[62] [1958] A.C. 301. See also *Duncan, Fox v. Schrempft & Bonke* [1915] K.B. 365 (contract involving trading with an enemy void in England notwithstanding its validity under proper law which was German), *ante*, §249.

law, the intention being that of deceiving the Indian authorities. As the contract was not carried out, because of the refusal of the Indian authorities to allow the exportation to Genoa, the buyer sued for damages for non-delivery under the contract. The claim was dismissed by the English courts who refused to recognise the validity of such a contract. The House of Lords held that it was against English public policy to enforce a contract which contemplated the performance of an illegal act in India, and that, since the contract could not be performed without such an act (there being no alternative source of supply for jute bags), it was illegal and void.

397   Where the contract provides for submission of disputes to arbitration, and the arbitrators have come to an erroneous decision on the issue of illegality, this does not constitute a misconduct on their part giving the court the power to set the award aside, unless the contract was illegal at its inception. In the latter case, the entire contract (including the arbitration clause) is void and the arbitrator would never have had jurisdiction to make an award. This was suggested by Mocatta J. in *Prodexport State Company for Foreign Trade v. E. D. & F. Man Ltd.*[63] where the plaintiffs were unable to complete delivery of a contract, the proper law of which was English, for the sale of sugar f.o.b. Constanza, because the Rumanian government, in consequence of calamitous floods, prohibited further exports of sugar. A motion to set aside a non-speaking award which ordered damages to the buyers was denied on the grounds that there was no misconduct or excess of jurisdiction in enforcing a claim for the non-performance of an illegal obligation. The right procedure in those circumstances would have been to request that the award be stated in the form of a special case but if this was not done for some reason the award was final.

398   As to refusal to stay proceedings where the parties have designated a different forum for the purpose (absent legislation requiring such stay)[64] this will, under English law, normally be confined to cases where the plaintiff moves that it is just and proper to permit the action to continue. In other words where enforcing the agreement depriving the English Courts of their jurisdiction would result in inconvenience or increased costs and thus be against the interests of the parties.[65] So for example in *Brazendale & Co. Ltd. v. Saint Freres S. A.*[66] the plaintiffs, an English company, bought some bales of Pakistani jute c.i.f. Apapa from the defendants, a French company having a place of business in London. The contract of sale stated that any dispute arising under it should be referred to arbitration in Pakistan and that the law of Pakistan was to apply. The defendants tendered to the plaintiffs two letters of indemnity to apply if the bills of lading were found to be "stale." The

---

[63] [1973] 1 Q.B. 389.
[64] *E.g.* s. 1. of the Arbitration Act 1975.
[65] See, *e.g. The Fehmarn* [1958] 1 W.L.R. 159 (C.A.).
[66] [1970] 2 Lloyd's Rep. 34.

plaintiffs claimed damages under the letters of indemnity, and then amended their claim so as to claim in addition, damages for breach of contract. The defendants applied to the court to stay the action under section 4(1) of the Arbitration Act 1950, because of the arbitration clause, and also under section 4(2) of that Act (now section 1 of the Arbitration Act 1975), which provided that if any party to a submission to arbitration under an agreement to which the Protocol on arbitration clauses in the First Schedule to the Act applied,

> "commences any legal proceedings in any court against any other party to the submission . . . any party . . . may apply to that court to stay the proceedings, and the court . . . shall make an order staying the proceedings."

It was held by Mocatta J. that the action would not be stayed under section 4(1) of the Act of 1950 because there was a danger of inconsistent findings of fact and holdings in law if the issues were split between the action under English law on the letters of indemnity and the arbitration in Pakistan under Pakistan law in relation to the claim for damages for breach of contract, and because on the balance of convenience and for the saving of costs it was in the interests of the parties that all the issues should be determined in one action in England. Moreover, the action would not be stayed under section 4(2) of that Act because the Protocol in the First Schedule to the Act only applied if (1) the parties resided and carried on business in different countries, and (2) the contract containing the arbitration clause resulted from business so conducted. In the present case the first requirement was, but the second requirement was not, satisfied. It should however be noted that under the 1975 Arbitration Act (giving effect to the New York arbitration Convention) there appears to be less latitude to order a stay where the contract contains an arbitration clause.

399   *Connecting factors.* Where the parties have failed to insert an express stipulation as to which law is to govern the contract, it used to be the task of the courts to determine what their intention would have been had their minds been directed to this question. More recently the courts have sought to establish an objective test to determine the applicable law in these situations, the test being the legal system with which the contract is most closely connected, and this is now expressly provided for in article 4 of the Rome Convention as embodied in the Contracts (Applicable law) Act 1990. As stated by McNair J. in *Rossano v. Manufacturers' Life Insurance Co.*[67]

> "The test to be applied in determining the proper law of the contract in the absence of any express provision in the policy or any provision in the policy as to jurisdiction has in my judgment been authoritatively determined in a manner binding upon me by the decision of the House of Lords in *In re United Railways of Havana and Regla Warehouses Ltd.*[68] . . . , where their lordships by a majority

---

[67] [1963] 2 Q.B. 352 at p. 360.
[68] [1961] A.C. 1007.

expressly accepted the test laid down in the judgment of the Privy Council delivered by Lord Simonds in *John Lavington Bonython v. Commonwealth of Australia*[69] . . . as being 'the system of law by reference to which the contract was made or that with which the transaction has its closest and most real connection.' Later Lord Simonds said, at p. 221: 'The question, then, is what is the proper law of the contract, or, to relate the general question to the particular problem, within the framework of what monetary or financial system should the instrument be construed. On the assumption that express reference is made to none, the question becomes a matter of implication to be derived from all the circumstances of the transaction.'''

In determining what is the proper law of a c.i.f. contract, two connecting factors were of particular relevance. The first is the law of the place where the contract was concluded, namely, the *lex loci contractus*. The second is the law of the place where the contract is to be performed, namely, the *lex loci solutionis.*

400   Where a contract is to be performed in the country in which it was concluded these two factors converge. By English law a contract is deemed to be concluded at the place where its definite acceptance is effected, for only then does a binding legal obligation come into existence. Thus, if an English manufacturer accepts a telephone order from abroad to ship goods c.i.f. a foreign port, the inference would be strongly in favour of presuming that the contract is to be governed by English law for it would both be concluded and performed in England, though complications could arise if payment was to be effected elsewhere. Where this is the case it may be decided that questions concerning the payment should be determined in accordance with the law of the place where it was to be made.

Thus, for example, Lord Phillimore stated in *N.V. Kwik Hoo Tong Handel Maatschappij v. James Finlay & Co.*[70] the facts of which have already been noted,[71] that, in the absence of the express agreement to submit to arbitration in London, implying that the proper law was to be English, "the *lex loci solutionis* would seem to be indicated as the governing law."[72] This, in the case under consideration, would have been the law of Java. However, since the contract was also concluded in Java the application of the *lex loci contractus* would have equally pointed to that law.

401   In cases where the place of performance of the contract is not identical with the *loci contractus* the factors pointing in favour of the law of the place of performance are obviously weaker. Clear authority favouring the *lex loci solutionis* under such circumstances where f.o.b. contracts are concerned is provided by the Privy Council's decision in *Benaim v. Debono*,[73] but no

---

[69] [1951] A.C. 201 at p. 219.
[70] [1927] A.C. 604.
[71] *Ante,* §394.
[72] [1927] A.C. 604 at p. 609.
[73] [1924] A.C. 514, see *post,* § 733.

corresponding decision appears to exist with respect to c.i.f. sales. Most commentators however have concluded that the same principles would apply. Thus it was stated by Dicey[74] that

"The paucity of decisions on conflicts of laws with regard to c.i.f. sales appears to indicate that commercial practice has brought about an international unification of the law going sufficiently far to make conflicts improbable. Should a conflict situation arise, much might be said in favour of the practice adopted by the Privy Council in *Benaim v. Debono* in the case of an f.o.b. contract, *i.e.* to apply the law of the port of shipment, from which presumably the documents will be forwarded by the seller. This appears to be the view taken by the French *Cour de Cassation.*"[75]

402   But in *H. Glynn (Covent Garden) Ltd. v. Wittleder*,[76] Pearson J. stated that there was no prima facie presumption under which the *lex loci solutionis* was the proper law in case of c.i.f. contracts. In this case the dispute arose in connection with a parcel of potatoes which were shipped from Hamburg to London. The seller contended that German law applied to the contract in question. In rejecting this contention Pearson J. said:

"The next question is whether English law or German law is proper for this contract. I am not sure in the end that it is going to make much difference. There are factors on both sides, obviously. As far as learned Counsel and I have been able to ascertain, there is no decided case which lays down any general rule as to what you can expect the proper law of c.i.f. contracts to be. Even if there was, one would still have to consider the particular facts and circumstances and provisions of the particular contract concerned. But, I understand that there is no prima facie rule. Here is a c.i.f. contract under which the sellers had performed their part of it by at first shipping the goods in Germany, and secondly, through their agents, handing over the bill of lading and other documents in England, so you get, so far as the sellers are concerned, performance partly in Germany and partly in England. So far as the buyers are concerned, they would perform their part of the contract by making the payment in London. I think that the payment was to be made, if I remember rightly, to a branch of Barclays Bank Ltd., at any rate, a payment in England, which they did, and they would take the shipping documents and they would so obtain possession of the goods.
Sometimes it is an important matter to ascertain in what country the contract was made. It is of less importance here, because it was largely made in the course of telephone conversations between Germany and England. There was the interview in England, and, strictly and technically, the view which I have expressed and adhere to is that the final conclusion of the contract was by the payment and acceptance of shipping documents which took place in England, but, to my mind, the most important factor is, again, that this was an English negotiation resulting in a predominantly English contract. By that, I mean expressed in the English language, which is an indication pointing towards English law being applicable, and, although there are factors on both sides, in my view, English law was the proper law of this contract" (at p. 420).

---

[74] Dicey & Morris, *Conflict of Laws* (8th ed., 1967), p. 793. Statement not repeated in later editions which merely state that: "There are very few English decisions on c.i.f. contracts in the conflict of laws" (9th ed., 1973), p. 814, (10th ed., 1982), p. 836.
[75] Battifol, s. 187 *bis*, quoting Cass. Req., March 1924, Sirey 1924, I, 252.
[76] [1959] 2 Lloyd's Rep. 409.

403   Moreover, in *Benaim v. Debono*[77] the sale was performed by shipment from the country in which the seller conducted his business. Whether the same presumptions would apply in the case of shipment from a neutral port where neither party is located is less clear. In such a case the connecting factor inference may be in favour of the *locus contractus* which may be the domicile of either party, depending on the facts of the particular case. A decision of the Swiss Federal Tribunal[78] cited by Rabel[79] suggests this view. In that case a London firm sold to a Swiss firm in Switzerland through a Swiss agent Ceylonese Orange Pekoe tea, c.i.f. Marseilles. Although both parties agreed to invoke Swiss law, the Tribunal stated that the London firm "had to expect that the acts of its representatives would be determined under Swiss law." The decision, however, caused Rabel to comment that "If the court had not been bound by stipulations of the parties on the applicable law, English rather than Swiss law ought to have determined the issue."[80]

404   Where both parties to the contract are English, English law is normally applied as the governing law of the contract even though the goods are to be shipped from some other place.[81] For the application of English law under these conditions presents no hardship or inconvenience to either party, and, consequently, the fact that the *locus solutionis* is abroad is immaterial to the legal relationship between them. But the courts may hold that although the applicable law of the contract is English, its mode of performance or the mode of the performance of particular parts thereof are to be regulated according to the law of the place of shipment. This could, for example, apply to obligations connected with the procurement of any necessary export licence which may have to be determined in the light of the law of the place of shipment.[82] The place of major performance under the usual c.i.f. contract is the port or place of shipment and not the place of arrival or the place where the documents were or should have been tendered.[83] As has already been

---

[77] [1924] A.C. 514.

[78] 46 BGE, 260 (July 20, 1920).

[79] *The Conflict of Laws; A Comparative Study*, Vol. III (2nd ed., 1964), p. 70.

[80] *Ibid.* at p. 71.

[81] The cases are too numerous to mention.

[82] See, *e.g. Société d'Avances Commerciales (London) Ltd. v. A. Besse & Co. (London) Ltd.* [1952] 1 T. L. T. 644; *A. V. Pound & Co. v. M. W. Hardy Inc.* [1956] A. C. 588 (f.a.s. contract); see *post*, § 491.

[83] Where payment is to be by a confirmed letter of credit, which is a usual practice nowadays, the place of shipment and payment are generally identical. In *Congimex Companhia Geral de Comercio Importadora e Exportadora S.à.r.l. v. Tradax Export S. A.* [1983] 1 Lloyd's Rep. 250 (C. A.), where a c.i.f. contract provided for final settlement to take place on delivered weights ascertained after discharge of vessel at Lisbon, the court held that Lisbon formed no part of the performance, and the contract was not frustrated when discharge there became unlawful because of an import ban, as the buyers could have accepted the documents and diverted the vessel. It was further stated that a minor impossibility would not suffice to justify non performance on the grounds of frustration. In this case payment was to be effected in New York (partly by means of letters of credit), and, since payment did not become illegal under New York law, supervening illegality could not be pleaded as a defence. For a more detailed description of the case, see *ante*, § 87.

noted, however, this view does not preclude the court from determining that the measure of damages for non-delivery or for delivery of non-conforming documents or goods under a c.i.f. contract should be measured by reference to the market price at their destination or place of tender of the documents or arrival of the goods.

Procedural aspects

405 Where a determination is made that foreign law governs the contract in question, that law has to be proved as a question of fact. Until the passage of the Civil Evidence Act 1972, this principle of English private international law meant that foreign law had to be proved in every case anew, although in a previous case in which exactly the same question arose the court may have found what the foreign law on the point in issue was and nobody contended in the later case that it was otherwise. This situation has now been remedied by section 4(2) of the said Act, which provides that any findings on foreign law made in civil or criminal proceedings in the English courts shall be admissible in evidence in civil proceedings for the purpose of proving the law of a foreign country if the following two conditions are satisfied:

(a) the finding on foreign law must be reported in an English series of law reports ''in a citable form'' i.e. authenticated by a member of the Bar; and

(b) the contrary is not proved, i.e. it is not established that the previous finding was wrong or the foreign law has changed.

Proprietary aspects

406 Although the contractual aspects of the transaction, namely the capacity, formalities, validity, construction, discharge and illegality of the contract, as also the question of remoteness of damages in case of breach,[84] are governed by the proper law, account being taken of the possibility that some other legal system may be invoked in respect of particular aspects thereof, the proprietary aspects of the transaction are by English conflict rules referred to the *lex situs*. In other words, questions relating to the transfer of property in the goods, the right of stoppage *in transitu* and other similar matters are governed by the law of the place where the goods are at the moment of transfer. An interesting illustration of this principle in relation to c.i.f. contracts is provided by *C.E.B. Draper & Son Ltd. v. Edward Turner & Son Ltd. and Ors.*,[85] where the sellers agreed to supply the buyers with a quantity of ground nut expeller cake, a commodity used in the preparation of cattle food,

---

[84] *Post* § 739.
[85] [1965] 1 Q.B. 424.

shipping it from Burma c.i.f. Liverpool. The contract contained a clause whereby the goods were not warranted free from latent defect. The bills of lading were transferred to the buyers before the goods reached Liverpool and some of the ground nut cake was sold by the buyers to third parties, who in turn sold it to the defendants. On the arrival of the ship in Liverpool, the defendants resold the ground nut cake to the plaintiffs, who used it in preparing cattle food. As a result of eating the mixture, which was contaminated, many cows became ill and some died. In the plaintiffs' action for damages against the defendants, the defendants made a claim against the third parties. The third parties thereupon claimed from the buyers, who in turn claimed from the sellers. Lyell J. entered judgment for the plaintiffs on the ground of a breach of the warranty contained in section 2(2) of the Fertilisers and Feeding Stuffs Act 1926, which provides that:

> "On the sale for use as food for cattle or poultry of an article included in the first column of the First or Second Schedule to this Act there shall be implied, notwithstanding any contract or notice to the contrary, a warranty by the seller that the article is suitable to be used as such, and does not, except as otherwise expressly stated in the statutory statement, contain any ingredient included in the Third Schedule to this Act."

407   The ground nut cake fell within the First Schedule and it in fact contained an ingredient specified in the Third Schedule. The Court of Appeal (Lord Denning M.R. Danckwerts and Diplock L.JJ.) allowed the appeal, holding that section 2(2) applied only to sales taking place within the United Kingdom and that in the present case the sale, namely, the transfer of property, as opposed to the contract of sale, was concluded at the time of transfer of the bills of lading and at a place outside the United Kingdom where the goods were then situated. The implied warranty in section 2(2) therefore did not apply and the buyers could not invoke it.

Diplock L.J. said:

> "If, at the time at which the documents are taken up by the buyer, the goods are outside the United Kingdom awaiting shipment or are afloat consigned to the United Kingdom but have not arrived at a United Kingdom port, the ''sale' of goods takes place outside the United Kingdom ... Prima facie an Act of the United Kingdom Parliament, unless it provides otherwise, applies to the whole of the United Kingdom and to nothing ouside the United Kingdom. ...
>
> "Section 2(2) of the Fertilisers and Feeding Stuffs Act 1926, does not apply to a sale of goods under which the property passes ... before the goods have arrived in the United Kingdom. This does not exclude from its application all sales on c.i.f. terms, for the property may pass by transfer of the bill of lading after the goods have arrived ... But did not happen in the present case" (at pp. 435, 436).

408   Referring to a choice of law clause in the contract[86] his lordship said:

[86] The clause provided, *inter alia* as follows:
"Buyers and sellers agree, that, for the purpose of proceedings either legal or by arbitration,

"I was at one time inclined to think that, notwithstanding that the warranty was not directly imposed by the Act itself, the parties might have incorporated it as a contractual warranty by virtue of [the foregoing] clause. . . . On further consideration, however, I am satisfied that the reference to the contracts being deemed to be performed in England in the first sentence is for the purpose of founding jurisdiction only. The second sentence deals with the law applicable. It does not import into the contract the statutory warranty contained in section 2(2) of the Fertilisers and Feeding Staffs Act 1926, because that warranty does not 'according to the law of England' apply to sales which take place outside the United Kingdom'' (at p. 436).[87]

Concurring, Lord Denning M. R. added:

"I know that oftentimes a contract for sale is spoken of as a sale. But the word 'sale' properly connotes the transfer of the absolute or general property in a thing for a price in money. . . . In this Act of 1926 I think that 'sale' is used in its proper sense to denote the transfer of property . . .'' (at p. 432).

409   Harsh criticism of these views was however voiced by Sellers and Davis L.JJ. in the subsequent case of *Hardwick Game Farm v. S.A.P.P.A. Ltd.*[88] There, the defendants supplied compounded meal which was fed to the plaintiffs' pheasants and partridges. Due to the presence of a poison in Brazilian ground nut extractions, which were an ingredient of the compounded meal, many of the plaintiffs' birds died while others suffered harmful damage. The defendants had bought their supplies from one or other of the two third parties to the proceedings who had in turn purchased the Brazilian ground nut extractions from the fourth parties. The third and fourth parties were members of the London Cattle Food Trade Association. The infected Brazilian ground nut extractions were imported under a number of c.i.f. contracts in the standard form of the Association, and at the time were aboard a variety of vessels in different positions. Some of the vessels had arrived at the dock but had not commenced unloading when the documents were transferred, while others were still on the high seas and one vessel had entered territorial waters but was not within the port area. It was noted that the question under consideration did not arise in the *Draper* case because all of the sales there took place while the vessels were a long way outside the territorial waters and that all that the court was there required to decide was whether or not the warranty contained in the Act applied if the sale took place outside the United King-

---

this contract shall be deemed to have been made in England, and to be performed there . . . and the courts of England . . . shall . . . have exclusive jurisdiction over all disputes which may arise under this contract [and] such disputes shall be settled according to the law of England, whatever the domicile, residence or place of business of the parties to this contract may be or become. . . .''

[87] To which the answer may perhaps be made that if the proper law is English then all warranties implied into English contracts are also imported into the contract.

[88] [1966] 1 W. L. R. 287 reversing [1964] 2 Lloyd's Rep. 227. The full name of the case is *Hardwick Game Farm v. Suffolk Agricultural and Poultry Producers' Association Ltd.; Wm. Lillico & Sons Ltd. (First third party); Grimsdale & Sons Ltd. (Second third party); Henry Kendall & Sons (First fourth party); Holland-Colombo Trading Society Ltd. (Second fourth party).*

dom. The present case required further refinement since documents in respect of some of the sales were tendered after the vessels had entered into the United Kingdom territorial waters though in all cases before unloading commenced. It was Havers J.'s view, in the court of first instance, that pheasants and partridges were "poultry" within the meaning of section 2(2) of the Fertilisers and Feeding Stuffs Act 1926. He held that it applied in all cases where the documents were tendered after the vessels had entered into United Kingdom territorial waters and that it was not necessary for the vessel to be within the boundaries of the port. Havers J. further held:

(1) that no breach of the warranty as to the suitability of the ground nut extractions for feeding the pheasants was to be implied as between the third and the fourth parties to the dispute; and

(2) that goods do not become unmerchantable within the meaning of section 14(2) of the Sale of Goods Act 1893 (as it then was, *i.e.* prior to the amendments introduced by the Supply of Goods (Implied Terms) Act 1973) merely because they were required for a particular purpose for which they were unfit, so long as they could be used for some other purpose.[89]

410   On appeal, Davies and Diplock L.JJ., Sellers L.J. dissenting, held that pheasants and partridges were not "poultry" within the meaning of this Act, and on this ground the appeal succeeded. The entire Court of Appeal concurred that the action must fail under (old) section 14(2) of the Sale of Goods Act 1893. The court, however, further divided on whether a warranty of fitness under (old) section 14(1) of the Act applies where both buyers and sellers are members of a trade association which specialises in a particular type of commodity. On this issue Diplock L.J. was in a minority, the majority holding that membership in such a trade association does not of itself rebut the inference that the buyers relied on the seller's skill and judgment for establishing his liability under (old) section 14(1), and on this ground the action succeeded. In addition, the court also divided on a number of other issues. Concerning the applicability of the Fertilisers and Feeding Stuffs Act 1926, to c.i.f. contracts and the effect, if any, of an English choice of law stipulation thereon, the court felt compelled to follow the *Draper* decision. The following extensive comments on the nature of a c.i.f. sale in general, and on the particular implications thereof to the issue which the appeal in this case raised, were however offered. Sellers L.J. stated.[90]

411   "The decision in *C.E.B. Draper & Son, Ltd. v. Edward Turner & Son Ltd.*[91] has been challenged as to its correctness by Kendall [the first fourth party] in so far as it holds that the warranty in section 2(2) of the Act of 1926 is not excluded from all c.i.f. contracts and is not inapplicable to them as such, and by Grimsdale [the second third party] in so far as it holds that the incidence of the warranty is

---

[89] As to this question generally, see *ante*, § 326.
[90] [1966] 1 W.L.R. 287 at p. 299.
[91] [1965] 1 Q.B. 424.

dependent on whether the goods are without or within the United Kingdom (which in relation to goods in transit by sea might be dependent on whether the ship was without or within our territorial waters) when the property in the goods passes to the buyer.

This court has heard sustained and interesting arguments from learned counsel who have stressed rightly the importance and far-reaching effect of this issue and the desirability for clarity and certainty in the application of the Act.

In *Draper's* case . . . Lyell J. had held that the warranty under section 2(2) should be implied. . . . The Court of Appeal reversed that decision and as this court is bound by the existing decision we are restricted in accepting some of the arguments addressed to us even if they might otherwise have prevailed. The arguments would have justified and merited a full review but if we cannot accept those in conflict with *Draper's* case no immediate purpose would be achieved in discussing them in detail, although some general observations may be permissible.''

412   Sellers L.J. then proceeded to examine whether, and to what extent, c.i.f. contracts were within the ambit of the Act. He could not accept the contention that its application was restricted to ''domestic'' transactions:

"There is no inherent difficulty in applying the Act to goods imported on a c.i.f. purchase. If what is aimed at—as clearly it is—is that food sold for use for cattle and poultry should be suitable to be used as such, the sooner the obligation is imposed in respect of goods which change hands from time to time the more likely is the object to be achieved. Shippers and exporters are not un-accustomed to meeting the requirements of importing countries in respect of goods shipped, for instance in respect of certificates of origin, licences, etc. The nature of the market and the transactions it undertakes are not factors which would tend to negative the application of the the the Act. 'It shall be the duty of every person who sells for use . . .'[92] has nothing exclusive about it. Things are grown for use as food and immediately on harvesting (or even before) are sold for the purpose for which they were cultivated and grown.

"Section 5 of the Act deals with consignments ex ship or quay: '(1) In the case of an article delivered or consigned direct from a ship or quay to a purchaser . . .' certain provisions shall apply in lieu of earlier provisions in the Act.

"That not only fits but might be said to contemplate the c.i.f. seller and to make special arrangements for him. It fits an importation from a foreign country. Sales on c.i.f. terms from one United Kingdom port to another may arise but I do not recall any such, and sales ex ship on a coastwise voyage would I think be rare.

"In 1926 and at the time of the predecessor[93] to this Act in 1906 and earlier, large importations of animal feeding stuffs from abroad were common. I see good reason for accepting fully the decision of Lyell J. and the Court of Appeal in *Draper's* case that the Act can be applied to c.i.f. contracts as such. The Act in its essence deals with goods delivered into or within the United Kingdom. Lord Denning M.R., however, said[94]. 'Once it is held that the Act of 1926 applies only to sales in which the property passes in this country, then it is very rarely that it will apply to a c.i.f. contract, like the present, where the goods are shipped at a port overseas for delivery here.'

"That seems to create an unfortunate uncertainty and unforeseeability and a serious limitation on the protection which the Act would otherwise give, for the goods will eventually arrive and be received at a United Kingdom port and then

---

[92]   See s. 1(1) of the Fertilisers and Feeding Stuffs Act of 1926.
[93]   The Fertilisers and Feeding Stuffs Act 1906.
[94]   [1965] 1 Q.B. at p. 432.

be distributed. It arises from the view taken by the Court of Appeal not as to when the property passes under a c.i.f. contract of sale, which is clearly established, but where the goods are to be held to be delivered under such a contract.

"The argument emphasised some of the curious results which may arise. If the shipper or seller dispatches the goods and then sends the relevant documents, if the documents arrive and are taken up by payment before the ship enters our territorial waters no warranty arises, but if the relevant documents, even for a parcel in the same ship, are delayed or there is delay in payment and the documents are not taken up until after the vessel and therefore the goods have arrived in the United Kingdom a warranty arises. The question, it would seem, is still open whether the mere presence of the goods in United Kingdom territorial waters is sufficient to attach the warranty.

"In support of his argument that the Act of 1926 applied only to inland sales counsel for Kendall analysed the Act and referred in particular to the administrative provisions, section 11 and section 27, and to the sections dealing with criminal liabilities, section 4, section 5 and section 7 in particular. As I am of the view that it is not open to this court to take a different view on this issue, I do not pursue that argument further and would say only that it in no way undermines, in my opinion, the decision reached by this court last year that the Act of 1926 may be applicable to contracts of sale on c.i.f. terms in respect of feeding stuffs imported from abroad.

"The difficulty arises under *Draper's* case that the Act of 1926 may apply in the case of goods imported on c.i.f. terms, but whether it does so or not depends on the fortuitous circumstance whether or not the goods at the time of the sale had reached the United Kingdom. A few minutes or a few miles may make all the difference. This leaves an absurd trading position and would seem to condemn legislation which produced such an unsatisfactory result. It arises if I understand it from the distinction which the court has applied between a contract for sale and a sale and to its requirement that the goods themselves should be within the United Kingdom when the property in them passes to the buyer under this particular type of contract. The unequal result of the decision is revealed in the judgment of Havers J., who had to apply it, and as a consequence some consignments came within the Act and some outside it.

"Mr. MacCrindle argued strongly in support of the transactions being within the ambit of the English statute and therefore of the warranty applying in respect of all the shipments irrespective of the actual position of the ship and the goods aboard her at the time the documents were taken up by the buyer. The facts are, as he pointed out, that in each case the contract was made in England; both parties are English and they carry on business in England; the contracts are expressly governed by English law; the documents were taken up and paid for in London and were required so to be by the terms of the contract, and he added, perhaps somewhat rhetorically, that it was in England that the animals and birds died or were damaged, and English farmers who suffered."

413   Addressing himself to the argument that the Act applied because English law was the "proper law" of the contract, his lordship observed[95]:

"By clause 26 of the contract it is provided that 'for the purpose of proceedings either legal or by arbitration this contract shall be deemed to have been made in England and to be performed there.' The documents were taken up and paid for in London and the sale and delivery of the goods either took place in London, as it was argued was the position under a c.i.f. contract, or if it did not it may

---

[95] [1966] 1 W.L.R. 287 at pp. 301. 302.

be said that the parties had agreed that it was deemed to be performed in England and delivery is part of performance.

"When goods secured in a hold of a ship are being moved inexorably across an ocean, their locality changing with every thrust of the propeller, it does not seem a necessary conclusion that the goods should be said to be 'delivered' at any particular moment of the voyage. There seems to be no good reason to apply the lex situs to goods so situated. The only delivery made under a c.i.f. contract is a delivery of documents. That enables the goods to be received at the port of destination. Here the delivery of the documents and the receipt of the goods thereunder from the ship took place in London.

"The goods bought by Lillico and Grimsdale by the documents being taken up in accordance with the contract of sale were goods consigned to them as purchasers, and section 26(2) of the Act provides that 'An article consigned to a purchaser shall not for the purposes of this Act be deemed to be delivered to him until it arrives at the place to which it is consigned whether the consignment is by direction of the seller or the purchaser.' In my view there is substantial argument in favour of the contracts in question being held to have been performed in the United Kingdom or if not so, by reason of clause 26 of the contract, being deemed to have been performed in the United Kingdom and by section 26(2) of the Act of 1926 by reason of delivery being deemed to take place at the place to which the goods were consigned, that is London.

"But *Draper's* case decided that the sale of the goods on such a contract as we have here takes place where the goods physically are when the property in the goods passes to the buyer, and if that place is outside the United Kingdom the Fertilisers and Feeding Stuffs Act 1926 does not apply to such a sale. We are invited by Mr. MacCrindle to say that *Draper's* case only misapplied the correct principle which it enunciated or that the decision was per incuriam. Certainly this court has had the benefit of arguments which were not before the court below.

"However, a decision is not to be treated as per incuriam because the court on the occasion of their decision did not have the benefit of the best argument."

414   While Davies L.J. concurring added:

"To what extent, if at all, did the Act of 1926 apply to the sales by Kendall and Holland Colombo on c.i.f. terms to Grimsdale and Lillico? . . . The point was directly in issue in *Draper v. Turner*. . . . It was held (a) that the Act applies only to sales which take place within and so pass the property within the United Kingdom, (b) that under a c.i.f. contract the property passes at the time when the buyer takes up the documents, but (c) that the property passes at the place where the goods are physically situate at the time when the property passes. . . . I have no doubt that that decision is binding on this court. It was strenuously argued by Mr. MacCrindle that proposition (a) was doubtful and that proposition (c) was wrong. He submitted that proposition (c) was not fully argued and that it need not be followed in the instant case, as having been laid down per incuriam. In my view it is not possible so to hold. All three propositions were essential to the decision. If one may venture to express an opinion about them, I would say this. As to proposition (b) there is no doubt. Proposition (a) is more debatable. From the terms of the Act and especially its administrative provisions and its creation of criminal offences there would seem to be the greatest difficulty in the way of holding that it can apply to transactions outside the United Kingdom. But as my Lord Sellers has pointed out, the Act seems to concentrate largely on delivery (see for example section 5, section 26(2) and (3)). And as delivery takes place under a c.i.f. contract when and where the documents are taken up, it would appear to be a convenient and simple rule to hold that the Act applies to any case where the documents are taken up in this country or the goods are physically delivered here. This in effect was the view of Lyell J. in *Draper.*[96]

"Proposition (c) is, I would respectfully suggest, still more doubtful. There is authority for the proposition that when on a c.i.f. contract the documents are taken up the property is deemed to have passed at the foreign port of shipment. If, therefore, the place where the property passes is the touchstone of the application of the Act, this would seem to exclude from its ambit all c.i.f. contracts where the goods are shipped from abroad.

"It was decided in *Draper's* case that the Act did not apply when the goods were outside territorial waters at the time when the documents were taken up. It is argued for Kendall and Holland Colombo that it does not follow that if the goods are inside territorial waters the Act does apply. The practical difficulties, the anomalies and the absurdities which would follow from applying the Act to all cases and only to cases in which the goods are inside territorial waters when the documents are taken up are too obvious to mention. It is for this reason, I apprehend, that Diplock L.J. has found it necessary to find a more restricted meaning and to hold that the Act does not apply where the property passes before the goods leave the ship's rail. This construction, however, might well leave room for considerable evasion of the Act.

"For myself, I should be prepared to hold, if it were open to us to do so, in agreement with Sellers L.J. and Lyell J., that the statutory warranty attaches to any c.i.f. contract where the documents are taken up or the goods are delivered in this country" (at pp. 315–316).

415   In his minority opinion Diplock L. J. defended the decision in the *Draper* case. His lordship, however, amplified the decision further and stated:

"In *Draper v. Turner* the Court of Appeal held that the Act did not apply to sales under c.i.f. contracts when the property in the goods passed before the vessel in which they were carried reached the United Kindom. The ratio decidendi can be expressed as follows:

(a) The Act does not apply to sales of goods which take place outside the United Kingdom.

(b) All sales of goods take place where the goods are when the property in the goods passes from the seller to the buyer.

(c) Upon a sale of goods under a c.i.f. contract the property in the goods passes from the seller to the buyer when the buyer takes up the documents.

(d) Therefore, if the buyer of goods under a c.i.f. contract takes up the documents when the ship in which the goods are carried is outside the United Kingdom the sale takes place outside the United Kingdom.

(e) Therefore the Act does not apply to a sale of goods under a c.i.f. contract if the buyer takes up the documents when the ship is outside the United Kingdom.

"(a) and (b) are both major premises. Both are essential to the conclusion reached in (d). This court is in my view bound by both of them. Mr. MacCrindle has contended that we are not bound by the major premise (b). He points out that in *Draper's* case, although major premise (b) was supported in argument by counsel for the appellants, who was in fact himself, it does not appear from the report that any argument to the contrary was advanced by counsel for the respondents. This part of the ratio decidendi, he contends, may be treated as

---

[96] [1964] 1 Lloyd's Rep. 169.

given per incuriam and for this reason is open to review by the Court of Appeal in a subsequent appeal such as the present. I do not think that it is open to this court at any rate to treat a decision as made per incuriam. . . .

"Mr. MacCrindle is unable to point to any statute or previous decision inconsistent with major premise (b) of the Court of Appeal's decision in *Draper v. Turner*. In my view the court is bound by it" (at pp. 328–330).

416   Having thus decided the issue before him, his lordship turned his attention to the more general aspects of the matter. He opined that in a c.i.f. contract governed by English law the property in the goods would pass by transfer of the bill of lading only if such transfer was recognised by the law of the place where the goods themselves were at the time. In other words that the "proper [or applicable] law" of the contract would, by English conflict rules, yield all questions relating to the proprietary aspects of the transaction to determination by the *lex situs* of the goods. His lordship stated:

"As this case will go further I may add that even if we were not bound by it I myself would unrepentantly adhere to it. Mr. MacCrindle's argument to the contrary is that under a contract of sale on c.i.f. terms the place where the property in the goods passes is where the documents are when they are taken up. A contract for the sale of goods is not a contract merely for the sale of documents relating to the goods, although the property in the documents as well as in the goods is transferred pursuant to the contract. The transfer of the documents is a symbolic act which has as a consequence in English law the transfer of the property in the goods wherever they may be. But it does not follow from this that the place where the property in the goods passes is the place where the symbolic act is done and not the place where it has its effect, that is to say the place where the goods are. The proper law governing the transfer of corporeal moveable property is the *lex situs*. A contract made in England and governed by English law for the sale of specific goods situated in Germany, although it would be effective to pass the property in the goods at the moment the contract was made if the goods were situate in England, would not have that effect if under German law (as I believe to be the case) delivery of the goods was required in order to transfer the property in them. This can only be because the property passes at the place where the goods themselves are. I think that the ratio decidendi of the Court of Appeal in *Draper's* case is not only binding on us, it is also right.

"But *Draper's* case did not decide the converse of the major premise (a), namely that the Act *does* apply to all sales of goods under contracts of sale on c.i.f. terms in which the property in the goods passes when they are within the territorial limits of the United Kingdom. There are dicta both by Lord Denning M.R. and by me to the effect that the Act may apply to goods sold under a contract of sale on c.i.f. terms if the property in such goods passes after the goods have arrived in the United Kingdom; but the particular circumstances in which the Act would apply was not considered in detail, the only circumstances given as an illustration of its applicability, and this only obiter, was one where the goods had been landed into warehouse before the property in them passed to the buyer.

"It is therefore open to this court to reach its own conclusion as to the applicability of section 2(2) of the Fertilisers and Feeding Stuffs Act 1926 to sales of articles under contracts of sale on c.i.f. terms when the property in the article passes from the seller to the buyer when the ship on which the articles are carried is within the territorial limits of the United Kingdom. The words of section 2(2) are in themselves wide enough to cover any such sale. The administrative sections of the Act, however (namely section 11 to section 14 and section 27 to section 29), reveal its policy to be the protection of those who feed cattle and poultry within the United Kingdom and it is I think legitimate to suppose that Parliament cannot have intended by the unqualified words employed in section 2(2) to make the Act apply to sales of goods on board a ship merely because at the moment the property in the goods passes from the seller to the buyer the ship happens to be within the territorial waters of the United Kingdom even though the goods are consigned to a foreign destination. So whimsical and ineffective an intention is not to be imputed to Parliament. But if the mere presence of the goods within the territorial limits of the United Kingdom at the time the property passes from the buyer to the seller does not suffice to bring the sale within section 2(2) of the Act some criterion of applicability in addition to the mere physical presence of the goods within the territorial limits of the United Kingdom must be sought in the Act. Clearly, I think, the goods must also be consigned to a port in the United Kingdom. But if these two were the only requirements the answer on the question whether section 2(2) of the Act applied to the sale might depend on the route the vessel took on the inward voyage and whether she happened to be sailing in territorial waters or not at the moment at which the property passed—a fact known only to the carrier and of which neither buyer nor seller would have any legal right to be informed by the carrier. Section 4 and section 5 of the Act, which deal with the marking and registration of parcels of feeding stuffs, appear to be intended to cover *all* parcels which are the subject of sales to which the Act applies. The latter section deals with sales ex ship, that is to say where the property passes from the seller to the buyer when the goods pass the ship's rail: neither section applies to parcels of feeding stuffs which are the subject-matter of a sale in which the property passes while the parcels are still abroad. It is true that these sections are dealing with criminal liabilities but the criminal and civil liabilities imposed by the Act are closely linked to one another and if necessary I should have been prepared, although not without considerable hesitation, to hold that section 2(2) of the Act did not apply to any sale under a contract of sale on c.i.f. terms under which the property in the article passed from the seller to the buyer before the goods had passed the ship's rail'' (at pp. 330–332).

When this dispute was finally resolved by the House of Lords,[97] similar divergent views were expressed. On one thing however the entire House agreed. The reasoning in the *Draper* decision could not be supported. For although their lordships were divided on whether or not the Fertilisers and Feeding Stuffs Act 1926 applied to c.i.f. contracts (the majority of the House answering this question in the affirmative), their lordships were unanimous in rejecting the view that the answer should depend on whether or not the goods at the time of sale had reached the United Kingdom or the territorial waters thereof. Such a holding would lead to "whimsical and illogical distinctions" between various cargoes on the basis of their fortuitous location, and the court could not agree that the Act was to be so construed. The application of the warranty under section 2(2) of the Act to c.i.f. contracts depended on other factors. The majority of the House (Lords Morris of

---

[97] *Henry Kendall & Sons v. W. Lillico and Sons, Ltd. and Oth and other consolidated appeals* [1968] 2 All E.R. 444.

Borth-y-Gest, Pearce and Wilberforce) found that the Act applied because the contracts in question were English contracts to be performed by delivery in England.

> "If," said Lord Morris of Borth-y-Gest,[98] "the word sale in section 2(2) of the Act is being regarded as the transaction which brings about a transfer of property, then in the present case there was such a transfer when, on payment in London, there was receipt of the documents in London. The sale was therefore in London. Nothing happened on the various ships. The particular location of a particular ship was an entirely irrelevant circumstance. The transaction which consisted of making payment in exchange for the documents was effective to pass property. The delivery of a bill of lading operated as a symbolical delivery of the goods that it covered.... If there was a sale in England of a chattel which was in a foreign country there might be questions whether there were provisions of the local law which would affect the passing of property. No such points here arise."

While Lord Pearce said[99]: "The c.i.f. contract is unlike other sales of goods. It is completed when the bill of lading is transferred (in this case in London) and this constitutes delivery.... The situation of the goods is irrelevant."

Unification of law

417　Clearly a situation that allows the rights and obligations of the parties to an international sales contract, as a c.i.f. contract normally will be, to fluctuate depending on its "proper (or applicable) law" is highly undesirable. Certainty above all is required in these circumstances, and the existence of several different legal systems with potential application to their contract is always a source of anxiety to parties engaged in international trade. The avoidance of conflict problems has, therefore, long been a major concern of the business world. Mention has already been made throughout this work to the International Chamber of Commerce's (the ICC) efforts to establish a uniform accepted definition of the c.i.f. and f.o.b. terms.[1] Where the contract incorporates this definition or *Incoterms* by reference, unnecessary disputes as to the precise scope of the obligations of the respective parties thereunder and their rights in respect of contractural performance of their c.i.f. bargain may be minimised or even avoided. Similar efforts have been undertaken by the United Nations Economic Commission for Europe. The Commission has issued General Conditions of Sale and Standard Forms of Contract for major commodities which are traded on the international market.[2] Finally, the member countries of what used to be the Council for Mutual Economic Aid

---

[98] *Ibid.* at p. 472.
[99] *Ibid.* at p. 488.
[1] *Ante,* § 24 and *post,* § 571.
[2] *e.g.* for cereals, citrus fruit, timber, the supply of plant and machinery. See Benjamin. "The ECE General Conditions of Sale and Standard Forms of Contract" [1961] J. B. L. 113.

accepted the *General Conditions of Delivery of Goods 1968*, which is a complete code of export trade law governing international trade between themselves.[3] All these efforts at unification may be taken, as one commentator has said,[4] "as an indication that we are witnessing in our time the emergence of a modern law merchant of distinctly international character."

Indeed a special unit of the United Nations, the United Nations Commission on International Trade Law (UNCITRAL), was established at the instance of the General Assembly in 1968 with the particular object of unifying and harmonising the legal règime applicable to international commercial and trade transactions. The Commission has already done a great deal of work in the field of General Conditions of Sale and standard contracts in an effort to promote further unification of the law in this area.

418 In addition to the efforts described in the preceding paragraph, an attempt by the governments of several states to achieve uniformity in international sales law by negotiating international conventions for the purpose ought to be mentioned. In April 1964 two conventions establishing uniform model laws on international sales were signed at a Diplomatic Conference at The Hague by representatives of several states including the United Kingdom. The Conventions on the *Uniform Law on the International Sale of Goods (ULIS)* and on the *Uniform Law on the Formation of Contracts for the International Sale of Goods (ULFIS)* originally sponsored by the International Institute for the Unification of Private Law (UNIDROIT) in Rome were introduced into the Municipal Law of England through the Uniform Laws on International Sales Act 1967 and, following the six required ratifications for their entry into force, were put into operation in respect of contracts concluded after August 18, 1973 by the Uniform Law on International Sales Order 1972.[5] The Uniform Laws however were subsequently revised by UNCITRAL on the grounds that there were too few state participants in the Conference which adopted their texts, and that further improvements were required therein before they could be expected to receive the broad recognition that would be necessary to enable them to serve the purpose they were designed to achieve. A new UN Convention on Contracts for the International Sale of Goods was therefore signed on April 11, 1980 and entered into force between the signatories that include most of the states of the European Union as well as the United States, Australia and Canada. However, at the time of writing, it has not been ratified by the United Kingdom. This is because ratification of the convention and its domestic implementation has encountered severe criticism. Particularly its mandatory features which are in contrast to the optional nature of the U.L.I.S legislation. For by section 1(3) of the 1967 Act it is provided that:

---

[3] See Eörsi. "The 1968 General Conditions of Delivery" [1970] J.B.L. 99.
[4] Schmitthoff, *The Sale of Goods* (2nd ed.), p. 35.
[5] S. I. 1972 No. 973.

"While an Order of Her Majesty in Council is in force declaring that a declaration by the United Kingdom . . . has been made and not withdrawn the Uniform Law on Sales shall apply to a contract of sale only if it has been chosen by the parties to the contract as the law of the contract."

This provision is designed to exclude the application of the Convention except in those cases when it has been expressly chosen as the applicable or "proper law" of the contract by the parties themselves. While previous drafts of the Convention on the Uniform Law on International Sale of Goods included definitions of terms such as c.i.f. and f.o.b.[6] they were omitted from the final draft as well as from the new (1980) version on the assumption that ICC's efforts in this field namely, *Incoterms*, adequately deal with the matter. Instead, both the old and new Uniform Laws refer to "usages" which prevail over provisions of the Convention, unless otherwise agreed by the parties.

[The next paragraph is 431.]

---

[6] Arts. 104 *et seq.* of the 1939 draft proposal for a Uniform Law on International Sale of Goods (Corporal Moveables). Recommendations to include an appendix to the final Convention in which the customary trade terms would be exactly defined (see Rabel, "The Hague Conference on the Unification of Sales Law" (1952) 1 *American Journal of Comparative Law* 58) were rejected.

Part Two

F.O.B. CONTRACTS

CHAPTER 8

THE VARIOUS TYPES OF F.O.B. CONTRACTS

Introductory

431   There is every reason to assume that the contract for the sale of goods "free on board" commonly known as the f.o.b. term has endured longer than any comparable instrument of international trade.[1] Indeed, the reported decisions in which the term f.o.b. is first mentioned date back to the very early days of the nineteenth century.[2] Thus, there exists a body of case law covering a span of close to 200 years.

It is not surprising that f.o.b. terms were the most suitable terms of the seaborne trade in the late eighteenth and early nineteenth centuries, when the rapid growth of international commerce had barely began. Prior to the establishment of regular shipping lines, and to the broad acceptance of documents as symbols of goods afloat, and before modern telegraph, radio and postal services were inaugurated, the means and methods of the overseas trade differed considerably from those today prevailing. The merchant of that epoch, close though it may be in historical terms, would normally have to charter a vessel to call at different foreign ports to purchase whatever goods were there available. He, or his agent, would personally have to oversee the adventure (and it was indeed an adventure) by being present on board throughout the entire voyage. If suitable merchandise was found he would order it to be delivered to "his" vessel where he would normally give it final inspection. If goods conformed to any sample he had previously seen, he would then and there tender the price or other consideration. It is probably to circumstances such as these that the f.o.b. term owes it inception. With technological progress, and as the means of communications developed, the

---

[1] All too often the term f.o.b. is regarded as a term of international or seaborne commerce only. This is inaccurate. The term f.o.b. frequently appears in domestic transactions, for instance between a manufacturer or wholesale merchant and an exporter. Furthermore in the U.S. and Canada, the term f.o.b. is commonly used with reference to transport by land as well as by water, and unless qualified by, *e.g.* the word "vessel" a contract calling for delivery "f.o.b. New York" could be held to refer to delivery at the railroad or truck terminal rather than at the harbour. The use of the words "shipment f.o.b." in an American contract may not be decisive for this purpose, although in a contract construed according to English law, it would normally indicate that the mode of transport was to be a vessel. See observations in *The "Mahia" No. 2.* [1959] 2 Lloyd's Rep. 433 at p. 438. See also the cases relating to c.i.f. sales, *ante,* §§ 52 *et seq.*

[2] See, *e.g. Wackerbarth v. Masson* (1812) 3 Camp 270; *Craven v. Ryder* (1816) 6 Taunt. 433; *Ruck v. Hatfield* (1822) 5 B. & Ald. 632.

conditions of international trade also rapidly changed. Regular shipping lines were established. Information was more readily available. Foreign contacts could be maintained on a permanent basis. Documents could be posted. The Bills of Lading Act 1855 was enacted conferring upon the indorsee the right to sue on the contract of affreightment where no such right, which he could in his own name enforce, previously existed.

432   New means of finance were devised, and banks began participating in transactions as "buyers of exchange." Business could now be transacted more easily calling for different methods more suitable to the conditions of the day and age. In short, the familiar pattern of international trade as currently known began to emerge. With the expansion of commerce the c.i.f. term evolved, though, as the first cases decided in 1862 and 1871,[3] respectively, illustrate, the initials were originally spelled out in a different order *viz.*: "c.f. & i." Where the buyer or his agent were not physically present at the point of delivery and payment was to be deferred to a subsequent date the c.i.f. term better served the interests of the seller, and it also had certain clear advantages for the buyer who was relieved of the responsibility of securing the necessary shipping space and of arranging for the insurance of the goods.[4] "Thus" as an early American decision described it "the purchaser ... transacts the various branches of business with one person instead of three, fixes his liability at a lump sum, and in case of loss will recover the amount of his interest under the policy."[5] Because of reasons such as these the c.i.f. contract soon gained ground, and gradually replaced the f.o.b. term as the most widely used form of contract in seaborne trade. By the beginning of the twentieth century the volume of business transacted on c.i.f. terms far exceeded that transacted on any other basis.[6] However, the f.o.b. term was not entirely abandoned. It still performed a useful function, for example, in situations where, because of the size or nature of the cargo purchased, or for any other reason, the buyer had chartered a vessel under hire. Consequently, the f.o.b. term survived and was still in relatively frequent use. And the same situation obtains to this very day, for example in the oil and other bulk trades where entire shiploads are bought.

---

[3] *Tregelles v. Sewell* (1862) 7 H. & N. 574, *ante*, § 14, *Ireland v. Livingston* (1872) L. R. 5 H. L. 395, *ante*, § 5.

[4] As the older cases show, the c.i.f. term probably evolved from the f.o.b. term through the efforts of buyers to shift the risk of fluctuations in the cost of freight to the sellers. Thus, *e.g.* in *Sparkes v. Marshall* (1836) 2 Bing. (N. C.) 761 the sale was f.o.b. "freight not to exceed 2s., if it does, [seller] to pay the addition ...," and in *Couturier v. Hastie* (1856) 5 H. L. Cas. 673, the sale was made at "27s. per quarter free on board, and including freight and insurance to a safe port in the United Kingdom." It is probably for this reason that the c.i.f. term developed as a "shipment" rather than a "destination" contract, the normal inference being that where the seller is to pay the cost of transport, delivery is postponed till arrival at the destination.

[5] *Mee v. McNider* 109 N. Y. 500, 17 N. E. 424 (1888).

[6] See Lord Wright's speech in *Ross T. Smyth & Co. Ltd. v. T. D. Bailey, Son & Co.* [1940] 3 All E. R. 60, 68, quoted *ante*, § 9.

433   With the scarcity of shipping space caused by the First World War, the
volume of trade transacted on c.i.f. terms soon began to contract. And, as
sellers were reluctant to undertake the onus and risk of securing tonnage with
the uncertainty of rapid fluctuations in the availability and price of freight,[7]
a corresponding increase of trade handled on f.o.b. terms soon began to manifest itself. In the 1920s this pressure abated, and with the re-establishment of
normal shipping conditions in the post-war period the c.i.f. contract regained
the position of prominence it had theretofore enjoyed. This revival (as the
reported cases indicate) lasted until the advent of the Second World War
when a new resurgence of f.o.b. trade, due to causes similar to those noted
with respect to the First World War, is again apparent. By the time this was
over, and sufficient tonnage was once again available, a new factor influen-
cing the preference of transacting business on f.o.b. terms had arisen, namely,
the development and establishment of many new national shipping and insurance industries and the scarcity of foreign exchange. In order to preserve
foreign currency or support domestic industries, governments have often
restricted the allocation of foreign currency to the f.o.b. value of the goods
at the foreign port of embarkation compelling the importer to procure carriage
and insurance in the local market and in domestic currency.[8] In the absence
of import regulations or other legal or administrative measures having a similar effect being introduced, pressure was nonetheless exerted to restrict
imports to f.o.b. terms in order to support and promote national shipping
and insurance industries. In addition, and throughout much of this period, a
substantial volume of domestic business was transacted on f.o.b. terms. This
was due to orders placed by exporters with domestic suppliers. Although the
exporter might be sending the goods to his clients abroad on similar (f.o.b.)
or other (c. and f., c.i.f. or ex ship) terms, the domestic supplier would frequently be requested to deliver the goods f.o.b. a vessel nominated by the
exporter. Since this was a transaction between parties situated in the same
country, the supplier has often successfully maintained that the f.o.b. point
was no different from any other place of delivery in the local market. Thus,
any duties or expenses which arose by virtue of the goods going further on
had to be regarded as the obligation of the buyer who must assume the costs
and risks pertaining thereto. Since sufficient attention has not always been
paid to the circumstances underlying particular disputes, conclusions purporting to be of general application to all f.o.b. sales, namely, to home market

---

[7] The situation is well described in *Blythe & Co. v. Richards, Turpin & Co.* (1916) 114 L.T.
753. During the period of hostilities, a similar situation prevailed with respect to insurance
premiums, in particular the cost of covering war risks, see observations in *The Kronprinsessan
Margareta & Other ships* [1921] 1 A.C. 486.

[8] See, *e.g.* the Report of the United Nations Conference on Trade and Development, on "Invis-
ibles: Insurance" (Doc. TD/B/C.3/107 of April 30, 1973) which states in para. 17 that:
    "Two developing countries, Brazil and Ghana, have decided that all insurance relating to
    imported goods must be effected with companies established in the importer's country.
    Consequently, both Brazil and Ghana have ceased to import on a c.i.f. basis; it has been
    estimated that, in Brazil, for example, this measure will increase the annual premium of the
    national insurance market by approximately U.S. $20 million."

as well as to export transactions, have sometimes been assumed to have emerged from particular decisions though no such general rule was in fact intended.

434 *Different variants of f.o.b. contracts.* The foregoing description, though brief, should suffice to indicate that any rigid and inflexible interpretation of the f.o.b. term which failed to take account of the various factors surrounding a particular transaction would be doing violence to reality. Like the c.i.f. term, the f.o.b. term is the out-growth of the custom and usages of merchants instead of the product of legislation. But unlike the c.i.f. term whose nature and object have undergone little fundamental change since first appearing more than a century ago (account being taken of express stipulations which may replace its ordinary meaning),[9] the f.o.b. term has been designed to serve different interests in different periods. Definitions applicable to one type of f.o.b. contract are therefore not necessarily applicable to another type of what might appear as an identical instrument. To pronounce upon the f.o.b. contract exclusively in the terms of the past and only on the basis of stereotyped notions would have done violence to reality and produced erroneous results. It would have defeated the prime object of the courts which is to give effect to the intention of the parties. And this intention, when unexpressed, would have to be inferred from the entire set of conditions and facts in which the transaction arose. It is to be noted with satisfaction that despite the pressure to uphold orthodox or traditional views which refuse to recognise or allow any variation in the interpretation of the f.o.b. term, English courts have been fully cognisant of the evolution of the term and have effectively acknowledged the realities of the change in circumstances. Consequently, in *Pyrene Co. Ltd. v. Scindia Navigation Co. Ltd.*[10] Devlin J. described the f.o.b. contract as a "flexible instrument," contrasting what he pronounced to be the "classic" type with more recent variants of this term, in the following manner:

> "The f.o.b. contract has become a flexible instrument. In . . . the classic type . . . for example in *Wimble, Sons & Co. Ltd. v. Rosenberg & Sons*[11] the buyer's duty is to nominate the ship, and the seller's to put the goods on board for account of the buyer and procure a bill of lading in terms usual in the trade. In such a case the seller is directly a party to the contract of carriage at least until he takes out the bill of lading in the buyer's name. Probably the classic type is based on the assumption that the ship nominated will be willing to load any goods brought down to the berth or at least those of which she is notified. Under present conditions, when space often has to be booked well in advance, the contract of carriage comes into existence at an earlier point of time. Sometimes the seller is asked to make the necessary arrangements; and the contract may then provide for his taking the bill of lading in his own name and obtaining payment against the transfer, as in a c.i.f. contract. Sometimes the buyer engages his own forwarding

---

[9] See *ante*, § 11.
[10] [1954] 2 Q.B. 402.
[11] [1913] 3 K.B. 743, see *post*, § 662.

agent at the port of loading to book space and to procure the bill of lading; if freight has to be paid in advance this method may be the most convenient. In such a case the seller discharges his duty by putting the goods on board, getting the mate's receipt and handing it to the forwarding agent to enable him to obtain the bill of lading.''[12]

In *The El Amria and The El Minia*,[13] Donaldson L.J. discussed the various types of f.o.b. contracts classified by Devlin J. in *Pyrene Co. Ltd. v. Scindia Navigation Co. Ltd.* In that case the endorsee wished to go behind the bill of lading to a contract concluded between an association representing the sellers and the shipowner, in order to benefit from a jurisdiction clause in that contract which was more advantageous than the jurisdiction clause contained in the bill. Donaldson L.J. observed:

> "In *Pyrene Co. Ltd. v. Scindia Navigation Co. Ltd.* Devlin J. instanced three types of f.o.b. contract. . . .
> In the first, or classic type, the buyer nominated the ship and the seller put the goods on board for the account of the buyer, procuring a bill of lading. The seller was a party to the contract of carriage and if he had taken the bill of lading to his order, the only contract of carriage to which the buyer could become a party was that contained in or evidenced by the bill of lading which was endorsed to him by the seller.
> The second is a variant of the first, in that the seller arranges for the ship to come on the berth, but the legal incidents are the same.
> The third is where the seller puts the goods on board, takes a mate's receipt and gives this to the buyer or his agent who then takes a bill of lading. The buyer was a party to the contract *ab initio*'' (at p. 32).

Donaldson L.J. held that, from what was known, the contracts of carriage in the present case were f.o.b. contracts of the second type of Devlin J.'s classification and the only rights given to the receivers of the cargo were those given by the bills of lading.

435   Although Devlin J. (as he then was) was the first to describe the three broad categories under which f.o.b. contracts could, and probably should, normally be classified, this is by no means the result of recent developments. To be sure conditions have changed so that the particular reasons for engaging in one form of contract instead of another are not necessarily similar, but the existence of these variant types of the contract for the sale of goods "free on board" could have probably been established much earlier. In actual fact in *Wimble v. Rosenberg*, the seller appears to have agreed not only to relieve the buyer of his obligation to nominate the vessel but to advance the freight also. Whereas the variant to which Devlin J.'s concluding remarks were addressed, under which the buyer and not the seller assumes the role of shipper of the goods, is probably the oldest form of f.o.b. contract and the original prototype thereof. The foregoing notwithstanding, Devlin

---

[12] *Ibid.* at p. 424.
[13] [1982] 2 Lloyd's Rep. 28.

J.'s act of recognition marks a turning point and thereafter the self-imposed constraint of the courts appears to have abated and a less dogmatic and more flexible approach was adopted.

436   Thus, in *N. V. Handel My. J. Smits Import-Export v. English Exporters (London) Ltd.,*[14] it was expressly said that a contract does not cease to be an f.o.b. contract by virtue of the fact that the seller has agreed to secure the shipping space. McNair J. stated that "that obligation" seemed to him

> ". . . to co-exist quite consistently with the contract being otherwise upon f.o.b. terms; the f.o.b. terms still remain effective and important for two purposes at least, namely, to specify the exact price and what is included in the price, namely all charges up until free on board, and, secondly those words are apt for determining the place and moment at which the property and risk passes; and there is nothing inconsistent in those provisions with the obligation to find shipping space which I have endeavoured to state."

And in *Carlos Federspiel & Co., S.A. v. Charles Twigg & Co. Ltd.*[15] where the seller in addition also agreed to pay for the freight and insurance of the goods, Pearson J. agreed that these c.i.f. features were not necessarily inconsistent with the f.o.b. term and

> "that fundamentally [this contract] is to be regarded as an f.o.b. contract. . . ."

Similarly, in 1956, the House of Lords concluded in *A. V. Pound & Co. Inc. v. M. W. Hardy & Co. Inc.*[16] that there could be no general rule to the effect that under every f.o.b. contract it was the buyer's duty to secure any export licence which might be necessary. This was a conclusion that most authorities imputed to *H. O. Brandt & Co. v. H. N. Morris & Co.,*[17] decided by the Court of Appeal (nearly 40 years earlier) on the grounds that the f.o.b. contract did not differ from the ordinary inland contract of sale except with respect to the place at which delivery was to be made.

Essence of f.o.b. contract

437   When turning to the various judicial pronouncements that have attempted to define the f.o.b. term, one may be struck by the general terms in which they are couched. Of these, the earliest is probably Brett M.R.'s statement in *Stock v. Inglis*[18] to the effect that:

---

[14] [1957] 1 Lloyd's Rep. 517 at p. 521, see *post*, § 519.
[15] [1957] 1 Lloyd's Rep. 240, see *post*, § 518, 595.
[16] [1956] A.C. 588, see *post*, § 491.
[17] [1917] 2 K.B. 784, see *post*, § 485.
[18] (1884) 12 Q.B.D. 564 at p. 573, affirmed by H.L. in (1885) 10 App.Cas. 263, see *post*, § 564.

"if the goods dealt with by the contract were specific goods, it is not denied but that the words 'free on board,' according to the general understanding of merchants, would mean more than merely that the shipper was to put them on board at his expense; they would mean that he was to put them on board at his expense on account of the person for whom they were shipped; and in that case the goods so put on board under such a contract would be at the risk of the buyer whether they were lost or not on the voyage.

Now that is the meaning of those words 'free on board' in a contract with regard to specific goods, and in that case the goods are at the purchaser's risk, even though the payment is not to be made on the delivery of the goods on board, but at some other time, and although the bill of lading is sent forward by the seller with documents attached, in order that the goods shall not be finally delivered to the purchaser until he has either accepted the bills or paid cash."

Almost a century later Lord Caldecote C.J. similarly stated in *J. Raymond Wilson & Co. Ltd. v. N. Scratchard Ltd.*,[19] that the f.o.b. term has:

"for a long time, certainly more than one hundred years, had a well-known meaning, and if a party sells goods 'free on board,' the meaning is that he has to put the goods on board and to pay the expense of doing so, and delivery is made and the goods are at the risk of the buyer when they are on board, the expense having been paid by the seller."

438 In both judgments the two basic features of the f.o.b. term are outlined, namely, that (i) the seller must pay the cost and bear the responsibility of putting goods "free on board," in other words, bear full liability for the cost and safety of the goods until the point of their passing the ship's rail, and (ii) that upon this being accomplished delivery is complete and the risk of loss in the goods is there and then transferred to the buyer.

Indeed there is little doubt that these are the essential ingredients of an f.o.b. contract. However, it has sometimes been construed to refer merely to the price of the goods, and not to delivery, while unnecessary complications have also arisen because of the bias of the English law of sales to determine a variety of issues on the basis of locating the right of property in the goods at any particular moment.

439 *Marginal responsibilities.* However, the above cited definitions are only directed to the essential features of the f.o.b. term. They do not include an extensive or detailed examination of a variety of marginal responsibilities and expenditures, many of which have been the subject of controversy and even litigation between parties to f.o.b. sales. For example, they do not indicate whether an obligation, monetary or other, which relates to the shipment or exportation of the goods, that must be complied with before the goods can in fact be loaded, is for the buyers' or for the sellers' account. And they probably refrain from so doing because no such general rule can be formu-

---

[19] 77 Ll. L. Rep. 373 at p. 374.

lated notwithstanding suggestions that such rules do in fact exist, and that the "crucial test is whether or not the expenses are payable prior to putting the goods on board,"[20] or that the determining factor is the phase of the transaction (delivery f.o.b. as against shipment and export) to which they relate.[21] In the absence of express contractual stipulations, judicial interpretations have had to rely on usage or custom (whether of general or particular application) and by implication attempt to ascertain what the intention of the parties with respect to performance must have been. It seems clear from what has already been said that there is no general agreement as to the precise division of responsibilities under an f.o.b. contract, applicable irrespective of the particular circumstances in which the actual transaction took place. Moreover, the parties are of course always at liberty to alter the nature of their transaction and thus some, or all, of the requisites of the f.o.b. term may be vitiated. The resulting agreement then loses the force and effect of an f.o.b. contract proper, and the rights and duties of the parties are to be ascertained according to the actual terms agreed upon. Similarly, the usage at different ports, the customs of the trade and the practice of steamship companies are all pertinent in considering on whom the incidence of certain charges in any particular f.o.b. contract falls. Consequently, the study of precedents should be undertaken with some caution.

440 *Detailed definitions.* Exhaustive and detailed definitions of trade terms, including in particular the f.o.b. term, have from time to time been suggested by various organisations and institutions. For example, by the Institute of Export[22] and by the British Association of Chambers of Commerce in the United Kingdom,[23] the latter being a periodically revised publication that outlines the practice which prevails in the various British ports with respect to the apportionment of liabilities under f.o.b. sales; by the Joint Committee representing the Chamber of Commerce of the United States, the National Council of American Importers, and the National Foreign Trade Council in the United States,[24] as well as by the International Chamber of Commerce.[25] In addition, standard f.o.b. contracts and conditions of sale designed to avoid uncertainty and add clarity have been drafted; not only by various national trade associations but some also on a bilateral or multilateral basis,[26] and in

---

[20] See, *e.g.* Halsbury, *Laws of England* (Simonds ed.), Vol. 34, p. 178, n. (*k*).

[21] See, *e.g.* the conclusion of the Institute of Export, *post*, § 442.

[22] See "Proposed Definition of the Term F.O.B." in 14 *Export*, p. 211 (1951), set out *post* § 442.

[23] "*F.O.B. Vessel*" (Rev. ed., January 1971).

[24] Entitled "Revised American Foreign Trade Definitions—1941." See definition of the term "F.O.B. Vessel (named Port of Shipment)" reproduced in 2 *Williston on Sales*, para. 280 (II-E)(Rev. ed.), New York, 1948.

[25] See Incoterms, set out *post*, § 551, and *Trade Terms*, ICC document No. 16.

[26] For example, the General Conditions of Delivery of Goods, 1958, between the then Comecon countries. See Berman, "Unification of Contract Clauses in Trade between Member Countries of the Council of Mutual Economic Aid" (1958) 7 *International and Comparative Law Quarterly*, p. 659.

the case of certain commodities under United Nations auspices.[27] Finally, the Uniform Commercial Code which is now enacted in all but one of the jurisdictions in the United States, includes in section 2–319 a definition of responsibilities applicable to the term f.o.b. vessel. Some of these interpretations and definitions will hereinafter be referred to from time to time. As far as can be ascertained however, English courts have rarely relied on any of this material. Possibly this is because the various proposed definitions themselves reveal a lack of consensus on many issues.

441   *Classification.* What follows is a detailed examination of the various types of f.o.b. contracts. For the sake of convenience they have been grouped under three major headings and will be referred to accordingly throughout this entire work. The classification is completely arbitrary. It is in the first place directed exclusively to the elaboration of the first of the two basic features of the f.o.b. contract mentioned earlier, namely, to the division of costs and responsibilities which putting goods "free on board" may actually entail in various instances. For this reason they have been termed respectively the "strict," the "additional services" and the "shipment to destination" variants. Where further refinements have been found necessary they are dealt with under appropriate subtitles. The second major feature of the f.o.b. contract, namely, "delivery," is considered in subsequent chapters, and since it is not entirely clear whether some of the principles and prima facie presumptions embodied in the Sale of Goods Act are applicable and relevant to f.o.b. contracts, an elaborate examination of these principles and the judicial pronouncements relating thereto has been considered advisable.

The "strict" interpretation

442   Under the interpretation of the term f.o.b., as defined by the Institute of Export,[28] the responsibilities of the seller entail the following specific obligations:

(1) To make available at the port of loading and to ship free on board goods answering in all respects the description in the contract of sale.

(2) To pay all handling and transport charges in connection with the above operation.[29]

(3) In cases of delivery of goods from bond or under drawback to complete declarations required by H.M. Customs and Excise.

---

[27] See Cummins, "The General Conditions and Trading Form Contracts of the United Nations Economic Commission for Europe," 38 N.Y. *University Law Review* 548, 552, nn. 18, 20 [1963].

[28] 14 *Export* [1951], pp. 211 *et seq.,* paras. 19. 20.

[29] *Cf. Joseph (D.) Ltd. v. R. Wood & Co. Ltd.* [1951] W.N. 224. Where the ship is not lying at the quay transport includes lighterage, see Maughan, *Trade Term Definitions* (London 1924), pp. 22 *et seq.,* and *cf. Hecht, Pfeiffer (London) Ltd. v. Sophus Berendsen (London) Ltd.* [1929] 33 Ll.L.Rep. 157.

    (4) To meet all charges arising in connection with the goods up to the time of their passing over the ship's rail.[30]

Whereas the buyer must:

    (1) Advise the seller in good time on what ship at the port of loading agreed in the contract the seller has to put the goods free on board.

    (2) Secure shipping space in the designated vessel.

    (3) Obtain an export licence where necessary.

    (4) Designate an effective ship in time to enable the seller to deliver within the period agreed in the contract.

    (5) Enter and declare the goods at Customs as provided in the Customs Acts, and meet all charges arising from the making of such entry.

    (6) Make entry and meet charges arising from the upkeep and the conservance of waterways used by the ship in her passage out of the port, for example, London Port Rates.

    (7) In the event of a breakdown of his arrangement with the ship arrange for substitute vessel or vessels with the least possible delay, and pay all additional cost of transport, rent, and other charges incurred on account of substitution and/or transfer.

443   To this interpretation, which is, because it entails the performance of a lesser number of responsibilities on behalf of seller than under any other interpretation or usage, hereinafter referred to as the "strict" variant of the f.o.b. contract, Schmitthoff has suggested the addition of the following obligation on part of the seller: "4(a) To comply with section 32(3) of the Sale of Goods Act 1893."[31] The subsection (substantively unchanged by the Act of 1979) provides[32] that the seller must give the buyer such notice as would enable him to procure marine insurance for the goods, failing which the risk of loss in them is not transferred.

    The buyer's duties of nominating the vessel and of bearing the expenses and duties incidental to the shipment and export of the goods are the two points in this definition which demand particular attention.

The buyer's duty to nominate the vessel

444   This duty of the buyer is a condition precedent to the obligation of the seller to load the goods under the contract.

    Hewart C.J. once definned it in the following manner with respect to a contract "f.o.b. Rotterdam, October shipment":

---

[30] Consequently this does not include the cost of stowage; see *post*, § 463.

[31] *The Export Trade* (7th ed. 1980), p. 16. Schmitthoff (*ibid.*) has also suggested the addition of an obligation on part of the seller to pass and pay the cost of customs entry for the goods on the grounds that it is a pre condition for placing them on board the vessel. But this omission from the Institute's definition is apparently deliberate, see *post*, § 464.

[32] See *post*, § 662.

"Under such an agreement it was the duty of the purchasers to provide a vessel at the appointed place, Rotterdam, at such a time as would enable the vendors to bring the goods alongside the ship and put them over the ship's rail so as to enable the purchasers to receive them within the appointed time.... The usual practice under such a contract is for the buyer to nominate the vessel and to send notice of her arrival to the vendor, in order that the vendor may be in a position to fulfil his part of the contract."[33]

Before the buyer has provided the necessary tonnage and has given the seller proper notice of the name of the ship and its expected arrival time the seller will be unable to perform his part of the contract. As stated by Pollock C.B., as long ago as 1863[34]:

"It had been decided, in a case where the expression 'free on board' was used, that it is the duty of the person who seeks to have the goods to point out the ship, or specify where they are to be delivered, before he can complain that the goods are not on board the ship."

For, as subsequently stated by Megaw J. in another case[35]:

"They [the sellers] are not under an obligation to take the goods away from their factory or warehouse and to start them in circulation in the hope, or expectation, that they may arrive at a place which, later, the buyers would have said was the place where the buyers' ship was going to be at some particular time."

Advance Notice. Many f.o.b. contracts nowadays provide that the buyer's notice of the vessel's nomination and readiness to receive delivery of the goods be given to the seller sometime (*e.g.* 15 consecutive days) in advance of delivery. If the buyer fails to do so on time, he is in breach of a condition of the contract and the seller may refuse to make delivery. This was decided by the House of Lords in *Bunge Corp. v. Tradax Export S. A.*[36] where the buyers agreed to buy from the sellers a quantity of U.S. soya bean meal f.o.b. one U.S. Gulf port at sellers' option stowed and trimmed. The sellers issued a separate contract in respect of the first of three monthly shipments which provided *inter alia* that the buyers were to give 15 days' loading notice. This contract incorporated the terms of GAFTA 119 including the notice provision of clause 7. No notice pursuant to clause 7 was initiated by the buyers to any sub-buyers until 14 days prior to loading. On appeal by the buyers, the House of Lords held that clause 7 was intended as a term, the buyers' performance of which was the necessary condition to performance by the seller of his obligations. It was clearly essential that both the buyers and sellers should know precisely what their obligations were particularly because the ability of

---

[33] *J. & J. Cunningham Ltd. v. R. A. Munro & Co. Ltd.* (1922) 28 Com. Cas. 42 at p. 45.
[34] *Sutherland v. Allhusen* (1866) 14 L. T. 666; *Armitage v. Insole* (1850) 14 Q. B. 728; *Stanton v. Austin* (1872) L. R. 7 C. P. 651. See also *per* Porter M. R. in *Hobson v. Riordan* (1886) 20 L. R. Ir. (Q. B.) 255 at p. 271.
[35] *Anglo African Shipping Co. v. J. Mortner Ltd.* [1962] 1 Lloyd's Rep. 81 at p. 92.
[36] [1981] 2 Lloyd's Rep. 1.

the seller to fulfil his obligation might well have been totally dependent on punctual performance by the buyers since until the 15 day notice requirement was fulfilled the sellers could not nominate the "One Gulf Port" as the loading port. Thus, Lord Wilberforce stated in the course of his judgment[37]:

> "[T]he statement of the law in *Halsbury's Laws of England* (4th ed.) Vol. 9 (Contract) paras. 481–482, including the footnotes to par. 482 . . . appears to me to be correct, in particular in asserting (1) that the Court will require precise compliance with stipulations as to time wherever the circumstances of the case indicate that this would fulfil the intention of the parties, and (2) that broadly speaking time will be considered of the essence in 'mercantile' contracts—with footnote reference to authorities which I have mentioned.
>
> "This relevant clause falls squarely within these principles, and such authority as there is supports its status as a condition—see *Bremer Handels–gesellschaft m.b.H. v. J.H. Rayner & Co. Ltd.*[38] and cf. *Turnbull & Co. (Pty.) Ltd. v. Mundas Trading Co. (Pty.) Ltd.*[39] In this present context it is clearly essential that both buyer and seller (who may change roles in the next series of contracts, or even in the same chain of contracts) should know precisely what their obligations are, most especially because the ability of the seller to fulfil his obligation may well be totally dependent on punctual performance by the buyer."

In *Gill & Dufus S.A. v. Societe Pour L'exportation Des Surcres S.A.*,[40] the question arose as to whether a term requiring the f.o.b. sellers of a shipment of sugar to give the buyers notice of the loading port (within the line Rollen/ Hamburg excluding Immingham) "at latest Monday 14.11.83", was a condition, the breach of which entitled the buyers to rescind the contract. Shipment under the contract was to be in December 1983/ January 1984, with 14 days notice in respect of the vessel's e.t.a. Because the market price of sugar fell, the buyers refused to accept a nomination (of Dunkirk as the load port) made on November 1983, that would still have permitted shipment on the first day of the shipment period with sufficient time to give the 14-day advance notice in respect of the vessels estimated arrival time. The sellers claimed U.S.$977.300 in damages for a repudiatory breach, and prevailed in a trade arbitration based on the finding that the words "at latest" were not to be construed as a condition. The award stated that in the refined sugar trade it would be customary for a trader, in such circumstances, to give a notice of default albeit short, *e.g.* 24 hours, prior to cancellation, before time became of the essence of the contract. But both Leggatt J., as well as the Court of Appeal, disagreed, and reversed the award ". . . there are no words in the English language by which a deadline can be appointed more concisely, more precisely and with more finality than the words "at latest" said Leggatt J.,[41] and the Court of Appeal concurred, adding that:

---

[37] *Ibid.* at p. 6.
[38] [1978] 2 Lloyd's Rep. 73, reversed on a different point by the Court of Appeal.
[39] [1954]2 Lloyd's Rep. 198.
[40] [1986]1 Lloyd's Rep. 322 (C.A.).
[41] [1985]i Lloyd's Rep. 621.

"There is no suggestion that the process of shipment under an f.o.b. contract for sugar or indeed contracts for the sale of sugar generally are in any relevant respect different from contracts for the sale of some other soft commodity" (*Per* Sir John Donaldson M. R. at p. 325).

In some trades there may be a custom in relation to the scope of the buyer's duty of notification. Thus, *e.g.* in the oil trade, considered in *Scandinavian Trading Co. A/B v. Zodiac Petroleum S.A. and William Hudson Ltd. (The Al Hofuf)*,[42] Mocatta J. noted that:

"It is common ground that in this interesting and relatively new trade it is the custom that the buyer who buys f.o.b. must give, in succession, notices of expected arrival of the vessel at the refinery or lifting port in question, 72, 48 and 24 hours in advance of the anticipated date of arrival."[43]

Where loading facilities are very limited, the contract may provide that the f.o.b. seller give the buyer a "terminal acceptance" within a stipulated period of time subsequent to nomination of the vessel by him so as to ensure him of timely delivery. The obligation of the seller to provide such a terminal acceptance within the time stipulated was construed as an imnominate term (and not as a condition justifying recission by the buyer) by Hobouse J. in *Phibro Energy A.G. v. Nissho Iwai Corp. and Bomar Oil Inc. ("The Honam Jade")*[43a] and the Court of Appeal was reluctant to reverse this decision.

The ship has to be available at the port of loading specified in the contract and, unless the seller agrees to deliver at a different place, the buyer is in default by designating a ship in another port. Accordingly, Rowlatt J. once observed[44]:

"In this case the parties have made a contract for the sale of coal to be shipped f.o.b. Hull, Grimsby or Immingham, and, of course, there can be no question at all but that the tender of a ship by the buyers at Goole would have been a bad tender."

Moreover, as time (see further *post*, § 455) is normally of the essence of the contract failure to provide the ship on time will release the seller from his obligation to deliver the goods. In *Olearia Tirrena S.p.A. v. N. V. Algemeene Oliehandel, The Osterbek*,[45] the sellers contracted to sell oil f. o. b. Anzio, shipment March, 1970 to the buyers. The contract incorporated London Oil and Tallow Trades Association contract No. 43 which provied by clause 2 that should the buyer not tender suitable tonnage within the contract time the sellers undertook to carry the goods for buyer's account at current rates for storage, interest, and insurance, for 28 days. There were no oil storage facilities at Anzio. The buyers failed to provide a vessel in March and the sellers

---

[42] [1981]1 Lloyd's Rep. 81.

[43] *Ibid.* at p. 84.

[43a] [1991] 1 Lloyd's Rep. 38, [1991] 1 Lloyd's Rep. 50 (C.A.).

[44] *Modern Transport Co. Ltd. v. Ternstrom & Ross* (1924) 19 Ll.L. Rep. 345 at p. 346.

[45] [1973] 2 Lloyd's Rep. 86. affirming [1972] 2 Lloyd's Rep. 341.

warned them that if a ship was not provided by April 28, the sale would be cancelled. The ship arrived on May 2, but the sellers refused to deliver. The Court of Appeal (Lord Denning M.R., Megaw and Scarman L.JJ.) affirmed Mocatta J. who, on a special case from an arbitration tribunal, held that the sellers were entitled to refuse to deliver late as time was of the essence of the contract and the buyers had failed to tender the vessel by April 28, and there was no evidence that the sellers had waived their rights. On the other hand the sellers were only entitled to those charges in respect of such part of the period and in respect of such goods as were actually held and insured.

445   In *Miserocchi and C. S. p. A. v. Agricultores Federados Argentinos S. C. L.; Same v. Bunge A. G.*[46] the problem in dispute was whether under an f.o.b. contract the risk of delivery to the carrying vessel (and costs incurred by virtue of congestion at the port of loading) falls on the buyer or the seller? Staughton J. considered the basic obligations of an f.o.b. contract and stated:

"It is the buyer's obligation to provide a ship at the place of shipment, on the day when shipment is to take place. The seller must then bring his goods to the ship's rail for loading. If there is not a single day fixed for shipment, but for example any of the 30 days in the month of June, then the question arises who will choose when a ship shall be provided. In these contracts the choice lay with the buyers. Similarly there may be more than one place of shipment. . . . Again the question arises who is to choose where the ship must be provided; in this instance . . . the choice lay with the sellers. Presumably the option as to the precise time of arrival is entrusted to the buyers, because it is their duty of providing a ship which will most require some flexibility; and the option as to a berth is entrusted to the sellers, because they are most affected by the choice. Those reflections must of course give way to the actual terms of the contracts."[47]

The buyers, who had chartered vessels and gave the required 15 days' notice of probable readiness to load, disputed their duty to present the vessels at the loading berths, but their contention was rejected as nothing could be found in the contracts distinguishing them from the ordinary f.o.b. contract "where the obligation [of the buyer] is to present the ship at the place of loading."[48] And while the sellers had in fact failed to nominate a berth as soon as they received notice of probable readiness to load (as they were obliged to do) this was held to be immaterial since by virtue of the port congestion it would have made no difference to the vessel's progress. Accordingly, it was held that the buyers had to bear the costs including those arising from storage and carrying charges.

In an attempt to avoid this situation some standard forms of contract provide that the expense of delay caused by congestion shall be borne by the f.o.b. seller.[49] But as such costs are generally due to an event for which

[46] [1982] 1 Lloyd's Rep. 202.
[47] At p. 207.
[48] *Ibid.* at p. 208.
[49] See, *e.g. Federal Commerce and Navigation Co. Ltd. v. Tradax Export S.A.* [1978] A.C. 1 at pp. 10–11.

neither party is directly responsible, the risk, in the absence of an express contrary provision in the contract, falls on the party whose performance it affected, and no implied obligation that there would be an available berth as would enable a duly nominated vessel to load within the contract period will ordinarily be implied.[50]

Carrying charges. On the other hand, where the contract permits or provides for an extension in the time of delivery, which will normally be limited to a definitive period, *e.g.* 21 days (after expiration of the original delivery period) in the event of the nominated ship being delayed (or all the goods not being on board by the end of the delivery period or for any other reason) it is usual to provide for carrying charges (*i.e.* the cost of storing the goods plus interest and insurance) to be for the buyers account.[51] Stipulations for the extension of the period of delivery in the event of a late nomination or arrival of the vessel nowdays appear in many standard f.o.b. contracts. They generally require the buyer to give the seller suitable notice of his intention to exercise his right of extension. Absent the required notice, the seller may (as previously noted) view of the buyers' failure to nominate, or the delay in the arrival of the vessel, or the delay in completing the loading of the contractual quantity, as a repudiation by the buyer, and escape his obligation to perform the transaction at the agreed contractual price. While extension clauses are to be strictly construed an extension clause need not be disregarded as contradicting a nomination clause.[52] So too a provision for carrying charges to be met by the buyers (who have exercised a right to extend the period of delivery) is not of itself inconsistent with time being of the essence, and if a specific advance notice of the vessel's arrival is required it must be complied with.[53]

Moreover, carrying charges may be inter dependent on the buyer exercising his option (where contractually stipulated) to claim an extension of delivery, and may not be due simply because delivery was delayed because of the vessel's late arrival where no extension of delivery was claimed, and where the f.o.b. seller did not treat that delay as a final default bringing the contract to an end. The sellers' failure to terminate implied a tacit variation in the terms of the original contract, and his readiness to load (beyond the original delivery date), in the absence of a claim to extend the delivery (by the buyer) based on the extension of delivery provision contained in the contract, deprived him of his ability to recover actual costs resulting from the delay for which the buyer is responsible. This was decided by Hirst J. in *Kurt A. Becker G.m.b.H. & Co. v. Voest Alpine Intertrading G.m.b.H. ("the Rio*

---

[50] *Ibid.* [1982] 1 Lloyd's Rep. 202 at p. 209.
[51] See, *e.g. R. Pagnan & Fratelli v. N.G.J. Schouten N.V. (The Filipinas I)* [1973] 1 Lloyd's Rep. 349.
[52] See *Bremer Handelsgesellschaft m.b.H v. J.H. Rayner & Co. Ltd.* [1979] 2 Lloyd's Rep. 216, where the Court of Appeal reversed Mocatta J. [1978] 2 Lloyd's Rep. 73 which held that an extension clause has to be disregarded as contradicting a nomination clause.
[53] See *The Osterberk* [1973] 2 Lloyd's Rep. 86 (in particular *per* Lord Denning M.R.).

Apa'').[54] On the other hand, in *Lusograin Comercial Internactional De Cereas Ltd. v. Bunge A.G.,*[55] the sellers failure to treat the contract as ended, due to buyers nomination of four (instead of "up to three") loading vessels, allowed the extension provision of the contract to be activated, thus entitling them to recover carrying charges until the extension period lapsed, and they were not limited to a claim in respect of such charges for a shorter period only, *i.e.* excluding the 60-day extension subsequent to the buyers breach. In other words, the sellers were entitled (under the terms of the particular contract) to leave the contract open for performance by the buyers until the end of the delivery period, as the same was prolonged by the extension clause. But the buyer may be excused from carrying charges where the vessel is prevented from getting to the loading port due to action of governmental authorities that control access to it, as was the case in *Bunge A.G. v. Sesostrad S.A. (The "Alkeose C."),*[56] where, however, an express stipulation regarding such a contingency was provided for in the contract.

Finally, it should be noted that where the f.o.b. buyer has nominated a vessel that may not be able to load the entire contract quantity (because of the buyers' obligation to accept other cargo) the seller may not assume a repudiatory breach as a matter of course. Absent a clear and unambiguous statement of unwillingnes or inability to perform by the buyer, the seller must show that on the balance of probabilities the buyer would not perform. Showing that the buyer may not be in a position to perform is insufficient. This was decided in *Alfred C. Toepfer International G.m.b.H. v. Hagrani Export S.A.*[57] where Saville J. refused to alter an arbitration award in favour of the buyers. In that case a cargo of 22,000 tonnes of Argentine Maize for delivery f.o.b. during August 1983 was sold. The buyers agreed to sell a like quantity of maize, on similar terms, to sub-buyers who nominated a vessel for carriage of the cargo that was passed on to the sellers. However, the sub-buyers also nominated the same vessel to load 6,100 tonnes up river under another contract, so that only 15,400 tonnes of the contract quantity could be loaded on the vessel. The sellers submitted that the buyers were guilty of a repudiatory breach. It was held that the mere fact of entering into inconsistent obligations (in the circumstances of the case) did not of itself necessarily establish inability or unwillingness to perform, and that the buyers did not wrongfully repudiate their contract with the sellers.

446   *Port of Shipment. In Cumming & Co Ltd. v. Hasell,*[58] an Australian case, it was held that an agreement for the sale of goods f.o.b. without any stipulation, express or implied, as to the port of shipment was too uncertain to constitute a binding agreement. But in *David T. Boyd & Co. Ltd. v. Louis*

---

[54] [1992] Lloyd's Rep. 586.
[55] [1986] 2 Lloyd's Rep. 654.
[56] [1984] Lloyd's Rep. 687.
[57] [1993] 1 Lloyd's Rep. 360.
[58] (1920) 28 C.L.R. 508.

Louca[59] Kerr J. held that in the absence of express agreement, trade custom or any inference which can be drawn from surrounding circumstances, the choice of loading port in an f.o.b. contract is that of the buyer if the contract does not name a port of shipment. In this case a contract for the sale of a quantity of Danish herring meal provided for delivery to be made by three instalments in successive months "f.o.b. stowed good Danish port." The buyers did not provide any shipping instructions or communicate with the sellers in any way, and towards the end of each month the sellers claimed that the buyers were in default. This was accepted by the court which held, as stated above, that naming the port of shipment in an f.o.b. contract was the buyer's duty.

Where no time for delivery is fixed, the duty of the parties is to comply with their respective obligations within a reasonable period of time. So that where the buyer delays to make his nomination until after a reasonable period of time has elapsed, the contract may be avoided by the seller.

It follows that, if the buyer is unable to designate a suitable or "effective" vessel (namely, a vessel which is not by virtue of some physical or administrative factor unable to receive and carry the contract goods and which will be available at the port of loading agreed in the contract on the date stipulated therein), he cannot enforce an action against the seller for non-delivery, since as Bucknill J. stated:

"I do not . . . assent to the proposition that when two persons have to do something, one person to deliver and another to accept, and the person whose duty it is to accept fails in the performance of that duty . . . he is entitled simply because the other has not been in a position to deliver, to any damages."[60]

447 *Seller's repudiation.* Failure to make prompt delivery and to load within the contract period is generally a breach of a condition entitling the buyer to treat the contract as at an end. He may then withdraw the vessel or its nomination (and not merely claim demurrage).[61] Alternatively, the buyer can affirm the contract, and claim damages (including demmurage) for any loss occasioned by the delay. The right of the f.o.b. buyer to treat the contract as at an end, and to reject the goods was recognized in *Tradax Export S. A. v. Italgrani di Francesco Ambrosio*[62] (Bingham J.) in relation to an f.o.b. contract expressly stipulating for delivery during a specified period "at buyers' call" (GAFTA Contract 119). But it is thought that the same rule would also apply in the absence of such express words.[63] Had the rule been otherwise,

---

[59] [1973] 1 Lloyd's Rep. 209.
[60] *Per* Bucknill J. in *Forrestt & Son Ltd. v. Aramayo* (1900) 83 L. T. 335, 337; *Société Coopérative Suisse des Céréales et Matières Fourragères v. La Plata Cereal Co., S. A.* (1947) 80 Ll. L. Rep. 530.
[61] Contrast the case of delay in loading which, if not amounting to a "frustrating period" is not usually treated as a breach of a condition *post*, § 455 .
[62] [1983] 2 Lloyd's Rep. 109.
[63] *Tradux Export S. A. 339 Italgrani di Francesco Ambrosio; Italgrani v. Sosimase S. P. A.* [1986] 2 Lloyd's Rep. 112, 116.

as Bingham J.'s judgment points out, the buyer may be required to keep the ship waiting in a falling market. Furthermore, where it is apparent that the seller is not going to deliver the cargo at the stipulated time and place, the buyer's duty of nominating the vessel is discharged.[64] In these circumstances the seller's conduct is normally deemed to be a repudiatory breach of the contract and a waiver of all conditions precedent thereto.

448   In *Peter Turnbull & Co. Proprietary Ltd. v. Mundas Trading Company (Australasia) Proprietary Ltd.*,[65] the High Court of Australia (Dixon C.J., Webb and Kitto JJ., Taylor J. dissenting), reversing the decision of the Supreme Court of New South Wales, held that the seller's conduct absolved the buyers from strict compliance with the terms of the contract and from their duty to give the required shipping instructions and have a vessel ready to load in the port of shipment during the delivery period set by the contract. The contract in question called for the sale of oats f.o.b. Sydney "to be loaded on ship or ships nominated by the buyer during the months of January and February, 1951. Buyer to give seller 14 days' notice of ship(s) and shipping date(s). . . ." The sellers for their own advantage induced the buyers not to insist upon loading in Sydney and an effort was made to have the goods shipped from Melbourne. This effort failed because the ship-owners had some technical objection against loading oats in Melbourne, but the sellers presistently maintained their inability to ship goods at Sydney throughout the contract period. In an action for non-delivery of the goods at Sydney, the sellers argued that as the buyers had failed to give shipping instructions by February 14, and, as the ship nominated by the buyers was in any event delayed and not ready to load in Sydney during the contract period, the action must fail. The court of first instance accepted this contention, but the judgment was reversed on appeal. Allowing the appeal, Dixon C.J. stated:

> "The reason why my conclusion differs from his Honour's is that I think that the [seller] unmistakably intimated to the [buyer] that it was useless to take the steps requisite if the [seller] was to deliver f.o.b. Sydney because the [seller] could not do so and so impliedly intimated to the buyer, when time still allowed the [buyer] to find another February ship and to give 14 days' notice of the ship and of the shipping date or dates, that the [buyer] need not do so" (at p. 208).

449   In an earlier case, *Nordisk Oversoisk Handelsselskab A/S v. Eriksen & Christensen*,[66] Rowlatt J., on a case stated by arbitrators, gave judgment for the buyers, whose right to reject a late delivery was contested by the sellers. The learned judge said:

> "The contract was for the sale of 8,000 tons of Argentine maize f.o.b. Buenos Ayres, delivery August and September, at buyer's option. That means that the buyers have August and September to declare their desire to take the maize, and

---

[64] *Wertheim v. Chicoutimi Pulp Co.* [1911] A. C. 301 at p. 313.
[65] [1954] 2 Lloyd's Rep. 198.
[66] (1920) 5 Ll.L.Rep. 71.

if they do it in August and give reasonable time to the sellers to do the necessary acts to transport the maize to the buyer's steamer, then September drops out of it altogether, the time for the delivery being then fixed by the exercise of the buyer's option.

"The facts are that . . . [the buyers] wrote on September 1, having then the steamer ready, asking for delivery at once. 'At once' in that letter really meaning as soon as you can, having regard to the exigencies involved in the handling of the goods. Then the reply came that they were without instructions, and they remained without instructions right up to September 15.

"Then there came to the sellers the cancellation of the buyers, and the question is whether they were justified in cancelling. The Arbitrators have found that 14 days is a reasonable time to allow to elapse after the request for delivery . . . it is not a question of an anticipatory breach, but of an occurred breach. A demand is made for delivery, a reasonable time for compliance with that demand has passed, and therefore it was not a case of it being intimated that the contract would be broken, the contract was already broken" (at p. 72).

In other words the seller, in such a case, must have the goods ready within a reasonable time after he has been advised of the expected delivery date.

450   *Delivery on shore.* Because the f.o.b. term is not to be regarded solely for the benefit of any one party, a failure to nominate a suitable[67] or "effective" ship in time is a breach of contract, and the buyer cannot normally insist on substitute performance, *e.g.* delivery on shore. Lord Ellenborough enunciated this principle as long ago as 1812, in *Wackerbarth v. Masson*,[68] where he stated:

"The delivery for which the [seller] undertook was—on board a ship to be named by the [buyer]. He was always ready to deliver . . . in this manner, and he offered to do so. But the [buyer] requires a *tertium quid*. Instead of naming a ship, he demanded to have the sugars weighed off and delivered into his own hands, or transferred to his own name in the warehouse-keeper's books. The seller might have been exposed to some risk, or might have lost some advantage by agreeing to this; and he had a right to refuse, as it was not the mode of delivery for which he had stipulated."

451   However in *Cohen & Co. v. Ockerby & Co. Ltd.*[69] decided by the High Court of Australia, Isaacs J. was less emphatic. Although he held that in the circumstances before him the buyer could not substitute for delivery f.o.b. delivery on shore, it was his "opinion" that:

"In the case of a simple f.o.b. contract the purchaser may in some cases . . . claim delivery short of the ship. The universal principle (subject, of course, to any requirement of public policy) is that a man may renounce a benefit, but he cannot, without consent, impose a burden or disadvantage on another. If I contract to pay a certain sum to carry my goods two miles, I may dispense with the carriage of them after a mile, provided I pay the agreed price and occasion no

---

[67] See, *e.g. Hecht, Pfeiffer (London) Ltd. v. Sophus Berendsen (London) Ltd.* (1929) 33 Ll.L.Rep. 157.
[68] (1812) 3 Camp. 270; see also *Wetherell v. Coape, ibid.* 272.
[69] (1917) 24 C.L.R. 288.

burden or inconvenience to the carrier. If I purchase goods for a specified price to cover the cost of putting them over the ship's rails for my benefit, I can pay the price and take them on the wharf or at the seller's warehouse, unless it can be shown that the seller thereby sustains some detriment. But is that the case having regard to the present contract? I am not prepared to go so far with the respondents as to say that there was an undertaking on the part of the appellants to export the flour. It is not necessary to go so far. It is one thing to limit the buyer's right as against the seller to delivery on board, and another to impose on the buyer the obligation of sending and keeping the goods out of the country. If the narrower interpretation is correct, it is sufficient; if it is not correct, it is useless to inquire further.''

Isaacs J.'s final words in the passage just quoted however do little to substantiate the foregoing hypothesis, for he concluded his judgment by saying that:

"In my opinion . . . the agreement as to delivery was 'free on board' a ship, to be provided by the buyers; that they were bound to provide such a ship, unless prevented by war, and in that event there was to be no delivery at all'' (at pp. 299–301).

Nor indeed, absent a specific agreement to this effect, will the seller be allowed to claim performance by delivery at the pier.[70] That performance became impossible due to a failure by the buyer to nominate a ship or because, as a result of circumstances beyond his control, the ship nominated by him was in fact unable to receive the goods, is immaterial.

452 Consequently, where the buyer fails to nominate the ship the seller may sue for damages without tender of performance if he alleges having been willing and able to perform; but he cannot normally tender delivery at the docks and sue for the price of the goods. In *Colley v. Overseas Experters*[71] the seller delivered for shipment f.o.b. Liverpool a consignment of leather bolting. However, the vessel originally nominated by the buyer was withdrawn from service by her owner, and four other vessels which were in turn substituted by the buyer were all prevented from receiving the goods by a series of misfortunes and as a result of a variety of causes. The seller contended that he was entitled to recover the contract price and not merely damages for breach. The claim failed. It was held that no action for the price of the goods could subsist even though it was due to the buyer's default that property failed to pass. McCardie J. said:

"It seems clear that in the absence of a special agreement the property and the risk in goods does not in the case of an f.o.b. contract pass from the seller to the

---

[70] See, however, *Burch & Co. Ltd v. Corry & Co.* [1920] N.Z.L.R. 69 (New Zealand) and *Meyer et al. v. Sullivan et al.* 40 Cal. App. 723, 181 Pac. 847 (1919) where the court held that the term "f.o.b." was used in connection with the price and was entirely for the benefit of the buyer, who could waive it and succeed in claiming damages for the seller's failure to deliver on shore.
[71] [1921] 3 K.B. 302.

buyer till the goods are actually put on board: see *Browne v. Hare*[72]; *Inglis v. Stock*[73]; *Wimble v. Rosenberg*.''[74]

But this, it is submitted, is not an entirely accurate statement. The risk of loss or damage to the goods may in such cases pass to the buyer, at any rate to the extent that the goods are appropriated and such risk is due to the breach. But the remedy for this, as for any additional charges resulting from the failure to nominate the vessel, is in damages.

It should be noted that many standard f.o.b contracts contain provisions entitling the seller to claim payment at the contract price (plus various carrying charges such as storage, insurance and interest) against tender of, *e.g* warehouse receipts, if the buyer should fail to provide suitable tonnage within the contract time, or any pre-agreed extension thereof. Sometimes such clauses allow deduction of loading charges that may have been saved.[75]

453 *Substitute vessel.* As already stated, time normally will be of the essence of the contract, and a failure to nominate a ship on time would amount to a repudiation by the buyer not just of a collateral warranty or mere representation but of a condition of the contract, the seller being entitled to cancel the same by virtue thereof. The buyer is not however (unless otherwise agreed) irrevocably bound by having nominated any particular vessel. The seller therefore cannot cancel the contract on the grounds that the vessel nominated has failed to arrive and that the buyer is prohibited from nominating another vessel. If his first nomination fails and the original vessel becomes unavailable for any reason, a substitute vessel may still be nominated by the buyer, provided loading can be completed within the contract period. This was so held in *Agricultores Federados Argentinos v. Ampro S.A.*[76] where the allegation that the buyer could not withdraw the vessel originally nominated and nominate a substitute vessel in performance of the contract failed. The sellers had sold a quantity of Plate maize f.o.b. Rosario, shipment to be from September 20 to 29, 1960. The buyers nominated the *Oswestry Grange* but she was delayed by rain, and it was apparent that she could not load until September 30, the day after the contract would expire. At 4 p.m. on September 29, the sellers informed the buyers that they intended to cancel the contract because the vessel nominated by them had not arrived. However at 4.30 p.m. the buyers managed to engage another vessel, the *Austral*, which was at Rosario and was capable of carrying the goods. The sellers however refused to co-operate and to undertake the arrangements which were required in order to enable the *Austral* to load within the contract time. There was a clear finding of fact that there was sufficient time for them to have done what was necessary in order to enable her to load in time. It was held, on a case stated,

---

[72] (1858) 3 H. & N. 484: (1859) 4 H. & N. 822, see *post*, § 566.
[73] (1884) 12 Q.B.D. 564. (1885) 10 App. Cas. 263, see *ante*, § 437.
[74] [1913] 3 K.B. 743, see *post*, §§ 625, 662.
[75] As was, *e.g.* the case in *Bremer v. Rayner* [1979] 2 Lloyd's Rep. 216.
[76] [1965] 2 Lloyd's Rep. 157.

that the sellers' behaviour evinced an intention not to perform their contract and that the buyers were entitled to treat this failure as an anticipatory breach and a repudiation of the contract. In the course of his judgment Widgery J. said:

> "There is nothing expressly in this contract to provide the circumstances in which a particular vessel shall be nominated, and the rights of the parties are to be regulated by the general law as it applies to an f.o.b. contract. As I understand it, the general law applying in such a contract merely is that the buyers shall provide a vessel which is capable of loading within the stipulated time, and if, as a matter of courtesy or convenience, the buyers inform the sellers that they propose to provide vessel *A*, I can see no reason in principle why they should not change their minds and provide vessel *B* at a later stage, always assuming that vessel *B* is provided within such a time as to make it possible for her to fulfil the buyers' obligations under the contract. I can see no principle at all to indicate in a case of this kind that when the buyers had nominated the *Oswestry Grange* they were in any way inhibited at any time from changing their minds and substituting the *Austral*, provided always, as was the fact here, that the *Austral* was capable of accepting the cargo within the time for shipment stipulated in the contract" (at p. 167).

Widgery J. further held that the buyers had failed to discharge the burden of proving an alleged custom at the port of embarkation (Rosario) allowing for an extension of up to five days beyond any shipment date stipulated in the contract. However, as stated, the decision was in their favour nonetheless because they were entitled to nominate a substitute vessel. The foregoing being the general rule, it is not uncommon for the parties to stipulate expressly in relation to the right of substitution. Thus, *e.g.* long-term contracts for delivery f.o.b. often specify that the buyer shall submit shipping schedules for the seller's approval some time in advance of the delivery dates, and nominate particular vessels for actual loading some time prior to expected arrival date. In these cases the right of substitution may be restricted by a specific term, *i.e.* to any time prior to 10 days before the expected date of arrival of the previously designated vessel at loading terminal. Or it may be denied completely by means of a provision that nomination "once given shall not be withdrawn,"[77] or that "nomination of vessel is irrevocable unless the seller agrees to substitution." The latter provision was considered in *Bremer Handelgesellschaft m.b.H v. J. H. Rayner & Co. Ltd.*[78] where Mocatta J. opined that it meant that a valid nomination was irrevocable but that "an invalid nomination [could] be replaced by a valid one."

In *Cargill U.K. Ltd. v. Continental U.K. Ltd.*[79] the contract was for the sale of 25,000 tonnes of English feed barley between August 5 and 31, f.o.b. Hull. The contract incorporated certain general conditions, one of which provided

---

[77] As was the case in *R. Pagnan & Fratelli v. N. G. J. Schouten N.V. (The Filipinas 1)* [1973] 1 Lloyd's Rep. 379.
[78] [1978] 2 Lloyd's Rep. 73 at p. 94. The decision was reversed on a different point in [1979] 2 Lloyd's Rep. 216 (C.A.).
[79] [1989] 2 Lloyd's Rep. 290 (C.A.).

that "buyers were to give notice of eight clear days of the date of arrival of the vessels e.t.a. at loading port. . . . Such notice to show vessel name, itinerary and approximate quantity to be loaded. The provisional notice must be followed by a final (definite) notice of four clear days of the date of presentation of the vessel for loading. . . . In the event of failure to give definite notice. . . . buyer will be deemed in default. . . ." The buyers gave a provisional notice nominating Cobetas *or sub,* and a definite notice nominating Cobetas e.t.a. of August 1986. The sellers acknowledged receipt of the definite notice. But a different vessel *The Finnbeaver* arrived at 23.35 on August 31, and was then ready to receive the contract goods. The sellers, however, refused to load the vessel on the ground that she was not the contractual vessel not having been nominated in accordance with the contract terms. They regarded the buyers in default and cancelled the contract. The dispute was referred to a trade arbitration which held for the buyers as the contract was not read to expressly preclude the buyers from nominating a substitute vessel, but this decision was reversed both by Evans J.[80] as well as by the Court of Appeal (Parker, Bingham and Taylor L.JJ.). It was held that in view of the stipulation above quoted it was impossible to attribute to the parties the mutual intention that the buyers could nominate another vessel with a different itinerary, notwithstanding that it was too late to give either a provisional or a final notice in respect of her. No such term could be implied into the contract and the sellers were entitled to refuse to load *The Finnbeaver.* The value to the seller of a clause limiting the buyers' right of substitution in f.o.b. contracts may be due to the fact that, absent such a clause, the seller could not recoup from the buyer any additional expenditure or loss incurred as a result of the substitution. No such problem arises if the substitution constitutes a breach of contract. If the buyer is not in breach of his basic nomination obligation, and the substitution is valid, is the seller able to recover for additional costs? In *J. & J. Cunningham v. Munro Ltd. R.A. & Co.*[81] Lord Hewart C.J. founded the sellers right to recovery (in such circumstances) on the ground that he had relied on the buyers' statement and acted upon it to his detriment. However, this was a *dictum,* and the proposition is not free from difficulty. Perhaps one could construe the buyer's right to substitute as subject to an implied restriction that any loss or damage attributed to it would be recoverable. But this too is not free from difficulty, and it has therefore been suggested that appropriate express terms are best suited to deal with the problem.[82]

Sometimes, a substitution provision is read as extending the shipment date as was held in *Thomas Borthwick (Glasgow) Ltd. v. Bunge & Co. Ltd.*[83] In other cases, the words are construed more restrictively as was done by the Court of Appeal in *Finnish Government (Ministry of Food) v. H. Ford & Co.*

---

[80] [1989] 1 Lloyd's Rep. 193.
[81] *Ibid.* n. 33, (1922) 28 Com.Cas. 42 at p. 46.
[82] As recommended by Bennett, "F.O.B. Contracts: Substitution of Vessels" [1990] L.M.C.L.Q. 466.
[83] [1969] 1 Lloyd's Rep. 17.

Ltd.[84] There an f.o.b. contract for the sale to the appellants of a quantity of
River Plate maize provided that shipment would be by "steamers expected
ready to load February and/or March 1920." The quantity clause specified
"14,750 tons, or sufficient to load the steamships *Pallada, Merkur,* and
Joulan or substitutes." Two out of the three named ships loaded part of the
contract goods though late, but the *Merkur* was sunk in May while she was
on her way to load. The court held that another ship could not be substituted
for her because in May it was quite impossible to replace her by another
vessel which was expected ready to load in February and/or March. Bankes
L.J., construing the shipment clause, said:

> "In order to make sense of the clause, it is necessary to read in the word 'by.'
> It would therefore read: 'shipment by steamers expected to load February and/
> or March 1920.' [it was] suggested that the words there used 'expected ready to
> load,' are not contractual words at all, that they are mere words of expectation.
> In my opinion, that is not the view of this clause at all. I am satisfied that these
> words were used as contractual words" (at p. 189).

Consequently, the seller was entitled to regard the contract as at an end so
far as the balance of the wheat was concerned, and could not be held liable
for breach in respect thereof.

454   *Time of nomination.* Similarly, where the buyer has an option of taking
delivery within a stated period of time, he cannot complain that the seller has
not completed delivery according to the contract if this is a direct result of a
last minute designation on his part.

This was decided in *F. E. Napier v. Dexters Ltd.*[85] The dispute arose under
a contract for the sale of twenty tons of London sweet fat. It provided for
"delivery during the month of October 1925, f.o.b. London steamer. Cash
against mate's receipt." The buyers failed to exercise their option until very
late, and did not give any instructions for forwarding the goods until October
27. On that date they informed the sellers that the goods were to be delivered
"alongside the steamship ... at Fennings Wharf on Friday ... for steamer
sailing Saturday"—which was the 31st. The sellers were unable to complete
delivery of more than seventeen out of the twenty tons because by 2.30 p.m.
on Friday, the wharf ceased receiving goods for the steamer. The buyers
purported to reject the goods on the grounds that the sellers failed to deliver
the quantity agreed to in the contract. But the Court of Appeal (Bankes,
Scrutton and Sargent L.JJ.), affirming the decision of an arbitrator and of two
lower courts, held that the buyers were not entitled to reject the goods. Moreover, it was held that the sellers notwithstanding their retention of the mate's
receipt, had a right to sue for the price of the goods and not merely for
damages.

---

[84] (1921) 6 Ll.L. Rep. 188.
[85] (1926) 26 Ll.L. Rep. 184, C.A., see *post,* § 634, *cf.* also *Carswell v. Donald & Jacobs, Re
an Arbitration* [1921] N.Z.L.R. 368.

455   Where therefore the vessel nominated by the buyer arrives at the port of shipment close to the expiration of the shipment period, the seller (if he does not wish to risk unjustified rescession) is under a duty to load as much as can be loaded within the delivery period specified in the contract but his obligation ceases at the end of that period, and he is under no obligation to continue loading after that period expires. In *Bunge & Co. Ltd. v. Tradax England Ltd.*[86] the contract was for the sale of 1,000 tons of barley for delivery f.o.b. from one good East Coast United Kingdom Port (to be declared before December 15, 1972) between January 1 and 20, 1973 (both dates inclusive) at buyers call. The sellers nominated the port of Berwick in due time. The buyers nominated a certain vessel but as she was delayed they nominated a substitute vessel (as to the right of substitution see *ante*, § 453), expected ready to load on Friday, January 19, 1973. The sellers protested that if the vessel arrived on January 19, there would be insufficient time to load the cargo within the shipment period which expired at midnight, January 20. In the event, only 110 tons of barley were loaded, and the balance of the contract quantity was never shipped. Donaldson J., upholding an award in favour of the sellers, on a case stated by a trade association Board of Appeal, *inter alia*, said:

> "Under an f.o.b. contract, the obligation to deliver and the obligation to accept delivery are mutual and both are confined to the shipment period. Even if the sellers waived their right to rely upon the buyers' failure to tender the vessel timeously as a ground for refusing to deliver, this waiver did not create a new right in the buyers to demand delivery outside the agreed shipment period."[87]

So too in the *Al Hofuf*,[88] Mocatta J. noted that "It was admitted between counsel that the provision in the ... contract for delivery between Feb. 20 and 28 was a condition of the contract and of its essence, and it was further admitted that timely notices of expected time of arrival of the vessel ... was also a condition and of the essence of the contract." But where, as in that case, there was insufficient time to load the entire contract amount (due to the late nomination of the vessel which the sellers did not have to accept to begin with and her arrival on Friday, February 28) the buyer is not entitled to complain if loading is not completed within the delivery period, and, unless the delay amounts to a "frustrating period," the delay is not a breach of a condition. Delay in loading (at least where due to late nomination) is thus to be distinguished from most other delays, and particularly from failure to deliver in time (*ante*, § 447), since generally time is of the essence in mercantile contracts and delay amounts to a repudiatory breach. Provisions are however often found in f.o.b. contracts under which the buyer may apply for an extension of the

---

[86] [1975] 2 Lloyd's Rep. 235.
[87] *Ibid* at p. 239.
[88] [1981] 1 Lloyd's Rep. 81 at p. 84.

shipping period (and—if the seller agrees to grant the extension—bear the costs and carrying charges including interest resulting therefrom) in which case, and to the extent that such costs are contractually fixed at a predetermined and onerous rate, the question has sometimes arisen as to whether they are to be considered as a penalty (and thus not binding) or as the price of the extension. In *T. P. Gonzalez Corp. v. F. R. Waring (International) Pty. Ltd.*[89] The Court of Appeal viewed such a clause as "a provision for an extension, so that the provision of a ship during that extended period would not constitute a breach of contract," and thus the charges stipulated were not to be viewed as penal in character but as a consideration for the variation in the contract terms. Likewise, where the f.o.b. buyer elects to affirm the contract, despite late delivery by the seller, and claim for the loss in lieu of cancellation, a provision in the contract, for the payment of a specified sum by way of demurrage, may be enforced as a liquidated damages claim.[90] In *Richco International Ltd. v. Alfred C. Toepfer International G.m.b.H.*[91] the question arose on an appeal from an arbitration award, as to the sellers' right to carrying charges where notice of an extension was served, and loading was delayed through the sellers' inability to load at the guaranteed loading rate, due to a breakdown of the loading elevator. The buyers argued that the sellers (who had settled the demurrage account due to late loading) could not recover the carrying charges since to allow such recovery would entitle them to profit from their own breach. The buyers' submission rested on the premise that breach of a loading rate guarantee in a f.o.b. contract can give rise to a claim for general damages in addition to an entitlement to demurrage provided for in the contract. Potter J., after viewing several charterparty cases, reached the conclusion that while demurrage provisions are not to be construed as if they excluded additional damages, the plaintiff could only recover such additional damages if he was able to demonstrate both that any additional loss was different in character from loss due to delay to complete loading on time, and also that such loss stems from the breach of an additional or independent obligation. His Honour opined that the same conclusion "should be drawn in respect of the rights and obligation of a seller and buyer under a f.o.b. contract into which provisions are imported in relation to rates of loading and payment of demurrage".[91a] In other words the buyers right to demurrage must be construed as the sole remedy for breach of the loading rate guarantee unless it could be shown that the seller was in breach of an additional obligation within the lay days. The buyers argued that there was a failure to deliver at the agreed contractual date and not only to load at the guaranteed rate. But Potter J. was unwilling to accept this:

---

[89] [1980] 2 Lloyd's Rep. 160.
[90] *Tradax Export S.A. v. Italgrani Di Francesco Ambrosio* [1986] 1 Lloyd's Rep. 112, 116.
[91] [1991] 1 Lloyd's Rep. 136.
[91a] *Ibid.* at p. 142.

"As a broad proposition", he said, "governing f.o.b. contracts for carriage by sea, it may be said that loading of the goods is delivery" (at p. 143).

456   The buyer must nominate the ship in reasonable time to enable the seller to send forward the goods in accordance with instructions.[92] However, where the contract called for delivery f.o.b. Rotterdam "October Shipment" of 200 tons of Dutch bran the buyers having secured freight for October 28, and the sellers having forwarded the bran to the port on October 14, it was held in *J. J. Cunningham Ltd. v. R. A. Munro & Co. Ltd.*[93] that the buyers were not deprived of their right to reject the bran. The bran had deteriorated in the interval between these two dates but since the buyers were not bound to take delivery under the contract before October 28, their rights were not prejudiced by the sellers' action. Obviously, where the buyer has the option to select the date of delivery within a stipulated period of time, *e.g.* January to March, the contract should provide for some advance notice of his readiness to load and for the declaration of the expected vessel's name in order to give the seller sufficient advance notice to enable him to perform his duty of delivery. As already noted provisions to this effect are to be found in most standard f.o.b. contracts, but failing them would in any event be implied.

457   *Port options.* The contract sometimes provides for delivery at one of several ports which are defined regionally, *e.g.* "f.o.b. United Kingdom port," or "f.o.b. European continental port."[94] In such a case, the buyer's duty is generally to elect the port of shipment within the stipulated range and to inform the seller where delivery will be expected in good time.[95] Where, however, the seller agrees to provide the vessel for and on behalf of the buyer (*post*, § 412), Schmitthoff has suggested that the duty of selecting the appropriate port will also fall on the seller for in his words "the party responsible for the shipment has normally the choice of the port of shipment."[96] Although no doubt there is much to be said for this view, it is not certain that any such general rule can be formulated. Clearly it is possible for the two issues to be separated and it might well be the case that the buyer may wish to reserve the choice of selecting the port of departure while delegating the responsibility of securing tonnage to the seller. In some cases the choice of the actual loading port may be determined by a governmental authority that enjoys an export monopoly of the product sold. In such a case the loading port will be dictated by a third party and any load port restrictions must be complied with by the buyer in respect of all permissible options.

---

[92] See *Bunge & Co. Ltd. v. Tradax England Ltd.* [1975] 2 Lloyd's Rep. 235, *ante*, § 455.
[93] (1922) 28 Com. Cas. 42.
[94] Such was the case in *Fielding & Platt Ltd. v. Najaar* [1969] 1 W.L.R. 357.
[95] *Muller Brothers v. G. M. Power Plant Co.* [1963] C. L. Y. 3114; *David T. Boyd & Co. Ltd. v. Louis Louca* [1973] 1 Lloyd's Rep. 209 *ante*, § 446.
[96] *Schmitthoff: Export Trade: Law and Practice (9th ed., 1993), pp 296–302.*

Where the buyer nominates a vessel that does not meet load restrictions of some of the ports, the seller may reject the nomination.[97]

458 *Time of delivery.* The seller must deliver the goods in time so that they may be put on board by the end of the contract period, though as already noted (*ante*, § 455), delay in loading may have to amount to a "frustrating event" in order to justify rescission.[98]

For example, in *All Russian Co-operative Society Ltd. v. Benjamin Smith & Sons*,[99] the Court of Appeal (Bankes, Scrutton and Younger L.JJ.) gave judgment for the appellant who was the purchaser of a cargo of oats. Under the contract which gave rise to the dispute in question, the oats were to be delivered f.o.b. London during the month of January. The respondents' case was that they tendered the oats in barges alongside the vessel nominated by the appellants, but that the appellants were guilty of a breach of duty in not taking deliveries on board of the last 105 tons of the oats sent alongside the steamer in one of the barges. This was caused by the fact that the last 105 tons were delivered alongside the steamer at 4.30 p.m. on January 31, whereas the working hours ceased fifteen minutes later. However, the county court judge and the Divisional Court both gave judgment for the seller on the ground that by a course of dealing between the parties the buyers undertook the obligation of taking the oats out of the barge. No attention was paid to the question of the seller's duty to tender the goods within the contract time. In allowing the appeal, Bankes L.J. said:

> "Now, what was the contract time? The contract time was to deliver the goods in January, the last day of January, being the 31st. In my opinion, that is an obligation to tender within working hours. The evidence showed that the last 105 tons were delivered alongside at 4.30 p.m. on January 31, and that working hours ceased at 4.45 p.m. I think it is clear, therefore, that there was no tender of the goods alongside within working hours. . . . If, as has been suggested, it was clear upon the evidence that there was no room in the ship for the last 105 tons of oats, a different complexion would have been put on the matter, because it would be no use to complain of late tender on January 31 if the ship had been full some hours before. But . . . the ship was not full . . . and if the oats had arrived in time on January 31 they would have been taken on board" (at p. 352).

Concurring with this opinion Scrutton L.J. added:

---

[97] Phillips J. reversing a GAFTA Board of Appeal award in *Richco International Ltd. v. Bunge & Co. (The "New Prosper")* [1991] 2 Lloyd's Rep. 93.

[98] See *The Al Hofuf* [1981] 1 Lloyd's Rep. 81 at pp. 89 *et seq.* and the authorities there quoted where it was decided that the principles derived from charterparty cases (that time taken for loading is not a condition or of the essence of the contract) are applicable to f.o.b. contracts. Given the fact that ports are inactive on weekends and holidays, and that customs formalities have to be complied with, loading may extend beyond the period originally envisaged or contemplated. In the *Al Hofuf* the vessel sailed away before the sellers had adequate time to load (due to its arrival on Friday which was the last day for delivery f.o.b. under the contract), and the buyers were deemed to have repudiated the contract by this act.

[99] (1923) 14 Ll.L. Rep. 351.

"The sellers' primary obligation is to deliver the goods on board in January, and the fact that the buyers do part of the work for themselves does not of itself relieve the sellers of the obligation to put the goods in such a position that the buyers can do part of the work and put the goods on board in January" (at p. 353).

459   However, where the contract provides for "delivery during October, shipment to Tokyo" and though it is a known fact that the last vessel for Japan sails on the 25th, the seller is probably not at fault if he delivers too late for shipment, but before November 1.[1] Again, where the seller is allowed to elect the date or place of delivery he must exercise his option and communicate the date or place, or both, at which he proposes to deliver to the buyer in proper time, before any obligation rests on the buyer, and before he can complain of the buyer's failure to nominate the ship.[2]

But where the seller notifies the buyer of the necessary particulars and the contract, in turn, provides for the buyer to then give advance notice to the seller of the name of the vessel and expected date of readiness to load, the buyer may become liable for late nomination though he is unable to send back the advance nomination notice within the time stipulated due to the arrival time of seller's notification. See, *e.g.* the facts in *T. P. Gonzales Corp. v. F. R. Waring (International) Pty. Ltd.*,[3] where sellers in South Africa nominated the loading port, and contract period of October 14 to 23, to buyer in Los Angeles on October 4. The buyer was required to give 10 days' advance notice of vessel but because of the time difference between South Africa and Los Angeles it was too late for buyers to comply with their obligation even if they had sent back their nomination on the very day of hearing from the sellers. Nevertheless, it was held that damages for extension in time of shipment requested by the buyer (in accordance with terms of the contract) as of October 4 would be allowed.

Although the usual time option in f.o.b. contracts (of the "strict" variant) is the buyer's, *i.e.* it is he who must decide the exact shipping date within the permissible shipping period and let the seller know on what date the vessel will arrive in good time to enable the seller to have the goods ready for shipment by the nominated vessel (contractual stipulations concerning how much advance notice the buyer is to give, and at what rate the seller is to load, are fairly common) there is nothing to prevent the parties from varying the usual position by granting the seller the right to determine the shipping date. Such was the case in *Harlow & Jones Ltd. v. Panex (International) Ltd.*[4] In these circumstances, however, the buyer must be informed when the goods are going to be ready so as to know when the ship is to arrive and load. If the parties fail to specify anything in relation to the latter point, it

---

[1] See Maughan, *Trade Term Definitions* (London 1924), p. 18.
[2] Semble, *per* Solomon J. A. in *Murray & Co. v. Stephen Bros.* [1917] A.D. 243 (South Africa); see also observations in *Stenhouse v. Oelrichs* [1914] W.N. (N.S.W.) 72 (Australia).
[3] [1980] 2 Lloyd's Rep. 160 (C.A.).
[4] [1967] 2 Lloyd's Rep. 509.

will be necessary to import such a term into the contract by implication in order "to make the contract work commercially" as was done by Roskill J. in the aforementioned decision.[5] There an f.o.b. contract for the sale of steel blooms "to be delivered during August/September [1966] in supplier's option" was considered. The question before the court was whether the contract had been repudiated by the seller or whether the buyers wrongfully failed to accept the goods on or before September 30, 1966. The sellers notified the buyers in July that the goods would be ready at the beginning of August and requested them to arrange for a vessel for August. The buyers did not reply to that communication or to subsequent reminders nor to offers for vessels which their chartering brokers had advised them of. On August 1, the buyers notified the sellers that they would be calling for the first of two shipping instalments (as contemplated at the time) for loading between August 12 and 22, and that the balance would be loaded by the end of August, requesting confirmation of them. On August 3, the buyers told the sellers that owing to their failure to confirm, the vessel for August 12 to 22 had been missed and that the buyers could not ship during August. On August 11, the buyers demanded a reply within 24 hours as to whether the sellers would guarantee the entire contract quantity for loading on August 24 to 27, and on the 22nd purported to cancel the contract on the ground of a repudiation by the sellers who then proceeded to claim damages for alleged breach. This claim succeeded. In the course of his judgment relating to the implied term which must read into the f.o.b. contract in question, Roskill J. said:

> "The only implication which, to my mind, it is necessary to make is an implication that before the buyers need nominate the ship the sellers will notify them when, or approximately when, the sellers expect to load."

In situations such as these, the buyer would be well advised to include an express stipulation in his contract whereby the seller assumes responsibility for any demurrage expenses due to late delivery as was indeed done in the aforesaid case. This would remove any commercial risk from the buyer should the ship be detained by late delivery of the cargo. The contract may then, or independently, also require the buyer to advise the seller what the demurrage rate is "not customarily treated by the trade as being a term of great or fundamental importance to the contract as to give a seller the right to reject the nomination or to refuse to ship the goods".[6]

Interdependent obligations:

459a   "The respective obligations of the parties" (in both the more common case where the buyer must give the notice so as to fix the time of shipment,

---

[5] *Ibid.* at p. 526.
[6] From the arbitration award quoted by Mocatta J. whose Judgment (on a different point) was reversed in *Bremer Handelegesellschaft m.b.H. v. J.H. Rayner & Co. Ltd.* [1978] 2 Lloyd's Rep. 73 at p. 81; [1979] 2 Lloyd's Rep. 216 (C.A.).

as in the less common case where the option of fixing the time of shipment is the seller's) "are" as stated by Kerr L.J. in *Tradax Export S.A. v. Italgrani Di Francesco Ambrosio*[7] "accordingly designed to bring about the concurrence of the vessel provided by the buyers being ready to load the contractual goods, and the sellers obligation to deliver the goods by loading them on board the vessel when so provided in accordance with the contract". Kerr L.J. went on to note that some of the respective f.o.b. obligations have been held to be in the nature of conditions, while others have not. In *Bunge Corporation v. Tradax S.A.*,[8] unanimously affirmed by the House of Lords,[9] it was held that the buyers' obligation to give 15 days loading notice is a condition of the contract.[10] It is also a condition that the vessel will arrive, and be ready to load in sufficient time to allow loading (at the contractual rate, if any) before the end of the shipment period.[11] So too is a term relating to the vessel's compliance with load port restrictions, and if several port options have been provided, and the designation of the particular loading port is not the buyers, such compliance must apply to all potential ports and the seller may reject the nomination of a non-complying vessel.[12] If these conditions are complied with, then the seller is obliged, also as a condition of the contract, to load the goods before the end of the shipment period (or any extension thereof). However, Kerr L.J. in *Tradax Export S.A. v. Italgrani Di Francesco Ambrosio*[13] (at p. 117) avoided answering the question which, he noted, is not covered by any authority, whether an f.o.b. seller can be in breach of a condition before the expiry of the shipment period if he in fact loads the contractual goods by that date, or is ready, able and willing to do so when the buyers nevertheless purport to declare him to be in default, *i.e.* in breach of contract, before that date? Kerr L.J. confessed that "he had never before heard any such contention as this that was pleaded in the present case", but concluded that since the issue did not really arise on the facts it was "unnecessary to express any concluded opinion on it". He could hold for the sellers on the grounds that the sellers could not be in default at any time when they were ready, able and willing to complete the loading of the vessel at the applicable contractual rate before the expiry of the shipment period. He (and the rest of the Court of Appeal with him) held that an f.o.b. seller is under "no obligation to have any goods available and ready for loading" at a date "earlier than the date on which the vessel is ready to receive the goods."[14] The appeal therefore had to be allowed since the initial award in this case, and confirming judgment in the case under appeal, were based on the erron-

---

[7] [1986] 1 Lloyd's Rep. 112.
[8] [1980] 1 Lloyd's Rep. 294.
[9] [1981] 2 Lloyd's Rep. 1.
[10] However where a notice under a c.i.f. contract had to be given "without delay", it was held by the House of Lords not to be in the nature of a condition in *Bremer Handelsgesellschaft M.b.H. v. Vanden Avenne- Izegem P.V.B.A.* [1978] 2 Lloyd's Rep.109, *ante*, § 317.
[11] *Bunge & Co. Ltd. v. Tradax (England) Ltd.* [1975] 2 Lloyd's Rep. 235.
[12] *Richco International Ltd. v. Bunge & Co.* [1991] 1 Lloyd's Rep. 98.
[13] [1986] 1 Lloyd's Rep. 112.
[14] *Ibid.* at p. 118.

eous premise that an f.o.b. seller is in default if, on receiving a notice of readiness from a buyers vessel, he does not, at that moment in time, have the goods ready for delivery. In the case in dispute, the buyers nominated the vessel, and the sellers nominated the loading port, in time. But the sellers failed to advise the buyers of the shipper's name. The vessel arrived at the loading port, and began loading other cargoes at the elevator, and the buyers purported to withdraw the nomination of the vessel before the shipment period had expired. In their view the sellers had defaulted in that they failed to disclose the shipper's name in time. The sellers, however, managed to advise the buyers of the shipper's name a few hours after the purported withdrawal, and in sufficient time to have permitted performance, but their advice was rejected by the buyers. The buyers view was supported in a trade arbitration, and also by Bingham J. on the grounds, *inter alia*, that the contract in question stipulated for delivery during a specified period "at buyer's call," which call, it was thought, was unheeded in the circumstances for lack of the sellers failure to promptly provide the shipper's name, and on the basis, above already noted, that a f.o.b. seller should have the contract goods ready for delivery at the moment in time he is in receipt of the buyers' notice of readiness to load. However, as the latter proposition was devoid of any legal basis, the appeal was allowed. The only relevant obligation of the f.o.b. seller was to deliver the goods by loading them, when the vessel was ready to receive them. The sellers were not under an earlier obligation, to promptly respond to the buyers call.[15] The purpose of the words "at buyer's call" was merely that the buyer's have the option of calling for the goods to be loaded at any time during the shipping period when the vessel provided by them is ready to do so. A requirement that the goods should be available at a time earlier than that required to permit loading within the contract period "would introduce a novel obligation into f.o.b. contracts" (at page 118). However Kerr L.J. was careful to add that there may indeed be cases where an f.o.b. seller may be obliged to have the goods ready for loading before the vessel is ready to receive them, namely, cases where the non-availability of the goods prevents the vessel from getting to the loading place or berth. Even in such cases, however, (and such were not the circumstances he had to consider in the dispute before him) the consequences would be that the buyers could contend that they should be placed in the same position as if the lay time had begun to run, and this would not entail a breach of condition by the sellers for which they could be held to be in default of fulfilment.

Where the contract contains a provision concerning the daily average loading rate which the seller is willing to be obligated to, the buyer will not be in a position to claim demurrage for failure to load at a faster rate in accord-

---

[15] *Cf. Bremer Handelsgesellschaft m.b.H. v. Vanden Avenne-Izegem P.V.B.A.* [1978] 2 Lloyd's Rep. 109, where the House of Lords held that where a notice under an f.o.b. contract had to be given "without delay" this did not import an obligation in the nature of a condition into the contract.

ance with the custom of the port of loading. This was decided by the Court of Appeal in *Kurt A. Becher G.m.b.H. & Co. K.G. v. Roplak Enterprises S.A. ("The World Navigator")*[16] where f.o.b. buyers of a cargo of maize claimed damages from their sellers for wrongful detention of the vessel, prior to loading. Their nominated vessel lost her place in the loading schedule due to some deficiency in the sellers (shipper's) documentation. While an f.o.b. contract probably implied (as held by Phillips J. whose decision was reversed) a term requiring the sellers to co-operate in providing the appropriate documentation to permit the buyers to present the vessel for loading (as to the duty to co-operate generally, see *post*, § 508), the specific contract considered contained a term of a minimum average loading rate of 500 tons per weather working day, and that obligation had been performed. In other words even if the vessel had not been detained, the sellers would not have been required to load more than 500 tons per day, which would have given them 24 loading days. Since the vessel was loaded before the expiry of that period, the buyers were denied the right to any damages resulting from the failure (if such was the case) of the sellers to enable the vessel to reach the loading berth after having received valid notice of readiness to load.

459b   That terms relating to the time of arrival of the vessel, or of the nomination of the port of loading, in f.o.b. contracts are to be construed as conditions, and not merely as warranties or as innominate terms was confirmed by the Court of Appeal in *Gill & Dufus S.A. v. Societe Pour L'exportation Des Surcres.*[17] There an f.o.b. contract for the sale of sugar at the seller's quay "one port within the line Rouen/Hamburg excluding Immingham, port to be specified by the [sellers] at latest Monday 14.11.83", was the subject of the dispute. The sellers failed to nominate the port until November 15, 1983 and, because the market price of sugar fell, the buyers refused to accept the late nomination on the grounds that it was out of time. The sellers treated this as a repudiation of the contract, and sought damages in an arbitration. The issue was whether the provision for the nomination of the port in time was a condition, an intermediate or innominate term (see *ante*, § 317), or a warranty. If it was a condition, or an innominate term having the same character as a condition, then the buyers were entitled to treat the contract as repudiated. Otherwise the sellers were entitled to damages which were agreed to amount to U.S.$977,300. The arbitrators held for the sellers on the grounds that the term was a warranty, and the buyer had to serve notice of an extension after the sellers were in default, since "in the refined sugar trade it would be customary for a trader, in such circumstances, to give such notice before treating, and being able to treat, the contract as repudiated". But this decision was reversed on appeal by Legatt J. whose opinion was confirmed by the Court of Appeal. In confirming Legatt J.'s decision, sir John Donaldson M.R. stated:

---

[16] [1991] 2 Lloyd's Rep. 23.
[17] [1986] 1 Lloyd's Rep. 322.

"For my part, like the learned judge, I am most reluctant to reverse or differ from a trade tribunal. Nevertheless, the issue is one of construction and thus of law. The arbitrators' finding of fact is part of the contractual matrix and a very important part, but it is no more than that. There is no suggestion that the process of shipment under an f.o.b. contract for sugar or indeed contracts for the sale of sugar generally are in any relevant respect different from contracts for the sale of some other commodity. All that is said is that those engaged in the sugar trade find strict punctuality difficult, which may well be true of other trades not to mention other individuals, and that in practice they adopt a more relaxed attitude. This seems to me to be quite insufficient to displace the construction which would usually be placed upon a term involving interdependent obligations in relation to the time of loading, reinforced, as in the present case, by the use of the imperative words 'at latest'."[18]

As the aforesaid review of the cases shows, problems as to the time of shipment in f.o.b. contracts abound. Indeed, few problems arising out of f.o.b. contracts give rise to as much difficulty. This is due to the fact that delivery under this type of contract is a joint operation. The seller must supply the goods, and the buyer the means of transporting them, *i.e.* the ship. In this situation it often becomes difficult to apply the rules which govern stipulations as to the time of delivery in contracts for the sale of goods generally. The difficulties are compounded by the fact that generally the time of delivery is not a given date, but rather a period within which performance is to take place. While it is settled that, unless the specific contract otherwise provides, any failure to make or take delivery within that time gives the injured party the right to rescind, so that the buyer need not accept if he can demonstrate that the seller could not complete loading,[19] nor need the seller ship if the goods could not be put on board the ship nominated by the buyer within the shipment period,[20] serious difficulties arise from the fact that the precise date or point within the period (which may be subject to extension) in which the goods are to be shipped, must first be determined. If the contract is silent on this matter, the option (in f.o.b. contracts) is the buyer's, but the contract may provide the reverse. In either case the question arises, what effect the option, conferred on one party, has on the obligations of the other. As stated by Professor Treitel[21] "It is clearly not sensible, where the option is the sellers, to require the buyer to have a ship ready to load for the whole of the shipment period; nor, conversely, for the seller to have the goods ready at the point of shipment for the whole of that period". Either the seller or the buyer (as the case may be) may find it difficult to estimate in advance whether loading can be completed within the contractual period (original or extended), or whether the ship must be nominated, and made available to load the goods. In an attempt to remove or mitigate this uncertainty express provisions on time tables are often stipulated. But such provisions may give rise to the further

---

[18] *Ibid.* at p. 325.
[19] *Tradax Export S.A. v. Italgrani Di Francesco Ambrosio* [1986] 1 Lloyd's Rep. 112, 117.
[20] *The Osterbek* [1972] 2 Lloyd's Rep. 341; *Bunge & Co. Ltd. v. Tradax England Ltd.* [1975] 2 Lloyd's Rep. 235.
[21] "Time of Shipment in f.o.b. Contracts" [1991] L.M.C.L.Q. 147, 148.

problem of the effect of the failure to comply precisely with the pre-agreed time tables. Is the failure a breach of a condition justifying rescission or not? In *Bunge Corporation v. Tradax Export S.A.*[22] the House of Lords held that a term requiring the f.o.b. buyers to give the sellers 15 days advance notice of the ships readiness to load was a breach of a condition entitling the sellers to rescind the contract. The buyers' duty to give the required notice was to enable the sellers to load the contract quantity, at the rate fixed by the contract, to be completed by the end of the shipment period, and his failure to give the required notice in time would have prevented this. In *The Naxos*[23] the contract was for 12,000 tons of sugar f.o.b. and stowed one nominated EEC port. Delivery was to be "to one or more vessels. . . . ready to load in May or June 1986. Buyer to give seller not less than 14 days advance notice of vessel(s) expscted readiness to load". The period of loading was also fixed. But the contract also incorporated certain rules of the London Refined Sugar Association and in particular, rule 14 stipulating, *inter alia*, that:

(1) "the seller shall have the sugar ready to be delivered at any time within the contract period";
(2) "the buyer, having given reasonable notice shall be entitled to call for delivery of the sugar between the first and last working days inclusive of the contract period";
(3) the buyer was to be responsible for the costs incurred by the seller if the vessel did not present herself within five days of the date specified in the buyers notice; and
(4) if the vessel presented herself as ready for loading within the contract period but loading had not been completed by the end of that period, the seller was nevertheless bound to make, and the buyer to take, delivery of the balance of the contract quantity.

This last provision varied the general and normal rule previously noted, under which the f.o.b. seller need not continue to load, after the period has expired.[24]

On May 15, 1986 the buyers gave the 14 days advance notice, calling on the sellers to load the sugar on board *The Naxos*, estimated to arrive at Dunkirk on May 29 to 31. Although the vessel arrived on May 29 the sellers did not commence loading. They advised the buyers that a cargo would be available on June 3, but on that day the buyers terminated the contract and bought a replacement cargo at a higher price. The question arose as to whether the buyers were justified in terminating, and in their claim for damages. While an arbitration tribunal held for them its decision was reversed by Gatehouse J. with whom a majority of the Court of Appeal agreed. But the tribunal's decision was restored and finally upheld by a majority of the House of Lords; Lord Ackner, speaking for the majority of the House, while Lord Brandon

---

[22] [1981] 2 Lloyd's Rep. 1, *ante*, § 444.
[23] *Compagnie Commerciale Sucres et Denrees v. C. Czarnikow Ltd.* [1990] 1 W.L.R. 1337.
[24] *Ante*, § 444 and § 455.

dissented. There were two questions that had to be answered. The first was what obligations were imposed by rule 14(1)? The entire House agreed that the obligations went beyond that imposed by the general law on an f.o.b. seller. Under general law, where the time of shipment is at the buyer's option, the seller is not required to have the goods ready at the port of shipment for the entire period. His only obligation is to have the goods ready within a reasonable time of the buyer's call for delivery (*ante*, § 449). Here rule 14 of the rules incorporated into the contract imposed on the seller an additional obligation "to have the sugar available to begin loading immediately upon the arrival after proper notice of the ship at the loading port ready to load". Was that a condition, the breach of which gave rise to right of termination? The answer is not simple as the lack of unanimity in their Lordships speeches clearly indicates. Generally time clauses are classified as conditions (unless otherwise agreed) so that the parties know that if performance was delayed they can safely enter into a substitute transaction, and this rule clearly promotes certainty. This is generally true where a specific date for performance is fixed. In *The Naxos* the position was that once 14 days' notice had been given by the buyers and the ship had arrived, the sellers' failure to have the cargo ready was a breach. Of this there could be no doubt. But what was the effect of this breach? The majority agreed with the buyers' contention in view of the utmost importance attached to the provision, *i.e.* because of the commercial significance of the term in question. Whereas Lord Brandon, in his dissenting opinion, relied on the intention of the parties. In his view other time stipulations in the contract were not conditions, *e.g.*, the fact that delay in loading only resulted in damages and the seller was bound to make, and the buyer to take delivery of the balance of the contract quantity contrary to the normal rule applicable to f.o.b. contracts. Lord Brandon regarded it as "illogical" to classify two obligations, the breach of which would cause delay in loading the ship as warranties, but a third, which would have a similar effect, as a condition. Interestingly, neither Lord Ackner (for the majority) nor Lord Brandon (in his dissent) even alluded to the existence of intermediate or innominate terms. But since this was not an issue, this silence cannot be taken to have put that "vital tertuim Quid" in doubt.[25]

Ancillary obligations of the seller

460   After the ship nominated has arrived, the seller must place on board goods answering the description of the contract in all respects. It is his duty to see to it that the goods are adequately packed, are carefully loaded (or to be more precise delivered to the ship's rail) and are in a proper and fit condition for their sea transit as the circumstances may warrant. *A. Hamson & Sons (London) Ltd. v. S. Martin Johnson & Co. Ltd.*[26] furnishes a good illustration

---

[25] See Treitel, *ante*, n. 21.
[26] [1953] 1 Lloyd's Rep. 553.

of the foregoing principle. The dispute raised the question of responsibility for damage caused by radiators that had not been drained to a consignment of tractors shipped during the cold weather. Jones J. held that normally this would have been the responsibility of the f.o.b. seller. However, in the present case, the evidence showed that the radiators were not drained because of instructions by the buyer's representative. Consequently, the sellers could not there be made to suffer the loss caused.

461 *Packing*. In so far as the provision of adequate packing is concerned, although the definition of the Institute of Export nowhere mentions such an obligation on part of the seller, it is probably to be implied from the fact that the goods are bought on f.o.b. terms with a seaborne voyage in mind. The omission by the Institute of Export from specifically mentioning any such duty may be due to any one of a number of reasons. Possibly because the contract will normally contain some specification relating to the particular type of packing to be provided to enable the seller to estimate the cost thereof in advance, and to adjust the price if necessary. But it may also be due to the particular type of f.o.b. contract to which the "strict" definition is most applicable. This may also explain the omission to mention certain other ancillary obligations such as the duty to provide the buyer with information enabling him to insure the goods.[27]

462 Since the obligation to provide packing adequate to the nature of the goods and the contemplated journey is designed to minimise the risks to which the goods may be exposed by virtue of their seaborne voyage, the seller must normally bear the responsibility for any loss or damage caused by defective or unsuitable packing.[28] Such losses may include expenses suffered from prolonged unloading as was the case in respect to cement bags shipped from India which had opened during unloading.[29] Whether a further obligation exists whereby the seller warrants that the goods will not deteriorate in transit and arrive at their destination in a merchantable condition in the event of no abnormal risk being encountered is less clear.[30] Thus for example, according to the Draft Standard Form of Contract for Sale of Consumer Goods on F.O.B./F.A.S. Basis, prepared for the Asian-African Legal Consultative Committee (1972) by Mr. S. S. Basnayak, Joint Rapporteur, the seller must only "deliver the goods in packing that is reasonably sufficient to prevent damage to or deterioration of the goods during transit assuming the packages are properly handled." The commentary to this provision expressly states that:

---

[27] See *post*, § 627.
[28] See, *e.g. George Wills & Sons Ltd. v. T. Brown & Sons and Ors.* (1922) 12 Ll.L.Rep. 292; *Sime, Derby & Co. Ltd. v. Everitt* (1923) 14 Ll.L.Rep. 120; *Board of Trade (Minister of Materials) v. Steel Bros. & Co. Ltd.* [1952] 1 Lloyd's Rep. 87. The carrier normally assumes no responsibility with respect to damage arising from inadequate packing since he can claim that it was caused by the "inherent vice" of the goods.
[29] See *Kollerich & Cie S.A. v. The State Trading Corp. of India* [1979] 2 Lloyd's Rep. 442.
[30] See *ante*, § 319.

"while an obligation on the seller to ensure that the packing is sufficient to prevent damage to the goods during transit is fair, it is a moot question whether an obligation to provide packing sufficient to prevent deterioration is not too stringent on the seller. Deterioration might occur in a number of unforeseeable ways, including natural process."

However, even if such a stringent condition is to be implied (and it is thought that normally it would not) the seller cannot be held liable for any deterioration in transit when the buyer's specifications as to the mode of the transit are the cause of the damage. Thus, where turnips were sold f.o.b. a shipping point in Ontario to be shipped to British Columbia "standard heat and vent," and on arrival had so deteriorated as to make them unfit for human consumption, the Ontario High Court upheld the seller's claim for the price on two grounds. First, because under an f.o.b. contract the transit is at the risk of the buyer, and, second, because the evidence showed that the damage resulted from the turnips having been shipped under standard heat and ventilation in accordance with buyer's instructions who disregarded the seller's suggestion that they be protected through waxing.[31]

Returning to the question of packing, the importance which ought to be attached thereto should not be minimised. This is so because insurers often succeed in avoiding liability for damage caused by inadequate packing on the grounds that the proximate cause of the damage in these cases is the inherent vice of the subject-matter insured to which the exception in section 55(2)(c) of the Marine Insurance Act 1906 applies.[32]

463 *Loading.*[33] As to the duty of loading, under the strict interpretation (and, absent an express stipulation or custom to the contrary probably under the other variants of the f.o.b. contract also), the sellers' responsibility for the goods terminates at the time of their passing the ship's rail.[34] Consequently, the cost of stowage, trimming, tallying and such other similar incidental expenses are for the account of the buyer under an f.o.b. contract. As stated by Avory J. in *Attorney-General v. Walford Ltd.*[35]: "I really do not know why all the evidence has been given to satisfy me that the words or letters 'f.o.b.' mean merely that the shipper has to pay the cost to the rail of the ship and has no further liability with regard to stowing or loading." Thus, where the parties desire to allocate expenses differently it is common to stipulate expressly in regard to these costs.

In certain commodity markets, stipulations such as "f.o.b. and stowed or trimmed" are frequently encountered with the intention of shifting the costs

---

[31] *Kelly, Douglas & Co. Ltd. v. Pollock* (1958) 14 D.L.R. (2d) 526.
[32] *Cf. Berk (F. W.) & Co. Ltd. v. Style* [1956] 1 Q.B. 180.
[33] See *post*, § 572.
[34] *Ante*, § 442: Institute of Export—definition of seller's obligations § 4.
[35] (1923) 14 Ll.L. Rep. 359 at p. 361.

connected therewith from buyer to seller.[36] In *Minex v. International Trading Company of Virginia v. SS Eirini, ex SS. Acgina and Oth.*,[37] a decision of the U.S. District Court, E. D. Virginia, the terms of the contract were "f.o.b. stowed Polish port." The cargo which was the subject matter of the sale, cement bags, had suffered some contamination, and the buyer contended that pursuant to the said clause the seller had a duty to make certain that the holds of the vessel were clean and fit for the reception of the cargo which they alleged the seller had failed to do attributing the contamination to this failure. This contention was rejected by the court which stated that under the agreement in question the seller:

> "had the duty to load and stow, but not the duty to clean, sweep and dry the holds, deck beams, etc. . . . The term 'stowed' merely gives emphasis to the . . . obligation under the contract. Clearly it would not have been sufficient to merely dump the bags of cement on the open deck. It required stowage under deck 'in an orderly compact manner'[38] and 'in such a manner as to protect the goods from friction, bruising, or damage from leakage.'"[39]

Two older cases[40] establish the principle that the buyer is to be furnished with documentary evidence of performance, namely, a receipt by the carrier that the goods have been received on board in apparent good order and condition. This will normally be a bill of lading, but since the "strict" definition apparently assumes the buyer to be the shipper of the goods,[41] the omission to mention any such duty on part of the seller in some of the standard definitions of the f.o.b. term may not be due to oversight. If the buyer requires additional or supplemental evidence such as certificates of origin, weight or quality, then, unless these are customarily provided in a particular trade, an express stipulation providing therefor would be required. The seller however is probably under a duty to co-operate with the buyer, and to extend such information or assistance as may be necessary to enable the buyer to obtain the necessary documents.[42]

---

[36] See, *e.g. President of India v. Metcalfe Shipping Co.* [1970] 1 Q.B. 289; *David T. Boyd & Co. Ltd. v. Louis Louca* [1973] 1 Lloyd's Rep. 209; *Pagnan & Fratelli v. N. G. J. Schouten N.V. (The Filipinas I)* [1973] 1 Lloyd's Rep. 349. For a case involving f.o.b. stowed interpreting the terms (in relation to the time permitted for loading) of "per workable hatch per day" and "pro rata," see *Cargill Inc. v. Rionda De Pass Ltd. (The Giannis Xilas)* [1982] 2 Lloyd's Rep. 511.

[37] 303 F. Supp. 205 (1969).

[38] Judgment citing Webster, *Third New International Dictionary*, p. 2253.

[39] *Ibid.* at p. 208.

[40] *Jack v. Roberts & Gibson* (1865) 3 M. (Ct. of Sess.) 554 (revised ed., p. 638); *Green v. Sichel & Ors.* (1860) 7 C.B. (N.S.) 747 at p. 754.

[41] See *post*, § 466.

[42] Some f.o.b. contracts provide that the buyer may (normally in the presence of the seller or his representative) satisfy himself as to quality of the shipment by taking samples of the cargo at the port of loading in which case the seller must naturally co-operate if a request for samples is made. See contract discussed in *Mantovani v. Carapelli S.p.A.* [1980] 1 Lloyd's Rep. 375 (C.A.) and see further on certificates of quality *ante*, § 325.

The buyer's duty to comply with the formalities and bear the cost of shipment and export

464   In support of this proposition it is said that the seller is responsible only for services and expenses relating to placing the goods f.o.b. Obligations not connected therewith which, due to administrative regulations or otherwise, may require arrangement before the goods can, in effect, be loaded are not really his concern and thus not for his account or risk. The decisive factor therefore is not the *time* of payment (or compliance with the relevant regulations) but rather a functional test, namely, whether the requirement pertains to the embarkation-delivery phase of the transaction as opposed to the shipment-export aspect thereof. Consequently, an examination of the precise nature of certain expenses such as customs entries and the like incurred in the course of many f.o.b. sales is necessary. The Institute of Export[43] has analysed the relevant provisions of the Customs and Inland Revenue Act 1881,[44] the Port of London Act 1908, and the Port of London (Port Rates on Goods) Provisional Order Act 1910. It concluded that the service charge for passing Customs entries and Port Rates are payable by virtue of the shipment and export of the goods. Since these expenses do not arise from or pertain to the act of delivery f.o.b. they are in the Institute's view the buyer's responsibility, even in cases where a pre-entry is necessary and where payment thereof is due before loading can commence.[45]

465   From the foregoing analysis it is doubtful whether the Institute of Export would concur with the statement of the Association of British Chambers of Commerce that "the legal liability of the seller . . . is that he is responsible for all charges made against the goods until the point of passing the ship's rail.[46] This overriding principle applies according to the Association regardless of any variation resulting from the different customs and usages prevailing in the various United Kingdom ports which may govern the incidence of f.o.b. charges in practice.

466   *Buyer as shipper.* The party named in the ship's manifest as shipper is responsible for the various entries required by the Customs and Excise authorities. The shipper, moreover, is also the party who must satisfy the Port of London Authority's regulations, and on whom the onus for meeting the charges levied in most other U.K. ports falls. Under the "strict" definition, therefore, the buyer is deemed to be the shipper of the goods. Accordingly, the bills of lading will be issued to his order, and performance by the seller

---

[43] 14 *Export* (1951), pp. 211, 212.
[44] Repealed, but now largely contained in ss.53 and 57 of the Customs and Excise Management Act 1979.
[45] *i.e.* in all cases where the goods are subject to Exchange Control Regulations or require an export licence. And of course this reasoning would *a fortiori* apply in cases where a post entry would be sufficient.
[46] *"F.O.B. Vessel"* (January 1971 ed.).

will have to be evidenced by some other document, usually a mate's receipt. This however does not in itself exclude a contractual relationship between the seller and the ship. For, as held by Devlin J. in *Pyrene Co. Ltd. v. Scindia Navigation Co. Ltd.*,[47] the shipowner is still entitled to plead the maximum limits of liability incorporated in the Carriage of Goods by Sea Act, if the goods are damaged by negligence of the shipowner or his servants at a time prior to their being placed f.o.b., namely, before having crossed the ship's rail.[48] In this case, a fire tender was dropped and damaged through the negligence of stevedores employed by the shipowners. The loading had commenced, but the tender had not crossed the ship's rail at the time of the accident. No bill of lading was ever issued, but the shipowners claimed a limitation of liability under the (1924) Act alleging that the transaction under which the goods were shipped was a "contract of carriage covered by a bill of lading" within the meaning of Article 1(b) to the schedule thereof. They succeeded before Devlin J. who held this contention to be correct.[49]

However, the fact that the buyer does assume the status of shipper may confer upon him certain liabilities *vis-à-vis* the ship that, because they are indispensable to the seller's performance and also relate to a time preceding the moment in which the goods actually cross the ship's rail, could be considered to be the seller's responsibility under an f.o.b. contract.

467   *Loading charges.* Although loading has traditionally been regarded as a joint operation of the shipper and shipowner, the division of duties at the ship's rail instead of alongside it has been described as "somewhat out of keeping with modern methods."[50] Moreover, there is nothing to prevent the parties from altering their respective responsibilities, as was stated by the House of Lords in *Renton (G. H.) Co. Ltd. v. Palmyra Trading Corporation of Panama*,[51] where Devlin J.'s dictum to this effect in the *Pyrene* case[52] was endorsed with approval. Either by virtue of some usage, course of dealing, or as a result of an express agreement, the buyer may consequently be charged with the cost of certain operations (loading and stevedoring for example) which are normally considered to be the seller's or the ship's responsibility.

468   For example, it has been stated that in the port of Bristol: "The point to which the shipper bears the charges depends upon the customs of the various shipping companies' conferences. Some conferences bear charges for part of the shore work out of the freight".[53] Similarly in the port of Glasgow the

---

[47] [1954] 2 Q.B. 402.
[48] See *post*, § 577.
[49] *Cf.* however *Scruttons Ltd. v. Midland Silicones Ltd.* [1962] A.C. 446 reasserting in full vigour the doctrine of privity of contract.
[50] See *Scrutton on Charterparties* (19th ed.), p. 169, n. 3.
[51] [1957] A.C. 149.
[52] [1954] 2 Q.B. 402 at p. 417.
[53] *"F.O.B. Vessel"* (January 1971 ed.).

following charges are said to be for the ship's account: "(i) Delivery from transit shed to alongside vessel; (ii) Making up slings and (iii) Hooking up and hoisting to rail of vessel"[54] all of which are presumably recompensed for by means of the freight. So that when the question arose as to whether a loading broker entered into any independent contractual relationship with the shipper (other than as agent of the shipowner) in the port of Liverpool, Devlin J. answered it in the negative in *Heskell v. Continental Express Ltd.*[55] He stated that:

> "the dock-owner who actually received the goods for shipment at No. 9 shed was the servant or agent of the shipowners to receive and handle them. He was paid for his services by the shipowners through their loading brokers, and, no doubt, the shipowner recouped themselves by means of the freight. Accordingly, in the circumstances of this case . . ., I think that the contract of carriage would normally be made when the goods were delivered at No. 9 shed and accepted there by the ship's agents, and that there would be no need for the shipper to take any further steps. There is, therefore, no need to assume that in supervising the handling and loading of the goods the loading brokers were discharging any duty towards the shipper."

469   *Glengarnock Iron & Steel Co. Ltd. v. Cooper & Co.*[56] furnishes an excellent illustration of the application of this principle to f.o.b. contracts. In that case, the buyer of goods f.o.b., who had chartered the vessel, claimed a reduction in the price of the contract equal to the amount paid by him for labour engaged in loading. In dismissing this claim, Lord Trayner said:

> "The counsel for the [buyers] argued, as far as I could follow him, as the only ground on which he could maintain this claim for deduction, that this was a contract 'free on board,' and that unless the deduction was allowed him we would be drawing no distinction between the contract f.o.b. and the contract f.a.s.[57] Now, I have been for a good many years very familiar with both these contracts, and I never heard until today that it was a distinction between these two contracts that in the one case a shipper was bound to pay the expense of shipment, and that in the other case he was not. The distinction between the two contracts is not very far to seek . . . The point of delivery under the two contracts is different, and the consequent risks and the necessary insurance to cover those risks may be very different . . . the risk in the one case lying upon one party, and in the other upon the other party; but as regards the question which is to be at the expense of putting the cargo on board, there is not any difference which I have heard between the one contract and the other. . . .[58]

Similarly, in *Meyer et al. v. Sullivan et al.*[59] Waste P. J. likewise commented with respect to the practice at the port of Seattle:

---

[54] *Ibid.*
[55] [1950] 1 All E.R. 1033 at p. 1041.
[56] (1895) 22 R. (Ct. of Sess.) 672.
[57] Free alongside ship.
[58] At pp. 675–676. Where extra charges for the loading of particularly heavy goods are imposed, the difference between the f.o.b. and f.a.s. terms is, however, significant. See Preciado, *Exporting to the World* (1921), pp. 144–145.
[59] 181 Pac. 847 at p. 849 (1919).

> "The witnesses on the part of the defendants testified as to the use of the terms
> f.o.b. and 'f.a.s.' (free-along-side) in contracts. The evidence discloses that con-
> tracts might be made, between buyer and seller, using either of those terms. . . .
> In both f.a.s. sales and f.o.b. sales, however, the seller of the goods pays the cost
> of all handling on the dock; and the cost of stevedoring, or transferring the cargo
> from the dock to the ship, is paid and absorbed by the shipowner from the freight,
> which in turn is paid by the buyer. The only [*sic!*] distinction between the two
> kinds of sales appears to be as to the time when the responsibility of the seller
> ends. In the case of f.a.s. sales, it seems to end with delivery on the dock. In the
> case of f.o.b. sales, the responsibility of the seller appears to end when the com-
> modity is on board ship. The element of cost, to either buyer or seller, does not
> appear to enter into the matter at all."

470   In *Blandy Brothers & Co. Lda. v. Nello Simoni Ltd.*,[60] the buyer appears
to have similarly failed in his attempt to enforce a claim for the recovery of
stevedoring charges. It was there held that the buyer did not discharge the
burden of proving an alleged usage at the Port of Funchal in the island of
Madeira according to which the cost of stevedoring and stowing should not
be for his account as charterer of the vessel. Nevertheless, regardless of
whether the cost of loading is borne by him, the seller is probably under a
duty to ensure skilful and careful loading of the goods, as the circumstances
of the case may warrant.[61]

Usages may also operate to the disadvantage of the seller. Thus, for
example, it is stated that the custom in the Port of Liverpool:

> "is that, under a Liverpool f.o.b. contract, the seller of the goods f.o.b. is
> responsible for the goods until placed on board the vessel; included in that
> responsibility is the payment of carriage to Liverpool, as also cartage, haulage,
> and lighterage, and wharf handling charges applied by certain conferences
> according to the method of delivery employed. The seller is moreover respons-
> ible for the payment of Dock and Town Dues and (in the absence of agreement
> to the contrary) the service charge for passing of Customs Entries."[62]

471   A party claiming the benefit of a usage must not only support his claim by
furnishing satisfactory evidence as to its existence (and wide and regular
acceptance) but must also establish that it is not repugnant or inconsistent
with the f.o.b. term generally. Where courts have declined to give effect to
an alleged usage because of lack of sufficient evidence, they have sometimes
added that in any event the usage would be of no avail because it could not
be reconciled with the f.o.b. term. This, for instance, was the case in Australia
in *W. Siemon & Sons Ltd. v. Samuel Allen & Sons Ltd.*[63] where the Supreme
Court of Queensland held that the buyer who had chartered the vessel must
succeed in a claim against the seller for recovery of a sum expended for
stacking and transferring a cargo of maize from a wharf where it was received

---

[60] [1963] 2 Lloyd's Rep. 24, 31; affirmed *ibid.* 393 (C. A.).
[61] See *A. Hamson & Son (London) Ltd. v. S. Martin Johnson & Co. Ltd.* [1953] 1 Lloyd's Rep.
553, *ante*, § 460.
[62] *"F.O.B. Vessel"* (January 1971 ed.).
[63] [1925] Q.S.R. 269 (Australia).

to the ship's slings. The seller's allegation that these operations were for the account of the ship by virtue of the usage at the port of loading, Brisbane, was not sustained on appeal. It was there held that the seller did not discharge his burden of proving the usage, and that even if he had met this requirement it would be to no avail since any such usage would be in conflict with the contract being on f.o.b. terms.

472   On the basis of the foregoing analysis, it has been concluded that shipping permits, dock and harbour dues and rates, export duties or licences, and any similar charges, fees and permits, where applicable, though matters which would normally have to be taken care of prior to the time in which the goods can be loaded, are the responsibility of the f.o.b. buyer. They relate not to the delivery on board but to a later phase of the transaction, namely, the shipment and export of the goods. This principle is borne out by the following passage from Scrutton L.J.'s opinion in *H. O. Brandt & Co. v. H. N. Morris & Co.*[64] in which the question arose as to whose duty it was to secure an export licence for goods to be shipped f.o.b. where he said:

> "The buyers must provide an effective ship, that is to say, a ship which can legally carry the goods. When the buyers have done that the sellers have to put the goods on board the ship. If that is so, the obtaining of a licence to export is the buyers' concern. It is their concern to have the ship sent out of the country after the goods have been put on board and the fact that . . . a prohibition against export includes a prohibition against bringing the goods on to any quay or other place to be shipped for exportation does not cast a duty of obtaining the licence on the sellers. Bringing the goods on to the quay is merely subsidiary to the export which is the gist of the licence."

473   The division of responsibilities as set out above is, however, often found to be unsuitable. The Institute of Export (*loc. cit. ante*) has stated that "there can be no variation in the interpretation of the term f.o.b.," and that absent an express agreement to the contrary,[65] circumstances or usages which require variation therein are to be regarded as mere concessions "since they are not based upon the legal interpretation of the term f.o.b." This statement is probably too rigid and misleading, and it is suggested that the f.o.b. term must always be interpreted in the light of surrounding circumstances. Since courts must give effect to the intention of the parties, commercial reasonableness and practice (from which the intention may be implied) must be considered before a conclusion based on, or derived from, a dogmatic interpretation of the term f.o.b. is enforced. F.o.b. contracts cannot be divorced from mercantile reality and surrounding circumstances, and it is wrong to cast them in so

---

[64] [1917] 2 K.B. 784 at p. 798, considered *post*, § 485.
[65] There has already been occasion to mention clauses such as "f.o.b. and stowed or trimmed" which shift certain of the buyers' responsibilities to the seller. Another clause which is frequently used is one placing on the seller the responsibility for the cost and risk of damage to goods "until they have been placed *actually* on board the vessel." See, *e.g.* in *President of India v. Metcalfe Shipping Co. Ltd.* [1969] 2 Q.B. 123; aff'd. [1970] 1 Q.B. 289 (C.A.).

rigid a mould by employing a mechanical test in every case. For example, the customs of the trade or the usage at the port of loading are, as already noted, factors that cannot be disregarded when the respective obligations of the parties are to be determined. And there are other factors, hereinafter discussed, which may similarly pertain to this question. It is submitted, therefore, that, where the circumstances surrounding the sale render the "strict" interpretation unsuitable or commercially impracticable, it may be inferred that the parties have agreed to modify their relative obligations accordingly.[66]

Internal and external sales

474 F.o.b. terms are found both in domestic contracts as well as in contracts for the export of goods. Under a domestic contract (hereafter sometimes referred to as an "internal sale"), goods are sold by a local manufacturer to a local merchant. Though the latter may order the goods for the purpose of an immediate resale to a foreign buyer, the contract is between two residents of the same country. Both parties are generally within easy access to the point of shipment, and neither is disqualified from undertaking the domestic formalities that shipment and export entails. The seller may be unaware of the overseas destination of the goods. Since there is no presumption of export in the mere offer to sell f.o.b. (although the exporter is well advised to put the manufacturer on notice of the contemplated resale abroad in order that he may claim any "loss of profit" in case of default, and in order to remove any doubts as to the duty to provide packing adequate to the oversea journey), he may legitimately allege that the purpose for which the exporter requires the goods is of no concern to him.[67] In other words, that all the responsibilities and any costs arising from the export and shipment of the goods are a direct result of an independent contract (*viz.*, the resale by the exporter), but for which they would not have arisen and to which, since he is no party, he can bear no liability. Moreover, in the event of a resale by the exporter, the manufacturer normally cannot even comply with some of the required formalities. For example, the manufacturer, who does not know at what price the goods have been resold, would be forced to make a false entry where it his duty to make the necessary customs declarations.

475 It seems fairly clear that in the case of internal sales the "strict" devision of responsibilities normally causes no undue hardship for either party. No doubt these are the typical circumstances in which this interpretation applies.[68] Indeed, it seems fairly clear that it is this type of transaction that underlies the Institute of Export's definition of the f.o.b. term. This may be

---

[66] See *ante*, § 434.

[67] See, *e.g. McMaster & Co. v. Cox, McEuen & Co.* 1921 S.C.(H.L.) 24, *post*, § 488.

[68] See Davies, "The Various Types of F.O.B. Contract" [1957] 3 *Business Law Review* 256 at p. 270. See also correspondence in *Export* (February 1950), p. 51.

concluded from the imposition of the duty to obtain an export licence on the f.o.b. buyer, and from the omission of any reference to a duty on the part of the seller either to (i) furnish the buyer with information such as will enable him to insure the goods during their sea transit, or (ii) bear the onus and cost of passing the necessary customs entry, or (iii) to provide adequate packing of the goods in a manner suitable to a seaborne voyage. The former obligation arises from section 32(3) of the Sale of Goods Act and does in principle govern f.o.b. contracts,[69] though it is applicable only "where goods are sent by the seller to the buyer by a route involving sea transit" which would not be the normal way of performing an internal f.o.b. contract. As to the latter obligation, it may perhaps be contested by the supplier where the ultimate destination of the goods has not been disclosed by the exporter who has bought them for resale to a client abroad. Both of these obligations and also the sellers' (rather than buyer's) obligation to obtain an export licence (where necessary) are expressly mentioned in most of the other proposed definitions of the f.o.b. term, for example, in "Incoterms"[70] which have been drafted with primary reference to external sales. The factors which must be taken into account in considering external sales differ however from those earlier related. The contract is between parties who are residents of different, and normally far apart, localities.

476 The overseas buyer is usually unable to arrange the necessary formalities connected with the shipment or export of the goods without employing an agent at the shipping point. Where export licences and customs formalities are considered, it is often virtually impossible for the foreign importer to act in person. Because the amount of work and expense involved is relatively small, the exporter frequently undertakes to meet some (or all) of these requirements. Moreover, the exporter is usually less willing to part with his interest in the goods before the purchase price (or adequate security thereof) is tendered. The reluctance of the manufacturer in the internal sale is generally more easily overcome and for the following reasons: first, he is better acquainted with the export merchant's financial and business integrity and, secondly, the (defaulting) buyer is always within the jurisdiction of the English courts, and the seller thus faces fewer complications in attempting to enforce his rights in the event of breach.[71] Consequently, the exporter normally procures the bill of lading and thereby maintains effective control over the goods until payment is made or assured. Where payment is arranged through a documentary letter of credit, as it normally will be in external sales, (see *post*, §§ 612 *et seq.*) the bill of lading must usually be procured in order to satisfy the terms of the credit. By procuring the bill of lading the seller renders himself responsible to the administrative authorities with regard to

---

[69] See *post*, § 662.
[70] A. 2 and A. 5, *post*, § 511.
[71] See *ante*, § 382, and *post*, § 731 with respect to the rules applying to jurisdiction over foreign defendants.

the shipment and export of the goods (see *ante,* § 466). In interpreting the
f.o.b. term, contemplation of export and the special implications which arise
from the buyer's foreign residence, must therefore be considered. For
although the symbol has the same basic meaning as under the "strict" interpretation, the apportionment of responsibilities may be different. In the words
of clause 13.1 of the standard form of F.O.B. Contracts for the Sale of Cereals,[72] the apportionment of responsibilities under an external f.o.b. contract
in the cereal trade may mean that:

> "All taxes, duties, fees and charges whatsoever relating to the conclusion and
> fulfilment of the contract shall be paid by the seller when they are levied in the
> seller's country, in the country of origin of the goods or in the country of ship-
> ment, and by the buyer when they are levied in the buyer's country or in the
> country of destination of the goods. All taxes, duties, fees and charges whatso-
> ever levied upon the freight shall be paid by the buyer."

"Additional services" variant (seller as shipper and exporter)

477 Over a century ago Lord Brougham stated in *Cowas-jee* v. *Thompson
Kebble*[73] that

> "It is proved beyond doubt, indeed it is not denied that when goods are sold in
> London 'free on board' the cost of shipping them falls on the seller but the buyer
> is considered as the shipper."

But this proposition does not meet all f.o.b. contracts. In cases where the
seller obtains the bills of lading, he and not the buyer is the shipper. Brett
M.R. stated that in *Stock v. Inglis*[74] when we said: "... the words 'free on
board,' according to the general understanding of merchants ... mean ...
that the shipper was to put them on board at his expense. ..."

It has therefore been said that:

> "in writing about the responsibilities of the parties to a f.o.b. contract, most
> authorities mention only the buyer and the seller, but it is suggested that a
> notional third party—the shipper—has duties to perform and expenses to bear.
> The shipper's duties and expenses have to be borne either by the seller or by the
> buyer, depending on the contract."[75]

Where the f.o.b. term appears in an external sale usually the seller is the
shipper.

478 Indeed the Association of British Chambers of Commerce admitted that
the nature of the transaction determines the liability for customs entries and

---

[72] Nos. 5A and 5B drawn under the auspices of the United Nations Economic Commission for
Europe.
[73] (1845) 5 Moore 165 at pp. 173, 174; see *post*, § 708.
[74] (1884) 12 Q.B.D. 564 at p. 573, *ante*, § 437.
[75] Davis, "The various Types of F.O.B. Contract" [1957] 3 *Business Law Review* 256 at p.258.

port charges, which, it will be recalled, is for account of the shipper. In practice, therefore, the issue is seldom resolved by mere reference to the f.o.b. term. The Association has accordingly drawn attention to the following distinction between internal and external f.o.b. contracts.

> "There is some confusion as to who bears the onus of passing Customs Entries. As H.M. Customs stipulate that the value to be declared to them is the final f.o.b. price chargeable to the buyer abroad, it follows that the Customs Entry must be made by the person who charges that price; so that a manufacturer selling direct f.o.b. to a customer abroad would have the onus of passing Customs Entry, but if he sells to a shipper who in turn is selling abroad, then the onus of passing Customs Entry lies with the shipper, and not with the manufacturing supplier."[76]

479   So, too, with respect to the custom in the Port of London, it is stated that:

> "It must be clearly understood that the ultimate seller—which is interpreted as the person who sells f.o.b. to a buyer overseas—is not necessarily the f.o.b. supplier of the goods. The only person who can pass the Customs Entry is the ultimate seller of the goods as he is the only one competent to quote the sales value to the overseas customer."[77]

The statement goes on to discuss the question of London Port Rates as follows:

> "The position is that they become payable upon export of the goods and are not payable in consequence of the goods being placed on board the ship. Therefore, the seller is responsible only for the charges incurred in placing the goods on the vessel. It is known, however, that there is in existence a fairly extensive practice under which the seller pays the Port Rates.
>   In order to avoid the possibility of any dispute as to the responsibility for the payment of Port Rates, the Chamber recommends that when it is desired that the Port Rates should be included in an f.o.b. transaction, the point should be covered in contracts or orders by the adoption of such a phrase as 'f.o.b. (including London Port Rules).'"

Whereas by the Custom at the Port of Belfast:

> "For goods shipped direct by *foreign going vessel*, the party selling f.o.b. Belfast is responsible for delivering the goods to the shed nominated by the Shipping Company and usually liable for the cost of Customs, Bill of Lading, and Harbour Due charges."[78]

480   Where payment calls for the presentation of bills of lading or shipping documents or where other terms indicating that the seller is to procure the bills of lading are stipulated, the inference is that he will assume the status

---

[76] *"F.O.B. Vessel"* (January 1971 ed.).
[77] *Ibid.*
[78] *Ibid.*

of shipper and the costs and responsibilities associated therewith. Accordingly, in *The Tromp*,[79] Duke P. held that, since the contract there provided for delivery f.o.b. Gothenburg payment against bills of lading, the sellers, and not the buyers, were in the circumstances to be regarded as the principals of the shippers. The buyers were therefore entitled to succeed in their claim against the carrier who, having been furnished with an indemnity by the shippers, agreed to misrepresent the condition of the goods upon delivery and issue clean bills of lading notwithstanding their defective appearance. It may be mentioned that although provisions calling for payment against bills of lading are normally associated with external sales they are commonly found in the case of internal sales also.

As already noted in some of the older cases, a usage was even established whereby the seller is under a duty to procure the bills of lading or some other document which furnishes evidence of the goods actually being placed on board.[80] It would therefore seem that, unless a contrary intention is apparent, the responsibilities and functions of shipper fall within the scope of the seller's performance in external sales. Although the Institute of Export maintains that departures from the "strict" interpretation are to be regarded as mere concessions, neither practice nor authority lend this statement much support. Where the seller acts as shipper, the cost of port rates and custom entries, and any expenses incurred on account of lodging the bills of lading themselves, are normally borne by him. He is well advised therefore to take the cost thereof into account in determining his f.o.b. price. Yet "it is no part of his duty to pay for the carriage, and the bill of lading he will get will usually be a 'freight collect' one. The freight is then collected from the foreign importer."[81] Should the carrier refuse to consent to freight collect terms then, absent any agreement to the contrary, the seller is normally under no responsibility, mandate, or implied authority, to extend freight on behalf of the buyer. An alleged usage to the effect that the seller is under a duty to prepay the freight was not recognised in *Green v. Sichel & Ors.*,[82] which, though over 100 years old, would still appear to reflect the commercial understanding of the f.o.b. term. Dismissing a claim by the buyer who alleged that the seller had failed to perform his f.o.b. contract, Erle C.J. stated:

"The only contest, therefore, between the parties was, whether, besides putting the goods on board, it was the duty of the vendor, under the contract of sale, to procure the bill of lading, and to prepay the freight, at all events if that should be necessary in order to obtain the bill of lading. But the jury have found, in answer to the second question put to them, that the [sellers] did not undertake to pay freight. . . ."

---

[79] [1921] P. 337.
[80] See, *e.g. Jack v. Roberts & Gibson* (1865) 3 M. (Ct. of Sess.) 554 (revised ed., p. 638); *Green v. Sichel & Ors.* (1860) 7 C.B.(N.S.) 747 at p. 754.
[81] See Syrett, *Finance of Overseas Trade* (2nd ed., 1949), pp. 25–26.
[82] (1860) 7 C.B.(N.S.) 747 at p. 754.

Time of presentation of shipping documents

480a Where the f.o.b. seller assumes the role of shipper, and the bill of lading is issued to him must he, like the c.i.f. seller (*ante*, § 242), tender the documents promptly to the buyer (which, depending on the circumstances, may nevertheless not precede the arrival of the goods at their intended destination), or is the rule otherwise? This question arose in *Concordia Trading B.V. v. Richo International Ltd.*,[83] where the buyers' disputed this proposition, with respect to f.o.b. contracts arguing there was no default until such time as the documents ceased to be marketable, and not earlier. It was Evans J.'s view that:

> "there is good reason . . . why the correct inference in the case of f.o.b. contracts should be derived from what is 'mercantiley reasonable' in these contracts rather than from a direct application of the c.i.f. rule. The contracts are of different kinds, and the analogy is not so close that a straight transfer should be made.
>
> "Nevertheless, there are compelling reasons why, in my judgment, the duty imposed on the f.o.b. seller should be to the same effect as has been established in the case of c.i.f. sales. The f.o.b. seller is required to obtain shipping documents and to tender them to the buyer, and the buyer is obliged to make payment against documents. . . . In the normal case, although the goods have been shipped on a vessel nominated by the buyer, the seller for his own protection will have reserved the right of disposing of the goods, as unpaid seller, and the bill of lading will require delivery to him or to his order. . . . So far as 'mercantile reasonableness' is concerned, I cannot see any reason why the f.o.b. seller should not be required to tender the documents forthwith. Neither party suggests that there is no duty, or that the seller can retain the documents indefinitely. The only reason for holding on to them is that he might have some intention of controlling the date of default, in the event of non-payment, in a way which appears advantageous to him. There is, on the other hand, an overwhelming weight of reasons, practical as well as ones of legal principle, why he should perform rather than delay performance of the contract. Not least, the buyer may want the documents promptly, rather than having to wait until the vessel discharges or is about to discharge the goods. Moreover, the more emphasis that is placed on the fact that the buyer has nominated and is in control of the ship, the more it seems to me that the seller has placed the goods on board that ship in a capacity which is analagous to that of agent for the buyer. . . . As such, he may be under a duty . . . of acting promptly and with reasonable regard to the buyer's interests." (at pp. 478–479.)

The rule therefore is that there rests on an f.o.b. seller, who is obliged by his contract to obtain and tender shipping documents, a duty to perform that obligation forthwith, that is to say, with all reasonable despatch, subject of course to any express provision or time limit which the contract may contain. For all practical purposes this duty is commensurate with that which rests upon the c.i.f. seller.

In the *Concordia* dispute the test was most difficult to apply since there was a series of contracts forming a circular string (including the sepervening insolvency of one of the parties), and the buyers were the original shippers.

---

[83] [1991] 1 Lloyd's Rep. 475.

Nevertheless, this did not, in Evans J.'s view, alter the general rule. There was need to take account of the time required for the documents to pass through several hands, but except for this allowance the general rule governed, and this meant that the duty was more stringent than that of merely passing on the documents as soon as they were received by the seller because he could not claim allowances for any previous breach (of the timely transfer of documents) which he may have suffered. The date of default was the day following the last date of performance of the obligation to tender the documents "forthwith".

Form of bills of lading

481   Where the seller assumes the role of shipper it is his duty, subject to any express specification contained in the contract, to procure and tender bills of lading in the "terms usual in the trade,"[84] namely, as may be customary in the circumstances of the case. These would then also normally constitute prima facie evidence of performance and delivery f.o.b. Since a "received for shipment" bill of lading does not acknowledge the goods to be on board at all it is not usually a good tender under a f.o.b. contract. Such a bill furnishes no proof of the date of goods being placed on board nor of the loading on any particular vessel, and its acceptance, moreover, would normally imply that the risk (and property) in the goods has been transferred prior to the goods having crossed the ship's rail (*post*, § 592). Section 2–323(1) of the American Uniform Commercial Code accordingly stipulates that "where the contract contemplates overseas shipment and contains a term ... f.o.b. vessel, the seller unless otherwise agreed must obtain a negotiable bill of lading stating that the goods have been loaded on board." The right of an f.o.b. seller to tender a "received for shipment" bill of lading was considered in *Yelo v. S. M. Machado & Co. Ltd.*[85] where the sellers alleged that they were entitled to satisfy the terms of a credit, and tender received for shipment bills by virtue of a trade custom. Sellers J. held that the burden of proof was not discharged and pronounced himself as follows with respect to this problem in general:

> "The plaintiff adduced evidence that 'Received for shipment' bills of lading were frequently used by shipowners whose vessels were chartered to carry fruit from the Spanish ports concerned ... I do not regard this evidence as establishing ... that for an f.o.b. shipment a 'Received for shipment' bill of lading was customarily accepted in the trade between the ports involved. It would, in my opinion, require strong evidence of an agreement, express or to be implied, to supplant the requirement of a 'Shipped' bill of lading in an f.o.b. contract where the seller undertook to find the ship. The date of shipment in this contract was vital, as it would normally be in an f.o.b. contract, and a 'Received for shipment'

---

[84] Devlin J. in *Pyrene Co. Ltd. v. Scindia Navigation Co.* [1954] 2 Q.B. 402.
[85] [1952] 1 Lloyd's Rep. 181.

bill of lading, unless specially indorsed with the date of shipment, is of itself no evidence of the date when the goods were put on board and acknowledged so to be by the shipowner.''

482   When payment is arranged through a documentary credit,[86] banking requirements and practice are also pertinent. In *Enrico Furst & Co. v. W. E. Fischer Ltd.*[87] Diplock J. held, on the evidence there submitted, that where a credit calls for payment against bills of lading, it is not satisfied by bills of lading signed by forwarding agents[88] nor by bills of lading claused to incorporate the terms of a charterparty. He added that he did not wish to comment upon the question whether these would constitute a good tender as between parties to an f.o.b. contract since this question was irrelevant to the dispute before him. His lordship was solely concerned, he said, with the terms on which the letter of credit was to be opened, and banking practice was the only relevant consideration in seeing what that meant. However, since it is the buyer's duty to make the necessary shipping arrangements in f.o.b. contracts, and, even where undertaken by the seller, it is only as agent of the buyer (see *post*, § 513), the f.o.b. buyer, it is thought, could normally not reject a bill of lading incorporating the terms of a charterparty, and the fact that the bank may refuse it under a documentary credit (if such was the agreed mode of payment) could be immaterial. The situation, of course, would be different where the seller was instructed not to ship under such terms. The *Furst* decision further makes clear that banks do not attach importance to the abbreviation "S.S.,"[89] in relation to instructions with respect to the form of the bill of lading against which they are to make payment. Provided the bill did not refer to the terms of any charterparty (*post*, § 483), it was immaterial whether the vessel was under charter, as the seller erroneously presumed this abbreviation to imply in the case above referred to, or was a regular liner. Although Diplock J. did not mention it, bankers (as well as buyers) also require clean bills of lading.[90] In other words, bills which contain no express declaration that the condition of the goods or their packaging was defective upon receipt.[91] Such a bill constitutes a representation that a reasonable inspection has revealed no defect in the goods so as to make the carrier liable for any damage which has not been excepted. Clearly, the seller is in default if he has tendered defective goods or inadequately packed ones, and it may therefore be concluded, at least as a general

---

[86] See generally *post*, § 612.
[87] [1960] 2 Lloyd's Rep. 340 at p. 346.
[88] For this would jeopardise the security of the bill.
[89] Steamship bill of lading.
[90] As to clean bills of lading generally see *The Problem of Clean Bills of Lading*, ICC publication No. 223 (1963). See also cases cited *post*, § 619.
[91] See *per* Salmon J. in *British Imex Industries Ltd. v. Midland Bank Ltd.* [1958] 1 Q.B. 542. The term is sometimes loosely used to describe "below deck" bills of lading also, namely bills of lading that do not contain a valid liberty to carry goods on deck.

proposition, that he is in default to the buyer where the carrier issues an unclean bill of lading.

483   *Relation of charterparty to bill of lading.* Where the seller acts as shipper, and the goods are dispatched on a vessel chartered by the buyer, questions have sometimes arisen as to which document embodies the contract of carriage between the carrier and the buyer. The question can be of considerable importance because the terms of the charterparty are sometimes inconsistent with or different from the terms of the bills of lading issued thereunder[92] and also because the body of one of these instruments is frequently incorporated by reference into the other. It has long been held that where the seller merely acts as agent of the buyer in procuring shipment under an f.o.b. contract, then the charterparty will be deemed to be the governing document as between the buyer (charterer) and the shipowner. The bill of lading which the seller will procure in such a case will be construed as a mere receipt and document of title for the goods but will not affect or alter the contractual provisions of the charterparty if inconsistent therewith.[93] Until recently, however, the position was less clear in situations where the seller was held to have reserved a right of property in the goods. In these circumstances, it was sometimes thought that since the seller could not be considered to be acting merely in a capacity of an agent of the buyer for purposes of procuring the bill of lading, any subsequent transfer of the bill of lading to the buyer (which would normally occur on payment of the purchase price) would alter the terms of the contract of carriage embodied in the charterparty in favour of the provisions in the bill of lading, which would then govern. This supposition, which found expression in various textbooks, was based on *Calcutta Steamship Co. Ltd. v. Andrew Weir & Co.*,[94] now distinguished or overruled by *President of India v. Metcalfe Shipping Co.* Ltd.,[95] where the facts were as follows:

By the terms of a charterparty the S.S. *Dunelmia*, was chartered for a voyage from the Italian ports of Ravenna and Ancona to Madras, carrying 8,000 tons of urea in bags. The charterparty provided expressly that the vessel should deliver the cargo at a safe berth in Madras on being paid freight at the rate of 70 shillings per ton. The cargo was to be loaded by the charterers free of expense and risk to the vessel. It was provided that the master should sign bills of lading at any rate of freight required by the charterers or their agents, without prejudice to this charterparty, but at not less than the chartered rate. Before the charterparty was made the charterers had entered into a contract with an Italian firm. By this contract the Italian firm agreed to sell to the charterers 8,000 tons of urea at a price of £31 17s. 3d. per ton "net F.O.B. stowed port of exit." The port of loading was Ravenna and the port of discharge was Madras. A clause headed "Shipping" provided that "the

---

[92] Which are to a considerable extent standardised by virtue of conference practice or the Hague Rules.

[93] See *Rodoconachi v. Milburn Bros.* (1886) 18 Q.B.D. 67 (C.A.).

[94] [1910]1 K.B, 759.

[95] [1969]2 W.L.R. 125. aff'd. [1969] 3 All E.R. 1549 (C.A.).

stores shall be delivered by the sellers free on board stowed on such vessels as may be nominated by the purchaser. . . .'' It was also provided that "Freight for the conveyance of the stores will be engaged by the chief controller of chartering . . . New Delhi, who will give due notice to the sellers, when and on board what vessels the stores are to be delivered.'' Later in the same clause there also appeared the following provision:

> "The term 'F.O.B. vessel port of loading' means: . . . (b) That it shall be the responsibility of the sellers to do the following: . . . (iii) Be responsible for any loss or damage, or both, until goods have been placed actually on board the vessel . . . and clean on board ocean bill of lading is delivered to the purchasers or the agent nominated by purchasers."

The sellers loaded the fertiliser on the ship and obtained a bill of lading which was signed "without prejudice to the charterparty'' and to order. They later endorsed it in blank, and in due course presented it to the charterers, who paid the price, and obtained delivery of the goods. The charterers however claimed that there was a shortage on delivery, and since this was contested by the shipowners, asked for arbitration in accordance with a clause in the charterparty. The shipowners refused. They maintained that the carriage was governed not by the charterparty but by the bill of lading, which did not contain an arbitration clause. The question before the court was which document was to govern this question? The charterparty as claimed by the charterers? or the bill of lading as the owners insisted?

Following a much ignored Scottish case,[96] the Court of Appeal (Lord Denning M.R., Edmund Davies and Fenton Atkinson L.JJ.) affirmed the decision of Megaw J. and held that, even though the charterers were not the shippers and only took possession of the goods as indorsees of the bill of lading, the charterparty governed the relations between the parties. The dispute was therefore determinable by arbitration. Whether or not a similar decision would have been made even absent the express bill of lading stipulation "without prejudice to the charter-party,'' remains to be seen. But the tenor of the judgment suggests that it would. The issue as to what is the appropriate language that should be used in order to effectively incorporate charterparty arbitration clauses into bills of lading (by reference) continues to trouble the courts in the United Kingdom and elsewhere. Two seemingly conflicting decisions by the commercial court were rendered by Hobhouse J. in *Skips A/S Nordheim v. Syrian Petroleum Co. and Another (The Varenna)*[97] on the one hand, and by Staughton J. in *Astro Valiente Compania Naviera S.A. v. Government of Pakistan (Ministry of Food and Agriculture (The Emmanuel Colocotronis) (No. 2)*[98] on the other. A review of the earlier authorities on this problem is to be found in Staughton J.'s judgment in the

---

[96] *Love and Stewart Ltd. v. Rowtor Steamship Co. Ltd.* [1916] 2 A.C. 527; reversing 1916 S.C. 223.
[97] [1982] 2 All E.R. 375.
[98] [1982] 1 Lloyd's Rep. 286.

latter case.[99] In the United States the courts have been more liberal in permitting incorporation by reference,[1] but even there the issue continues to provoke litigation.[2]

Terms of the contract of carriage. Since the f.o.b. seller's obligations are discharged once the goods cross the ship's rail, a question may arise (though oddly enough it does not seem to have been the subject of a reported dispute until now), as to whether he has committed a breach where the carrier issues a bill of lading, indicating that the goods are carried ''on deck'' at receiver's risk. Clearly a bank, unless authorised by the buyer, would have to reject such a bill if tendered to it under a documentary credit. But, as *Enrico Furst & Co. v. W.E. Fisher Ltd.*[3] shows, the terms of the letter of credit transaction are not necessarily identical with those of the underlying sales contract, and a bad tender under the letter of credit thus need not constitute a bad tender under the sales contract. Clearly, where the buyer has made the shipping arrangements, he may instruct the carrier not to carry on deck but could he claim from the seller if the carrier does not abide (or if no such instructions were given) and the goods are lost or damaged, and are uninsured for this reason? The carrier may argue that the seller (or his agent) were fully aware of the on deck carriage, and did not object when the bill of lading was issued. While the seller could argue that under the terms of the f.o.b. contract, he had performed once the goods crossed the ship's rail, and that where the goods were actually placed by the carrier (on board, or under deck) was none of his business. Since the question does not appear to have arisen until now, an attempt to give a definitive answer will not be made. Suffice it to say that the parties should be aware of the difficulties that may arise, and should attempt to guard themselves against the consequences in the appropriate circumstances, *e.g.* through an express term requiring the seller to ensure ''under deck'' carriage. For, unless an obligation can be imported that the seller must obtain an under deck carriage bill of lading, the buyer may be exposed to a risk that is not (or was not) insurable under the terms of the marine policy. Possibly, a term should be implied that the seller is under a duty at least to advise the buyer of the ''on deck'' carriage in order to enable him to obtain appropriate insurance coverage.

484 It has been noted that formalities and expenses which pertain to the export of the goods, such as customs entries, are for the account of the shipper. The performance of an f.o.b. contract, however, often gives rise to further obliga-

---

[99] See also E. Marshall, ''Incorporation of Arbitration Clauses into Charterparty Bills of Lading'' [1982] J.B.L. 478.
[1] See J. P. McMahon ''The Hague Rules and Incorporation of Charterparty Arbitration Clauses into Bills of Lading'' (1970) 2 J.M.L.C. 1.
[2] See, *e.g. Coastal States Trading Inc. v. Zenith Navigation S.A.* (1977) 446 F. Supp. 330 and *Amoco Oil Co. v. M.T. Mary Ellen*, 529 F. Supp. 227 (S.D.N.Y. 1981).
[3] [1960] 2 Lloyd's Rep. 340, *ante*, § 482.

tions which are even more directly related to the act of export, and for which the shipper is not necessarily responsible. These include in particular the payment of export duties and the application for and procurement of export licences, obligations which, though they form no part of delivery f.o.b., must be met before loading can legally commence. It was therefore once presumed that, absent an express agreement to the contrary which is commonly to be found, export licences or duties are always the responsibility of the f.o.b. buyer.

Export licences

485 The buyer's duty to apply for and obtain a licence to export, where necessary, in the case of f.o.b. contracts was considered to have been decided by the Court of Appeal in *H. O. Brandt & Co. v. H. N. Morris & Co. Ltd.*[4] There, the plaintiffs, Manchester merchants who acted as agents for an American firm, placed an order with the defendants, a Manchester manufacturer, for the purchase of sixty tons of aniline oil f.o.b. Manchester. After the contract was signed, an order was issued prohibiting the export of aniline oil except under a licence. The buyers left it to the sellers to apply for the licence but they were unable to perform the contract. Their first application was refused and another was granted after the contract period had expired. In an action for non-delivery, the Court of Appeal, reversing Lawrence J., held that the obligation of applying for and obtaining the necessary licence lay upon the buyers and not upon the sellers, and the action therefore failed.

Scrutton L.J. declared that the buyers had to provide "an effective ship, that is to say, a ship which can legally carry the goods" (see *ante*, § 472). As his lordship explained in the portion of his judgment immediately preceding this citation:

> "This is a contract to sell 60 tons of aniline oil f.o.b. Manchester. At the date of the contract there was no prohibition against the export of aniline oil. In *In re Anglo-Russian Merchant Traders Ltd. and John Batt & Co.*[5] the contract was a c. and f. contract, and at the date thereof there was an existing prohibition against export except under a licence. . . . Bailhache J. held that the person who had contracted to sell undertook to obtain the licence or to pay damages. This Court held that, as there was a finding of fact that the seller had done all in his power to get a licence, at any rate his obligation was not higher than that, and that therefore he was not liable. In this case it becomes necessary to go further and to decide whether in this f.o.b. contract the obligation to obtain a licence, in case there should after the making of the contract be a prohibition against export, lies upon the sellers or the buyers. In my opinion it lies upon the buyers" (at p. 798).

---

[4] [1917] 2 K.B. 784.
[5] [1917] 2 K.B. 679, see *post*, § 501.

486   Significantly, the decision in this case was to a large extent based on the relevant export regulations. These stated, and this is still the practice today,[6] that application for the necessary permit may only be made by a U.K. domiciled person. In *Brandt v. Morris*, both parties were equally competent to apply for the permit. The buyers, however, were better qualified to do so. It was, as Viscount Reading C.J. explained, their duty:

> ". . . to find the ship, and the facts which it was necessary to state when a licence had to be applied for were known to them and not to the defendants. All that the sellers know in such a case is that they have sold the goods to their buyers" (at p. 795).

487   Under these circumstances, it is not unreasonable to determine that the onus of securing the necessary licence is upon the buyer. The conclusion, however, is not supported by a dogmatic distinction between the two independent phases of the f.o.b. transaction, or from juxtaposing delivery and export, but from an examination of the conditions surrounding the contract, from which the intention of the parties was inferred. The decision, therefore, establishes no general rule that the f.o.b. term is not an export term at all; that it merely creates an ordinary contract requiring delivery at a particular point, and that under all circumstances, and irrespective of the surrounding conditions, export requirements are at the cost and risk of the f.o.b. buyer, though these consequences were sometimes imputed to it.

488   *In McMaster & Co. v. Cox, McEuen & Co.*,[7] the sale was of jute f.o.b. Dundee between two Scottish merchants, and the prohibition of export subject to licence was subsequent to the contract. The buyers who wished to export the jute were refused a licence and purported to cancel the contract. The House of Lords held that the buyers had no right to cancel merely because the necessary export licence could not be secured. That the buyers had done everything in their power to obtain such a licence (though it is an excuse which would, it is submitted, normally suffice to establish commercial frustration)[8] was immaterial. It was no answer to a claim by the seller for non-performance. The House concurred with the contention that, since the contract provided for complete performance in Scotland, what the buyers planned to do with the goods after delivery f.o.b. was of no concern to the

---

[6] In certain basic materials there might be a control of supply exercised by some Ministry other than the Board of Trade, and these Ministries sometimes allocate an export quota to particular manufacturers. Where this is the case, the manufacturer will have to procure a certificate from the sponsoring Ministry (that the goods fall within the quota), but this does not necessarily affect the question of the export licence, since the certificate can be submitted with an application for export by any other resident of the U.K., *e.g.* the buyer (export merchant).

[7] 1921 S.C. (H.L.) 24.

[8] As was held by the Court of Session in this case, 1920 S.C. 566. See *Re Anglo-Russian Merchant Traders Ltd. v. J. Batt & Co. (London) Ltd.* [1917] 2 K.B. 679, *post,* § 501; *Mayer & Lage Inc. v. Atlantic Sugar Refineries Ltd.* [1926] 2 D.L.R. 783 (Canada). Sometimes a party undertakes an absolute responsibility: see *Peter Cassidy Seed Co. Ltd. v. Osuustukkukauppa I.L.* [1957] 1 W.L.R. (seller); *Austin, Baldwin & Co. v. Turner & Co.* (1920) 36 T.L.R. 769 (buyer).

sellers. The sellers, being unaware of the contemplated export, were entitled to regard the f.o.b. point as if it were no different from any other point of delivery in the domestic or local market. Accordingly, they could not be made to bear the risk which they had not assumed simply because the buyers were prevented from accomplishing the purpose for which they intended to use the goods.

489   As Lord Dunedin, who addressed himself to this point, stated:

> "The right to dispose of the goods when and where they [the buyers] chose is a right due to the fact that after delivery they were the owners of the goods ... the duties of the respondents [the buyers] under this contract were only two, namely, to accept the goods and to pay the price; and nothing that the government did with respect to preventing goods going abroad, or imposing conditions on their going abroad, interfered with either of those duties" (at p. 28).

Lord Finlay made a point of noting that his opinion was motivated not by the f.o.b. term but by the contract in question and the surrounding circumstances. His lordship said:

> "Something was said about the words 'f.o.b.' They, of course, would be equally applicable to any transit by sea whether coastwise or to foreign ports, but it appears to me quite impossible to find in the documents or in the surrounding circumstances any sufficient foundation for making it a term of the contract that liberty of export should exist at the time it was to be performed" (at p. 27).

There was therefore no basis for drawing from *McMaster v. Cox, McEuen*, a general rule with respect to all f.o.b. contracts. The decision could hardly be justified in the case of most external sales, and, had it so been applied, it would have led to a serious discrepancy between the law and practice. The courts therefore were bound to restrict its applications sooner or later.

490   *Brandt v. Morris* was first distinguished in *Ga Galia Kotwala & Co. Ltd. v. K. R. L. Narasimhan & Bro.*,[9] decided by the Madras High Court in 1952. There the plaintiffs contracted to buy from the defendants certain quantities of tapioca starch f.o.r. ("free on rail") Sankaridrug. The starch was subject to an export permit under the Madras Tapioca (Movement Control) Order. The defendants (sellers) applied for the licence but, the plaintiffs alleged, subsequently withdrew their application with the intention of resiling from the contract and reselling at a higher price. The plaintiffs claimed for breach of contract. The lower court denied the claim, relying *inter alia* on *Brandt v. Morris*, but the judgment was reversed on appeal. It was there pointed out that since permits were being granted on the basis of the tapioca held in stock by the applicant prior to a certain date:

---

[9] [1954] A.I.R. (Madras) 119.

"... the defendants only could make the application for permits and, realising the situation in which they were placed, they rightly applied for the permit and allowed the stock to be inspected and verified by the revenue officials. In this case, therefore, we have no hesitation in holding that the duty of applying for the permits ... was undoubtedly on the defendants" (at p. 122).

Referring to the judgment below, Krishnaswami Nayudu J. said:

"The lower Court adopted the reasoning in this decision [*Brandt's* case] and purported to apply it to the present case by placing the duty to arrange for the wagons upon the plaintiffs and stated that, in the absence of the railway wagons, it was not possible for the defendants to deliver the goods at the railway station and that the railway wagons could not be had unless the railway authorities were shown the Collector's export permit. We are unable to see how the question of the availability of the wagons or otherwise arises in the present case, since nowhere in the correspondence is there any indication that the defendants were prevented from carrying out their part of the contract by reason of the non-availability of the railway wagons. The lower Court failed to note that in the decision cited above [*Brandt's* case], there was no prohibition on the date of the contract, and the buyer therefore could not have expected to arrange for a licence as it could not form part of the bargain. In an f.o.b. contract unlike in an f.o.r. contract a ship has to be found before the goods can be exported whereas in an f.o.r. contract the railway authorities generally receive the goods for despatch as and when wagons are available; but it cannot be laid down as an absolute proposition of law that in all cases, whether in an f.o.b. or f.o.r. contract, where either the ships or the wagons are required, it is the duty of the buyer to secure export permits where a prohibition exists against export without a licence. As to whose is the duty will mainly depend upon the terms and the nature of the contract as also whether the prohibition was in force on the date of the contract or supervened subsequently and other facts and circumstances of each case . . . in the present case, there was a prohibition at the time when the parties entered into the contract and it can reasonably be held that the sellers agreed to sell subject to being able to export the goods to the destinations mentioned in the contract which implied an obligation on their part to apply for and obtain the necessary licence. If the defendants had used their best endeavours and did whatever was reasonably required and if eventually they did not succeed in securing the licence, it must be held that the defendants had performed their part of the obligation as regards the export permits. It is clear that the defendants in this case had not only applied for export permit, but had been sincerely endeavouring their utmost to secure the same, and if they had not withdrawn their application, which they did in May 1946, but allowed the application to be disposed of either in favour of the granting of the permit or otherwise, they would have absolved themselves from any blame in the export permit not being granted, because the granting or otherwise of the export permit rested with an outside agency over whom none of the parties have any control" (at p. 123).

Three years later *Brandt's* case was likewise distinguished by the English Court of Appeal and by the House of Lords thereafter.

491 In *A. V. Pound & Co. Ltd. v. M. W. Hardy & Co. Inc.*,[10] an American firm agreed to purchase from an English company 300 tons of Portuguese gum

---

[10] [1955] 1 Q.B. 499 (C.A.); [1956] A.C. 588 (H. L.). See also *D. H. Bain v. Field & Co. Fruit Merchants* (1920) 5 Ll.L.Rep. 16 at p. 17.

spirits of turpentine "f.a.s. Lisbon," during the second half of May 1951. The American firm concluded the contract through its London branch. The sellers knew that the buyers contemplated East Germany as the destination of the goods. Under Portuguese law, an export licence which could only be obtained by a supplier registered by the Portuguese authorities was necessary. Neither the buyers nor the sellers were suppliers registered under Portuguese law for the purpose of obtaining the necessary licence. The sellers, therefore, contracted to buy the turpentine from Portuguese suppliers on similar terms except for the price. The contract between the parties was silent as to whose duty it would be to obtain the necessary export licence, nor was there any provision as to the liability (or lack thereof) ensuing from a failure to obtain the necessary licence. As a result of the "Iron Curtain" destination, the sellers (through their suppliers) failed to obtain the required permit. Since the buyers were unwilling to nominate a substitute or alternative destination, the contract could not be performed. The sellers thereupon claimed damages for breach of contract. The action succeeded before McNair J. who found himself bound by *Brandt v. Morris (ante,* § 485), and *McMaster v. Cox, McEuen (ante,* § 488), but his judgment was reversed both in the Court of Appeal and in the House of Lords. The House held that in the circumstances of the case the duty to secure the necessary export licence was cast on the sellers and not on the buyers. Viscount Kilmuir L.C. said:

> "In my opinion, the decision in *H. O. Brandt & Co. v. H. N. Morris & Co. Ltd.*[11] is authority only for the proposition that where a British buyer has bought goods for export from Britain, and a British prohibition on export except with a licence supervenes, then there is a duty on such a buyer to apply for a licence, because not only is he entitled to apply to the relevant British authority but he alone knows the full facts regarding the destination of the goods.
> ... I cannot extract from *H. O. Brandt & Co. v. H. N. Morris & Co. Ltd.* a general rule that on every f.o.b. or f.a.s. contract the buyer must supply a ship into which, or alongside which, the goods can legally be placed where there exists a prohibition on export except with a licence" (at pp. 602, 603).

492   Quoting from Scrutton L.J.'s judgment in *Brandt's* case, wherein the buyer's duty to provide an "effective" ship was laid down, Lord Somervell of Harrow stated:

> "The[se] observations, if general, must be confined to cases where both parties are within the jurisdiction of the licensing authority. I do not say the conclusion is necessarily different if they are not, but different considerations arise. Even so, I think this is an area in which it is impossible to lay down general rules. There might be a licence system based not on destination but on the proportion of a manufacturer's product to be sent out of the country. In such a case the fact necessary to be stated would be known to the producer and not to the buyer. It would seem obvious that in such a case it would be for the seller to apply.... The appellants invited your Lordships to lay down some general rule. There can be no general rule."[12]

---

[11] [1917] 2 K.B. 784.
[12] [1956] A.C. 588 at p. 611.

His lordship then referred to the facts in *McMaster v. McEuen* and proceeded:

"Jute might be sold f.o.b. Dundee if the jute was intended for coastwise traffic, and this was, presumably, a normal way of transporting jute to other parts of the country. The contract was, therefore, treated as one to sell goods in Scotland. Whether the buyer was precluded from disposing of them in a particular way did not, in that view, bring the contract to an end. That decision has no application to the point which I have been considering. Here the seller could only buy from the suppliers for export and knew at the time of the contract that the goods were to go to East Germany."[13]

493   While Viscount Simonds made the following observations:

"I do not dissent from the view entertained by the Court of Appeal that that case [*Brandt's*] is in material respects distinguishable from the present case. But I think that it is proper to note that, just as in this case it is not primarily the seller's obligation which has to be determined, so in *Brandt's* case it was not primarily the buyer's obligation, and to that extent—perhaps a limited extent— the observations of Scrutton L. J. upon the latter's obligation may be regarded as *obiter*. If they are to be read as laying down a general proposition of law that in every f.o.b. contract, and *a fortiori*, I suppose, in every f.a.s. contract, the duty of obtaining any necessary export licence primarily falls on the buyer in the absence of any relevant provision in the contract, then with the greatest respect to a very learned judge, I cannot assent to such a proposition. It appears to me to beg the question to state that it is the duty of the buyer to provide an 'effective ship,' meaning thereby a ship which can lawfully carry the contract goods to a named destination. It is equally the duty of the seller to deliver f.o.b. or f.a.s. 'effective goods,' meaning thereby goods which can lawfully be carried to that destination."[14]

494   *Pound v. Hardy*, therefore, carefully avoided laying down any rule for general application.[15] What it does show is that the respective obligations of parties to an f.o.b. contract depend on the surrounding conditions in the light of which the contract will be read. Accordingly, if the application of the "strict" definition is commercially unreasonable, reason or business efficacy must prevail. It is a:

"... great merit of the decision that it introduces into the law of f.o.b. sales a much needed element of flexibility which will enable it to develop in accordance with mercantile practice."[16]

Each case therefore depends on its particular circumstances from which the necessary inferences must be drawn.

In external sales, however, the inference that the buyer assumes the obliga-

---

[13] *Ibid.*
[14] *Ibid.* at pp. 607, 608.
[15] But "*Incoterms*" definitely state that an export licence (in external sales) is the responsibility of the f.o.b. seller, see *post,* § 511.
[16] Gower, "F.o.b. Contracts" M.L.R., Vol. 19, pp. 417, 419 (1956).

tion to procure any export licence which may be necessary would, it is submitted, usually call for some explanation.

This, apparently, is also true in the United States where the position has been described to be as follows[17]:

> "Although American courts have held that under an f.o.b. contract it is normally the buyer's, not the seller's, duty to obtain export permits, the cases have involved sales by American sellers to American buyers, delivery being made within the United States,[18] and recently an American Court interpreted a bare statement of the seller that he understood it to be his responsibility to obtain the export permit as imposing an absolute liability for failure to do so and not merely a duty to use diligence."[19]

495   Where the seller assumes the duty of securing an export licence *Banking & Trading Corporation v. Reconstruction Finance Corporation*[20] held that he does not perform his contract by placing the goods f.o.b. in contravention of any export regulations. In this instance, contravention of the regulations had subjected the cargo (rubber of Indonesian origin) to risk of seizure and confiscation by the Dutch Navy and, consequently, the court held that "the loading of the rubber under the circumstances was ineffective to constitute delivery."[21] Indeed, that the buyer is under no obligation to accept delivery f.o.b. which is defective at the place of performance, as would invariably be the case if it was unlawful or illegal according to the law of the country in which it is to be made, cannot be doubted.

Export duties

496   The rule in *H. O. Brandt & Co. v. H. N. Morris & Co. Ltd.*,[22] which purported to treat the f.o.b. contract as differing from the ordinary domestic sale only in respect of the place of delivery, has often been taken to apply to the question of liability for export duties also.[23] That this runs counter to commer-

---

[17] Berman, "Force Majeure and the Denial of an Export Licence under Soviet Law" 73 Har.L.R. 1128 at p. 1141 (1960).

[18] *Amtorg Trading Corp. v. Miehle Printing Press & Mfg. Co.*, 206 F. 2d 103 (2d Cir. 1953); *Bardons & Oliver, Inc. v. Amtorg Trading Corp.*, 301 N.Y. 622, 93 N.E. 2d 915 (1950) (Memorandum decision).

[19] *Banking & Trading Corp. v. Reconstruction Fin. Corp.*, 147 F.Supp. 193 (S.D.N.Y. 1956). See however the observation to the effect that:

> "Even though it may be assumed that the usual rule under an f.o.b. ocean vessel contract is that the buyer is to obtain export permits and pay export duties, this responsibility may be shifted to the seller by agreement of the parties. It is my conclusion that, in fact, the parties did intend to shift it and that they contemplated [the buyer's] obligation as subject to the condition precedent that [the seller], . . . obtain the export permit" (at p. 208).

[20] 147 F.Supp. 193 (S.D.N.Y. 1956).

[21] *Ibid.* at p. 210.

[22] See *ante*, § 485.

[23] See *Halsbury's Laws of England* (Simonds ed.), Vol, 34, p. 178, n. (*k*), commenting on the buyer's duty to the effect that: "Export duties are not common in practice, but it is conceived that the reasoning in *H. O. Brandt & Co. v. H. N. Morris & Co. Ltd.* [1917] 2 K.B. 784, C.A.,

cial practice in the case of external sales is clear from *"Incoterms"* which in earlier editions stated that "the seller must bear all costs . . . including any taxes, fees or charges levied because of exportation."[24] This was also the view of the Scottish Court of Session in *Bowhill Coal Co. Ltd. v. A. Tobias.*[25] The dispute there related to an f.o.b. contract for the sale of coal between Scottish sellers and a German buyer. Subsequent to the signature of the contract, a duty of a shilling per ton was imposed on any coal sold for export. The buyer, who paid the tax under protest, sought recovery thereof. The court held (Lord Young dissenting) that the export tax was the sellers' responsibility and the buyer's claim, therefore, succeeded. The decision, like *Brandt's* case, is largely based on the language of the relevant statute, in this instance the Finance Act 1901, but parts of the reasoning of the court are nonetheless of general interest. Lord Trayner said:

> "The Statute imposes no duty on foreigners—only upon subjects—or the property of subjects of the king. If it was necessary to the [buyer's] case to maintain that the duty fell upon the exporter, I think a good deal might be said in support of the view that the [sellers] were the exporters. They were sending their coal out of the country, under a contract stipulation that it must not be taken to, or delivered at, any home port. It was expressly sold for exportation" (at p. 267).

497   But in the same case, Lord Young[26] took exception to the argument that, under an f.o.b. contract, it was for the sellers to pay a tax which is due before the coal can be placed on board by curtly saying: "Now I cannot assent to that as even a sensible argument" (at page 266). On the assumption that the *Bowhill* decision rests on the foregoing passage from Lord Trayner's speech, no problem arises of reconciling it with a subsequent English judgment in which the same Act was considered, but which held that it was the f.o.b. buyer's responsibility to pay this tax.[27] For in the English decision the dispute arose in an internal sale, and the English buyer was the exporter of the goods. In the United States on the other hand, the decision in *Krauter v. Menchasatorre et al.*[28] held—following the presumed *Brandt v. Morris* rule—that it was the foreign buyer's responsibility to pay all export duties, since the contract being on f.o.b. terms it was to be performed by delivery on board. The seller, in other words, was to be relieved from any concern with respect to responsibilities arising from the additional or independent (export) phase of

---

would apply to these." Though it is there submitted that "The crucial test is whether or not the expenses are payable prior to putting the goods on board," the statement is subsequently followed not by a time but by a functional test so that the material question is not when the payment is due but the phase of the transaction to which it relates. "In the case of export duties pure and simple the duties are payable in respect of a transit which takes place after the goods are on board." See also *Krauter v. Menchasatorre*, 195 N.Y.S. 361; 202 App. Div. 200 (1922) *post*, § 497.

[24] These words are omited from the latest edition, see *post*, § 511.

[25] (1902) 5 F. (Ct. of Sess.) 262.

[26] Who would have dismissed the claim.

[27] *Insole & Son v. Gueret* (1907) 23 T.L.R. 294 (C.A.).

[28] 195 N.Y.S. 361; 202 App.Div. 200 (1920).

the transaction although in the instant case he actually undertook the further obligation of furnishing the vessel.

498 In this latter case the buyer sued the seller for failure to ship a cargo of Spanish olive oil that became subject to an export tax which he refused to pay. The judgment of the Appellate Division of the Supreme Court of New York in part reads:

> "The main question for consideration is as to whether the buyer was compelled to pay this [export] tax in execution of the contract. It seems to me clear that . . . the duty of paying the tax in the performance of the contract was on the buyer. Delivery was to be made f.o.b. Seville; the title of the goods passed when the [seller] had put the goods on board the steamer. The seller's duty then stopped. The actual exportation [to the United States] was the concern of the buyer alone. It seems to be assumed by the [buyer's] counsel that these goods could not be put on board the steamer without the payment of this tax. . . . The export tax is a tax upon goods which actually go out, which actually leave the country, and would seem to fall upon the party which took them out, and in this case the buyer was the one. Having received title at Seville upon the loading of the goods, the export tax should properly be paid by the buyer, who thereupon sought to take them out of the country. The contention of the purchaser seems to be that the seller was required to ship the goods. This is a general expression and simply means that the seller was required to place them on board the steamship for shipment.
>
>   If we assume, however, that they could not be put on board . . . we are still of the opinion that the duty was upon the buyer to pay this tax. In the case of *Brandt & Co. v. H. N. Morris & Co. Ltd.* . . . . This case is, I think, a clear authority for holding that it was the duty of the buyer in this case to pay the tax and even if the payment of the tax was a necessary pre-requisite to the placing of the goods on board or bringing them on the wharf, and the contract was an f.o.b. contract, nevertheless, it became the duty of the buyer to pay this tax, which is, in fact, a tax upon the actual exportation of the goods, with which the seller had no concern. It is here claimed that the seller did, in fact, obtain the steamer and assumed its obligation to obtain the steamer, which otherwise, would rest upon the buyer, and the contract is thus interpreted by the parties to cast the burden of furnishing an effective ship, authorised to export, on the seller. It is evident, however, that the sellers, living in Spain, could more easily do this, and the fact that they assumed part of the duty of the buyer in obtaining the ship to carry the goods without contract requirement cannot change the legal obligation of the sellers in case the buyer refuses to pay the tax which it is necessary to pay in order to have the goods exported under the contract" (195 N.Y.S. at pp. 363, 364).

499 Where the seller includes the amount due on account of export duty in the price of the goods, and at a date subsequent to the contract a reduction or exemption is introduced, is the buyer entitled to claim the benefit thereof, in the absence of stipulation to this effect? The question is not covered by direct authority, but it is thought the answer is negative. *In Compagnie Continentale d'Importation Zurich S.A. v. Ispahani Ltd.,*[29] the plaintiff purchased from the

---

[29] [1962] 1 Lloyd's Rep. 213; [1961] 1 Lloyd's Rep. 293.

defendant hessian goods f.o.b. Calcutta under a contract which contained the clause "Export Duty based on current rates; any alterations to be on buyer's account." Export duty was abolished after part of the shipment was made and the plaintiff requested that a letter of credit which he opened in favour of the seller be reduced by the amount of export duty. The seller refused to accede to this demand whereupon the action was commenced. The claim was upheld by Diplock J. whose judgment was affirmed by the Court of Appeal on the ground of the special clause.

500   From all that as already been said, it will appear that where the seller is the exporter, and is aware of the overseas destination of the goods and of the foreign domicile of his buyer, the "strict" division of f.o.b. responsibilities is frequently unsuitable.

In most external sales, therefore, the seller is probably responsible over and above his minimum performance for any requirements arising from the shipment and export of the goods also. He must then bear the cost of all taxes, fees or charges levied by the country in which delivery f.o.b. takes place because of the exportation of the goods as well as the cost of any formalities which he has to fulfil in order to load the goods on board. In other words, the buyer normally bears the costs and assumes liabilities for the goods only after they are actually on board, including stowage, freight, and those charges and responsibilities which the importation of the goods at their destination give rise to. Where, therefore, the seller fails to add shipment and export expenses to his f.o.b. price, no subsequent recovery would normally be allowed.[30]

Export prohibition

501   The parties often insert an express stipulation that the contract is deemed cancelled where the seller is unable to perform because of a cause beyond his control including a denial or withdrawal of export licences. In the absence of such an agreement, is the contract cancelled if reasonable effort to obtain the licence has achieved no result? It has sometimes been stated that the seller bears the risk of a denial of an export licence.[31] This appears to imply that, in the absence of a contrary agreement, an absolute warranty (and not merely a duty to use his best endeavours) is imposed on him.[32] It has been suggested that this view[33] "though not accepted in all countries, finds consid-

---

[30] Thus, in *The Tromp* [1921] P. 337, where the question arose as to whether a forwarding agent, who was the shipper in this case, was acting on behalf of the buyers or the sellers, it was held that the buyers were quite right in supposing him ". . . to be the seller's agent paid by a commission for his services in selling goods which they bought f.o.b. at Gothenburg" (at p. 349).

[31] *e.g.* by the International Chamber of Commerce in *"Incoterms"* A. 3, *post*, § 511.

[32] See Eisemann, "Keine Haftung des FOB-Verkäufes für die Beschaftung der Ausfuhrgenehmigung nach Sowjetischem Recht?" Verkehr (Vienna) January 10, 1959, pp. 41–42.

[33] Berman, "Force Majeure and the Denial of an Export Licence under Soviet Law" 73 Har. L.R. 1128 (1960), p. 1141, see also p. 1142 (n. 29) quoting the respective authorities for this proposition.

erable support in the practice of courts and arbitral tribunals throughout the world." Nevertheless, it would seem that under English law a party normally undertakes not the absolute duty to procure a licence, but merely a conditional obligation to do his best to obtain it. If his endeavours fail, no liability for breach of contract attaches. This view was taken by the Court of Appeal in *Re Anglo Russian Merchant Traders and John Batt & Co. (London)*[34] (a c. and f. contract) where Viscount Reading C.J. accordingly stated:

> "The buyers contend that the implied obligation is that the sellers will obtain a licence to ship, and that if they do not they will pay damages. . . . There was at the time of making the contract and at all material times a prohibition against the export of aluminium except under licence. If a licence cannot be obtained aluminium cannot be shipped, and I cannot see why the law should imply an absolute obligation to do that which the law forbids. A shipment contrary to the prohibition would be illegal, and an absolute obligation to ship could not be enforced. I cannot agree that, in order to give the contract its business efficacy, it is a necessary implication that the sellers undertook an absolute obligation to ship whether a licence was or was not obtained. . . . The reasonable view of the contract . . . is that the sellers sold subject to their being able to ship under a licence and that they impliedly undertook to use their best endeavours to obtain a licence" (at p. 686).

502   A similar opinion was expressed by Devlin J. in *Peter Cassidy Seed Co Ltd. v. Osuustukkukauppa I. L.*[35] There a contract to purchase a quantity of ants' eggs, f.o.b. Helsinki provided for "Delivery: prompt, as soon as export licence is granted." The sellers who admitted that it was their duty to obtain the necessary licence were unable to secure it. On a case stated by an umpire, Devlin J. held that the sellers were liable in damages to the buyers because of the particular language of the contract. His lordship added, however, that where the contract fails to stipulate any term relating to export prohibition, the obligation to procure any licence which may be required is best considered conditional and not absolute.

It was his view that[36]:

> "If the contract said nothing at all about the obtaining of a licence, it is clear that some provision would have to be implied into it about it. The contract could not be fulfilled legally under the law of Finland unless one or the other, either the buyer or the seller, obtained a licence, and it would, therefore, be necessary to imply a term as to whose duty it was to apply for a licence, and it would then further be necessary to imply a term as to what the nature of his obligation was. In this case it is accepted (and I think rightly) that it was the sellers' duty to apply for a licence. The person whose duty it is to apply for a licence may either warrant that he will get it—that is an absolute warranty; or he may warrant that he will use all due diligence in getting it. When nothing is said in the contract it is usually, indeed I think it is probably fair to say almost invariably, the latter class of warranty that is implied, but there can be no doubt that each case must

[34] [1917] 2 K.B. 679.
[35] [1957] 1 W.L.R. 273.
[36] At pp. 278–279.

be decided according to its own circumstances and the question of implication settled in the ordinary way in which implied terms are settled.''

503   The learned judge then surveyed a number of decisions, in which the nature and scope of the obligation to procure any necessary licence was examined, and went on to conclude:

> "There is here no clause 'Subject to licence.' If there had been, then I think, on the authorities, that that would conclude the matter; but in the absence of those words, and if there were no clause at all it would be necessary for me to determine, in relation to all the circumstances of the case, what I thought would be the appropriate terms to be implied. There is, however, a clause, and, in my judgment, that clause, upon its true construction, gives very considerable assistance to the contention of [the buyer's counsel] that it is the absolute obligation which was intended in this case. That clause, which I have read, is: 'Delivery: prompt, as soon as export licence granted.' There is no 'Subject to'—a piece of phraseology with which all commercial men must be very familiar—it is: 'Delivery: prompt, as soon as export licence is granted.' That seems to me to show quite clearly that the assumption underlying the contract which was in the minds of both parties was that an export licence certainly would be granted, and the only question was, when was the precise moment of time likely to be, because it was not until the licence was in fact granted that delivery could be made . . .'' (at pp. 278–279).

The undertaking is not to perform an illegal act but quite the contrary. Where therefore export is prohibited and the duty to obtain the licence is construed as an absolute duty it is not on the failure to perform that which is illegal that the action lies, but on the breach of the promisor's warranty that the doing of the act that he has contracted to do will be legal and that performance shall not become illegal.

In *Walton (Grain) Ltd. v. British Italian Trading Co.*[37] where there was a *force majeure* clause and export licences became unobtainable, the arbitrators found that as export licences were not explicitly mentioned, the contract was a "clean contract" and the sellers were in default in failing to ship. However, Mr. Justice Diplock (as he then was) held that prohibition of export (which was mentioned in the *force majeure* clause) included a general refusal of export licences and the seller was not therefore in default. Had a quota licensing system been introduced, the position might have been different.[38]

In *Czarinkow Ltd. v. Centrala Handlu Zagranicznego "Rolimpex,"*[39] the House of Lords held that a clause in a contract for the sale of Polish sugar f.o.b. "one safe Polish port during October/November 1974" (stipulating that "the seller shall be responsible for obtaining any necessary export licence," and, that, "the failure to obtain such licence shall not be sufficient grounds for a claim of *force majeure* if the regulations in force at the time the contract

---

[37] [1959] 1 Lloyd's Rep. 223, following *Ralli Brothers v. Compania Naviera Sota y Aznar* [1920] 2 K.B. 287.
[38] See *ante*, § 115.
[39] [1978] 2 Lloyd's Rep. 305.

was made, called for such licence to be obtained'') did not imply an unqualified duty to maintain the export licence in force at the time of delivery. Hence, the sellers were excused from performance where the Polish Minister of Foreign Trade and Shipping issued a decree banning the export of sugar. The *force majeure* clause of the contract which provided an escape in the event delivery was prevented by any cause beyond the seller's control was operative, and the seller could not be deprived of its protection by virtue of being an organ of the Polish State, since their status as a state trading company (and the object of the export ban in question) did not preclude them from relying on the contractual *force majeure* exception clause.

But in *Atisa S.A. v. Aztec A.G.*[40] Parker J. upheld a trade arbitration award in favour of f.o.b. buyers of Kenyan white crystal sugar agreeing that non-performance was not excused in the circumstances. The contract in question contained a provision placing the responsibility for any export licence on the seller, stating the failure to obtain any such licence would not be sufficient grounds for a claim of force majeure if the regulations, in force at the time when the contract was made, called for such licence(s) to be obtained. At the time the contract was made export licences were required, but no difficulties were foreseen. Subsequently, however, the contract could not be performed because of political developments that led to a denial of the licence. It should be mentioned that the sole supplier to the sellers was the Kenyan Government. The sellers argued that the contract was frustrated due to "governmental intervention", but, as aforesaid, the buyers prevailed. The judgment confirmed the award that the export licence denial was not due to the exercise of sovereign powers but was properly to be regarded as having been done under private law. The sellers, it was held, "had specifically undertaken the risk that the government would refuse an export licence which would render them unable lawfully to perform the contract" (at page 584).

On the other hand in *Pagnan S.p.A. v. Tradax Ocean Transportation S.A.*[41] the Court of Appeal (Dillon, Woolf and Bingham L.JJ) held that the f.o.b. seller of Thai tapioca was excused from performance under an export prohibition clause, notwithstanding an agreement (construed as imposing an absolute obligation and not merely a due diligence duty on the seller) to obtain an export licence. The contract in question also provided that special terms and conditions would prevail over printed clauses, and the clause imposing the duty to procure the export licence was such a special term, whereas the export prohibition clause was part of the standard (GAFTA 119) form of contract adopted by the parties. The judgment notes that one should not start with an "*a priori*" assumption that parties are likely to have had a due diligence duty in mind, and that it is always a question of construction, not implication, whether the duty to procure the licence was absolute or not. Nevertheless the buyers claim failed because there was no inconsistency between the two provisions. The contract provided for its cancellation if an executive or legis-

---

[40] [1983] 2 Lloyd's Rep. 579.
[41] [1987] 2 Lloyd's Rep. 342.

lative act done by or on behalf of the Government of Thailand restricted export, and the absolute duty to procure the licence was to be read subject to that escape clause.

A distinction must be drawn between cases where the export prohibition is absolute and total, and cases where the prohibition is only partial. In the former case, and in the absence of a construction placing the risk of the licence's denial on the seller, the export prohibition operates to exonerate the seller from any further duty and performance is excused. But in the case of a partial prohibition (*e.g.* where exports are only permitted on the grant of a licence) the seller is under a duty to apply for a licence, and is further obliged to use all reasonable endeavours to obtain permission to export.

504   Whether or not the seller has used his best endeavours or efforts to obtain the licence (if such be his duty) is a question of fact. In *Agroexport State Enterprise for Foreign Trade v. Compagnie Européene De Céreales*[42] the sellers (by a contract dated June 24, 1970) agreed to sell about 50,000 metric tons of Rumanian yellow maize f.o.b. stowed and trimmed Constanza and/or Braila/Galatzi and/or Franco border, delivery during the months of October to December 1970. The contract contained a clause cancelling the contract in the event of inability to perform due to export prohibition. At all material times an export licence was required. Because of heavy rainfall and flooding in Rumania, a licence was only obtained by the sellers (in September 1970) for about half the contract quantity. On October 14, 1970 the sellers advised the buyers that they could not deliver any maize. Meanwhile, and without informing the buyers, the sellers continued to press for a licence for the balance of the contract quantity but they were unsuccessful. Finally, on December 21, the sellers advised the buyers that they could only supply 24,197,460 tons under the contract, and for the first time informed them that there was a prohibition because of natural calamities. A dispute arose which was referred to arbitration, and Ackner J., on a case stated, held that from the moment the contract was made the sellers were under an obligation to use their best endeavours to overcome the partial export prohibition. The sellers must thus show that despite their having taken all reasonable steps to obtain permission to export, they were unable to achieve success or alternatively that it was useless for them to take any steps, because they were foredoomed to failure. Such is their duty where the export prohibition is partial and not absolute or total (for in the latter case the provision in the contract operated to exonerate the sellers from performance). In the present case there was a combination of a partial, and of a total, prohibition. Until October 28, the prohibition was partial. The sellers therefore were under a duty to take all reasonable steps to get an export licence for the entire contract quantity. The sellers, however, failed to prove that they had discharged this duty. They may well have known about the possible crop difficulties at the time the contract was concluded yet they did not apply for an export licence until

---

[42] [1974] 1 Lloyd's Rep. 499.

August 28. Having received a partial export licence they made no further application for some six weeks for the balance. This second application, moreover, was made only after the sellers had expressed their intention not to export any maize at all. Since the sellers were unable to show that their failure to apply earlier for a licence, or to re-apply for it promptly when their application was only partially successful, occurred without any fault on their part they were in breach, and liable for damages. The sellers effort to rely on *Ross T. Smyth Ltd. v. W. N. Lindsay*[43] (a case of a supervening export prohibition that operated to exonerate the seller from performance) failed. Ackner J. distinguished that case on the ground that the sellers duty there only arose at the time of shipment, and that they were under no obligation to do anything until the time they were faced with the supervening obstacle of the prohibition. As explained by him:

> "Here the sellers have been unable to show that their failure to apply earlier for the licence, or to re-apply promptly when their application was only partially successful, occurred without any fault on their part. In short their failure to ship is only excusable if they can show that at all times after the conclusion of the contract until the imposition of the absolute prohibition on October 28 they used their best endeavours to overcome the obstacle of the licensing system or that their failure to do so was in no way responsible for the failure to obtain, prior to October 28, permission to export the full contract quantity. This they failed to do. Accordingly, I am satisfied that the sellers are liable to the buyers in respect of their failure to supply the whole of the contract quantity" (at p. 507).

505   Where unascertained goods are sold, it is sometimes said that the seller could have fulfilled his contract by providing goods from some source of supply other than the one contemplated by him when entering into the agreement.[44] Moreover, the fact that performance would be more costly, and that the seller would have to acquire the goods at a price exceeding the one he agreed to sell them for, is not sufficient to frustrate the contract. Thus, where the Brazilian Government had, in effect, fixed a minimum price limit for certain commodities, which resulted in an increase in the price of the contract goods so that export licences could not be procured if the transaction were to be based on the price prevailing at the date of the agreement, the court did not consider the contract frustrated. Nor was the contract in this case cancelled by virtue of an express stipulation that the contract was "subject to any Brazilian export licence."[45] But where export, albeit not officially prohibited, was effectively barred by virtue of the Argentine Government having monopolised the grain trade, the seller was relieved from his duty to deliver maize f.o.b. Buenos Aires in *Société Co-opérative Suisse des Céréales et Matières Fourragères v. La Plata Cereal Company, S.A.*[46] Having carefully

---

[43] [1953] 1 W.L.R. 1280.
[44] *Beves & Co. Ltd. v. Farkas* [1953] 1 Lloyd's Rep. 103, applying *Blackburn Bobbin Co. v. Allen (T.W.) & Sons* [1918] 1 K.B. 540; [1918] 2 K.B. 467. *Cf.* also *George Wills & Sons Ltd. v. R.S. Cunningham Son & Co. Ltd.* [1924] 2 K.B. 220.
[45] *Brauer & Co. (Great Britain) Ltd. v. J. Clark (Brush Materials) Ltd.* [1952] W.N. 422.
[46] (1947) 80 Ll.L.Rep. 530.

examined many of the earlier precedents with respect to frustration Morris J. said:

> "It becomes necessary therefore to decide whether on the particular facts of this particular case there must be an implied term or, stated otherwise, whether the basis of the contract became overthrown. In my judgment, the basis of the contract did become overthrown. Although there was no prohibition of export in the sense that any exporting was absolutely forbidden, there was on the facts as found a *de facto* prohibition which prevented the sellers from exporting. They were by law prohibited from exporting any maize that they had not purchased from the Argentine Agricultural Products Regulating Board, and that Board had no maize which they were willing to sell. The sellers had 6,750 tons of maize. It became illegal for them to export that.[47] The new conditions created by the changes in the law fundamentally altered the situation. Exportable maize was, by law, removed from the scope of private obligation. The parties ought not to be regarded as having contracted to impose upon the seller a continuing obligation to export goods, even at a time when such exporting would be contrary to the law of the land. That would be unreasonable and not creditable" (at p. 543).

While the implied term test is no longer valid,[48] the prohibition there was a result of a change in the law, and the decision, it is thought, is still correct on that basis.

Where the effect of the government monopoly is merely to increase the price of the goods so that the seller can only fulfil his (resale) obligation at a loss, the seller, as already noted, cannot rely on an exemption clause relieving him from liability for non-performance because of an impossibility created by an export prohibition. This was decided in *Exportelisa S.A. v. Rocco Giuseppe & Figli Soc. Coll.*[49] where a contract for the sale of 5,000 tons of Argentine Candeal/Taganrog wheat at a price of U.S. \$230 per ton f.o.b. Necochea was not performed. The sellers invoked an exemption clause which was to relieve him of liability in the event of performance being rendered impossible by virtue of an export prohibition. But both Donaldson J. and the Court of Appeal, as well as a trade arbitration panel, found in favour of the buyers. In the course of his judgment Megaw L.J. said:

> ". . . it is impossible for the sellers to establish as a matter of law that, on the facts of the present case, they are excused from performance. They are not so excused merely because, by reason of a change in Argentine law or by the act of the executive government in the Argentine, they may have been precluded from buying from a particular seller from whom they intended to buy in order to perform the contract: the circumstances being that, on the facts as found, they could have bought the goods, albeit at a much higher price, from another seller in the Argentine."[50]

---

[47] No attempt was made to argue that it was the buyer's duty to see to the export of the goods. All parties assumed throughout that the Argentine seller and not the Swiss buyer had to suffer all (if any) of the consequences resulting from inability to perform the contract.

[48] See *per* Parker J. in *Atisa S.A. v. Aztec A.G.* [1983] 2 Lloyd's Rep. 579 at p. 586.

[49] [1978] 1 Lloyd's Rep. 433, affirming Donaldson J. in [1977] 2 Lloyd's Rep. 494.

[50] *Ibid.* at p. 437.

506   Where by virtue of the outbreak of war, performance of the contract involves trading with the enemy, similar principles apply. The contract is *ipso facto* dissolved and no liability attaches. But where export is merely suspended by a temporary embargo, performance is not necessarily excused. In *Andrew Millar & Co. Ltd. v. Taylor & Co. Ltd.*,[51] the plaintiffs agreed to supply the defendants with confectionery f.o.b. Liverpool for export to Morocco. The contract was entered into in July 1914, but no fixed date for delivery thereunder was specified. Upon the outbreak of the First World War, the exportation of confectionery was forbidden. The prohibition subsisted for 15 days (August 5 to 20) and was removed thereafter. It was held by the Court of Appeal, reversing Rowlatt J., that the plaintiffs were not entitled to repudiate the contract. The contract involved no trading with the enemy as both parties were English. The effect of the proclamation prohibiting the export of confectionery was not to annul subsisting contracts, but merely to suspend them. Although it was not necessary to wait for an indefinite period for the prohibition to be relaxed, the contract would be invalidated only if, having regard to its terms, it could not be carried out in reasonable time. In the case under consideration the plaintiffs acted prematurely.[52] Since no delivery date had been specified and since the prohibition had been removed before a reasonable time for delivery had expired, the plaintiffs had committed a breach. Warring L.J. stated:

> "Now, as I have already said, the particular contract which we have to consider is one which was to be performed within a reasonable time. Has the act of state in fact rendered the contract impossible of performance within a reasonable time? It plainly has not; it expired on August 20, before the time had arrived within which, even according to the ordinary practice in peace time, the contract would have been performed, and there is nothing to indicate that it would have been impossible to perform this contract after the removal of the prohibition on August 20. The plaintiffs—the defendants in the counter-claim, the plaintiffs in the action—have chosen to run the risk that of course they were entitled to do, and if the prohibition had lasted so long that the contract in fact turned out to be impossible of performance then they would have been right. Having taken the course of not waiting the reasonable time before they chose to treat the contract as at an end, they had to take the consequences of it having turned out as it in fact has turned out, that the contract was capable of performance" (at pp. 416, 417).

507   However, this being an internal f.o.b. contract, the defendants (buyers) also

---

[51] [1916] 1 K.B. 402 (C.A.).
[52] *Cf. Provimi Hellas A. E. v. Warinco A. G.* [1978] 1 Lloyd's Rep. 373 (C.A.), where the sellers advised the buyers two days prior to the expiration of the contractual shipping period that, due to an export prohibition imposed on the contract goods (shortly before the ship arrived to load), the contract could not be performed, claiming the benefit of a *force majeure* clause. The buyers' contention that this notice was an unequivocal declaration by the sellers that they no longer regarded themselves as being bound by the contract, and that the notice should therefore be regarded as a repudiation by the sellers, failed. The notice was construed not as one purporting to prematurely terminate the contract, but as one asserting the sellers' contention that they assumed no liability in respect of non shipment under the contract.

argued that no condition binding them to export the goods could be implied. In their opinion, therefore, the plaintiffs would have committed a breach even if the prohibition was not lifted before the period of delivery had expired. Bray J., who was the only member of the court to address himself to this argument, noted the seller's interest in the export of the confectionery which arose from his drawback rights in respect of the import duty paid on the sugar used in the confectionery. The learned judge said:

> "It is quite clear that the contract did contemplate that the goods would be exported, and the course of business showed that, in that event, after they had been exported the plaintiffs would receive the drawback. It may be a question, and a difficult question, as to what was the implied term of the contract with reference to exportation, but I will assume in favour of the plaintiffs, without deciding it, that there was an implied term of the contract by which the defendants promised to export the goods so that the plaintiffs might get their drawback. That being so, two points arose; the first question was whether such a promise was a condition or an independent promise. One must look at the general circumstances to see which it was. Now the breach first of all involves only a question of money, a comparatively small amount of money, but only a question of money, namely, the amount of the drawback. The next circumstance is that the breach would not under ordinary circumstances occur until after the plaintiff had delivered the goods to the defendants at Liverpool. These considerations lead me to the clear conclusion that it was not a condition, but merely an independent promise" (at p. 417).

Duty to co-operate

508   Finally, it may be added that, before the seller can be made liable for breach of any obligation to obtain an export licence, the buyer must have furnished to him all the details which may be necessary for such purpose. So that when Lord Simonds said in *Pound v. Hardy*[53] that the buyer has a duty to co-operate with the seller in these matters by telling him "the destination of the goods and otherwise as may be reasonable" he was in effect stating that this duty (of co-operation) is a condition precedent which the buyer must perform before the seller's liability to obtain the export licence arises.[54] Under the American Uniform Commercial Code, this duty is made the subject of specific statutory provision: The code provides in section 2–311(3) that:

> ". . . where one party's co-operation is necessary to the agreed performance of the other but is not seasonably forthcoming, the other party in addition to all other remedies
>   (a) is excused for any resulting delay in his own performance; and
>   (b) may also either proceed to perform in any reasonable manner or after the

---

[53] [1956] A.C. 588 at p. 608, *ante*, § 491.
[54] *Cf. Kyprianou v. Cyprus Textiles Ltd.* [1958] 2 Lloyd's Rep. 60; and see Bateson, "The Duty to Co-operate" [1960] J.B.L. 187.

> time for a material part of his own performance treat the failure to . . .
> co-operate as a breach by failure to deliver or accept the goods."

So too in *Metro Meat Ltd. v. Fares Rural Co. Pty Ltd. and Ano.*,[55] an appeal to the Judicial Committee of the Privy Council, Lord Diplock likewise opined that "A contract for the sale of goods for export on f.a.s. terms, more particularly when it provides for delivery by instalments from more than one port of shipment, calls for co-operation between the buyer and the seller in arranging for loading and shipping schedule so as to accommodate it to the reasonable business interests of each party".[56] Their Lordships concluded that such a term of co-operation was to be implied in relation to fixing the shipping schedule for the last two of five shipments that were envisaged to take place under the (oral) contract (for delivery by instalments) that the parties had entered into, and which was repudiated by the sellers, committing an anticipatory breach of a fundamental term, which the buyers treated, as they were entitled to do, as rescinding the contract.[57]

Is destination a term of the contract?

509   Where the seller is unable to obtain the export licence by virtue of an export prohibition which applies to the particular destination of the goods, a question may arise as to the buyer's duty to nominate another destination for which a licence can be secured. In *Pound v. Hardy*,[58] where the sellers so alleged, the question was only briefly considered. Some of the speeches in the House of Lords seem to indicate that the destination contemplated (Rostock in East Germany) had become a term of the contract,[59] but this view does not appear to have been shared by the entire House. Lord Somervell, for example, observed that it was clear that under the contract in question the buyers were not restricted as to the choice of destination, but that it was too late to require them to nominate an alternative port.[60] It is doubtful whether any general rule can be formulated as to whether or not the destination for which the buyer requires the goods and which he has in mind upon entering into an f.o.b. contract becomes a term thereof. And the converse is probably equally valid there being no necessary implication in an offer to sell goods f.o.b. that the goods originate in the country where the port of delivery is

---

[55] [1985] 2 Lloyd's Rep. 13 (P.C.). And in *Kurt A. Becker G.m.b.H. & Co. K.G. v. Roplak Enterprises S.A. ("The World Navigator")*, previously noted (see *ante*, § 459a n. 16), the Court of Appeal, affirming Phillips J. (on this point) agreed that an f.o.b. contract probably implied a duty of co-operation by the seller in providing the appropriate documentation that might be required in order to enable the buyer to present the vessel for loading.
[56] At p. 14.
[57] [1985] 2 Lloyd's Rep. 13.
[58] See *ante*, § 491.
[59] See, *e.g. per* Viscount Simonds in [1956] A.C. 588 at p. 607.
[60] At p. 612.

situated. Whether or not the destination or source of supply is a term of the contract probably depends on the circumstances of any given case.[61]

510 Any attempt to invoke the f.o.b. term as one from which the answer is to be derived would be extending its meaning beyond permissible limits. There is nothing to suggest that the f.o.b. term is to be construed as one under which the movement of the goods subsequent to delivery f.o.b. at the port of embarkation is of no concern whatsoever to the seller. To be sure there is probably even less to say in favour of an inference that a guarantee of import into a particular market is implied as there is to say in favour of stating the reverse. Generally speaking, it would probably be more difficult to imply any such term in the case of internal sales than would be the case in an external sale, though no rule of general application is to be drawn from *Pound v. Hardy* which is best considered as a decision on its special facts. Moreover, where the import prohibition is due to the nature or origin of the article sold the buyer must probably bear the risk of any impossibility to deal with the goods at their destination. For the seller does not warrant that there is no local legislation prohibiting their resale (or use) at the destination contemplated.[62] Similarly, if the destination cannot be reached due to a breakdown of arrangements with the carrier, the risk is generally for account of the buyer and he cannot usually claim that performance became impossible because the carrier is unable to deliver the goods at the contemplated port of discharge.[63] Where the destination is made a term of the contract, there can be no question of nominating an alternative destination. Express provisions to this effect are sometimes inserted in f.o.b. contracts as the following excerpt from the General Produce Brokers' Association of London standard form of f.o.b. contract illustrates:

---

[61] See *Schijveschuurder and Ors. v. Canon (Export) Ltd.* [1952] 2 Lloyd's Rep. 196 in which it was decided that no contract for the sale of Rongalite f.o.b Rotterdam was concluded for the parties were not *ad idem*, the buyer intending to obtain Rongalite of Dutch origin, the seller intending to supply American Rongalite which the buyer could not accept.

[62] See, *e.g. Sumner Permain & Co. v. Webb & Co.* [1922] 1 K.B. 55, Indian tonic sold f.o.b. London is not rendered unmerchantable within the meaning of (old) s.14(2) of the Sale of Goods Act because it cannot be resold in Argentina regardless of the seller's knowledge that the tonic was acquired with this purpose in mind.

[63] In *J. S. Hatcher et al. v. Barlow Ferguson*, 33 Idaho 639, 198 Pac. 680 (1921), the Supreme Court of Idaho held that the buyer assumes the risk of refusal on part of the carrier to bill the goods to the contemplated destination. The contract in question was for the delivery during the month of August of a consignment of livestock f.o.b. railcar in the American interior. The intention was to carry the livestock to Chicago. On August 30, when delivery was made the railroad company refused to accept any livestock for shipment to any point in the east because of a threatened strike of railroad employees all over the system unless delivery at destination could be made before noon on September 2. In delivering judgment for the seller, Dunn J. said:

> "The aim of the [buyers] in this case has been to show that the contract imposed upon the [seller] the burden of billing the lambs to an Eastern market, and that in the absence of such billing delivery according to the contract was not possible, but we think no such construction can fairly be placed upon said contract. There is in the contract nothing that would warrant this construction, and the evidence shows no agreement outside of the contract by which the [seller] was to become in any sense responsible for the destination of the lambs. When he loaded them on cars at Ketchum without expense to the buyer he discharged the obligation of his contract, and the fact that the buyers were unable, on

"*Licences*. Whenever an Import Licence is necessary Buyers undertake to be responsible for obtaining such Licence. Buyers further undertake to accept the consequences resulting under this Contract from their inability to obtain the necessary Licence and from the revocation or annulment of such Licence granted; provided always that no act on the part of the Sellers has prevented or prevents the granting of the Licence required. Should, however, revocation or annulment or refusal hereafter to grant the Licence result from a Government Order made before shipment prohibiting unconditionally the importation of the goods contracted for, this Contract shall be cancelled forthwith without allowance or penalty to either party. The foregoing stipulations shall be construed to apply equally to the Sellers regarding an Export Licence if such Licence is necessary."

It may be added that a provision by which the contemplated destination becomes a term of the contract is not to be regarded as one which operates entirely for the benefit of the buyer. The seller frequently also has a legitimate interest in curtailing the movement of goods supplied or manufactured by him. He may *e.g.* wish to restrict them from reaching markets which are undesirable either from his own business or personal point of view or where the national interests of his government so dictate. Conversely, he may have an interest in a particular destination.

Thus, *e.g.* in *Port Sudan Cotton Co. v. Govindaswamy Chettiar & Sons*[64] the Court of Appeal had to consider whether an f.o.b. seller was in breach for his refusal to ship 9,000 bales of Sudanese cotton to a destination other than India. For some years (prior to the dispute) there was a trade agreement between India and Sudan, and the sellers claimed that the contract in question (which was concluded with an Indian purchaser) was in implementation of that trade agreement. The Indian buyers said that no limitation as to the destination of the cotton was incorporated in the final contract, and nominated a vessel destined for Rumania. The purchase was the result of a bid (in response to a public tender) which indicated that the buyers had hoped to sell the cotton to certain Indian mills, and the original contract forms prepared and signed by the sellers indicated the destination as India. But the buyers took exception to this, and obtained a telexed confirmation from the sellers that no limitation as to the destination would apply and that the destination could be "anywhere," provided payment was effected in freely convertible currency. The sellers, however, were unable to secure permission to ship to any destination but India, and purported to justify cancellation on the ground that the buyers had misrepresented the destination in their bid, and that the contract provided for an Indian destination. But the Court of Appeal (Denning M.R. and Browne and Pennycuick L.JJ.), reversing an arbitration award and Donaldson J., held that there was no misrepresentation, and that the sellers were in breach for refusing to perform since the buyer could nominate any destination and no limitation thereon applied in the circumstances.

---

account of the embargo, to ship farther than Shoshone, was not sufficient reason for them to refuse to accept the lambs and pay for them."
[64] [1977] 2 Lloyd's Rep. 5 (C.A.).

International Chamber of Commerce definition

511   ''Incoterms'' has often been referred to in the preceding pages. Since the allocation of responsibilities between the parties to an f.o.b. contract thereunder is closer to the ''additional services'' variant than to either of the other two variants of f.o.b. contract here considered, it may now be useful to set forth the definition of the International Chamber of Commerce in full. According to ''Incoterms 1990'' the respective obligations of the parties are as follows:

A. The Seller Must:

1.   *Provision of goods in conformity with the contract*

Provide the goods and the commercial invoice, or its equivalent electronic message, in conformity with the contract of sale and any other evidence of conformity which may be required by the contract.

2.   *Licences, authorisations and formalities*

Obtain at his own risk and expense any export licence or other official authorisation and carry out all customs formalities necessary for the exportation of the goods.

3.   *Contract of carriage and insurance*

   a) Contract of carriage No obligation.
   b) Contract of insurance No obligation.

4.   *Delivery*

Deliver the goods on board the vessel named by the buyer at the named port of shipment on the date or within the period stipulated and in the manner customary at the port.

5.   *Transfer of risks*

Subject to the provisions of B.5., bear all risks of loss of or damage to the goods until such time as they have passed the ship's rail at the named port of shipment.

6.   *Division of costs*

Subject to the provisions of B.6.
   • pay all costs relating to the goods until such time as they have passed the ship's rail at the named port of shipment;
   • pay the costs of customs formalities necessary for exportation as well as all duties, taxes and other official charges payable upon exportation.

423

7. *Notice to the buyer*

    Give the buyer sufficient notice that the goods have been delivered on board.

8. *Proof of delivery, transport document or equivalent electronic message*

    Provide the buyer at the seller's expense with the usual document in proof of delivery in accordance with A.4.

    Unless the document referred to in the preceding paragraph is the transport document, render the buyer, at the latter's request, risk and expense, every assistance in obtaining a transport document for the contract of carriage (for example, a negotiable bill of lading, a non-negotiable sea waybill, an inland waterway document, or a multimodal transport document).

    Where the seller and the buyer have agreed to communicate electronically, the document referred to in the preceding paragraph may be replaced by an equivalent electronic data interchange (EDI) message.

9. *Checking—packaging—marking*

    Pay the costs of those checking operations (such as checking quality, measuring, weighing, counting) which are necessary for the purpose of delivering the goods in accordance with A.4.

    Provide at his own expense packaging (unless it is usual for the particular trade to ship the goods of the contract description unpacked) which is required for the transport of the goods, to the extent that the circumstances relating to the transport (e.g. modalities, destination) are made known to the seller before the contract of sale is concluded. Packaging is to be marked appropriately.

10. *Other obligations*

    Render the buyer at the latter's request, risk and expense, every assistance in obtaining any documents or equivalent (electronic messages (other than those mentioned in A8. Issued or transmitted in the country of shipment and/ or of origin which the buyer may require for the importation of the goods and, where necessary, for their transit through another country.

    Provide the buyer, upon request, with the necessary information for procuring insurance.

B. The Buyer Must:

1. *Payment of the price*

    Pay the price as provided in the contract of sale.

2. *Licences, authorisations and formalities*

    Obtain at his own risk and expense any import licence or other official authorisation and carry out all customs formalities for the importation of the goods and, where necessary, for their transit through another country.

3. *Contract of carriage*

Contract at his own expense for the carriage of the goods from the named port of shipment.

4. *Taking delivery*

Take delivery of the goods in accordance with A.4.

5. *Transfer of risks*

Bear all risks of loss of or damage to the goods from the time they have passed the ship's rail at the named port of shipment. Should he fail to give notice in accordance with B.7., or should the vessel named by him fail to arrive on time, or be unable to take the goods, or close for cargo earlier than the stipulated time, bear all risks of loss of or damage to the goods from the agreed date or the expiry date of the period stipulated for delivery provided, however, that the goods have been duly appropriated to the contract, that is to say, clearly set aside or otherwise identified as the contract goods.

6. *Division of costs*

Pay all costs relating to the goods from the time they have passed the ship's rail at the named port of shipment.

Pay any additional costs incurred, either because the vessel named by him has failed to arrive on time, or is unable to take the goods, or will close for cargo earlier than the stipulated date, or because the buyer has failed to give appropriate notice in accordance with B.7. provided, however, that the goods have been duly appropriated to the contract, that is to say, clearly set aside or otherwise identified as the contract goods.

Pay all duties, taxes and other official charges as well as the costs of carrying out customs formalities payable upon importation of the goods and, where necessary, for their transit through another country.

7. *Notice to the seller*

Give the seller sufficient notice of the vessel name, loading point and required delivery time.

8. *Proof of delivery, transport document or equivalent electronic message*

Accept the proof of delivery in accordance with A.8.

9. *Inspection of goods*

Pay, unless otherwise agreed, the costs of pre-shipment inspection except when mandated by the authorities of the country of export.

10. *Other obligations*

Pay all costs and charges incurred in obtaining the documents or equivalent electronic messages mentioned in A.10. and reimburse those incurred by the seller in rendering his assistance in accordance therewith.

"Shipment to destination" variant

512   It has been noted that in an f.o.b. contract the nomination of the ship is the duty of the buyer; that it is in point of fact a condition precedent to the contract, and that before the buyer has complied with this duty, the seller need not, indeed cannot, deliver f.o.b.

In external sales, however, it is often more convenient for the seller to arrange shipping space at the f.o.b. point than for the buyer abroad to do so. And pressure to assume this task is also exerted by liner conference shipowners who occasionally condition rebates under loyalty agreements on "active support" or "exclusive patronage" provisions which cover f.o.b. as well as c.i.f. shipments. Thus, an f.o.b. seller may risk being penalised (or at least be denied a benefit) by the regular shipping lines servicing his country if engaged in a transaction wherein his buyer designates a non-conference vessel for the shipment of goods under a contract to which he is a party. Clearly there is no justification for this conference practice, and it is extremely doubtful whether the provision would be enforced where the seller has no right to select the carrier. Nonetheless the practice persists[65] (except in trade to and from United States ports where it is expressly prohibited) and it probably encourages some f.o.b. sellers to agree to secure shipping space for their buyers. In some cases the seller might further agree to prepay the freight and insurance charges also.

513   As stated by Diplock J. in *Ian Stach Ltd. v. Baker Bosley Ltd.*[66]

> ". . . it may be a matter of doubt as to whose was to be the responsibility for finding shipping space and for determining shipping port and shipping date. Prima facie, under an f.o.b. contract that is the duty and responsibility of the buyer; but there are probably as many exceptions to the rule as there are examples of it."

Where the seller agrees to secure the vessel (hereafter referred to as the f.o.b. "shipment to destination" variant[67]), further complications arise, especially since in these cases, the bordeline between the f.o.b. and the c. and f. or c.i.f. terms, is often difficult to determine. It is suggested that the capacity in which the seller acts while procuring the shipment and/or prepaying freight and insurance (if so be the case), provides the necessary differentiating factor between the f.o.b. and any other similar shipping contract. It has already been mentioned (*ante*, § 480), that the additional services undertaken by the seller as shipper or exporter are in the case of external f.o.b. sales executed by him in his capacity as seller, *i.e.* as principal, and not in his capacity as agent of

[65] See *The Liner Conference System*, United Nations document TD/B/c.4/62/Rev. 1, paras. 133 *et seq.* (N.Y. 1970).
[66] [1958] 2 Q.B. 130 at p. 138.
[67] Not to be confused with an f.o.b. point of destination contract which is a contract for the sale of goods after arrival at their destination, the seller having to transport the goods at his own expense and risk to that place as provided for, for example in s.2–319(1)(b) of the Uniform Commercial Code.

the buyer. Where the f.o.b. "additional services" type of contract is employed, the seller therefore invariably acts as principal. A *converse* rule applies here. It is suggested that for a sale to be on f.o.b. terms, all services connected with the provision of the vessel and/or prepayment of freight or insurance, *are always on account and risk of the buyer*, and if undertaken by the seller it is as agent of the buyer.

514   There is, of course, "nothing unusual in one party being both a principal in one capacity and an agent, [and] he may have these two functions arising out of the same transaction."[68] In the case of *The Tromp*[69] Duke P. held that the f.o.b. seller (through a forwarding agent) was the shipper of the goods, and he further held that the same forwarding agent acted on behalf of the buyer "for a variety of purposes" including, it would appear, the securing of the tonnage and the insurance of the cargo. This decision thus aptly illustrates the foregoing proposition showing that in shipping the goods the consignor acted for the seller, but that the position was reversed in regard to securing the shipping space and insuring the voyage, in respect of which he acted as agent for the buyer.

It would, however, be incorrect to assume that the proposition above set forth enjoys universal recognition as the following passage from the judgment of Herring C.J. (Sup.Ct. of Victoria) in *The "Mahia" (No. 2)*[70] clearly illustrates:

> "In any event even if [the seller] was not bound by its [f.o.b.] contract, or the course of dealing between the parties, to make these arrangements [freight and insurance], but made them merely because it desired to be accommodating, it would be proper to regard it as having made them in its capacity as seller under and in performance of the contract of sale. There is nothing here to suggest a new contract or a new transaction, separate from the contract of sale, such as a mandate to send the goods or a new contract to forward them. See *Wimble, Sons & Co. v. Rosenberg & Sons* [1913] 3 K.B. 743 at p. 758, *per* Hamilton L. J. as he then was."

515   With respect this view is not tenable in the case of f.o.b. contracts proper. Indeed the *Mahia* court itself did not conceal its doubts as to the precise nature of the contract in question, though it appears that it ultimately decided to treat it as an f.o.b. contract. The case involved an action by the shipowner against various parties for damage caused by an explosion resulting from a consignment of sodium chlorate which was shipped in unsuitable containers. If it could have been shown that the property had passed to the consignees prior to loading and shipping the chlorate in Montreal, the consignees could have been held liable. This contention the court rejected, *inter alia*, on the grounds above stated, namely, that the shipment was not arranged by the seller as agents of the buyers, and that as a result the buyers could not be

---

[68] McNair J. in *Sobell Industries v. Cory Bros.* [1955] 2 Lloyd's Rep. 82.
[69] [1921] P. 337.
[70] [1960] 1 Lloyd's Rep. 191 at p. 197.

held to be vicariously responsible as principals for any breach of duty towards the ship. But this conclusion would have in any case applied to an f.o.b. contract of the type here considered. The difficulty the court encountered in this case resulted from the fact that this was an American type of f.o.b. contract featuring f.o.r. elements.[71] The risk in the goods was actually transferred to the consignee from the moment the goods were placed in the hands of the railroad in the Canadian interior at Buckingham, with the seller undertaking to arrange their passage and insurance up to the point of destination by means of a through bill of lading involving both land and sea passage.

516   However, the question of whether the seller performs, or undertakes to perform, certain duties as principal or as agent is further complicated by an additional factor. Had the f.o.b. term furnished conclusive evidence as to the intention of the parties, it could perhaps have been concluded that where the seller agrees to procure shipment or to prepay the freight or the insurance, or both, he is acting as agent for the buyer. However, in certain instances the parties have been held to apply the f.o.b. term as a basis for calculating the price of the goods only and not as a basis for defining their respective obligations under their contract. The problem is succinctly described by Williston[72] in commenting on *Hackfeld v. Castle*[73] wherein he stated:

> "the question being whether the buyer or the seller should secure the necessary transportation, the answer was held to depend on the intention of the parties as to what they contemplated and the expression f.o.b. was made to throw no light on the question, such expression merely making it the seller's duty to load at his own expense."

Thus, export price lists are of necessity normally expressed in f.o.b. terms, *i.e.* on an f.o.b. basis, this being the highest common denominator of general application. The cost of shipment, namely, freight and insurance, must vary from case to case since it is subject to the circumstances—distance, etc.—of any particular sale. This incidentally is also the practice of the United Kingdom Customs ad Licensing Authorities. The export value of goods is always calculated on an f.o.b. basis irrespective of the particular terms of sale. This value is defined as: "the cost of the goods to the purchaser abroad, including packing," and covers:

> "Inland and coastal transport in the United Kingdom, dock dues, loading charges, and all other costs, profits, charges and expenses (*e.g.* insurance and commission) accruing up to the point when the goods are deposited on board the exporting vessel or aircraft or at the land boundary of Northern Ireland. In all cases, outward sea or air freight and marine or air insurance to the purchaser abroad should be excluded and cash and trade discounts to the purchaser abroad deducted."[74]

---

[71] See *ante*, § 431, n. 1.
[72] *Williston on sales* (Rev. ed.), para. 280a, n. 5.
[73] 186 Cal. 53, 198 P. 1041 (1921).
[74] See *Export List*, 1969 Notes, para. (c).

517   This practice of employing the f.o.b. term only in conjunction with the price may cause confusion. By obtaining various price lists, the buyer is able to compare different offers from the same source of supply, but when he decides with whom to place his order he often expects the seller to provide the necessary tonnage and sometimes also to advance the freight and insurance for the carriage of the goods to their destination. In effect, a transaction on a c. and f. or c.i.f. basis may be contemplated. Since these variant terms differ not merely in price, *viz.*, one including, and the other excluding, freight and insurance expenses, the correct description of the contract is extremely important. Under both types of contract, the buyer assumes the risk of the goods being destroyed or damaged during their sea transit,[75] but there the resemblance sometimes ends. From a practical point of view, the difference between a contract f.o.b. (seller acting as agent), and any other similar contract (seller acting as principal), could be said to relate to the question of certain incidental risks, *e.g.* the risk involved in procuring shipment and insurance, or the risk of a fluctuation in the price thereof.

518   It is thought that in a genuine f.o.b. contract these risks should not be for the account of the seller whereas in the case of other contracts, and c.i.f. contracts in particular, they normally would.

As stated by Pearson J. in *Carlos Federspiel & Co., S. A. v. Charles Twigg & Co. Ltd.*[76]

> "I agree ... that fundamentally [this contract] is to be regarded as an f.o.b. contract, but one has to add that it has some c.i.f. features attached to it. ... It would seem that the intention is that the sellers are, in the first instance, to arrange the insurance and the contract of affreightment, and they are to pay the freight and insurance and charge them as extras to the buyers; and the intention seems to be that they should charge the cost price to the buyers, so that any rise or fall in rates of freight or insurance would be for the account of the buyers and of no interest to the sellers."

519   And in *N. V. Handel My. J. Smits Import-Export v. English Exporters (London) Ltd.*,[77] the question being whether the sellers undertook an absolute

---

[75] It may be useful to point out that, although both are shipment terms, and neither is a destination term, the normal c.i.f. contract does not directly identify the point of delivery whereas an f.o.b. contract invariably does. This distinction is reflected in the following passage from Lord Trayner's judgment in *A. Delaurier & Co. v. J. Wyllie & Ors.* (1889) 17 R. (Ct. of Sess.) 167, where he dismissed the argument that the term c.i.f. was a destination term and said:
> "But the defenders maintain that a contract for the sale of goods c.i.f. imports an obligation to deliver at the port of discharge. ... It was said that the view submitted by the defenders of the effect and import of a contract c.i.f. was that which mainly distinguished it from a contract f.o.b. These contracts are no doubt different and distinguishable. The contract f.o.b. directly stipulates for delivery at a certain place, namely, on board ship, and delivery there (free of charge to the buyer) is fulfilment of the seller's obligation. But granting that, the defenders are no further forward; for it still remains that the contract c.i.f. does not stipulate for delivery at a certain place."

[76] [1957] 1 Lloyd's Rep. 240 at p. 246. The facts of the case are set out *post*, § 515.
[77] [1957] 1 Lloyd's Rep. 517.

obligation to secure the shipping space, McNair J. held the answer to depend on the agreement of the parties concluded by means of an exchange of letters. In the course of his judgment the learned judge said:

> "The only doubt in my mind, at all, is whether those letters, taken together, are sufficiently clear to impose upon the sellers an absolute obligation to find and nominate a ship in the sense that if they fail to find and nominate a ship they will be in contractual default. I think the buyers' letter of April 24, and particularly the paragraph reading: 'It has been agreed that you will do your best to obtain shipping space,' indicates clearly that all that had been undertaken by the sellers was to do their best to obtain shipping space, and that involves two things: first it relieves the buyers of the necessity of taking steps themselves to obtain shipping space and communicating their nomination to the sellers; and, also, it imposes upon the sellers the limited obligation of doing 'their best to obtain shipping space'" (at p. 521).

520   Replying to the argument put forth by the seller that when in a written contract the symbol f.o.b. is used that necessarily imports, or imports unless excluded by very clear language, that there shall rest upon the buyers the obligation to nominate the vessel, McNair J. noted that "as has been observed in a number of cases,[78] these expressions 'f.o.b.' and 'c.i.f.,' as applied to sale contracts, do not of themselves standardise the legal incidents falling upon one party or the other" (at page 519).[79] He further went on to say that "an f.o.b. contract—may, as a matter of construction, contain obligations which are not those normally associated with [it]" (at page 520). On the basis of the foregoing, McNair J. concluded that he must "approach the question of the construction of those . . . letters to see whether there is anything in them which does displace the normal incidents of an f.o.b. contract."

The first letter, he said, contained a very striking stipulation which would not normally be found in an ordinary f.o.b. contract, for in it one finds the sellers and not the buyers saying:

> "We are now arranging shipment for Hong Kong as early as possible in June and as soon as we are in the position to give you the name of the steamer we shall not fail to do so immediately" (at p. 521).

---

[78] He referred in particular to the following: *Pyrene Company Ltd. v. Scindia Navigation Company Ltd.* [1954] 2 Q.B. 402 (see *ante*, § 434; *Comptoir d'Achat et de Vente du Boerenbond Belge. S.A. v. Luis de Ridder, Limitida* [1949] A.C. 293 (see *ante*, § 16; *A. V. Pound & Co. Ltd. v. M. W. Hardy & Co. Inc.* [1956] A.C. 588 (see *ante*, § 491.

[79] The statement should perhaps be qualified. The terms do determine the legal incidents to the extent that their meaning has not been altered by some agreement, express or implied, to the contrary. Thus, *e.g.* in *Frebold and Sturznickel (Trading as Panda O.H.G.) v. Circle Products Ltd.* [1970] 1 Lloyd's Rep. 499, the Court of Appeal reversing Nield J. held that notwithstanding the fact that the sellers paid for transport to destination (explained as "an act of grace" by themselves), and that the goods were not to be handed over to the buyers by sellers' agents at destination until payment, the f.o.b. term still governed. "Prima facie," said Widgery L. J. (at p. 504) "when two commercial men use a well known phrase of this kind (f.o.b.) they must be presumed to give it its established meaning. I do not think that this presumption is rebutted by the fact that the sellers instructed Schenkers not to hand over the goods until payment had been secured."

521   Though McNair J. clearly based his decision that the seller did not undertake an absolute obligation to procure shipment on the terms of the letter
which constituted the agreement between the parties in the case just considered, it is thought that the normal case would call for a similar inference. In
other words that, unless an express agreement to the contrary can be shown
to exist, the seller would, in the case of f.o.b. shipment to destination contracts, always undertake merely a conditional obligation to do his best to
secure the ship. Put differently, that he does not assume the further obligation
of warranting that a ship will be available, and that if he has discharged his
duty diligently he is not liable to pay damages for failing to ship.

This was so held by the Supreme Court of Canada in relation to a contract
for the sale of goods f.o.b. railway cars. The decision however may have
been in part motivated by the particular circumstances of the case, there being
no alternative carrier available. For as stated by Anglin C.J.[80]:

> "There may be some ground for . . . [the] contention that the authorities holding
> that under a contract for the sale of goods . . . f.o.b. a vessel the purchaser is
> bound to have a ship ready to receive the goods at the designated place of ship-
> ment do not govern such a case as this. The number of owners having ships
> open for charter is large: here C.P.R. cars were the only available means of
> carriage."

It is suggested that whatever the merit of this distinction may be in respect
to the buyer's duty to nominate the vessel, in so far as the seller's duty is
considered, its qualified nature would also be due to the fact that in undertaking this duty under an f.o.b. contract he should, in effect, be considered as
acting as the agent of the buyer.

522   Similarly, in *J.S. Hatcher et al. v. Barlow Ferguson*[81] where goods sold
f.o.b. railroad cars could not be carried to their contemplated destination
because of an embargo placed by the railway company prior to delivery, the
risk was held to fall on the buyer. The fact that the seller was to secure the
carriage was immaterial. For it was said that when the f.o.b. seller enters into
a contract with the carrier for shipment to a particular destination he acts
agent for the buyer. He has done his duty when he demands of the carrier a
contract to the destination requested by the buyer, and if any loss results from
the refusal of the carrier to make a contract to deliver at the desired destination, the loss must be borne by the buyer and not by the seller.

523   The foregoing principles, it is thought, would not apply in the normal case
of a c.i.f. contract, where the seller's obligations with respect to the shipment
of the goods, undertaken by him in the capacity of principal, would have a
more stringent flavour. Likewise an additional difference between an f.o.b.
contract proper and any similar contract may pertain to the risk of a denial
of any export licence which may be necessary. As will be recalled, there is

---

[80] *Vancouver Milling & Grain Co. v. C.C. Ranch Co.* [1925] 1 D.L.R. 185 at p. 187.
[81] 33 Idaho 639, 198 Pac. 680 (1921).

no clear authority (except *"Incoterms"*) for the proposition that in *all* external sales this responsibility rests with the seller. Where (i) the risk is borne by the buyer, and (ii) the contract is not deemed cancelled in the event of an export prohibition or any similar supervening impossibility, this difference is equally crucial, because in a c.i.f. sale there is no doubt that it is always the duty of the seller to furnish the necessary export documents and pay the relevant tax. An additional difference could possibly be found in connection with the "proper" insurance documents with more flexibility allowed than the c.i.f. contract would normally permit.[82] Similarly, the place at which tender of the documents should be made may be different and it may be that, in the absence of an express stipulation, the f.o.b. buyer could not demand that the documents be tendered at his place of business.[83] Finally, there might also be a variation in price. For it would appear that only in the case of the sale f.o.b. is the seller allowed subsequently to add an unexpressed commission for services rendered and expenses incurred in connection with the shipment and insurance of the goods.

524   Since these differences, which frequently do not lend themselves to clear recognition, are usually quite insignificant, the importance of the foregoing distinction is not always fully realised. Consequently, it is often difficult in the extreme to determine what the dominant features of the transaction are, and whether the contract is in fact on c.i.f. or f.o.b. terms.[84]

525   Recognising the wide-spread practice of contracting on f.o.b. "shipment to destination" terms, Bailhache J. was once even led to remark that[85]

> "This case shows, as all these cases do now, that as a matter of fact the practice in f.o.b. contracts for the sale of comparatively small parcels, as distinguished from cargoes, it is the universal practice now for the sellers at the port of shipment, when that port is abroad, to busy themselves in securing the shipping space, and I am inclined to think that the Court, in holding the view that the duty is still on the buyer and that the seller is acting merely in a friendly way or as an *agent* for the buyer, is deciding in a manner not in accordance with the commercial practice or the views of commercial men. Some day I shall expect that point to be raised, but if it is one will have to have evidence of the universality of the practice. My own view is that in the case of small parcels sold f.o.b. it is the duty of the seller to take the necessary steps to provide the shipping accommodation. That is contrary to what is always held in these Courts, and it will be interesting—if anybody has enterprise enough to raise the point—to know what view this Court will take of the matter.

---

[82] *Ante*, § 209.

[83] *Ante*, § 244.

[84] See, *e.g. The Parchim* [1918] A.C. 157, *post*, § 534, and *Re An Arbitration Between Comptoir Commercial Anversois and Power, Son & Co.* [1920] 1 K.B. 868, *ante*, § 187 (a sale f.o.b. including freight and insurance, which Bailhache J. apparently treated as an f.o.b. contract observing that "the practice appears to be for the sellers to arrange for or nominate the carrying steamships" (at p. 876)).

[85] *D. H. Bain v. Field & Co. Fruit Merchants Ltd.* (1920) 3 Ll.L.Rep. 26 at p. 29; affirmed 5 Ll.L.Rep. 16 (C.A.).

"It is desirable that a decision of the Court should be in accordance with the practice and views of commercial men, except where these views infringe upon or are contrary to some settled principle of law. But there is no settled law about this. It is merely a question of what is the settled commercial practice as to f.o.b. sales of small parcels of goods, not being cargoes, when the sellers are abroad. I invite somebody at some time to be enterprising enough to raise that point in order to see how the matter stands, and to ascertain if the view of the Court is contrary to the practice of commercial men, or if the two cannot be reconciled.

"I am not able to do it in this case, and I am not sure I should say it could be done, and it could not be done without a very considerable body of evidence as to the general practice, but I do say that these cases are decided on a somewhat artificial basis, having regard to the commercial practice."

526   Bailhache J.'s challenge (on which the Court of Appeal in confirming his judgment conspicuously refrained from commenting)[86] is yet to be acted upon, though from all available information his suspicion that there is a discrepancy between the law and commercial practice does not seem warranted. For although, as is clearly apparent from the foregoing, it is quite common for the seller to engage the shipping space, whenever this is done (and the contract is on f.o.b. terms proper), the seller probably acts *not* on his own behalf, but as the agent of the buyer. And this is equally true when the advancement of freight and insurance is considered. This is clearly the view of the business community. Neither of the publications of the International Chamber of Commerce which define the f.o.b. term supports Bailhache J.'s contention, no distinction being drawn between consignments large or small.[87] Thus, there appears to be no divergence between the legal and commercial interpretations of the f.o.b. term, and the distinction between a genuine f.o.b. contract and c. and f. or c.i.f. contracts (where the symbol "f.o.b." is used as a measure of the price only) can, it is therefore thought, be expressed in the following manner: In the case of an f.o.b. "shipment to destination" contract, the shipping space is secured by the seller on behalf of the buyer for whom he acts as agent. Whereas, in the case of these other contracts, the seller secures the shipping space for his own behalf, and only thereafter sells the contract of carriage (together with the goods) to the buyer.

527   Accordingly, the seller's capacity probably reflects a basic differentiating factor between these various similar shipping contracts, and provides a useful guideline for a scientific inquiry attempting to classify the contract. In view of the two possible meanings of the f.o.b. term, however, and because of the

---

[86] (1920) 5 Ll. L. Rep. 16.

[87] *"Incoterms"*; *"Trade Terms,"* notes to B. 1, pp. 58 *et seq.* (see esp. Italy, n. 6); see also comment 6 on all f.o.b. terms by Joint Committee representing the U.S. Chamber of Commerce *et al.* in 2 *Williston on Sales* (Rev. ed., 1948), para. 2801, p. 133, to the effect that "under f.o.b. terms . . . the obligation to obtain ocean freight space, and marine and war risk insurance, rests with the buyer. Despite this obligation on the part of the buyer, in many trades the seller obtains the ocean freight space, and marine and war risk insurance, and provides for the shipment on behalf of the buyer. Hence, seller and buyer must have an understanding as to whether the buyer will obtain the ocean freight space, and marine and war risk insurance, as is his obligation, or whether the seller agrees to do this for the buyer."

misunderstandings which still prevail in this field, the foregoing distinction has not always been applied.

Absent a specific agreement,[88] trade usage or course of dealing between the parties by virtue of which the seller could be said to have relieved the buyer of his duty of securing the shipping space (and no such agreement ought to be implied from a term in the contract which merely provides for "free on board December shipment, seller's option," for, as held in *Darling v. Gurthrie & Co. Ltd.*,[89] such a provision refers only to the time of delivery and does not transfer the onus of securing the shipping space to the seller) an f.o.b. term proper, definitely requires some subsequent arrangement in order to throw the onus of securing freight or insurance, or both, from the buyer to the seller. In the absence of any such special arrangements, the seller may normally disregard any request from the buyer to incur any of these additional obligations, and he may insist on the buyer providing shipping space on the penalty of default. Where, however, the f.o.b. seller is held to have assumed some or all of these obligations, it is as agent of the buyer that he assumes them. In such a case, the seller will probably be allowed to claim the usual commission and charge the buyer for any such service over and above the original contract price.[90]

528   Since the invoice furnishes some evidence as to the terms of the contract the suggestion has been made that[91]

> "where the f.o.b. seller undertakes to ship and insure the goods sold, he may make out two invoices, one invoice showing the f.o.b. values of the goods including all expenses up to the delivery of the goods over the ship's rail, and another invoice showing the additional services which he performed by request of the buyer, and in particular the costs of prepaid freight and marine insurance and any commission which might be due to him."

Though it has frequently been the subject of differing opinions between parties to an f.o.b. contract, the question whether, in cases such as these, where the seller agrees to prepay the freight for account of the buyer, the benefit of any conference rebates should accrue to the seller or to the buyer does not appear to have been the subject of litigation up to now. The better view is for the buyer to enjoy the benefit of any rebate. Since as suggested the seller in assuming this duty under a genuine f.o.b. contract merely acts for the buyer as his shipping agent. He therefore should not be entitled to

---

[88] See, *e.g. Warin & Craven v. D. Forrester* (1876) 4 R. (Ct. of Sess.) 190, where an f.o.b. contract containing the clause "the sellers will use every endeavour to engage freight-room and expedite shipments, but are not liable for delay caused by want of tonnage" was considered. The court held that in performing this task the sellers were acting as agents for the buyers.

[89] (1907) S.A.L.R. 152 (Australian decision).

[90] See Lord Blackburn's definition of the c.i.f. contract in *Ireland v. Livingston* (1872) L.R. 5 H.L. 395 at p. 406 *ante*, § 5 which he concluded by remarking that "Each party there takes upon himself the risk of the rise or fall in price and there is no contract of agency or trust between them, and therefore no commission is charged."

[91] Schmitthoff, *The Export Trade* (7th ed., 1980), p. 20.

debit the buyer for an amount which is higher than the actual sum which he has expended on account of the freight.[92] In the absence of any agreement, the seller would be ill advised to take any rebates into consideration in calculating his sale price. Consequently no assumption should be made that any allowance in the price will in due course be covered by a rebate from the carrier which he would be entitled to withhold. The foregoing notwithstanding, in practice conference rebates are in such circumstances sometimes added to the account of the seller and not passed on to the buyer. This is particularly so when the rebate is deferred (shipowners obviously prefer deferred rebates because of the advantage it gives them in case of breach of loyalty) rather than immediate, a practice permitted almost everywhere except in the United States, where it is proscribed by law.[93]

529   Wherever the seller agrees to procure shipment, he must ensure that the goods are delivered f.o.b. within the period of time allowed by the contract. A failure to meet the delivery date would generally permit the buyer to cancel the transaction and reject the goods.[94] Conversely, the buyer's duty is to declare the port of discharge in time in order to enable the seller to comply with the foregoing duty. A failure to communicate the port of discharge to the seller before the earliest day on which shipment can be effected is a breach of a condition precedent, and the seller can terminate the contract by virtue thereof.[95]

530   *Purchase through a confirming house.* Where the buyer orders goods through a confirming house[96] for delivery within a stated period of time—not by a specific date—*Anglo African Shipping Company of New York, Inc. v. Mortner Ltd.*[97] shows that period of time to run from the date the confirming house entered into a contract to fulfil the order, not from the date on which the order is placed with, or received by, the confirming house. The facts there were as follows: On November 24, 1964, the defendants airmailed an order for 5,000 yards of plastic vinyl sheeting f.a.s. New York "delivery two or three weeks"; the contract called for confirmation by the plaintiffs and further stipulated that "complete delivery must be made by the time stated or goods shall be refused . . . time shall be of the essence of this contract."[98] The

---

[92] See correspondence in the *Merchant Shipper*, November 1959 at p. 573.
[93] s.12 of the Shipping Act 1916. In the U.S. the "dual rate" system (under which shippers who agree to use only conference tonnage benefit from lower rates) is used to reward loyalty of shippers.
[94] *Wilson v. Wright* (1937) 59 Ll.L.Rep. 86; *Yelo v. S. M. Machado & Co. Ltd.* [1952] 1 Lloyd's Rep. 183; *Nortier & Co. v. Maclean, Sons & Co.* (1921) 9 Ll.L.Rep. 192; *cf.* also *Stenhouse v. Oelrichs* (1914) 41 W.N.(N.S.W.) 72 (Australia), and *Warin & Craven v. D. Forrester* (1876) 4 R. (Ct. of Sess.) 190.
[95] *Ante*, § 508.
[96] The legal nature of a confirming house, its principal functions, and the rights and liabilities thereof, are discussed in detail in Hill, "Confirming House Transactions in Commonwealth Countries," 3 *Journal of Maritime Law and Commerce* 307 (1972).
[97] [1962] 1 Lloyd's Rep. 81; *ibid.* 610 (C.A.).
[98] [1962] 1 Lloyd's Rep. 610 at p. 611.

plaintiffs received this order on November 28, and their confirmation took the form of an order to certain suppliers who received it on November 30. On December 18, the defendants purported to cancel their order by cable to the plaintiffs. The plaintiffs in turn immediately sought to cancel their contract with the supplier but the latter refused to abide by or accept the cancellation and sent the plaintiffs an invoice for the goods on the following day. The plaintiffs promptly arranged for shipping space for the goods which were loaded on December 29, and shipped to the defendants in London. Megaw J. gave judgment for the plaintiffs, and was upheld by the Court of Appeal (Sellers and Danckwerts L.JJ.; Diplock L.J. dissenting). The stipulated period for delivery of "two to three weeks" was held not to commence on November 24, the date of dispatch of defendants' order, but on November 30, the date on which the suppliers accepted the plaintiffs' order. Consequently, the contract period did not expire until December 21. It was further held that there was no breach, on the part of the suppliers, in placing the goods alongside the vessel on December 29. The ship was only nominated by the plaintiffs on the preceding day, and the plaintiffs, in their capacity as shipping agents for the buyers, did not act in a dilatory or negligent fashion when they reserved space on the vessel they had elected for carriage. This vessel was the fastest in terms of arrival in London, though not the earliest to leave New York for England. Megaw J. noted:

> "An early sailing date is not the only thing that the plaintiffs have to consider in doing their duty as shipping agents" (at p. 94).

531   Diplock L.J., in his dissenting judgment in the Court of Appeal, however, considered that the contractual relationship between a confirming house and its client was one of buyer and seller and that, accordingly, plaintiffs, as confirming house, were bound by the terms of their contract with the defendants and were under an absolute duty to deliver the goods f.a.s. New York within the shipment period. But this view, it is submitted, is in most instances an erroneous characterisation of the confirming house-client relationship which is more correctly to be construed as one of agency though in respect of the right of *stoppage in transitu* (*post*, § 706) and possibly in some other respects also, it may resemble a contract of sale. As to the problem of reconciling the personal responsibility of the confirming house to the seller under the contract, with the transfer of property in the goods to the buyer, other solutions are available.[99]

532   *Divisible contracts.* When the contract is divisible, the buyer must pay for each instalment delivered within the time limits specified in the contract even if the seller is prevented from completing delivery of the entire contract quantity by virtue of some event beyond his control. In *L. Osborn & Co. Ltd.*

---

[99] See Hill, *ibid* at p. 318 and the authorities there cited, in particular, *Bolus & Co. Ltd. v. Inglis* [1924] N.Z.L.R. 164.

v. Davidsons Bros.,[1] the plaintiffs agreed to sell the defendants 2,000 bags of maize f.o.b. Melbourne with shipment to be *spread* over January and February, at a rate of 1,000 bags each month. Subsequently, but before any shipments were actually made, the defendants suggested that only 500 bags be shipped in January and that the balance should be deferred to February. The seller shipped 296 bags on January 28, but was unable to ship more because of a strike of wharf labourers. The Victoria Supreme Court held that the defendants wrongly refused to pay for the quantity shipped. It was the court's view that the word "spread" still applied to the contract as altered and that having regard to it the plaintiffs were at liberty to deliver in more than one instalment. The defendants therefore were bound to pay for each instalment and could not reject the goods.

533   Whether the fact that the seller undertakes some or all of the shipping and insurance arrangements from the start, rather than by virtue of some subsequent arrangement, alters the character of the contract is not easy to answer. It is suggested, however, that where the contract is to be construed as an f.o.b. contract proper, the seller in undertaking these obligations would invariably act as agent for the buyer. In other words, the contract is improperly described as an f.o.b. contract where any of these obligations are construed to be undertaken by the seller in his capacity as principal though the contract may so be designated or labelled by the parties. This view appears to be shared by the authors of the comment appended to the *Revised American Foreign Trade Definitions—1941* who accordingly stated that[2]:

> "Under F.O.B. terms . . ., the obligation to obtain ocean freight space, and marine and war risk insurance rests with the buyer. Despite this obligation on the part of the buyer, in many trades the seller obtains the ocean freight space, and marine and war risk insurance, and provides for shipment on behalf of the buyer. Hence, seller and buyer must have an understanding as to whether the buyer will obtain the ocean freight space, and marine and war risk insurance, as is his obligation, or whether the seller agrees to do this *for* the buyer."

Hybrid contracts

534   In addition to contracts which have the appearance of being on f.o.b. terms, but which are not in fact f.o.b. contracts proper, contracts expressed as c. and f. or c.i.f., but which are mainly composed of f.o.b. elements are sometimes encountered. "This," as Lord Parker observed in *The Parchim*,[3] a prize case:

> ". . . is not an ordinary c.i.f. contract. The insurance is separately provided for and the premium is not included in the price, and, although the price includes freight, it is only the freight under the charterparty which the buyer is to take

---

[1] [1911] V.L.R. 416.
[2] Comment No. 6 of Comments On All F.O.B. Terms.
[3] [1918] A. C. 157 at pp. 163, 164. See also *ante*, § 11.

over. If the right to cancel that charterparty arises . . . the buyer has the responsibility of finding another ship. . . . He has to pay any excess of freight over the chartered freight. . . . As the sum included for freight in the price is a mere matter of calculation . . . the price is really for cost only, and the contract has far more of the characteristics of a contract f.o.b. Taltal, than it has of a contract c.i.f. European port.''

Finally, the words ''free on board'' have sometimes been used merely to describe the condition of the goods as being afloat. In these cases the f.o.b. term is neither a term of delivery nor a stipulation of price.[4]

Summary and conclusions

535   The f.o.b. term imports a particular division of responsibilities in a contract of sale, and defines the respective obligations of the parties thereto.

From a purely academic point of view, the ''strict'' interpretation has, perhaps, much to commend itself as the most satisfactory definition of the term f.o.b. Circumstances have, however, rendered this interpretation unsuitable in many cases. A practice has consequently developed whereby the respective obligations are adjusted somewhat. Because judicial pronouncements have seldom gone much beyond the general statement, that in a f.o.b. contract the seller bears all charges and responsibilities up to and including delivery on board, the question of marginal liabilities, ranging from barely putting the goods on board to c.i.f. terms (with or without pre-payment of freight and insurance) remains a matter of doubt in many instances, and the subject of conflicting opinions. The result of this situation is reflected in the diversity of views about the precise interpretation of the f.o.b. term.

536   For presentation purposes these differences are probably best reflected in the seller's capacity while performing certain (additional) services, which according to the ''strict'' definition are regarded as the responsibility of the buyer. Where the seller undertakes these as agent of, and for and on behalf of the buyer, the latter assumes the cost and risk, and also the ultimate liability therefor. On the other hand, where the seller as principal undertakes these additional obligations, the position is reversed. He personally bears responsibility therefor, and unless exempted by virtue of the operation of some legal principle (*e.g.* frustration, illegality, etc.) or protected by an appropriate exception clause, is therefore liable for any failure of performance.

537   The view that the seller invariably acts as agent of the buyer in undertaking any duties beyond those presented under the ''strict'' definition finds no support in jurisprudence or commercial practice. This view is tenable only where the question of procuring shipment (and/or of prepaying for the freight and

---

[4] See *Couturier v. Hastie* (1856) 5 H. L. Cas. 673 (a sale of corn, shipped ''free on board,'' and including ''freight and insurance . . .''); also *Tamvaco v. Lucas* (1861) 1 B. & S. 185.

insurance) is considered. It follows therefore that the seller's capacity in securing the shipping space provides the key for differentiating between the f.o.b. contract and other similar shipping contracts. This distinction is, however, often overlooked. The seller normally debits the buyer with the cost of these additional and marginal services regardless of his status. In any event the amount concerned is relatively small and would seldom become a subject of litigation. Nevertheless, in theory at least, there is more than one f.o.b. price depending upon whether the shipper's and/or the exporter's expenses are included or excluded. Moreover, where non-performance is not justified, the capacity of the seller may be crucial for determination of liability. In other words, this is not merely a matter of labelling the contract though it may so appear in most cases.

Because of the foregoing uncertainty, misunderstandings are best eliminated by incorporating into the contract a set of established standard rules wherein the respective obligations of the f.o.b. parties are defined in detail. Where the parties fail to express their intention, it will have to be imputed. The contract will then be read by the court in the light of the surrounding circumstances and an effort will be made to extract the parties' intention therefrom. The significant factors to be considered in such a case are the nature of the transaction (*i.e.* internal or external), the terms of payment, any established course of dealing between the parties, and he relevant port usages and trade customs.

F.O.B. airport

538   In 1976, a special trade term was introduced by the International Chamber of Commerce into Incoterms for cases where the goods are intended to be transported by air (a mode of transport that has become increasingly significant). This term was called "f.o.b. airport" and is based on the same main principles as the ordinary f.o.b. term. The current 1990 edition of Incoterms has however discarded this particualar term in favor of a more general F.C.A. (free carrier) term under which the seller fulfils his obligation to deliver by handing the goods, cleared for export into the charge of the carrier named by the buyer at the named place or point.

In light of different factual situations and practices in air transport compared with sea transport, f.o.b. airport or f.c.a airport differs from f.o.b. in that the point of delivery has not been tied to the means of conveyance, since there is nothing on the aircraft that could be given the same importance as the ship's rail in traditional sea transport. Thus, the point of delivery is reached when the goods are delivered to the air carrier (or his agent) at the transport terminal.

A second major difference between the f.o.b. and f.o.b. airport terms lies in the practice of the seller arranging for air transport. Under f.o.b., this is an "additional service." However, this is specifically regulated in f.o.b. airport. The buyer however has the option to name the air carrier. This could be important to him if he enjoys favourable conditions with a particular airline or has adequate facilities for booking the cargo in the country of dispatch through a freight forwarder or confirming house. If the buyer does not exercise this option (which normally he does not) the seller may not remain idle.

Unless the buyer gives contrary instructions, the seller must either arrange for transportation at the buyer's risk and expense (which he normally does) or give prompt notice to the buyer that he does not wish to do so. The buyer must give the seller any instructions necessary to have the goods carried to the desired destination, and the seller must notify the buyer of the delivery of the goods to the air carrier.

When the seller makes the contract of carriage with the air carrier in his own name (which is normally done), he and not the buyer becomes the contracting party (the "shipper") in the contract of carriage. The seller must assist the buyer to claim any compensation from the air carrier and surrender his rights under the contract of carriage to the buyer since the buyer bears the risk of loss of or damage to the goods after they have been delivered to the air carrier at the airport of departure. If the goods are lost or damaged after delivery to the air carrier but prior to their being lifted into the carrying aircraft, such loss or damage is for the buyer's account who should insure this exposure.[5]

According to "Incoterms," the respective obligations of the parties to a contract containing the "f.o.b. airport" term were as follows:

A. *The Seller must:*

1. Supply the goods in conformity with the contract of sale, together with such evidence of conformity as may be required by the contract.

2. Deliver the goods into the charge of the air carrier or his agent or any other person named by the buyer, or, if no air carrier, agent or other person has been so named, of an air carrier or his agent chosen by the seller. Delivery shall be made on the date or within the period agreed for delivery, and at the named airport of departure in the manner customary at the airport or at such other place as may be designated by the buyer in the contract.

3. Contract at the buyer's expense for the carriage of the goods, unless the buyer or the seller gives prompt notice to the contrary to the other party. When contracting for the carriage as aforesaid, the seller shall do so, subject to the buyer's instructions as provided for under article B. 1, on usual terms to the airport of destination named, to the nearest airport available for such carriage to the buyer's place of business, by a usual route in an aircraft of a type normally used for the transport of goods of the contract description.

4. At his own risk and expense obtain any export licence or other official authorisation necessary for the export of the goods.

5. Subject to the provisions of articles B. 6 and B. 7 below, pay any taxes, fees and charges levied in respect of the goods because of exportation.

---

[5] The term "f.o.b. aircraft" should thus be avoided.

6. Subject to the provisions of articles B. 6 and B. 7 below, bear any further costs payable in respect of the goods until such time as they will have been delivered, in accordance with the provisions of article A. 2 above.

7. Subject to the provisions of articles B. 6 and B. 7 below, bear all risks of the goods until such time as they will have been delivered, in accordance with the provisions of article A. 2 above.

8. Provide at his own expense adequate protective packing suitable to dispatch of the goods by air unless it is the custom of the trade to dispatch the goods unpacked.

9. Pay the costs of any checking operations (such as checking quality, measuring, weighing, counting) which shall be necessary for the purpose of delivering the goods.

10. Give the buyer notice of the delivery of the goods without delay by telecommunication channels at his own expense.

11. In the circumstances referred to in articles B. 6 and B. 7 below, give the buyer prompt notice by telecommunication channels of the occurrence of said circumstances.

12. Provide the buyer with the commercial invoice in proper form so as to facilitate compliance with applicable regulations and, at the buyer's request and expense, with the certificate of origin.

13. Render the buyer, at his request, risk and expense, every assistance in obtaining any document other than those mentioned in article A. 12 above issued in the country of departure and/or of origin and which the buyer may require for the importation of goods into the country of destination (and, where necessary, for their passage in transit through another country).

14. Render the buyer, at his request, risk and expense and subject to the provisions of article B. 9 below, every assistance in bringing any claim against the air carrier or his agent in respect of the carriage of the goods.

B. The Buyer Must:

1. Give the seller due notice of the airport of destination and give him proper instructions (where required) for the carriage of the goods by air from the named airport of departure.

2. If the seller will not contract for the carriage of the goods, arrange at his own expense for said carriage from the named airport of departure and give the seller due notice of said arrangements, stating the name of the air carrier or his agent or any other person into whose charge delivery is to be made.

3. Bear all costs payable in respect of the goods from the time when they have been delivered in accordance with the provisions of article A. 2 above, except as provided in article A. 5 above.

4. Pay the price invoiced as provided in the contract as well as the cost of air freight if paid by or on behalf of the seller.

5. Bear all risks of the goods from the time when they have been delivered, in accordance with the provisions of article A. 2 above.

6. Bear any additional costs incurred because the air carrier, his agent or any other person named by the buyer fails to take the goods into his charge when tendered by the seller, and bear all risks of the goods from the time of such tender, provided, however, that the goods will have been duly appropriated to the contract, that is to say, clearly set aside or otherwise identified as the contract goods.

7. Should he fail to provide proper instructions (where required) to the seller for the carriage of the goods, bear any additional costs incurred because of said failure and all risks of the goods from the date agreed for delivery or from the end of the period agreed for delivery, provided, however, that the goods will have been duly appropriated to the contract, that is to say, clearly set aside or otherwise identified as the contract goods.

8. Bear all costs, fees and charges incurred in obtaining the documents mentioned in article A. 13 above, including the costs of consular documents, as well as the costs of certificates of origin.

9. Bear all costs, fees and charges incurred by the seller in bringing and pursuing any claim against the air carrier or his agent in respect of the carriage of the goods.

[The next paragraph is 551.]

CHAPTER 9

DELIVERY F.O.B.

Introductory

551   The principles that govern the transfer of property in the goods under the Sale of Goods Act, have already been described in relation to c.i.f. contracts.[1] Briefly recounted they are as follows: in the case of specific or ascertained, *i.e.* identified, goods, the property in them is transferred to the buyer at such time as the parties intend it to pass, which intention may be gathered from the terms of the contract, the conduct of the parties and the circumstances of the case (section 17). By section 18 of the Act, unless a different intention appears, certain presumptions apply with respect to the transfer of property. In the case of specific goods, which are in a "deliverable state," the presumption is that property passes at the time of the contract (section 18(1)); but where the seller has to do something to the goods for the purpose of putting them into a deliverable state, the property does not pass until such thing is done (section 18(2)). Where there is a contract for the sale of unascertained or future goods by description, the property does not pass unless goods of that description which are in a deliverable state have been unconditionally appropriated to the contract (section 18(5)(1)). By section 18(5)(2), unconditional appropriation is presumed to occur where, in pursuance of the contract, the seller delivers the goods to a carrier for the purpose of transmission to the buyer. However, the seller may reserve his right of disposal in the goods until certain conditions are fulfilled (section 19(1)). And where goods are shipped, and by the bill of lading the goods are deliverable to the order of the seller or his agent, the seller is prima facie deemed to reserve the right of disposal in relation thereto (section 19(2)). The latter presumption has sometimes been extended by the courts to include situations where the bill of lading is issued in the name of the buyer but is retained by the seller for the purposes of security prior to payment,[2] such extension being inferred from the provision in section 19(3) of the Act. The latter provision states that where the seller draws on the buyer for the price of the goods and transmits both the bill of exchange and bill of lading to the buyer to secure acceptance or payment of the bill of exchange, the buyer is bound to return the bill of lading if he does not honour the bill of exchange, and if he wrongfully retains

---

[1] See *ante* §§ 274, *et seq.*
[2] See *The Kronprinsessan Margareta, The Parana and other ships* [1921] 1 A.C. 486 at p. 517.

443

the bill of lading the property does not pass to him. Finally, according to section 20 of the Act:

> "(1) Unless otherwise agreed, the goods remain at the seller's risk until the property in them is transferred to the buyer, but when the property in them is transferred to the buyer the goods are at the buyer's risk whether delivery has been made or not.
>
> (2) But where delivery has been delayed through the fault of either buyer or seller the goods are at the risk of the party at fault as regards any loss which might not have occurred but for such fault.
>
> (3) Nothing in this section affects the duties or liabilities of either the seller or buyer as bailee or custodian of the goods of the other party."

552   From all that has already been said, it is clear that the words "free on board" do more than merely determine the allocation of costs and relevant responsibilities of the parties to the contract. Without exception, all the proposed definitions of the term f.o.b. clearly state that the seller must bear the risk of loss or destruction of the goods, whether they be identified or unascertained up to the moment of delivery f.o.b. Upon placement on board the ship, and subject to any duty of notification to enable the buyer to insure the sea transit,[3] the risk is transferred to the buyer, who, except as otherwise agreed, then becomes liable to pay their price. Because both the risk in the goods and the right to claim their price as well as a variety of other rights and obligations are prima facie the consequence of the right of ownership under the Sale of Goods Act, the applicability of the foregoing principles to f.o.b. contracts has sometimes been doubted. The editor of Carver, for example, has questioned whether the presumption incorporated in section 19(2) of the Act "is justifiable under a contract f.o.b.," and has stated that "the fact that it is f.o.b. should logically reverse the presumption; since the seller is in breach of his contract if he does reserve the right of disposal."[4] He has consequently taken issue with those judgments in which an opposite view was expressed. He has for example, stated that:

> "Since it is ... clear that (despite Parke B.'s dicta in *Wait* v. *Baker*[5]) the fact that an f.o.b. contract provides only for handing over the bills of lading against payment does not affect the seller's obligation under the contract to pass the property to the buyer on shipment, it is difficult to justify, in the case of f.o.b. contracts, the presumption, mentioned by Lord Parker,[6] that property is to pass only on payment."

553   None of the proposed definitions of the term f.o.b. which intentionally refrain from dealing with the question of the transfer of property (but concentrate instead on the rights and remedies of the parties pursuant to the various stages of performance of the transaction) is of any assistance in clarifying

---

[3] See Sale of Goods Act 1979, s.32(3) and generally *post*, § 662
[4] *Carriage by Sea* (13th ed.), *British Shipping Laws, Vol. 2 para. 1620.*
[5] (1848) 2 Ex. 1, see *post*, § 555.
[6] In *The Parchim* [1918] A.C. 157 at p. 170, see *post*, § 566.

this problem. The view that property passes to the buyer under an f.o.b. contract when the goods have been placed on board the vessel no doubt enjoys a certain amount of support. It must also be added, however, that a reservation by the seller of a property interest in the goods, rather than a mere right to their possession, prior to being paid their price and for the sole purpose of obtaining the price or enforcing any rights relating thereto is not necessarily inconsistent with the f.o.b. term. Moreover, since the question of transfer of property is always subordinated to the intention of the parties, which is a question of fact, the view that the f.o.b. term in itself furnishes conclusive evidence as to such intention, because it is one of the very elements of the transaction that the seller undertakes an irrevocable obligation to transfer the property in the goods at the f.o.b. point come what may, is, with all respect, open to some question.

554   The entire difficulty appears to emanate from the somewhat outmoded notion of "property" which underlies the Sale of Goods Act. Clearly, if a retention of property by the seller entails results which cannot be reconciled with the f.o.b. term (*e.g.* that the risk of loss in the goods has not been transferred, or that their price is not recoverable, or that the buyer has no beneficial interest in the goods and no remedy if the seller withdraws and resells them to a third party by transfer of the bills of lading), then the conclusion is unavoidable that the property must be deemed to pass upon delivery f.o.b. However, as such an unconditional and irrevocable transfer of property has been held to jeopardise the position of the seller, when payment has not been tendered, or to curtail his rights of raising money on the documents by means of pledging them with a bank, courts have sometimes been forced into the position of declaring that property has not been transferred. These rulings have been made despite the consequences for the contract which is otherwise on f.o.b. terms. Since a decision as to who has property in one case would normally constitute authority for predicting who will be held to have the property in the goods in a subsequent case, irrespective of whether or not the issues to be determined in both cases are identical or different, the practical problems involved in the application of property concepts to f.o.b. transactions becomes apparent. It was presumably to escape the undesirable results arising from property notions that courts have, particularly in the United States, sometimes reached the conclusion that the f.o.b. term was used solely in conjunction with the price of goods and what is included therein. Where this interpretation has been adopted the f.o.b. term is taken to mean that the goods would be loaded free of expense to the buyer who would be responsible for the cost of transport subsequent to the f.o.b. point. In such a case, it is normally held that the f.o.b. term has no bearing on when, where or in what manner or fashion delivery to the buyer is to be effected under the contract. The difficulties inherent in this approach are, however, considerably greater than the difficulties encountered as a result of the proprietary approach, since a greater area of uncertainty will inevitably be promoted and because it patently contradicts the delivery aspect of the term. Without a doubt the f.o.b. term is a term of delivery. It should, therefore, unless the parties expressly manifest a contrary intention, be so construed. However, there can be no hope of solving the difficulties arising under the Sale of Goods Act, and from the various precedents, satisfactorily until such time as "property" thinking is entirely abandoned.[7] Indeed, it seems that this approach, which is now embodied in the most recent and modern of commercial codes,[8] has not escaped the attention of the courts. Thus, the courts, disregarding the problems which this may cause for the theoretician, and with the possible exception of disputes arising in connection with prize cases where special rules apply,[9] have on the whole enforced the rights of the parties in a manner consistent with sound commercial practice. Moreover, as international trade is to an increasing extent being financed by means of documentary letters of credit the entire problem of property transfer between seller and buyer has lost much of its significance. Between seller and buyer, performance is complete upon presentation of the required documents to the bank. There is no question as to the seller reserving any property rights in the goods after he has been paid their price.

It is now therefore relevant to discuss the various decisions and outline the difficulties which "property" thinking has imported into f.o.b. contracts, with respect to some of the issues which have been the source of serious controversy.

Double sale

555   It has sometimes been suggested that where the seller f.o.b. has had bills of lading issued in his own or his agent's name, he retains the absolute and unconditional right of disposal in the goods. He may, therefore, withdraw the goods from the contract and transfer the property in them to a third party, the buyer having no remedy in an action for conversion. In *Wait v. Baker*,[10] the earliest of these cases, the terms of payment of a sale of barley f.o.b. Kingsbridge or some neighbouring port called "for cash, on handing bill of lading or by acceptance. . . ." By the bills of lading the cargo was deliverable to the order of the seller who refused the tender of cash by the buyer and instead transferred the bill of lading to the plaintiffs. The defendants, who were the original buyers, managed to obtain some of the barley on the arrival of the vessel at Bristol, which was the port of disembarkation. In an action for trover by the plaintiffs, for the value of the barley so obtained, the court held that no property passed to the defendants either at Bristol or upon ship-

---

[7] See the illuminating note "Significance of the Concept Title Where the Seller Retains the Bills of Lading to Goods" 29 Columbia L. R. 1100 (1929).
[8] See, *e.g.* the American Uniform Commercial Code, Scandinavian Laws of Sale; Uniform Law on the International Sale of Goods.
[9] See *ante*, § 282, n. 66.
[10] (1848) 2 Ex. 1.

ment of the cargo on board by the seller, and that therefore the plaintiffs were entitled to recover.

556   In the course of his judgment Parke B. said:

> "It may be admitted, that if goods are ordered by a person, although they are to be selected by the vendor, and to be delivered to a common carrier to be sent to the person by whom they have been ordered, the moment the goods, which have been selected in pursuance of the contract, are delivered to the carrier, the carrier becomes the agent of the vendee, and such a delivery amounts to a delivery to the vendee; and if there is a binding contract between the vendor and the vendee . . . then there is no doubt that the property passes by such delivery to the carrier. It is necessary, of course, that the goods should agree with the contract. In this case, it is said that the delivery of the goods on ship-board is equivalent to the delivery I have mentioned, because the ship was engaged on the part of [the seller] as agent for the defendant. But assuming that it was so, the delivery of the goods on board the ship was not a delivery of them to the defendant, but a delivery to the captain of the vessel, to be carried under a bill of lading, and that bill of lading indicated the person for whom they were to be carried. By that bill of lading the goods were to be carried by the master of the vessel for and on account of [the seller], to be delivered to him in case the bill of lading should not be assigned, and if it would, then to the assignee. The goods, therefore, still continued in the possession of the master of the vessel, not as in the case of a common carrier, but as a person carrying them on behalf of [the seller]. There is no breach of duty on the part of [the seller], as he stipulates under the original contract that the price is to be paid on the delivery of the bill of lading. . . . The act of delivery, therefore, in the present case, did not pass the property. Then, what subsequent act do we find which had that effect? It is admitted by the learned counsel for the defendant, that the property does not pass, unless there is a subsequent appropriation of the goods. . . . I must own that I think the delivery on board the vessel could not be an appropriation in that sense of the word. . . . It is clear that [the seller's] object was to have the contract repudiated, and thereby to free himself from all obligations to deliver the cargo" (at pp. 7–9).

Under this construction the only remedy available to the buyer, is a personal action against the seller for non-fulfilment of his contract.

557   As has been pointed out by the editor of Carver,[11] the accuracy of the foregoing proposition is doubtful unless it is based (as it apparantly was by Parke B.) on the finding of the court that the seller had repudiated the contract. It is impossible to assume that commercial practice would condone the right (to be distinguished from the *power* based on the negotiability of the bill of lading) of a seller f.o.b. to betray the original buyer by allowing him to withdraw the goods after delivery to the carrier. It is suggested, therefore, that whether the correct inference in f.o.b. sales is that property passes forthwith subject only to an unpaid seller's lien, or conditionally upon payment (these alternatives are later discussed in more detail), a retention of the bills of lading by the seller, even if they are issued to his own order, should not

---

[11] See *ante*, § 552.

be construed in a manner which is inconsistent with commercial practice. In other words, that any such retention should be regarded in conjunction with the object of securing the purchase price of the goods only. In the absence of a default by the buyer, the seller should therefore not be considered as having reserved a right which not merely enables but actually entitles him to withdraw the goods from the contract. Indeed already in *Ogg v. Shuter*,[12] the seller's right was apparently so qualified. In this case the plaintiffs, who bought a quantity of potatoes f.o.b. Dunkirk payment cash against bill of lading, erroneously supposed the shipment to be short and refused to accept the seller's draft upon presentation. The defendant, to whom the bill of lading was transferred under instructions from the seller, then sold the goods to a third party. The plaintiffs subsequently brought an action against the third party for conversion on the grounds that the property in the goods had passed to them. The plaintiff's claim succeeded in the Court of Common Pleas but was reversed on appeal (Lord Cairns C.; Kelly C.B.; Bramwell B.; and Blackburn J.) on the grounds that in refusing to pay for the goods the plaintiffs were in default. In allowing the appeal Lord Cairns said:

> "The transactions in which merchants shipping goods on the orders of others protect themselves by taking a bill of lading, making the goods deliverable to the shippers' order, involve property of immense value, and we are unwilling to decide more than is required by the particular case. But we think this much is clear, that where the shipper takes and keeps in his own or his agent's hands a bill of lading in this form to protect himself, this is effectual so far as to preserve to him a hold over the goods until the bill of lading is handed over on the conditions being fulfilled, or at least until the consignee is ready and willing and offers to fulfil these conditions, and demands the bill of lading. And we think that such a hold retained under the bill of lading is not merely a right to retain possession till those conditions are fulfilled, but involves in it a power to dispose of the goods on the vendee's default, so long at least as the vendee continues in default. It is not necessary in this case to consider what would be the effect of an offer by the [buyer] to accept the draft and pay the money before the sale, for no such offer in this case was ever made" (at pp. 50, 51).

558   In *Mirabita v. Imperial Ottoman Bank*,[13] decided only a few years later, the buyer was held to have acquired the property in the goods by offering to pay their price against receipt of the bill of lading. The defendants, a bank with whom the sellers discounted their bill of exchange, refused to accept this offer alleging that since they had taken possession of the cargo they had become liable to pay the freight. Thereupon the buyer offered to give them a guarantee with respect to the freight but this offer also was declined. The defendants then sold the cargo which was worth more than the amount of the bill of exchange, freight and other expenses. The court held the defendants liable for conversion.

559   Bramwell L.J.'s judgment in part reads:

---

[12] (1875) 1 C.P.D. 47.
[13] (1878) 3 Ex.D. 164.

"I think it is not necessary to inquire whether what the shipper possesses is a property, strictly so called, in the goods, or a just disponendi, because I think, whichever it is, the result must be the same, for the following reasons. That the vendee has an interest in the specific goods as soon as they are shipped is plain. By the contract they are at his risk. If lost or damaged, he must bear the loss. If specially good, and above the average quality which the seller is bound to deliver, the benefit is the vendee's. If he pays the price, and the vendor receives it, not having transferred the property, nor created any right over it in another, the property vests. It is found in this case that as far as intention went the property was to be in the plaintiff on shipment. If the plaintiff had paid, and the defendants had accepted the amount of the bill of exchange, it cannot be doubted that the property would have vested in the plaintiff. . . . It follows that it vested on tender of the price. . . . There is nothing in the authorities inconsistent with this. The only case that may be thought to seem so is *Wait v. Baker*[14] where, though the vendee tendered the price, he was held to have acquired no property. But it is manifest that in that case the vendor originally took the bill of lading to order, and kept it in his possession, to deal with as he thought fit, and never intended that the property should pass until he handed the bill of lading to the vendee on such terms as he chose to exact. . . " (at pp. 169, 170).

560   While Cotton L.J., with whose judgment Bramwell L.J. expressly concurred, said[15] as follows:

"Under a contract for sale of chattels *not specific* the property does not pass to the purchaser unless there is afterwards an appropriation of the specific chattels to pass under the contract, that is, unless both parties agree as to the specific chattels in which the property is to pass, and nothing remains to be done in order to pass it. In the case of such a contract the delivery by the vendor to a common carrier, or (unless the effect of the shipment is restricted by the terms of the bill of lading) shipment on board a ship of, or chartered for, the purchaser is an appropriation sufficient to pass the property. If, however, the vendor, when shipping the articles which he intends to deliver under the contract, takes the bill of lading to his own order, and does so, not as agent or on behalf of the purchaser, but on his own behalf, it is held that he thereby reserves unto himself a power of disposing of the property, and that consequently there is no final appropriation, and the property does not on shipment pass to the purchasers. When the vendor on shipment takes the bill of lading to his own order, he has the power of absolutely disposing of the cargo, and may prevent the purchaser from ever asserting any right of property therein; and accordingly in *Wait v. Baker*,[16] *Ellershaw v. Magniac*[17] and *Gabarron v. Kreeft*[18] (in each of which cases the vendors had dealt with the bills of lading for their own benefit), the decisions were that the purchaser had no property in the goods, though he had offered to accept bills for or had paid the price. So, if the vendor deals with or claims to retain the bill of lading in order to secure the contract price, as when he sends forward the bill of lading with a bill of exchange attached, with directions that the bill of lading is not to be delivered to the purchaser till acceptance or payment of the bill of

---

[14] (1848) 2 Ex. 1. See *ante*, § 555.
[15] *Ibid* at p. 172.
[16] (1848) 2 Ex. 1. *Ante*, § 555.
[17] (1843) 6 Ex. 570. Buyer of linseed sent a ship to load it and paid part of the price. Seller took a bill of lading *"to order or assigns."* and obtained advances by transferring it to a *third party*. Held, that seller had reserved the right of property.
[18] (1875) L.R. 10 Ex. 274. *Post*, § 562.

exchange, the appropriation is not absolute, but, until acceptance of the draft, or payment, or tender of the price is conditional only, and until such acceptance, or payment, or tender, the property in the goods does not pass to the purchaser; so it was decided in *Turner v. Trustees of Liverpool Docks*[19]; *Shepherd v. Harrison*[20]; *Ogg V. Shuter*[21]. But if the bill of lading has been dealt with only to secure the contract price, there is neither principle nor authority for holding that in such a case the goods shipped for the purpose of completing the contract do not on payment or tender by the purchaser of the contract price vest in him. When this occurs there is a performance of the condition subject to which the appropriation was made and everything which, according to the intention of the parties, is necessary to transfer the property is done; and in my opinion, under such circumstances, the property does on payment or tender of the price pass to the purchaser.''

Mirabita v. Imperial Ottoman Bank, therefore, may be taken to establish the principle that when the seller deals with the bills of lading in the course of performing the sale, normally nothing less than a default by the buyer would give rise to his right to withdraw the goods from the contract.

561   It is, however, important to note that notwithstanding this principle, third parties are able to acquire valid rights when the seller, albeit in violation of his contract, transfers the bills of lading to a bona fide purchaser for value. In these cases the seller has by virtue of retaining the right of possession, exercised through control of the bills of lading, a *power* (if not a right) to convey ownership in the goods. The buyer cannot invoke the classic maxim *nemo dat quod non habet* since it is specifically excepted by statute. Both section 8 of the Factors Act 1889, and section 24 of the Sale of Goods Act 1893 and 1979,[22] state that the seller can, solely by virtue of his right over the bills of lading, transfer a valid and effective title in the goods to any person that acquires them in good faith and without notice of the previous sale. Consequently, decisions which concern themselves with the rights third parties may have acquired from the seller[23] need not be determined by reference to the seller's right of property.

---

[19] (1851) 6 Ex. 543. Sellers of cotton loaded it on buyers' ship, took bills of lading *to their own order*, "he or they paying freight, *nothing, being owner's property*," and sent an invoice to the buyers, drew bills of exchange on the buyers and sold them to a bank to whom they transferred the bills of lading as security, so informing the buyers. Held, that the *jus disponendi* had been reserved.

[20] (1871) L.R. 5 H.L. 116. Bill of lading to *Sellers' order* sent with bill of exchange to their agents.

[21] (1875) 1 C.P.D. 47 (C.A.). *Ante,* § 557

[22] See also s.48(2) of the Act which provides that where an unpaid seller who has exercised his right of lien, retention or stoppage resells the goods the buyer acquires a good title thereto against the original buyer.

[23] The converse case, where the buyer had obtained possession of the bills of lading without having met the conditions of payment and transfers them to an innocent party, can be solved in a similar fashion notwithstanding the fact that the documents or the goods must be shown to have been obtained "with the consent of the seller" for this exception applies to larceny by trick but not to simple fraud (Sale of Goods Act, s.25(1), Factors Act, s.9, see *ante*, §§ 267 *et seq.*). But in this case also courts have sometimes based their decision on the ground that property to the buyer was transferred at the f.o.b. point. See, *e.g.* Pennsylvania Ry. Co. v. Bank of the United States, 212 N.Y.S. 437 (1925).

562   Moreover, the fact that the seller transfers the bill of lading to a third party may indicate that he has no intention of performing his contract. In *Gabarron & Another v. Kreeft and Others*,[24] the contract called for delivery of ore f.o.b. ships at Cartagena. The contract stipulated that upon payment the ore would be considered as the property of the buyer. It was decided that a third party to whom the seller had transferred the bills of lading acquired all rights to the ore shipped notwithstanding prepayment by the buyer. The decision was rendered prior to the enactment of the Factors and Sale of Goods Act by Bramwell and Cleasby BB., on the ground that the manner in which the seller shipped the ore and the form in which the bills of lading were taken, showed that the property in the ore did not pass to the original buyer before or after shipment; and by Kelly C.B., on the ground that the charterparty to which the original buyer was a party gave the master the power to sign bills of lading in a form which gave the third party a title to the goods. Kelly C.B. appears to have been motivated by considerations of estoppel similar to those which underlie the provisions now incorporated in the Factors Act and Sale of Goods Act. *Gabarron v. Kreeft*, however, was decided by the majority of the court on the ground that the seller repudiated his contract, hence the goods were in no sense appropriated to the contract. The reservation of the seller's right of disposal there was not a right exercised in conformity with but rather in spite of the contract. This furnishes a completely different explanation for the seller's *right* of disposal. For it is obvious that where the seller deliberately breaks the agreement and does not place the goods f.o.b. in performance of his contract but in pursuance of some other intention, he can do whatever he pleases with his *own* goods. As aforesaid, *Wait v. Baker* lends itself to a similar construction and, though it was decided prior to the passage of the Bills of Lading Act 1855, which first gave statutory recognition to the negotiable nature of bills of lading, that principle had already been recognised by the courts over half a century earlier.[25]

It can, therefore, be concluded that the mere retention of the bills of lading does not *per se* entitle the seller to exercise absolute dominion over the goods. Only where the buyer has defaulted, or where the manner of shipment is inconsistent with an intention to perform the f.o.b. contract, and regardless of his actual power to convey ownership, should the seller be considered to have vested in him such an unqualified right. Consequently, section 20(2) of the American Uniform Sales Act superseded by the Uniform Commercial Code which is largely, but not entirely, modelled on the Sale of Goods Act, provided that:

> "If, except for the form of the bill of lading,[26] the property would have passed to the buyer on shipment of the goods, the seller's property shall be deemed to

---

[24] (1875) L.R. 10 Ex. Cas. 274.

[25] See, *e.g. Lickbarrow v. Mason* (1793) 6 East 21n.

[26] The Uniform Sales Act clearly distinguishes between cases where the bill of lading is drawn to the seller's order (referred to in this subsection), and cases where the bill is drawn to the order of the buyer, where the seller is expressly held to reserve possession only: see s.20(3) of the Act.

be only for purposes of securing performance by the buyer of his obligations under the contract.''

Transfer of risk

563 Section 2 (a) of the said Uniform Sales Act was the natural corollary of section 20 (2) above cited. It provided that where—

> "the property in the goods has been retained by the seller merely to secure performance by the buyer of his obligations under the contract, the goods are at the buyer's risk from the time of . . delivery.''

Despite the fact that no similar provision is to be found in the Sale of Goods Act, this provision, like section 20(2) of the same American Act, does little more than restate principles of which English courts have long been cognisant. The prima facie presumption incorporated in section 20 of the Sale of Goods Act that risk is an attribute of property is, therefore, rebutted. It does not apply when the seller reserves property in the goods for the purpose of securing the contract price only; which, it is submitted, would be the normal inference to draw in the case where the seller ships goods in performance of his contract of sale and issues the bills of lading to his own order merely to secure payment. In other words, in all cases where the seller has in the performance of his contract put the goods f.o.b., the risk, subject to compliance with any duty of notification for the purposes of insurance contained in the Act,[27] is immediately transferred to the buyer.[28] And if the goods have gone astray or have been lost the buyer must suffer any damage resulting therefrom. The foregoing conclusion is based on a simple premise: The seller has shipped the goods f.o.b. as required by the agreement; it is the buyer who insures them; upon payment in the stipulated manner the buyer acquires, and the seller loses, all[29] interests in the goods. The mere retention of the bill of lading by means of which the seller only endeavours to protect himself against a hypothetical default cannot, therefore, lead to the conclusion that the risk of loss or damage to the goods has not been transferred. As already mentioned, English jurisprudence does not reject this notion. On the contrary, it lends it much support. The much-cited opinion of Brett M.R. in *Stock v. Inglis*[30] is clear authority to this effect.

564 In that case sugar merchants in London agreed to sell to the plaintiff, a Bristol merchant, 200 tons of sugar of a certain description. The sugar was

---

[27] See *post*, § 662.
[28] *Cf. Para-Type Stationary Corp. v. Brandtjen & Kluge*, 108 N.Y.S. 2d 377 (1951) in which the Appellate Division of the Supreme Court of New York held that the fact that the transaction was a conditional sale did not alter this conclusion.
[29] If payment is by bill of exchange and the buyer goes insolvent, the seller might still enjoy a limited right of stoppage *in transitu*, see *post*, § 708.
[30] (1884) 12 Q.B.D. 564 at p. 573, cited *ante*, § 437.

to be shipped f.o.b. Hamburg, payment in cash to be made in London in exchange for the bill of lading. In order to satisfy the contract, and also a similar contract with another purchaser, the seller's agents in Hamburg shipped 400 tons in 3,700 bags of sugar of the description contracted for, and consigned the same to "order Bristol." It was the usual course of business in the sugar trade between the respective ports not to appropriate specific bags of sugar to any particular contract at the time of shipment. The bags and the bills of lading representing them were apportioned between the various buyers only after the sellers had obtained the bills of lading. The vessel on which the sugar was loaded was lost prior to the sellers having appropriated any of the consignment to the plaintiffs. The goods were however subsequently appropriated, and the plaintiffs paid the contract price and obtained the bills of lading representing the same. The defendant was an underwriter with whom the plaintiff had an open-cover policy. The defendant declined to honour the policy on the grounds that since no property passed to the plaintiff before the loss occurred he had no insurable interest in the goods on which he could rest his claim. The Court of Appeal held, and the judgment was confirmed by the House of Lords, that notwithstanding the fact that no property in the sugar had passed prior to the loss, the term f.o.b. in a contract made in the circumstances described meant that the sugar was shipped at the risk of the plaintiff who was liable to pay their price against the bill of lading whether the sugar arrived or not.

565   The decision of Brett M.R., a portion of which has already been cited,[31] goes on in part to read as follows:

> ".. one must, with regard to that contract, give some meaning to those words 'free on board.' What meaning can be given to them with regard to the unseparated part of the goods which is the subject-matter of the contract, but the same meaning as is given to those words with regard to goods attributed to the contract? What is there unreasonable or contrary to business or law in those words 'free on board,' meaning in such a contract 'I sell you twenty tons out of fifty upon the terms that you shall pay such a price for those twenty, I paying the costs of shipment, that is "free on board," and you bearing the risk of whether they are lost or not?' It does not seem to me that there is anything more inconsistent with business or law that parties should make such a contract with regard to a portion of a cargo than that they should make it with regard to a whole cargo or with regard to a specific part of a cargo. . . ." (at pp. 573, 574).

Whereas Bagallay L. J. added:

> "It has not been denied that, where the contract deals with specified goods, the introduction of the provision that they are to be 'free on board' places the goods at the risk of the buyer. But it has been suggested that such is not the case where the goods are not specific. . . . What authority is there for [such] a suggested difference. . . . Why should there be any difference between the two? I think it very difficult indeed to suggest any. . . ." (at p. 575).

---

[31] See *ante*, § 437.

In the earlier decision of *Williams* v. *Cohen*,[32] Bramwell B. similarly observed with respect to the goods in question:

> "If they were shipped on board in conformity with a contract between the parties, I am inclined to think that it is not material that the [seller] retained the *jus disponendi* of them, for, if the coals were shipped in accordance with a contract and were lost at sea, the plaintiff would be entitled to recover" (at p. 303).

566   Likewise, it was stated in *The Parchim*[33] (goods shipped, bills of lading deposited with seller's bank) that: "The goods then most certainly were at [the buyer's] risk, and he had an insurable interest whether he had the property or not." In most cases, however, the correct inference that risk is with the buyer, from the moment of delivery f.o.b., has been based on property thinking. Thus, in *Browne* v. *Hare*,[34] Pollock C.B. who delivered the judgment of the Court of Exchequer[35] (Pollock C.B., Martin and Channell BB.; Bramwell B. dissenting) said:

> "If, at the time the oil was shipped at Rotterdam, the [sellers] had intended to continue their ownership, and had taken the bill of lading in the terms in which it was made for the purpose of continuing the ownership and exercising dominion over the oil, they would in our opinion have *broken their contract to ship the oil* 'free on board,' and the *property* would not have passed to the [buyer]; but if and when they shipped the oil they intended to perform their contract and deliver it 'free on board' for the [buyer], we think they did perform it, and the *property in the oil passed from them to the [buyers]*" (at pp. 498–499).

567   In this latter case, the dispute arose on a contract for the sale of oil f.o.b. Rotterdam, to be paid for by acceptance of a bill of exchange on delivery of the bill of lading. The seller shipped on board a general vessel ("additional services" variant) part of the contract goods. The bill of lading was issued to his order and then endorsed to the buyer and posted together with an invoice and bill of exchange to a broker through whom the transaction was effected for presentation to the buyer. Thereafter, and before the documents were presented to the buyer, the ship upon which the oil was placed became a total loss. The buyer refused to pay the price on the grounds that the oil was not delivered free on board within the meaning of the contract because the bill of lading was made out deliverable to shipper's order. He argued moreover that because the seller had control over the oil and the contract of carriage was made with him, he, and not the buyer, should suffer the risk of loss. The majority of the court held that this contention must fail since property, and not merely risk, passed to the buyer on shipment. In the view of the court, the seller did not issue the bill of lading in the form he did in order

---

[32] (1871) 25 L.T. 300. But Bramwell B. might be drawing a distinction between "property" and *jus disponendi*; see his decision in *Mirabita* v. *Imperial Ottoman Bank, ante,* § 559.
[33] [1918] A.C. 157, *per* Lord Parker at p. 167.
[34] (1858) 3 H. & N. 484.
[35] Affirmed by the Court of Excheque Chamber (1859) 4 H. & N. 822.

to retain the property or for purposes of defeating the contract, but only to secure the price of the goods which was not inconsistent with the f.o.b. term. As was summarised by Pollock C.B. "As to the contract in the bill of lading being originally made with the [seller], we do not think it at all effects the terms as to the shipment 'free on board'. . . ." (at page 500).

568 Similarly, in *Joyce v. Swann*,[36] a decision concerning the f.o.b. buyer's insurable interest in goods lost which was contested by the underwriter, it was held that the property and not merely the risk had passed notwithstanding the fact that the bills of lading were drawn to the sellers' order and that the price had not been definitely agreed upon between the parties. Williams J. said:

> "It is true that the correspondence does not show any express assent to the price; but, in substance, it seems to me to amount to a grumbling assent . . . the buyer in substance says, I will take the guano you have shipped or contracted to ship, but I trust you will not insist on the price you mention. . . . It is true that the bill of lading was taken in the names of the sellers, and at the time the insurance was declared was unindorsed. . . . The cases of *Wait v. Baker*[37] and *Browne v. Hare*,[38] appear to me clearly to establish . . . that, if from all the facts it may fairly be inferred that the bill of lading was taken in the name of the seller in order to retain dominion over the goods, that shows that there was no intention to pass property; but that, if the whole of the circumstances lead to the conclusion that that was not the object, the form of the bill of lading has no influence on the result" (at p. 101).

Willes J. concurring added however that he was prepared to go further saying that "even if by reason of some special circumstances the property did not pass on shipment, yet, by reason of the risk, the buyer might insure the cargo in respect of the interest he had in it" (at page 104).

Finally, in *Frebold and Sturznickel (Trading as Panda O. H. G.) v. Circle Products Ltd.*[39] a much more recent case, the Court of Appeal, reversing the judgment of Nield J., reiterated the principle. There, a West German firm sold toys to an English company on f.o.b. terms. It was agreed that the toys should be delivered in time for the buyers to catch the Christmas market. Payment was to be made by cash against documents through the sellers' bank in London, and the sellers instructed the forwarding agents that the goods must not be handed over to the buyers until payment of the price.

The toys were despatched from Germany on November 1, 1967. They were shipped via Rotterdam and arrived at the London International Trade Terminal at Stratford on November 13. This was in time for the Christmas trade, but unfortunately the buyers were not informed of their arrival until

---

[36] (1864) 17 C. B. (N. S.) 84.
[37] (1843) 2 Ex. 1., *ante*, § 555.
[38] (1859) 4 H. & N. 822, affirming (1858) 3 H. & N. 484, *ante*, § 566.
[39] [1970] 1 Lloyd's Rep. 499.

January 17, 1968. To be sure, they constantly asked the representatives of the forwarding agents and British Rail whether the goods had arrived but they were always informed that the whereabouts of the goods, which were stored at Stratford, were unknown. On December 27, 1967, the buyers cancelled the order but the sellers refused to accept the cancellation. The sellers claimed damages for non-acceptance of the goods. Nield J. dismissed their claim on the ground that the contract, although described by the parties as an f.o.b. contract, was in fact an arrival contract by virtue of the sellers' reservation of the right of disposal until they had received payment in London.

The Court of Appeal reversed this decision and gave judgment for the sellers. The court held that the contract was a genuine f.o.b. contract. In this type of contract there could be delivery of the goods before payment was made, and delivery and payment did not have to be concurrent conditions. Since all the indications were that the parties intended the contract to be f.o.b., the term as to payment did not suffice to alter the contractual intention. The risk, then, passed to the buyers on delivery of the goods on board ship in Rotterdam, and the goods were delivered in time for the Christmas trade. As stated by Edmund Davis L.J.:

> "Is it, irreconcilable with the fundamental conception of an f.o.b. contract that physical possession is not to be given to the buyer until payment? Adverting to the rule of section 18[40] Mr. Justice Nield held that there had been no unconditional appropriation of this consignment to the contract, for the term that documents were to be handed over only against payment rendered it a *conditional* appropriation and that, therefore, a right of disposal had been reserved in the seller. But that property may pass although possession is made conditional is clear from *The Parchim*[41] [where] the point now being considered was authoritatively disposed of by Lord Parker of Waddington. . . ." (At p. 503).

On the other hand at least one case[42] held that where an f.o.b. contract stipulates for a transfer of risk subsequent to delivery free on board there is a similar delay in the transfer of property. This, of course, is the reverse of the situation here discussed. In that case the contract provided for the seller assuming responsibility for the goods (risk of damage and/ or loss) until a clean bill of lading was delivered to the buyers, and it was there held that the seller reserved a right of disposal in the goods until that time.

The authorities, therefore, hold practically without exception that under a contract f.o.b. the buyer bears the risk of loss, damage, or misplacement in transit. However in so holding they have sometimes referred to property considerations instead of confining themselves to the independent and narrower issue of transfer of risk.

---

[40] Of the Sale of Goods Act 1893.
[41] See *post*, § 569.
[42] *President of India v. Metcalfe Shipping Co. Ltd.* [1970] 1 Q.B. 289, (C.A.), *ante*, § 483.

Right to price[43]

569   The seller is able to recover the price of the goods (as distinct from damages for breach of contract), only if the *property* in the goods has already been transferred to the buyer; Sale of Goods Act 1893 and 1979 versions, section 49.

The several decisions in which consideration was given to the question of the retention of the bills of lading by the f.o.b. seller were reviewed by Lord Parker of Waddington in his speech in *The Parchim*.[44] This was a prize case,[45] where, having regard to the terms of the contract (a hybrid f.o.b.-c.i.f.) and the particular circumstances of the case, if was held that property passed on shipment. His lordship said:

> "The English cases . . . on which the Sale of Goods Act was founded seem to show that the appropriation would not be such as to pass the property if it appears or can be inferred that there was no actual intention to pass it. If the seller takes the bill of lading to his own order and parts with it to a third person, not the buyer, and that third person, by possession of the bill of lading, gets the goods, the buyer is held not to have the property so as to enable him to recover from the third party, notwithstanding that the act of the seller is a clear breach of the contract: *Wait v. Baker*,[46] *Gabarron v. Kreeft*.[47] This seems to be because the seller's conduct is inconsistent with any intention to pass the property to the buyer by means of the contract followed by the appropriation. On the other hand, if the seller deals with the bill of lading only to secure the contract price, and not with the intention of withdrawing the goods from the contract, he does nothing inconsistent with an intention to pass the property, and therefore the property may pass either forthwith subject to the seller's lien or conditionally on performance by the buyer of his part of the contract: *Mirabita v. Ottoman Bank*[48]; *Van Casteel v. Booker*[49]; *Browne v Hare*[50]; *Joyce v. Swann*.[51] The prima facie presumption in such a case appears to be that property is to pass only on the performance by the buyer of his part of the contract and not forthwith subject to the seller's lien. Inasmuch, however, as the object to be attained, namely, securing the contract price, may be attained by the seller merely reserving a lien, the inference that property is to pass on the performance of a condition only is necessarily somewhat weak, and may be rebutted by the other circumstances of the case."

570   A choice must therefore be made between the various alternatives described by Lord Parker. We have already had occasion to refer to statements by the editor of Carver questioning the accuracy of Lord Parker's proposition which maintained that in the case of f.o.b. contracts the presump-

---

[43] See further *post*, § 699 *et seq.*
[44] [1918] A.C. 157 at p. 170.
[45] As to the principles which govern the transfer of property in time of war, see *ante.* § 282 n. 66.
[46] [1848] 2 Ex. 1 *ante*, § 555.
[47] [1875] L.R. 10 Ex. 274, *ante*, § 562.
[48] [1878] 3 Ex.D. 164, *ante*, § 558.
[49] [1878] 2 Ex. 691.
[50] [1858] 3 H. & N. 484. [1859] 4 H. & N. 822, *ante*, § 566.
[51] [1864] 17 C.B.(N.S.) 84, *ante*, § 568.

tion that property is to pass only on payment and not forthwith is hard to justify.[52] As the question of the transfer of property ultimately depends on the intention of the parties, it may be useful to examine how their respective interests find expression within the framework of either of these possibilities. If the view that the transfer is conditional were to prevail, would the seller be entitled to recover the price of the goods or would he then be allowed an action for damages for nonacceptance only? For example, assuming that they are of the kind and amount ordered can the seller force the buyer to accept the goods upon a proper tender of the bills of lading and claim the purchase price even though the buyer has wrongfully refused to accept them or the goods? This is a matter of some importance because generally it is far simpler to establish the purchase price of goods than to prove the amount of damages caused by default of the buyer when questions of foreseeability, mitigation, and remoteness may have to be considered. There is little doubt that, as the law presently stands, English courts would reply to the foregoing question in the negative. For, if the seller is held to have reserved the property in the goods, and the transfer of the property is an indispensable condition precedent to the establishment of a right of action for the purchase price, how is it also possible to say, at the very same time, that property has passed? Furthermore since by the definition (contained in the Sale of Goods Act) property means the general property, and not merely a special property, the recognition of a beneficial interest in the buyer should be to no avail in this connection. Indeed, under the prevailing notion of "property," it is very difficult to escape this conclusion. The only possible argument against it derives from the preamble to the definition in the Act (section 62 of the 1893 version and section 61 of the 1979 version), under which all the definitions in the Act are inapplicable where "the context or subject-matter otherwise require." It has therefore sometimes been suggested[53] that the Act's definition of "property" be disregarded in the type of situation here considered and that a beneficial interest (such as the buyer f.o.b. invariably possesses) would suffice to support an action for the purchase price, and thus enable the seller to force the buyer to accept the goods. Otherwise, as Williston has pointed out, the absurd conclusion is unavoidable that the price is recoverable when the goods are destroyed since the risk is borne by the buyer[54] "and yet denied ... when the elements of ownership are the same and the goods are actually tendered." Persuasive as it is, this argument has not as yet met with much success. Consequently, both American and English courts have either decided that the seller's action must fail[55] on the grounds that property was retained or that it

---

[52] See *ante*, § 552.

[53] *Williston on Sales* (Rev. ed., 1948), para. 560b.

[54] Although the correct form may be an action for damages (and the difference would, therefore, only be procedural), and see *post*, § 699, n. 38.

[55] See note in 22 Col.L.R. 462 (*Rosenberg Bros, & Co. v. F. S. Buffum*, which is the subject of the commentary, was however reversed on appeal, on the ground that the general property passed in 234 N.Y. 338 (1922)); and see *Muller Maclean & Co. v. Leslie & Anderson* (1921) 8 Ll.L.Rep. 328.

must succeed on the grounds that, notwithstanding the retention of the bill of lading by the seller, the true intention was to pass absolute property.[56] The latter alternative, naturally having more appeal in circumstances such as these, tends to outweigh the prima facie inference suggested by Lord Parker, and would appear to support the alternative theory under which the seller has only reserved an unpaid seller's lien (a right of possession in the goods). Whether the establishment of such an "intention" adversely affects the interests of the seller even where the seller's right to claim the price is not the issue raised, depends upon examining the consequences which attach to a possessory rather than proprietary interest in the goods in such circumstances.

571   As has already been noted, in *Ross T. Smyth & Co. Ltd. v. T. B. Bailey Son & Co.*[57] Lord Wright expressed the view that the whole machinery for raising money on documents would be threatened if it were established that the seller who controls bills of lading issued to his own order reserves only a right of possession or even a special property by way of security in the goods rather than the general property therein. Significantly this statement, purporting to reflect the commercial or business point of view, has encountered criticism from those very quarters.[58]

Mercantile contracts seldom, if ever, connect the retention of the bills of lading with the question of the transfer of property. It is "the possession of the goods as distinguished from the property (which) strikes the parties as being the more important."[59] Thus, clause 14 of the Wood Trade Uniform f.o.b. Contract (1929) states:

> "property in the goods to be deemed for all purposes, except retention of the vendor's lien for unpaid purchase price, to have passed to buyers when goods have been put on board."[60]

572   It has already been noted that by section 24 of the Sale of Goods Act 1979 the seller's possession of the bills of lading enables him to dispose of them

---

[56] See *F. E. Napier v. Dexters Ltd.* (1926) 26 Ll.L.Rep. 62, 184. In this case the stipulation was "cash against mate's receipt." Roche J. held that the seller was entitled to waive the condition precedent in his favour so that the price would become payable after delivery f.o.b. even if by the original terms of the contract the seller intended to reserve the right of disposal until payment. In the Court of Appeal on the other hand the emphasis was put on the fact that there was no intention to reserve the right of property. See also note entitled "The Tripartite Ownership Resulting From the Transfer of a Bill of Lading to Seller's Order to a Discounting Bank" in 26 Col.L.R. 63 at p. 69, n. 46 (1926). And see "Transfer of Title in F.O.B. Shipments when Bill of Lading is drawn to the Sellers Order" (1923) 8 Cor.L.Q. 276.

[57] [1940] 3 All E.R. 60 at p. 68, cited *ante*, § 9.

[58] See Lagergren, *Delivery of the Goods and Transfer of Property and Risk in the Law of Sale* (Stockholm 1953), pp. 115 *et seq.* and the authorities there cited.

[59] *Ibid.*

[60] *The Wood Trade C.I.F. Contract* (Lond. 1930), p. 179. The contract was employed by the Timber Trade Federation of the U.K., The Swedish Wood Exporters' Association, and the Finnish Saw-Mill Owners' Association. Commenting on the identical provision in the uniform c.i.f. contract, the anonymous author says: "It will be noticed that the transfer of property is described as being for all purposes. The most obvious of the purposes arising out of the transfer of the property in the goods, deemed to have taken place, is the matter of payment" (at p. 84).

and to effectively confer rights in the goods to any innocent third party which includes a pledge thereof with a bank. Consequently, the rights of a bank with whom the documents have been pledged ought not to entail a consideration of the property rights in the goods since its security rests on the documents and on the seller's power to pledge them. The bank can then also sue for wrongful conversion of the goods if they are undelivered by the carrier. And it is of course quite clear that the bank for its part is not interested in obtaining the general property in the goods for otherwise it may be held liable and responsible to any third parties for claims they may have against the owners of the goods. The point is well illustrated by the judgment of the House of Lords in *Sewell v. Burdick*.[61] There the bank could only exonerate itself from a claim by the carrier for unpaid freight on the ground that it acquired not the proprietary but merely a possessory right to the goods.

573   A further examination of the authorities will, it is submitted, be to no avail. The question of the transfer of property in f.o.b. sales must thus remain open for determination in relation to the relevant issues raised in particular disputes and according to the circumstances of each individual case.[62] The most adequate way in which the principles embodied in the Act can be reconciled with the commercial meaning of the term, taking into account the various interests involved, is probably to construe the contract as one under which property is transferred to the buyer at the f.o.b. point subject to a condition subsequent of payment in time. Thus, when the buyer fails to tender the price in accordance with the terms of the agreement, the property revests to the seller as a result of a breach of condition. Indeed the normal inference with respect to the transfer of property is that it is deemed to be merely a conditional transfer subject to the conformity of the goods to the contract. The buyer may still reject the goods where inspection, which often takes place at their destination, reveals that the seller has defaulted by shipping f.o.b.

---

[61] (1884) 10 App. Cas. 74.

[62] In *President of India v. Metcalfe Shipping Co.* [1969] 2 Q.B. 123, the question before the court was whether a charterparty arbitration provision was applicable to the dispute in question. This was, *inter alia*, to be determined by answering another question, namely whether the charterparty or the relevant bill of lading issued thereunder constituted the contract of carriage between the parties. The charterers argued that the charterparty governed because the bill of lading was issued after the property in the goods had passed, and should therefore be construed as a mere receipt and document of title but not as a document constituting the contract of carriage. In this case, the f.o.b. contract of sale expressly provided that the sellers were to bear the risk of loss or damage, or both, to the goods until they had been placed "actually on board the vessel . . . and clean on board ocean bill of lading is delivered. . . ." Megaw J. stated that this provision:

"which provide[s] that the risk shall not pass until a time which necessarily is later than the completion of loading, provide[s] a powerful indication that the property in the goods was not intended by the parties to the sale contract to pass, and did not in law pass, until the later date when the bill of lading was received by the charterers in London. The bill of lading cannot, therefore, be treated as having been a mere receipt for the goods as it would have been if the property in the goods had passed immediately on the completion of loading so that the shippers would have held it, not in their own right but only as agents of the charterers" (at p. 138).

non-conforming goods in which case the property therein revests to the seller if the buyer so elects.[63] It follows that if the seller is nevertheless to be deemed to have reserved the property in the goods, such a reservation should be construed as effectual only for the purposes of securing him against default so as to prevent the buyer from obtaining possession of the goods if the conditions of payment are not met.[64] And Carver's statement notwithstanding, a reservation of property for this limited purpose would not, it is submitted, destroy the nature of a f.o.b. contract.

574   Under present conditions, where payment is normally arranged by an irrevocable and confirmed letter of credit in the country of origin, the entire problem of the seller's reservation of any rights in the goods is avoided. As between seller and buyer the transaction is fully consummated when collection is made upon presentation of the documents to the bank which acts for the buyer.[65]

Nevertheless, the problems which arise as a result of the underlying principles of the Sale of Goods Act cannot hope to be solved until such time as thinking along proprietary lines is entirely abandoned, as has for example been done in the American Uniform Commercial Code under which the reservation of a "security interest" in the goods by the unpaid seller "must be regarded as a means given to the seller to enforce his rights against the buyer which is unaffected by and in turn does not affect the location of title generally. The rules set forth . . . are not to be altered by any apparent 'contrary intent' of the parties as to passing of title, since the rights and remedies of the parties to the contract of sale . . . rest on the contract and its performance and not on stereotyped presumptions as to location of title."[66]

575   Finally, it is important to note that questions concerning the transfer or retention of property in the goods are not necessarily confined to cases where the seller acts as shipper of the goods. In the case of "strict" f.o.b. contracts, when the seller has delivered the goods against a mate's receipt the terms of the receipt may bear upon his rights and remedies in the case of default. For although the bills of lading are not usually surrendered by the carrier except in exchange for the mate's receipt,[67] it has been held that where the receipt acknowledges the buyer to be the shipper of the goods the shipowner is not at fault if he issues the bills of lading to the buyer who then has both the

---

[63] As to this problem generally, see *post*, § 637, *et seq.*
[64] As construed in *The Sorfareren* (1916) 114 L.T. 46, a prize case.
[65] As to payment under a letter of credit, see generally *post*, §§ 612 *et seq.*
[66] See comments to s.2–505 of the Code in Uniform Commercial Code. Official Text and Comments. s.2–505(1)(a) of the Code provides as follows:
"Where the seller has identified goods to the contract by or before shipment his procurement of a negotiable bill of lading to his own order or otherwise reserves in him a security interest in the goods. His procurement of the bill to the order of a financing agency or of the buyer indicates in addition only the sellers' expectation of transferring that interest to the person named."
[67] As to mate's receipts, see also *ante*, § 133.

property and the possession in the goods. Any unpaid seller's lien would then be merely an equitable charge which would be ineffectual against third parties.[68] The seller is therefore well advised to obtain the mate's receipt in his own name. The carrier cannot thereafter issue the bill of lading to the buyer without the consent of the seller,[69] and if he does so he will normally be liable for conversion of the goods.[70] This procedure will also enable the seller to raise money from a bank to finance the contract for the supply of the goods sold in advance of receipt of the purchase price from the buyer. But if the bank merely relies on the promise of the seller to have the shipping documents put in its name without this actually being done, it will normally be in no position to enforce any rights in respect of the goods against the carrier or the buyer.[71] Where the goods are loaded by shipping agents, it is their duty to see to it that the mate's receipt and the bills of lading are not misdelivered and consequently they are liable for any breach of this duty on their part.

576 In *A. R. Brown, McFarlane & Co. v. C. Shaw Lovell & Sons and Walter Potts & Co.*,[72] the plaintiffs sold to the second defendants a quantity of pig iron f.o.b. Liverpool, payment against shipping documents or mate's receipt. The goods were loaded by the first defendants in their capacity as shipping agents and they obtained the mate's receipt. The receipt was subsequently exchanged by them for a bill of lading which was delivered to a third party to whom the iron was resold by the second defendants. The plaintiffs claimed for the price inasmuch as they were unable to obtain the documents. The second defendants denied liability on the ground that their duty to pay depended on the production of the mate's receipt which was never delivered. Rowlatt J. held the first defendants liable and, in the course of his judgment, stated:

> "I was under the impression that when goods are sold f.o.b. it results in the buyer being the shipper, because the seller has done all he has to do when he delivers the goods to the buyer at the place of delivery. But the contract of affreightment is made on behalf of the buyer. The mate's receipt, although it shows the person who is likely to get the contract of affreightment, and the

---

[68] See *Nippon Yusen Kaisha v. Ramjiban Serowgee* [1938] A.C. 429.
[69] If the terms of payment have been met, the seller is probably unable to recover from the shipowner who has issued the bills of lading to the buyer. See *Cowas-Jee v. Thompson & Kebble* (1845) 5 Moo.P.C. 165, where the buyer accepted a bill for the price drawn by the sellers and became insolvent. The Judicial Committee of the Privy Council held that an action for trover could not lie against the carrier regardless of the fact that the bills of lading were not issued in exchange for the mate's receipt (which was held by the sellers) inasmuch as the transaction was fully consummated when the conditions of payment were met.
[70] See *Craven v. Rayder* (1816) 6 Taunt. 433; *Ruck v. Hatfield* (1822) 5 B. & Ald. 632 and more recently *Kum and Ano. v. Wah Tat Bank Ltd. and Ano.* [1971] 1 Lloyd's Rep. 439 (P.C.). Where the mate's receipt is not surrendered an indemnity from the person to whom the bill of lading is issued is therefore normally required by the shipowner.
[71] See *Chase Manhattan Bank v. Nissho Pacific Corporation*, 254 N.Y.S. 2d 571 (1964), aff'd 265 N.Y.S. 2d 660 (1965), where the seller encountered financial difficulties with the purchase price becoming the subject of a set-off and the bank's action failed.
[72] (1921) 7 Ll.L.Rep. 36.

person whom the shipowner regards as the owner of the goods, still is not a contract for affreightment. It is exactly what it says it is, *viz.*, a receipt by the ship that these goods have been brought on board the ship by someone, and it seems to me that he gives that receipt to the person who brings them, as the person who brings them, and not as the person who necessarily will be a party to the contract of affreightment.

So I think it was given to Messrs. Shaw Lovell & Sons, as the agents of plaintiffs. But I do not know that it very much matters, because, looking at it more broadly, Messrs. Shaw Lovell & Sons were clearly engaged by the series of sellers in their capacity of sellers to take the goods to the ship and put them on board, and they must have known when they got to the ship there would be a mate's receipt; and a mate's receipt is an important thing to get into the right hands. Messrs. Shaw Lovell & Sons ought, I think, to have asked their successive employers what they were to do with the mate's receipt, and if they chose to deliver it into the wrong hands I think they do that at their own risk.''

When delivery f.o.b. is completed

577   Delivery f.o.b. is consummated when the contract goods cross the ship's rail at the named port of shipment.[73] As stated by Devlin J. in *Pyrene Co. Ltd. v. Scindia Navigation Co. Ltd.*[74]

"He [the seller] treats the word 'on' [in the Carriage of Goods by Sea Act 1924] as having the same meaning as in 'free on board'; [namely] goods are loaded *on* the ship as soon as they are out across the ship's rail . . .''

So that although, as Devlin J. proceeded to describe it:

"only the most enthusiastic lawyer could watch with satisfaction the spectacle of liabilities shifting uneasily as the cargo sways at the end of a derrick across a notional perpendicular projecting from the ship's rail.''[75]

apparently this in fact is precisely what happens in so far as the seller is concerned. In other words, the unsound situation that Devlin J. attempted to avoid with respect to determining the liability of the carrier under the contract of carriage, obtains in regard to delivery and the passage of risk in the goods under the contract of sale between the f.o.b. seller and his buyer. Thus, loading might well have a different meaning in the context of these two types of contract. Should the goods therefore suffer damage after they have left the ground but before they cross the ship's rail the loss would normally be for account of the seller. But if the goods have crossed the rail and the damage occurs before they are safely on board, say as a result of an accident while still in mid-air, that damage would probably be held to be for the account of the buyer and not of the seller. Though this is no doubt true as a general

---

[73] See "Incoterms" A. 4, *ante*, § 511.
[74] [1954] 2 Q.B. 402 at p. 414.
[75] *Ibid.* at p. 419.

proposition, an exception may apply in cases where the accident disrupts
normal loading conditions and interferes with the seller's ability to deliver
the quantity stipulated by the contract within the period fixed thereunder. For
in these circumstances, the seller may be held not to have performed his
agreement. However the question does not seem to have arisen and there is
no definite authority for the proposition. The suggestion has also been made
that an exception should apply to contracts for the sale of liquid or gaseous
products and that where these products are sold on an f.o.b. basis risk transfers when the subject matter enters the ship's fittings (whether the same be
fixed or flexible). This apparently is the rule applied in the port of Antwerp
and elsewhere,[76] presumably on the ground that in these circumstances the
connecting point of the shorebased, and the ship's, pipes, are to be considered
as the ship's rail. Under an f.o.b. contract the fact that the shipowner has
accepted the goods on shore,[77] does not relieve the seller of his responsibility
for their safety towards the buyer which continues until they have crossed
the ship's rail. Though the cost of loading may, and often is, by the usage of
the port borne by the ship, the time of delivery under the contract is not
thereby advanced. That the seller is relieved from meeting any charges in
connection therewith because the ship reimburses itself for the entire loading
operation by means of the freight, ultimately throwing the cost thereof on the
buyer, is equally immaterial. The same obviously applies to lighterage
expenses where the responsibility and cost of conveying the goods to the ship
by lighters is borne by the ship and is subsequently recovered by means of
the freight.[78] The importance which attaches to the place of acceptance by
the shipowner may thus, as Lord Trayner acknowledged in *Glengarrock
Iron & Steel Co. v. Cooper Ltd.,*[79] be only in regard to the point at which
delivery occurs. In other words, it may be the only distinguishing factor
between an f.a.s. and an f.o.b. contract in many cases, the allocation of forwarding costs between seller and buyer being identical under both types of
contract.[80] For this reason the f.o.b. seller must tender a shipped, or an on

---

[76] Information obtained from the ICC.
[77] And irrespective of whether he assumes full responsibility therefore from that moment, see
British Columbia and Vancouver Island Lumber and Sawmill Co. Ltd. v. Nettleship (1868) 37
L. R. (N. S.) C. P. 235.
[78] See Maughan, *Trade Term Definitions* (London, 1929), pp. 22–24.
[79] (1895) 22 R. (Ct. of Sess.) 672, see *ante*, § 469.
[80] Reference may also be made to the following passage from Schwind, "F. A. S. clauses in
American and Comparative Law" 32 *New York Univ. Law Review* (1957) 1243 at p. 1250 to
the effect that:

> "F.a.s. must be distinguished from the more widely used term f.o.b., which requires delivery
> on board the vessel at the port of departure. From the definitions of the two terms the
> difference appears clear; and in fact an American court has held that a contract which uses
> the expression 'f.o.b.-f.a.s.' is too vague to be enforced, the two terms being inconsistent
> with each other. But this distinction cannot always be maintained. In practice ... both in
> America and abroad f.o.b. shipments are delivered on the docks to the shipping company,
> which arranges to bring the goods on board, so that in the case of both f.o.b. and f.a.s.
> shipments the shipping company handles the loading and pays for it, the expenses being
> covered by the freight charges which in turn are paid by the buyer. In some countries the
> seller's obligation to pay expenses ceases in all cases with delivery at the docks, while the

board, bill of lading and he does not satisfy the contract by furnishing a "received for shipment" bill of lading.[81] No contrary inference is to be drawn from the fact that the buyer has obtained insurance on "warehouse to warehouse" terms.[82] It has therefore been stated by Schmitthoff[83] that:

> "in f.o.b. contracts, the ship's rail is the dividing line to which lawyers and businessmen attach equal importance. The ship's rail determines not only the charges which have to be borne by the seller or buyer respectively but it is also the legal test adopted for the performance of the contract, *viz.*, the passing of property, the delivery of the goods, and the passing of risk, except where a different intention of the parties is evident. The ship's rail is, thus, the legal frontier between the seller's and buyer's lands . . ."

However, the parties are always at liberty to modify the f.o.b. contract in which case the seller's liability may be terminated prior to the time of delivery over the ship's rail. Where, for example, the buyer agrees to accept a "received for shipment" bill of lading there is a strong implication that delivery has been performed as soon as the goods have been taken into the custody of the shipowner on shore. The inference is based on the nature of the document. For such a bill is a document of title. Otherwise an express agreement will generally be required in order to vitiate the ordinary meaning of the f.o.b. term. This is often concluded with one of the following two objects in mind. It is designed either to enable the seller to claim the price of the goods where performance becomes impossible as a result of the buyer's default in providing a ship on time, or, in order to give the buyer an option to accept performance by substituting for delivery f.o.b., delivery at a warehouse on shore. As has already been noted (*ante*, § 450), no such option is to be presumed or implied in the normal case of f.o.b. contracts.[84] However, these exceptions are so common that they appear in virtually all the standard forms of f.o.b. contracts. A typical provision of this kind reads:

> "Should the buyer consider that the vessel he has chartered will not arrive in time, and in all cases where the vessel would be unable to load within the time-limits specified in the contract, which would make it impossible for the goods to be delivered within those time-limits, the buyer may ask the seller to deliver the goods to him at the place where they are situated within the time-limits specified in the contract and in accordance with the provisions of . . .; from the time when the buyer takes over the goods they shall be considered to have been delivered

---

risk of loss passes to the buyer after loading under f.o.b. contracts, but before loading under f.a.s. contracts. The distinction between f.o.b. and f.a.s. provisions is especially blurred in France and the Netherlands. Older commentaries to the French Commercial Code expressly state that under f.o.b. contracts delivery is made alongside the ship. The cases, however, are divided, and a more recent commentary maintains that the expression 'on board' has no technical meaning but depends on the usage in the port of departure. . . ."

[81] See *Yelo v. S. M. Machado & Co. Ltd.* [1952] 1 Lloyd's Rep. 183, *ante*, § 481.

[82] See *post*, § 666.

[83] *Legal Aspects of Export Sales* (1953), p. 43.

[84] *Wackerbarth v. Masson* (1812) 3 Camp. 270; *Wetherell v. Coape, ibid.* at p. 272; *Maine Spinning Co. v. Sutcliffe.* (1917) 23 Com. Cas. 216; *J. Elton & Co. Ltd. v. Chas Page & Co. Ltd.* (1920) 4 Ll.L. Rep. 226; *Cohen & Co. v. Ockerby & Co. Ltd.* (1917) 24 C.L.R. 288 (Australia).

and shall lie at the buyer's cost and risk. If the buyer does not exercise this right, the seller shall be entitled, upon expiry of the time-limits specified in the contract, to place the goods, or such portion thereof as has not been loaded, in storage at the buyer's cost and risk, and the buyer shall make payment against a certificate from the warehouse or dock authority, or other authorised body in the port of shipment, attesting that the goods have been stored at the port of shipment with a body entitled to deliver such certificates. The buyer shall bear the whole cost of storage and insurance, and also the cost of delivering the goods to the warehouse and from the warehouse to the vessel. Only the normal cost of loading, based on the form of delivery adopted by the parties, shall be paid by the seller. The date of the certificate shall be considered to be the date of delivery."[85]

578 In addition, an option allowing the buyer to claim delivery on shore is sometimes recognised by the usage of the trade. Paragraph 4(a) of the Broker's Notes of Copenhagen on Delivery of Corn F.O.B. clearly reflected this usage. This paragraph reads:

"Instead of obtaining the goods free on board, the purchaser is entitled to demand of the seller that he should effect delivery wholly or in part on land within the boundaries of the place of loading, against payment in cash on the receipt of the goods, and subject to obtaining compensation in respect of expenses which the seller may eventually have saved through this mode of delivery."[86]

Where the buyer enjoys such an option, the contract, unless cancelled by virtue of some other provision,[87] does not necessarily become invalid or void by virtue of an embargo on the export of the goods. As Lord Cozens-Hardy M.R. stated in *Smith Coney & Barrett v. Becker, Gray & Co.*[88]:

"It is, according to the terms of the contract and of the documents incorporated therewith, for the buyer to say whether his sugar which he has purchased is to be delivered on board a vessel at Hamburg or whether it is to be warehoused there. It seems to me that there is nothing in the embargo to prevent a purchaser saying to the seller, if he so minded, 'I do not want my sugar shipped to be exported; warehouse this for me at Hamburg.' That being so, I fail to see any ground for holding that the contract is . . ., of such a nature that both parties are relieved from its obligations on the principle of *Taylor v. Caldwell*[89] and cases of a similar class" (at p. 93).

579 If the seller fails to stipulate (in a contract containing such an option) that the purchase price will become due and payable on a certain date, regardless

---

[85] Clause 9.7 of the standard form of F.O.B. Contracts for the Sale of Cereals (Nos. 5A and 5B) drawn up under the auspices of the United Nations Economic Commission for Europe.
[86] *Commercial Laws of the World*, Vol. 20 (Denmark), pp. 91–92.
[87] See *Bach & Vig. v. M. L. Meyer and Bach & Wagner v. Meyer* (1921) 7 Ll.L. Rep. 63, contract including option clause deemed cancelled by virtue of events to which exception of cancellation applied.
[88] [1916] 2 Ch. 86, contract for the purchase of sugar f.o.b. Hamburg not terminated by virtue of war with Germany. See further *Jager v. Tolme & Runge and The London Produce Clearing House Ltd.* [1916] 1 K.B. 939.
[89] (1863) 32 L.J.Q.B. 164.

of whether an effective ship has arrived, he can only claim damages for breach if the buyer wrongfully fails to provide the required tonnage within the time limits fixed in the contract. He cannot normally insist on acceptance on shore. For as held by McCardie J. in *Colley v. Overseas Exporters*[90] though

> "The [Sale of Goods] Act does not deal specifically with f.o.b. or c.i.f. contracts. Judicially settled rules exist ... with respect to them ... It seems clear that in the absence of special agreement the property and risk in goods does not in the case of an f.o.b. contract pass from the seller to the buyer till the goods are actually put on board" (at p. 307).

In *Henderson & Glass v. Radmore & Co.*,[91] Bankes L.J., allowing an appeal from Branson J. who held that the sellers had a right to recover the price of the goods from the time of their receipt by the wharfinger onshore, said:

> "The learned judge below has dealt with three points and come to a conclusion ... upon the first point he says that by the practice of the shipping company, directly the shipping instructions are given by the buyers, it is the buyers' agents who really have control of the goods; and if the sellers have delivered the goods to the wharfinger, from the moment the goods arrive at the wharfinger's and the shipping company refuse to deal with them except on the instructions of the buyers' agents, he (Mr. Justice Branson) considered, in a contract of this kind for sale, f.o.b., that the sellers have performed their part of the contract directly they have delivered the goods to the wharfinger.
> I do not think that can be a fair interpretation of a contract f.o.b., unless there be some custom of the port binding upon both buyers and sellers, and which will vary a f.o.b. contract to the extent indicated by the learned judge ...
> I think, therefore, that the sellers have failed to show performance by them of their part of the contract, a failure of performance of which, unless waived by the buyers, would indicate that there had been no passing of the property from the sellers."

Bankes L.J. later proceeded to examine the question of whether or not it could be said that the buyers accepted the goods because, in the language of section 35 of the Sale of Goods Act (as it then stood), they had done acts in relation to them which were inconsistent with the ownership of the seller and held that no such acts were in this instance proven.[92]

However, provided the goods are identified, all risks as regards any loss in them which would not have occurred but for the buyer's failure to provide the vessel in time, and any costs incurred as a result therefrom (*e.g.* warehous-

---

[90] [1921] 3 K.B. 302; and see note entitled "Sales—When Title Passes in F.O.B. Transactions" in 12 *Tennessee Law Review*, pp. 61 *et seq.* (1933–1934) with respect to the American decisions on the subject. Contrast, however, *Burch & Co. Ltd. v. Corry & Co.* [1920] N.Z.L.R. 69, a New Zealand decision, where the seller succeeded in recovering the price of the goods and storage charges upon the buyer's failure to provide the vessel. The court did not address itself to the question of the transfer of property in the goods.

[91] (1922) 10 Ll.L.Rep. 727.

[92] As to this question generally, see *ante*, § 332, *post*, § 640.

ing and insurance) are for the account of the buyer in such a case.[93] Moreover, and as we have already seen,[94] the seller is normally free to treat any such failure as a repudiation of the contract. But he is not, in the absence of any agreement to this effect, authorised to engage freight for account of the buyer. Consequently, it has been stated that[95]:

> "Where the nominated ship is withdrawn or the nomination fails for another reason the buyer is obliged to name a substitute vessel as soon as possible and to bear the additional expense caused by the substitution. This rule is, however, subject to a qualification; if the contract of sale provides that the buyer shall nominate a ship within a stated time or shall[96] deliver the goods to the ship within a stated time, it is thought that he can nominate a substitute ship only if he is within the contract time. Unless a term can be implied into the contract allowing the substitution beyond the contract time or a trade custom or practice exists to that effect—which in any event would allow the substitution only within a reasonable time—the buyer would be in default if the second nomination carried him beyond the contract time."

[The next paragraph is 591.]

---

[93] See Sale of Goods Act 1979, s. 20. *"Incoterms" ante*, § 511.
[94] See further, *ante*, §§ 444 *et seq.*
[95] Schmitthoff, *The Export Trade* (7th ed., 1979), p. 22.
[96] The words "that the seller" which should precede the word "shall" seem to have been omitted inadvertently.

CHAPTER 10

THE F.O.B PRICE TERM

Introductory

591   Quite apart from the presumptions that arise from a retention of the bills of lading by the seller, the provisions of the Sale of Goods Act would, normally, militate against a finding that the property or risk in the goods has been transferred prior or subsequent to their being placed f.o.b. the vessel. Consequently, any attempt to construe the f.o.b. term as one of price only, and not as a term of delivery, must overcome the general principles of the English Law of Sales. It is beyond question that any such argument runs counter to the commercial understanding of the f.o.b. term under which the delivery aspect of the symbol (of which the courts generally take judicial notice) is clearly established. Yet, the parties are of course at liberty to vitiate this meaning by special agreement. Though very strong evidence should be required to support such a departure from what is universally regarded as the underlying characteristics of the f.o.b. term, such departures have periodically been enforced in various jurisdictions. It is therefore proposed to consider briefly the general principles of the English law of sales in order to show that they do not easily lend themselves to a construction which seeks to displace the technically and universally accepted meaning of the f.o.b. term.

Transfer prior to the f.o.b. point

592   It has already been noted that the transfer of property is in English law governed by the intention of the parties, and that where this intention is unexpressed the presumptions incorporated in section 18 of the Sale of Goods Act apply. With respect to specific goods the Act requires that they be in a "deliverable state" before property is deemed to pass. Unascertained or future goods further require unconditional appropriation to the contract as is generally deemed to take place upon delivery to a carrier for the purposes of transmission to the buyer. Because of the "deliverable state" requirement which must be met in all events, efforts to construe an f.o.b. contract as one under which the seller merely bears the charges made against the goods up to the time of delivery to the vessel, while discharging him from guaranteeing their safe arrival there, are normally unsuccessful. In other words, there is little chance of succeeding with the contention that any damage caused to the

469

goods prior to delivery f.o.b. is to be sustained by the buyer even in cases where the goods have been identified as the contract goods at some earlier point of time.[1] This is clearly demonstrated by *Underwood v. Burgh Castle Brick & Cement Syn.*,[2] in which such an argument failed with respect to a contract for the delivery of a specific engine f.o.r. ("free on rail") no reliance having been placed on the delivery aspect of the term.[3]

593   Dismissing a claim for the price of the engine that was damaged during loading before delivery f.o.r. took place, Rowlatt J. said:

> "The sale was that of a specific chattel to be delivered by the plaintiffs, but the fact that it was to be delivered by them is not the test whether the property passed. The test is whether anything remained to be done to the engine by the sellers to put it into a deliverable state; and by that I understand a state in which the thing will be the article contracted for by the buyer . . ." (at pp. 124–125).

The Court of Appeal (Bankes, Scrutton and Atkin L.JJ.) upheld Rowlatt J. but the foregoing observation (which describes "deliverable state" as referring to the quality of the goods only) was criticised, Bankes L.J. said[4]:

> "A 'deliverable state' does not depend upon the mere completeness of the subject matter in all its parts . . . where the vendors have to expend as much trouble and as much money as the appellants had to expend before this engine could be

---

[1] An exception may apply where the seller has forwarded the goods to the port of loading, on the strength of a representation by the buyer that the ship was ready for loading and the goods deteriorate because the ship has been delayed. But in this case the responsibility of the buyer arises from his misrepresentation. As suggested by Lord Hewart C.J. in *J. & J. Cunningham Ltd. v. R. A. Munro & Co. Ltd.* (1922) 28 Com.Cas. 42:

> "There may also be circumstances where, although the purchaser may be entitled to reject when the goods are being placed over the ship's rail, yet the vendor may be entitled to recover damages in respect of the deterioration of the goods. Assume the sale of a perishable cargo, say, of fresh vegetables for October shipment. Suppose the purchasers nominate their vessel and write to the vendors saying: 'She will be at the quayside in three days' time.' The vendors gather their vegetables and send them to the quayside, but the nominated ship does not arrive for a fortnight, during which time the vegetables go bad. It may be that the purchasers are entitled to reject the vegetables which have so deteriorated, but the vendors are then entitled to rely upon and bring into play another legal principle. It is not exactly an estoppel which prevents the purchasers from rejecting, but it is the doctrine that where one person makes a statement to another, meaning that statement to be relied upon and acted upon by that other, if the other suffers damage by so relying and acting upon it, he is entitled to recover such damage from the person making the statement. In the case put the damage would be the loss of price which the vendors would otherwise have obtained from the purchasers" (at p. 46). See also cases cited *ante.* § 330.

[2] [1922] 1 K. B. 123.

[3] This corresponds with the f.o.b. term in most respects save for the place in which delivery is to be made. *Cf. Young (T.) & Sons v. Hobson & Partner* (1949) 65 T.L.R. 365, where the Court of Appeal did rely on the commercial meaning of the f.o.r. clause but nevertheless rejected the sellers' claim for the price of goods delivered f.o.r. because he failed to comply with s.32(2) of the Sale of Goods Act 1893, inasmuch as the contract of carriage which he arranged stipulated that the goods were to be sent at owner's risk when they could have been sent at the same cost, subject only to inspection by the railways, at carrier's risk.

[4] [1922] 1 K. B. 343 at p. 345.

placed on rail, I cannot think that the subject matter can be said to be in a deliverable state."

Only where the cost and trouble connected with the movement of the goods is negligible, and the demarcation line is obviously not easy to draw, can the goods be properly described as being in a deliverable state. For example:

> "A man may select and agree to buy a hat and the shopman may agree to deliver it at the buyer's house. There notwithstanding the obligation to deliver the hat, the property passes at the time of the contract."[5]

Thus, the performance of any substantial duty on the part of the seller is usually not merely a collateral obligation under the contract, but a condition precedent to the transfer of property and risk thereunder. The responsibilities connected with the movement of the goods to the ship would, therefore, normally be fatal to a claim that the goods were in a "deliverable state" before they are actually put on board.[6] Moreover, the seller's obligation to pay the cost of transporting the goods to the f.o.b. point furnishes a strong presumption that safe arrival there is a condition of transfer of property under the contract.[7]

594   Though delivery is not, in theory, relevant to the determination of the passing of property in the goods:

> "where the seller agrees to deliver the goods at a particular place, *prima facie* he takes the risk during the transit, as the property does not pass till delivery."[8]

Notwithstanding the emphasis put on "intention" in the Sale of Goods Act, in practice therefore, the time of transfer is, usually, determined by reference to concrete action.

In the vast majority of f.o.b. sales, however, the goods are not specific and require ascertainment by way of unconditional appropriation. This would not obviate the requirement that the goods be in a "deliverable state" (section

---

[5] *Ibid.* at pp. 344–345.

[6] *Cf.* also *Anderson v. Morice* (1876) 1 App. Cas. 713, holding that the buyer of a "cargo" of rice of which only a part was loaded has no insurable interest therein and cannot recover on a policy if the part which was loaded be lost (c. & f. sale). The House of Lords was divided on the issue, with the result that the judgment of the Exchequer Chamber (Quain J. dissenting) which reversed the judgment of the Court of Common Pleas stood affirmed. The decision was distinguished in *The Colonial Insurance Company of New Zealand v. The Adelaide Marine Insurance Company* (1886) 12 App. Cas. 128; see *post*, § 668.

[7] This rule is expressly stated in s.19(5) of the American Uniform Sales Act, which thus provides: "If the contract to sell requires the seller to . . . pay the freight or cost of transportation to the buyer or to a particular place the property does not pass until the goods have been delivered to the buyer or reached the place agreed upon."

Although the Sale of Goods Act contains no similar provision, this is a presumption taken from the common law, and has been followed by English courts. Clearly however it does not apply to the case of c.i.f. contracts because of a contrary intention.

[8] Benjamin, *Treatise on the Law of Sale of Personal Property* (8th ed., London 1950) p. 648, and the authorities there cited.

18(5)(1) of the Act). The presumptions concerning the payment and responsibility of conveying and putting the goods on board therefore equally apply
to unascertained goods. In addition, however, appropriation by way of an
irrevocable attachment of the goods to the contract is necessary. This would
normally be evidenced only by the execution of the *last* of the seller's obligations, namely, the actual putting of the goods on board the ship—since:

> "where several things are to be done by the seller to the goods, it is to be
> presumed that the parties intend the appropriation to be deferred until the last of
> these acts has been done."[9]

This rule affects seller and buyer alike. It normally disallows an action for
the price (as distinct from damages for breach) where performance becomes
impossible due to a breakdown of the buyer's arrangement with the ship.
Equally it may be an obstacle to the buyer in cases where the purchase price
has been prepaid, and he seeks to obtain the goods.

595   Thus, in *Carlos Federspiel & Co., S.A. v. Charles Twigg & Co. Ltd. &
Anor.*,[10] where the purchase price for eighty-five bicycles f.o.b. British port
had been prepaid by the plaintiffs (a Costa Rica company) a plea for specific
performance of the contract in view of the seller's impending insolvency was
denied. Pearson J. held that no property in the bicycles had passed to the
buyer. The fact that the bicycles had actually been set aside, duly packed for
export and named with the buyer's name, the seller also having reserved
shipping space for the same was held to be immaterial. For it was said, *inter
alia*, that:

> ". . . the last two acts to be performed by the seller, namely, sending the goods
> to Liverpool and having the goods shipped on board, were not performed" (at
> p. 256).

And "the analogy naturally presents itself of the rule that, where something
remains to be done to put the goods in a deliverable state, the property presumably does not pass."[11]

596   In *Pentel & Co. (London) Ltd. v. Lastextile Ltd.*,[12] the plaintiffs sought
to obtain an injunction restraining the defendants—who were buyers of a
consignment of certain clothes—from parting with the possession of those
clothes. The plaintiffs alleged that the property in the goods, which were due
to arrive in London on the day the motion was heard, had previously passed
to them in pursuance of a contract of sale f.o.b. Marseilles. Pennycuick J.
held that there was no prima facie evidence of such passing of property since
as he is reported to have said:

---

[9] *Williston on Sales* (Rev. ed., 1948) para. 278.
[10] [1957] 1 Lloyd's Rep. 240.
[11] See Williston, *ibid.*
[12] *The Times*, September 8, 1960.

"The contract must have been subject to the implied condition that a licence would be obtained from the French authorities for the export of the goods from France [and as] No such licence was obtained ... the property in the goods never passed. It was very doubtful if it was the common intention ... that the property in the goods should pass to the plaintiff company at the date of the contract. The plaintiffs had not shown a *prima facie* ownership of the goods such as would require the court to interfere by injunction to restrain the defendants from dealing with the goods."

597   Delivery to the ship, therefore, appears to be not merely a collateral or ancillary obligation but normally also a condition precedent to the transfer of property in the goods, and of appropriation (where necessary). In the absence of special considerations these presumptions would, therefore, militate against a claim of transfer prior to the f.o.b. point even without having to fall back on the special meaning of the f.o.b. term.[13] American courts have however sometimes concluded that transfer took place prior to the f.o.b. point[14] in order to enable recovery of the price where performance became impossible due to default by the buyer. Desirable as it may be, this view finds little support in precedent and raises more problems than it solves.[15]

Therefore in order to obtain such relief, an express agreement to the effect that the price shall be deemed due and payable on a certain day even if performance becomes impossible as a result of default by the buyer is recommended.

The foregoing principles of the common law do not enjoy universal application. Indeed, under some legal systems, precisely reverse rules apply.

598   Under German law, for example (B.G.B., Article 447), the risk of loss shifts when the goods commence their journey at the inland point of dispatch, so that the buyer must bear the risk during the subsequent transmission to the ship. As a result, under German law the f.o.b. term was for many years construed as referring to the price merely, no effect being given to the "delivery" aspect thereof. Not until 1924 (R.G.Z., Volume 106, pp. 212 *et seq.*), and after a long and obstinate struggle by business circles and the commercial community,[16] were German courts prepared to recognise and enforce the business meaning of the term which contravened the normal inferences of their own legal system. Today,[17] as universally recognised,[18] the technical meaning

---

[13] See Note "F.O.B. Contracts and Proposed Sales Legislation" 41 Col.L.R. 892 at pp. 904 *et seq.* (1941).
[14] *Ibid.*
[15] See *ante*, §§ 569 *et seq.*
[16] See *Rechtsvergleichendes, Handwörterbuch für das Zivil- und Handelsrecht* (Berlin, 1931), Vol. III, pp. 444 *et seq.*, and "Risk of Loss in Sales" (1932) 6 Tul.L.R. 272, n. 35 and the authorities there cited.
[17] See *Manual of German Law* (H.M.S.O.), Vol. 1, para. 254(c).
[18] But see Caeymaex, *Les Principes de la Vente F.O.B.* (Bruxelles, 1948) who persistently contends (paras. 14–21, 28, 42) that the passage of property (and risk) is subject to the specification of the goods—which does not necessarily occur as late as delivery on board. Similarly, it is stated by Wessel, *Law of Contract in South Africa* (2nd ed., 1951), para. 4522 that in South Africa risk attaches to the buyer from the moment the sale is concluded. The accuracy of these

of the f.o.b. contract is upheld, and is, in the absence of an express agreement to the contrary, fully binding on the parties thereto. Theoretically, however, it would probably be easier to establish a passing of risk prior to the f.o.b. point in a German court than in a court applying common law principles.

599   It may be noted that notwithstanding the attempt to reconcile civil law with common law principles in the Uniform Law on International Sales, and in the newer UN Convention on contracts for the International Sale of Goods (*ante*, § 418), the omission of a definition of specific trade terms such as f.o.b. and c.i.f., which were included in earlier drafts, may (conceivably) raise similar problems in future.

The original and unrevised Uniform Law, as already noted,[19] has been incorporated into the law of England by The Uniform Law of International Sales Act 1967. Its application is limited to "international contracts," a condition which under Article 1 is satisfied in any one of the following three circumstances:

(1) If the goods are to be carried from one country to another; or
(2) if the acts constituting offer and acceptance have taken place in more than one country; or
(3) if the goods are to be delivered in a country other than the one where the acts constituting offer and acceptance took place, and for the time being is only applicable to such contracts "if it has been chosen by the parties as the law of the contract" (section 1(3) of the 1967 Act).

Later transfer

600   In this case the proposition is that the burden of expenses after the f.o.b. point is on the buyer, but that otherwise the seller is responsible for the safe delivery of the goods at their destination (or some other place) and bears the risk of loss in transit. Common law principles do not easily lend themselves to this construction either. In the absence of an express and unambiguous stipulation to the effect that the seller has undertaken such a responsibility, the normal inference of the Sale of Goods Act is that where the seller has delivered goods to a carrier for the purpose of transmission to the buyer, delivery is then and there performed, *a fortiori* when the carrier is nominated by the buyer and freight and insurance are paid by him. However, because no property can pass in unascertained goods, and because of the presumptions which apply in cases where the bill of lading is to the order of the seller (or his agent) or has been retained by the seller, problems may arise in the following types of cases:

---

authorities is however questionable. As to the position under French law, see Juglart, "Les obligations des parties dans la vente f.o.b." *Droit Maritime Français* (1958), p. 51.
[19] *Ante*, § 418.

(1) where the contract goods are shipped in bulk and have not been segregated from a consignment of similar goods which have simultaneously been shipped to various consignees; and

(2) where the seller is held to have reserved a right of property in the goods.

601   Should either of these circumstances lead to the conclusion that the risk of loss was not transferred to the buyer at the f.o.b. point (which is by no means an inevitable and inescapable conclusion since, although as a rule *res perit domino*, risk and property are not inseparable), the inference would be that the parties have replaced the ordinary and business meaning of the f.o.b. term. The contract could not then properly be described as an f.o.b. contract. Instead it would be a destination contract in which the f.o.b. symbol was used merely as a price stipulation. However, as one observer has stated in relation to certain decisions of American courts, although:

> "There are some decisions . . . placing the risk of loss of shipment on [the seller] which cases can be explained only on the ground that 'absolute title' remained in the seller . . . it is surprising that there should be so few of these cases in view of the fact that there are so many cases which supposedly adopt the 'absolute title' rule."[20]

602   Nevertheless such decisions do exist and they had led at least one commentator to state that

> "The difficulties in the f.o.b. field cannot hope to be cleared up until the difference between an f.o.b. price term and an f.o.b. delivery is not only recognised but enforced . . . it may be hazardous to put a duty on contracting parties to state what they mean, but that duty seems justified if otherwise neither party can know what his rights are . . ."[21]

This comment is open to objection in so far as it assumed that the f.o.b. term lacked a definite and acknowledged meaning. It most certainly does have such a meaning, and courts have generally taken judicial notice of it. Thus, where by the general presumptions of the Act different results may appear to ensue (and as the foregoing examination reveals, this would rarely happen) they must yield to the contrary intention of the parties which the f.o.b. symbol clearly imports. Consequently in *Stalik v. United States*[22] the court refused to allow evidence on what the f.o.b. term implied, holding that its meaning "is too plain to call for or permit judicial construction" (at page 138).

---

[20] See Note, "Significance of the Concept Title when the Seller Retains the Bill of Lading to Goods" 29 Col.L.R. 1100 at p. 1109 (1929).

[21] "F.O.B. Contracts and the Proposed Sales Legislation" 41 Col.L.R. 892 at p. 907 (1941).

[22] 247 Fed. 136 (1957). See also *Minex v. International Trading Co. of Virginia v. SS. Eirini ex SS. Acgina and Oths.*, 303 F. Supp. 205 (1969) where various cases are cited in all of which summary judgments were obtained denying the right to present oral evidence for the purpose of interpreting the term f.o.b.

603   For this reason the parties if they so desire must unambiguously indicate
their intention to vitiate the ordinary meaning of the f.o.b. term. And there
is, of course, nothing to prevent parties from so agreeing. But in situations
where the evidence is not overwhelming in favour of displacing the ordinary
meaning of the term f.o.b. the usual construction will prevail. So, *e.g* in
Frebold and Sturznickel (trading as Panda O.H.G.) v. Circle Products Ltd.,[23]
which has already been mentioned,[24] the Court of Appeal reversed the judgment of Nield J., and held that the fact that goods (which had to be delivered
in time for the Christmas trade) were not to be released to the buyer until
after payment, were nevertheless to be regarded as sold on f.o.b. terms proper,
and that the contract there was not to be viewed as an arrival contract as a
result of it. In this case, the buyer for some reason never learned of the arrival
of the goods in mid November until mid January, and the court held that he
bore the risk of this mishap because, *inter alia*, where the term f.o.b. is used
the presumption is that it will be given its established and well-known meaning. Widgery L.J. noted that Nield J.:

> "gave insufficient weight to the fact that this was a contract on f.o.b. terms.
> Prima facie, when two commercial men use a well known phrase of this kind
> they must be presumed to give it its established meaning. I do not think that this
> presumption is rebutted by the fact that the sellers instructed . . . not to hand
> over the goods until payment had been secured" (at p. 504).

While Sir Frederic Sellers L.J. added:

> "It was not possible, in my view, to change what was clearly a contract on f.o.b.
> terms to one which required delivery by the sellers, Panda, in London . . . A term
> which required delivery in London would be totally inconsistent with an f.o.b.
> contract, and in my view there was no evidence which supported an overthrow
> of the agreed f.o.b. terms.
>   It was also contended that the provision . . . that the goods should not be
> handed over . . . to the buyers altered the essential terms of the contract. This
> provision is quite a customary one under an f.o.b. contract. If, as here, the
> arrangement is merely to secure the contract price by requiring cash before
> the goods are handed over, and is not made with the intention of withdrawing
> the goods from the contract, it shows, and it does, nothing inconsistent with the
> intention to pass the property on shipment" (at pp. 504 and 505).

Absent a clear agreement to the contrary, the term f.o.b. will therefore be
construed as a delivery term.[25] This is clearly stated in section 2–319(1) of
the Uniform Commercial Code which accurately reflects the present state of
the law as universally recognised:

---

[23] [1970] 1 Lloyd's Rep 499.
[24] *Ante*, § 520 (footnote) and § 568.
[25] See *A. M. Knitwear v. All America Export Import Corp.*, 41 N.Y. 2d 14 (1976) holding that
such an agreement is not to be inferred (from the term f.o.b. appearing in a price column) but
requires "an express statement varying the ordinary meaning" of the term.

Later transfer

"Unless otherwise agreed the term F.O.B. (which means 'free on board') at a named place, even though used only in connection with the stated price, is a delivery term under which

 (a) when the term is F.O.B. the place of shipment, the seller must at that place ship the goods in the manner provided in this Article[26] and bear the expense and risk of putting them into the possession of the carrier; . . .
 (c) When . . . the term is also F.O.B. vessel, . . . the seller must in addition at his own expense and risk load the goods on board. If the term is F.O.B. vessel the buyer must name the vessel and in an appropriate case the seller must comply with the provisions of this Article on the form of bill of lading . . .[27]

[The next paragraph is 611.]

---

[26] s. 2–503.
[27] s. 2–323, see *ante*, § 781.

CHAPTER 11

PAYMENT AND ACCEPTANCE

Introductory

611   Failure to stipulate the time, place, currency and method of payment is most uncommon. In the case of f.o.b. contracts the form this usually took until fairly recently was payment (in cash or by acceptance of a bill of exchange) against certain specified documents. Generally, the custom was to specify an invoice and a bill of lading (for which a mate's or wharfinger's receipt was occasionally substituted) and sometimes also a certificate of quality or weight or both. The place of payment is either at the seller's or the buyer's place of business. It is unclear whether in the absence of an express agreement a provision to pay "cash against documents" would imply that the place of payment is the buyer's overseas address, and the authorities in respect of this stipulation have already been reviewed in relation to c.i.f. contracts.[1]

Documentary letters of credit

612   More recently, the foregoing method of payment has in many cases been replaced by calling for the establishment of a documentary letter of credit. As there are various types of documentary credits, *e.g.* revocable and irrevocable, confirmed and unconfirmed, transferable and non-transferable to mention only the most important variants, it is best for the contract of sale to specify the precise and particular form of credit desired. Because the irrevocable (and confirmed) letter of credit is the most widely accepted form of payment in international trade, it is primarily to this type of credit that the text hereunder is addressed. Indeed it has been said that:

> "International trade has to an increasing extent ... been financed by bankers' confirmed credits. So much so that the classic f.o.b. and c.i.f. contracts of the textbooks providing for cash or acceptance against documents without the intervention of the banker are now probably the exception rather than the rule."[2]

---

[1] *Cf. ante*, § 244.
[2] *Per* Diplock J. in *Ian Stach Ltd. v. Baker Bosley Ltd.* [1958] 2 Q.B. 130 at pp. 137–138. For the facts of the case, see *post*, § 615.

Payment by means of an irrevocable and confirmed documentary credit has many advantages over any other method of payment.[3] It resolves the problem of the seller's security and thus the entire issue of his retaining any interest in the goods which has given cause to so much difficulty in the past (see *ante*, §§ 551 *et seq.*). It will usually also enable the buyer to borrow money for the period of transport thus relieving him of the duty to mobilise the necessary funds until after the arrival of the goods at their destination. The banker in issuing an irrevocable credit usually undertakes to honour drafts negotiated (if drawn on him) or to guarantee payment.[4] The furnishing of the credit (and sometimes also a further deposit guarantee that it will be available in time[5]) is a condition precedent to the obligation to deliver the goods, and any failure to furnish it in time is a breach not of a separate collateral agreement but a default under the contract.[6] So, for example, where a contract for the sale of coffee provided, *inter alia*, that the buyers should pay by a letter of credit confirmed by a Lisbon bank their failure to do so in conformity with the provisions of the contract was rightly held to be a repudiation of the contract in *Wahbe Tamari & Sons and Jaffa Trading Co. v. "Colprogeca" Sociedade Geral de Fibras, Cafes e Productos Coloniais, Lda.*[7] The buyers delayed in opening the letter of credit and eventually tendered one in the name of A Co. which did not conform to the terms of the contract. The buyers denied that they were parties to the contract, and they and A Co. alleged that the latter were the true parties to the deal. Finally the sellers treated the contract as having been wrongfully repudiated and submitted the matter to arbitration. On an award in favour of the sellers, a special case was stated on the question as to whether the sellers were entitled to treat the contract as repudiated. Megaw J. held that the sellers were correct in their assumption and on the following three different counts. First, the continued assertion by the buyers that they were not the parties to the contract; second, on the grounds that the credit did not conform to the terms of the contract, and, third, the delay in providing the letter of credit coupled with their refusal to extend the shipping period to correspond with such delay. Each and every one of these separate events was held to constitute a wrongful repudiation by the buyers.

---

[3] See further, (*post*, § 624), as to the buyers' inability of pleading illegality, and thus discharge, in the event he is unable to obtain the foreign exchange required for furnishing the credit. Under English law he can only invoke illegality at the place of payment as an excuse for non-performance.

[4] But where the draft is used to finance an illegal transaction, *e.g.* to exchange Peruvian currency for foreign exchange in contravention of the Bretton Woods Order in Council, the illegal portion will not be enforced and the bank will be relieved of its obligation in respect thereof. See *United City Merchants (Investments) v. Royal Bank of Canada* [1982] 2 W.L.R. 1039 (H.L.) There the draft covered both a legal and an illegal transaction, and the House of Lords held that the credit was severable and was enforceable in respect of the legal part but not in respect of the illegal part.

[5] See, *e.g. S.C.C.M.O. v. Société Générale de Compensation* [1956] 1 Lloyd's Rep. 290.

[6] See *Dix v. Granger* (1922) 10 Ll.L.Rep. 496; *Cohen & Co. v. Ockerby & Co. Ltd.* (1917) 24 C.L.R. 288 (Australia).

[7] [1969] 2 Lloyd's Rep. 18.

But though it be a condition precedent to the seller's duty to deliver or ship the goods, the furnishing of the credit may, by the terms of the contract, depend upon an act of the seller so that it is not necessarily a condition precedent to the performance of all of the duties of the seller. In *Knotz v. Fairclough, Dodd & Jones Ltd.*,[8] the defendants agreed to purchase copra from the plaintiff and to pay by means of a confirmed credit to be opened for 97 per cent of a provisional invoice which the plaintiff never furnished. Sellers J. (as he then was) held that unless and until this invoice was received the defendants were not obliged to open the credit.

613   Likewise where the seller waives strict compliance with this condition he is not entitled to rely upon the furnishing of the credit as a condition precedent to his obligation of delivering the goods and he is liable to the buyer for any failure in performance. This was held by the Court of Appeal (Singleton, Denning and Hodson L.JJ.) in *Plasticmoda Societa per Azioni v. Davidsons (Manchester) Ltd.*[9] involving a sale by an English firm to Italian buyers of two consignments of fifty tons each of cable strippings f.o.b. English port. The first consignment was to be shipped on or about March 2, 1950, and the second 60 days later. Payment was to be by letter of credit in Manchester against proper shipping documents. There was a delay in shipping the goods which was requested by the sellers and various negotiations took place between the parties. The buyers then opened a letter of credit which covered the price of 30 tons only because they had the feeling that more time was needed for delivery than had been expected and there was little sense in letting their money lay idle in an English bank. They were, however, ready to open a new credit immediately upon obtaining assurance that the sellers were able to deliver a larger consignment. The buyers were never informed by the sellers of the amount likely to be shipped and in fact no shipment ever took place. The buyers then brought an action against the sellers to which the defence was raised that since the buyers violated a condition precedent of the contract, *viz.*, opening a letter of credit for the full amount, the sellers were discharged from performance. The Court of Appeal dismissed this defence. Denning L.J. said:

> "the evidence shows that the seller, by his conduct, led the buyer to believe that he would not insist on the credit being established until the seller had told the buyer that the goods were ready. There was nothing in writing on the matter. The conduct consists of an oral conversation . . . just after the contract was signed, when it was orally agreed that, as soon as the seller had given notice that the goods were ready, the buyer would provide a letter of credit. Then there was a long series of letters in which the buyers asked the sellers when the goods would be ready, and those letters were never answered. Finally, there was a conversation . . . when the seller said that the goods were not ready owing to difficulties with the machinery. It was due to that conduct of the seller that the

---

[8] [1952] 1 Lloyd's Rep. 226.
[9] [1952] 1 Lloyd's Rep. 527.

buyer never established a letter of credit for the 100 tons. He was never told the goods were ready. So he never established the letter of credit.

What is the effect of that conduct in law?

It is this: If one party, by his conduct, leads another to believe that the strict rights arising under the contract will not be insisted upon, intending that the other should act on that belief, and he does act on it, then the first party will not afterwards be allowed to insist on the strict rights when it would be inequitable for him so to do" (at pp. 538–539).

614   The credit must comply with the terms stipulated by the contract. In *Enrico Furst & Co. v. W. E. Fischer*,[10] Diplock J. held that where an irrevocable letter of credit to be opened in London is called for, this requirement is not met if the credit is irrevocable only in so far as the issuing bank in the buyer's country is concerned but has not been so confirmed by a bank in London.

Where the exact shipping date is not specified in the contract, but an option allowing the buyer or—in "shipment to destination" contracts—the seller to determine this date within a given period of time is afforded thereunder, and no specified date for the opening of the credit is provided, the credit must be furnished by the beginning of this period, prior to the earliest permissible shipping date.

615   This was decided in *Ian Stach Ltd. v. Baker Bosley Ltd.*[11] The sellers, who were dealers in steel, negotiated on July 6, 1956, a contract to sell to the buyers five hundred metric tons of ship plates of West German origin at 205 dollars a ton. On the same day the sellers entered into a contract to purchase the steel from suppliers at the price of 190 dollars a ton. By the terms of a written contract signed by the sellers and the buyers on July 10, the goods were to be delivered f.o.b. a Benelux port for shipment to Canada. Delivery was to be in August/September 1956, and payment was to be by confirmed irrevocable transferable and divisible letter of credit in favour of the sellers' nominees. The buyers had the right to select the port and the date of shipment, and the responsibility of making arrangements for shipment. Except in regard to the purchase price and the quantity, the terms of the contract between the sellers and their suppliers were similar to those of the contract between the sellers and the buyers, and the sellers required the letter of credit to be opened by the buyers before the sellers could obtain the goods from their suppliers. Although the sellers repeatedly asked the buyers to open their letter of credit, the buyers had failed to do so by August 14, and the sellers then treated the contract as repudiated and began to try to sell the goods elsewhere. On September 14, they entered into a contract to sell the goods to other buyers at the price of 194 dollars a ton, which was the market price at the time. In an action by the sellers for damages against the buyers for breach of contract, the buyers contended that, as they were entitled to call for shipment at any time within the shipping period and the sellers were not required to com-

---

[10] [1960] 2 Lloyd's Rep. 340 at p. 345.
[11] [1958] 2 Q.B. 130.

mence the performance of any of their obligations under the contract until they had received the shipping instructions, it was unnecessary for the buyers to open the letter of credit until a reasonable time before September 30, the end of the shipping period. This defence failed and Diplock J. held the buyers liable in damages for breach of contract because it was their duty to open the letter of credit by August 1, 1956 (the earliest contractual shipping date). It was further held that, as the buyers must have known that their failure to provide the letter of credit would make it impossible for the sellers to carry out the transaction, the measure of damages was the sellers' loss of profit on the transaction.

616   The following extracts from Diplock J.'s judgment explain the grounds upon which the decision was based.

"There is clear authority binding upon me that in c.i.f. contracts the confirmed credit must be opened at latest by the beginning of the shipment period. That was decided by the Court of Appeal in *Pavia & Co. S.p.A. v. Thurmann-Nielsen*,[12] where Somervell L.J. said[13]: 'I think when a seller is given a right to ship over a period and there is machinery for payment, that machinery must be available over the whole of that period'; and Denning L.J. put the matter succinctly in the following words[14]: 'The question in this case is this: In a contract which provides for payment by confirmed credit, when must the buyer open the credit? In the absence of express stipulation, I think the credit must be made available to the seller at the beginning of the shipment period. The reason is because the seller is entitled, before he ships the goods, to be assured that, on shipment, he will get paid. The seller is not bound to tell the buyer the precise date when he is going to ship; and whenever he does ship the goods, he must be able to draw on the credit. He may ship on the very first day of the shipment period. If, therefore, the buyer is to fulfil his obligations he must make the credit available to the seller at the very first date when the goods may be lawfully shipped in compliance with the contract.' That, I think, is as far as the binding authorities upon c.i.f. contracts go.

"It is, however, to be observed that in the *Sinason-Teicher* case,[15] in the Court of Appeal, Denning L.J. said this[16]: 'We were referred to *Pavia & Co. S.p.A. v. Thurmann-Nielsen*.[17] I agree with what Devlin J. said about that case. It does not decide that the buyer can delay right up to the first date for shipment. It only decides that he must provide the letter of credit at latest by that date. The correct view is that, if nothing is said about time in the contract, the buyer must provide the letter of credit within a reasonable time before the first date for shipment. The same applies to a bank guarantee: for it stands on a similar footing.'

"I think that those observations, although entitled to great respect, are obiter, and they were not necessary for the decision in that case—as indeed appears from the judgment of Devlin J.[18] in the lower court, where he refers to the matter

---

[12] [1952] 2 Q.B. 84.
[13] [1952] 2 Q.B. 84 at p. 88.
[14] *Ibid.*
[15] [1954] 1 W.L.R. 1394; see for the facts of this case *ante*, § 344.
[16] *Ibid.* at p. 1400.
[17] [1952] 2 Q.B. 84.
[18] [1954] 1 W.L.R. 935 at p. 939.

and says it is unnecessary to decide it. Neither of the other Lords Justices appears to me to express any view on the matter.

"Those being the cases upon c.i.f. contracts, Mr. Kerr,[19] to whom for his researches among the case law I am much indebted, has drawn my attention to five cases which concern f.o.b. contracts. They are: *Plasticmoda Societa per Azioni v. Davidsons (Manchester) Ltd.*[20]; *Trans Trust S.P.R.L. v. Danubian Trading Co Ltd.*[21]; *Etablissements Chainbaux S.á.r.l. v. Harbormaster Ltd.*[22] a cryptic judgment by Bailhache J. in *Dix v. Grainger*[23] and, finally, *N. V. Handel My J. Smits Import-Export v. English Exporters (London) Ltd.*[24] In each of these cases it was either held or assumed that the confirmed credit had to be opened at latest by the shipment date. It does not, however, seem to me that any of them is an authority for Mr. Kerr's proposition. In the *Plasticmoda* case[25] there was a date of shipment fixed—not a period of shipment, as in this case. In the *Trans Trust* case[26] the provision was that the letter of credit should be opened forthwith. In the *Smits* case[27] it was not a classic f.o.b. contract in that the seller had the duty and responsibility of fixing the shipping; and in the *Etablissements Chainbaux* case[28] it was rather an exceptional contract, and a manufacturer's contract at that.

"The distinction between those cases and the present case is that this is a classic f.o.b. contract in that the buyer is entitled to call for shipment at any time within the shipping period and up to the end of the shipping period. The authority for that (if any be wanted) is to be found in *J. & J. Cunningham Ltd v. Robert A. Munro & Co. Ltd.*[29] So it is said that there is a distinction to be drawn between a c.i.f. contract and a classic f.o.b. contract, and a distinction to be drawn between a classic f.o.b. contract and those f.o.b. contracts which where the subjects of the cases to which Mr. Kerr referred, namely, that in the classic f.o.b. contract, where the buyer can dictate the date of shipment, the seller is not obliged to commence any of the operations directed to performing his obligations under the contract until he has had shipping instructions or calling forward instructions from the buyer. It is urged by Mr. Lawson[30] that, applying the ratio decidendi in the c.i.f. contract cases—the *Pavia*[31] line of cases—the time at which the confirmed credit must be opened is a reasonable time before the shipping instructions take effect. The rival contention by Mr. Kerr is that the credit must be opened a reasonable time (as he put it) before the earliest shipping date; but in his reply he was prepared to put it as at latest by the earliest shipping date. Mr. Lawson, on the other hand, says that it must be a reasonable time before the actual shipping date.

"There is no authority which guides me in this matter. It seems to me, however, that the contention for which Mr. Kerr argues is the sensible one, and, since it is the sensible one, and since there is no authority to the contrary, the one which I am inclined to hold, and do hold, is good law.

---

[19] Counsel for the sellers.
[20] [1952] 1 Lloyd's Rep. 527; *ante,* 613
[21] [1952] 2 Q.B. 297.
[22] [1955] 1 Lloyd's Rep. 303.
[23] (1922) 10 Ll.L.Rep. 496.
[24] [1957] 1 Lloyd's Rep. 517.
[25] [1952] 1 Lloyd's Rep. 527.
[26] [1952] 2 Q.B. 297.
[27] [1957] 1 Lloyd's Rep. 517.
[28] [1955] 1 Lloyd's Rep. 303.
[29] (1922) 28 Com. Cas. 42; *ante,* 456.
[30] Counsel for the buyers.
[31] [1952] 2 Q.B. 84.

"I am fortified in this view by the fact that it is quite apparent from the correspondence and from the conduct of the parties in this case (and, so far as one can see, from that of the parties to the other contracts) that it is their view that that was the requirement of the contract. It seems to me that, particularly in a trade of this kind, where, as is known to all parties participating, there may well be a string of contracts all of which are financed by, and can only be financed by, the credit opened by the ultimate user which goes down the string getting less and less until it comes to the ultimate supplier, the business sense of the arrangement requires that by the time the shipping period starts each of the sellers should receive the assurance from the banker that if he performs his part of the contract he will receive payment. That seems to me at least to have the advantage of providing a definite date by which the parties know they have to fulfil the obligation of opening a credit.

"The alternative view put forward by Mr. Lawson, namely, that the credit has to be opened a reasonable time before the actual shipping date, seems to me to lead to an uncertainty on the part of buyer and seller which I should be reluctant to import into any commercial contract . . .

"It seems to me that on Mr. Lawson's argument the obligation that arises on the buyer does not arise until a date which he could not possibly know, because it is a date which must depend on circumstances which would not normally be known to him; he does not know, and would not normally know, how long a chain there was between him and the actual manufacturer or stockist to whom the credit or some subsequent back-to-back credit founded upon it has to be transferred: he would not know how long it would take to bring the goods from the place where they were and transport them to the port: he would not know in a case of this kind, and did not know, whether or not the goods had to be rolled to order or whether they were in stock or whether they were partly rolled. It seems to me that in a case of this kind, and in the case of an ordinary f.o.b. contract financed by a confirmed banker's credit, the prima facie rule is that the credit must be opened at latest (and that is as far as I need go for the purposes of this case) by the earliest shipping date. In that way one gets certainty into what is a very common commercial contract. In any other way one can, I think, only get a position in which neither buyer nor seller knows what his rights are until all the facts have been ascertained, and one, and possibly two or three courts have directed their minds to the question whether in all the circumstances that was a reasonable time for the credit to be opened.

"I therefore hold that it was the duty of the defendants under this contract to open their letter of credit or to get a banker's pre-advice of it by August 1, 1956, at the latest. That makes it necessary for me to consider the second line of defence, namely, that the plaintiffs waived their right to treat the contract as repudiated by the defendants when they failed to open their letter of credit within the appropriate time. The defendants rely for that waiver first on the letter of August 8, 1956, which calls upon the defendants to open the letter of credit immediately. I think there is no doubt that that letter did amount to a waiver of their right to treat the contract as repudiated by breach of condition until such time had elapsed after receipt of that letter by the defendants as could reasonably be called "immediately." Certainly that time had elapsed by August 14, on which date a letter was sent which said: "In view of your failure to adhere to the conditions of the above-mentioned contract we must hold you responsible for all consequences arising out of this and have no option but to place the matter into the hands of our legal advisers." It is, in my view, perfectly plain that at that date the plaintiffs accepted the breach of condition by the defendants in failing to open a credit as a repudiation of the contract. It was obviously a term which went to the root of the contract, and they were entitled so to do in law" (at pp. 140–144).

Moreover, the buyer's duty to open the credit, and have it communicated to the seller or his agent in time,[32] is an absolute one. It is no excuse for him to do all that is in his power to do because if he fails he is in default. This was decided in *Lindsay (A. E.) & Co. Ltd. v. Cook*[33] where due to a delay in inter-bank communications the credit was not opened in time. Pilcher J. expressed his sympathy with the plaintiffs who had done their best to establish the credit in time, but found that he could do little to actually assist them. The seller, in his opinion, was entitled to repudiate the contract.

617   Should the buyer wish to avoid having to put the credit machinery into motion at this early date and defer it until shortly before the actual shipping date, he must insert some express stipulation in the contract by which the provisions of the credit shall be so conditioned, *e.g.* 14 days before notice of shipment is received or dispatched.[34] Where the buyer is concerned as to the quality of the goods shipped, and is unable to arrange for satisfactory proof in relation thereto until arrival at destination, he might be able to stipulate that the seller would be entitled to draw only a partial amount of the price, *e.g.* 30 per cent against presentation of the documents to the bank, with the remaining balance to be paid after inspection at the destination to take place within an agreed period after discharge. But the much more common arrangement would be to call for a certificate of inspection attesting to the quality of the goods purchased.

It has already been noted that the time of establishing the credit is a condition of the contract so that a failure to meet it may be treated as a repudiation by the seller. It has been further held that when this time has been waived (and has not properly been reinstituted), the buyer cannot sue on the contract if the seller is able to show that, irrespective of any such reinstitution, the buyer could not have possibly complied with it.[35]

618   Once communicated to the beneficiary the credit, if irrevocable (as it undoubtedly will normally be), imposes upon the bank an absolute obligation to pay upon the tender of the stipulated documents[36] subject only to limitations as to the period of time for which it is available, from which it cannot resile. No subsequent instructions from the buyer (unless approved by the beneficiary), and no controversy between buyer and seller as to whether the contract of sale has been performed can release it therefrom.

In other words, the defences of the buyer arising out of the sale contract in connection with which the letter of credit was issued (and subject to the

---

[32] See *Bunge Corp. v. Vegetable Vitamin Foods (Private) Ltd.* [1985] 1 Lloyd's Rep. 613.
[33] [1953] 1 Lloyd's Rep. 328.
[34] See *per* Somervell L.J. in *Pavia & Co., S.p.A. v. Thurmann-Nielsen* [1952] 2 Q.B. 84 at p. 88.
[35] See *Etablissements Chainbaux S.à.r.l. v. Harbormaster Ltd.* [1955] 1 Lloyd's Rep. 303. With regard to the question of waiver, *cf.* *"Baltimex" v. Metallo Chemical Refining Co.* [1956] 1 Lloyd's Rep. 450 (C.A.).
[36] See *Urquhart Lindsay & Co. Ltd. v. Eastern Bank Ltd.* [1922] 1 K.B. 318. See also *Hamzeh Malas & Sons v. British Imex Industries Ltd.* [1958] 2 Q.B. 127.

possible fraud exception)[37] do not concern the bank and in no way affect its liability. The bank is concerned only in the terms of the credit itself being complied with, *i.e.* in drafts and documents which are to be furnished by the seller.[38] Had the rule been otherwise, one of the strongest reasons for making use of this mode of payment, namely a desire to avoid any obstacle to payment which the buyer might raise after the goods have been put in transit, would be inoperative.

A case in point is *Hamzeh Malas & Sons v. British Imex Industries Ltd.*[39] where the plaintiffs contracted to buy from the defendants a quantity of reinforced steel rods, to be delivered in two instalments. Payment was to be made under two confirmed credits, one for each instalment to be opened with a London bank. Both credits were duly opened and confirmed by the bank to the defendants. The first credit was duly realised on shipment of the first instalment but a dispute arose with respect to the second credit. The buyers alleged that the quality of the first shipment was not in accordance with the contract specifications and applied for an injunction restraining the sellers from realising the second credit or recovering any money thereunder. The Court of Appeal upheld Donovan J., and refused to grant the injunction, on the grounds stated in the following portion of Jenkins L.J.'s judgment:

"... it seems to be plain enough that the opening of a confirmed letter of credit constitutes a bargain between the banker and the vendor of the goods, which imposes upon the banker an absolute obligation to pay, irrespective of any dispute there may be between the parties as to whether the goods are up to the contract or not. An elaborate commercial system has been built upon the footing that bankers' confirmed credits are of that character, and, in my judgment it

---

[37] Attempts to incorporate the terms of the sales contract into the credit have failed. So, *e.g.* in *Davis O'Brian Lumber Co. Ltd. v. Bank of Montreal* [1951] 3 D.L.R. 536 an effort to construe a credit that called for documents evidencing a shipment "in accordance with contract dated 22.12.47 no. 47450" as adding to the normal obligations of the banker failed. The situation, however, is different where the buyer is able to establish (and not merely allege) that he was a victim of fraud, *i.e.* that the documents tendered are forged or worthless because of fraudulent misrepresentations contained in them. See *Sztejn v. J. Henry Schroder Banking Corp.* 31 N.Y.S. 2d 631 (1941); *Discount Records Ltd. v. Barclays Bank Ltd.* [1975] 1 W.L.R. 315. See also as to the meaning of fraudulent documents *United City Merchants (Investments) v. Royal Bank of Canada* [1982] 2 W.L.R. 1039 (H.L.), and generally on the fraud exception Ellinger, "Fraud in Documentary Credit Transactions" [1981] J.B.L. 258.

[38] The credit may, however, alter the terms of the contract of sale, in which case the terms of the letter of credit will govern and prevail. In *Ficom S. A. v. Sociedad Cadex* [1980] 2 Lloyd's Rep. 118, the contract (for the sale of Bolivian coffee f.o.b. Matarani) incorporated the terms of the European Coffee Contract which, *inter alia*, provided that, in the absence of fraud or gross negligence, differences in quality (of the coffee tendered) shall never give rise to a right of rejection, but shall only be a basis for a price allowance. Yet the letter of credit (by which payment was to be effected) called for a certificate of quality. Since the certificate noted that the coffee did not meet the contractual specification the bank (after consultation with the buyer) refused payment. The question arose as to whether the buyer (in the circumstances) was entitled to reject the documents, and Goff J. (reversing a trade arbitration) answered it in the affirmative. The letter of credit terms (which were left undefined in the contract of sale) were agreed to by the parties and were binding on them notwithstanding any inconsistency between them and the terms of the sale contract.

[39] [1958] 2 Q.B. 127.

would be wrong for this court in the present case to interfere with that established practice.

   There is this to be remembered too. A vendor of goods selling against a confirmed letter of credit is selling under the assurance that nothing will prevent him from receiving the price. That is of no mean advantage when goods manufactured in one country are being sold in another'' (at p. 129).

   However, it has been suggested that where circumstances subsequent to the issue of the credit are such as to clearly divest the beneficiary of the legal right to perform and receive payment, the court should restrain him from obtaining payment, *e.g.* where a credit is issued for the purpose of paying a seller who ships under an instalment contract calling for a number of monthly shipments, and one or more deliveries are so defective as to constitute a material breach, the buyer, having a legal right to treat the entire contract as broken, would seem to be entitled to a court order which would restrain the seller from obtaining further payments under the credit.[40] The point, however, does not seem to have been taken up before the courts till now, and whether or not this view will prevail, if and when the matter is raised, is unclear.

619   On the other hand, if the bank violates the terms of the credit and erroneously makes payment without strict adherence to the instructions it received or to the specific documents required thereunder, it is in default towards the buyer who is released from his obligations towards the bank.[41] In other words, the bank is under an obligation of strict performance that is rigorously adhered to and the *de minimus* maxim is generally inapplicable to documentary credit transactions. Thus, in *English, Scottish & Australian Bank Ltd. v. Bank of South Africa*,[42] Bailhache J. said:

> "It is elementary to say that a person who ships in reliance on a letter of credit must do so in exact compliance with its terms. It is also elementary to say that a bank is not bound or indeed entitled to honour drafts presented to it under a letter of credit unless those drafts with the accompanying documents are in exact accord with the credit as opened."

This statement was cited with approval by Mackinnon L.J. in *Rayner & Co. Ltd. v. Hambro's Bank Ltd.*,[43] where the Court of Appeal held that a bank acted at its peril if it departed from the precise terms of its customer's mandate and, accordingly, that it was justified in refusing payment where the credit specified "Coromandel groundnuts" and the bill of lading referred to "machine shelled groundnut kernels." Evidence that this latter description was universally understood in the trade to be identical with Coromandel

---

[40] McGowen, "Assignability of Documentary Credits" *Law and Contemporary Problems* (1948) 665.
[41] *Midland Bank Ltd. v. Seymour* [1955] 2 Lloyd's Rep. 147.
[42] (1922) 13 Ll.L.R. 21 at p. 24.
[43] [1943] K.B. 37 at p. 40. See also *Bank Melli Iran v. Barclays Bank* [1951] 2 T.L.R. 1057; *Moralice (London) Ltd. v. E. D. & F. Man* [1954] 2 Lloyd's Rep. 526; *Soproma S.p.A. v. Marine & Animal By-Products Corpn.* [1966] 1 Lloyd's Rep. 367.

groundnuts was rejected, for it was held that the bank was under no duty to know the trade customs and terms of all its customers and that, even if it has such knowledge, the seller had not complied with the exact terms of the credit. In other words the documents must be those called for, and not documents which are almost the same or which might do just as well.[44] However, it is often impossible for the bill of lading to contain all the descriptive terms of the credit and, as a result, it is generally sufficient if it describes the goods in general terms and there is no conflict between that description and the credit description while any missing particulars are contained in the other documents, *e.g.* the invoice.[45]

So too, where the credit called for a "full set" of bills of lading, a tender of two bills and an undertaking to produce the third or an indemnity in respect thereof was held not to be a compliance with the conditions requiring production of the full set.[46]

620   In *British Imex Industries Ltd. v. Midland Bank Ltd.*,[47] Salmon J. considered the extent of the duty of a bank in relation to the tender of documents and gave it as his opinion that its obligation was to satisfy itself that the correct documents had been presented and that no endorsement appeared on the bill of lading which might indicate some defect in the packing or the goods. It was not concerned with the clauses printed on the back of the bill or their legal implications. His lordship held that where a letter of credit called for a bill of lading without further qualification, the seller had to tender a "clean" bill of lading, which he tentatively described as one without any reservation as to the apparent good order or condition of the goods or the packing.[48] The view has been expressed that a bill of lading containing the statement "freight paid by cheque" is a bad tender under a c.i.f. contract, and one which the bank is justified (and presumably required) to reject as a bad tender.[49]

---

[44] *Per* Lord Sumner in *Equitable Trust Co. of New York v. Dawsons Partners Ltd.* (1927) 27 L1.L.R. 49 at p. 52 (H.L.); and see *Kydon Compagnia Naviera SA v. National Westminster Bank, The Lena* [1981] 1 Lloyd's Rep. 68.

[45] *Midland Bank Ltd. v. Seymour* [1955] 2 Lloyd's Rep. 147. The principle is now embodied in the I.C.C.'s Uniform Customs and Practices that are incorporated and govern letter of credit transactions.

[46] *Scott & Co. Ltd. v. Barclays Bank Ltd.* [1923] 2 K.B. 1 at p. 11. *Cf. Dixon Irmaos & Cia v. Chase National Bank* (1944) 144 F. 2d 759, *ante*, § 259, where a custom to accept less than a full set of bills of lading in return for an indemnity by a reputable bank was established, and the court held that the custom did not contradict the express terms of the credit but explained the meaning of the condition and was incorporated by implication therein.

[47] [1958] 1 Q.B. 542.

[48] Salmon J. held that a bill of lading endorsed "shipped in apparent good order and condition, weight, measure, marks, numbers, quality, contents and value unknown" was a "clean" bill. Apparently, it was not a reservation as to the apparent good order of the goods but simply a statement denying all knowledge of the contents. In the subsequent case of *M. Golodetz & Co. Inc. v. Czarnikow-Rionda Co. Inc., The Galatia* [1980] 1 W.L.R. 495 (C.A.) it was held that a bill of lading is clean if there is nothing in it to qualify the carriers' admission that *at the time* of shipment the goods were in apparent good order and condition; it is irrelevant that the bill of lading records the fact that the goods were subsequently discharged on account of fire damage.

[49] Gutteridge and Megrah, *The Law of Banker's Commercial Credits* (6th ed., 1979), p. 97.

As far as insurance is concerned, an insurance *certificate* will not do if an insurance *policy* is specified.[50]

The documents which the seller must furnish and which the bank must examine with reasonable care to ascertain their compliance with the terms of the credit are usually specified in the contract of sale.

Great caution is required in drafting provisions relating to the documentary evidence which the buyer requires as a condition of payment, because it is an established principle in relation to documentary credits that if the instructions given to the issuing banker as to the documents to be tendered are ambiguous or capable of covering more than one kind of document, the banker is not in default if he acts upon a reasonable meaning of the ambiguous expression or accepts any kind of document which fairly falls within the wide description used.[51]

Aside from that however, and as already stated, unless the documents tendered under the credit are those for which it called, the beneficiary (*i.e* the seller) cannot claim against the bank, and it is the bank's duty to refuse payment.

621   *Credit not exclusive source of payment.* Whether the credit furnishes the exclusive or merely the primary source of payment so that the seller is not deprived of all rights of claim for the purchase price when payment has not been met out of the letter of credit proceeds for one reason or another was at one time an open question. With the decision of *W.J. Alan & Co. Ltd. v. El. Nasr Export & Import Co.,*[52] the matter was resolved in favour of the view suggested in the first edition of this book. Namely that failure of the method of payment agreed (and it is immaterial whether the credit is both irrevocable and confirmed or only irrevocable but unconfirmed) normally does not release the buyer from his liability for the purchase price. As stated by Lord Denning M.R. after review of the various authorities on the point (in the aforementioned case at page 210):

> "In my opinion a letter of credit is not to be regarded as absolute payment unless the seller stipulates, expressly or impliedly, that it should be so. He may do it impliedly if he stipulates for the credit to be issued by a particular banker in such circumstances that it is to be inferred that the seller looks to that particular banker to the exclusion of the buyer. If the letter of credit is *conditional* payment of the price, the consequences are these: the seller looks in the first instance to the banker for payment; but, if the banker does not meet his obligations when the time comes for him to do so, the seller can have recourse to the buyer."

Obviously this does not mean that the mode of performance of the contract or any part thereof can be unilaterally altered by either party. It merely enables the seller to claim the price direct from the buyer if the bank which

---

[50] *Scott & Co. Ltd. v. Barclays Bank Ltd.* [1923] 2 K.B. 1, *ante*, § 212.
[51] See *Commercial Banking Co. of Sydney Ltd. v. Jalsard Pty. Ltd.* [1973] A.C. 279, *ante*, § 325.
[52] [1972] 2 Q.B. 189. C.A., discussed in *ante*, § 272.

has opened or confirmed the irrevocable credit is for some reason unable to pay the agreed purchase price upon presentation of the documents. This view is consistent with the Australian decision in *Saffaron v. Société Minière Cafrika*[53] where an irrevocable but unconfirmed credit was considered. In that case an f.o.b. contract provided for payment against a letter of credit which was not honoured because of failure to present the required documents to the bank. The seller nevertheless delivered the goods and the buyer was able to obtain the bill of lading without payment being met. Upon suit for recovery of the price the buyer alleged that according to the agreement the obligation to pay was discharged by furnishing the credit and that if payment did not come therefrom the seller lost his right to be paid. The High Court of Australia dismissed this argument, describing the events which led to the dispute in the following terms:

> "In this case the seller had nothing to do with arrangements for the carriage or the insurance of the goods to be shipped or with the payment of freight; its obligations were fulfilled when it put the goods on board and allowed the buyer by virtue of his possession of the weight certificate to obtain such bill of lading as he wanted ... It is true that the course which the seller adopted was, as the events show, an improvident one. It put the buyer in a position to procure a bill of lading which would give him control of the goods and yet would not comply with the terms of the letter of credit, so that the seller unnecessarily lost all control of the goods without payment or assurance of payment" (at pp. 241, 242).

However, in *Shamsher Jute Mills Ltd. v. Sethia (London) Ltd.*,[54] the sellers were less fortunate. There 200 tons of jute yarn of a specified quality were sold f.o.b. by sellers in Bangladesh to buyers in London. The case involved what Bingham J. described as a "novel" problem.

> "If an f.o.b. seller who has contracted for payment under a letter of credit to be opened by the buyer ships the goods but fails to obtain payment under the credit because of a failure on his part to comply with its terms, may he recover the contract price or damages for non-acceptance against the buyer?"

It was argued that the documents presented by the sellers contained discrepancies, and that the bank was entitled to refuse payment, but unlike the *Saffaron* decision, the buyer never took delivery of the goods that were eventually sold in Antwerp in order, it was assumed, to satisfy freight and warehousing claims from which proceeds "neither the buyers[55] nor sellers", in the language of the decision, "derived any benefit". The sellers action failed. While it was admitted that the credit was only the conditional means of payment agreed between the parties, the sellers could not proceed against the buyer personally if the non-payment under the letter or credit was due to a failure

---

[53] (1958) 100 C.L.R. 231.
[54] [1987] 1 Lloyd's Rep. 388.
[55] Query, however, whether, this being an f.o.b. contract, the payment of freight was not in effect a benefit derived by the buyer as he would have been liable to the carrier.

on his part to comply with its terms. Bingham J. (at page 392) said he "knew no (such) case". But this, with respect, appears to overlook the *Saffaron* decision which, however, may be distinguished on the grounds that there the buyers took possession of the goods, whereas in *Shamsher* they did not. Presentation of documents to the bank was not equivalent to presentation to the buyers, since the bank "was not the buyers agents to receive the documents otherwise than under the letter of credit" (at page 393). The decision notes the result to be "harsh" for the sellers who appear to have set out to perform the contract in an honest, efficient and businesslike way but concludes in noting that "the law and practice of international commerce cannot be modified by the Courts to meet particular cases, however hard".

622 In *Newman Industries Ltd. v. Indo-British Shipping Industries Ltd. (Govindram Bros. Ltd., Third Parties)*,[56] which predates the decisions establishing that the credit is merely the primary, and not exclusive means of payment, Sellers J. expressed a similar view:

> "The action is against the buyer, not against the bank, and the question of importance is whether the seller must look only to the bank who issued the letter of credit; that is, whether the method of payment agreed releases the buyer from direct liability for payment under the contract of sale. There does not seem to be any definite authority on the matter.[57] When it has been agreed that payment is to be by a bill of exchange, the payment would normally be a conditional payment and it would require very clear terms to make it an absolute payment . . . I do not think there is any evidence to establish, or any inference to be drawn, that the draft under the letter of credit was to be taken in absolute payment. I see no reason why the plaintiffs . . . should not look to the defendants, as buyers, for payment" (at p. 236).

Where the credit is made transferable and thus divisible and assignable it provides the most convenient machinery for finance. It can pass along a string-line of transactions from the ultimate consumer to the original manufacturer, enabling the various participants to handle transactions far beyond their own financial resources. To minimise frauds and abuses of the letter of credit mechanism, the buyer can as a measure of precaution insist that, preceding the furnishing of the credit or immediately thereafter, the seller provide him with a bond of performance, or a guarantee of delivery issued by a well-known financial or similar institution. In the absence of such a provision, the buyer may end up with purchasing a personal claim against an insolvent or fraudulent party because of the rule already mentioned[58] (*ante*, § 618) that payment under an irrevocable credit must be made irrespective of whether the contract of sale has or has not been performed. Since bills of lading are

---

[56] [1956] 2 Lloyd's Rep. 219. The judgment was reversed on appeal in [1957] 1 Lloyd's Rep. 211, on the ground that the terms of the different proposals were too vague to constitute a binding agreement and there being no consensus *ad idem* no contract was concluded.

[57] This was prior to the decision in *W. J. Alan & Co. Ltd. v. El Nasr Export and Import* Co., *ante*, § 621.

[58] *Ante* § 618.

always qualified by words such as "said to contain" in order to absolve the carrier from any responsibility for a representation that the goods which the bills of lading purport to represent have actually been received and shipped, the buyer may be exposed to serious risks which can normally be minimised by the requirement of a certificate of inspection (issued by a reputable third party)[59] as to the quality of the goods (see *ante*, § 325).

623   *Currency provisions.* Mention has already been made of the problem of currency provisions in international sales contracts.[60] Similar difficulties are frequently transported into the letter of credit transaction as was the case in *W. J. Alan & Co Ltd. v. El Nasr Export and Import Co.*[61] There the plaintiffs, coffee merchants carrying on business in Kenya, sold to the defendants, an Egyptian State trading company with offices at Nairobi and Dar-es-Salaam, 250 tons of coffee f.o.b. Mombasa under two contracts of sale made in Nairobi. Shipment under the first contract was to be during September/October 1967, and shipment under the second contract was to be during October/November 1967. The price was fixed at Sh. 262/- per cwt. and payment was to be by confirmed irrevocable letter of credit to be opened at sight one month prior to shipment. The defendants resold the coffee to Spanish sub-buyers, who opened an irrevocable letter of credit in sterling in Madrid, and the buyers procured the transfer of the sub-buyers' letter of credit in favour of the sellers up to a limit of £131,000, and the credit transfer was confirmed by the National Bank of Commerce at Dar-es-Salaam. The sellers accepted payment under that arrangement in respect of the full amount of the price under the first contract. Thereafter, and prior to completion of performance under the second contract, the pound sterling was devalued but Kenyan currency was not. The sellers then claimed that the currency of account was Kenyan or East African shillings (not sterling) and that the buyers, having paid under the letter of credit a sterling equivalent which was no longer effective, were liable to pay such an additional sum as would bring the price up to 262 Kenyan shillings per cwt. The buyers, however, contended that the currency of account as distinct from the currency of payment[62] was sterling. This contention was rejected on the ground that the currency of account which fell to be determined by the proper law (by virtue of an express stipulation that the contract be interpreted according to English law)[63] was Kenya shillings. But it was also held by the Court of Appeal that the action must fail because the sellers by accepting payment under a sterling letter of credit had waived their right to be paid that currency or had agreed to vary the contract to that extent.

---

[59] See *Heisler v. Anglo-Dal Ltd.* [1954] 1 W.L.R. 1273, holding that a personal guarantee of the seller (not endorsed by any third party) would satisfy the requirement, and the word "guarantee" should therefore be qualified if the intention is that it be given by a third person, *e.g.* a bank.
[60] *Ante*, § 272.
[61] [1972] 2 Q.B. 189.
[62] As to this distinction, see *ante*, § 272.
[63] As to this aspect, see *ante*, §§ 393 *et seq.*

624   *Illegality.* Where, because of foreign exchange restrictions, the buyer requires permission to open a letter of credit the question has sometimes arisen as to whether his inability to do so may excuse performance (and liability) on grounds of illegality. This issue first arose in *Toprak Mahsulleri Ofisi v. Finagrain Compagnie Commerciale Agricole et Financière S. A.*[64] where the buyers (a Turkish state trading corp.) bought a large quantity of American wheat, and payment was to be "by irrevocable, divisible and transferable letter of credit ... to be confirmed by a first class U.S. or West European bank." The letter of credit could not be opened because of a refusal by the Turkish Ministry of Finance to allocate the necessary foreign exchange. The contract provided for arbitration in London in accordance with the law of England, where, on a special case stated, the court held the buyers liable in damages for breach. In the course of his judgment Lord Denning M. R. said:

> "It seems to me in this contract, where the letter of credit had to be a confirmed letter of credit ... the sellers are not in the least concerned as to the method by which the Turkish buyers are to provide that letter of credit. Any troubles or difficulties in Turkey are extraneous to the matter and do not afford any defence to an English contract. ... This illegality—or impossibility—by the law of Turkey is no answer to the claim."[65]

In fact the formalities which the buyer may have to go through to obtain funds (including any foreign exchange permits) are normally regarded as entirely at the buyer's risk and responsibility, and absent an express stipulation which may protect him against default in the event of his failure to obtain the necessary permits, he will normally be liable for breach if payment is unaffected through his inability to obtain the necessary exchange authorisation. This precedent was later followed in *Congimex Compania Geral de Comercio Importadora e Exportadora S.à.r.l. v. Tradax Export S.A.*[66] where a contract for the sale of soya bean meal c.i.f. Lisbon provided for payment by letter of credit, and another for cash against shipping documents in New York. The buyer was unable to obtain necessary import and exchange permits that he had to procure. Under Portuguese law it was illegal to conclude such transactions without the necessary permits but the court held that supervening illegality was only a defence if it arose by the proper law of the contract or by law of the place of performance (New York), and under New York law payment by the buyers did not become illegal. The contract further provided that final settlement should take place on delivered weights ascertained after

---

[64] [1979] 2 Lloyd's Rep. 98 (C. A.).
[65] At p. 114 following *Klienwort, Sons & Co. v. Ungarische Baumwolle Industrie Aktiengesellschaft & Ano* [1939] 2 K. B. 678. For illegality to provide a good defence under a contract governed by English law it must be an illegality under the proper law or one emanating from the law at the place of performance. See. *e.g. Ralli Bros. v. Compagnia Naviera Sota y Anzar* [1920] K. B. 287.
[66] [1981] 2 Lloyd's Rep. 687. aff'd by C.A. [1983] 1 Lloyd's Rep. 250. See also *Congimex S.à.r.l. (Lisbon) v. Continental Grain Export Corp.* [1979] 2 Lloyd's Rep. 346.

discharge at Lisbon but while the performance of this obligation became impossible this was not considered sufficient to frustrate the contract in question. The court further held that as the buyers could have accepted the documents and diverted the ship, discharge at Lisbon formed no part of the performance, and that the contract was not frustrated when discharge there became unlawful.

Likewise, where the buyer obtains an injunction prohibiting the issuing bank from making payment under the letter of credit this may be ineffectual to prevent payment to the beneficiary exporter since in the normal course of events the proper law that governs the transaction is the law of the place of performance where the exporter is to tender the documents.[67]

Time of payment

625   It has sometimes been held that an f.o.b. term implies that payment is due on receipt of the bill of lading, and that any attempt to vary this rule requires agreement by the parties. In *Jack v. Roberts and Gibson*,[68] the Scottish Court of Session held, affirming a decision of the Lord Ordinary, that where an f.o.b. contract had been concluded subject only to agreement on specification of the goods the seller, in approving the specification, cannot demand payment against the invoice. If the seller refuses to tender the goods except against payment the buyer can succeed in an action for non-delivery under the contract. In that case the contract was entered into through an exchange of letters. The sale was to be f.o.b. Newport, Cardiff or Swansea; a price was quoted, and delivery was required within four weeks. The seller accepted the offer subject to approval of the specification by him which he later approved, requesting the buyer to note that payment would be against invoice "as we cannot keep such a small quantity on hand waiting a vessel to receive it for Glasgow." The buyer resisted this demand and succeeded in recovering damages for non-delivery. The judgments are based on a finding of fact by the Lord Ordinary that an f.o.b. term implies, by usage, that payment is due upon receipt of the bill of lading and that the sellers are not entitled to introduce a new condition as to payment after the contract has been concluded. While it is doubtful whether any such usage could today be invoked, advance payment is rare and would likewise be subject to agreement. When the contract contains no specific provision relating to the time of payment the matter is controlled by section 28 of the Sale of Goods Act, which provides that "delivery and payment are concurrent conditions."[69] According to section 32(1) of the Act, delivery to a carrier for purposes of transmission to the buyer is prima facie deemed to be delivery to the buyer. Whether section

---

[67] *Power Curber International v. National Bank of Kuwait* [1981] 1 W.L.R. 1233; *European Asian Bank A.G. v. The Punjab and Sind Bank* [1981] 2 Lloyd's Rep. 651.

[68] (1865) 3 M. (Ct. of Sess.) 554.

[69] Delivery in this context refers to the transfer of possession (see s.61 of the Sale of Goods Act 1979), and should not be confused with the technical term "delivery f.o.b." discussed earlier.

32(1) applies to f.o.b. contracts of the "strict" type has sometimes been questioned, for as Hamilton L.J. pointed out in *Wimble Sons & Co. v. Rosenberg & Sons*[70]

> "It is well settled that, on an ordinary f.o.b. contract, when 'free on board' does not merely condition the constituent elements in the price but expresses the seller's obligations additional to the bare bargain of purchase and sale, the seller does not 'in pursuance of the contract of sale' or as seller send forward or start the goods to the buyer at all except in the sense that he puts the goods safely on board, pays the charge of doing so, and, for the buyer's protection but not under a mandate to send, gives up possession of them to the ship only upon the terms of a reasonable and ordinary bill of lading or other contract of carriage. There his contractual liability as seller ceases, and delivery to the buyer is complete as far as he is concerned. In such a case the goods are not 'sent by the seller to the buyer,' though they then begin a journey which will end in the buyer's hands. In law, as between buyer and seller, they are then and there delivered by the seller to the buyer, and thereafter it is by the buyer and his agent, the carrier, and not by the seller, that the goods are 'sent' to their destination."

However, whether this is a correct or incorrect description matters little in this context, for in either case there should be no doubt about the seller's right to claim the price upon delivery of the goods to the ship, or, when he comes into possession of the bills of lading, upon their surrender. But the seller clearly cannot defend an action for non-delivery by raising the defence that payment was not tendered. All the buyer must do in such a case is to show that he was ready and willing to pay.[71]

626 Indeed, had it not been for a serious qualification suggested by Williston, further speculation on this question would be unnecessary. Williston apparently suggests that in these cases account must be taken of other factors, and that the seller is normally unable to claim the price before the buyer has had an opportunity to examine the goods.[72] As the right of examination is often exercised not at the port of shipment but at the point of destination (*post*, § 631), the obligation to pay does not, according to this view, mature concurrently with delivery to the carrier but only after the buyer has exercised or waived his right of examination. For, as Williston argues:

> "Where the rule otherwise, contracts to pay the price against the bill of lading ... instead of being favourable to the seller would be beneficial to the buyer who would otherwise be liable for the price as soon as the goods were shipped."

---

[70] [1913] 3 K.B. 743 at p. 756. This was a dissenting judgment; see *post*, § 662, where the decision is discussed in detail; but the observation here cited is probably an authoritative view of the law; see *per* Sellers J. in *Newman Industries Ltd. v. Indo-British Industries Ltd, (Govindram Bros. Ltd., Third Parties)* [1956] 2 Lloyd's Rep. 219 at p. 235.

[71] See *H. J. Macauley and C. J. Cullen v. T. J. Horgan* [1925] 2 Ir.R. 1 (f.o.r. contract).

[72] *Williston on Sales* (Rev. ed., 1948), para. 448a. The Uniform Sales Act, s.42, repeats, verbatim, the provision of the Sale of Goods Act, s.28.

627   There appears to be no direct English authority on the point since it is
most uncommon for the contract not to specify how and when payment is to
be effected. While the view above set forth has never really been challenged,[73] it seems clear from the few dicta and the various textbooks[74] that
no one has ever entertained much doubt that in cases where the seller has
never had the control over the bills of lading, payment is due immediately
upon the delivery of the goods f.o.b. without this in any way impairing the
buyer's right of examination or subsequent rejection (*post*, § 631). The rule
is thus summarised in Halsbury: "Although if nothing is said, payment is
due upon delivery of the goods by the seller to the ship, in ordinary practice
the f.o.b. contract contains special terms for payment analogous to those
common in c.i.f. contracts. . . ."[75] This view is also supported by most American authorities, and is borne out by the statement of the *Corpus Juris* which
concludes that:

> "While there is some authority to the effect that the term f.o.b. has nothing to
> do with the fixing of the time of payment, payment is usually not due for goods
> shipped f.o.b. until the goods reach the place where they are f.o.b. . . . *but when
> the goods reach the proper place*, payment is due, regardless of the right of
> inspection."[76]

The Uniform Commercial Code now contains a specific provision with
respect to contracts providing for payment against bills of lading. Section 2–
513(3)(b) of the code states that "the buyer is not entitled to inspect the
goods before payment of the price when the contract provides . . . for payment against documents of title, except where such payment is due only after
the goods are to become available for inspection." The position under the
code is however less clear with respect to f.o.b. contracts in which the buyer
acts as shipper and the documents of title never come into the hands of the
seller because of the general rule under the code (which probably does not
apply to export transactions) that appears to permit a right of inspection prior
to payment where the agreement is silent on the point.[77]

---

[73] See however *Biddell Bros. v. E. Clemens Horst Co.* [1912] A.C. 18 with respect to c.i.f.
contracts; *ante*, § 261.

[74] See *Green v. Sichel* (1860) 29 L.J.(N.S.)C.P. 213; *King v. Reedman* (1883) 49 L.T. 473, defendant, seller of goods f.o.r., could not insist on payment as a concurrent condition of delivery by
virtue of a course of business between the parties which vitiated the normal rule. Plaintiff therefore not debarred from claiming in respect of non-delivery; Schmitthoff, *Legal Aspects of Export
Sales* at p. 47; Davis, "The Various Types of F.O.B. Contract" (1957) 3 *Business Law Review*
256 at p. 259.

[75] *Laws of England* (Simonds ed.), p. 177, para. 303. See further para. 12 on p. 10 where it is
stated that under an f.o.b. contract it is "the duty of the seller to deliver the goods on board ship
at his own expense, upon which . . . payment for the goods becomes due."

[76] C.J.S., p. 998, para. 230. Similarly, where credit is allowed, it has been held to run from the
moment of delivery f.o.b. at the port of shipment; see 77 C.J.S., p. 1011, para. 235. An exception
does, however, apply with respect to the sale of certain agricultural commodities which are
subject to the regulations issued pursuant to the Federal Perishable Agriculture Commodities
Act (7 Code Fed. Regs., para. 46.24) which state that "the buyer shall have the right of inspecting
at destination before the goods are paid for . . ."

[77] See s. 2–310.

628   Whether the term of payment is to be of the "essence" of the contract in such a case is a more difficult question to answer. The presumption of the Sale of Goods Act that stipulations with regard to the time of payment are not normally deemed to be of the essence[78] is a harsh one to apply in the usual circumstances of f.o.b. transactions. It has already been noted[79] that the furnishing of a letter of credit is always a condition precedent of the contract. Similarly, an American decision has held that the seller was entitled to rescind the contract when he delivered the goods f.o.b. at the place of shipment at the specified time and the buyer refused to make payment as he had been notified he would be required to do pursuant to the contract.[80] It is suggested that this makes sense especially if it is borne in mind that stipulations as to the time of delivery are, as a rule, construed to be conditions justifying repudiation, and not warranties, for the breach of which, only damages can be claimed.

Right of rejection

629   Section 34 of the Act to which reference has already been made in connection with c.i.f. sales[81] gives the buyer a right to reject the goods if they do not conform to the contract. In order to exercise this right, the buyer must be given a reasonable opportunity to examine the goods for the purpose of ascertaining whether they are in conformity with the contract. Prima facie, the proper place of examination is the place of delivery, *viz.*, the f.o.b. point.

630   In *Perkins v. Bell,*[82] decided before the enactment of the Sale of Goods Act, the sale was of barley by sample to be delivered at a railway station near the seller's farm. The seller was aware at the time of the sale that the buyer would resell, and probably to brewers, though when or to whom the resales would take place he did not know. The buyer on the same day resold the barley to a brewer. The barley sold was by mistake subsequently mixed with inferior barley, and the seller on discovery of the fact notified the buyer of it. The barley so mixed was delivered at the station, and, while it was there, the buyer procured a bulk sample and then directed the stationmaster to send the bulk on to the brewer. The brewer rejected it as not being according to sample, and the buyer then claimed to reject. It was held by the Court of Appeal (Lindley, Bowen and A. L. Smith L.JJ.), reversing Lawrence J., that there was nothing in the contract or the circumstances to rebut the presumption that the place of delivery was to be the place of inspection, and that as the buyer had inspected a sample at the place of delivery and sent the

---

[78] Sale of Goods Act, s.10. This presumption has often been criticised; see, *e.g.* "Untimely Performance in the Law of Contract" (1955) 71 L.Q.R. 527 at p. 539.
[79] *Ante,* § 612.
[80] *Burden (C.A.) v. Elling State Bank,* 76 Mont. 24 (1926).
[81] See *ante,* § 332.
[82] [1893] 1 Q.B. 193 (C.A.).

bulk on to his purchaser, he must be considered to have accepted the barley and could not afterwards reject it.

> "'We find no evidence in this case,' said A. L. Smith L.J., delivering the judgment of the court,[83] "to dislodge the presumption which prima facie arises, that the place of delivery is the place for inspection. To hold otherwise would be to expose the vendor to unknown risks, impossible of calculation, when the contract was entered into. The vendee might consign the barley not only to one, but to different sub-vendees living in different places ... and until arrival at these places the barley would be at the risk of the vendor. If the barley was rejected by these sub-vendees upon arrival, the vendor would have at his own risk and cost to take the barley back from whatever places it might happen to be in ... or to arrange for its sale at the places where it then was. As to these risks the contract is silent, and in our judgment it is impossible to read into it that the vendor undertook these risks. . . .''

But the intention of the parties may be that inspection shall be postponed. So too, where it is not reasonably practicable on account of the unsuitability of the place of delivery or the nature of the article to inspect at the place of delivery, inspection may be deferred. If on such later inspection there is revealed a breach of condition, the buyer is then entitled to reject the goods.

631 In *Molling v. Dean*,[84] a firm of colour printers in Germany contracted to supply buyers in England with a number of books. They supplied a parcel of 40,000 books, which they knew were intended for America. The buyers, without inspecting the books, sent them to America, where they were inspected and rightly rejected as not being of the contract quality. The buyers claimed to reject. It was held by the Divisional Court (Lord Alverstone C.J., Darling and Channell JJ.), affirming the decision of the Official Referee, that as the sellers knew that the books were intended for America, that was the proper place for the inspection, and the buyers were entitled to reject them and could recover as damages the cost of sending them to America and back to England.

In *Bragg v. Villanova*,[85] the Court of Appeal relied on *Molling v. Dean* as authority for the proposition that an f.o.b. contract does not involve acceptance at the shipping point, and that the buyer is entitled to reject where no reasonable opportunity for inspecting the goods arises prior to delivery at the destination.

632 In *Van den Hurk v. Martens*,[86] the question was as to the measure of damages, namely, whether they were to be assessed at the price prevailing at the time of original delivery or at the price obtaining at the time of discovery

---

[83] *Ibid.* at p. 197.
[84] (1901) 18 T.L.R. 217. It does not appear from the report why the goods could not have been examined in England. See the comments of Bankes L.J. in *Hardy & Co. (London) Ltd. v. Hillerns and Fowler* [1923] 2 K.B. 490 (C.A.). at p. 497, quoted *post*, § 640.
[85] (1923) 40 T.L.R. 154.
[86] [1920] 1 K.B. 850.

of breach. There were two sales of sodium sulphide in drums *ex* store Manchester and f.o.b. Manchester respectively. The sellers knew that the drums were intended for export. The buyer resold the drums and, owing to congestion on French railways and other causes, the drums did not reach the ultimate consignees at Lyons and Genoa until some months later. They were there examined and found not to contain sodium sulphide and were rejected, and the original buyer then claimed to reject. Disputes followed, not as to the right to reject, which was not disputed, but as to the measure of damages. The umpire in an arbitration found that owing to the difficulty of opening and reclosing the drums it was, to the knowledge of both parties, impracticable to open them until they were required for actual use. On a case stated as to whether damages were to be assessed with reference to prices ruling at the time of delivery to the buyer or at the time of discovery of the defects, Bailhache J. held that the proper basis was the date at which the goods arrived at their ultimate destination, namely, Lyons and Genoa. Dealing with this case in *Hardy & Co. (London) Ltd. v. Hillerns and Fowler,*[87] Greer J. commented:

> "The question was as to the measure of damages, and the case seems to me to be only an authority for the proposition that when it is reasonable and in the ordinary course of business for goods to be sent on to sub-purchasers without examination, either because of good reasons connected with business, or because the nature of the goods is such that they ought not to be opened till they have reached the consumer, in that case the damages arising at the later date, when they have got to the consumer, are damages which naturally arise from the breach, and are therefore within the legal measure of damages and recoverable."

633 In *Saunt v. Belcher and Gibbons,*[88] Bailhache J. explained the reasons for his decision in *Van den Hurk*'s case. There, owing to the nature of the cargo (breeze) and the facilities for examination at the place of immediate destination, Deptford, the buyer lost his right to reject by failure to inspect at Deptford. The sellers in that case knew that the breeze was to go on to France, and it was argued that, because they were aware of that fact, the place for examination and acceptance must be extended from the place at which they were to deliver the goods, *viz.*, Deptford, to France. In support of that contention, Bailhache J.'s judgment in *Van den Hurk v. Martens* was cited as showing that where goods are sold by a seller who has to deliver them at a destination which, to his knowledge, is not their final destination, but only a place from which there is to be a further transit, the place of inspection and acceptance is removed from the place at which the seller has to make his delivery to the place which is the ultimate destination of the goods.

> "But that proposition is not by any means universally true; it depends upon this further fact, whether the place at which the seller has to make his delivery, although it is not the ultimate destination of the goods, is a place where, having

---

[87] [1923] 1 K.B. 658 at p. 665.
[88] (1920) 26 Com.Cas. 115.

regard to the nature of the goods and the way in which they are packed, inspection can reasonably be had. . . . I want to say quite clearly, if I did not sufficiently make it clear in that case, that, in my opinion, in order to postpone the place for inspection it is necessary that there should be the two elements; the original vendor must know, either because he is told or by necessary inference, that the goods are going further on, and the place at which he delivers must either be unsuitable in itself or the nature or packing of the goods must make inspection at that place unreasonable."[89]

Consequently, the fact that examination is often postponed in the case of f.o.b. contracts does not replace the prima facie presumption contained in the Act so as to give rise to any converse presumption for as Lord Sterndale M.R. once said:[90]

"I was at first inclined to think that on a f.o.b. contract there would be a *prima facie* rule that the goods should be examined at the place of destination. But looking at the cases, I doubt very much whether there is any *prima facie* rule at all. I am inclined to think there is not, and I am inclined to think the question of whether there has been reasonable opportunity of examination before shipment where the goods are to be put free on board is a question to be decided in the particular case on its circumstances."

634 In *Boks and Co. v. J. H. Rayner and Co.*,[91] the respondents contracted to purchase from the appellants a quantity of palm oil f.o.b. Antwerp, and in pursuance of the contract seventy-nine casks were shipped to Liverpool. Both parties had representatives at Antwerp, but the oil was not inspected until arrival at Liverpool where it was found that the oil was not of the contract quality. The arbitrators ruled that by a usage of the trade as applied to f.o.b. contracts of the type under consideration it was the regular custom for the buyer to examine the goods before instructions to put them on board were given, and that therefore the right to reject expired when the goods were placed f.o.b. Antwerp, and the respondents could only claim damages. The Court of Appeal (Bankes, Scrutton and Atkin L.JJ.), affirming Bailhache J., held on a case stated that the custom was so vaguely stated that it did not extend to exclude the respondents from rejecting the goods at Liverpool.

Scrutton L.J. is reported to have said:

"It was a question whether the arbitrators meant to find that there was a custom of trade, or were annexing an incident of law to an f.o.b. contract, but assuming they meant to find a custom, then the question of the reasonableness of such a custom would arise.

The judgment of Mr. Justice Bailhache proceeded on the footing that the arbitrators were not finding a custom of trade, but were annexing an incident of law to an f.o.b. contract. His Lordship was not [*sic*] dissatisfied with that view. But he concurred in dismissing the appeal on the ground that the custom was not

[89] *Ibid.* at pp. 118, 119.
[90] *J. W. Schofield & Sons v. Rownson, Drew and Clydesdale Ltd.* (1922) 10 Ll.L. Rep. 480.
[91] (1921) 37 T.L.R. 800.

sufficiently found by the arbitrators; and, if found, it would be unreasonable"
(at p. 801).

And where goods sold f.o.b. New York were by reason of Admiralty orders
diverted from their original port of discharge to some other port (Glasgow
instead of Liverpool), the buyer is not deemed to have accepted them merely
because he does not examine them at the unexpected port, but examines them
on arrival at his place of business.[92]

In *Toepfer v. Warinco*,[93] the question of whether loading superintendents
appointed by the buyers had implied authority to waive a condition relating
to the description of soya bean meal in a contract for sale f.o.b. Hamburg
was considered. Brandon, J. held that the loading supervisors had no implied
authority from the buyers (by whom they were employed) to vary or waive
the terms of the contracts of sale between the buyers and the sellers especially
so far as a condition of correspondence with the description was concerned.
However, although it was not within the implied authority of the supervisors
to vary or waive a condition in the contract of sale, it was entirely within
their authority as soon as it was, or should have been, apparent to them that
the wrong kind of meal was being delivered to protest about it, and their
failure to do so had to be regarded so far as the question of mitigation of
damages was concerned as the failure of the buyers. Thus, Brandon, J. stated
in the course of his judgment:

> "It may well be that, if a cargo superintendent, appointed by a shipper or char-
> terer to supervise or take an interest in stowage on his behalf, consents, expressly
> or by implication, to bad stowage, his principal will be bound by that consent.
> The reason for this is that it is within the implied authority of such superintendent
> to make representations to the shipowners or their agents with regard to such
> matters. In my view, however, this does not lead to the conclusion that super-
> visors appointed by f.o.b. buyers to supervise loading as in the present case
> have implied authority to waive altogether a condition of the relevant contract
> or contracts of sale relating to the description of the goods. On the contrary, I
> think that they have no such implied authority."

The buyers, through their failure to mitigate damages, were therefore entitled
to nominal damages only.

635   Where the goods are rejected at their destination, the buyer is of course
entitled to recover the freight and insurance and other expenses incurred by
him in respect of the goods after the f.o.b. point in addition to return of the
purchase price.[94] Although postponement of examination is normally associated with external sales, and particularly with cases where the bills of lading
are to be tendered by the seller (in which case it may even be correct to say
that "delivery," in its ordinary meaning of transfer of possession, has not

---

[92] *Scaliaris v. E. Ofverberg & Co.* (1921) 37 T.L.R. 307.
[93] [1978] 2 Lloyd's Rep. 569.
[94] *Post*, § 693.

been effected merely by placing the goods f.o.b.), a postponement of examination is not uncommon, even in the case of internal contracts, and the
burden of proof that opportunity of examination has been afforded rests with
the seller.[95] The fact that examination is postponed does not alter the rule as
to transfer of the risk of loss. The conformity of the goods to the contract,
save as may otherwise be expressly agreed or implied with respect to any
inevitable deterioration in transit,[96] is therefore to be determined according
to their condition upon shipment at the f.o.b. point.[97]

Unless the fact that the seller has defaulted is abundantly clear, if the goods
perish after delivery f.o.b., and inspection becomes impossible, the buyer
cannot invoke his right of examination and, thereby, escape liability for the
price. The position of the seller (where payment is postponed and the proper
place of examination is at some distant, sometimes unknown, place overseas)
is, to say the least, not a happy one. In the case of perishable goods, a rejection abroad normally results in total or heavy loss. Even in other cases the
situation is not much better since:

> "It is a matter of common knowledge that where goods are shipped to a foreign
> country the buyer not infrequently rejects them unreasonably and uses his rejec-
> tion, coupled with the fact that the goods are a long way off, as a lever to extort
> a reduction in the price. . . ."[98]

636 Above all, it must be borne in mind, as a matter of simple economics, that
goods which are commercially in accordance with the contract are seldom
rejected on a rising market. The prospect of profit usually induces acceptance
of a legally defective tender—and rejection is, therefore, more a means of
evading the contract in case of a drop in the market and a resulting adverse
price movement. To avoid the perils of a wrongful rejection it is very

---

[95] *Per* Scrutton L.J. in *Service Reeve & Co. (London) v. Central Iron & Metal Co.* (1926) 24
Ll.L.Rep. 340. See, however, *Commercial Fibres (Ireland) v. Zabaida and Zabida (T/A Lenmore
Trading) and Oth.* [1975] 1 Lloyd's Rep. 27 where Donaldson J. held that the buyer lost his
right of rejection once he obtained constructive possession of the goods. The plaintiffs sold 109
cartons of cotton yarn to defendants ex warehouse in the U.K. The defendants in turn sold it
f.o.b. Ipswich for shipment to a buyer in Nigeria. The goods were badly packed and this was
noted by the Ipswich port authority (on the receipt it issued) as well as by the carrier (on the
bill of lading) upon arrival of the cartons and their shipment from Ipswich. The defendants were
apparently unaware of this, and the yarn was shipped to Lagos where it was rejected. The
defendants then purported to reject *vis-à-vis* the plaintiffs but failed. It was held that the right
of rejection should have been exercised at the latest when the goods arrived at Ipswich. At that
point, constructive possession was obtained by the defendants, and the port authority as well as
the carrier were considered to be agents of the defendants for the purpose.
[96] Caused, *e.g.* by bad packing or inferior quality; see *ante*, § 448 and § 449.
[97] See *Lord v. Edwards*, 12 Am.St.Rep. 581 (1889) ("Warranty—sugar on basis of 88 pol'r—
means in a sale f.o.b., of quality at the port of shipment"). *Cf.* the express provision to this
effect in s. 62 of the Danish and Norwegian Laws of Sale. In *California Vegetable Growers v.
U.S.*, 194 F. 2d 929 (1952), it was, however, expressly agreed that the inspection should relate
to the condition of the goods at the destination, and not at the time of delivery at origin.
[98] *Per* Scrutton L.L. in *Szymonowski & Co. v. Beck & Co.* [1923] 1 K.B. 457 at p. 467. The
contract under discussion expressly provided for credit, but on this particular point it can, perhaps, be argued with equal force that the buyer's position is just as precarious in the converse
case of a proper rejection after the price has been tendered.

common for the seller to insert in his contracts what are known as "rejection clauses." The clauses aim at excluding or limiting the buyer's right of rejection (usually by substituting for this right an allowance in the price of the goods, or by allowing a "reasonable" tolerance and percentage of deficiency). These clauses are generally construed against their draftsmen, so where a contract provided that:

> "the goods delivered shall be deemed to be in all respects in accordance with the contract, and the buyers shall be bound to accept and pay for the same accordingly unless the sellers shall within fourteen days after arrival of the goods at their destination receive from the buyers notice of any matter or thing by reason whereof they may allege that the goods are not in accordance with the contract"

the Court of Appeal held in *Szymonowski & Co. v. Beck & Co.*[99] that the exception applied only to the right of rejection. This was precluded once the period specified had expired. But the right to claim damages was not foreclosed thereby if the goods delivered were not according to the contractual description. Commenting on this clause Scrutton L.J. observed:

> "It is not very clear what is the destination in the case of goods to be delivered f.o.b., which cannot ordinarily be examined while being put on board the ship" (at p. 467).

And where a contract for the sale of goods to a New York buyer, f.o.b. Le Havre, provided for cash against documents in London by confirmed credit and that "Any claims in relation to weight, quality, or otherwise must be made in writing and delivered to the sellers within ten days of the date of delivery to the purchaser of the delivery order or other documents of title," Bankes, Atkin and Younger L.JJ. held (in *G. F. Taylor & Co. v. E. Ofverberg & Co.*[1]) that the period of time therein specified began to run from the moment the documents were handed over to the purchaser in New York and not to the bank in London.

Occasionally trade usages may limit the right of rejection, or possibly purport to determine the proper place of examination.[2] In the United States, a federal statute—the Perishable Agricultural Commodities Act[3]—was introduced "primarily to prevent consignees from taking advantage of consignors

---

[99] [1923] 1 K.B. 457.

[1] (1923) 39 T. L. R. 637.

[2] See, however, Scrutton L. J.'s query as to the "reasonableness" of such customs in *Boks v. Rayner* (1921) 37 T.L.R. 800; *ante*, § 634.

[3] 7 U.S.C., paras. 499a *et seq.*, followed by administrative regulations (7 Code Fed. Regs., para. 46.24), which include definitions of many trade terms, *e.g.*: "f.o.b. acceptance"—a term which confines the purchaser's right for the seller's default to an action for damages. "F.o.b. acceptance final" means that the purchaser accepts the goods as shipped without recourse (but this has been liberally interpreted to exclude not only cases of fraud, but of major breach also; see 21 A.L.R. 2d at p. 845). It may be of interest to note that the basic term "f.o.b. point of shipment" implies a right of inspection at the destination prior to payment; see *ante*, § 627, n. 76.

where distance makes enforcement of legal rights troublesome and expensive."[4]

Where, for the right of rejection is substituted the lesser remedy of a claim for damages the suit will usually be brought before the courts in the seller's country "which is much more satisfactory for [him] than [his] having to sue in a foreign country in Courts with which he is not familiar."[5]

Delivery f.o.b. does not constitute acceptance

637   In the past, the question of the buyer's right of rejection invoked some theoretical difficulty in circumstances where the right of examination was not exercised until arrival and receipt of the goods at their destination abroad. Although the law was changed by section 4(2) of the Misrepresentation Act 1967,[6] the general rule earlier embodied in the Sale of Goods Act was that the right of rejection was lost upon acceptance of the goods (in which case the breach of condition had to be treated as a breach of warranty which would sound in damages only)[7] irrespective of whether an opportunity for examination of the goods had existed or not. It was therefore sometimes alleged that delivery to the carrier involved such an irrevocable acceptance at the f.o.b. point, as would defeat a right to reject overseas. Dismissing this contention, Bigham J. once said, in relation to an f.o.b. contract which included the stipulation that property shall be deemed to have passed for all purposes except retention of vendor's lien for unpaid price as and when the goods are placed on board, as follows:[8]

> "Two other points were taken by the plaintiffs. It was said that by the terms of the contracts the property in the goods had passed on shipment, or, in the alternative, that the property had passed by reason of the defendants having accepted the goods by receiving them on board their ship, and that, therefore, the defendant must keep the goods and be satisfied with an allowance in respect of their inferiority. I think there is nothing in either of these points. The provision in the contracts as to the passing of the property only applies to a shipment of goods which come within the meaning of the contract; it cannot apply to any others; and the receipt of the goods by the captain is no acceptance at all of the goods as a delivery under the contract. The captain of the ship is merely an agent to receive the goods for the purpose of carriage; he knows nothing of the contract of purchase, and he is not an agent to accept delivery under it."

638   Although this is a correct analysis of the situation, namely, that where the seller performs property passes so that acceptance cannot be refused and any attempt to reject will not revest property in the seller, whereas if the seller repudiates it does not, Bigham J.'s statement is unavailing in conditions

---

[4] *Williston on Sales* (Rev. ed., 1948), *Cumulative Supplement* (1957), para. 280q, pp. 21 *et seq.*
[5] *Per* Scrutton L. J. in *Szymonowski v. Beck* [1923] 1 K. B. 457 at p. 468.
[6] See *ante*, § 334.
[7] See *ante*, § 316.
[8] *Vigers Bros. v. Sanderson Bros.* [1901] 1 K.B. 608 at p. 612.

where the rights and remedies of the parties depend on the location of property at any given moment.[9] Following what has previously been said, the conclusion seems unavoidable that, prima facie, property does in fact pass to the buyer at the f.o.b. point. However, so as not to prejudice the buyer's right of rejection, or validate an unauthorised appropriation by the seller, this transfer of property is to be construed as a conditional transfer only. In other words the transfer is subject to a condition subsequent of conformity to be asserted at the proper place of examination. If upon examination the goods are found to be not in accordance with the contract the property in them revests to the seller. The principles which apply to c.i.f. contracts as stated by Devlin J. in *Kwei Tek Chao v. British Traders & Shippers Ltd.*[10] are it is thought applicable in the case of f.o.b. sales also, as the following American authorities clearly illustrate.

639 In *Pierson v. Crooks*,[11] iron was sold f.o.b. and the English seller argued that the American buyer accepted the goods upon shipment. Andrews J. said:

"Assuming that the title ... vested in the [buyers] on delivery to the steamers, it was, as between the vendor and the vendee, a conditional title subject to the right of inspection and rejection of the inferior quality at New York."

So too in *Delaware Railroad Co. Ltd. v. U.S.*[12] it was stated that:

"There are two types of acceptance—one of quality, and the other of title. They are not necessarily contemporaneous.... The contract ... meant that the title should pass when delivery was accepted ... but that the [buyer] might rescind if, on later inspection, the quality was found to be different from what had been described in the contract of sale."

640 *Acceptance.* Section 35 of the Act has already been noted in relation to c.i.f. contracts where the relevant authorities were noted.[13] In brief, and prior to the passage of the Misrepresentation Act 1967, the weight of the more recent authority indicated that the right of rejection was lost if the f.o.b. buyer did an act inconsistent with the ownership of the seller in the goods. Where, for example, the buyer resold the goods and the sub-purchaser assumed possession thereof (a mere resale not accompanied by disposal of the goods or inquiries whether the goods are saleable would not have prejudiced the right

[9] In *Anderson & Coltman Ltd. v. Universal Trading Co.* [1948] 1 S.A.L.R. 1277 (South Africa) the buyer sought to found jurisdiction against the English seller by attempting to attach goods delivered f.o.b. U.K. port in which he alleged the property had not passed by virtue of their failure to conform to the contract. The court dismissed the allegation and held that the buyer failed to show that the goods belonged to the seller. The property passed upon delivery f.o.b. and the buyers are to be considered the owners until the goods are redelivered to the seller.
[10] [1954] 2 Q.B. 459. See *ante*, § 335.
[11] 12 Am.St.Rep. 831 (1889).
[12] 231 U.S. 363 (1913); and *cf.* further the many decisions to a similar effect cited in *Easton v. Blackburn*, 132 Am.St.Rep. 705 (1908).
[13] See *ante*, § 332.

of rejection[14]) the right to reject was lost even where a reasonable opportunity of examination had not yet arisen. The authority of earlier decisions such as *Molling v. Dean*[15] or *Morton v. Tibbett*[16] which allowed a right of rejection regardless of a resale (where examination was postponed and exercised by the sub-purchaser abroad) was questioned. As Bankes L.J. stated in *E. Hardy & Co. (London) Ltd. v. Hillerns & Fowler*[17]: "In *Molling v. Dean* it does not appear clear upon what ground the court proceeded."[18] Referring to this judgment in *Pelhams (Materials) Ltd. v. Mercantile Commodities Synd.*[19] Roxburgh J. candidly confessed:

> "Fortunately . . . I have guidance . . . from *Hardy & Co. v. Hillerns & Fowler* . . . I am very glad to have this guidance because I am satisfied that there are earlier cases which cannot be wholly reconciled with this decision . . . [and] I am very glad that I have not had to make up my own mind as to the manner of reconciling some of the earlier cases" (at p. 284).

641   The Privy Council ruled similarly on an appeal from Malta in *Benaim & Co. v. Debono*.[20] There under a contract concluded in Malta anchovies were sold f.o.b. Gibraltar. The Maltese buyer purported to reject after the anchovies had been refused by his sub-purchasers, on the ground of inferior quality. The Sale of Goods Act applied in Gibraltar but by the civil law of Malta the buyer's right to rescind was saved. The Privy Council advised that the law of Gibraltar was the proper law of the contract and that the buyer had lost his right of rejection because of the provisions of section 35 of the Act.

642   The foregoing rule produced harsh results and was not in accord with commercial practice. It delayed the turnover of goods and unnecessarily increased their price. In particular if, as was apparently the case, this result ensued simply by virtue of property considerations (based on the doing of an act inconsistent with the ownership of the seller), and not by reason of the hazards to which the seller may be exposed where the goods have been so

---

[14] See, *e.g. J. & J. Cunningham v. R. A. Munro & Co.* (1922) 28 Com.Cas. 42 where the buyer was able to exercise a right of rejection at the ship's rail notwithstanding the resale of the goods.
[15] (1901) 18 T. L. R. 217; see *ante*, § 631.
[16] (1850) 15 Q. B. 428.
[17] [1923] 2 K. B. 490 at p. 497; see *ante*, § 333.
[18] See, however, Bankes L. J.'s decision in *Scaliaris v. Ofverberg & Co.* (1921) 37 T. L. R. 307 where the learned judge appears to have held that the buyer did not lose his right of rejection by virtue of a resale and delivery of the goods to a sub-purchaser. In this case the sale was f.o.b. New York and the goods which were sold to an English buyer were sent to the sub-purchaser before examination took place. Bankes L.J. said:
> "[the seller] had contended that the [buyer] had never made any examination at all nor had he ever attempted to make an examination and that consequently he was not entitled to reject the goods. The answer for that contention was that the [buyer] for this purpose adopted the not unreasonable [*sic*] attitude that his sub-purchaser had examined the goods at a reasonable place—namely, London, and, if that was a reasonable place for him, it was also a reasonable place for the [buyer] who was consequently entitled to reject the goods" (at p. 308).
[19] [1953] 2 Lloyd's Rep. 281.
[20] [1924] A. C. 514; and see *post*, § 733.

dealt with by the buyer that they cannot be put immediately at his disposal upon notice of rejection being given.[21] But efforts to restrict its application met with little success before the courts. In *E. & S. Ruben Ltd. v. Faire Bros. & Co.*,[22] a contention that the buyer should have obtained physical custody of the goods prior to their resale[23] in order for the principle embodied in section 35 of the Act (prior to its amendment by the Misrepresentation Act) to become operative failed before Hilbery J. He held that where on the instructions of the buyer the seller forwarded the goods directly to the sub-purchaser, the buyer was deemed to have accepted the goods and forfeited his right of rejection. Constructive delivery at the seller's premises was sufficient and the resale thereafter was an act inconsistent with the ownership of the seller. Yet in *Kwei Tek Chao v. British Traders and Shippers Ltd.*,[24] Devlin J. held that a transfer of the bills of lading which is not followed by an actual delivery of the goods to a sub-purchaser did not prejudice the buyer's right to reject the goods. He held that a distinction must be drawn between two different rights of rejection arising from two different breaches, *viz.*, a right pertaining to the documents where these are not in order and a right to reject the goods where the goods do not conform to the contract. It was his view that the property in the goods passed only conditionally on the acceptance of the documents and all dealings with the documents were dealings merely with the conditional property so that the right of rejection was upon transfer of the documents lost in respect of the documents alone. This did not necessarily entail the loss of a right to reject the goods. Although Devlin J. was considering the rights under a c.i.f. contract, there is no reason why the foregoing principles should not equally apply to the case of f.o.b. sales even where the bills of lading had never been in the hands of the seller but had originally been issued by the shipowner to the order of the buyer. It is of course true that in such a case no question of acceptance of the documents could arise but this, it is submitted, need not destroy the validity of the distinction drawn between dealings with the documents and dealings with the goods themselves. The premise is that in the absence of an opportunity to examine the goods, only conditional property in the goods passes upon delivery f.o.b. Aside from this mitigating distinction, and save for cases of latent defects where a reasonable examination would not, even were it to have taken place, have revealed the defective quality of the goods where different principles may apply,[25] the state of the law (until amended in 1967)

---

[21] See Branson J.'s comments on *Hardy v. Hillerns & Fowler* in *Jordeson & Co. v. Stora Kopparbergs Bergslags Aktiebolag* (1931) 41 L1. L. Rep. 201 at p. 204. The latter approach is at least not mechanical. It could be justified on the ground that any such delay increased the risk of the seller.
[22] [1949] 1 K.B. 254; see *ante*, § 333.
[23] See *per* Atkin L. J. in *Hardy v. Hillerns & Fowler* [1923] 2 K.B. 490 at p. 498.
[24] [1954] 2 Q.B. 459; see *ante*, § 335.
[25] See *per* Brett J. in *Heilbutt & Ors. v. Hickson & Ors.* (1872) L.R. 7 C.P. 438; a sale of shoes to be delivered free at a wharf in London where inspection was to be made before shipment to France, which, to the knowledge of the seller, was their final destination. The shoes were inspected in London but their soles were not opened there and since suspicions arose as to the quality

was such that an exporter who had bought goods from a supplier f.o.b. and resold them to a foreign party on similar terms probably could not exercise a right of rejection in respect thereof if they were rejected by the sub-purchaser after an examination abroad revealed their non-conformity. To be sure the rule probably did permit an exception in cases where, having regard to the nature of the goods and the way in which they were packed, inspection at any place except that of ultimate destination would expose the goods to some risk which may destroy their utility to the ultimate consumer. For as stated by Greer J. in *Hardy & Co. (London) Ltd. v. Hillerns & Fowler*[26]:

> "It is true that there may be cases in which rejection is justified after the goods have been sent on from the place of delivery to a sub-purchaser. . . . It may be that the goods were in such a condition that they could not, without destroying their utility for the consumer, be examined before they got to the consumer, and that under those circumstances there might be a right of rejection, notwithstanding the fact that they had been sent on to the consumer . . ."

643   Referring to this passage, Branson J. stated in *Jordeson & Co. v. Stora Kopparbergs Bergslags Akiebolag*[27]:

> "I think the true position is that apart from the very special cases which Greer J . . . recognises as possibly existing . . . the mere fact that the buyer has handed over the goods to a sub-purchaser is sufficient to put an end to his right to reject. I think that, that being so, where the umpire has, as he had in this case, no suggestion by anyone that this was in any way a special case—that these goods were goods the examination of which before they were handed over to the sub-purchasers might have spoiled them or might have endangered them in any way, or were goods the examination of which according to the contract was not to take place until they got into the hands of the sub-purchaser, as in the case of *Heilbutt v. Hickson*[27a]—he was entitled to come to the conclusion as a matter of law upon the facts . . . that the buyers had lost their right of rejection" (at p. 205).

The question therefore was one of fact and depended on whether or not the nature of the goods or their packing made inspection at the f.o.b. point or at their destination abroad, and before delivery to the sub-purchaser, feasible or not. If objectively unfeasible, the right of rejection subsisted notwithstanding the resale, as was for example held by Roche J. in *James Southern & Co. v. Austin & Son.*[28] There the plaintiffs bought from the defendants scrap

---

of the shoes, the sellers subsequently wrote a letter in which they expressly agreed to take back any shoes should any paper be found in their soles. Upon arrival in France an examination showed the shoes contained paper in their soles. The majority of the court held that the buyers did not lose their right to reject the shoes by virtue of the specific agreement of the seller, but by Brett J. on the ground that apart from the special agreement the buyer would have been entitled to reject inasmuch as any inspection in London would have been ineffectual by reason of a latent defect and that the shoes were rejected immediately upon opportunity occurring for the discovery of such defect.

[26] [1923] 1 K.B. 650 at pp. 665–666.
[27] (1931) 41 Ll.L.Rep. 201.
[27a] See note 25 *ante.*
[28] (1921) 6 Ll.L. Rep. 24.

mixed bagging delivery f.o.b. London for resale to buyers in Finland. The defective quality of the goods was discovered in Finland and the plaintiffs succeeded in reclaiming the purchase price and also the cost of sending the goods to Finland. The learned judge said in the course of his judgment:

> "The plaintiffs had not the opportunity of seeing the goods they were going to buy before they bought. They had an inspection here in England prior to purchase of specimens of goods or a large number of goods which were said to be the class of goods to be delivered to them. But as to the inspection of the deliveries, the goods were to be an f.o.b. shipment of pressed bales, and it is impossible to avoid any other conclusion than that the material place to examine the deficiencies in delivery was in Finland, when the goods were taken from the ship" (at p. 26).

644   So too the fact that the buyer had claimed and recovered under his insurance policy in respect of loss to the goods during transit was held not to be an act inconsistent with the ownership of the seller by the High Court of Australia.[29] As there stated by Williams J.:

> "A person who has th[e] conditional property in goods for which he had paid the price and of which he has taken the delivery must have the right to receive the goods without forfeiting his right to reject the goods ... By insuring the goods he does nothing which is inconsistent with the ownership of the seller. If a loss occurs and he makes a claim on the insurance company for the loss and receives payment, the payment takes the place of the goods that have been lost and, if the buyer subsequently became entitled to reject the goods, he would have to credit the seller with the insurance monies" (at pp. 59, 60).

645   Since suggestions which would have had the effect of broadening the exception yet further received little support from the courts,[30] a relaxation of the rule required legislative intervention. This was achieved, in respect of England and Scotland, through section 4 of the Misrepresentation Act which amended section 35 of the Sale of Goods Act.[31] The amendment provides that a buyer is not deemed to have accepted goods which have been delivered to him, even if he has done an act in relation to them inconsistent with the seller's ownership, unless he has had a reasonable opportunity to examine them.[32]

The question thus is a factual one. Where the buyer (or his representative at the f.o.b. point) has had a reasonable opportunity to examine the goods, or it is (or should have been) apparent that non-contractual goods have been supplied, he loses his right of rejection, and if the defect could have been

---

[29] *J.S. Robertson (Aust.) Pty. Ltd. v. Martin* (1956) 94 C.L.R. 30.
[30] See, *e.g. Pelham's (Materials) Ltd. v. Mercantile Commodities Synd.* [1953] 2 Lloyd's Rep. 281.
[31] The amendment was based on the recommendations of the Law Reform Committee in its Tenth Report: see Cmnd. 1782 (H.M.S.O., July 1962).
[32] See *ante* § 332, where s.35 of the Sale of Goods Act, as amended, is quoted.

remedied at that point his remedy may be reduced to nominal damages only.[33]

So too, where the buyer accepts documents that indicate a default that gives rise to a right of rejection, and resells the cargo in order to minimize the loss (on a falling market), he looses his right to claim substantial damages (unless such resale is the subject of a special "without prejudice" agreement with the seller), and can only claim for the difference between the value of the goods as warranted and their value in fact, if any.[34]

[The next paragraph is 661.]

---

[33] See, *e.g. Commercial Fibres (Ireland) Ltd. v. Zabida and Zabida (T/A Lenmore Trading) and Others* [1975] 1 Lloyd's Rep. 27, where a buyer who had purchased ex warehouse and resold f.o.b. for shipment to Nigeria was held to have lost his right of rejection *vis-à-vis* his supplier since the defective condition of the goods was apparent both to the port authority and to the carrier who received the goods, and their possession was deemed to be a constructive possession by the buyer (*ante* § 635, n. 95): *Toepfer v. Warnico A. G.* [1978] 2 Lloyd's Rep. 59, where f.o.b. buyer appointed superintendent to supervise loading of fine ground soya bean meal, and since superintendent was negligent in not detecting that coarse ground meal was loaded buyer could not recover except for nominal damages because if superintendent would have acted diligently and reasonably the defect could have been corrected, and the damage would have been avoided (*ante*, § 634, n. 93).

[34] *Vargas Pena Apezteguia & Cia SAIC v. Peter Crewer G.m.b.H.* [1987] 1 Lloyd's Rep. 1 394.

CHAPTER 12

INSURANCE

661 Since the buyer bears the risk of destruction to the goods (from the moment of delivery f.o.b.), he will normally seek to protect himself against their loss or damage by way of insurance. In the ordinary course of events this insurance will cover—apart from the contract price—the freight and a margin of profit, as well as the insurance premium. Frequently provision is also made for perils other than marine (*i.e.* war, seizure, strikes, etc.) that the goods may encounter on their sea journey.

However, unless there is an agreement to the contrary, the buyer cannot be under any legal obligation to procure such a cover. This might be a source of serious concern to the seller. For, so long as he remains "unpaid,"[1] his fears that in the absence of insurance recovery of the price may be prejudiced, where loss or damage has ensued, are by no means idle. In order to overcome this undesirable situation, the seller therefore frequently inserts a provision in the contract, whereby the buyer undertakes to confirm his insurance before loading commences.[2] Occasionally, the buyer agrees to hold the policy at the seller's disposal and to deposit it with him—until the price has been tendered.[3] Moreover, in some cases where the seller acts as the buyer's agent for the purpose of procuring insurance, he may even be allowed to procure a policy of his own, which will be assigned to the buyer, only upon the termination of his interest in the goods.[4] Where the seller is acting in this capacity, the question may arise as to whether he is under a duty to tender any particu-

---

[1] If provision is made for payment by an irrevocable credit the seller will normally be assured of payment, but the f.o.b. buyer may have to deposit a policy with the bank, or the bank may be authorised to issue a cover on his behalf.

[2] See, *e.g.* cl. 11 of the standard form of F.O.B. Contracts for the Sale of Cereals (Nos. 5A and 5B) drawn under the auspices of the ECE which provides that "The buyer shall satisfy the seller, *before* loading of the vessel begins, that he has taken out marine insurance on the FPA conditions of the Institute of Underwriters or on equivalent conditions with reputedly first-class underwriters, but shall not guarantee the solvency of any underwriter."

[3] See, *e.g.* Chap. 5 of the standard form of F.O.B. Contract for Sale and Purchase of Rice drawn under the auspices of the London Rice Brokers' Association which provides that "The Rice to be at Buyers' risk from warehouse to warehouse and they engage to effect Marine Insurance, including War Risk (in Accordance with London Underwriters' Institute War Clause), at their own expense covering the full amount of Invoice and to hold the policies at Sellers' disposal until documents are required. Cover note of insurance to be lodged with Sellers, if required, unless it is already mentioned in the Letter of Credit that the insurance has been effected." See *The Sorfareren* (1916) 114 L.T. 46, where such a provision existed.

[4] *The Exporter's Year Book* (1953).

lar form of policy (see the case of the sale c.i.f.).[5] Whatever authority exists on the matter appears to indicate that the contract will probably be satisfied by a certificate or letter of insurance and that f.o.b. contracts are not necessarily subject to the rules which govern c.i.f. contracts.[6]

The seller's duty of notification

662   Section 32(3) of the Sale of Goods Act, which is derived from Scottish rather than English sources, provides that:

> "Unless otherwise agreed, where goods are sent by the seller to the buyer by a route involving sea transit, under circumstances in which it is usual to insure, the seller must give such notice to the buyer as may enable him to insure them during their sea transit, and, if the seller fails to do so, the goods are at his risk during such sea transit."

In *Wimble, Sons & Co. v. Rosenberg & Sons*,[7] the majority of the Court of Appeal (Buckley and Vaughan Williams L.JJ.; Hamilton L.J. dissenting) held that this provision applied to f.o.b. contracts. It was there noted that there was some difficulty in reconciling this view with the previous law relating to f.o.b. contracts where no such duty had been mentioned.[8] Moreover, the decision does not appear to be confined to any particular variant of f.o.b. contract since exception was taken to Bailhache J.'s view in the court below,[9] to the effect that the duty set forth in subsection (3) of section 32 would only be applicable to those types of f.o.b. contract in which the seller agreed to secure the shipping space for the buyer. In other words, that the duty imposed under the Act applied exclusively to the "shipment to destination" type of f.o.b. contract, the type upon which the *Wimble v. Rosenberg* dispute arose.[10]

---

[5] *Ante*, §§ 207 *et seq.*

[6] *Per* Roche J. in *Muller Maclean & Co. v. Leslie & Anderson* (1921) 8 Ll.L.Rep. 328, *ante*, §216 and see "Export Documentation" *Export* (March, 1948), p. 41 at p. 44.

[7] [1913] 3 K.B. 743.

[8] No authorities were cited but reference may perhaps be made to *Browne v. Hare* (1858) 3 H. & N. 484; (1859) 4 H. & N. 822, *ante*, §§566, 567, where one of the arguments advanced by the f.o.b. buyer in support of his contention that he could not be made liable for the price of a cargo of oil shipped under a bill of lading to the order of the seller and lost soon after shipment was his inability to procure insurance in respect thereof. In rejecting this proposition, Pollock C.B. said:

> "It was said that the [buyers] could not insure the oil. This is not so in fact, for by a letter of the 7th, which was communicated to them on the 9th [the day on which the ship and its cargo became a total loss] they were informed that the shipment would take place on the following day; but whether they had the opportunity to insure or not is immaterial to the present question, which depends upon the law as to contracts and the transfer of property to a vendee upon a sale" (3 H. & N. at p. 500).

[9] [1913] 1 K.B. 279.

[10] Though Bailhache J. apparently took the view that under the terms of the contract the sellers "might have disregarded the shipping instructions and might have required the [buyers] to procure and provide their own shipping room" (*ibid.* at p. 283) and for this reason gave judgment for the sellers.

In that case the plaintiff sold to the defendant goods "f.o.b. Antwerp to be shipped as required by buyers." The defendant instructed the plaintiff to ship the goods to Odessa leaving it to him to select the ship and also requesting him to advance the freight on his account. The goods were shipped in accordance with these instructions but became a total loss two days thereafter, prior to any notice of shipment being received by the defendant. The seller's action for the price nevertheless succeeded, the court holding (Vaughan Williams L.J. dissenting) that no liability for the failure to comply with the duty of notification attaches if, irrespective of such failure, the buyer already has in his possession sufficient information to enable him to obtain an effective cover. The defence failed on the ground that, although section 32(3) of the Act which applied "notwithstanding the previous law laid down in the cases relating to the carriage of goods under an f.o.b. contract" could be invoked, it provided no relief in the present case. The defendant could have insured the goods despite the fact that the name of the vessel and its sailing date were unknown to him. In Buckley L.J.'s view, however, the buyer had waived his right to receive certain information. It was his opinion that the contract of sale:

> "gave the buyer knowledge of all the necessary particulars other than knowledge which rested with himself, or was determinate by himself, namely, first, the port of discharge, and, secondly, the name of the ship. The former was within his own knowledge and was supplied by him. . . . The latter was not necessary to enable him to insure, and in fact he waived knowledge of it by leaving it to the seller to select the ship" (at pp. 754, 755).

663   This final remark seems to place a most unsatisfactory construction on what amounts to a "shipment to destination" type of f.o.b. contract, because it is for cases such as these that the rule embodied in the Act is most directly relevant.[11] Consequently, the decision is best considered on the ground that adequate insurance could have been obtained in that case regardless of the information withheld.

664   In *Northern Steel and Hardware Company (Limited) v. John Blatt and Company (London) (Limited)*[12] the Court of Appeal (Lord Reading C.J., Scrutton L.J. and Neville J.) pointed out that despite the cogent reasoning of Hamilton L.J., they felt "compelled" to follow the majority decision in

---

[11] This conclusion is based on a practical consideration. In the case of other variants of f.o.b. contract, the buyer will generally be in the possession of more information, and circumstances under which he would be unable to insure are hard to conceive. Yet whether or not a sanction attaches to its nonfulfilment the duty exists, and as such it is also mentioned in *Incoterms* (A.2). (See Eisemann, *Die Incoterms in Handel und Verkehr*, p. 107, Vienna 1963, who states that the notification required by *Incoterms* A.2 corresponds with the duty imposed under the Sale of Goods Act.) The omission of the Institute of Export to incorporate any such duty in their definition led Schmitthoff to propose an amendment relating thereto (see *ante*, 443. This may be due to the fact that the definition contemplates internal sales and the assumption that in such a case the goods are never sent by the seller to the buyer by a route involving sea transit (see *ante*, 475

[12] (1917) 33 T.L.R. 516.

Wimble v. Rosenberg and hold that an f.o.b. contract came within section 32(3). Lord Reading C.J. stated the rule therein contained to be:

> "that knowledge of facts, although not given by the seller, sufficient to enable the buyer to insure, would prevent the operation of the subsection. That would be the case if the buyer knew of material facts which would enable him to effect an insurance on goods shipped or to be shipped by the seller" (at p. 517)

His lordship further pointed out that "In the case cited (*Wimble v. Rosenberg*) Lord Justice Buckley and Lord Justice Hamilton also held that the contract itself gave the buyer sufficient notice, and that to give further notice would be unnecessary." The plaintiffs, in this subsequent action, sold to the defendants a quantity of nails f.o.b. New York. The nails were shipped from New York on August 24, 1916. On September 18, the ship was struck by a submarine. The defendants refused to pay the price relying on section 32(3) of the Act. The court held that the provision in the Act would not assist them. It was clear on the evidence that insurance could have been effected before the loss, the fact of shipment having been communicated to the defendants at least fourteen days before the ship was torpedoed.

From the above, it is apparent that there will be relatively few cases in which the buyer could in fact avail himself of the provision in the Act where the seller failed to comply with his duty thereunder. But the obligation nevertheless stands, and the seller must consider the heavy penalty of being made to suffer the risk of destruction or loss to the goods that may result from a breach thereof.

Insurable interest

665   In order to procure and effect a valid cover by way of insurance, the assured must have an interest in the goods at the time of the loss. When the assured has no insurable interest in the subject matter insured, the policy is void in law and cannot be enforced against the insurer.[13]

666   Where goods are sold on f.o.b. terms the seller normally has the sole interest in them up to the time they have crossed the ship's rail since they are his property and at his risk. The fact that the buyer has already obtained insurance under "warehouse to warehouse" terms does not, in the absence of stipulation that the risk in the goods is to be borne by him prior to delivery f.o.b.,[14] alter the legal position. Nor can it provide protection or indemnity for the benefit of the seller. For, as has been pointed out, "the buyer having no pecuniary interest in the goods at the time has no claim for indemnity which he can transfer . . . ."[15] Though the point is not covered by authority, an

---

[13] Marine Insurance Act 1906, ss.4–8.
[14] See provision cited in n. 3, *ante*.
[15] Gow, *A Handbook of Marine Insurance* (5th ed., 1931), p. 79.

intention to assume the risk in the goods at any point prior to that at which delivery f.o.b. was to be completed is not to be implied from the mere fact that the buyer's insurance extends beyond the ship's rail and covers certain preshipment risks. Consequently, the seller is strongly advised to procure insurance for the period of transmission to the ship.[16] The seller must personally see to this insurance. For it has been held that where the seller has arranged for the goods to be conveyed to the ship by forwarding agents this does not place upon them the obligation to insure or even to inquire whether the seller had himself arranged for insurance.[17] If the goods therefore are lost or damaged through no negligence and no cover exists they are at the seller's risk. The terms of the cover are for the seller to determine but protection against the eventuality that delivery f.o.b. will not take place due to a breakdown of the buyer's arrangements with the designated vessel would be advisable. The buyer who has prepaid for the goods or has made an advance payment in respect thereof, may also wish to insert a condition in the contract whereby the seller undertakes to insure the goods for this period.

667   Upon delivery of the goods f.o.b., the buyer immediately acquires an insurable interest in them. This is, undoubtedly, the case once property has been transferred and regardless of whether it was a conditional or irrevocable transfer.[18] But it is equally true of the situation (as e.g. where the seller reserves a security title, or when the goods are as yet unascertained) in which the inference is that a partial interest only has been transferred.[19]

In the latter case as well as in circumstances where the seller is held to have retained only a right of possession in the goods, the seller, or a discount bank with whom the documents are deposited, also have an insurable interest in the goods.

668   Moreover, where a loss occurs before the entire contract quantity has been loaded f.o.b. the insurer cannot refuse to honour a policy effected by the buyer on the grounds that he did not acquire an insurable interest in the goods prior to complete performance. A case in point is *The Colonial Insurance Company of New Zealand v. The Adelaide Marine Insurance Co.*[20] where the subject matter of the sale was a cargo of wheat. The cargo consisted of 13,000 bags, but before completion of loading the vessel, whatever wheat had been

---

[16] See *The Exporter's Year Book* (1957)p. 47; *Export* (1951) at p. 213.
[17] *W.L.R. Traders (London) Ltd. v. British & Northern Shipping Agency Ltd. and I. Leftley Ltd.* [1955] 1 Lloyd's Rep. 554, *per* Pilcher J. But the forwarding agent may effect insurance if he so desires and in such a case his right of cover is not limited to his own interest in the goods. He may cover the whole value of the goods in his custody, holding in trust for the owner anything beyond the amount attributable to his own interest therein. *Hepburn v. A. Tomlinson (Hauliers) Ltd.* [1966] A.C. 451.
[18] *J. S. Robertson (Aust.) Pty. Ltd. v. Martin* (1956) 94 C.L.R. 30 (Australia), *ante,* §644
[19] *Inglis v. Stock* (1885) 10 App. Cas. 263, affirming (1884) 12 Q.B.D. 564, see *ante,* § 564 *Cf.* also *Castle v. Playford* (1872) L.R. 7 Ex, 98, and further *The Parchim* [1918] A.C. 157 at p. 167 cited *ante,* §566.
[20] (1886) 12 App.Cas. 128.

loaded on board was lost by the stranding of the vessel. The insurers denied their liability on the grounds *inter alia* that the plaintiffs who were the purchasers under the contract had no insurable interest in the goods at the time of the loss since they had contracted to purchase a cargo and not part of a cargo of wheat. The Judicial Committee of the Privy Council held that the action must succeed. Sir Barnes Peacock, delivering the judgment of their lordships, considered the evidence accepted by the Supreme Court of South Australia, to the effect "that the letters 'f.o.b.' in the particular contract were used with the meaning that the bags were to be at the buyer's risk immediately they were put on board," as inadmissible in this case. He preferred to rest the decision on what the court must have presumed to be broader grounds. It was the opinion of their lordships:

> "that the delivery of the wheat from time to time was a delivery to the purchasers, that it vested in them the right of possession as well as the right of property, and that at the time of the loss it was at their risk. The right which they had to return the wheat which had been delivered, in the event of the sellers neglecting, without lawful excuse, to complete the supply, did not prevent them from having an insurable interest. The interest in this case was defeasible, not by the vendors, but at the option of the vendees in the event of the vendors not completing the contract" (at p. 140).

Although the Judicial Committee proceeded to base its decision on property considerations derived from the fact that the buyer was the shipper in this case, it is thought that the same would hold true regardless of who is the shipper, that is to say even in cases where the facts show that the seller was to have issued the bill of lading to his own order.

669   A question arises, however, with respect to the seller's right of insurance in the case where he has parted with both the right of property in the goods and the right of possession in them. Clearly upon a revesting of any recognised interest in the goods as would for example happen where the unpaid seller exercises the right of stoppage *in transitu*,[21] the seller acquires an interest which can be made the subject of insurance. On the other hand, the insurable interest of the buyer is not thereby brought to an end. The exercise of the right of stoppage (*per se*) does not amount to a rescission of the contract and the buyer continues to remain the owner of the goods subject only to the lien of the seller.

670   It is less clear however whether the unpaid seller has an insurable interest in the goods before he has given notice of stoppage. This might be a matter of some concern to an f.o.b. seller who has sold on credit terms and has not received payment of the purchase price. The question has apparently not been settled conclusively by judicial authority and forms the subject of differing opinions among the commentators. Where Arnould[22] maintains that "it would

---

[21] *Post*, §§ 708, *et seq.*
[22] *On Marine Insurance* (16th ed.), British Shipping Laws, Chaps. 12 *et seq.*

be contrary to the principles on which an insurable interest depends if a seller who has parted with the property and possession could insure the goods and, if they were lost and the buyer afterwards became insolvent, recover their value, since at the time of the loss he had no right to take possession''; Schmitthoff is of the opinion[23] "that the unpaid seller has in these circumstances an insurable interest." This, it is thought, is the sounder position. And, were the question to be approached purely from the business point of view, there is no reason to suppose that it would be open to serious challenge. Indeed it seems clear that a recognition of the seller's interest in these circumstances is not within the mischief which the Marine Insurance Act was designed to cure. Furthermore, the decision in *Moran Galloway & Co. v. Uzalli & Ors.*[24] also appears to lend the proposition some support. In that case the English agents of a foreign ship effected an insurance for a voyage from Vancouver to any ports in the United Kingdom "on disbursements." The owners of the ship were indebted to the agents for advances in respect of necessary ship's disbursements, and Walton J. decided that the agents had an insurable interest in the ship to the extent of their advances by virtue of their right to enforce their claim by an action *in rem.*[25]

On the other hand, an American decision, *Home Ins. Co. v. Chang*[26] appears to be in the opposite direction. There an insurer brought an action to recover insurance premiums allegedly due and owing under an ocean marine cargo open policy. The New York Court of Appeals held that with respect to contracts providing for delivery of Taiwanese foodstuffs to New York imported on f.o.b., Taiwan or c. and f., U.S. port terms, coverage was specifically excluded by the terms of the policy. In addition, the court found that the seller did not have a covered insurable risk between the time of receipt of the merchandise from Taiwanese producers and the time of ocean shipments. Finally, the court held that the warranty that the foodstuffs would pass United States customs and food and drug inspection, which could revest title in seller only after the ocean voyage was concluded, did not create an insurable interest under the policy.

But the issue in that case was whether the seller had any obligation to pay premiums with respect to the transactions in question, which based on the foregoing reasons, the court found he did not.

Contingency insurance

671 The question, however, may be largely academic by virtue of the arrangements for contingency insurance which have been approved by the Institute

---

[23] Schmitthoff: *Export Trade*: *Law and Practice* (9th ed., 1993), pp 296–302.
[24] [1905] 2 K.B. 555.
[25] In *Seagrave v. The Union Marine Insurance Co.* (1866) L.R. 1 C.P. 305 the Court of Common Pleas overruled Martin B, who decided that "the plaintiff had an insurable interest as an unpaid vendor" on the grounds that he was neither a "vendor" nor "unpaid."
[26] 41 N.Y. 2d 288 360 N.E. 2d 1089.

of London Underwriters. This form of insurance, which *inter alia* is designed to meet the requirements of sellers under f.o.b. terms and to avoid the necessity of paying twice for full insurance protection, is now readily available. It provides that claims in respect of loss or damage to the goods shall be payable only to the extent that the buyer fails to pay for the goods lost or damaged. As stated by Schmitthoff[27]:

> "This type of insurance is used nowadays by many exporters although it entails additional cost. . . . If the payment of freight is the buyer's liability, as is *e.g.* the case under an f.o.b. contract, it is advisable to include in the valuation of the goods for the purposes of contingency insurance some provision for freight because not only is the value of the goods increased by the carriage to the port of destination but the seller might have to satisfy the carrier's lien for freight before being able to resume possession of the goods."[28]

Contingency insurance of this type would also provide protection for the seller in case the goods are rightfully rejected by the buyer, whereupon the buyer's interest in the goods comes to an end. But where the buyer's policy has not expired he can probably assign it to the seller before rejection.[29] Whereas if the buyer recovers under his policy, and subsequently exercises a right of rejection, he must credit the seller with the proceeds of the policy.[30]

672 Where contingency insurance is for some reason inconvenient, the seller can arrange to have the buyer's insurers extend cover to him for the period between the commencement of the risk, and the time of payment or acceptance of the documents. A particular form for this latter kind of arrangement which has been worked out with primary reference to c. and f. sales is apparently also used occasionally in the case of f.o.b. sales.[31] Finally, in cases where the seller effects the insurance for the buyer as for example under an f.o.b. "shipment-to-destination" contract, no problems arise on account of the buyer's insurable interest not having been disclosed to the insurer. By an express provision of the Marine Insurance Act (section 26(2)) the nature and extent of the insurable interest need not be disclosed at the time of the contract so that it is immaterial whether the identity of the principal is or is not revealed at the time the cover is effected.

Export credit guarantees

673 When commercial insurance is unavailable because, for example, the legal principles appertaining to insurable interest do not permit it the seller may

---

[27] Export Trade: Law and Practice at pp 488–532.
[28] As to the obligation of the seller who exercises a right of stoppage to discharge the carrier's lien for unpaid freight see *Booth Steamship Co. Ltd.* v. *Cargo fleet Iron Co. Ltd.* [1916] 2 K.B. 570.
[29] See Chalmers. *Marine Insurance Act* (5th ed., 1956), p. 15.
[30] See *Robertson (Aust.) Pty. Ltd.* v. *Martin* (1956) 94 C.L.R. 30 (Australia).
[31] Dover and Calver. *The Bankers Guide to Marine Insurance of Goods* (London, 1960), pp. 230, 232.

be able to protect himself to some extent by means of an export credit guarantee cover. The scheme is in England administered by a government department and is designed to promote exports. It offers cover (though not complete) which is not normally available by means of commercial insurance including the buyer's insolvency, default in payment and refusal to accept the goods where such refusal is not excused by or arises from the seller's breach. Other risks for which cover is obtainable, include the risk of denial of export or import licences under certain conditions, and exchange restrictions risks which prevent the effective remittance of the purchase price.[32]

[The next paragraph is 691.]

---

[32] As to this subject generally see Schmitthoff, *Export Trade! Law and Practice* (9th ed., 1993), pp 488–532.

CHAPTER 13

REMEDIES

Breach of contract by seller

691   *Failure to deliver.* The principles applicable to breach of contract by
the seller have already been reviewed (see *ante*, Chapter 6) in relation to
c.i.f. contracts. They, including the principles applicable to contracts calling
for delivery by instalments, also govern f.o.b. contracts *mutatis mutandis.*
When the seller fails to deliver the goods within the period stipulated
under the contract, the remedy of the buyer is to claim damages for
non-delivery. The measure of damages is calculated in accordance with
the provisions set forth in section 51(2) and (3) of the Sale of Goods
Act. Prima facie damages are to be computed with reference to the market
price of similar goods at the date of the breach at the place of delivery
f.o.b. including any reasonable expenses incurred by the buyer for the
purpose of performing his obligations under the contract, *e.g.* amounts
payable on account of demurrage or dead freight.[1] The principle was
stated by Cardozo J. in *Standard Casing Co. v. California Casing Co.*[2]
where a contract for the delivery of goods f.o.b. San Francisco was not
performed and the buyer alleged that damages were to be calculated on
the market price at their intended destination, New York. Rejecting this
allegation, the learned judge explained:

> "We hold, then, that the risk of transit was the buyer's, whether the bill of lading
> was made out to him or to the seller. . . . If that is so, the seller's performance
> would be complete upon the beginning of the transit. There was no undertaking
> that the goods would reach their destination. . . . The undertaking was merely
> that they would be delivered to the carrier. The place where that was to be done,
> as it would be the place of final performance by the seller if the contract had
> been kept, must be the place also of default when performance was refused.
> Market values in California, and not market values in New York, must therefore

---

[1] *O. H. Perry Tie & Lumber Co. v. Reynolds & Bros.*, 100 Va. 264 (1902); *Garfield & Proctor
Coal Co. v. Pennsylvania C. & C.*, 199 Mass. 22 (1908) (U.S.). But in the absence of a demurrage
provision in the charterparty "a seller who has delayed the loading of a ship provided by the
f.o.b. buyer cannot be brought to book for holding the vessel up and causing the buyer to pay
hire for the time lost," so held by Mocatta J. in *The "Al Hofuf"* [1981] 1 Lloyd's Rep. 81 at
pp. 86, 87. See also cases noted *post*, n. 15.
[2] 233 N. Y. 413 (1922).

be the measure of the value of the bargain. . . . No doubt, in any case of delivery to a carrier, the expectation of the buyer is that the goods will reach their destination. That is not enough to transfer to the point of destination the computation of the damages resulting from the consignor's default'' (at p. 418).

Where the seller is guilty of an anticipatory breach (*ante* § 313) the buyer may in the appropriate case elect to rescind the contract, as was, *e.g.* the case in *Metro Meat Ltd. v. Fares Rural Co. Pty Ltd. and Ano.*[3] And where the buyer has resold, and the resale was a term of the contract, the buyer may recover his loss of profit as well as any damages to which he would be liable for breach of the contract of resale.[4] But this may be subject to the buyer's duty to mitigate his damages.

692 *Delivery of non-conforming goods.* Nevertheless, there are many cases in which the market price at the contemplated destination of the goods would have to be invoked in order to establish the basis for computing the measure of damages. This would particularly be the case when the seller has delivered non-conforming goods, the default not being discovered until the goods have reached their destination. This was held in a subsequent case, *Perkins v. Minford et al.,*[5] by the Court of Appeal in New York where a claim for damages under a contract for the sale of sugar f.o.b. Cuban ports consigned to New York was considered. The claim alleged a deficiency in quality which only became known on arrival.

> ''Generally [the measure of damages] is fixed by the difference between the contract and the market price at the time and place when and where the delivery should have been made. . . . Such was the rule here applied in *Standard Casing Co. Inc. v. California*[6] and under somewhat similar circumstances in *Seaver v. Lindsay Light Co.*[7] . . ., in both of which cases there was a total failure to deliver any part of the goods sold.[8] The reason is clear. Usually, knowing of the breach of contract, the buyer may protect himself against the consequences of a rising market by buying from others. But what if he does not know? What if the delivery being made at a distance the buyer neither knows nor has the means of knowledge that the contract has not been completed until he actually receives the goods or bill of lading stating the amount shipped to him? What is the loss then directly and naturally resulting from the breach of contract? This situation is one of those as to which an exception is made . . . 'special circumstances' are present, showing 'proximate damages of a greater amount' than those provided by the general rule. The time as to when the damages are measured is shifted. It is now the date on which the buyer knew or ought to have known of the default'' (at p. 305).

---

[3] [1985] 2 Lloyd's Rep. 13 (P. C.).
[4] *Re. R. and H. W. Hall Ltd and H. Pin (Junior) & Co's. Arbitration* [1928] All E. R. 763 (H. L.).
[5] 235 N.Y. 301 (1923).
[6] *Ante,* §691.
[7] C.i.f. sale, 233 N.Y. 273 (1922), *ante,* §305.
[8] See however *Disch v. National Surety Co.*, 196 N.Y.S. 833 (1922) following the *Standard Casing* decision where non-conforming goods were shipped.

693   If the buyer rejects (as to the buyer's right of rejection, see *ante*, §§ 629 *et seq.*) because of the non-conformity, freight, insurance and other forwarding charges incurred by him are also recoverable.[9] The destination market price then governs as was decided by Bailhache J. in *Van den Hurk v. R. Martens & Co.*[10] which has already been noted.[11] The same however is true even if the buyer elects to accept the goods, waiving the breach of condition or of his right of rejection and claiming an allowance in their price in lieu thereof, as was decided by Lord Goddard C.J. in *Obaseki Bros. v. Reif & Son, Ltd.*[12] In that case he confirmed the decision of an umpire on a case stated that the measure of damages for non-conforming goods shipped f.o.b. from Africa equalled the difference between the market value in England of goods as should have been tendered under the contract and the market value of the goods actually delivered on the date on which the defective quality was established. Because the seller was also in default with respect to delay in delivery, the buyer, moreover, recovered the increase in freight costs resulting therefrom. The same would of course apply where the goods arrive in a defective condition for which the seller is held liable, for example, where they have not been adequately packed or loaded or where a warranty is implied that they will arrive in a merchantable condition.[13] Where the goods deteriorate as a result of a breach of duty on the part of the ship an action against the carrier will lie which, if any risks remain with the seller, can also be enforced by him irrespective of whether or not the property in the goods has passed.[14]

But the buyer cannot reject, unless the seller is guilty of a breach of condition amounting to a repudiation. The principles that apply have already been discussed in relation to c.i.f. contracts, and little purpose would be served by reiterating them here. Suffice it to say that the view that contractual terms may be neither conditions proper nor warranties proper, and that the severity of the breach may determine the remedy in appropriate cases equally applies (albeit the uncertainty involved) to f.o.b. contracts. Thus, in *Tradax Internacional S. A. v. Goldschmidt S. A.*[15] it was held that an impurity of 0.10 per cent over the tolerance permitted by a contract for the sale of 8,000 tonnes of white Syrian barley would not be treated as a breach of a condition. The courts should—it was said—lean in favour of construing the provision as an intermediate term, only a serious and substantial breach of which entitled rejection. In that case the seller was to provide a certificate of quality attesting to the percentage of impurities and foreign matters in the barley. The certificate was furnished and indicated the excess impurity already noted but the buyers' plea that they could have rejected the certificate as non-conforming

---

[9] *Southern v. Austin & Son* (1921) 6 Ll. L. Rep. 24.
[10] [1920] 1 K.B. 850.
[11] *Ante* §632.
[12] [1952] 2 Lloyd's Rep. 364. *Contra: Bronstone v. Burdett* [1928] 1 D.L.R. 877, where the Manitoba Court of Appeal held that damages are to be calculated with reference to the date and place of delivery f.o.b. though the deficiency was only discovered upon arrival at the destination.
[13] *Ante*, § 318, *et seq.*
[14] *Den of Airlie SS. Co. Ltd. v. Mitsui & Co. Ltd.* (1912) 106 L. T. 451.
[15] [1977] 2 Lloyd's Rep. 604.

was dismissed. Slynn J. noted that commercial men considered this type of deviation in quality as insignificant. The seller was thus entitled to damages for the buyers' unjustifiable recision.

In the course of his judgment Slynn J. said:

> "It is accepted that the provision as to impurities was not part of the description of the goods so there was no implied condition under s.13 of the Sale of Goods Act, 1893, entitling rejection on non-compliance. Nor is any condition implied by s. 14 of the Sale of Goods Act, 1893, relied on. Accordingly it seems to me that on the basis of what was said in the case of *The Hansa Nord* [1975] 2 Lloyd's Rep. 445; [1976] Q.B. 44 at pp. 451 and 61 by Lord Denning, M.R., and at pp. 457 and 70H–71B by Lord Justice Roskill and what was said in *Hong Kong Fir Shipping Co. Ltd. v. Kawasaki Kisen Kaisha Ltd.* [1961] 2 Lloyd's Rep. 478; [1962] 2 Q.B. 26, in the absence of any clear agreement or prior decision that this was to be a condition, the Court should lean in favour of construing this provision as to impurities as an intermediate term, only a serious and substantial breach of which entitled rejection."

Furthermore, Slynn J. went on to state:

> "The buyers here had to consider whether the breach established by the quality final certificate was substantial and serious or went to the root of the contract or, on the other hand, whether it was of such a kind that they should have been satisfied with a price adjustment. There was, on the findings of the Board of Appeal, only one answer to that. Those findings are in strong terms and show that commercial men (to whose conclusions on these matters I must and do attach great weight) considered that this kind of deviation in quality would not be treated as entitling a rejection either of a quality final certificate (being otherwise valid) or the goods. Accordingly I hold that the buyers were not entitled automatically to reject the document because of this statement in the quality final certificate that the goods contained 4.1 per cent. impurities" (at p. 612).

694   *Late delivery.* When the breach consists in a delay in the date of delivery the damages may equal the increase in the cost of the goods due to a devaluation in the currency of payment, if such a result was forseeable by the parties at the time when the contract was made, as a "likely" consequence of the breach.[16] The increased cost of transport including demurrage[17] or the difference between the amount realised on a resale and the amount that could

---

[16] See *Aruna Mills Ltd. v. Dhanrajamal Gobindram* [1968] 1 Q.B. 655, *ante*, § 310.

[17] But where an f.o.b. contract contained a clause by which the goods were to be delivered to the ship in accordance with the custom of the port, any delay excusable thereunder excludes the seller's liability even though the buyer incurs demurrage to the owner of the vessel. See *Einar Bugge A.S. v. W. H. Bowater Ltd.* (1925) 31 Com.Cas. 1. And when demurrage is stipulated in the form of liquidated damages at a fixed rate it was held that the stipulation applies even when loading commenced after the shipping period and was not merely delayed beyond it. See *Trading Society Kwik-Hoo-Tong v. Royal Commission on Sugar Supply* (1923) 16 Ll.L.Rep. 250; (1924) 19 Ll.L.Rep. 70, 343. (Delay caused by failure to nominate the port of loading and vessel kept awaiting instructions at some other port.) See also case noted *ante*, n. 1. The inclusion of a specific demurrage clause is strongly recommended but in view of the foregoing authorities should be drafted with great caution.

have been realised had the contract been performed on time will normally be recoverable as damages.[18] But if the market price at the destination has fallen below the price at which the buyer was able to resell the goods then he will not be entitled to recover more than the loss actually sustained by him.[19]

695 *No market.* The destination (or any other reasonable market) will normally also furnish the basis for computing damages in cases where there is no available market at the f.o.b. point. For as stated in *Spargue v. Northern Pacific Railway*[20]:

> "He [the seller] must have apprehended that if he failed to make delivery according to agreement and [the buyer] could not supply himself with the same amount and quality of lumber at or in the vicinity of the delivery point, he would probably suffer damages to the extent of the difference of the market price of such lumber at [the destination] at the agreed time of delivery, and the contract price less what it would have cost [the buyer] for inspection fees and freight had the contract been performed. . . ."[21]

In yet other cases the contract may expressly provide for damages to be computed with reference to the market value of the goods ruling on the date of default at the destination contemplated.[22]

In *Esteve Trading Corp. v. Agropec International ("The Golden Rio")*[23] the question arose as to the meaning of the term in a FOSFA string and circle contract for the sale of Brazilian and/or Paraguayan soya beans f.o.b. Rio Grande concerning the bankruptcy or insolvency of one of the parties. The provision in question provided for immediate closure of the contract (the suspension of payment would or might not ordinarily be an anticipatory breach, and the affected party may be compelled to wait until the time of performance, by delivery or otherwise, when an actual default, if there was one, would occur),[24] on the basis of "the market price then current for similar goods" or, "at a price to be ascertained by repurchase or resale. . . ." The act of insolvency occured on July 28 1987, while the goods were afloat and the vessel was in the course of its voyage to its destination in Belgium. Since there was no repurchase or resale it became necessary to fix the market price then current for similar goods. The GAFTA Board of Appeal decided this question by reference to the Antwerp/Ghent c.i.f. price, from which the cost of freight and insurance were deducted. The buyers disputed this decision. In their submission the reference point should have been the prices established

---

[18] *Joseph I. Emanuel Ltd. v. Cardia and Savoca* [1958] 1 Lloyd's Rep. 121.
[19] *Wertheim v. Chicoutimi Pulp Co.* [1911] A.C. 301 (P.C.).
[20] 106 Am.St.Rep. 997 at p. 998 (1904).
[21] See also *H. J. Macauley and C. J. Cullen v. T. J. Horgan* [1925] 2 Ir.R. 1.
[22] See, *e.g.* stipulations in the contracts considered in *James Laing, Son & Co. (M/C) Ltd. v. Eastcheap Dried Fruit Co.* [1961] 1 Lloyd's Rep. 142; *Joseph (D) v. Ralph Wood & Co. Ltd.* [1951] W.N. 224. As to the meaning of "value of the goods" see *The Calorio ante*, §309.
[23] [1990] 2 Lloyd's Rep. 273.
[24] See *Simmonds v. Millar & Co.* (1898) 4 Com. Cas. 64; *Shipton Anderson & Co. (1927) Ltd. (In Liquidation) v. Micks Lambert & Co.* (1936) 55 Ll.L. Rep. 384.

by the Chicago Board of Trade, for which the last day on which a July soya beans contract was quoted was July 22, and which was, in their contention, some ten per cent. higher than that found by the Board. Evans J. opined, in the course of his judgment that rejected the buyers contention (and affirmed the Board's award), that the difficulty of there not being a Chicago Board of Trade reference price for July 28 could probably be overcome by the reference to the price for the August shipment. But he added:

> "there remains an underlying problem which is one of principle, because the act of insolvency could have occured after July 31, or rather after the latest time when a prompt f.o.b. price for July goods could possibly be obtained. Once July has passed, July shipment becomes impossible. Then there can only be a market f.o.b. price for August or later shipment, that is, for non-contractual goods.
>
> In truth, once the shipment period is over, there cannot be a market f.o.b. price for goods to be shipped during that period. The seller cannot agree to ship goods anymore than the buyer can agree to nominate the carrying vessel, during a period which has already passed. So, as a matter of legal theory, there cannot be an f.o.b. sale after the time for shipment has expired". (At p. 276).

In his view "the existence of a market is not limited to a recognised exchange or similar place of business, nor is 'market price' limited to a published or recorded price. It is enough that there are 'sufficient traders who are in touch with each other to evidence a market' (per Sellers J. in *ABD Metals & Waste Ltd.* [1955] 2 Lloyd's Rep. 456 at p. 466)."[25] He therefore concluded that so long as it remained possible to buy goods f.o.b. for July shipment at Rio Grande that would be the appropriate retrence price. Thereafter the price for goods of the contractual description, and which are either afloat and bound for the contractual destination, or which can be bought for delivery there at about the time the vessel was scheduled to arrive, would provide the test. Evans J. declined to accept the plaintiff's contention that even after it became impossible to conclude f.o.b. purchases for July shipments the Rio Grande market price (for later shipment and adjustment where necessary) was the relevant market price. Because, in his words, "this is the current market for goods which have not been shipped and which, even if they are then shipped to the same destination, will be carried on a different voyage, with all that that involves in terms of arrival date and risks. If they are shipped in August rather than July they will not be 'similar goods' either in fact or in law."[26]

696   When there is no market for the goods in question the general principles embodied in section 51(2) of the Sale of Goods come into operation. In these cases a resale price or loss of profit will almost invariably be considered as furnishing the proper value of the goods for the purpose of determining the amount of damages. In *Société Co-op. Suisse des Céréales et Matières Fourragères v. La Plata Cereal Co., S.A.*,[27] where delivery f.o.b. was prevented

---

[25] *Ibid.* at p. 279.
[26] *Ibid.*
[27] (1947) 80 L1.L. Rep. 530.

as a result of an export ban imposed by the Argentine Government,[28] Morris J. observed that had he held the seller liable in damages, which in the circumstances he had not (on the grounds that the contract was discharged because of the export prohibition), he would have been dissatisfied with the damages awarded by the Appeal Committee of the London Corn Trade Association. These were measured by the difference between the contract price, and the internal price of the goods in the Argentine plus the f.o.b. charges relating thereto on the date of default. His view was that in a case such as this where no market exists by virtue of an export prohibition, section 51(3) was inapplicable and damages should be assessed by reference to the more general provisions of section 51(2).

697   *Rights against the goods.* Before the goods have been delivered f.o.b. the buyer will normally not be in a position to obtain specific relief, regardless of the fact that he has prepaid for the goods. Thus if the seller becomes insolvent the buyer's rights are normally confined to those appertaining to any other unsecured creditor.[29] Specific relief may also be denied, even when the goods have already been shipped, should it be decided that they have not been appropriated to the contract for one reason or another.[30] However, if the seller wrongfully withholds delivery (after the property in the goods has passed to the buyer) the buyer may sue in tort for conversion. Since the transfer of the bill of lading to a bona fide purchaser for value would defeat the original buyer's claim, such an action would not necessarily enable the buyer to obtain the possession of the goods but only damages (or restitution of the profits made by the seller on the resale)[31] in the computation of which anything he owes on account of the purchase price must be accounted for. Generally, therefore, an action in tort or in contract would amount to the same thing. The measure of damages would be the difference between the contract price and the market price on the date of the conversion.[32]

698   *Actions against the carrier.* In certain circumstances, an action may lie both against the seller and the carrier. Where, for example, the "f.o.b. calling for additional services" variant is employed, and the seller assumes the status of shipper, and the carrier, notwithstanding the apparent defective condition of the goods, agrees to issue a "clean" bill of lading therefor,[33] the buyer

---

[28] See *ante*, §505.
[29] See *Carlos Federspiel & Co. S.A. v. Charles Twigg & Co. Ltd. & Anor.* [1957] 1 Lloyd's Rep. 240, *ante*, §595.
[30] See, *e.g. Re Wait* [1927] 1 Ch. 606, *ante*, §§275 *et seq.*
[31] *Ante*, §315.
[32] See, *e.g. Empresa Exportadora De Azucar v. Industria Azucarera Nacional S.A. (The Playa Larga and Marble Islands)* [1983] 2 Lloyd's Rep. 171 (C.A.), a c. & f. sale holding seller (a Cuban state enterprise) liable in conversion for diverting ship containing a cargo of sugar sold to the respondents.
[33] The practice of issuing false bills of lading against indemnities has, presumably, been curtailed by the decision in *Brown Jenkinson & Co. Ltd. v. Dalton (London) Ltd.* [1957] 2 Q.B. 621, which held that where the carrier is guilty of fraud he will not be permitted to enforce the indemnity.

may prefer to bring an action against the ship instead of claiming for breach of the contract of sale. Thus, where a consignment of potatoes was shipped in wet bags, in consequence of which many rotted, and the master issued a clean bill of lading (under an indemnity from the consignor), the buyers' action against the owners of the vessel was upheld.[34] Sir H. Duke P. dismissed the submission that in law the plaintiffs themselves were the shippers of the goods, and that they, by their agents, therefore, not only knew of the state of the potatoes, but knowingly stowed them in wet bags and agreed to be responsible for any damage which might be thereby caused. He held that the buyers—correctly—supposed the consignor "to be the sellers' agent paid by a commission for his services in selling goods which they bought f.o.b. at Gothenburg" (at page 349). In this case the buyers elected to pursue their claim in England by means of *in rem* proceedings against the vessel instead of suing the seller personally for the following reasons:

> "The financial position of the [seller] and the situation in point of domicil of the various parties concerned are sufficient to explain the election of the plaintiffs to proceed here under the jurisdiction *in rem*, instead of pursuing elsewhere remedies against individuals" (at p. 347).

And where as a result of the carrier's unjustifiable deviation the goods arrive late the carrier may be liable to the buyer for the damages sustained including, in the appropriate cases, loss of profit. Thus in *Satef–Huttenes Albertus S.p.A. v. Paloma Tercera Shipping Co. Ltd. (The Pegase)*[35] the vessel, which was chartered by the sellers for the buyers to whom they sold 3,100 tons of chromite sand f.o.b. Lourenco Marques, deviated and arrived at the port of destination after a delay of 65 days. It was held by the commercial court, on a case stated by an arbitrator, that the carrier may be liable to the buyers for loss of their profits provided this loss was not too remote, namely, provided it could reasonably have been contemplated in the circumstances, and the award was remitted for a finding on this question. Goff J. noted in the course of his judgment that:

> "... before assessing the damages on the basis of the resale profits actually lost by the receivers [the buyers], the arbitrator ought, in my judgment, to have considered two questions in particular. First, since the actual resale contracts were not known to the owners [of the vessel], he should have considered whether the actual profits lost by the receivers were out of the ordinary; clearly, they should not be entitled to recover the profits for 'extravagant or unusual bargains,' but only at a reasonable level. Second, and more important, the arbitrator should have taken into account the fact that the owners had no knowledge of the limited storage space available to the receivers or of their having run down their stocks, and (as I understand the position) had no knowledge that the receivers had an immediate need of these goods for processing and resale. That being so, it was necessary for the arbitrator to make some allowance for a period during which stocks might have been used for the purpose of meeting commitments, in order

---

[34] *The Tromp* [1921] P. 337.
[35] [1981] 1 Lloyd's Rep. 175.

to assess the loss of resale profits only by reference to the period during which, on the knowledge available to them, the owners (had they considered the position) ought reasonably to have contemplated that it was not unlikely that the receivers would lose resale profits for want of these goods'' (at p. 186).

However, as to the additional claim of the buyers for loss of goodwill, his honour considered them to be too remote in the circumstances.

Breach of contract by buyer

699 *Non-acceptance.* Unless there is an express stipulation in the contract by which the price shall become due and payable on a day certain, the purchase price is not recoverable unless the property in the goods has passed to the buyer, which will almost never occur prior to delivery f.o.b.[36]
For this reason, as Wright J. once stated, the rule[37]:

"... in the case of ordinary c.i.f. and f.o.b. contracts ... where buyers refuse goods the sellers cannot claim the price, but only damages for non acceptance under section 50 of the Sale of Goods Act."

The same applies after delivery f.o.b. where the seller is held to have reserved the property by means of the bill of lading even if the goods meet with some disaster and perish as a result therefrom. For although the risk of loss will be borne by the buyer so that the redress will be the same whether he proceeds to claim damages or the price, the proper remedy and course of action in such a case is an action for damages. By proceeding from the wrong course the seller may thus incur the cost of the litigation and be forced to commence an action *de novo.*[38]

700 Normally the amount of damages will be ascertained by the difference between the contract price and the market price of similar goods at the place of delivery f.o.b. and at the time when the buyer ought to have taken delivery of the goods or of the documents. However, where the goods have already been loaded and it is impracticable to unload them, or where the voyage has commenced, it would be unreasonable to relate the damages to the date or

---

[36] *Ante,* § 592 *et seq.*
[37] *Shell Mex Ltd. v. Elton & Dyeing Co. Ltd.* (1928) 34 Com.Cas. 39 at p. 44, where a contract for the sale of oil by instalments to be delivered in sellers' road tank wagons as required by the buyers contained the clause that the sellers should have the right at any time to invoice to the buyers the due quantities of oil not taken up and to demand payment of the invoice price. The court held that no action for the price would lie, the seller being confined to an action for damages for non-acceptance which were nominal since the market had risen. But see *Burch & Co. v. Corry & Co.* [1920] N.Z.L.R. 184, *ante,* §579, n. 90.
[38] See *per* Bankes L.J. in *F. E. Napier v. Dexters Ltd.* (1926) 26 Ll.L.Rep. 184. The reverse however is not necessarily true. When property has passed the seller can apparently sue for the price by claiming damages equal to the price. See, *e.g. Frebold and Sturznickel (Trading as Panda O.H.G.) v. Circle Products* [1970] 1 Lloyd's Rep. 499, C.A.

place of delivery f.o.b. In these circumstances the damages will often be assessed with reference to the market price ruling at the contemplated destination at the time of arrival, due allowance being made for the cost of freight, insurance and other expenses incident to their movement thereto. This principle was favoured by Roche J. *in F. E. Napier v. Dexters Ltd.*,[39] where he observed that had he decided to dismiss the sellers' action for the price, which he upheld (on the grounds that the property in the goods had passed notwithstanding the retention of the mate's receipt by the sellers), he would have awarded the damages on the basis of the difference between the contract price and the price of the goods in Hamburg, their destination, and not in London, the place of delivery f.o.b., as the buyers alleged. Addressing himself to this problem, the learned judge said[40]:

> "The first point is whether, if the price were not recoverable, which of two measures of damages is the proper measure. . . . If I had to decide it I think I should have decided without doubt that the proper measure of damages is the Hamburg measure of damages, the larger sum, and for this reason, that it seems to me that the goods when taken on board this ship nominated by the buyers were irrevocably committed—if I may use that expression—to the voyage to Hamburg, and that the proper measure [of damages] is the difference in price they would realise there."

701 But the seller must act expeditiously. If he delays the resale of the goods on a falling market he does not recover the difference between the contract and the resale price but only the difference between the contract price and what would have been obtainable had he resold when he should have.[41]

Where the seller waives the date of fulfilment by the buyer he cannot claim damages for non-acceptance unless he reinstates some other date therefore by reasonable notice in which case damages will be assessed with reference to the market price on that later date.[42]

In the appropriate circumstances, damages may be awarded by applying a different yardstick such as the "loss of profit" resulting from the buyer's default. It has even been said that in the case of string-transactions to be financed by confirmed credits, "prima facie the measure of damages is the loss of profit," regardless of whether the market goes up or down.[43] This is so because the failure to provide the credit usually makes it impossible to carry on with the transaction. In other words, because the buyer normally knows that the sellers "[can] not obtain the goods at all unless the credit [is]

---

[39] (1926) 26 Ll.L.Rep. 62; affirmed by C.A., *ibid.* at p. 184; for the facts of the case see *ante* § 454.
[40] (1926) 26 Ll.L.Rep. 62 at p. 64.
[41] See *Warin & Craven v. Forrester* (1876) 4 R. (Ct. of Sess.) 190.
[42] See *S.C.C.M.O. (London) Ltd. v. Société Général de Compensation* [1956] 1 Lloyd's Rep. 290.
[43] See *Ian Stach Ltd. v. Baker Bosley Ltd.* [1958] 2 Q.B. 130 at p. 145; *ante,* § 615, for the facts of this case; following *Trans Trust S.P.R.L. v. Danubian Trading Co. Ltd.* [1952] 2 Q.B. 297 (C.A.), f.o.b. buyer who failed to open a letter of credit held liable for seller's loss of profit, despite a rise in the market price.

provided."[44] The seller may of course also recover any expenses caused by the breach (*e.g.* in respect of extra storage charges incurred because of the buyer's failure to take delivery)[45] and interest on the amounts due.

702   *Anticipatory breach.* An accepted anticipatory breach *i.e.* where the seller treats such a breach as a repudiation of the contract,[46] ought, it is thought, crystallise his rights as of the time of this acceptance. Damages should, therefore, normally be awarded with reference to that earlier date. Case law however, does not always support this proposition, and a later date has sometimes been preferred, namely when the goods ought to have been delivered, though the buyer may recover mitigation costs as of the earlier date.[47] It is incumbent upon the seller who accepts the repudiation to act reasonably in order to mitigate his damages. But the buyer's repudiation is ineffective unless it is accepted by the seller. Under English law, the seller can therefore continue to insist on performance, the buyer's anticipatory breach notwithstanding.[48] Thus, in a contract for the supply of coal at 16s. a ton f.o.b. English port, where the buyers found that they could not furnish their vessel in time and, wishing to cancel their bargain, offered the seller an alternative purchaser at an even higher price (namely, at 16s. 3d.), the Court of Appeal,[49] reversing Phillimore J., held that the sellers were not bound to accept the substitute. The court ruled that the sellers were entitled to keep the contract alive until the time of delivery had expired, and that the damages should be computed on that date on which the market had fallen to 15s. per ton, and a difference of 1s. per ton was recoverable. The seller, therefore, is under no duty to

---

[44] *Per* Denning L.J. in *Trans Trust S.P.R.L. v. Danubian Trading Co., ibid.* at p. 306.
[45] See, *e.g. Phoebus D. Kyprianou Co. v. Wm. H. Pim Jnr. & Co. Ltd.* [1977] 2 Lloyd's Rep. 570.
[46] The seller, however, is not bound to make his election forthwith; he is entitled to consider the buyer's suggestion. If he has not "delayed unreasonably," he will not forfeit his rights to accept and take advantage of the buyer's repudiation: *Sudan Import & Export Co. Ltd. Société Générale de Compensation* [1957] 2 Lloyd's Rep. 528; affirmed in [1958] 1 Lloyd's Rep. 310 (C.A.). The seller, moreover, is not required to communicate his acceptance to the buyer. His actions may demonstrate his acceptance, e.g. his selling the goods to a third party, see *Vitol S.A. v. Norelf Ltd (The "Santa Clara")* [1993] 2 Lloyd's Rep. 301. Where a contract for the sale of oil f.o.b. Genoa was to be in two instalments, and the buyer rejected the first shipment on the grounds of discoloration and alleged unsatisfactory quality, the seller is under no duty to ship more of the same type of oil for the additional instalment, and may treat the buyer's rejection of the first instalment as a repudiation of the entire contract: *Warinco A.G. v. Samor S.p.A.* [1979] 1 Lloyd's Rep. 450 (C.A.), reversing Donaldson J. in [1977] 2 Lloyd's Rep. 582. As to the general principles that determine the right to repudiate contracts calling for delivery by instalments they are as follows: first, if the buyer commits a breach before all deliveries have been made which is so serious as to go to the root of the contract, the seller is not expected to go to the trouble and expense of tendering later instalments if he does not want to. Second, if it becomes clear that the buyer will be unable to accept or pay for later instalments the seller, if he so wishes, is discharged from any further obligation to perform. And, finally, if the buyer acts or speaks in a manner which declares in clear terms his failure to future perform his part of the contract the seller has the option of being discharged from further obligations.
[47] See *Melachrino v. Wickallf Knight* [1920] 1KB. 693, *ante,* § 314.
[48] See *White and Carter (Councils) Ltd. v. McGregor* [1962] A. C. 413 (H. L.).
[49] *Tredegar Iron & Coal Co. Ltd. v. Hawthorn & Co.* (1902) 18 T. L. R. 716. See also *Brooker, Dore & Co. v. Keymer, Son & Co.* (1923) 15 Ll.L. Rep. 23.

mitigate his damages by accepting a wrongful repudiation. So that where a New York confirming house refused to sell in the U.S. goods that its U.K. principals ordered for the English market under a contract which they subsequently purported to cancel, it was held in *Anglo–African Shipping Co. of New York, Inc. v. J. Mortner Ltd.*[50] that there was no obligation to mitigate the damages by selling in New York. They had every right to proceed to engage shipping space in the name of their principals ("f.o.b. shipment to destination" variant) and to ship the goods across the Atlantic pursuant to the terms of the contract, though they had been informed that the goods would not be accepted. And in *Phoebus D. Kyprianou Coy v. Wm. H. Pim Jnr. & Co. Ltd.*,[51] where under three contracts the sellers agreed to sell to the buyers 1,250 tons, 1,500 tons and 5,000 tons, respectively, of English Horse and/or Tic Beans f.o.b. Lowestoft for shipment between February 1 and April 15, 1975 and the buyers took delivery of 919 tons under the second contract, but were in default with respect to the remainder, Kerr J. (on a case stated in an arbitration award) rejected the buyers contention that since they were in default on dates earlier than the final permissible shipment dates (*i.e.* March 15, March 31 and April 15) under the respective contracts (because, *inter alia*, of contractual provisions relating to spreads between each shipment and the limited loading facilities at Lowestoft) damages should be assessed on the basis of the earlier default dates by deciding by what dates the buyers should reasonably have lifted what quantities. The court held that it was open to the sellers to keep the contracts alive, as they did, and that the sellers were under no duty (indeed it would be extremely risky on their part) to treat the buyers as having repudiated their obligations before termination of the respective shipment dates, and to resort to the market to sell the unaccepted goods prior thereto. Since the market was falling rapidly, the buyers alternatively sought to advance the date of assessment of the damages to, at least, before the end of the respective shipment periods when insufficient time remained to nominate and load the necessary ships. But this contention also failed. The breach is not final until the end of the shipment period; at any rate the sellers are not obliged to treat it as final until then.[52]

Finally the buyers claimed that since the contracts were for 10 per cent. more or less "at buyer's option" the amount of damages which were assessed on the contractual or "mean" quantities was wrong as the damages should only have been assessed on the basis of 90 per cent of the contract quantities because this was the limit of their legal obligation. The court conditionally agreed to remit this question back to the arbitral tribunal as it was not raised before it, and there was never any opportunity of dealing with it adding that trade tribunals have traditionally awarded damages on the basis of mean contract quantities disregarding such options in the past.

[50] [1962] 1 Lloyd's Rep. 81 affirmed, *ibid.* 610 (C. A.); for the facts of the case, see *ante*, §§ 530 *et seq.*
[51] [1977] 2 Lloyd's Rep. 570.
[52] See also *Lusograin Comercio Internacional de Cereas Ltda v. Bunge A.G.* [1986] 2 Lloyd's Rep. 654.

703   Whether the buyer has repudiated is a question of fact, namely is the breach
such as can be described as going to the root of the contract. In *Panchaud
Frères S.A v. R. Pagnan & Fratelli*[53] the appellants sold two cargoes of
Brazilian yellow maize (each consisting of 20,000 tons) to the respondents,
the terms being f.o.b. Santos. Since the respondents, who had nominated the
necessary vessels, were apprehensive about the quality of maize coming to
Italy from Brazil they sent a representative to Santos to examine the shipments. The representative was dissatisfied with the condition of the maize
being loaded by the appellants and as a result, issued instructions to stop
loading unless the situation was remedied, and the consignments were up to
contract quality. The appellants protested this action and insisted on performance but subsequently purported to call off the contract on the ground of
alleged repudiation. The Court of Appeal confirming a decision of Kerr J.
and of two arbitral tribunals (an umpire and an appeal board) held first, that
the respondents' action in suspending loading in the circumstances did not
amount to a repudiation, as the breach did not go to the root of the contract
and, second, that even if there was a repudiation the appellants did not accept
it but elected to treat the contract as subsisting. The appellants rather than
the respondents were thus liable for repudiation in their refusal to go on with
the contract.

On the other hand the buyer's right to repudiate may be in question. Where
the seller's breach does not amount to a breach of a condition the buyer may
not repudiate. Whether he does or does not have this right will depend on
the circumstances of individual cases. In *Bunge Corporation v. Tradax
Export S.A.*[54] Parker J. held that a term requiring an f.o.b. buyer to nominate
the vessel by giving the seller 15 days advance notice of the vessel's readiness to load was an innominate term,[55] but the House of Lords (as well as
the Court of Appeal) disagreed.[56] In that case the notice was delayed by three
days and the seller was left with 12 clear days to permit him to perform.
Parker J. took the view that this was an insignificant breach.

In so holding the judge quoted the following passage from Roskill J.'s
decision in *The Hansa Nord*[57] as support for the proposition that some contractual terms could be regarded as neither conditions nor warranties proper,
and that the severity of the breach would determine the consequences following therefrom.

"... In my view, a court should not be over ready, unless required by statute or
authority so to do, to construe a term in a contract as a 'condition' any breach
of which gives rise to a right to reject rather than as a term any breach of which
sounds in damages. ... In principle contracts are made to be performed and not
to be avoided according to the whims of market fluctuation and where there is a
free choice between two possible constructions I think the court should tend to

---

[53] [1974] 1 Lloyd's Rep. 394.
[54] [1979] 2 Lloyd's Rep. 477.
[55] *Ante*, § 693.
[56] [1981] 2 Lloyd's Rep. 1 (H.L.); [1980] 1 Lloyd's Rep. 294 (C.A.).
[57] [1976] Q.B. 44 at p. 70.

prefer that construction which will ensure performance and not encourage avoidance of contractual obligations.''

The House of Lords and the Court of Appeal, however, disagreed with his
conclusion in the case. The higher courts opined that in mercantile contracts
such as c.i.f. and f.o.b. contracts, stipulations as to time not only might be,
but usually were to be treated as being ''of the essence of the contract,'' even
though this was not expressly stated in the words of the contract. Where, in
such contracts, an act or term had to be performed by one party as a condition
precedent to the ability of the other party to perform another term (especially
an essential term such as the nomination of a single loading port) the term
as to time for performance of the former obligation would be treated as a
condition.[58] But this might even be true where the other party's ability to
perform is unaffected, if the contract includes appropriate words, as where
the nature of a load post by the f.o.b. seller was to be given ''not later'' than
a specified date.[59]

704   *No market.* Where there is no market for the goods at the relevant date,
the general principles embodied in the Sale of Goods Act section 50(2)[60]
must be applied. The measure of damages in such cases is the estimated loss
directly and normally resulting, in the ordinary course of events, from the
buyer's breach. Whether, however, the seller f.o.b. is entitled to his loss of
profit or not is always governed by the particular circumstances of the case
and he must always take all reasonable steps to mitigate his loss.[61] But the
seller:

> ''is not bound to nurse the interests of the contract breaker, and so long as he
> acts reasonably at the time it ill lies in the mouth of the contract breaker to turn
> round afterwards and complain, in order to reduce his own liability to a plaintiff,
> that the plaintiff failed to do that which perhaps with hindsight he might have
> been wiser to do.''[62]

In the case from which this citation is taken, a defaulting buyer argued that
the plaintiff seller should have accepted an alternative offer for repurchase
of the goods from his own supplier at a price which was below the original
contract price and which, if accepted, would have reduced the loss actually
sustained because it would have saved mounting storage costs that ultimately
absorbed more than the difference between the repurchase price offer and the
price subsequently obtained from a resale. Roskill J. dismissed the allegation

---

[58] *Ante,* § 444.
[59] *Gill & Dufus S.A. v. Societe Pour L'esportation Des Suceres S.A.* [1986] 1 Lloyd's Rep. 322
(C.A) affirming a lower court decision that reversed a trade arbitration award influenced no
doubt by the fact that the breach did not prevent performance by the buyer, *ante,* § 444.
[60] Sale of Goods Act 1979.
[61] See, *e.g. J. D'Almeida Araujo Limitada v. Sir F. Becker & Co. Ltd.* [1953] 2 Q.B. 329.
[62] *Per* Roskill J. in *Harlow & Jones, Ltd. v. Panex (International) Ltd.* [1967] 2 Lloyd's Rep.
509 at p. 530.

holding that, there being no available market (the market having fallen drastically), the measure of damages was the difference on the date of breach—the last permissible shipping date—between the contract price of the goods and the then value of the goods to the sellers, plus the storage charges which were incurred as a consequence of the breach. However, with regard to a small portion of the goods (1,500 out of 10,000 tons of steel) that the suppliers agreed to retake at no cost, the damages were equal to the loss of profit sustained by the seller.

705 Where the price is payable in foreign currency, the damages for the purposes of an English judgment used to be converted into pounds sterling, according to the rate of exchange prevailing at the date of default, since that was the material date for computing damages.[63] But this is no longer true. The instability caused by the weakness and floating of sterling has led to the doctrine that English courts can now give judgments in foreign currencies so that justice can be done to plaintiffs with claims that are payable in foreign currencies. This was decided by the House of Lords in *Miliangos v. George Frank (Textiles) Ltd.*[64], which reversed the previous (contrary rule) proclaimed in *Re United Railways of Havana and Regla Warehouses Ltd.*,[65] and further decided that the appropriate rate of exchange, if settlement of a claim expressed in a foreign currency is made in sterling, is the rate at the date of payment and not at the date of default when the claim accrued. This had previously been possible only in respect to arbitrations held in England,[66] but, as aforesaid, the distinction between the two was abolished in 1976. Whether there is a duty to mitigate damages by negotiating forward exchange contracts (and the effect of such contracts if entered into) on claims resulting from fluctuations in exchange rates is still undecided.

Finally, where the buyer has not acquired the right of possession, the seller can institute an action for the conversion of the goods if the buyer wrongfully deals with them (*e.g.* by obtaining and/or transferring the bills of lading). The amount recoverable under these circumstances is, however, limited to the seller's interest (even where property is held to have been reserved), and does not automatically extend to the "value" of the goods.[67]

706 *Rights against the goods.* By the provisions of the Sale of Goods Act, the "unpaid seller"[68] is afforded three rights against the goods, namely:

(a) a lien on the goods while he is still in possession;
(b) a right of stoppage *in transitu* after he has parted with possession (but before the buyer takes possession); and

---

[63] *Barry v. Van den Hurk* [1920] 2 K.B. 709.
[64] [1976] A.C. 443.
[65] [1961] A.C. 1007.
[66] See *Jugoslovenska Oceanska Plovidba v. Castle Investment Co. Inc.* [1973] 3 W.L.R. 877 (C.A.).
[67] *Rew v. Payne, Douthwaite & Co.* (1885) 53 L.T. 932.
[68] See definition, s.38 of the Act.

(c) a right of resale if the conditions set forth in section 48(3) or 48(4) have been met.

Strictly speaking, the seller can enjoy these rights only after the property in the goods has been transfered to the buyer, since, "It is a contradiction in terms to say a man has a lien on his own goods, or a right to stop his goods *in transitu.*"[69] The Act itself, however, does not always make, or follow, this distinction. Consequently, there is some confusion between the seller's right of "withholding delivery" (which is, in effect, only an attribute of his owner-ship in cases where property has not yet passed to the buyer (section 39(2) of the Sale of Goods Act), and the statutory rights of lien and stop page *in transitu* which derive from the right to the possession of the goods where the property has already passed to the buyer (section 39(1)). The right of with-holding delivery is therefore more than a right which is "co-extensive and similar" (section 39(2)) to the rights of the unpaid seller where the property in the goods has passed, and may be distinguished therefrom on the following grounds:

707   First, where property is retained, the seller is always entitled to a right equivalent to a lien, and never to the more limited right of stoppage.[70] But since a question of invoking the right of stoppage could only arise where the seller's control over the bills of lading has ceased, and since this would in itself normally indicate an intention by the seller to transfer the property in the goods, this difference is of no practical significance.[71] Secondly, in a limited number of cases where the goods are considered to come into the buyer's custody and possession immediately upon delivery f.o.b. (for example, because the ship belongs to him or is under a demise charter to him),[72] a retention of anything less than a right of property in the goods would defeat any claim to the goods. Finally, where the seller is held to have reserved the property in the goods, there can be no question as to the ultimate non-consummation of the transaction, and his right to retain any profits realised on a resale of the goods.

A further point to bear in mind is that the provisions of the Act which deal with the situations where property has not passed do not appear to refer to cases where the seller has retained the *absolute* dominion over the goods, but only to situations such as, for example, where the seller is held to have reserved the right of property by means of the bills of lading for the limited

---

[69] *Per* Buller J. in *Lickbarrow v. Mason* (1793) 6 East 22 at p. 27. Also *per* Lord Wright in *Nippon Yusen Kaisha v. Ramjiban Serowgee* [1938] A.C. 429 at p. 444.

[70] *Cf. Wilmshurst & Anor. v. Bowker & Anor.* (1841) 10 L.J.C.P.(N.S.) 161 (reversed on a point of fact by the Court of Exchequer Chamber in (1844) 7 Man. & G. 882); *Ogle v. Atkinson* (1814) 5 Taunt. 759.

[71] But notwithstanding that the buyer has a power to transfer the property to a bona fide third party, there remains a distinction (although usually only theoretical) with respect to rights over the purchase money since the unpaid seller's right of stoppage can only be exercised against the *actual* goods. See *post*, § 714.

[72] See *post*, § 708.

purpose of securing the purchase price, and where his right of disposal is in fact qualified.[73] It is not here proposed to deal with these remedies[74] except the right of stoppage which was in earlier times often invoked in the case of f.o.b. contracts.

708   *Stoppage in transitu.* This right was defined by Lord Reading C.J. as[75]:

> "the right of the unpaid vendor, on discovery of the insolvency of the buyer, and notwithstanding that he has made constructive delivery of the goods to the buyer, to retake them . . . before they reach the buyer's possession."

The goods must be in a state of transit, namely, "in the custody of a third intermediate between the seller who has parted with, and the buyer who has not yet acquired, actual possession."[76] Since the transfer of the bills of lading to the buyer does not of itself invest him with the actual possession of the goods, the question of the duration of the transit in f.o.b. contracts has been the source of controversy from time to time. It has sometimes been stated that where the seller puts the goods "free on board," the goods have arrived at their destinations, have been delivered to the buyer, and the seller's right of stoppage is lost.[77] Thus, in *Cowas–Jee v. Thompson & Kebbel*,[78] the Judicial Committee of the Privy Council, overruling a decision of the Supreme Court of Judicature at Bombay, advised that the transit came to an end immediately the goods were delivered f.o.b. (and a bill of exchange given for the price). Lord Brougham said[79]:

> "The argument of the [sellers] and of the Court below, we must presume . . . is, that . . . the sale was not completed, the delivery was imperfect . . . and the transaction was not finished, nor the *transitus* determined . . . there was evidence in the present case that by the custom of the trade, when goods were sold 'free on board,' the buyer is considered as the shipper. . . . The question in all the cases between buyer and seller . . . is, whether, or not, anything remained to be done as between these two parties."

With the greatest respect, this does not seem to have been the correct test to apply in these circumstances, and if the decision rests on this ground alone its authority is open to serious question. Thus, in the later case of *Berndtson*

---

[73] This is because it is obvious that the unpaid seller's right of "withholding delivery" is co-extensive with his right of lien only where the buyer has already acquired some beneficial interest in the goods. In other circumstances the seller's powers are much wider and do not depend on the buyer's default.

[74] See *ante*, §§346 *et seq.*

[75] *Booth Steamship Co. Ltd. v. Cargo Fleet Iron Co. Ltd.* [1916] 2 K.B. 570 at p. 580.

[76] *Per* Rolfe B. in *Gibson v. Carruthers* (1841) 8 M. & W. 321 at p. 328.

[77] Aitken, *The Principles of the Law of the Sale of Goods* (1921), p. 154; Syrett, *Practice and Finance of Foreign Trade* (1st ed., 1938), p. 11.

[78] (1845) 5 Moore P.C. 165, where *Craven v. Ryder* (1816) 6 Taunt. 433 is questioned on a misunderstanding of the term f.o.b.

[79] (1845) 5 Moore P. C. 165 at pp. 174, 176 and 177.

v. Strang,[80] the unpaid seller's right of stoppage under an f.o.b. contract was recognised to subsist until the arrival of the goods at their destination abroad. Commenting on *Cowas-Jee v. Thompson & Kebbel*, Wood V.-C. said:

> "There a ship was sent out, goods were ordered for that ship *and that ship being the property of the person who sent her out* . . . that was the full *transitus* . . ." (at p. 885, italics supplied).

709   If these were the circumstances in the *Cowas-Jee* case, and the carrier qualified not merely as an intermediary and transporter of the goods but was also considered to be the agent of the buyer for the purpose of taking delivery of the goods, he (the f.o.b. buyer) being the owner of the ship, the decision falls into harmony with the general rule.[81] In such a case the buyer-principal has, undoubtedly, come into possession upon delivery of the goods f.o.b. his own vessel so that the transit is at an end, and, unless there is a reservation of property by the seller, he cannot exercise any rights against the goods thereafter.[82] Only where the carrier is an intermediary between the parties (and his possession does not correspond to the actual possession of the goods by the buyer) can the right of stoppage be invoked. Thus, in *Ex p. Rosevear China Clay Co., Re Cock*,[83] the Court of Appeal (Brett, James and Cotton L.JJ.), reversing the decision of the Chief Justice, held that delivery f.o.b. the buyer's chartered vessel did not terminate the transit. Nor was the fact that the destination of the goods was not communicated to the seller a ground for distinguishing *Berndtson v. Strang*[84] since this was immaterial and could not prejudice his rights. The only pertinent question upon which the right of stoppage depended was whether the goods had in fact arrived at their destination, or had come into the actual possession of the buyer.

710   In *Cowdenbeath Coal Co. Ltd. v. Clydesdale Bank Ltd.*,[85] however, it was held that the seller was not entitled to exercise a right of stoppage after the goods were delivered f.o.b. the export vessel at Burntisland. In this case, a string transaction, namely an internal sale between two Scottish merchants, followed by a resale (on similar f.o.b. terms) to a Danish consignee was considered, and the Scottish Court of Session held that as between the first two parties the ship was the final destination and, furthermore, that the buyer through having obtained the bills of lading was in valid possession of the

---

[80] (1867) 36 L. J. Ch. 879. Decree, varied on different point, in (1868) 37 L. J. Ch. 665.

[81] The *Cowas-Jee* case could, perhaps, further be explained on the ground that the payment by the acceptance of the bill of exchange in that case was absolute and not merely conditional — as it would normally be.

[82] In *The Australia* (1916) 2 Bri. & Col. Prize Cas. 315 (Ceylon), however, Wood Renton C.J. quotes the *Cowas-Jee* case as authority for the proposition that "as a general rule" the effect of a shipment of goods f.o.b. "is to put an end to the right of stoppage *in transitu*." With the greatest respect this view, which is *obiter*, is, as explained above, questionable.

[83] (1879) 11 Ch. D. 560, on appeal, *ibid.* 565.

[84] *Ante*, §708, n. 80.

[85] (1895) 22 R. (Ct. of Sess.) 682, following *Morton & Co. v. Abercromby & Co.* (1858) 30 Sc.Jur. 193.

goods. The *Rosevear* judgment was distinguished on the ground that as the destination in that case was Glasgow, and no bill of lading was ever issued (coastal traffic) the buyer had not, in that case, come into possession of the goods upon delivery f.o.b.

In an attempt to consolidate the principles emerging from the earlier cases, section 45(1) of the Sale of Goods Act now provides that:

> "Goods are deemed to be in course of transit from the time when they are delivered to a carrier ... for the purpose of transmission to the buyer, until the buyer or his agent ... takes delivery of them from the carrier. ..."

and section 45(2) of the Act further provided that:

> "When goods are delivered to a ship chartered by the buyer it is a question depending on the circumstances of the particular case whether they are in the possession of the master as a carrier or as agent to the buyer."

Thus, the distinction between the normal case, where the carrier qualifies as a transporter only (notwithstanding the fact that delivery to him operates, prima facie, as delivery to the buyer), and the less common case, where the carrier also qualifies as the agent of the buyer (so that his possession is synonymous with an immediate and actual possession by the buyer), is made clear.

711   The question, therefore, is as a rule a question of fact, and is normally resolved by references to the status of the carrier. In sales f.o.b. the unpaid sellers' right of stoppage would consequently be precluded only in two relatively rare cases. These are:

(1) where the f.o.b. point is deemed to be the destination of the goods, and the following carriage by sea a new transit; and
(2) where the carrier qualifies as a representative of the buyer not merely for the carriage of the goods but also for taking actual possession thereof.[86]

For example, cases where the buyer is the owner of the ship,[87] or, possibly, where the vessel is on a charter by demise hire,[88] or where in the course of transit the buyer intercepts the goods. Since these circumstances are rare, it has been stated that:

---

[86] In these circumstances a reservation of a right of property in the goods has clear advantages for the seller. See *Turner v. Trustees of Liverpool Docks* (1851) 6 Ex. 543. And see Lord Chelmsford's comments in *Schotsmans v. Lancashire and Yorkshire Rv.* (1867) L.R. 2 Ch. App. 332 at p. 337.
[87] *Van Casteel v. Booker* (1848) 2 Ex. 691; *Schotsmans v. Lancashire and Yorkshire Rv., ante.* But not merely because he travels as a passenger on the same ship; *cf. Lyons v. Hoffnung* (1890) 15 App.Cas. 391.
[88] See *Fowler v. Kymer & M'Taggart* (1797) 7 Term Rep. 442, referred to in *Inglis v. Usherwood* (1801) 1 East 515 at p. 522.

"Where goods are sold f.o.b., the transit is not at end when the goods have been shipped, but continues until the termination of the voyage, and the goods may be stopped at any time before such termination, although the vendor may not have known at the time of the sale for what port they were destined."[89]

712   But although this would, undoubtedly, appear true as a general proposition, it is subject to certain exceptions. In particular, in the case of string transactions the f.o.b. point may well be deemed to be the destination of the goods, in so far as the rights of the original supplier are concerned. Where the unpaid seller exercises his right of stoppage, the carrier must act upon the notice by delivering the goods to, or according to the directions of the seller. If he fails to do so he is liable to an action for wrongful conversion.

713   But in such circumstances the seller for his part, although he may not be a party to the contract of affreightment (as would be the case under the "strict" variant of f.o.b. contract), is bound to take the goods or give directions for their delivery on arrival, and to discharge the carrier's lien for unpaid freight, and if he refuses to admit responsibility for freight and the other expenses payable for the landing of the goods, he is liable for damages to the carrier for the same amount.[90]

714   *Disposition by the buyer.* The unpaid seller's rights against the goods are not proper rights *in rem*, and are normally defeated by third parties to whom the bills of lading have been transferred.[91] Prior to the enactment of the Sale of Goods Act, there existed some uncertainty as to whether the seller could intercept purchase money if the insolvent buyer had resold but had not yet received the price from his sub-purchaser. In *Ex p. Golding Davis & Co. Ltd., re Knight*,[92] in which a string transaction was considered, it was held that the seller was entitled to do so. In that case goods were sold f.o.b. The buyer resold the goods and took a bill of lading making them deliverable to the sub-purchaser. The bill was not forwarded to the sub-purchaser. The buyer stopped payment prior to the vessel's departure from the port of loading. The seller served notice on the master, stopping the goods *in transitu*. The court held that the seller was entitled to be paid his price out of the sums owing to the buyer by the sub-purchaser. James L. J. said:

"... on the facts of the present case, full effect can be given to the right of the vendors to stop *in transitu*, without in the slightest degree affecting any right or equity of *Taylor & Sons* [the sub-purchasers] because it does not prevent *Taylor & Sons* from getting the goods in performance of the contract into which

---

[89] See Cohen, "Stoppage *in Transitu*" (1885) 1 L.Q.R. 398 at p. 399, quoted with approval in *Kennedy v. Leyland & Co.* (1923) 16 Ll.L. Rep. 339 at p. 400.

[90] *Booth Steamship Co. Ltd. v. Cargo Fleet Iron Co. Ltd.* [1916] 2 K.B. 570 (C.A.).

[91] But the seller has an equity to oblige a bank, with which the documents have been pledged, to pay itself out of other securities which are the absolute property of the bankrupt, before resorting to the goods on which the right of stoppage is claimed. See *Re Westzinthus* (1833) 5 B. & Ad. 817.

[92] (1880) 13 Ch. D. 628.

they had entered, upon their paying their purchase-money, and the only question is whether the money which they gave for the goods is to be subject to the stoppage *in transitu*'' (at 634–635).

Without specifically mentioning *Ex p. Golding*, the correctness of the latter proposition was questioned by the Court of Appeal two years later[93] on the ground that, where the sub-buyer gets a good title,[94] the seller cannot apply the right of stoppage to the purchase money, since this right exists as against the goods only.[95] Section 47 of the Sale of Goods Act affirms this view, and there is nothing in its terms to suggest that the seller, whose right of stoppage has been defeated, has any right to intercept sub-purchase money.

[The next paragraph is 731.]

---

[93] *Kemp v. Falk* (1882) 7 App. Cas. 573, *per* Lord Selborne at p. 577.
[94] It is possible that in *Ex p. Golding* the sub-purchasers had not, in fact, defeated the right of stoppage, since the bills of lading (though made out in their name) had not yet been transferred to them.
[95] Thus the right does not extend to insurance money which may be due under the buyer's policy; see *Berndtson v. Strang* (1868) 37 L. J. Ch. 665.

CHAPTER 14

CONFLICT OF LAWS

Because of what has already been said with respect to the changes resulting from the United Kingdom's membership in the European Union (*ante* Chapter 7), this chapter has not been rewritten to take account of the Civil Jurisdiction and Judgments Act 1982 (that came into full force on January 1, 1987), as amended by the Civil Jurisdiction and Judgments Act 1990, which would apply where the plaintiff brings an action in a United Kingdom Court and the defendant is domiciled or deemed to be domiciled in Scotland, Northern Ireland or a State party to the conventions embodied in the Civil Jurisdiction and Judgments Acts. Likewise, the provisions of the Contracts (Applicable Law) Act 1990 have been disregarded since, and apart from different terminology and emphasis, ('applicable' instead of 'proper' law, and replacing the presumed intention test, which in any event had weakened, with the objective connection test) they do not appear to conflict with the common law principles.

Jurisdiction and process

731   The exercise of jurisdiction upon a defendant who is resident abroad was governed by Order 11, r. 1(1)(d) and (e) of the Rules of the Supreme Court, already described in relation to c.i.f. contracts.[1]

The paucity of litigation on the application of the relevant principles to f.o.b. transactions is in sharp contrast to the many disputes that arose in the case of c.i.f. sales over attempts to support the serving of writs upon foreign defendants. However, account must be taken of the fact that the typical c.i.f. dispute concerns a buyer in this country suing a seller abroad for breach of a contract requiring shipment c.i.f. British port with tender of the documents in England, while in the case of f.o.b. transactions the entire contract will often be performed (or breached) at the place of shipment. Nevertheless the principles are identical and c.i.f. decisions apply *mutatis mutandis*, to f.o.b. contracts. A dispute with respect to jurisdiction under an f.o.b. sale arose in the Australian case of *Wainwright & Son Pty. Ltd. v. Gibson*,[2] and the Victoria Supreme Court held that a contract concluded in Sydney, between the

---

[1] *Ante*, 382 *et seq.*
[2] (1921) V.L.R. 8.

defendant and the agent of the plaintiff, providing for the shipment of goods f.o.b. Melbourne in accordance with instructions to be given by the defendant but which were never given, involved a breach within the jurisdiction. The plaintiff was therefore able to sue for damages resulting from the defendant's failure to give the necessary instructions and it was held that the writ had been properly served.[3] More recently in the New Zealand case of *Witt & Scott Ltd. v. Blumenreich*,[4] the question arose as to the place of making of a contract for the sale of 150 pieces of Cauretex Heavy Coating in accordance with sample. The contract was made through Tozer Kemsley & Millburn, a confirming house in Melbourne, pursuant to an offer by the defendants to this firm. The plaintiff buyer gave a signed order in Wellington to Tozers "goods to be bought and shipped by Tozer Kemsley & Millburn, Melbourne, as buying agents merely, ship to Wellington as soon as possible." Tozers ordered the goods from the defendants "for and on account of" the plaintiff f.o.b. Melbourne, in Australian currency together with a covering letter. The goods were invoiced by the defendants. When the goods arrived in Wellington it was discovered that they did not conform to the contract description, and an action was commenced by the buyer against the seller. In order to obtain service out of the jurisdiction it was necessary to show that the contract was either made, performed or broken in New Zealand. The plaintiff argued that the contract was made in Wellington by Tozers as the defendants' agents. But the court rejected this submission and held that the contract of sale was in fact made in Melbourne by the defendants with Tozers. Leave for service out of the jurisdiction was therefore denied. O'Leary C.J. stated that Tozers, although probably acting as agents of the plaintiffs, were not in his view empowered to enter into relationships which would impose contractual liabilities on the defendants direct. They bought goods in their own name and on their own responsibility. However, under the present version of Order 11, r. 1(1) (d) (ii) (*ante*, § 382) of the Rules of the Supreme Court an order for service out of the jurisdiction under such circumstances would probably be granted.

In *Clarke v. Harper and Robinson*,[5] a Northern Ireland case, leave to serve a writ on the English defendant was sought. The contract was for the purchase of turkeys which were delivered f.o.b. Belfast by the Irish seller and were subsequently rejected in London, their destination, and the *locus contractus*. The court held that, although the Sale of Goods Act applied in both jurisdictions, the proper law of this contract was English and not Irish, and jurisdiction could therefore not be invoked on the basis of the rule which empowered the court to issue a writ where the proper law of the contract was Irish.

---

[3] So too the Court of Appeal for East Africa held in *Karachi Gas Co. Ltd. v. H. Issaq* [1965] E.A. 42, that a refusal to accept goods "f.o.b. Mombasa" and further neglect to provide a ship to carry the goods were a breach of contract committed in Kenya for the purposes of the Kenya Rules corresponding to Ord 11. The Supreme Court of Kenya accordingly had jurisdiction to order service upon an absent defendant.

[4] [1949] N.Z.L.R. 806.

[5] [1938] N.I. 162.

In *Gill and Duffus Landauer Ltd. v. London Export Corporation GmbH,*[6] English sellers sold to German buyers 20 tons of California almonds f.a.s. California with payment against presentation of documents in New York. The buyers rejected the documents and refused to pay for the goods alleging a breach by the sellers. The sellers obtained leave to issue and serve proceedings out of the jurisdiction on the basis that the contract was made within the jurisdiction (R.S.C., Ord. 11, r. 1(1)(f)(i))[7]; or the contract was made by or through an agent trading or residing within the jurisdiction on behalf of a foreign principal (R.S.C., Ord. 11, r. 1(1)(f)(ii))[8]; or the contract was by its terms or implication governed by English law (R.S.C., Ord. 11, r. 1(1)(f)(iii))[9]; or the action was brought in respect of a breach of contract committed within the jurisdiction (R.S.C., Ord. 11, r. 1(1) (g).[10] But the permission was set aside on the grounds that the contract was not governed by English law, but by California law with which it was most closely connected, and that there was no breach of the contract in England. The only grounds on which leave could therefore arguably be maintained were under R.S.C., Ord. 11, r. 1(1)(f)(i) or (ii). However Goff J. seriously doubted whether either of the two latter principles applied to the case, and therefore determined that it was not a proper case for service out of the jurisdiction on any of the grounds stated in R.S.C., Ord. 11, and he thus set aside the writ.

Proper (applicable) law of the contract

732   On the other hand, controversies in which the proper or applicable law of the contract has been in dispute appear to have arisen with more frequency in the case of f.o.b. contracts than in the corresponding case of c.i.f. sales. *Clarke v. Harper and Robinson*[11] has already been noted. Although the issue there was the question of assuming jurisdiction, the exercise of jurisdiction depended, as it would under the present rule 1(1)(d)(iii) of Order 11, upon a determination that the *lex fori* was the law of the contract. In rejecting the plea to exercise jurisdiction, Andrews L.C.J. referred to the presumptions in favour of the *lex loci contractus* and the *lex loci solutionis*, as (the then prevailing) indications of the proper law of the contract where the parties fail to make an express stipulation relating thereto. The contract in that case was concluded in England but was to be performed in Belfast where delivery f.o.b. was to take place. It was the learned judge's view that in seeking to replace the presumption in favour of the law of the place of the contract the claimant had to show that at the place of the performance a different law would be applicable to the dispute. Where both laws were identical, as in the

---

[6] [1982] 2 Lloyd's Rep. 627.
[7] Now r. 1(1)(d)(i).
[8] Now r. 1(1)(d)(ii).
[9] Now r. 1(1)(d)(iii).
[10] Now r. 1(1)(*e*).
[11] *Ante*, n. 5.

case before him, the inference in his opinion was irrebuttable that the contract is governed by the *lex loci contractus*. It is a little difficult to see the justification for this determination on the part of Andrews L.C.J. because, apart from other considerations, the mere fact that the same law will be applied in both jurisdictions contains no assurance whatsoever that the outcome of the dispute would be similar in either case. As is eminently clear from the advice of the Judicial Committee of the Privy Council in *Grant v. Australian Knitting Mills Ltd.*[12] courts of different jurisdictions often disagree on the interpretation of the same law.

In order to determine the applicable law of the contract (in the absence of an express choice of law agreed by the parties),[13] the courts at one time used to employ a number of presumptions to assist them. More recent decisions have indicated and this is today provided expressly the Contracts (Applicable Law) Act 1990, that the only relevant question is the following: What is the system of law with which the transaction has the closest and most real connection?[14] In one sense this is not dependent on the intention of the parties at all as they never thought about it. Moreover, it is often a quite indecisive test and thus one which is difficult to apply. In such a case, precedent will no doubt provide a pointer, and it is with this in mind that the following review of the various decisions is presented.

733   The leading authority on the law that governs an f.o.b. contract in which no direct or indirect stipulation as to a choice of the applicable law is contained is *Benaim v. Debono.*[15] In that case the appellants, residents in Gibraltar sold to the respondents in Malta a quantity of anchovies f.o.b. Gibraltar. Gibraltar was also the place of payment. The contract, however, was made in Malta from where acceptance of the offer was cabled. When the anchovies arrived in Malta, the respondents complained about their inferior quality but did not reject them. They delivered them to their sub-purchasers, who refused acceptance on quality deficiency grounds. At this stage the respondents claimed to rescind the sale. The action was first tried in Malta, where the civil law, which allows rescission in such a case, applies. Since no one in those proceedings contended that the law of Gibraltar applied, the courts

---

[12] [1936] A.C. 85.
[13] The question whether a contract containing a choice of English law clause, as the governing law of the contract, contains an arbitration agreement (or not) is to be resolved by the English courts, and the Civil Jurisdiction and Judgments Act, 1982 could not be invoked to deny such jurisdiction (by way of a stay of proceedings) on the grounds that another EEC member state court was first seized with the matter, since arbitration (including the preliminary determination of the validity of the arbitration agreement itself) was excluded from the scope of the Convention on the basis of which the 1982 Act was enacted. See *Marc Rich & Co. A.G. v. Societa Italiana Impianti P.A. ("The Atlantic Emperor")* [1992] 1 Lloyd's Rep. 342 (E.C.J.), where this question arose in connection with an f.o.b. contract for the sale of oil.
[14] See *per* Lord Simonds in *Bonython v. Commonwealth of Australia* [1951] A.C. 201 at p. 209; *In Re United Railways of Havana and Regla Warehouses Ltd.* [1961] A.C. 1007; and *Re Compagnie d'Armement Maritime S.A. v. Compagnie Tunisienne de Navigation S.A.* [1971] A.C. 572, H.L.
[15] [1924] A.C. 514.

decided that there was no acceptance of the anchovies in question, and both the courts of first and second instance upheld the respondents' plea, judgment being entered accordingly. The seller appealed, and the Judicial Committee of the Privy Council reversed the decision on the ground that as:

"the contract was to be performed by the delivery of the goods on board a ship at Gibraltar selected by [the buyer]"

the law applying in Gibraltar, that is to say the Sale of Goods Act, and not that of Malta, was the proper law. In support of this conclusion it was pointed out that from the moment of delivery f.o.b. the seller had lost control over the goods and had parted with the property and possession in them. The respondents, therefore, were deemed to have lost their right of rejection by doing an act inconsistent with the ownership of the seller in relation to the goods.[16]

734   Earlier editions of Dicey and Morris stated the principle that emerged from this decision as follows:

"In many instances, especially of contracts f.o.b., the place of delivery will, however, in fact be in the country in which the seller carries on his business. According to English law (and to many other systems of law) this is also the *locus solutionis* for the buyer,[17] so that much is to be said for the selection of the law of the country of delivery as a subsidiary proper law in the absence of a choice of law by the parties."[18]

However the current edition of Dicey (12th ed., 1993) has reworded the principle: (in Rule 185, Vol. 2 at p. 1327) to take account of the Contracts (Applicable Laws) Act 1990. Despite the different wording it is thought there is no change in substance.

This view has much to commend itself from the commercial and business viewpoints. It enables the export firm to conduct its transactions on the basis of one law, *i.e.* the law of the place of shipment which is normally its own *lex domicilli*, and accordingly this principle is, as a rule, followed in many jurisdictions.[19] Thus, *e.g.* in *The Nile Co. for the Export of Agricultural Crops v. H.J.M. Bennett (Commodities) Ltd. & Oth.*[20] Evans J. held that Egyptian, and not English law, was the proper law of an f.o.b. contract for the sale of Egyptian potatos. In his view Egypt was "the business centre of the relation-

---

[16] *I.e.* by delivery to the sub-purchaser; see *ante*, § 629 *et seq.*
[17] Since in the absence of an agreement to the contrary, this is also the normal place for payment; see *ante,* § 611 and Kahn–Freund, *Conflict of Laws in Foreign Trade* (1955), n. 27.
[18] *The Conflict of Laws* which in the 1980 edition (10th ed., 1980), p. 836 cites the earlier edition of this work (2nd ed., 1975) as authority for this proposition. *Cf.* also note in the *South African Law Journal* (1925) at p. 63.
[19] Rabel, *The Conflict of Laws; A comparative Study* (2nd ed., 1964), Vol. III, pp. 61–62; Batiffol, *Les Conflits de Lois en Matière des Contrats* (1938), ss. 186–187; 77 *Corpus Juris Secundum*, para. 6 (n. 30); and para. 70.
[20] [1986] 1 Lloyd's Rep. 555.

ship'', and the fact that the contract was in the English language, that the buyers were English companies operating in the English markets, that the subject of the contract was to import and establish the sellers' brand potatos in England, that payment was to be in England, and that the sellers undertook liability for the condition of the potatos when they arrive in England, in the sense that the price was fixed in relation to such condition, were insufficient to support a contrary finding. But the inference in favour of the law of the place of shipment or delivery in the case of f.o.b. contracts is not confined to such cases only and is sometimes applied even where the goods are to be delivered in the buyer's country or in some third country.[21] However, although there is much to be said in favour of selecting the law of the place of shipment in the absence of a contrary intention[22] as the applicable law of the contract, this is by no means an indispensable presumption. Quite often a different inference had to be drawn from the circumstances of the case. Thus, where a provision in the contract was invalid according to the *lex loci solutionis* the *lex loci contractus* was preferred.[23] This is so because a contract (and this includes the terms and provisions thereof) is to be construed so as to make it valid rather than invalid in accordance with the well-known Latin maxim according to which a stipulation must be construed as *res magis valeat quam pereat*. Thus where the court has to infer the proper law which the parties have failed to expressly provide for, and where the circumstances point to more than one particular country's legal system as the potential proper law, and the contract contains a provision which is valid under one law but invalid under another, that legal system which saves the provision was usually selected as the proper law of the contract.[24] *N. V. Handel My. J. Smits Import-Export v. English Exporters Ltd.*,[25] that held that the proper law of a contract calling for delivery "f.o.b. Rotterdam" was English and not Dutch illustrates the application of the foregoing principle. In that case, the dispute arose with respect to the seller's undertaking of the additional obligation of shipment. The parties entered into a contract which was not performed and the sellers claimed in respect of the breach. By an exchange of letters between the parties it appeared that the onus of securing the necessary shipping space was transferred to the sellers. They however claimed that Dutch law governed. It appeared that according to the law of Holland, the transfer of this onus from the buyer to the seller (where the f.o.b. term occurs in a written contract) could not be effected in such an informal manner as was adopted in this case. Consequently, a decision applying Dutch law to the contract in question would have entailed the commission of a breach on part

---

[21] See *Re Viscount Supply Co. Ltd.* (1963) 40 D.L.R. (2d) 501. But see *post*, § 737.

[22] Which may, *e.g.* be inferred from an agreement to submit to a particular jurisdiction (including arbitration) in which case the maxim of *que elegit jus elegit judicem* was generally applied. It should be noted that even under the new Act the intention (as to the applicable law) may be either expressed or "demonstrated with reasonable certainty."

[23] *Cf. Hamlyn & Co. v. Talisker Distillery & Ors.* [1894] A.C. 202.

[24] *Cf. Coast Lines Ltd v. Hudig & Veder Chartering N.V.* [1972] 2 Q.B. 34.

[25] [1955] 2 Lloyd's Rep. 69; 317 (C.A.). *Benaim v. Debono* was not mentioned in either instance.

of the English buyer for failure to provide the shipping space though it was the clear intention of the parties to relieve him from this obligation. McNair J., who heard the case at first instance, decided that the proper law was English and based this inference on the following connecting factors[26]:

">... first, that ... the contract was made in this country; secondly, that the financial obligation was expressed in pounds sterling; thirdly, that an English form of contract was used when the order form was despatched; and, fourthly, that the [sellers] have elected to choose this forum it being suggested that there is some suggestion that they appreciated that the law of this court was the proper law of the contract."

735   The Court of Appeal affirmed this decision but emphasised different grounds for the selection of the law of England as the proper law of the contract. Singleton L.J., with whose judgment Jenkins and Parker L.JJ. concurred, said that because of the provisions of Dutch law heretofore mentioned, an acceptance of the plaintiffs' contention would have led to the conclusion that they themselves had[27]:

"entered into a contract which is in a sense repugnant to the law of Holland. One must not assume they would enter into a contract with English buyers which they knew was a bad contract."

736   *Law governing mode of performance.* In certain cases, different aspects of the contract may be held to be governed by different laws. Thus, the *mode* of performance might be determined by a different law from that governing the substance of the obligation applicable; so that where the proper law is not the law of the place of shipment, but some other law, there may nevertheless be questions which will have to be surrendered to determination by the former law. The extent and precise scope of what falls into the category of "mode," as distinct from "substance," is, however, not always clearly stated. In *Mann George & Co. v. J. & A. Brown*,[28] there was a contract for the sale of coal f.o.b. Newcastle (New South Wales), with provision for payment in London against bills of lading. After the contract was made, the Australian Government issued certain regulations pursuant to which all contracts for the sale of coal subsisting on the date when the regulations were issued were to be varied by an increase of the selling price in a specified sum amounting in the case under consideration to an increase of 4s. per ton above and beyond the price agreed to by the parties in the contract. The buyers, having paid this excess sum in order to obtain the coal, sought to recover it from the seller. The Court of Appeal upheld the claim on the ground that the proper law of the contract was English and that according to English law, the seller was not entitled to demand any rise in the contract price. In support of

---

[26] [1955] 2 Lloyd's Rep. 69 at p. 72.
[27] [1955] 2 Lloyd's Rep. 317 at p. 324.
[28] (1921) 10 Ll.L.Rep. 221.

the application of English law as the proper law of the contract, the court cited the following factors:

(1) that it was made in England;
(2) that it involved two firms domiciled in England; and,
(3) that since tender of the documents and payment of the price took place in London part performance of the contract was also in England.

Lord Sterndale M.R. added, however, that in so far as the sellers' obligation to deliver and ship the coal in New South Wales was concerned, that part of the agreement "would naturally be governed by Australian law" (at page 223).

In *W. J. Alan & Co. Ltd. v. El Nasr Export & Import Co.,*[29] on the other hand, where the proper law of a contract for the sale of Kenya coffee f.o.b. Mombasa was English, by virtue of an express provision to submit disputes to arbitration in London and in such event to interpret the contract according to the law in force in England, it was stated that it was permissible to look at the law of Kenya as well as to the law of England on a point concerning the construction to be put on the currency of payment provisions of the contract. The learned judge pointed out that Kenya was the place where all the terms of the contract save one were to be performed. The sellers claimed that payment was to be in Kenya currency whereas the buyers alleged that payment in sterling was effective to discharge their obligation. When the contract was signed, both currencies were on par, but by the time of performance sterling was devalued in relation to Kenya currency.

In *M. W. Hardy & Co. Inc. v. A. V. Pound & Co. Ltd.*, which likewise has already been noted,[30] the Court of Appeal similarly invoked the law of Portugal as justification for the conclusion that the obligation to obtain the necessary export licence was cast upon the seller and not upon the buyer though the proper law of the contract was held to be English law. Singleton L.J. affirmed with approval McNair J.'s observation to the effect that:

> "Of course it must be borne in mind that, even on such a finding [that] the proper law of the contract is English, it may still be the fact that in so far as the performance is to be carried out in Portugal that part of the contract has to be regulated by Portuguese law."[31]

737   These statements, however, would appear to require some qualification. It should clearly be understood that (although there might well be more than one relevant law), the application of the *lex loci solutionis* to the exclusion

---

[29] [1972] Q.B. 189 reversing; [1971] 1 Lloyd's Rep. 401. The case is discussed at § 272 and § 623 *ante*.
[30] See *ante*, § 491: *sub nom. A.V. Pound & Co. Ltd. v. M. W. Hardy & Co. Inc.*
[31] [1955] 1 Q.B. 499 at p. 510; see also remarks by Lord Goddard C.J. at p. 512 to the same effect, and see "F.a.s. Contract—Failure to Obtain Export Licence—Conflict of Laws" (1955) 18 M.L.R. 405 *et seq.* In the House of Lords, however the seller's duty to obtain the necessary licence was not supported by drawing a distinction between Portuguese and English law: see [1956] A.C. 588.

of the proper or applicable law, generally refers only to questions falling under the heading of "mode of performance." It cannot be applied to alter a matter of substance, which is usually governed by the proper or applicable law exclusively.

The inference that the applicable law is the law governing at the port of delivery f.o.b. is always weak where the shipping point is not situated in the country of the seller or the place from which he conducts his business since:

> ". . . neither the hypothetical intention of the parties nor an objective evaluation of such cases can refer the determination of the applicable law merely to the place of shipment."[32]

The presumption, that the *lex loci solutionis* is the proper law of the contract f.o.b. is, therefore, true only as the general proposition, and, as is apparent from the foregoing review, a different legal system may be applied because of special circumstances.

738   Where the proper or applicable law is the law of England, the contract may nonetheless be invalid in so far as it is illegal according to the law of the country where it is to be performed.[33] Thus, where a French buyer entered into a contract for the purchase of coal f.o.b. English ports, and French law made it illegal to purchase coal at a price exceeding a certain amount which was lower than the contract figure, Sankey J. held, confirming the decision of arbitrators in a case stated in *Harrison Sons & Co. Ltd. v. J. Cavroy*,[34] that the effect of the French decree was to discharge the contract. The decision, it is thought, is not in conflict with the principle later stated by the Court of Appeal in *Kleinwort, Sons & Co. v. Ungarische Baumwolle Industrie Aktiengesellschaft*,[35] because, although it may appear as if the effect of the French decree was to prohibit the acceptance of coal in England, part performance of the contract was to take place in France, Paris being specified as the place of payment.[36] Furthermore, it was held that, since the coal was

---

[32] Rabel, *loc. cit.*, p. 67, and the cases there discussed. In *J. D'Almeida Araujo Lda. v. Sir F. Becker & Co.* [1953] 2 Q.B. 329, a shipment f.o.b. Angola, payment in Lisbon (the residence of the seller), it was agreed that the proper law was Portuguese, but it is not clear from the case whether the law of Angola and Portugal were identical. On the other hand in *Gill and Duffus Landauer Ltd. v. London Export Corp. GmbH* [1982] 2 Lloyd's Rep. 627 where English sellers sold to German buyers f.a.s. California with payment in New York, Goff J. held the contract to be governed by California law with which it was "most closely connected."

[33] See Foster v. Driscoll [1929] 1 K.B. 470, and *Regazzoni v. K. C. Sethia* (1944) [1958] A. C. 301. See also with respect to illegality *ante*, § 396, and *ante*, § 624.

[34] (1922) 12 Ll.L.Rep. 390.

[35] [1939] 2 K.B. 678.

[36] So too the fact that it became unlawful for f.o.b. sellers to export on the terms of the contract (cash against documents) and a requirement that payment would have to be by means of a letter of credit was held to be a supervening illegality or impossibility sufficient to frustrate the contract in *The Nile co. for the Export of Agricultural Crops v. H. J. M. Bennett (commodities) Ltd.* [1986] 1 Lloyd's Rep. 555, on the ground that in the *Kleinwort* decision, and similar subsequent cases "there were no acts which the contract required to be performed in the foreign country concerned" (at p. 581).

bought for import into France, the destination was in the circumstances of this case an implied term of the contract, and the buyer could plead the decree as a cause which made it impossible for him to take delivery thereunder. As already noted, however,[37] it is questionable whether in the absence of special circumstances a contract for delivery f.o.b. implies a guarantee of transport to a particular market. Where such a term is not implied (and it usually ought not to be) or expressly provided, the manner in which the buyer proposes to deal with the goods after they have been delivered f.o.b. is of no concern to the seller. Moreover, there are cases where, in order to succeed on the defence of illegality, the defendant may have to show that the plaintiff was implicated in the illegality, that he was aware of the illegal purpose, and that he *agreed* to participate actively in that purpose. Where the evidence fails to support such an implication, as where the buyer requested the f.o.b. seller to falsely describe goods in the invoice in order to mislead the customs authorities regarding their true nature but such request had not in the opinion of the court been made a term of the contract, the defence of illegality failed. In addition, the illegal term may be severable leaving the rest of the contract intact and enforceable. This was explained in *Fielding and Platt, Ltd. v. Najjar*[38] where Lord Denning M.R. further opined that:

> "even if there was a term that these goods should be invoiced falsely in order to deceive the Lebanese authorities, I do not think it would render the whole contract void. The term would be void for illegality. But it can clearly be severed from the rest of the contract. It can be rejected, leaving the rest of the contract good and enforceable. The English company would be entitled, despite the illegal term, to deliver the goods f.o.b. English port, and send a true and accurate invoice to the Lebanese buyer. The Lebanese buyer could not refuse the goods by saying 'I stipulated for a false invoice.' He could not rely on his own iniquity so as to refuse payment" (at p. 362).

739   The foregoing principles apply to matters of substance. Questions relating to procedure, including the remedies for breach of contract, are governed by the *lex fori*, but the question of remoteness of damage, such as whether the kind of loss resulting from a breach of contract is actionable, as distinct from its quantification, has been held (and is now expressly stated to be so governed by the Contracts (Applicable Law) Act, 1990) to be a matter of substance to be governed by the proper or applicable law. This principle emerges from *J. D'Almeida Araujo Lda. v. Sir F. Becker & Co. Ltd.*[39] There the plaintiffs, a Portuguese company, agreed to sell to the defendants in England a quantity of palm oil f.o.b. Angola. In order to fulfil their undertaking, the plaintiffs agreed to buy the palm oil from another firm under a contract which provided that in the event of a default the party in breach should indemnify the other to the extent of five per cent. of the total value of the contract, a

---

[37] *Ante*, § 509.
[38] [1969] 1 W.L.R. 357.
[39] [1953] 2 Q.B. 329. See however an *obiter dictum* to the contrary by McNair J. in *N. V. Handel My. J. Smits Import–Export v. English Exporters Ltd.* [1955] 2 Lloyd's Rep. 69 at p. 72.

sum that amounted to the equivalent of £3,500. The defendants failed to open a letter of credit in payment of the price as agreed, and as a result thereof the plaintiffs had to pay the above-mentioned sum to their suppliers which they sought to recover from the defendants. The contract between the plaintiffs and the defendants was governed by Portuguese law. Under English law, such a payment establishes no claim for damages since it is not the kind of loss that normally results from such a breach of contract. However, Pilcher J. held that English law was irrelevant. He said:

> "... I conclude that the question whether the plaintiffs are entitled to claim from the defendants the – £3,500 which they have paid to [their supplier], depends on whether such damage is or is not too remote. In my view, the question here is one of remoteness, and therefore falls to be determined in accordance with Portuguese law" (at p. 338).

On the other hand, once what must be taken into account in assessing the damages has been decided, in accordance with the applicable law, the quantification thereof must be governed, in an English court, by English law as the *lex fori* and not by the applicable law.

Proprietary aspects

740   A distinction is to be drawn between the contractual and proprietary aspects of the transaction. It has been noted that where a question of conflict arises the contract is governed by what used to be called the "proper law," and today the "applicable" law which (in the absence of an express choice of law clause) is normally inferred from a variety of connecting factors, of which the *lex loci solutionis* and the *lex loci contractus* are possibly of the most importance. But this is true only in so far as the obligatory part, *i.e.* the *jus in personam* element of the contract is considered. Where the conflict involves a question of "property" (or to use the technical terminology a question of "transfer"), *i.e.* in all the *jus in rem* manifestations of the transaction, a different principle applies.

741   The law governing the transfer is the *lex situs* of the goods. It follows that the contractual rights can often be enforced only to the extent that they are valid and recognised by that law. So as to give full effect to the relevant principles here involved, the applicable law of transfer, *i.e.* the *lex situs*, must then also determine whether the conflict involves a proprietary or obligatory question. The parties, therefore, cannot select the law applicable to the transfer and their own intention must be ignored in this connection. It is wrong, however, to assume that the hypothetical (static) conflict between the law of the contract and the *lex situs*, which would at first sight appear inherent in all these cases, is really problematic in practice. As a result of a variety of reasons, much of this static conflict is in fact avoided. In the first place, the *lex situs* and the applicable law of the obligation are often identical. This is particularly the case in f.o.b. sales, where the law of the shipping point is normally both the *lex situs* and the applicable law of the contract.[40] Second, even if the primary laws are different, a great number of these potential conflicts are eliminated by a co-ordination (whether of private international, or domestic rules) between the two competing systems. Thus, for example, it is quite common for the *lex situs* to surrender such questions as the intention to transfer[41] or the validity of the transfer to determination by the applicable law, and likewise for the applicable law to refer contractual questions as, for example, the transfer of risk to the *lex situs*.[42] Finally, it is important to remember that the more or less universally accepted meaning of trade terms (such as f.o.b.) on the one hand, and the recognition of the negotiable quality of bills of lading on the other, have considerably reduced the significance of selecting a particular law in this sphere.

742 *The right of stoppage.* It has been noted that the *lex situs* determines the extent of the transfer; in this connection the right of stoppage (or more precisely the corresponding right of re-vindication of the civil law)[43] is of particular interest. For, although it is sometimes classified as proprietary, it is not a pure right *in rem*, nor a chose in possession proper, but rather a border case between a contractual and property interest. In *Inglis v. Usherwood*[44] a London merchant instructed a factor in Russia to procure and deliver goods f.o.b. a vessel he had chartered for the purpose. Before the ship left Russia the purchaser became insolvent. By English law the right of stoppage was lost, by Russian law it was not. The court held that Russian law governed. However since the sea transit had not in fact begun, the application of Russian law was eminently reasonable since it was not only the *lex situs* but also; (a) the *lex loci actus*; (b) the *lex domicilii* of the consignor and (c) (since this was the law of the place of shipment) most probably also the applicable law of the contract. Where, however, the transit has already commenced, the reasons for applying the original *lex situs* are not so strong. Although the weight of existing authority would in these circumstances appear to lean in favour of the *lex loci destinationis* as the relevant governing law, it has sometimes been held that the law of the place of shipment (*i.e.* the proper law, the *lex loci expeditionis*, and the previous *lex situs*) must nevertheless apply.[45]

---

[40] *Inglis v. Usherwood* (1801) 1 East 515; *Benaim v. Debono* [1924] A.C. 514.

[41] "No doubt the municipal law with reference to which the parties enter into a particular transaction is material in considering their intention as to the passing of property ..." See Lord Parker's speech in *The Parchim* [1918] A.C. 157 at p. 161.

[42] Zaphiriou, *The Transfer of Chattels in Private International Law* (1956), pp. 97 *et seq.* The author's query (at pp. 100–103), as to why risk had not passed according to German law in *O.L.G. Hamburg*, October 24, 1907, when the meaning attributed to the abbreviation f.o.b. is similar in both the relevant jurisdictions, is not difficult to explain. At that time (*i.e.* 1907) B.G.B., para. 447, was rigidly applied, and as a result the symbol f.o.b. was construed as a price stipulation, see *ante*, § 598.

[43] As to the similarity and difference between the civil and common law rights, see comment, "Stoppage *in Transitu* in the Province of Quebec" (1936) 14 Can.B.Rev. 177 *et seq.*

[44] (1801) 1 East 515.

[45] *Rogers v. Mississippi & Dominion Steamship Co.* (1888) 14 Quebec L.R. 99.

Certainly where the goods have not only left their original *situs*, but have also acquired a new one, an application of the original *lex situs* seems illogical. The unusual Canadian decision in *Re Hudson Fashion Shoppe*[46] is therefore open to serious question. The case concerned a sale f.o.b. Montreal, and was tried in Ontario—the new *situs* of the goods. The court held that the sellers were entitled to exercise a right of dissolution (by way of stoppage or re-vindication) which was conferred by Quebec law, but which was unknown to Ontario law. Had the matter been treated as a contractual question, the decision could easily be explained on a proper or applicable law basis (Quebec law being the *lex loci solutionis*).[47] Unfortunately, it is impossible to so explain the decision, for the court unambiguously stated that the dispute involved a question of property. Consequently, the reasoning of the court in this case, if not the ultimate result, does not, with all respect, seem convincing.

As even the very brief foregoing commentary illustrates, the problems confronted in this particular area are very complex. And since the application of the (original or acquired) *lex situs* may present difficulties which are hard to support in the field of international trade, advocates of a more flexible approach have emerged. They suggest cutting back the operation of the *lex situs* as the governing law for proprietary issues affecting tangible moveables—generally in favour of the contractual proper law.[48] Whether or not this unorthodox approach will find support in the English courts, only time will tell.

---

[46] [1926] 1 D.L.R. 199.
[47] *Cf.* Falconbridge, *Essays on the Conflict of Laws* (1947), p. 398, and compare *Lowery & Co. v. Ulmer*, 1 Pennsylvania Sup.Ct. 419 (1896).
[48] See Chesterman, *Choice of Law Aspects of Liens and Similar Claims in International Sale of Goods* 22 I.C.L.Q. 213 (1973).

INDEX

All references are to paragraph numbers

555

Index

QUALITY,
certificate. *See* CERTIFICATE OF
QUALITY.
terms as to. *See* TERMS OF CONTRACT.
variation on, 693
QUIET POSSESSION, 318

RAIL, CARRIAGE BY, 147
"RECEIVED FOR SHIPMENT" BILL OF
LADING, 141–142, 144–145, 159,
164, 481
REJECTION. *See also* ACCEPTANCE;
REMEDIES.
acceptance barring, 332–334
clause, 636
documents, 638, 642
effect of, 635
estoppel by conduct, 338
inconsistent acts, 332–333
insurance cover after, 637, 640–645
loss of right of, 635n, 637, 640–645
market influence, 636
mitigation of damages after, 331
multiple grounds, 146
passing of property and, 638
place of, 332–334
right of,
custom limiting, 636
double nature of, 336, 638, 642
generally, 629, 693
loss of, 635n, 637, 640–645
waiver of, 338
time of, 332–334
waiver of, 338
wrong ground, on, 338–341
REMEDIES. *See also* DAMAGES.
action in rem, 698
breach of contract,
buyer, by, 699–714
seller, by, 302–334
carrier's liability, 2, 304, 698
damages. *See* DAMAGES.
devaluation losses, 310
deviation and loss of profit, 76n
disposition by buyer and, 714
expenses, recovery of, 693
f.o.b. contract non-performance, 691–
714
goods, rights against, 346–350, 697,
706–714. *See also* RESALE:
STOPPAGE IN TRANSIT.
injunctions, 618, 624
insurance contract, 2
lex fori governing questions of, 739

Remedies *See also* Damages—*cont.*
non-acceptance of goods, for, 345
payment not precluding, 2
price, action for. *See* PRICE.
rejection. *See* REJECTION.
resale,
acceptance, as, 640–645
unpaid seller's right of, 346, 350
ship, failure to, 302–309
specific performance. *See* SPECIFIC
PERFORMANCE.
stoppage in transit. *See* STOPPAGE IN
TRANSIT. tender of valid
documents, failure to, 302–309
unpaid seller's, 346–350
withholding delivery, 347, 706
RESALE,
acceptance, as, 640–645
unpaid seller's right of, 346, 350
RESERVATION OF RIGHT OF DISPOSAL.
See DISPOSAL.
RISK,
carrier, delivery to, and, 563–568
c.i.f. contract, in, 274
deterioration in transit, of. *See*
DETERIORATION.
f.o.b. contract,
passing under, 551–552, 563–568
seller, on, 462
vessel, delivery, 445
general rule, 4, 274
I.C.C. definition, 24
insurable interest and, 566–568
meaning of, 190–193
passing of, 164, 274, 481, 551–552,
563–568, 600–603
received for shipment bill of lading
and, 481
ROAD, CARRIAGE BY, 147
ROUTE OF SHIPMENT,
designation effect, 72–73
absence of, 74–83
importance of, 79
liberty of shipowner to, 76
reasonable, 74, 83
seller's obligation, 73, 83
transhipment, 83
unavailability of, 74
usual, 73, 75–77

SALE,
banker's commercial credit and, 618
common law on, 317
statutory preservation of, 59
internal, 318

571

Index

Index

574